D0313992

LE NORD AND PICARDY

Château Fort de Sedan

Parc Astérix

Reims Cathedral

The Battlefield of Verdun

Disneyland Resort Paris

PARIS *see map left*

ALSACE AND LORRAINE

CHAMPAGNE

ÎLE DE FRANCE

Colmar

lois

Vézelay

Dijon

BURGUNDY AND FRANCHE-COMTÉ

Parc Régional Naturel du Haut-Jura

Cluny

Chamonix

Château de Murol

Lyon

THE RHÔNE VALLEY AND FRENCH ALPS

THE MASSIF CENTRAL

Le Puy-en-Velay

Briançon

Gorges de l'Ardèche

Aven Armand

Pont du Gard

Fontaine-de-Vaucluse

Nice

LANGUEDOC-ROUSSILLON

Palais des Papes, Avignon

PROVENCE AND THE CÔTE D'AZUR

bi

Canal du Midi, Béziers

Marseille

St-Tropez

rcassonne

Mediterranean Sea

Golfe de Porto

CORSICA

Bonifacio

EYEWITNESS TRAVEL
FAMILY GUIDE
FRANCE

EYEWITNESS TRAVEL

FAMILY GUIDE

FRANCE

LONDON, NEW YORK,
MELBOURNE, MUNICH AND DELHI
WWW.DK.COM

MANAGING EDITOR Aruna Ghose

SENIOR EDITORIAL MANAGER
Savitha Kumar

SENIOR DESIGN MANAGER
Priyanka Thakur

EDITORS Shreya Sarkar, Bidisha
Srivastava, Priya Rajendran,
Ashwin Ahmad

PROJECT DESIGNER Amisha Gupta

DESIGNER Meghna Baruah

PICTURE RESEARCH MANAGER
Taiyaba Khatoon

PICTURE RESEARCH Sumita Khatwani

SENIOR DTP DESIGNER
Azeem Siddiqui

DTP DESIGNER Rakesh Pal

SENIOR CARTOGRAPHIC MANAGER
Uma Bhattacharya

CARTOGRAPHER Schchida Nand
Pradhan

PHOTOGRAPHY Alex Havret,
Kathryn Tomasetti, James Tye

CARTOONS Roland Ungoed-
Thomas

ADDITIONAL ILLUSTRATIONS
Arun Pottirayil, Stephen Conlin,
John Lawrence, Maltings
Partnership, John Woodcock

DESIGN CONCEPT Keith Hagan at
www.greenwich-design.co.uk

Reproduced by MDP Ltd, UK
Printed and bound by South China
Printing Co. Ltd., China

First published in Great Britain in 2012
by Dorling Kindersley Limited, 80 Strand,
London WC2R 0RL. A Penguin Company

12 13 14 15 10 9 8 7 6 5 4 3 2 1

**Copyright 2012 © Dorling
Kindersley Limited, London**

MIX
Paper from
responsible sources
FSC™ C018179

Contents

*The Eiffel Tower soaring above the
Champ-de-Mars, Paris*

View over the town and bay of St-Tropez, Côte d'Azur

How to Use this Guide

This guide is designed to help families to get the most from a visit to France, providing expert recommendations for sightseeing with kids along with detailed practical information. The opening section contains an introduction to France and its highlights, as well as information on how to plan a family holiday (including how to get there, getting around, health, money and communications), a guide to family-friendly festivals and a historical overview.

The main sightseeing section is divided into areas, each consisting of two or three regional chapters. A "best of" feature is followed by the key sights and other attractions to visit in each region, as well as options for where to stay, eat, drink and play and have more fun. At the back of the book are detailed maps of France and Paris, as well as a language section listing essential words and phrases for family travel.

INTRODUCING THE AREA

Each area chapter is opened by a double-page spread setting the area in context, with a brief introduction, locator map and a selection of area highlights.

Locator map locates the region.

Brief highlights give a flavour of what to see in the area.

THE BEST OF...

A planner to show at a glance the best things for families to see and do in the area, with themed suggestions ranging from seasonal visits to short stays, cultural holidays and the great outdoors.

Agencies' box lists the region's best accommodation agencies.

WHERE TO STAY

Our expert authors have compiled a wide range of recommendations for places to stay with families, from hotels and B&Bs that welcome children to farmstays, self-catering and camping.

Easy-to-use symbols show the key family-friendly features of places to stay.

Price Guide box gives details of the price categories for a family of four.

SIGHTSEEING IN FRANCE

Each area chapter is divided into 3–4 smaller regions, all of which are shown on the map at the start of the chapter. These feature a number of "hub" destinations (see below): practical and enjoyable plans for a half-day or day's visit, giving adults and children a real insight into the destination, balanced with chances to let off steam, "take cover" options for rainy days, suggestions for where to eat, drink and shop with kids, ideas for where to continue sightseeing, and all the practicalities, including transport.

Introductory text describes the key characteristics and geography of the area, and gives information on the transport infrastructure.

The Lowdown gives all the practical information you need to visit the area.

The map shows the regions covered and all the hubs, colour-coded by area.

The "hub" destinations pick out the best places to visit in each region, using lively and informative text to engage and entertain both adults and children.

Key sights uses illustrated artworks to show the most interesting features of each destination, highlighting elements likely to appeal to children.

The Lowdown provides comprehensive practical information, including transport, opening times, costs, activities, age range suitability and how long to allow for a visit.

Eat and drink lists recommendations for family-friendly places to eat and drink, from picnic options and snacks to proper meals and gourmet dining.

Kids' Corner is featured on all sightseeing pages (see below).

Letting off steam suggests a place to take children to play freely following a cultural visit.

Find out more gives suggestions for downloads, games, apps or films to excite children about a place and help them to learn more about it.

Next stop... suggests other places to visit, either near the key destination, thematically linked to it, or a complete change of pace for the rest of the day.

Further sights around each hub destination are described on the following pages. Each sight or destination is selected to appeal to both adults and children.

Town or sight gives details of the places of interest to visit, with an emphasis on the aspects most likely to attract children, incorporating quirky stories and unusual facts.

Kids' Corners are designed to involve children with the destination, with things to look out for, games to play, cartoons and fun facts. Answers to quizzes are at the bottom of the panel.

The Lowdown provides the usual comprehensive practical and transport information for each sight.

The richly sculpted interior of the spectacular Gothic Cathédrale Notre Dame de Chartres

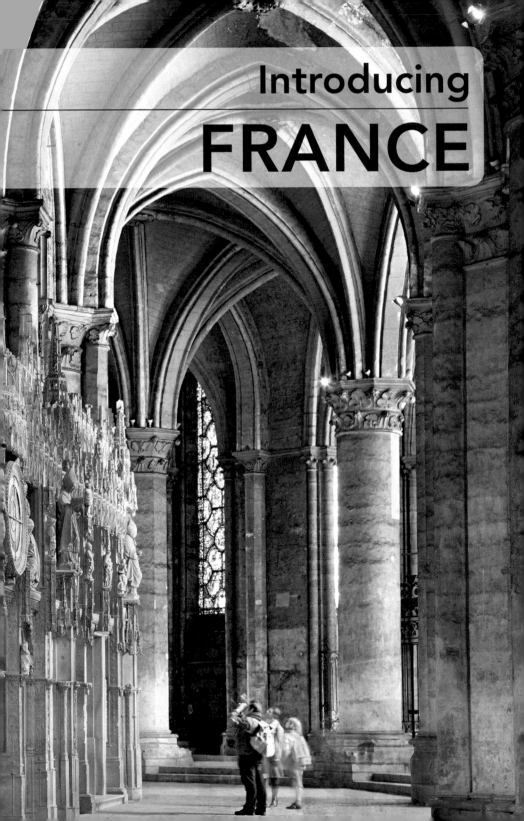

Introducing
FRANCE

The Best of France

France's remarkable diversity ensures that every member of the family is entertained. Breathtaking mountains, spectacular caves, meandering rivers and scenic national parks lie alongside grand castles, medieval villages and sun-kissed beach resorts. Art and culture abound in and around the beautiful cities, as Roman glories compete with Renaissance charms and an impressive collection of galleries and museums. The food is pretty good, too!

Kids' favourites

Some places have a special wow factor for kids, and candy wonderlands such as the **Musée des Bonbons** in Uzès (see p335), and the **Atelier du Chocolat**, a chocolate factory in Bayonne (see p302), score high on the list. Kids will also love the imaginative inventions and fun-filled rides at

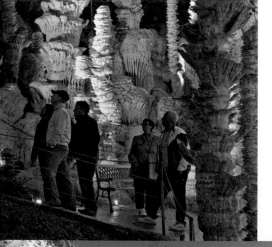

Les **Machines de l'Île** in Nantes (see pp174–5), or exploring, on a more modest scale, one man's crazy mechanical creations at the **Univers du Poète Ferrailleur** in Lizio (see p167).

One of the best spots for dinosaur-loving kids is **Dinosauria** in Espéraza (see p326), and the discovery of fossilized dinosaur eggs inspired the life-sized models of the giant lizards at the **Musée Parc des Dinosaures** in Mèze (see p333).

Pay homage to Jules Vernes' *Journey to the Centre of the Earth* in the fantastic stalactite chambers of the **Aven d'Orgnac** (see p232) and the **Aven Armand** (see pp240–41). The **Gouffre de Padirac** (see p270) and **Les Grottes de Médous** in Bagnères (see p307) can be explored on unforgettable boat rides.

France offers many train rides, and three of the most exciting are **Le Petit Train Jaune** (see p329) year-round into the Pyrenees, the steam train to the **Eco-musée de la Grande Lande** in 19th-century Marquèze (see p297) and the **Train du Montenvers** from Chamonix (see p224) up to France's largest glacier, the Mer de Glace.

Left *Fascinating stalactites and stalagmites at Aven Armand*
Below *The little red Train du Montenvers, Chamonix*

Magnificent façade of the immense Renaissance Château de Chambord, in the Loire Valley

Culture vultures

A treasure chest of art and architecture, France boasts splendid samples from every era. Start in the Dordogne with **Lascaux II** *(see pp262–3)*, a replica of the cave famous for its palaeolithic paintings. The **Standing Stones of Carnac** *(see pp166–7)* in Brittany form the world's greatest collection of Neolithic monuments. At **Filitosa** *(see p372)*, in Corsica, the standing stones have haunting faces.

Among Roman masterpieces, the **Pont du Gard** *(see pp334–5)* aqueduct, the **Maison Carrée** and **Les Arènes** in Nîmes *(see p336)*, as well as the **Théâtre Antique** in Orange *(see p345)* are truly exceptional. For France's most striking medieval citadel, head to **Carcassonne** *(see pp324–5)*. The cliffside church of **Rocamadour** *(see pp268–9)* and the spectacular island abbey of **Mont-St-Michel** *(see pp152–3)* never fail to amaze visitors. The massive **Palais des Papes** in Avignon *(see pp342–3)* is a superb example of Gothic architecture, as is the **Cathédrale Ste-Cécile** of Albi *(see p274)*.

Experience the splendour of the French Renaissance in the Loire Valley at the **Château de Chambord** *(see p185)* and the **Château Royal de Blois** *(see pp184–5)*. In the 17th and 18th centuries, much of France's budget went into glorifying **Versailles** *(see pp124–7)*.

The Impressionists and Post-Impressionists of the 19th century star in Paris's **Musée d'Orsay** *(see pp108–9)*, and in the museums of **Rouen** *(see pp144–5)* and **St-Tropez** *(see pp354–5)*. The towns along the Côte d'Azur are filled with 20th-century art. See some of the best collections in **Nice** *(see pp358–9)* and in the **Fondation Maeght** in St-Paul-de-Vence *(see p359)*.

The interactive Biospace Mission exhibit in the informative Cité de l'Espace, Toulouse

The great indoors

Travelling in the late autumn or winter, there is still plenty to see indoors, particularly in France's numerous museums. Many of these also appeal to children, such as the **Musée de la Tapisserie** in Bayeux *(see p149)*, home to the Bayeux Tapestry – that great comic strip version of the Norman Conquest. Watch the magic unfold at the **Maison de la Magie Robert-Houdin** in Blois *(see p185)*, or explore outer space at the **Cité de l'Espace** in Toulouse *(see p276)*. At St-Nazaire's **Escal'Atlantique** *(see p176)*, the simulated voyage aboard legendary ocean liners is memorable. Honfleur's **Maisons Satie** *(see p147)*, devoted to the composer Erik Satie, is quirky and fun.

Animals are always child pleasers, and some of them live indoors too. France's exceptional array of child-friendly aquariums includes **Mare Nostrum** in Montpellier *(see p333)*, **Nausicaá** in Boulogne-sur-Mer *(see pp66–7)*, the **Aquarium** in La Rochelle *(see p286)* and Brest's **Océanopolis** *(see pp162–3)*.

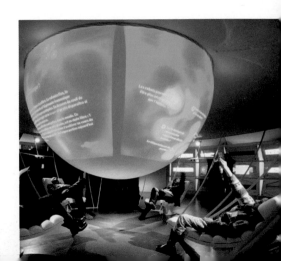

The great outdoors

France's spectacular mountain ranges attract families throughout the year, as much for their beauty as for the mountain sports. Head to the French Alps for a thrilling ride up a cable car to the **Aiguille du Midi** (see p224), under Mont Blanc (see p224), Western Europe's highest peak. For a relaxed excursion, explore the **Parc National de la Vanoise** (see p230) and its many lakes or the picture-perfect **Lac d'Annecy** (see p227).

If visiting the Pyrenees, take the cableway up to the **Pic du Midi de Bigorre** (see pp306–7) for a splendid view, or admire the waterfalls at the **Parc National des Pyrénées** (see p308). The natural marvels of the Massif Central include the majestic **Gorges du Tarn** (see p242) and extinct volcanoes in the lush **Parc Naturel Régional des Volcans d'Auvergne** (see p250).

Burgundy's **Parc Naturel Régional du Morvan** (see pp206–7) has a special idyllic quality, while Alsace's **Route du Vin** (see p56) passes through the region's prettiest villages. The world famous landscapes of Provence include the olive groves of the Alpilles, painted by Van Gogh, and equally delightful are the lazy charms of Languedoc's **Canal du Midi** (see pp330–31).

Above Paddling in the river below the Pont du Gard
Below Cafés in the Place des Terreaux, Lyon

Best cities

While Paris steals the limelight, France has a wealth of great cities, many of which can easily be the focus of a family holiday. Basking on a long beach, **Nice** is crammed full of arty museums and fun activities all year round. **Marseille** (see pp350–51), with its stunning coast, is within easy distance of Cézanne's Aix-en-Provence. **Lyon** (see pp220–21) offers plenty of culture and entertainment for kids, and day-trip options.

The Atlantic seaports of **La Rochelle** (see pp286–7), **Bordeaux** (see pp294–5) and the Basque port of **Bayonne** (see pp302–3) are great for families, and have easy access to beaches. Among the best smaller cities are the capital of Burgundy wine, **Beaune** (see p202), and **Nîmes** (see p336), the "Rome of France". Exceptional monuments abound in **Strasbourg** (see p57), with its cathedral and the European Parliament, in wealthy medieval **Bourges** (see pp186–7), and in **Dijon** (see pp200–1). **Rouen** (see pp144–5) charms with its medieval timbered houses and Monet's cathedral. There is also a fine clutch of historic towns in the Loire Valley, such as **Tours** (see pp180–81), **Chinon** (see p182), **Le Mans** (see p179) and **Saumur** (see p178).

Letting off steam

Kids adore running through mazes, and will have quite a few to choose from in France, including the beechwood maze in **Château de Villandry** (see p181), the one at **Artmazia** near Rouen (see pp144–5) and the maze at the **Château de Vendeuvre** (see p151). Solve the enigma of the Templars at the **Château d'Usson** in Pons (see p293). At Niaux's **Parc de la Préhistoire** (see p311), kids can polish their Stone Age skills.

Kayaking and canoeing on the country's many rivers is another family pleaser. Some beautiful waterways include the Sorgue, near **Fontaine-de-Vaucluse** (see pp346–7), and the Tarn through its winding gorge. Families can paddle on the Cher, right under the **Château de Chenonceau**

(see p183), while on the Gardon, they can easily glide under the **Pont du Gard** (see pp334–5). Punting is fun on the emerald canals of **Marais Poitevin** (see p285), as is white-water rafting on the long-winding Aude (see p326). From the age of 7, kids can learn how to surf near **Bayonne** (see p303), sand-yacht at **St-Jean-de-Monts** (see p177) or rock climb in Corsica.

Theme and animal parks

While there is no doubt that **Disneyland Resort Paris** (see pp130–33) is by far the largest theme park in France, there are several others. **Parc Astérix** (see pp74–5) has attractions based on the two popular Gaulish heroes of French comic-strip fame, and the **Parc d'Attraction Walygator** (see p52) has some of the scariest rides. **Marineland** in Antibes (see p360) is a Wild West theme park with a water park and dolphin shows. For something different, head to **Vallon du Villaret** (see p243), a non-commercial theme park set in the forest, designed by artists.

Futuroscope (see pp282–3) offers the ultimate high-tech experience, taking visitors into the future; even into the fourth dimension. The **Grand Parc Puy de Fou** (see p177) has no rides at all, but rather offers total immersion into different historical periods; families can even spend the night in a Dark Age village on stilts in a lake. **Terra Botanica** in Angers (see p179) is the first botanical theme park in the world.

Among the best zoos and animal parks in the country are the **Parc de la Coccinelle** near Bordeaux (see p295), especially designed for

kids aged under 12, with a petting zoo as well as rides, and **Le Récré des Trois Curés** in Brest (see p163), complete with a huge water park.

By the sea

There is something for all tastes along France's coastline. The fashionable resorts of **St-Tropez** (see pp354–5) and **Deauville** (see p147), the walled old port of **St-Malo** (see p161), Corsica's breathtaking **Réserve Naturelle de Scandola** (see p366) and the giant **Dune de Pyla** (see p295) overlooking the Bassin d'Arcachon are only some of the most enjoyable places around the country's shores. Explore the stunning granite coast of cliffs, beaches and fishing ports in Brittany; or soak in the sun on the sandy beaches at **Le Grau de Roi** in the Camargue (see p345).

Families can remember World War II at the **D-Day Beaches** (see pp148–9) in Normandy. The **Île Ste-Marguerite**, just off Cannes (see p360), is where the Man in the Iron Mask was imprisoned.

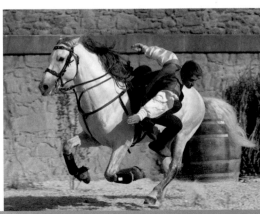

Right A show in progress at the Grand Parc Puy de Fou
Below The natural arch at the pebble beach in Étretat, Normandy

France Through the Year

The beauty and appeal of France is evident throughout the year. While the pleasant days of spring bring with them a myriad of flowers and pavement cafés, summer is chock-a-block with fêtes, festivals and parades, such as the one on Bastille Day. Autumn slips in with golden leaves, open-air fairs and skies filled with colour at the world's largest kite festival, and winter glitters in lit-up cities with midnight feasts, carnivals and snow holidays in the Alps.

Spring

One of the most beautiful seasons in France, with comfortable and mild temperatures, spring is just perfect for exploring the country. A riot of colours fills its many gardens and parks, and the markets overflow with fresh and juicy cherries, strawberries and asparagus in late-May. March is usually the last month to find good travel bargains and packages to France, before the main tourist period gets underway. By April, the fine weather is ideal for touring, hiking and horse-riding; pack an umbrella to protect against April showers.

MARCH

This is when the skiing season is winding down in the mountains, just as the fruit trees in the lower altitudes are opening their first buds. In late March or early April, the **Carnaval de Marseille** (see p350) is held in the city's Vieux Port area, featuring a traditional parade with singing, dancing, colourful floats and tasty food and drink, while the huge **Carnaval de Nantes** (see p175) includes floats and bands, and a special children's carnival.

APRIL

The country opens its arms wide for the first big wave of visitors arriving during the Easter holidays. Tables and chairs re-appear on the terraces of cafés and restaurants, as the shops fill with Easter chocolates. Arles puts together the big **Feria Pascale** (see p345) for Easter; while families may want to skip the actual bull fighting, they can take pleasure in good music and food, and the lively atmosphere on the streets.

Towards the end of the month, Orléans (see p187) celebrates **Les Fêtes Jeanne d'Arc** in honour of one of France's patron saints, Joan of Arc. Military parades, historical re-enactments, medieval markets and concerts are just some of the festivities that ensure a well-spent day.

MAY

Many French families take extended breaks during this month, thanks to three national holidays. Hardy souls brave their first annual dips on the beaches of the Côte d'Azur, Languedoc-Roussillon and Corsica. Others make a beeline for one of the most prestigious and anticipated events in May: the **International Grand Prix de Monaco** (see p360). This grand affair shares the limelight with the glamorous **Festival de Cannes** (see p361). Head over for an afternoon to see the movie stars if staying nearby. Children may also like the colourful costumes, drums and processions of the **Fête de la**

Below left A match in progress at the Roland Garros tennis tournament, the French Open, Paris
Below right Annual procession celebrating Les Fêtes Jeanne d'Arc in Orléans

Bravade in St-Tropez (see p354). **Jazz Sous Les Pommiers**, the jazz festival in Coutances, will delight music lovers. In Paris, May sees the beginning of the **Roland Garros** tennis tournament.

Summer

This is the busiest season in France, especially for families. Days tend to be hot, but are rarely unbearably so. Water parks and beaches are perfect for cooling off; the temperatures in the evenings are ideal for staying out late. June offers a slight calm before the great summer rush, and relative bargains for flights and hotel rooms can still be had before prices shoot up. By July and August, reservations are a must for accommodation and restaurants. Popular sights get busy, so make online bookings whenever possible to avoid long queues.

In August, many offices, shops and restaurants are shut as most of the country goes on holiday. The national holiday on 15 August, when people start their vacations, is a bad day to be on the road because traffic on the main *autoroutes* is backed up for miles. This month brings afternoon and evening thunderstorms, which can take the thermometer down a few degrees, although this is a bit of a bore for campers.

JUNE
Much singing, dancing and street celebrations are in evidence at one of Nîmes's (see p336) most important festivals, **Feria de Pentecôte**.

The commemorations on the D-Day Beaches of Normandy (see p148) are worth catching, and the sports car race, **24 Heures du Mans** (see p179), is thrilling to say the least. On 21 June, the **Fête de la Musique** features musical events in the streets across the country; **Les Feux de la St-Jean** marks the summer solstice with bonfires, especially in the Pyrenees, such as in Montségur (see p312).

JULY
The month of July is marked with hundreds of festivals and village fêtes, culminating on the 14th with La Fête Nationale or **Bastille Day**. Festivities include dances, often on the night of the 13th, and enormous fireworks displays in Paris and other cities. News of the **Tour de France** fills the airwaves. Go watch if the race is passing nearby; although the cyclists whiz by in a blur, kids love the freebies tossed into the crowd by the parade that precedes the racers.

The **Festival d'Avignon** (see p342), with its many street events, is great fun, as is the musical and cultural **Festival de Cornouaille** in Quimper (see p169). July and August see many family events in castles, gardens and châteaux. The superb night-time show, **Cinéscénie**, plays at the Grand Parc Puy du Fou (see p177), and is on a spectacular scale, with stunning fireworks. Kids enjoy the jousting show, **Chevaliers de la Foi**, in Carcassonne (see p324). Step into the **Centre de l'Imaginaire Arthurien**, King Arthur's legendary world in Broceliande (see p160), or marvel at the theatrical creativity of **A la Cour du Roy François**, at the Château d'Amboise (see p186), as hundreds of actors present a grand Renaissance spectacle, with fireworks.

AUGUST
One of the liveliest family-friendly events, **Mimos** is a mime festival held in Périgueux (see p265). The **Fête de St-Louis** in Sète (see p333) is a rousing water-jousting tournament. Celtic music, tradition and games are celebrated at the **Festival Interceltique** in Lorient and at **Les Celtiques de Guérande** (see p176). The traditional **Festival de Force Basque** at St-Palais, near Grottes d'Isturitz et Oxocelhaya, involves ancient Basque contests of strength, such as boulder-carrying races and mass tugs-of-war. In Dax (see p297), families may also enjoy bloodless bullfights (courses landaises).

Below left Jordan-Ford Formula 1 driver Giancarlo Fisichella speeding past the spectators during the International Grand Prix de Monaco *Below right* Tour de France cyclists racing through St-Jean-de-Maurienne

Autumn

As schools reopen and the locals return to work, autumn combines rich colours in the countryside with thinner crowds at the most popular sights. In many ways, September is the ideal month to visit France. The weather is generally warm and clear, perfect for exploring outdoors.

In October, plane fares and hotel prices tumble, but rain gear and umbrellas may be needed as it tends to get wet. Still, the reds and golds of the woods and vineyards, and the soft river mists add a lovely dimension to the countryside and mountains.

November marks the real end of the holiday season. Seasonal sights begin to close. The weather now is generally cold and wet. Restaurant owners, shopkeepers and everyone who has been working full tilt since spring take a break before gearing up for Christmas.

SEPTEMBER

Sunny days make this an excellent month for taking a ride on Le Petit Train Jaune *(see p327)* or Le Petit Train d'Artouste *(see p305)* to the top of the Pyrenees, or visiting Monet's gardens in Giverny *(see p146)*, with their autumn blooms. In Marseille *(see p350)*, all eyes are raised to the skies for the **Fête du Vent**, a kite flying festival. In even-numbered years, Dieppe *(see p146)* raises the bar with the **Festival International de Cerf-Volants**, the world's biggest kite flying festival.

Take a trip to the Renaissance era with Le Puy-en-Velay's *(see p244)* **Roi de l'Oiseau**, a fair with open-air feasts, period costumes, fireworks and acrobats. The **Deauville American Film Festival** *(see p147)* is a glittering event.

The third weekend of September offers a special bonus, as it brings the **Journées du Patrimoine**, a heritage weekend all across the nation, when historic monuments usually closed to the public are opened to visitors.

OCTOBER

This a great time to visit Paris and the sights that get jam packed in summer such as Pont du Gard *(see pp334–5)*, Lascaux II *(see pp262–3)*, Mont-St-Michel *(see pp152–3)* and Carcassonne *(see pp324–5)*, or cities such as Dijon *(see pp200–1)* in the lovely Burgundy countryside. It is a great time to take the kids to Rouen *(see pp144–5)*, with Monet's cathedral and the **Foire St-Romain**, the biggest fun fair in France.

NOVEMBER

Some attractions remain open until 11 November, the last public holiday before Christmas, commemorating the end of World War I – an evocative time to visit Verdun *(see pp50–51)*, the Somme *(see p72)* or other battlefields, memorials and cemeteries. Grown-ups may enjoy trying the new wines and autumn cuisine – mushrooms, game, truffles, *foie gras* – although kids are generally less than impressed.

Winter

Home to some of Europe's highest mountains, France is a gold mine for winter sports. The resorts in the Alps, the Vosges, the Massif Central and the Pyrenees are filled to capacity. The holidays begin just before Christmas, and extend into late-January and through February. French schools close for two weeks to allow families to hit the slopes; these breaks are nationally staggered into three groups, to keep everyone from crowding in on holiday spots at the same time. Christmas is a season of great revelry as the streets are alive with festivities, overflowing markets, carnivals, concerts and exhibitions. Some city squares are flooded and frozen for ice-skating parties.

DECEMBER

France becomes a glittering world as cities are adorned with gorgeous Christmas lights and decorations.

Below left Beginners gearing up for a skiing lesson at a ski resort in the Pyrenees *Below centre* Le Petit Train d'Artouste chugging along a hairpin bend, on its way up to the Lac d'Artouste in the Pyrenees

The display on the Champs-Elysées in Paris is justifiably famous, and the **Fête de la Lumière** held in Lyon (see p220), is a dazzling spectacle.

Richly stocked Christmas markets offer handicrafts, cakes, and other goodies – the market in Strasbourg (see p57) is one of the largest. The 200-year-old **Foire aux Santons** in Marseille is a great place to buy Provençal Christmas crib figures.

The traditional feast of Christmas, the **Réveillon de Noël** is celebrated on an elaborate scale on Christmas Eve, with many restaurants preparing and serving special meals.

JANUARY

New Year's Eve festivities in France are known as the **Réveillon de St-Sylvestre** and are accompanied by lavish midnight feasts, plenty of champagne and fireworks. The area around the Eiffel Tower is abuzz with activity, as restaurants put on special parties with music and dancing.

The end of the holiday season is marked on 6 January by Epiphany or **La Fête des Rois**. To celebrate, people buy a flat flaky pastry (galette des Rois) filled with almond paste (frangipane). Whoever gets the object hidden inside gets to wear a king's crown which comes with the cake. At the end of the first week of the month, the semi-annual January

sales begin, offering bargains galore. The **Festival International de la Bande Dessinée** (see p291) draws comic-book fans to Angoulême, while the **Festival International du Cirque de Monte-Carlo in Monaco** (see p360) is a breathtaking showcase for circus skills.

FEBRUARY

Among winter festivals, the curious, medieval carnival-like **Los Fécos** (see p325) in Limoux is one that might most appeal to families. Held

only on weekends, from January through March, it has teams of masked dancers, music and confetti battles. The largest post-Christmas gala is Carnival, usually in February but sometimes earlier. Many towns and villages have their own parades and parties for kids in costumes. The most splendid are in Dunkerque north of Lille (see p70) and the **Carnaval de Nice** (see p359), the largest in France, with huge flower-decked floats in ten days of celebrations before Mardi Gras.

The Lowdown

Public holidays
New Year's Day (1 Jan)
Easter Sunday & Monday (Mar/Apr)
Labour Day (1 May)
VE Day (8 May)
Ascension Day (6th Thu after Easter)
Pentecost (2nd Mon after Ascension)
Bastille Day (14 Jul)
Assumption Day (15 Aug)
All Saints' Day (1 Nov)
Remembrance Day (11 Nov)
Christmas Day (25 Dec)

Spring
Festival de Cannes www.festival-cannes.fr
Les Fêtes Jeanne d'Arc www.fetes jeannedarc.fr
International Grand Prix de Monaco www.monaco-grand-prix.com
Roland Garros www.rolandgarros.com

Summer
24 Heures du Mans www.lemans.org
Le Festival d'Avignon www.festival-avignon.com
Festival de Force Basque www.saint palais-tourisme.com/découverte/force-basque
Tour de France www.letour.fr

Autumn
Deauville American Film Festival www.festival-deauville.com
Festival International de Cerf-Volants www.dieppe-cerf-volant.org

Winter
Festival International de la Bande Dessinée www.bdangouleme.com
Festival International du Cirque de Monte-Carlo www.montecarlo festival.mc
Fête de la Lumière www.fetedes lumieres.lyon.fr

Below right Participants decked up in lavish costumes at the sumptuous parade and festivities celebrating the Carnaval de Nice, the biggest carnival in France

Getting to France

With excellent air, rail, sea and road connections, getting to France is easy. There are several economical and convenient options, many of which are child-friendly as well. However, finding them can require some research, as new connections are opening up all the time to new hubs across the country. Direct flights are available to many places, but families wishing to get to the heart of the country should consider the scenic routes by rail, sea or car.

Arriving by Air

While those coming to France from within Europe have many different transport choices, families travelling from the Americas, Australasia, Africa and Asia will have to fly. Fortunately, there are several options to choose from, including **Air France**, the national airline, with flights from many destinations across the world.

Other main carriers offering frequent flights from major European cities include **British Airways**, **Iberia**, **Lufthansa**, **KLM** and **Alitalia**. These airlines serve the two main airports of Paris – Roissy-Charles-de-Gaulle and Orly – and sometimes larger regional airports such as Nice, Toulouse, Bordeaux or Marseille. Several budget airlines, including **bmibaby**, **easyJet**, **Flybe**, **Jet2**, and **Ryanair**, also serve some of these airports, as well as many of the country's smaller airports. These airports are mainly linked to the UK, Ireland, Germany, Belgium, the Netherlands and Scandinavia.

Families flying in from the United States can pick from the many direct flights offered by major airlines, such as **American**, **Continental**, **United** and **Delta**. These fly in to Paris (Charles-de-Gaulle), with frequent connections from nearly 20 cities, including New York, San Francisco, Washington DC, Los Angeles and Chicago. In summer, Delta also offers direct flights from New York to Nice.

Those travelling from Canada can get excellent connections from Montreal and Toronto on **Air Canada**, United and Air France.

If the Paris area is not your final destination, look into flights to regional French airports by way of other European hubs – London, Frankfurt, Munich and Amsterdam are the primary ones. This can help save time and money. Also check flights by the Canadian charter, **Air Transat**. These fly regularly from Montreal to Bordeaux, Lyon, Nice, Marseille, Nantes and Toulouse.

There are no direct flights from Australia or New Zealand. However, **Qantas** has many connections with one or more stops, usually in Hong Kong, Dubai, Singapore, Frankfurt or London. Be aware that these usually take close to 24 hours.

Complete information on regional airports and getting from the airport to the nearest town is provided in each regional chapter within this guide.

Arriving by Sea

France is served by several car ferry and catamaran companies sailing from the UK and Ireland, and for families, they can be the most

Below left Arrivals board displaying flight information in Terminal 2 at Charles de Gaulle International Airport, Paris
Below right A Brittany Ferries ferry crossing the Channel between England and France

economical, practical and also a comfortable way of travelling. Ferry terminals and ferries have cafés, snack bars, restaurants and shops; many have video games or play rooms for kids as well.

While most ferries sail during the day, others sail overnight, allowing passengers to rest in their cabins before arriving at their destination.

The most popular cross-Channel ferry route is between Dover and Calais, which takes around 1 hour 15 minutes. **P&O Ferries** and **Seafrance** compete on this route and both have frequent sailings every day. P&O also has an overnight service from Hull to Zeebrugge in Belgium, a short drive from France. **DFDS Seaways'** ferries sail between Dover and Dunkerque, which is a longer crossing than Calais (2 hours) but often cheaper. **Brittany Ferries** offer many options: from Portsmouth to Caen (6 hours or overnight), to Cherbourg on a fast-craft service (3 hours) and to St-Malo (overnight). Ferries also depart from Plymouth to Roscoff (6 hours or overnight); those travelling late in the year can try the mid-November to mid-March ferry services from Plymouth to St-Malo (overnight). Ferries also sail from Poole to Cherbourg (2½ or 4½ hours) and from Cork in Ireland to Roscoff (once a week, 14 hours).

Irish Ferries run overnight from Rosslare in Ireland to Cherbourg and Roscoff, with several sailings each week (more frequently in summer).

The ferries of **LD Lines** sail from Newhaven to Dieppe and from Portsmouth to Le Havre in just a few hours. A service also runs from Gijón in Spain to St-Nazaire.

Condor Ferries sail from Poole to St-Malo (6 hours). They also offer year-round links from Weymouth to St-Malo, via the islands of Guernsey and Jersey. **Corsica Ferries** link Corsica to Italy, travelling from Savona to Bastia (6 hours), Île Rousse (6 hours) and Calvi (6 hours), as well as from Livorno to Bastia (4 hours).

TAKING PRIVATE VEHICLES

All ferries have vehicle-carrying facilities. If you want to really explore the French countryside at your leisure, taking your own car is the best option, and need not be expensive. Fares are now generally per vehicle.

For a fast alternative, check out **EuroTunnel's** rail service, Le Shuttle. Traversing the 52-km (31-mile) long Channel Tunnel, the shuttle allows motorists to drive aboard specially-constructed trains and travel from Folkestone in the UK to Calais in France. The high-vehicle carriages can accommodate camper vans, cars, roof racks with bikes and mini-buses.

The terminals on either end have cash dispensers (bureaux de change), food outlets, shops, baby-changing facilities and toilets. The Folkestone terminal has an outdoor playground and picnic tables. One ticket covers the car and up to nine passengers. The trip takes only 35 minutes; there are four departures an hour in peak season. Book in advance and, if possible, journey in off-peak times to get the most competitive rates.

Arriving by Rail

One of the best ways for families to travel to France from Europe is via train. You get to see more of France before arriving at your destination and kids have a good time.

The high-speed train service, **Eurostar**, links England to France. The journey starts off from London St-Pancras and reaches Paris in just 2 hours and 15 minutes. Some Eurostar trains to Paris stop in Calais and Lille and many run directly to Disneyland Resort Paris, as well as from London to Brussels via Lille. With Eurostar, it is easy to get to any part of France, by changing on to the TGV French high-speed rail network. Trains run frequently and year round, except on Christmas Day. In winter, direct Eurostar "ski trains" run from London to the French Alps.

Below left Signs indicating lanes for cars, coaches, motorbikes and other traffic at the entrance to the Channel Tunnel
Below right A high-speed Eurostar train swishing through the French countryside en route to Paris

HIGH-SPEED LINKS FROM EUROPE

There are several other international rail services with high-speed links to France and its national rail network, **Société Nationale des Chemins de Fer (SNCF)**. This excellent network operates high-speed TGVs (Trains à Grand Vitesse), which connect Paris and other main French cities to Luxembourg, Brussels, Strasbourg, Berlin, Munich, Geneva, Zürich and Basel, among others. Many TGVs run in conjunction with other European services, such as **DB Bahn**, **ICE** and **TGV Lyria**. Trains run from Paris to Brussels, Amsterdam, Cologne and several other German cities on the **Thalys** network. **Elipsos** trains link Barcelona and Madrid to Paris; while **Artesia** trains link Rome, Milan and Florence to Paris and Lyon. To find out more about these services and their routes, check the **TGV Europe**, **Railteam** and **Rail Europe** websites.

The SNCF and TGV services also act as tour operators, offering great discounts on hotels, ski packages, flights and rental cars and bikes.

FARES AND RAIL PASSES

Families travelling with children can take advantage of the many special discounts and deals offered by rail services. Eurostar fares are cheapest if bought up to 120 days in advance. They are easy to book on Eurostar's website; but be aware that the very cheapest fares are non-refundable and not-changeable in case of any change in plans.

SNCF fares are based on periods: blue (Monday 10am to Friday 3pm); white (Monday 5–10am, and Friday and Sunday 3–8pm); and red (Friday night, Saturday, Sunday morning and night and holidays); most discounts are offered only in the blue period. TGV tickets come with a compulsory reservation charge; those travelling in peak hours pay an added rate.

TGV Europe is a good website to check for discounts. Couples get a 25% discount on return tickets on TGVs and other trains as long as their journey starts in a blue period (Découverte à Deux); the same 25% reduction applies to a group of up to four people travelling with a child under 12 (Découverte Enfant Plus), to under 26s (Découverte 12–25) and over 60s (Découverte Senior).

Also look into **InterRail** passes, valid for 3–8 days of unlimited travel within a month; children (ages 4–11) get a 50% discount. These passes are only for European residents. Non-Europeans are eligible for a similar **Eurail** pass. There are many options on offer, as well as several discount deals on travel and hotels. For more details on these services, check the Rail Europe website.

By Car

European visitors coming to France with kids and all the equipment they require may well find it cheaper and easier to drive their own motorhome or car. Motorways (autoroutes) in France are perfectly integrated into the European system. Vehicles can be transported across on ferries and trains as well (see p19). Information on general rules, speed limits, toll fares and petrol can be found on pp22–3.

WHAT TO TAKE

Car insurance is a legal requirement in France; drivers must carry their vehicle's insurance policy, along with the original registration document, a European Accident Statement and a full driving license (drivers not from Canada, the USA, the EU or EEA should bring an international driving license). If you are not the registered owner, carry a letter from the owner giving you permission to drive the car. It is compulsory to carry passports or national ID cards too.

By law, the vehicle must carry within it a red warning triangle and a reflective waistcoat for any person who may step out of the car at the scene of an accident (this has to be kept in the car, not the boot). Snow chains are essential during winter if travelling in the mountains.

Below left The Gare du Nord, one of Paris's several international train stations
Below right Regional maps useful for driving to and around France

CAR HIRE

All major international car-hire firms are present in France. It is generally cheaper to book and pay for the car before arrival and absolutely vital in the summer, when cars are in short supply, especially in Corsica. When buying air tickets to France, look for fly/drive deals. The SNCF also offers train/drive packages, with pick-up points in all major train stations. See the Rail Europe website for details.

To hire a car, drivers have to be at least 21, and have held a full license for over a year. Be prepared to pay supplementary charges for a child seat, Sat-Nav (GPS), snow chains or automatic transmission. **Motorhome Hire France** and **Avis Caraway** hire out motorhomes and RVs.

MAPS AND PLANNING

Even if the car has Sat-Nav, it is a good idea to carry a road atlas or maps for the area being visited. These are available at petrol stations or at any newsstand: **ViaMichelin** is an excellent route planner.

Sunday can be the best day to drive, since large trucks are banned from 10pm on Saturdays and days prior to public holidays, as well as Sundays and public holidays from midnight–10pm year round. Try to avoid the massive traffic congestion around major French holidays.

Drivers wishing to avoid Paris should stick to the outer motorways, rather than trying the confusing routes closer to the city. Check the **Bison Futé** website for traffic forecasts and live information in English.

The Lowdown

Arriving by Air
Air Canada www.aircanada.ca
Air France www.airfrance.com
Air Transat www.airtransat.ca
Alitalia www.alitalia.com
American Airlines www.aa.com
bmibaby www.bmibaby.com
British Airways www.britishairways.com
Continental www.continental.com
Delta www.delta.com
easyJet www.easyjet.com
Flybe www.flybe.com
Iberia www.iberia.com
Jet2 www.jet2.com
KLM www.klm.com
Lufthansa www.lufthansa.com
Qantas www.qantas.com.au
Ryanair www.ryanair.com
United www.united.com

Arriving by Sea
Brittany Ferries www.brittany-ferries.co.uk
Condor Ferries www.condorferries.co.uk
Corsica Ferries www.corsica-ferries.fr
DFDS Seaways www.dfdsseaways.co.uk
LD Lines www.ldlines.co.uk
P&O Ferries www.poferries.eu
Seafrance www.seafrance.com

Arriving by Rail
Artesia www.artesia.eu
DB Bahn & ICE www.bahn.com

Elipsos www.eipsos.com
Eurail www.eurail.com
European Rail www.europeanrail.com
Eurostar www.eurostar.com
EuroTunnel www.eurotunnel.com
Rail Europe www.raileurope.com
Railteam www.railteam.co.uk
SNCF www.sncf.com/en_EN
TGV Europe www.tgv-europe.com
TGV Lyria www.tgv-lyria.com
Thalys www.thalys.com

By Car
Auto Europe www.autoeurope.com
Autoroutes www.autoroutes.fr
Avis www.avis.com
Avis Caraway www.aviscaraway.com
Bison Futé www.bison-fute.equipement.gouv.fr
Budget www.budget.com
Carrentals www.carrentals.co.uk
easyCar www.easycar.com
Europcar www.europcar.com
France Car Hire www.france-car-hire-rental.com
Hertz www.hertz.com
Motorhome Hire France www.motorhome-hire-france.com
National/Citer www.citer.fr
Travel Supermarket www.travelsupermarket.com
TT Car Hire www.ttcar.com/uk
ViaMichelin www.viamichelin.com

Below left A mountain road leading through the Pyrenees, one of France's many scenic routes
Below right A local car-hire station in Corsica

Getting Around France

France's comprehensive and efficient national rail network is great for inter-city travel, and offers convenient connections even to remote corners. Trains are often a better and more economical option than domestic flights, but there is still a good choice of flights linking many cities. Those travelling in their own vehicles will enjoy driving through the country, with plenty of rest areas catering to families along the way. Local public transport varies from superb to sketchy.

Domestic Flights

Many domestic flights run to one of Paris's two main airports – Orly and Roissy-Charles-de-Gaulle. These include the shuttle (navette) flights departing every hour, or even every 15 minutes, from Paris-Orly west to Bordeaux, Marseille, Toulouse and Nice. Direct flights also connect many cities to the nation's 45 airports (listed on the regional airport pages in this guide). Air France and its subsidiaries, such as **Brit Air** or **Air Corsica**, provide most connections, but many regional airlines – **Twin Jet**, **Chalair Aviation** and **Airlinair** – also ply some routes.

By Train

France's high-speed TGVs provide access to most of the nation from their Paris hub. The trains head out in four directions from the capital's stations: the Gare du Nord to Lille and points north, the Gare de l'Est for Alsace and Champagne in the east, the Gare Montparnasse for Brittany, the west and southwestern France, and the Gare de Lyon serves Burgundy and southeast.

In addition to the TGVs, there are many non-TGVs or regular trains that not just run the same routes, but also servicing smaller towns and villages. The fares are cheaper, and unlike the TGVs, reservations are not required, except for overnight trips. Travelling through the night on sleeper trains, with their bunks (couchettes), is an easy way to save on hotel bills. First class has four berths per car and second class has six berths per car.

The national rail network **SNCF** has a very useful online service for booking tickets. Before boarding, ensure all the tickets are validated in a composteur, a yellow machine at the station; or be subject to a fine. SNCF's AutoTrain service allows motorists to transport their cars from Paris to many points, including Lyon, Toulouse, Bordeaux, Biarritz, Brive, Avignon and Nice. Motorail also offer similar services from cities in the Netherlands and Germany. Check the SNCF website for details of all these services; information on discounts, car hires and hotel deals is also available.

By Car

Roads in France are well maintained and usually well signposted. Most motorways (autoroutes) are toll roads (péage), charging an average €.07 per kilometre for cars and more for caravans, motorhomes and RVs. Motorways can be expensive over long distances, but the N (Nationale) and D (Départmentale) roads offer a pleasant, low-traffic alternative.

Below left Trains leaving Gare St-Lazare in Paris, an inter-city station and the oldest in France
Below right Bus negotiating a narrow and winding road in Corsica

The headlights of right-hand drive cars must be adjusted for left-hand driving, or be fitted with deflectors (available at all ports and ferries). Kids aged 10 and below are not allowed to sit in the front seat. A special rear-facing baby seat is allowed as long as the airbag is disabled. The speed limit on motorways is 130 kmph (80 mph), but is reduced to 110 kmph (70 mph) on rainy days, or 50 kmph (30 mph) in case of fog or snow. On N and D roads, the limit is 90 kmph (55 mph), regardless of the road's width. After passing a white sign with a town's name, the limit is 50 kmph (30 mph). Speeding fines start at €68, going up to €4,500 for a failed breathalyzer test. Non-French drivers may have to pay any fine in cash on the spot.

It is always cheaper to buy petrol at supermarkets. Many have 24-hour machines that accept credit cards. Full-service areas, with cafés, petrol stations and toilets are set up every 40 km (25 miles) on the motorways; unmanned rest areas are located every 10–20 km (6–10 miles). In case of a breakdown or accident, walk to the orange SOS phone boxes every 2 km (1 mile). For serious accidents, dial 15 or 18 for an ambulance.

City centres, with their traffic and one-way systems, can be frustrating; follow the handy *Toutes Directions*

signs to get out of any town. Car parks in most towns (many underground) cost €3–5 an hour.

By Bicycle

While the French have great respect for cyclists, bike lanes are a relatively new concept. It is best to avoid the busier roads; check out suggestions and maps on bike-oriented websites.

The SNCF generally carries bicycles for free on regional trains. In some cities, they operate the **Train+Velo** service and arrange for a rental bike on arrival at the station. For extra child seats, use a private company; local tourist offices can supply names.

Buses and Coaches

Rural bus services fan out from the main towns into the countryside, serving most villages. But beware: quality and frequency of the service varies from one area *(département)* to another. Routes usually begin at rail stations. Check local tourist offices for information on the services. **Eurolines** run a number of coaches connecting France's main cities; these are often cheaper than travelling by train. Local buses are mostly for schools or weekly markets, so routes run once or twice a day.

Within Cities and Towns

In the cities, most of the important sites are close enough to visit on foot. For those that are not, taxis are convenient and quite cheap, but ensure that the meter has been turned on. Taxis can be hailed on the street, or found in city centres. Radio taxis can also be booked.

Public transport is often excellent. Most large cities have metros, and some, such as Strasbourg and Bordeaux, have high-tech tramlines. The same tickets usually work for trams, buses and metros. Discount passes differ with each city.

The Lowdown

Domestic Flights
Air Corsica *www.aircorsica.com*
Airlinair *www.airlinair.com*
Brit Air *www.britair.com*
Chalair Aviation *www.chalair.eu*
Twin Jet *www.twinjet.fr*

By Train
SNCF *www.sncf.com/en_EN*

By Bicycle
Bikely *www.bikely.com*
Bikemap *www.bikemap.net*
Train+Velo *www.velo.sncf.com*

By Bus
Eurolines *www.eurolines.com*

Below left Cycling along the picturesque banks of Lac d'Annecy, in the Alps
Below right Taxis queuing up outside the Gare du Nord, Paris

Practical Information

With a little bit of planning, a family trip to France can be a very comfortable experience. Make sure passports and insurance policies are up-to-date, and photocopy them. Consider the best options for carrying and changing money; travel currency cards are a good bet. While the country is mostly safe, apply the usual precautions. Health and emergency services are excellent, and tourist offices in every town provide comprehensive information.

Passports and Visas

There are no visa restrictions for EU nationals visiting France, and there are no limits on the length of the trip either, but passports or national ID cards still have to be carried. Those with Canadian, US, Australian and New Zealand citizenship also do not need visas if they plan to stay for less than three months; their passports must be valid till three months after the end of their trip. A visa will be required for stays longer than three months. Visitors from other countries need a tourist visa, and can apply for it at their local French consulate.

Insurance

It is absolutely essential to get travel insurance, and especially when travelling with family. A good one will top up medical expenses, and insure against cancellations or lost property. Before purchasing a policy, however, make sure you are not already covered by your bank account or credit card.

European citizens are eligible for the same healthcare as the French if they possess a **European Health Insurance Card (EHIC)**. This covers 70 per cent of the costs of visits to doctors and dentists, 80 per cent of hospital costs, and from 15 to 100 per cent of prescription drug costs. Although treatment fees have to be paid for at the time, they can be reclaimed later from the local Caisse Primaire d'Assurance Maladie (CPAM) office. A refund confirmation will be sent to your home address. EHIC cards can easily be obtained online; every member of the family should have their own.

People from other countries must check their insurance policies to see if they are properly covered.

Health

There is a hospital in every major town and city. Head to the *urgences* in the nearest hospital if faced with an emergency; call **SAMU** (Service d'Aide Médicale Urgence) for an ambulance, or **Sapeurs Pompiers** (the fire brigade), who are generally faster, and trained in first aid. This is especially relevant in rural areas, as the fire station is usually closer than the nearest hospital. Most doctors speak at least a little English.

Pharmacies can be recognized by the green neon crosses outside their windows. They are open Monday to Saturday, from 8:30am–7:30pm, and often on Sunday mornings as well. Many close for lunch, although in shopping centres and large towns, they stay open all day. At least one area pharmacy always remains open when others close; check for details of the nearest in pharmacy windows

Below left *At the beach next to Nausicaá in Boulogne-sur-Mer on a hot summer day, a great place for outdoor fun*
Below right *The distinctive green neon sign of a pharmacy*

or call 32 37. While no vaccinations are needed to enter France, bring any prescriptions and medications required by family members.

Summer can be very hot, so carry essentials such as hats, water, and sunblock. In July and August, harvest mites (aoûtats) can be a real nuisance in rural areas. If bitten, wash the area with soap and warm water; ask at the pharmacy for Aspivenin, Ascabiol or Tiq'Aouta to relieve the itch. For other insect bites and stings, apply mosquito cream (crème apaisante après-moustiques). When walking in forests, beware of ticks; on finding one, use fine-tipped tweezers to pull it out gently, without rotating it. Grip the head and not the body.

Babysitting

Except in expensive hotels, some resorts and camp sites aimed at families, babysitting services (garde enfant) can be hard to find in France, especially if you need an English-speaking sitter at a short notice. Contact your hotel or the tourist office, in advance, to arrange for one.

Personal Safety

France is a safe country for visitors, but it is always advisable to follow the same precautions as you would at home – be careful when carrying valuables such as phones, cameras, and wallets; and avoid isolated areas and major city suburban areas after dark.

Victims of a crime should report it at the nearest police station (gendarmerie). Jot down the numbers of credit cards, and keep photocopies of all passports in case they are lost and stolen. Misplaced or lost property may turn up at the local town hall (mairie); check there first. French law requires adults to carry an ID at all times. Police are allowed to stop anyone without any specific reason and ask to see it.

In an emergency, make sure you can give an address before calling the police. You will have to make a statement called a procès verbal. Do take a certified copy of this for insurance purposes. For what to do in case of a car accident see p23.

Money

Like many European nations, France also uses the euro (€); each euro is divided into 100 centimes or cents.

Most banks are open Monday to Friday or Tuesday to Saturday 8:30am–noon and 1:30–4:30pm. Many will not exchange bank notes, so obtain cash from an ATM, or exchange money at a bureau de change in Paris or another major city. The only other option may be to try the exchange at the central post office of a major city. Visitors are allowed to bring up to €10,000 in cash into France.

ATMs are widespread in airports, train stations, cities, nearly all towns and supermarkets. **MasterCard** and **Visa** are the most widely accepted cards; **American Express** and **Diners Club** can incur extra charges. French credit and debit cards are smart cards with a microchip (puce), which requires that you enter a PIN for each transaction. Cards that do not have a chip can be used in French ATMs, and in hotels, shops and other businesses where someone can swipe the magnetic strip. However, they cannot be used at automated petrol stations, autoroute toll booths and train-station ticket machines. An alternative is to have a travel currency card (also known as a cash passport), which you charge up in advance with a set amount of currency from your bank account at home. It can then be used at ATMs, hotels and shops like an ordinary card. Many international companies sell currency cards.

Be sure to report lost or stolen cards immediately, so that they can be blocked by the bank. Inform the police as well. Bring at least two cards and keep one in a safe place.

Below left Police on bicycles at a pony-riding event for children in a French park
Below right Sign of the Banque de France, France's central bank

Communication

Mobile phone coverage improves every year, but there is a possibility of hitting a black spot in very rural areas, the mountains or in gorges. European phones work normally in France; US tri-band cellphones with GSM will also work. Since roaming charges can be high, check the rates with your own service provider before using the phone. If you have a smart phone, make sure automatic data roaming is turned off, so that you only connect to the Internet when you want to. Be sure to keep an eye on older kids with their own phones! If expecting to make frequent calls while visiting France, it is worthwhile carrying an unlocked phone. It can then accept a SIM card from one of the country's three main providers – Orange, Bouygues or SFR. Any of these cards can easily be purchased online before leaving for France; a French mobile number, starting with 06, will be provided for use. Another option is to pick up a pre-paid SIM card on arrival.

As most French people now have mobiles, public telephones are not very common. However, they can still be found at airports and in train stations. Most accept phonecards (*télécartes*), available at newsstands, tobacconists (*tabacs*) and the post office; many also take credit cards.

It is getting increasingly rare to find a telephone booth that accepts coins. A push button on the phones offers instructions in English. Internet access is widely available, mainly in cafés in larger towns; most offer free Wi-Fi. Many hotels and B&Bs provide free Wi-Fi access too; most cottage rentals (*gîtes*), on the other hand, still do not provide any. Camp sites may have a Wi-Fi zone or computer access that guests can use near the reception. Using a video call service such as Skype is, by far, the cheapest way to phone home.

There is a wide variety of British and international English-language newspapers and magazines on offer at newsstands; they may be a day late in some of the more remote districts. Many hotels and *gîtes* are equipped with satellite TV that will pick up CNN, EuroNews, and the BBC. Kids may find it amusing to watch their favourite cartoons dubbed in French.

Opening Hours

Generally, shops in France are open from 9am–7pm, closing briefly for two to three hours for lunch. In big cities, however, shops and many supermarkets stay open without a break. In many parts of the country, shops are open on Sunday mornings, but are usually shut on Monday. The timings for major museums and sights may vary, and should be checked before visiting. They are mostly open from 9am–5pm, often during lunch too, and stay open late one evening in a week as well. Their closing days are usually Monday or Tuesday and on public holidays.

Visitor Information

Every city, town and most villages have either an Office de Tourisme or a Syndicat d'Initiative that offers local information for visitors. Most such offices have websites as well. The French government's official tourist office website, **FranceGuide**, is in English, and is another good place to get information.

Disabled Facilities

Each year, France improves wheelchair access to holiday areas, including beaches and ski slopes. Sites such as historical châteaux and medieval villages, however, usually have limited accessibility. Most modern hotels and B&Bs have at least one room that is especially equipped for wheelchair users. Restaurants are usually on the ground floor and easily accessible, and nearly all have disabled toilets (although cafés rarely do).

Below left *Tourist office with a variety of travel information on display*
Below right *A bright yellow French post box*

Public Conveniences

There are pay toilets in automatic cubicles, in many town squares. Car parks and markets have public toilets too, but they may not be very clean. Airports, shopping malls, large train stations and *autoroute* rest areas usually have baby changing tables.

Time

France is an hour ahead of Greenwich Mean Time (GMT) as it uses Central European Time (CET). It goes on daylight saving time from the last Sunday in March to the last Sunday in October. Timings are usually given according to a 24-hour clock.

Electricity

French electricity is run on 220 volts, so a transformer may be needed for non-European electrical equipment. Also, since the plugs have two round prongs, an adaptor will be required.

What to Pack

Apart from prescription medicines, French shops will have everything visitors may have forgotten to pack. Baby monitors are handy for young ones; easy-to-carry water bottles, baby wipes and basic medical and sewing kits are essential too.

Etiquette and Attitudes

The French are very polite, and it is customary, especially in rural areas, to greet everyone in a shop, café, or even public transport with a pleasant "Bonjour Messieurs/Mesdames" on entering the premises, and wishing goodbye *(au revoir)* when leaving. Always remember, and teach kids, to say thank you *(merci)*. Be sure to shake hands when introduced to someone; women and children can offer air kisses *(les bises)*.

The French are very fond of kids and greet them warmly, but expect them to be both well behaved and respectful. Since they do not put up with much nonsense or bad manners from their own offspring, they rather frown on parents who do.

The Lowdown

Emergency Numbers
All Services 112
Police 17
SAMU (ambulance) 15
Sapeurs Pompiers (fire brigade) 18

Embassies
Australian Embassy 01 40 59 33 00; *www.france.embassy.gov.au/pari/home.html*
Australian Consular Emergency Service 00 61 2 6261 3305
British Embassy 01 44 51 31 00; *www.ukinfrance.fco.gov.uk*
UK Citizens 24-hour Consular Assistance 00 44 20 70 08 1500
Irish Embassy 01 44 17 67 00; *www.embassyofireland.fr*
New Zealand Embassy 01 45 01 43 43; *www.nzembassy.com/france*
US Embassy 01 43 12 22 22; *www.france.usembassy.gov*
American Citizens Services Crisis Management 00 1 202 501 4444

Health Insurance
EHIC *www.ehic.org.uk*

Currency Cards
Travdex *www.travdex.com*
Travel Currency Cards *www.cashpassport.com*

Lost or Stolen Cards
American Express 00 1 905 474 0870
Diner's Club 08 10 31 41 59
MasterCard 08 00 90 13 87
VISA 08 00 90 11 79

Dialling Codes
To call a French number from abroad, omit the first 0. The prefix when calling from the UK is 00 33; from the US 011 33; from Australia, Ireland and New Zealand 00 11 33

To call out of France, dial 00 and then the country code: UK 44; Canada and US 1; Australia 61; Ireland 353; New Zealand 64

Directory Inquiries in France 118 218 or *www.pagesjaunes.fr*

Visitor Information
FranceGuide *www.franceguide.com*

Below left Shoppers at the swanky Carrousel du Louvre, an underground shopping mall in Paris
Below right Wheelchair accessibility on La Vapeur du Trieux steam train, Brittany

Where to Stay

From luxury villas with private pools to quaint bed and breakfasts, and from comfortable self-contained homes to cheap and cheerful camp sites, France offers a variety of inviting accommodation for families, suited to all budgets. Plan ahead as far as possible, especially if travelling during July and August, when popular hotels and resorts fill up fast. Early birds will not only have the most choice, but can often get great deals on rooms, and travel fares.

Hotels

French hotels are rated from one to five stars, based on the amenities and facilities being offered – more stars equal higher rates. Since nearly all hotels now have websites, it is a good idea to do some research and choose according to personal needs.

French hotels increasingly offer rooms designed for an entire family. Some have inter-connecting rooms, bunk beds, or a mezzanine, while others even have three or four beds in a room. Infant cots are available as well, often for a small fee; enquire when booking. Among the country's many chain hotels, one of the most family-friendly is **All Seasons**; they offer great family deals too. **Logis Hotels**, a network of family-run inns in villages and towns across France, are comfortable and usually of a reliable standard. Most also have decent restaurants.

A family of four can expect to spend about €70–150 per day if staying in a one- to three-star hotel; a four- or five-star hotel will easily cost around €200 and more. Breakfast is usually extra and can be slightly expensive, although kids may get a discount. However, some hotels provide *gîte d'étape* deals for travelling families, which include a set dinner and breakfast. Many hotel-booking websites offer discounts too, so it is worth checking them out as well.

Bed and Breakfast

Known as *chambres d'hôtes* in France, bed and breakfasts (B&Bs) are often the most atmospheric places to stay. Most are set in town houses, châteaux, or farms; not all are suitable for families as some are home to fragile antiques or designer furnishings. That said, many, such as the B&Bs on farms, have a suite or cottage rental (*gîte*) furnished with young children in mind. A family of four will need to budget between €70–150 per day for a stay.

One of the best features of a B&B is their owners. Most of them are great sources of local knowledge; some will pick up guests at train stations and airports and prepare home-cooked meals (*table d'hôtes*) on request, with special dishes for kids. The national self-catering networks, **Gîtes de France** and **Clévacances** provide detailed lists of B&Bs around the country.

Self-Catering

Available in many guises, from rural farmhouses to apartment hotels to villas, self-catering *gîtes* can be an economical and convenient option when travelling with kids. Among

Below left The turreted Château de la Motte, a B&B near Poitiers *Below centre* Family at a camp site on L'Île Rousse, Corsica
Below right Family room with a separate child's bed in Hôtel de l'Océan, Biarritz

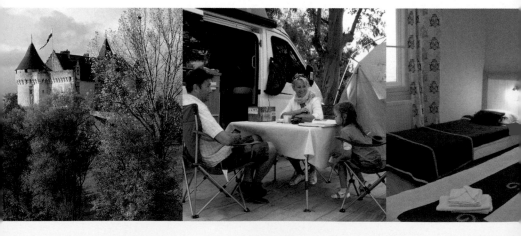

their advantages are a kitchen and, usually, laundry facilities. Many places also come with highchairs, toys, games and kids' DVDs. Check if linen is included, and read the fine print on deposits for breakages.

Most ski packages in France offer self-catering apartments and chalets suitable for families. Early-bird deals can include lift passes and discounts. A luxury villa can be expensive, but often have several rooms, allowing two or three families to share. The downside of self-catering homes is that many require at least a week's stay. Thousands of units are listed on Gîtes de France and Clévacances.

Holiday Villages

Holiday villages (villages vacances or résidences clubs) combine some of the best features of hotels, gîtes and camp sites. These resorts offer self-catering houses or apartments, along with on-site restaurants and cafés. The rooms are cleaned and linen provided; there are pools, kids' clubs and crèches as well.

Camping

One of the most popular ways of visiting France, camping is also the most affordable. There are thousands of sites to choose from, ranging from a basic municipal site to five-star luxury parks. Many rent out tents (already erected), chalets, bungalows, mobile homes or even tree houses.

Families looking for a low-cost option can carry a tent, a camping-gas burner, sleeping bags, and air mattresses, and stay in municipal or local camp grounds, or on farms. At the higher end are four- or five-star camp sites. With facilities that include air-conditioned houses with kitchens, evening entertainment and water parks, these are self-contained resorts in themselves. Holiday packages for such sites often offer discounts on flights and Channel crossings.

The **Fédération Française de Camping et de Caravaning (FFCC)** publishes the names of their 11,000 members, certified to meet certain standards, on their website. It may be worth it to get an international camping card (carnet); some camp sites offer a discount of up to 20% for cardholders. Only members of a national camping association can purchase the card. Those with their own tent or motor home should budget about €30–40 a night for a pitch and electricity. The most basic self-catering chalet for four starts at about €400 a week in the summer. Be aware that camp sites can be noisy at night.

House Swapping

This may be a good option for an affordable holiday. Online agencies charge a small fee to list your house. All offer the chance to browse available listings in France to see what is on offer before paying.

The Lowdown

Hotels
All Seasons www.all-seasons-hotels.com
Logis Hotels www.logishotels.com

Bed and Breakfast
Clévacances www.clevacances.com
Gîtes de France www.gites-de-france.com

Self-Catering
French Connections www.french connections.co.uk
Home Away Holiday Rentals www.holiday-rentals.co.uk
Pure France www.purefrance.com

Apartment Hotels
Appart City www.appartcity.com
Citadines www.citadines.com

Holiday Villages
M Vacances www.mvacances.com
Odalys www.odalys-vacances.com

Camping
FFCC www.ffcc.fr, listings on www.campingfrance.com

House Swapping
HomeExchange www.home exchange.com

Below Palm trees and pines surrounding a swimming pool at an upmarket self-catering villa in St-Tropez
Below right Entrance to one of the many Citadines apartment hotels in Paris

Where to Eat

Renowned internationally, and justly so, French cuisine offers a flavourful experience for every taste. Families travelling with children can choose from a huge range of family-friendly places, from gourmet restaurants to quick and easy snack bars, cheerful bistros or pleasant roadside cafés. Even the fussiest kids will enjoy the many sweet delights on offer. Remember to try the classic specialities from each region; ask locally for suggestions.

Restaurant Basics

The French keep fairly strict dining hours: lunch is served from noon–1:30pm and dinner from around 7:30–9pm. In some cases, especially in the countryside, those arriving after 1pm may not be served. Once you have sat down and ordered, you can eat unhurriedly and stay as long as you like, but you need to plan on arriving at a restaurant within these times. It is a good idea to reserve a table, especially at more popular or upmarket places, and definitely at weekends. Most restaurants close at least one day a week, and finding a place to eat on a Sunday night or Monday can be difficult.

In French restaurants, the full menu is called *carte*, which is always expensive, whereas a *menu* is a set, fixed-price lunch or dinner with a more limited choice of two, three or four courses; a *formule* is similar, but usually suggests a cheaper, simpler menu that is often available only for weekday lunches. Simpler restaurants also often have a dish of the day (*plat du jour*) chalked up on a blackboard (*ardoise*) for lunch. Many simpler restaurants and brasseries also offer mixed salads (*salades composées*).

Most French restaurants have an excellent wine list (*carte des vins*). A bottle of water can also be ordered with the meal: *gazeuse* is sparkling, and *plat* is flat. Asking for tap water (*carafe d'eau*) is also acceptable; it is safe and served free. Service and tax are included in the bill (*l'addition*), but if the service has been good, it is customary to leave a little extra tip.

Regional Specialities

One of the great joys of travelling in France is discovering the dishes and cuisine special to each region. Kids are sure to enjoy the journey too, especially in the northeast, which is the land of custard tarts (*tarte à gros bords*) and waffles. Alsace and Lorraine is famous for its *choucroute garni* (sauerkraut with sausage) and *pain d'épices* (gingerbread). In the west, try the pâtés and *tarte tatins* (apple pies) of the Loire Valley, or the *galettes* (savoury buckwheat pancakes) and shellfish in Brittany.

In Lyon, be sure to have its potato and cheese-based dishes *tartiflette* and *raclette*; while in Burgundy, try the *boeuf bourguignon* (beef stew). A classic dish in the Massif Central is *aligot* – melted Tomme cheese with mashed potatoes. In the southwest, expect to find *cassoulet* (a stew of beans and pork or duck) and plenty of succulent melons and fruit. The south produces olive oil, fresh herbs and vegetables that are so essential to its cooking, along with plenty of

Below left *Ten tiers of tempting macaroons in a pâtisserie window*
Below centre *Street cafés on the Cours Saleya, one of Nice's most popular attractions*

lamb and fish. It is also the land of good pasta dishes – Nice is famous for its ravioli.

Eating out with Kids

Most restaurants in France welcome children, but few will have highchairs, so consider taking a portable one for very young kids. French kids are well behaved and are treated as adults in restaurants; running about is not appreciated. Make sure kids do not disturb the other patrons.

An economical children's menu (menu enfant) – two or three courses in kid-sized portions, often specified for "under 10s" – is often on offer. Classic entries include steak haché (burger without the bun), chicken or ham with frites (chips) or spaghetti bolognese and ice cream. Or ask for a portion enfant, a scaled-down version of food on the regular menu. Since French dinner hours may be too late for young kids, brasseries that serve meals all day are always a good bet for an earlier meal. In summer, evening picnics are an option.

Cafés, bistros or restaurants with outdoor seating tend to be ideal for families, offering some distractions for squirmy children. The menus are always posted outside, so check that there is something for everyone in the family before sitting. There is no dearth of fast-food chains such as McDonalds, Buffalo Grill and the French hamburger outlet Quick, while bakeries, sandwicheries and kebab stands offer a range of kid-friendly food (pizza slices, pies and quiches). Present in all towns, cafés offer hot chocolate, fruit juices (jus de fruit) and sirops (fruit-flavoured syrups mixed with water) to choose from.

Shopping for Food

French markets (marchés) are a feast for the senses and fun to visit. Cities have at least one covered market (halle); most are open daily except on Mondays. Towns and villages will have one or more weekly outdoor market days and often farmers' markets selling organic produce (bio). See also page 32.

Supermarkets (supermarchés or hypermarchés) sell all types of foods and drinks, but the French treasure their traditional shops too, especially bakeries (boulangeries), which bake breads and croissants, and pastry shops (pâtisseries). Meats can be bought from a butcher shop (boucherie). Supermarkets usually also have a type of delicatessen (traiteur) that sells prepared meat and seafood dishes, as well as salads. Smaller villages have a family-run grocer (épicerie) or a convenience store, such as Vidal, Proxi or Casino.

Below left Farm-fresh strawberries (fraises) for sale at a local market stall
Below right Using long-stemmed forks to dip bread into cheese fondue

Shopping in France

Shopping in France will tantalize the senses. From chocolates to perfumes, speciality foods and wines to fashionable clothing, "Made in France" signifies quality. Leisurely shopping can be a challenge with children, but even they will enjoy exploring the fresh and varied goods on offer at the colourful outdoor markets. Check out the flea markets for a special memento that is distinctly French.

Opening Hours

The big chain stores usually remain open all day, but most other shops in France, especially those outside big cities, still operate traditionally, which means a break for lunch. Shops open sometime between 8–10am, close at noon or 12:30pm for lunch; they reopen around 2–3pm until 6–7pm; (some later in summer). Most shops, except supermarkets, are closed on Mondays. Most supermarkets and other shops do open on Sunday morning, however.

Food and Wine

Almost everything is available in the supermarchés and hypermarchés such as Carrefour, Leclerc, Auchan, Intermarché and others. Some of the world's best breads and pastries can easily be bought from the local boulangerie or pâtisserie; select from a wide range of cheese at the local fromagerie. Chocolate lovers should try out the many artisan chocolatiers who make their own creations. Speciality shops provide gift baskets or packaging for those who want to carry food items home. Besides these, look out for farms selling fresh produce directly – olive oil in Provence, pâtés and foie gras in southwest France.

But the best source for food and a must-try experience is the weekly market, whether it is on a city street or in a central village square. Most big towns have a permanent covered market halle, which is usually open six days a week. An outdoor market opens around it one or more days a week and is regarded as a social event. Look out for special farmers' markets in the summer; these are often held on Sunday mornings. Wine touring is very popular among those who visit France's many wine regions. Pick up bottles at rates often lower than in the shops. At smaller vineyards, guests are welcome to sample a glass and have a chat, but châteaux in Bordeaux and Burgundy mostly require prior notice for a visit.

Other Markets

Once a month or so, a local market may expand into a big affair, selling clothes, pots and pans, cowbells or even tractors. Permanent speciality markets, such as bird and flower markets, can be found on the Île de la Cité in Paris. Christmas markets in Strasbourg and Alsace continue an old tradition, with cakes, chocolates, Christmas decorations and a variety of other gifts on offer.

Find an odd memorable souvenir at an antique market or at a flea market (marché au puces). Probably

Below left Selection of fruit liquers displayed for sale **Below centre** The famous Galeries Lafayette department store in Paris **Below right** Colourful toys and souvenirs on a market street in Conques the best permanent flea market is the **Marché au Puces de St Ouen** on the edge of Paris. Porte de Vanves and Porte de Montreuil, two other flea markets in Paris, are worth a visit too.

Look for the posters announcing *vide greniers* (a kind of attic sale). These can be great fun for kids; the most astonishing things can come out of an old French attic, including an amazing array of toys.

Clothes and Accessories

The French love their department stores, and in Paris, they have some of the world's most famous: Le Bon Marché is the oldest and currently the most fashionable. Printemps and Galeries Lafayette have branches all around France.

The capital city's fashion enclaves include the famous designer shops of Rue du Faubourg St-Honoré and Avenue Montaigne. Many trendy places are appearing in the stylish Marais as well. In provincial towns, the best shopping is in the small and independent boutiques, especially and expensively on the Côte d'Azur, in Cannes and St-Tropez. Everyday items can be purchased at the many national chains and supermarkets such as Auchan, Monoprix, Géant Casino and Carrefour. For these, look out for signs to a *Centre Commercial*.

Factory Outlets

There are several factory outlets (*magasins d'usines*) in France that often specialize in discounts on a specific company's items: Le Creuset pots at Fresnoy-le-Grand, silks at the Atelier de Soie in Lyon, Mephisto shoes in Sarrebourg or even Royal Limoges china in Limoges.

The outlet centres (*centres de marques*) feature discount boutiques of designer brands, mostly clothing, shoes, sportswear and houseware, under one roof. Most of these outlets are in the suburbs of Paris – La Vallée Village, close to Disneyland Resort, is popular. Troyes, however, is the main centre in France, with three big design outlets – **McArthur Glen**, **Marques Avenue** and **Marques City**.

Books, Music, Art and Surprises

It is fairly easy to find at least a small selection of books (these are mostly bestsellers) in English in bookstores or newsstands. The **FNAC** chain has branches in many cities and is ideal for browsing and picking up books, music and electronics.

Artists, woodcarvers, glassmakers, potters and craftsmen of all kinds congregate in summer, selling their creations from their studios or at local markets. Check online national directories and at the tourist offices for details.

Sales Tax and Refunds

Non-European Union residents can claim back 12 per cent of the 19.6 per cent TVA (sales tax) as long as they spend over €175 in a single day in a single participating shop; there will be a "Tax Free" sign in the window. Ask for a tax refund cheque (*bordereau de détaxe*) to present at customs when leaving the EU.

The Lowdown

Markets
Marché au Puces de St Ouen
marchesauxpuces.fr

Factory Outlets
Marques Avenue www.marques
avenue.com
Marques City www.marquescity.com
McArthur Glen www.mcarthurglen.fr

National Directories
French antiques districts www.
curiositel.tm.fr/marches-villages-
antiquaires-fr
Shopping centres www.centres-
commerciaux.com
Wines and farm products www.
marchesdepays.fr

Books and Music
FNAC www.fnac.com

Below left *Glittery window displays at a Louis Vuitton store in Paris*
Below right *Stalls selling a variety of knick-knacks at the annual Braderie de Lille, Europe's biggest flea market*

Entertainment in France

France has plenty to see and do, and goes out of its way to entertain both visitors and locals. Besides the many festivals, there are high-energy music and dance concerts and impressive theatrical shows. Spectacular sound and light productions set in châteaux transcend language difficulties and have huge family appeal, as do the lively puppet shows. There is no dearth of sporting events and activities either. Visit the local tourist office to see what's on.

Music and Dance

From Easter to September, the calendar is packed with outdoor music and dance events, including the nationwide street music festival, **Fête de la Musique** in June. Folk festivals are popular with kids: notably the lively song and dance concerts at the **Festival Interceltique** in Lorient (see p15) and Bayonne's **Basque Folklore Festival**. The **Festival International de Folklore d'Issoire**, featuring dancers and musicians from around the world, take place in Issoire, near Puy-le-Dome, and Lourdes.

Theatre and Film

Although language may prove a barrier to theatrical productions in France, even kids are sure to enjoy the street performances during the **Festival d'Avignon** (see p342).

Look out for summer spectacles such as **A La Cour du Roy François**, a Renaissance-era inspired show at the fine Château d'Amboise (see p186); **Cinéscénie**, the torch-lit historical pageant at Grand Parc Puy du Fou (see p177); and **Promenade Nocturnes**, a charming sound and light show at the Château de Chenonceau (see p183).

Films are highly appreciated in France. Family films are often shown during the school holidays. It is rare to find movies in English or in another foreign language outside the bigger cities; look out for films designated VO (Version Originale).

Circuses

France has a proud circus tradition, and at least once or twice a year, little travelling circuses visit villages. For larger events, head to Monaco (see p360) in January or February for the energetic **Festival International du Cirque de Monte-Carlo**; or witness a colourful affair at the **Festival International du Cirque de Bayeux** in March. Kids will love the clowns and the incredible acrobatics at the **Cirque d'Hiver Bouglione's** winter performances in Paris.

Puppet Shows

The classic and much-loved French marionette, Guignol, is brought to life at the **Théâtre de la Maison de Guignol** in Lyon (see p221) in the form of exceptional performances by the Compagnie des Zonzons. Regular marionette performances also take place in Paris at many venues on Wednesday, Saturday and Sunday afternoons; check local listings or the tourist office for details. If visiting Charleville-Mézières

Below left Illuminations at the Château de Versailles during the annual Fête de la Musique
Below right Children watching a puppet show in the Jardins des Champs-Élysées, Paris

(see p65) in September, be sure to check out the Institut International de la Marionette for their international puppet event, the **Festival Mondial des Théâtres de Marionnettes**.

Sports

In the south and west, especially, rugby occupies many weekends from autumn to spring, from inter-village matches to league and international competitions. Football, though, is the most popular sport across France; find out about upcoming matches on the **Ligue 1** website, and book tickets through **Fnacspectacles**. Known as **Roland Garros** in France, the French Open tennis tournament (see p17) in Paris is a huge event in May–June. The **Fédération Française du Surf** organizes many surfing events around the French coasts.

Village Fêtes

These take place throughout the summer and can be a lot of fun for the whole family, especially children. In small villages, the annual fête usually lasts two or three days; in larger ones, festivities can go on for an entire week. There are often rides, games, food stands and some competitions – races or *pétanque* matches. There will also be at least

one communal dinner, so remember to book in advance for it. The meal is followed by live music – anything from accordions to rock 'n' roll – and dancing and a fireworks display.

Family Activity Holidays

There are many ways to see France a bit differently when travelling as a family. **Roulottes de Campagne** lists firms, all over the country, that offer leisurely vacations in horse-pulled wooden caravans or *roulottes*. Check **Anes et Randonnées** for the names of nearly 80 farms that provide short or week-long treks on donkeys through scenic routes. **Un Lit au Pré** provides options for authentic farm holidays, a short distance from Paris; **Ski Famille** specializes in arranging family skiing holidays; or tour the waterways of France on barges and houseboats with **Le Boat**.

Travel and Learn French allows families to combine French lessons with their holiday in Fréjus (see p357) on the Côte d'Azur. Fun-filled weeks of family adventures are on offer by **Activities Abroad**; enjoy white-water rafting and kayaking in the Ardèche (see pp232–3) in the Alps. Details of sports that are available on many of France's rivers are given in the regional chapters. Learn to sail at the Landes with **Rockley Watersports**.

The Lowdown

Music and Dance
Basque Folklore Festival
www.fetes.bayonne.fr
Festival International de Folklore
d'Issoire www.festival-issoire.fr

Circuses
Cirque d'Hiver Bouglione
www.cirquedhiver.com
Festival International du Cirque de
Bayeux www.festivalcirquebayeux.fr

Puppet Shows
Festival Mondial des Théâtres
de Marionnettes www.festival-
marionnette.com
Puppet Shows in Paris www.paris
paris.com/fr/enfant/marionnettes.html

Sports
Fédération Française Surf
www.surfingfrance.com
Fnacspectacles
www.fnacspectacles.com
French Football League
www.ligue1.com

Family Activity Holidays
Activities Abroad www.activities
abroad.com
Anes et Randonnées www.ane-et
rando.com
Le Boat www.leboat.com
Rockley Watersports www.rockley
watersports.com
Roulottes de Campagne www.
roulottes-de-campagne.com
Ski Famille www.skifamille.com
Travel and Learn French www.travel
andlearnfrench.com
Un Lit au Pré www.unlitaupre.fr

Below left Street performers in front of the Palais des Papes during the Festival d'Avignon
Below right Kayaking on the Ardèche near the Pont d'Arc, Gorges de l'Ardèche

The History of France

The one theme that marks France's past is the nation's resilience – a tireless ability to bounce back from disasters. From being the most powerful country in Europe to fighting for survival and then rebuilding to attain its former glory, France has seen her fair share of ups and downs. But along with the wars and the revolutions also emerged ideals of chivalry, Gothic cathedrals, the metric system, the *Declaration of the Rights of Man*, pasteurization and modern art.

Prehistory to 121 BC

Humans have occupied France since around 2 million BC. Cro-Magnon Man is credited with the creation of great art at Lascaux (*see pp262–3*) and other Palaeolithic-era painted caves in southwest France. By 5000 BC, France was at the centre of the Neolithic civilization; Brittany saw the erection of the famous stones of Carnac (*see pp166–7*).

The onset of the Bronze and Iron Ages around 1,500 BC brought in the Celts, or Gauls, who spread across the country in different tribes.

Roman Gaul

In 121 BC, the Romans took Marseilles, a Greek maritime colony, and pushed inland from there. Their

Stone Age cave art depicting a woolly mammoth and horse, Lascaux

new province is called Provence even today. The rest of Gaul fell to Julius Caesar, in a brilliantly-led six-year campaign (58–51 BC). Under the Romans, new cities, including Lugdunum (Lyon) and Lutetia (Paris), emerged, and imposing temples, forums and amphitheatres were built.

Christianity arrived in Gaul in the 3rd century. Under the Emperor Constantine, in 313, it became the principal religion of the Empire. At the same time, the Roman Empire was beginning its decline; its armies could no longer protect Gaul from barbarian invasions.

The Dark Ages

In 406, Germanic tribes crossed the Rhine frontier; the Visigoths settled in Tolosa (Toulouse) and the Burgundians founded Burgundy. The Franks set up base in the Seine river valley, now the Île de France. Politics and power became local affairs, although the Franks proved to be the most powerful: Clovis (482–511) conquered much of Gaul, Charles Martel stopped the Arab

The Gaulish chieftain Vercingetorix's surrender to Julius Ceasar

invasion in 732, and Charlemagne (768–814) seized most of Western Europe and was crowned Holy Roman Emperor by the pope. By 843, the empire was divided between Charlemagne's grandsons. A period of invasions followed, notably from the powerful Vikings, who founded a state on the Channel – Normandy.

Medieval France

At the turn of the millennium, the first indications of an economic and cultural explosion could already be seen in Europe, with the Frankish

Timeline

Cave paintings at Lascaux		Germanic tribes overrun the Rhine frontier		Charlemagne is crowned Holy Roman Emperor		First Crusade declared at Clermont-Ferrand
15,000 BC	**52 BC**	**AD 406**	**496**	**800**	**987**	**1095**
	Caesar defeats the Gauls at Alesia in a brilliant campaign		Clovis, king of the Franks, converts to Christianity		Hugh Capet founds the Capetian dynasty, which will reign until 1328	

Kingdom at its heart. Hugh Capet's dynasty, established in 987, saw his descendants increase their royal domain bit by bit. In 1095, Pope Urban II declared the first of many crusades to the Holy Land, in all of which France played a leading role. In the 12th and 13th centuries, the Franks' capital, Paris, emerged as Europe's art and intellectual centre. Gothic architecture began to take the shape of grand cathedrals.

Meanwhile, England's conquest by the Duke of Normandy in 1066 tied the two nations in war for years. In 1152, Henry II of Normandy wed Eleanor of Aquitaine and gained a mighty French duchy. The ensuing war between the kings of France and Henry II ended 60 years later, with victory for the French king, Philip II Augustus, who doubled the size of his realm.

The kingdom of France, however, signified only the north, the duchies of the south differing politically and culturally. But in 1209, the pope and Philip II Augustus led the Albigensian Crusade against the south, using the growing heresy of the Cathars there as a pretext, and absorbed the lands of the south into France's realm.

End of the Middle Ages

By the 14th century, France was the most powerful country in Europe, but turmoil was about to strike. Edward III, king of England, laid claim to the French throne in 1337, and invaded in force, signalling the start of the Hundred Years' War.

In 1347, France was devastated by the Black Death; millions died. Yet, the war continued. After victory at Agincourt in 1415, the English took Paris; they felt they had won. But the arrival of Joan of Arc in 1429 inspired the French to rise up. By 1453, they had recaptured all the English possessions, except Calais. France's recovery was quick, and by the 1490s, they were at war again, this time in Italy. It was during this time that the artistic influence of the Italian Renaissance spread to the country. But more troubles were on the way. The Protestant Reformation divided the French, as many became Huguenots, or converts to the reformed faith of John Calvin. The nation was wrecked by the Wars of Religion which broke out in 1562, leading to many atrocities, including the six-day St Bartholomew's Day massacre of Protestants in Paris. Finally, Henri IV fought his way to the throne and ended the war by decreeing religious tolerance with the Edict of Nantes in 1598.

Joan of Arc leading her men against the English during the Hundred Years' War

FACTS & FIGURES

The rooster emblem
Gallus, in Latin, can mean either a Gaul or a chicken. In the Middle Ages, the enemies of the country joked that the French were as proud and feisty as roosters. Instead of being insulted, the French made the *coq* a national emblem – you will often see them carved on top of war memorials.

Politics vs cheese
President Charles de Gaulle gave the best explanation for French politics, "How can anyone govern a country that makes 246 different kinds of cheese"? In fact, there may be more than a thousand!

Riding the bus
In 1662, mathematician and philosopher Blaise Pascal gave Paris the world's first city bus - a horse-drawn carriage. It was a big success, until common people were banned from using it.

The "humane" guillotine
The "national razor" or the guillotine of the Revolution was actually meant as a more humane means of execution. It was still being used as late as 1977.

More perfume please
The French nobility during the reign of Louis XIV believed that washing was bad for them. So they never did! They just piled on more perfume and powder.

Name that pig
In France, it is against the law to name your pig Napoleon.

What did you say?
In 1880, only a quarter of the French spoke French as their native language.

Hundred Years' War starts, taking a toll on France for the next 116 years

St Bartholomew's Day massacre of thousands of Protestants

| 209 | 1337 | 1431 | 1572 | 1598 |

lip II Augustus and pope decree the gensian Crusade

Joan of Arc burnt at the stake in Rouen

Henry IV decrees Edict of Nantes, granting religious tolerance

The Grand Siècle and Age of Enlightenment

After the assassination of Henri IV in 1610, four kings named Louis followed. The first, Louis XIII, ascended the throne very young. He was guided by Cardinal Richelieu, a powerful minister who transformed France into an absolute monarchy.

The 17th century is called France's Grand Siècle (Grand Century). It reached its peak under King Louis XIV (1634–1715). He built the spectacular palace at Versailles (see pp124–7). French music and Baroque architecture thrived. At the same time, the King's endless wars nearly bankrupted France, while his misrule caused famines and revolts in the countryside. He also revoked the Edict of Nantes, leading to an exodus of Protestants from France.

In Louis XV's reign (1715–74), 18th-century France entered an Age of Enlightenment. Philosophers such as Voltaire and Rousseau put forth

Louis XIV and his entourage stroll through the gardens of Versailles

ideas of equality and the inalienable rights of man – principles that went against the aristocratic order. But the nobility and church resisted any change. Louis XVI ascend the throne in 1774 and attempted to pass some half-hearted reforms, but it was too late.

The French Revolution

Spurred by economic ills and ideas of equality, the French Revolution began when the king convened the Estates-General, the French parliament, in 1789. Tired of being disregarded, the Third Estate (commoners) broke away from the main body and declared itself a National Assembly of the People. They then swore to give France a constitution. With growing support, mobs gathered in Paris; on 14 July, they stormed the Bastille, seizing the royal fortress and its cache of arms.

France became a Republic and the royal family were executed in 1793 by the newly-invented guillotine. A Reign of Terror followed, marked by the massacre of thousands of people thought to be enemies of the Revolution. Meanwhile, monarchies across Europe were alarmed at the situation in France and in 1799 declared war, setting the stage for the rise of Napoleon Bonaparte.

Two Napoleons

Napoleon, as France's leading general and strategist, went on to conquer and control much of

Napoleon and his officers watch the burning of Moscow in 1812

Western Europe and even Egypt in the name of the Revolution. At the start of the 19th century, he took over France as First Consul. In 1804, he declared himself Emperor, and extended his empire, giving his brothers and sisters thrones across Europe. He set about building roads, improved education, established the metric system of measurements, decreed freedom of religion and reformed both taxation and civil law. His legal system, the Napoleonic Code, is still used in France today.

Napoleon's empire was constantly at war with other European countries. For years he seemed invincible, but in 1812 he invaded Russia. He captured Moscow, but was unable to defeat the Russian armies. In 1814, Napoleon was deposed and exiled to Elba, but escaped to seize power yet again before his reign finally ended at the Battle of Waterloo in 1815.

After Napoleon, the Bourbon monarchs were restored under Louis XVII, but France's turbulent politics

Timeline

Reign of Louis XIV
marks a golden age of art and culture

Reign of Terror
begins; thousands executed by guillotine

July Revolution
brings Louis-Philippe to the throne

Prussia invades France; the Third Republic is formed

1643–1715	1789	1793	1815	1830	1848	1870–

French Revolution
sparks off in Paris

Napoleon faces his final defeat at the Battle of Waterloo

Second Republic soon becomes the Second Empire under Napoleon III led to another revolution in July 1830. This resulted in a constitutional monarchy under King Louis-Phillipe. France began to modernize, but Parisians, in particular, were still dissatisfied, and in 1848 yet another revolution led to a Second Republic. It elected Napoleon's nephew as its president. He soon proclaimed himself Emperor Napoleon III. His "Second Empire" was marked by the remaking and modernization of Paris. In the war of 1870, Prussia and other German states overran northern France and besieged Paris. The armstice terms left Parisians humiliated. Riots led to the creation of a Paris Commune, which was brutally crushed by the French Army.

The Third Republic

France finally found political stability under the Third Republic. The new regime passed long-needed reforms in education and social welfare, but political agitation still rocked the Republic. This period is also referred to as the *belle époque* (Beautiful Era), known for its Art Nouveau style and technological advancements.

Millions of Frenchmen and women died during World War I, and large parts of the country were devastated. The exhausted nation was slow to recover. The avant-garde 1920s saw the arrival of Art Deco, experimental writers, Surrealism and jazz. The grim 1930s were a time of depression and the threat of war. France was invaded once again in 1940. Northern France fell under a bitter Nazi occupation;

the south, left alone for a while under the Vichy regime, was occupied in 1942. A strong resistance network aided the liberation, and Free French troops entered Paris in August 1944.

France since 1945

The nation struggled to regain its bearings under an unstable Fourth Republic of squabbling politicians and short-lived governments. More trouble came in the form of colonial liberation movements; France lost both Vietnam and Algeria after years of fighting. In 1958, General Charles de Gaulle was established President, and constituted the Fifth Republic.

Angry with social inequalities and an inflexible state, students and workers came together in 1968 in a revolt that demanded political and economic reform. De Gaulle restored order once more. Since then, France has become a more open society.

Today, France is a prosperous and egalitarian society. Its innovative technologies have caught the world's imagination. With a rich cultural heritage and carefully-tended cities, the country attracts nearly 80 million foreign visitors a year.

Allied troops on the Champs-Élysées in August 1944

	World War I devastates Eastern France		Fifth Republic is established by President de Gaulle	
1874	1914–17	1940–44	1958	2012
st exhibition of the ressionists: beginning modern art		Nazi Germany occupies France		Presidential elections

Enjoying the Mediterranean sun
at Calanque de Marseilleveyre,
near Marseille

Exploring
FRANCE

Northeast France

Northeast France is a huge area: almost 650 km (400 miles) separate Boulogne on the coast from Mulhouse in Alsace, yet these regions tend to get overlooked by people who are on their way to somewhere else. The regions boast the rugged shores and beaches of the Côte d'Opale, magnificent cathedrals and castles, big open landscapes, a host of world-class museums and two great theme parks.

Le Nord and Picardy

Champagne

Alsace and Lorraine

Highlights

Nausicaá, Boulogne-sur-Mer
Patrolling sharks, performing sea lions and glittering tropical fish are the highlight of this giant aquarium, which offers superb holiday fun *(see pp68–9)*.

Parc Astérix
The comic-book characters from Ancient Gaul come to life in one of the top theme-park attractions of France *(see pp74–5)*.

Château Fort de Sedan
Explore the largest medieval castle in Europe, with massive walls honeycombed by spiral stairs, arrow slits and vaulted halls *(see pp64–5)*.

Reims Cathedral
Spot angels at this medieval masterpiece that is lit up by its stained glass, like a magic lantern made of stone *(see pp60–61)*.

Colmar
Straight out of a fairy-tale picture book, this gem of a town has half-timbered houses lining crooked streets *(see pp54–5)*.

Verdun
This symbol of French resolve in World War I is vividly recalled by its battlefield site, museums, cemeteries and eerie bone vault *(see pp50–51)*.

Left The west façade of the magnificent Gothic Cathédrale Notre-Dame, Reims
Above left A steam engine on display at the Cité du Train, Europe's biggest railway museum, in Mulhouse

The Best of
Northeast France

World War I battlefields such as Verdun and the Somme stand out across Northeast France, and their memorials and monuments are among the most fascinating and moving sights. But this part of France has many brighter sides too – such as the natural wonder of the Baie de Somme, superb Gothic cathedrals at Reims and Amiens, and the splendid Château de Chantilly. There is something for everyone to enjoy here.

Memorable museums

This region offers plenty of child-friendly museums; kids who do not have an inclination for art museums are in luck. **Mulhouse** (see pp56–7) has two wonderful, world-class museums, so large that they call them "cities": the Cité du Train and the Cité de l'Automobile. Nearby, the **Ecomusée d'Alsace** (see p56) at Ungersheim is a whole museum village. At **Troyes** (see p62), there is the unusual Musée de l'Outil et de la Pensée Ouvrière. In **Chantilly** (see p76), the Musée Vivant du Cheval features a collection of horses and riding displays. **Nausicaá** (see pp68–9) in Boulogne is effectively a museum of sealife.

Be sure not to miss the excellent art museums at **Reims** (see pp60–61), **Amiens** (see p73) and **Chantilly**, while **Strasbourg** (see p57) and **Troyes** each have a Musée d'Art Moderne that stretches back to the late 19th century. At **Colmar** (see pp54–5), the Musée d'Unterlinden has something for everyone, from Matthias Grünewald's splendidly gruesome Isenheim altarpiece to crossbows and jelly moulds.

The great outdoors

The Northeast boasts immense and dramatic expanses of protected landscape, such as the **Parc Naturel Régional de la Montagne de Reims** (see p61). The magnificent old hunting forests – the **Forêt de Chantilly** (see p76), **Forêt de St-Gobain** (see p77) and **Forêt de Compiègne** (see p77) – cast an enchanting spell. There are plenty of information centres and marked walks to help visitors explore them.

The **Côte d'Opale** (see p69) is the name given to the English Channel coastline of the Northeast. There are cliff-top walks with views right over the Channel and excellent beaches for swimming and watersports, such as at **Le Crotoy** (see p72). Visit the marshlands of the

Above Vineyards in the Parc Naturel Régional de la Montagne de Reims Left The Isenheim altarpiece in the Musée d'Unterlinden

Left The fairy-tale Château de Pierrefonds **Right** *Goat shed at the Ecomusée d'Alsace, Ungersheim*

Parc du Marquenterre *(see p72)*, a famous bird sanctuary, or take a boat trip to see the seals in the **Baie de Somme** *(see p72)*.

Hop on to a river cruise along the Meuse at **Verdun** *(see p51)*, or on branches of the Somme river that lead through the "floating gardens" of the Hortillonnages at **Amiens**. Near **Langres** *(see p63)*, ride a pedalo on the Lac de la Liez – one of the region's many artificial lakes.

Fortresses and châteaux

For the biggest and mightiest medieval castle, go to the **Château Fort de Sedan** *(see pp64–5)* and witness the evolution of castle architecture. The brilliance of Louis XIV's military architect, Vauban, is in evidence here and especially at his masterpiece, the star-shaped garrison town of **Neuf-Brisach** *(see p55)*. Head for the wonderful fortified hilltop towns at **Langres**, **Laon** *(see p77)*, **Montreuil-sur-Mer** *(see p71)* and **Boulogne-sur-Mer** *(see p69)*. See superb châteaux, notably the

Château de Compiègne *(see p76)*, the **Château de Chantilly** *(see p76)* and the fantastic 19th-century **Château de Pierrefonds** *(see p77)*.

Memories of World Wars

The most potent symbol of World War I, **The Battlefield of Verdun** *(see pp50–51)*, is marked by a scarred landscape, a museum and the Ossuaire de Douaumont. The **Battlefields of the Somme** *(see pp72–3)* evoke similar memories, with numerous battle-torn sites around Albert.

Memories of World War I go underground at the Carrière Wellington in **Arras** *(see pp70–71)*, part of the intriguing honeycomb of centuries-old tunnels beneath the city.

This region also became a battle zone in World War II. **The Maginot Line** *(see p52)* was an extraordinary chain of forts built in vain by the French to defend their border with Germany. La Coupole, the German V2 rocket-launching site, looms near **St-Omer** *(see p70)*.

Below *Poppies in full bloom across the battlefields of the Somme*

Northeast France

The landscape of Northeast France varies from the cliffs, coastal beaches and marshes of the Côte d'Opale in the west to the forested hills and mountains of the Ardennes, Lorraine and Alsace in the east. Efficient road and rail services connect all corners, but there are still plenty of quiet, winding roads and paths through unspoilt landscapes to explore, revealing scenes barely touched by tourism and the modern world.

Vintage pedal cars in the Cité de l'Automobile, Mulhouse

Places of interest

ALSACE AND LORRAINE
1 The Battlefield of Verdun
2 The Maginot Line
3 Parc d'Attraction Walygator
4 Metz
5 Nancy
6 Colmar
7 Enchanted towns of Alsace
8 Ecomusée d'Alsace
9 Mulhouse
10 Strasbourg

CHAMPAGNE
1 Reims Cathedral
2 Épernay
3 Troyes
4 Chaource
5 Langres
6 Château Fort de Sedan

LE NORD & PICARDY
1 Nausicaá, Boulogne-sur-Mer
2 St-Omer
3 Lille
4 Arras
5 Montreuil-sur-Mer
6 Baie de Somme
7 Grottes-Refuges de Naours
8 Battlefields of the Somme
9 Amiens
10 Parc Astérix
11 Chantilly
12 Compiègne
13 Château de Pierrefonds
14 Laon

Half-timbered houses with flower-bedecked balconies in Eguisheim, one of the "enchanted towns" of Alsace

The Lowdown

🚗 **Getting there and around**
Air *(see p48)*. **Ferry** Ferries from the UK sail to Calais, Dunkerque, Dieppe and Boulogne. **Train** Eurostar passenger rail services from the UK (via the Channel Tunnel) serve Lille and Paris; some also stop at Calais. There is a good network of trains: at local level they are operated by the TER division of the SNCF *(www.ter-sncf.com)*; the region is also served by the high-speed TGV network *(www.tgv.com)*, with lines via Lille (Thalys) to London and Brussels, as well as TGV Est Européen east from Paris to Strasbourg. **Bus** Bus services are operated by various companies on a departmental or local basis – Soléa operates only in and around Mulhouse; Artis around Arras. **Car** Major international car hire firms are present in the larger cities, such as Strasbourg, Lille and Nancy, and in many smaller ones, such as Boulogne and Arras. *Autoroutes* (motorways) link all the major cities; most of these are *péage* (toll roads). EuroTunnel enables cars to travel through the Channel Tunnel, emerging south of Calais.

🍽 **Supermarkets** Large, modern and well-stocked supermarkets are found on the outskirts of all the major towns and cities. The main companies are Leclerc, Auchan, Super U and Intermarché. **Market days** Most towns and cities have markets; some are open once a week, others take place daily. Contact the tourist offices for details.

🕙 **Opening hours** Most shops open from Monday to Saturday, often with a break for lunch. Supermarkets generally have longer hours. *Boulangeries* (bread shops) and *pâtisseries* open earlier and are often the only shops open on Sundays.

✚ **Pharmacies** There is at least one pharmacy, identified by a green cross outside, in each town and many villages. A list in the window will give details of the nearest *pharmacie de garde* open outside normal hours (on Sundays and at night). They are listed in local newspapers and on *www.pharmaciesdegarde.com*.

🚻 **Toilets** Most towns and cities have public toilets in the central areas, often staffed.

Detail of sculpture on the north door of Reims Cathedral

Rugged coastline of the Côte d'Opale

Northeast France Regional Airports

Most international air travellers to Northeast France will fly to Paris (see p86), although Ryanair goes to Paris Beauvais in Picardy. Distances across the region are substantial, justifying two major regional airports close to the eastern border with Germany, at Strasbourg and Mulhouse. All airports offer more or less the full range of services.

Metz-Nancy-Lorraine

Lying 15 km (9 miles) south of Metz and 35 km (22 miles) north of Nancy, this airport operates direct flights to and from a limited number of French airports (Lyon, Marseille, Nice, Toulouse and Corsica), and serves passengers from further afield travelling via those destinations. The main carrier is Air France.

Shuttle buses take passengers to the rail stations of Metz and Nancy (€4.60). Several major car hire companies have offices at the airport. There is a bar/cafeteria and also a self-service restaurant with views over the runways. Hotel accommodation can be found at Metz, Nancy and closer at hand at Pont-à-Mousson.

Mulhouse (Basel-Mulhouse-Freiburg EuroAirport)

This airport is in French territory, 25 km (15 miles) southeast of Mulhouse, but is the main airport for Basel in Switzerland and Freiburg in Germany. It serves many European destinations, including London (Heathrow and Gatwick), Manchester and Edinburgh. The airport is used by Air France, British Airways, bmi, Swiss International Airlines, KLM and easyJet. There are no train services from the airport. For links to Mulhouse, take the *navette* (shuttle service) to St Louis (€4.60) and then a train; for Strasbourg, there are shuttle buses. Most major car hire firms have offices at the airport, and there are several shops, cafés and

Planes on the airfield of Aéroport International de Strasbourg

restaurants. Hotels are available at Mulhouse, across the border in Basel and in towns just by the airport.

Strasbourg

The Aéroport International de Strasbourg, located just to the southwest of the city, has links to 22 destinations within France, in continental Europe and around the Mediterranean, but not currently the UK. Carriers include Air France, Iberia and Brussels Airlines. A train shuttle service (€3.60), with four departures an hour, takes just 9 minutes to reach the Gare de Strasbourg in the city centre, with onward links across the region. Most major car hire firms have offices at the airport. There is a bistro and café, as well as a couple of shops, including one selling specialities of Alsace.

Lille

Located just to the south of Lille, this airport serves mainly flights from within France, continental Europe and the Mediterranean, but not currently the UK. Airlines include Air France, Ryanair and Air Maroc. A *navette* (€7) takes 20 minutes to transport travellers into the centre of the city, from where there are rail links to places across the region. The main car hire firms are present. There is a

snack bar and a restaurant with views over the runways and there are plenty of hotels nearby and in Lille.

Le Touquet

L'Aéroport Le Touquet Côte d'Opale is a small airport virtually in Le Touquet, serving private flights and scheduled flights from the UK, operated only at weekends by LyddAir. Transport links are provided by bus, taxi (€8), car hire, and bicycles. There is a restaurant at the airport and hotels at Le Touquet.

Paris Beauvais

This is Ryanair's main Paris airport, located 80 km (50 miles) north of Paris and conveniently positioned for Chantilly, Parc Astérix and Amiens. Shuttle buses run to Paris and there is a separate *navette* to Disneyland, via Paris-Charles-de Gaulle airport. There are also bus links to Beauvais town, from which there are train links to Paris Gare du Nord and Amiens. Most major car hire firms have offices at the airport.

There is a restaurant in the airport and also a snack bar/pizzeria in the departure lounge, as well as several shops, including a mini-supermarket. The airport website lists details of hotels in Beauvais that are linked to the airport by a shuttle service.

The Lowdown

Lille 08 91 67 32 10; www.lille. aeroport.fr

Metz-Nancy-Lorraine 03 87 56 70 00; www.metz-nancy-lorraine. aeroport.fr

Mulhouse (Basel-Mulhouse-Freiburg EuroAirport) 03 89 90 31 11; www.euroairport.com

Paris Beauvais 08 92 68 20 66; www.aeroportbeauvais.com

Strasbourg 03 88 64 67 67; www.strasbourg.aeroport.fr

Le Touquet 03 21 05 03 99; www.aeroport-letouquet.com

Duty-free shop at the Basel-Mulhouse-Freiburg EuroAirport

Alsace and Lorraine

Hills, mountains and forests have shaped the character and history of this border region, which has swapped rulers and allegiances over the centuries, often through war. Picturesque half-timbered villages and town centres distinguish Alsace, including that of cosmopolitan Strasbourg. Lorraine remains rural outside of the dynamic fizz of Nancy and Metz.

Below Strollers on the Grand Rue in the old town of Colmar

The Battlefield of Verdun
p50

Colmar
p54

① The Battlefield of Verdun

The town that became a symbol of World War I

Much of World War I was fought along the Western Front, a line of trenches and defences that snaked down through Belgium and eastern France. On 21 February 1916, the Germans launched a ferocious artillery bombardment near the old fortress town of Verdun. But the French were determined to hold the town. Over the next 300 days, more than 300,000 soldiers died and a further 400,000 were wounded. Today a series of monuments both outside and inside Verdun evoke the desperate battle.

Miniatures in Le Mémorial de Verdun

Key Sights

① **Fort de Douaumont** Built in 1855, this fort, reinforced by a roof of concrete and sand, fell to the Germans, but was later recaptured by the French.

② **Tranchée des Baïonnettes** A monument was built over a trench buried by a shell explosion, killing 57 French soldiers, leaving their bayonets sticking out of the ground. No bayonets are visible now.

⑤ **Le Mémorial de Verdun** In Fleury-devant-Douaumont, one of nine villages that were wiped out in the conflict, this museum displays artefacts and other reminders of the battle.

③ **Ossuaire de Douaumont** The bones of 130,000 unidentified French and German soldiers lie in the vault of this monument, completed in 1932. Its tower, rising to 46 m (151 ft), offers panoramic views over the battlefield from the top.

④ **War graves** Neat rows of crosses outside the Ossuaire mark the graves of 15,000 identified French soldiers, each bearing a name.

⑥ **Monument du Lion** This poignant sculpture of a wounded lion marks the southernmost point of the German advance.

⑦ **Fort de Vaux** This was the second fort to be lost by the French. The troops were forced to surrender on 7 June, having run out of essential supplies.

The Lowdown

🌐 **Map reference** 5 D4
Address 55000 (Meuse). Ossuaire de Douaumont: 55100 Fleury-Devant-Douaumont; www.verdun-douaumont.com. Tranchée des Baïonnettes, Fort de Douaumont & Fort de Vaux: www.en.verdun-tourisme.com. Le Mémorial de Verdun: 1 Ave du Corps Européen, 55100 Fleury-Devant-Douaumont; 03 29 84 35 34; www.memorial-de-verdun.fr

🚗 **Train** from Nancy, Metz & Châlons-en-Champagne; TGV from Paris or Strasbourg to the TGV Meuse station, then shuttle

bus to Verdun. In summer, there is a hop-on-hop-off tour bus that covers the main battlefield sights. It leaves from the tourist office in Verdun.

ℹ️ **Visitor information** Pl de la Nation, 55106 Verdun; 03 29 84 14 18; www.verdun-tourisme.com

🕐 **Open** Ossuaire de Douaumont: daily (Feb: school hols only); closed Jan. Le Mémorial de Verdun: year round; closed first three weeks of Jan. Forts: check tourist website for details

💲 **Prices** Ossuaire de Douaumont: free; tower and 20-min film in

English & other languages €14–24; under 8s free. Le Mémorial de Verdun: €18–30; under 8s free. Forts: €12–24; under 8s free

🧍 **Skipping the queue** Buy the Battlefield Museum Pass that allows access to the main battlefield sights – Ossuaire de Douaumont, Le Mémorial de Verdun, Fort de Douaumont and Fort de Vaux. Contact the tourist office for details.

🚩 **Guided tours** The tour bus offers tours in English, French, German & Dutch; tickets valid for 24 hours

🧒 **Age range** 6 plus

Boats on the Meuse river through the town of Verdun

Letting off steam

Run about in the immense **Forêt Domaniale de Verdun** around the battlefield. In July and August, head down to the Meuse river and hire a canoe (www.meusecanoe.com) for excursions by the hour or for half-day. Schedules available at tourist office.

Eat and drink

Picnic: under €20; Snacks: €20–45; Real meal: €45–90; Family treat: over €90 (based on a family of four)

PICNIC Pause Picnic (*5 Rue de la Grange, 55100 Verdun; 03 29 85 34 41*) sells salads, quiches, ready-made sandwiches and also savoury tarts to take away. There are plenty of quiet woodland places with tables to picnic near the battlefield.
SNACKS L'Abri Des Pélerins (*Pl Monseigneur Ginisty, 55100 Douaumont; 03 29 85 50 58*) is a bar-café-restaurant close to the Ossuaire de Douaumont. It offers simple brasserie food, plus pancakes and ice cream.

REAL MEAL Pom'Samba (*7 Ave Garibaldi, 55100 Verdun; 03 29 83 49 34; pomsamba.free.fr*) focuses on potatoes cooked in all forms, and accompanied by meat, fish or vegetables.
FAMILY TREAT Le Clapier (*34 Rue des Gros-Degrés, 55100 Verdun; 03 29 86 20 14*), a charming small restaurant, proudly boasts of its "cuisine traditionnelle". The set-meal prices are modest, given the quality of the cooking.

Shopping

The main hub of Verdun runs along the north side of the river, with shops in the Rue Mazel and its arteries. Go to the splendid **Maison Braquier** (*50 Rue du Fort de Vaux, 55100; 03 29 84 30 00; www.dragees-braquier. com*) for the famous *dragées* (sugared almonds) and other confectionery.

Find out more

DIGITAL Look up "Verdun: Symbol of Suffering" in the BBC's section on World War I: *tinyurl.com/ae2v*.

Next stop...

VERDUN In the surprisingly pretty historic town of Verdun itself, visit the **Citadelle Souterraine** (*Ave du 5eme RAP, 55100; 03 29 83 44 28*) housed in a massive fortress dating originally from the 17th century. Visitors tour a huge network of tunnels in self-guided vehicles stopping at scenes that recall the experiences of French recruits at Verdun in World War I.

The "Voie Sacrée" (Sacred Way) to the southwest of Verdun was the road along which millions of French troops reached the battlefield.

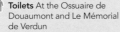
⏱ **Allow** A day

☕ **Café** Les Pélerins is the only café in the battlefield area.

👫 **Toilets** At the Ossuaire de Douaumont and Le Mémorial de Verdun

🎭 **Festival** Des Flammes à la Lumière, 300 French and German volunteers perform a *son-et-lumière* re-enactment of the events of the battle (Jun & Jul)

Good family value?
An important historic place to visit, but the ticket prices mount up to a considerable sum.

② The Maginot Line

A giant disappointment

To prevent the Germans from ever mounting a surprise attack again after World War I, in 1930 the French began building a huge chain of forts along their border with Germany. Named after André Maginot (1877–1932), the minister of war at the time, it was equipped with up-to-date armaments: pop-up gun turrets and lookout posts rose above the ground, with concrete bunkers and tunnels underground. But on 10 May 1940, Germany did invade France through neutral Luxembourg, north of the Maginot Line, skirting around it. A month later they attacked the line from the French side – most forts did not fall but surrendered nine days after the Second Armistice at Compiègne of 22 June 1940. Several of the forts are open to the public. **Fermont**, **Hackenberg** and **Simserhof** are the most striking, full of historic artifacts, with restored machinery, workshops and accommodation: all three have little trains scuttling through tunnels.

A train chugging through a tunnel of one of the forts of the Maginot Line

Whirling around on one of the thrilling rides at Parc d'Attraction Walygator

Letting off steam

The forts are located in rural or wooded areas, so there is plenty of space to romp about in.

③ Parc d'Attraction Walygator

Thrills in a top theme park

The biggest theme park in this part of France, Walygator has 40 rides to suit all ages: from gentle trains and roundabouts to heart-in-mouth roller coasters, including the wooden "Anaconda", splash rides and the "Terror House" ride, restricted to kids 14 plus. A schedule of shows – puppets, circus, high-diving – makes for a superb outing.

Located 4 km (3 miles) north, the privately owned **Zoo d'Amnéville**, has some 2,000 animals of 350 species, many in large open-air pens

The Lowdown

🌐 **Map reference** 6 E4
Address 57000 (Moselle). Voie Romaine, 57280 Maizières-les-Metz; 03 87 30 70 07; www. walygatorparc.com. Zoo d'Amnéville: 1 Rue du Tigre, 57360 Amnéville; 03 87 70 25 60; www.zoo-amneville.com

🚗 **Train** from Metz Ville

ℹ **Visitor information** 2 Pl d'Armes, 57007 Metz; 03 87 55 53 76; tourisme.mairie-metz.fr

🕐 **Open** Jul–Aug: daily (until 10pm Sat); Apr–May & Sep–Oct: Sat–Sun and school hols; Jun: Fri–Sun. Zoo d'Amnéville: daily

🍽 **Eat and drink** *Snacks* Croco'Crep (on site) is a little crêperie that serves pancakes, sandwiches, hot dogs and ice creams. *Real meal* Croco'Grill (on site) is a table-service restaurant with a full menu. It specializes in Mexican food and grilled meat. The terrace overlooks the central lake.

set in a vast forested area. It runs shows, featuring birds-of-prey, seal lions and polar bear feeding time.

Take cover

If it rains, head for one of the sights that are indoors such as the Terror House. There are also four scheduled indoor shows.

④ Metz

City of bridges

Metz is an enchanting city at the confluence of the Seille and Moselle rivers, with canals and islands and 20 bridges, including the castle-like Porte des Allemands. The pedestrianized centre of the Vieille Ville makes the city a pleasure to wander about, especially beneath its night-time illuminations. Pop into the Cathédrale St-Étienne, one of the finest Gothic cathedrals in the country, to admire the stained glass. A scary dragon

One of the 20 bridges spanning the river in Metz

The Lowdown

🌐 **Map reference** 5 D4, 6 E4 & 6 G5
Address 54000 (Meurthe-et-Moselle). Fermont: 9 Rue Albert Lebrun, 54260 Longuyon; ligne-maginot-fort-de-fermont.asso.fr. Hackenberg: Route du Hackenberg, 57920 Veckring; maginot-hackenberg.com. Simserhof: Rue André Maginot, Le Légeret, 57410 Siersthal; www.simserhof.fr

🚗 **Car** The forts are best reached by car. There is no public transport to or between the forts.

ℹ **Visitor information** Fermont: ot-longuyon.pagesperso-orange.fr; Hackenberg: www.ot-thionville.com; Simserhof: www.ot-pays debitche.com

🕐 **Open** Fermont: Apr–Oct. Hackenberg: year round. Simserhof: mid-Nov–mid-Mar. Days vary, check websites. Guided tours take 2–3 hours. Wear warm clothes as it gets cold in the underground tunnels.

🍽 **Eat and drink** *Real meal* L' Auberge du Lac (Rue Etang Hasselfurth, 57230 Bitche; 03 87 96 96 00; www.laubergedulac.fr), near Simserhof, offers well-priced buffets, plus a playground. *Family treat* La Brasserie des Caves (19 Rue de Sètes, 54260 Longuyon; 03 82 23 15 41; www.resto.fr/labrasseriedescaves) does reasonably priced market-based cooking.

Handsome buildings surrounding the splendid Place Stanislas, Nancy

The Lowdown

- 🌐 **Map reference** 6 E4
  Address 57000 (Moselle).
  Musée de la Cour d'Or: 2 Rue
  du Haut Poirier, 57007; 03 87 20
  13 20
- 🚗 **Train** TGV from Paris, Nancy,
  Strasbourg and Verdun
- ℹ️ **Visitor information** 2 Pl d'Armes,
  57007; 03 87 55 53 76; *tourisme.
  mairie-metz.fr*
- 🕐 **Open** Musée de la Cour d'Or:
  Wed–Mon
- 🍴 **Eat and drink** *Picnic* Marché
  Couvert (*Pl de la Cathédrale,
  57007*) has superb food stalls.
  Picnic at the Plan d'Eau de Metz.
  Family treat L'Aloyau (*3 Rue de la
  Fontaine, 57007; 03 87 37 33 72*)
  is the place for meat lovers, with
  traditional French cuisine on offer.

hangs from the ceiling of the crypt:
Graoully by name, it used to terrorize
Metz until it was slain by St Clement
in Roman times. The **Musée de la
Cour d'Or**, an archeological museum
set in a 17th-century monastery,
is noted for its Gallo-Roman and
Frankish collection. For an adventure
into modern architecture, visit the
tent-like Centre Pompidou-Metz, near
the station, inaugurated in 2010,
which mounts a programme of high-
profile temporary art exhibitions.

Letting off steam
Head for the **Plan d'Eau de Metz**,
just west of the city centre, a wide
expanse of water surrounded by
parks and walks, with beaches,
pedalos and playgrounds.

⑤ Nancy
Home of a new kind of art
Once the capital of the Dukes of
Lorraine, Nancy is a grand city. Its
central square is the stately Place

Stanislas, built in the 1750s for Duke
Stanislas Leszczynski. Nancy is also
known for its superb Art Nouveau
glass – the sparkling creations of
Emile Gallé, the Daum brothers and
others, on show at the **Musée de
l'Ecole de Nancy**, along with pottery,
furniture and accessories. From the
same era, the **Musée des Beaux-Arts**
has a visually stunning presentation
of Daum glass in its medieval cellar,
and houses a great collection of
19th- and 20th-century paintings.

Letting off steam
Located north of the Place Stanislas,
La Pépinière is a huge park. Just to
the west of the ring road around
Nancy is the **Parc de Loisirs de la
Forêt de Haye** (*www.parcdeloisirs-
haye.com*), with playgrounds, picnic
areas and guided walks.

The Lowdown

- 🌐 **Map reference** 6 E5
  Address 54000 (Meurthe-et-
  Moselle). Musée de l'Ecole de
  Nancy: 36–38 Rue Sergent
  Blandan, 03 83 40 14 86; *www.
  ecole-de-nancy.com*. Musée des
  Beaux-Arts: 3 Pl Stanislas, 54000;
  03 83 37 96 50; *mban.nancy.fr*
- 🚗 **Train** TGV from Paris; from
  Verdun, change at Conflans-
  Jarny or at Hagondange
- ℹ️ **Visitor information** 14 Pl
  Stanislas, 54000; 03 83 35 22 41;
  www.ot-nancy.fr
- 🕐 **Open** Musée de l'Ecole de
  Nancy & Musée des Beaux-Arts:
  Wed–Mon
- 🍴 **Eat and drink** *Snacks* Flunch
  (*Rue Grand Rabbin Haguenauer,
  54000; 03 83 32 65 85*) sells tasty
  snacks. *Family treat* Brasserie
  Excelsior (*50 Rue Henri-Poincaré,
  54000; 03 83 35 24 57; www.
  brasserie-excelsior.com*) boasts a
  classic Art Nouveau decor and
  fine French cuisine. Book ahead.

⑥ Colmar
A fairy-tale town

If Hansel and Gretel ever lived in a town, this is what it would have looked like. The winding little streets are filled with brightly painted houses, crisscrossed with half-timbering, hanging shop signs and the kind of projecting upper storeys from which a Rapunzel might let down her hair to the cobbled street below. This lively, beautiful little town is a great place to shop and find tasty things to eat, but it has a deep history that has given it some fabulous cultural treasures.

Wooden statue on the Maison Pfister

Key Sights

② **Musée du Jouet** The museum contains not only historic toys such as dolls, doll houses and puppets, but also working model train sets. Look out for its schedule of evening concerts and events.

④ **Musée Bartholdi**
This museum occupies the house where sculptor Frédéric-Auguste Bartholdi was born. It focuses above all on his most famous creation: the Statue of Liberty in New York.

⑤ **Maison Pfister** This classic Colmar house was built in 1537 for a hatmaker from Besançon. The tower, with a bell-shaped roof, contains the staircase.

| 0 metres | 200 |
| 0 yards | 200 |

① **Musée d'Unterlinden**
Set around the cloisters of an old convent, the town's main museum houses great medieval art and the Isenheim altarpiece by Matthias Grünewald.

③ **Collégiale de St-Martin**
Built in the 13th–14th centuries, this atmospheric church has several beautiful carved and painted altarpieces.

⑥ **Musée d'Histoire Naturelle et d'Ethnographie**
A delightful jumble of stuffed animals, mummies and masks are on display here.

The Lowdown

🌐 **Map reference** 6 G6
Address 68000 (Colmar). Musée d'Unterlinden: 1 Rue d'Unterlinden; www.musee-unterlinden.com. Musée du Jouet: 40 Rue Vauban; www.museejouet.com. Collégiale de St-Martin: Pl de la Cathédrale. Musée Bartholdi: 30 Rue des Marchands; www.musee-bartholdi.com. Maison Pfister: Rue des Mercière. Musée d'Histoire Naturelle et d'Ethnographie: 11 Rue Turenne; www.museum colmar.org

🚗 **Train** TGV from Paris (direct links or change at Strasbourg)

ℹ️ **Visitor information** 4 Rue d'Unterlinden, 68000; 03 89 20 68 95; www.ot-colmar.fr

🕐 **Open** Musée d'Unterlinden: May–Oct: 9am–6pm daily; Nov–Apr: 9am–noon & 2–5pm Wed–Mon. Musée du Jouet: Jan–Jun & Oct–Nov: 10am–noon & 2–6pm Wed–Mon; Jul–Aug: 10am–7pm daily; Sep: 10am–noon and 2–6pm daily; Dec: 10am–6pm daily. Musée Bartholdi: Mar–Dec: 10am–noon & 2–6pm Wed–Mon.

Musée d'Histoire Naturelle et d'Ethnographie: 10am–noon & 2–6pm Wed–Mon, closed 25 Dec–31 Jan

💶 **Prices** Musée d'Unterlinden: €16–32; under 12s free. Musée du Jouet: €9–18; under 8s free. Musée Bartholdi: €9–18; under 12s free. Musée d'Histoire Naturelle et d'Ethnographie: €10–20; under 7s free

👪 **Skipping the queue** A popular destination throughout the year, particularly in summer hols, during Easter and Dec. So arrive early.

Prices given are for a family of four

Letting off steam

A short walk from the town centre, the **Parc du Champ de Mars** (*2 Ave de la Marne, 68000*) is a tree-shaded park with formal paths, lawns and fountains. There is a beautiful 1920s carousel – choose between sitting in a carriage, a hot-air balloon, a bi-plane, or on a horse, stork or bull.

A child playing at the edge of a fountain in the Parc du Champ de Mars

Eat and drink

Picnic: under €20; Snacks: €20–45; Real meal: €45–90; Family treat: over €90 (based on a family of four)

PICNIC Marché Couvert (*Rue des Écoles, 68000; closed Sun & Mon*) is a 19th-century covered market offering charcuterie, cheese, bread, fruit, pastries and ready-made sandwiches. A good picnic spot is the Parc du Champ de Mars.
SNACKS Claude Wucher (*Marché Couvert de Colmar, 13 Rue de Écoles, 68000; 03 90 50 52 31*), set in the middle of the busy and beautifully restored covered market, is a good place to stop for a quick bite of Alsatian savouries or well-priced *plat du jour* (daily special).
REAL MEAL Le Comptoir de Georges (*1 Pl des 6 Montagnes Noires, 68000; 03 89 20 60 72;*

www.le-comptoir-de-georges.fr) is a bright restaurant that serves a great range of Alsatian dishes, from salads and quiches to steaks and Alsatian specialities; includes a kids' menu.
FAMILY TREAT Chez Hansi (*23 Rue des Marchands, 68000; 03 89 41 37 84*) is housed in a half-timbered building dating from 1532, with a beamed interior to match and staff in traditional dress. This is the place to eat in true Alsatian style: excellent *choucroute* (sauerkraut with sausages and often potatoes), savoury tarts, Alsatian stews and wines.

Shopping

Colmar is a delightful place to shop, with plenty of upmarket boutiques and curious speciality shops. Hunt in the streets around the Place de la Cathédrale and Rue des Marchands. Head for **Le Hameau** (*23 Rue des Serruriers, 68000*), a great, old-fashioned toyshop. Drop in to **Du Pareil...au même** (*5 Rue des Clefs, 68000*), which is an excellent kids' clothes chain.

A selection of cuddly toys at Le Hameau, a toyshop

Find out more...

DIGITAL Go to www.ot-colmar.fr for a range of pictures and short texts about the town, including sections called "Down the Road of History" and "Colmar for Children".

Next stop...

NEUF-BRISACH This octagonal 17th-century military town, located 18 km (11 miles) east of Colmar, has buildings laid out on a neat grid, surrounded by a star-like formation of fortifications. Constructed in 1698–1707 by Louis XIV's great military engineer Vauban, this masterpiece was built to guard the French border with Germany. Admire its perfect shape on the model in Porte Belfort or explore it on the ground.

KIDS' CORNER

Art activity
Try making a set of paintings on folding wings, with pictures on every surface – like the Isenheim altarpiece (1512–16) in the Musée d'Unterlinden. This masterpiece has a complex construction, with two sets of folding wings and three layers. In the museum, there are moveable models on the walls to show how the whole piece worked. There are paper models on sale at the museum shop.

THE CRAZY CLUBMEN
Legend has it that the ancient Greek hero Hercules, on his way home back from one of his Twelve Labours, stopped in Colmar to quench his thirst with the wine of Alsace. He drank vast amounts, fell asleep, woke up and stumbled off in a daze, leaving his club behind. The town put the club in its coat of arms and the inhabitants are known as as *Kolbnarren* (mad clubmen).

Hansi the French hero
The restaurant Chez Hansi is named after the artist and children's book illustrator Jean-Jacques Waltz (1873–1951), who was born in Colmar and used the pen-name Hansi. Colmar was in German territory from 1871 to 1918, and Waltz used his skills as a caricaturist to criticize German rule, for which he was arrested and imprisoned, making him a popular hero in France. Look out for his books – some are available in English – such as *My Alsace*, or *My Village*, and *L'Histoire d'Alsace*, which show his distinctive style.

Children performing a traditional handkerchief dance, Eguisheim

⑦ Enchanted towns of Alsace

A world of knights and ladies

This car journey follows the Alsace Route du Vin (wine road), but it offers much more than wine. The route winds its way through a hilly landscape dotted with picture-book towns and villages, redolent of a medieval past of knights, ladies, ogres and villains.

Travel on the D83 to Eguisheim, a beautifully preserved town, filled with half-timbered houses, surrounded by 13th-century ramparts. Riquewihr is perhaps the fairest of them all, with cobbled streets, geranium-filled balconies and ramparts crowned by watchtowers. Ribeauvillé is overlooked by three ruined hilltop castles. Pay a visit to the **Château du Haut-Koenigsbourg**, north of Ribeauvillé and just west of the town of Sélestat. It was rebuilt as an exact copy of the original for Kaiser Wilhelm II in 1900–1908, with ornate Neo-Renaissance interiors. Outside, the battlements stand at nearly 750 m (2,500 ft), offering a bird's-eye view over the plain of Alsace.

Letting off steam

Go to **Cigoland** (*www.cigoland.fr*), a theme park 9 km (5 miles) north of Ribeauvillé. There are animals to watch, a stork info-centre and rides particularly for younger children.

⑧ Ecomusée d'Alsace

Travel back in time

Some 70 historic traditional Alsace buildings have been reconstructed in this open-air museum, 4 km (2 miles) from the village of Ungersheim, creating a time-warp village set out in a lake-filled park. The buildings are brought to life by costumed volunteers who demonstrate crafts and professions from daily life in the 19th and early 20th centuries. Visitors can see the working mills, the forge, pottery, shoemaker's, cartwright's and saddlemaker's workshops, a barber's shop and a farm. There is also a rare, historic indoor merry-go-round. Shops and stalls sell the products of the potter, baker, blacksmith, beekeeper and perfume distiller.

Letting off steam

Take a Soléa bus from Ungersheim to **Le Bioscope** (*www.lebioscope. com*) a "leisure and discovery" park,

A rustic horse-drawn cart at the Ecomusée d'Alsace, Ungersheim

The Lowdown

🌐 **Map reference** 10 G1
Address 68000 (Haut-Rhin). Chemin Grosswald, 68190 Ungersheim; 03 89 74 44 74; *www.ecomusee-alsace.fr*

🚆 **Train** to Mulhouse, then Soléa bus 54. Best reached by car

ℹ **Visitor information** Hôtel de Ville, Pl de la Réunion, 68100 Mulhouse; 03 89 35 48 48; *www.tourisme-mulhouse.com*

🕑 **Open** 2 Apr–2 Nov: daily

🍽 **Eat and drink** *Picnic* Hypermarché Cora (*130 Route de Soultz, 68271 Wittenheim; 03 89 52 84 84*), located 5 km (3 miles) south of the museum, has provisions for an excellent picnic at the park. *Real meal* Restaurant La Taverne (*on site; 03 89 74 44 54*) specializes in a full range of Alsatian dishes.

that teaches kids lessons about nature and physics through games, shows, activities and 3D films.

⑨ Mulhouse

Steam engines and pedal cars

In a pocket of eastern France, close to the Swiss and German borders, Mulhouse had a long history as an independent republic and later became an industrial powerhouse. It has two top-ranking museums, both on an industrial theme – the **Cité du Train** is Europe's biggest railway museum, filled with impressive steam engines, sumptuous carriages, machines and memorabilia. It offers plenty of activities, interactive exhibits and audio-visual presentations. The **Cité de l'Automobile** claims to be the biggest museum of motor vehicles in the world, with 400 vintage cars. The museum has antique children's pedal cars, a pedal go-kart track plus tours on the "petit train". The main draw is the

Glamorous vintage cars on display at the Cité de l'Automobile

The Lowdown

🌐 **Map reference** 10 G1, 6 G6 & 6 G6
Address 68000 (Haut-Rhin) & 67000 (Bas-Rhin). Château du Haut-Koenigsbourg: Lièpvre, on N59, 67600; 03 88 82 50 60; *haut-koenigsbourg.fr*

🚗 **Car** from Colmar or bus from Sélestat railway station

ℹ **Visitor information** Eguisheim: 22A Grand Rue, 68420; 03 89 23 40 33; *www.ot-eguisheim.fr*. Riquewihr: 2 Rue de la 1ère Armée, 68340; 03 89 73 23 23. Ribeauvillé:

1 Grand'Rue, 68153; 03 89 73 23 23; *www.ribeauville-riquewihr.com*

🕑 **Open** Château du Haut-Koenigsbourg: daily

🍽 **Eat and drink** *Snacks* Au Péché Mignon (*5 Rue de Dinzheim, 68340 Riquewihr; 03 89 49 04 17; www.peche-mignon-riquewihr.com*) is open from midday for Alsatian snacks, tea, waffles or a full meal. *Real meal* Wistubzum Pfifferhüs (*14 Grand'Rue, 68150 Ribeauvillé; 03 89 73 62 28*) offers regional cuisine.

Exquisitely carved statues ornamenting the Cathédrale Notre-Dame, Strasbourg

The Lowdown

🌐 **Map reference** 10 G1
Address 68100 (Haut-Rhin). Cité du Train: 2 Rue Alfred Glehn; 03 89 42 83 33; *www.citedutrain. com*. Cité de l'Automobile: 15 Rue de l'Épée; 03 89 33 23 23; *www.collection-schlumpf.com*. Musée Historique: Hôtel de Ville, Pl de la Réunion; 03 89 33 78 17; *www.musees-mulhouse.fr*

🚗 **Train** TGV from Colmar, Strasbourg, Dijon & Paris

ℹ **Visitor information** Hôtel de Ville, Pl de la Réunion, 68100; 03 89 35 48 48; *www.tourisme-mulhouse.com*

🕐 **Open** Cité du Train & Cité de l'Automobile: daily (Jan: Mon–Fri). Musée Historique: Wed–Mon

🍴 **Eat and drink** *Real meal* Cafétéria "La Piste" (on site, Cité du Train) is a self-service restaurant offering a broad choice of dishes; mid-range among five food outlets at the museum. *Family treat* Tour de l'Europe (3 Blvd de l'Europe, 68100; 03 89 45 12 14; *www. restaurant-tour-europe.com*) has a sky-high revolving restaurant with a good menu.

Schlumpf collection of Bugattis and other fantastic vehicles. The **Musée Historique** in the splendidly painted old Hôtel de Ville presents a superb mix of grand civic rooms and folk culture, with reconstructed interiors, toys, board games and dolls houses.

Letting off steam

Go to the **Parc Zoologique et Botanique** (51 Rue du Jardin Zoologique, 68100; 03 69 77 65 65; *www.zoo-mulhouse.com*) with 1,200 animals of all kinds.

⑩ Strasbourg
Bright, brisk and prosperous

Strasbourg is a capital city of the European Union. The old town, on an island surrounded by branches of the Ill river, is a medieval web of streets, lined with half-timbered houses. At the western end is the lovely fishermen's and tanners' district called "La Petite France", with its three bridges with watchtowers, the "Ponts Couverts". For a bird's-eye view, climb the 332 steps to the spire-platform of the superb Gothic **Cathédrale Notre-Dame**; look out also for its famous 16th-century astronomical clock. The **Palais de Rohan** has three museums: Musée Archéologique, Musée des Beaux Arts and Musée des Arts Décoratifs, displaying 18th-century interiors, arts and crafts, particularly ceramics. The **Musée Alsacien** presents folk art and traditions, while the **Musée d'Art Moderne et Contemporain** has an excellent collection of European art, from 1850 to now.

Letting off steam

The **Parc de l'Orangerie**, northeast of the cathedral, has plenty of space to run about, along with a small zoo, with resident storks.

The Lowdown

🌐 **Map reference** 6 G5
Address 67014 (Bas-Rhin). Cathédrale Notre-Dame: Pl de la Cathédrale, 67082; *www. cathedrale-strasbourg.fr*. Palais de Rohan: 2 Pl du Château, 67000; 03 88 88 50 68. Musée Alsacien: 23–25 Quai St-Nicolas, 67000; 03 88 52 50 01. Musée d'Art Moderne et Contemporain: 1 Pl Hans Jean Arp, 67000; 03 88 23 31 31; *www.musees-strasbourg.org*

🚗 **Train** TGV from Paris

ℹ **Visitor information** 17 Pl de la Cathédrale, 67082; 03 88 52 28 28; *www.otstrasbourg.fr*

🕐 **Open** Palais de Rohan & Musée Alsacien: closed Tue. Musée d'Art Moderne et Contemporain: closed Mon

🍴 **Eat and drink** *Real meal* Zuem Strissel (5 Pl de la Grande Boucherie, 67060; *www.strissel.fr*) serves a range of Alsatian dishes; there is a kids' menu. *Real meal* Pommes de Terre et Cie (4 Rue de l'Ecurie, 67060; 03 88 22 36 82; *www.pommes-de-terre-cie.com*) offers potato and cheese dishes.

Picnic under €20; **Snacks** €20–45; **Real meal** €45–90; **Family treat** over €90 (based on a family of four)

Where to Stay in Alsace and Lorraine

Camp sites and rural *chambres d'hôtes* make the most of this region's rolling, forested, deeply rural landscape, while historic, half-timbered hotels – or their sleekly efficient modern counterparts – match the history and dynamism of the cities. Chain hotels step up where more individual options are lacking.

AGENCY
Gîtes en Alsace
www.gite-en-alsace.net
The French website provides a list of 370 properties for rent and B&Bs, presented by their owners, with links to their websites.

Colmar
Map 6 G6

HOTEL
Hôtel St Martin
38 Grand'Rue, 68000; 03 89 24 11 51; www.hotel-saint-martin.com
Located in the city centre, this is a smart, well-run hotel in an 18th-century mansion. Rooms are elegant and bathrooms modern. Free public parking sometimes available nearby.

€€

BED & BREAKFAST
Chez Leslie
31 Rue de Mulhouse, 68000; www.chezleslie.com
A 15-minute walk from the city centre, this characterful, cosy B&B offers four bedrooms with en-suite bathrooms, sleeping two, three or five. There is a garden to relax in during summer.

€

CAMPING
Camping des Amis de la Nature
Map 10 F1
4 Rue du Château, 68140 Luttenbach-près-Munster; 03 89 77 38 60; www.camping-an.fr
Located 20 km (12 miles) west of the city, in the foothills of the Vosges mountains, this spacious camp site is for tents and caravans. Shop and restaurant on site. Activities include mini-golf and *boules* pitch.

€

Longuyon
Map 5 D4

HOTEL
Hotel de Lorraine
63 Rue Augistrou, 54260; 03 82 26 50 07; tinyurl.com/3qmyhrd
An attractive, flower-bedecked hotel, well placed for visiting the Maginot

Medieval sign outside the Hôtel St Martin, Colmar

Line (Fermont). Rooms are basic, but the restaurant is great: outdoor terrace in summer and a kids' menu.

€

Metz
Map 6 E4

HOTEL
Novotel Metz Centre
Pl des Paraiges, Centre St-Jacques, 57000, 03 87 37 38 39; www.novotel.com
Smooth, modern and centrally located, this hotel has superior rooms for two adults and two kids.

€€

Mulhouse
Map 10 G1

HOTEL
Kyriad Mulhouse Centre
15 Rue Lambert, 68100; 03 89 66 44 77; www.hotel-mulhouse.com
Well located in the city centre, this hotel retains the sleek modern style that the Kyriad chain of hotels are known for. Free for under 12s when sharing with parents.

€€

Nancy
Map 6 E5

HOTEL
Best Western Hotel Crystal
5 Rue Chanzy, 54000; 03 83 17 54 00; www.bestwestern.com
A short walk from Place Stanislas, this is a smart, modern hotel. Two suites and two family rooms are on offer. Kids' beds are free for under 12s.

€€

Strasbourg
Map 6 G5

HOTEL
Hôtel du Dragon
2 Rue du Dragon, 67000; 03 88 35 79 80; www.dragon.fr
A set of brightly-painted 17th-century mansions, located just to the south of the Ill river and old town, has been thoroughly modernized to create a comfortable 32-room hotel with a patio. Family rooms sleep up to five.

€€

Verdun
Map 5 D4

HOTEL
Le Montaulbain
4 Rue de la Vieille Prison, 55100; 03 29 86 00 47
Centrally located, close to the Meuse river, this is a two-star hotel with ten somewhat basic rooms, including a family room that sleeps four to five. Public parking is a short walk away.

€

CAMPING
Camping Les Breuils
8 Allée des Breuils, 55100; 03 29 86 15 31; www.camping-lesbreuils.com
Just to the west of the town, the site has pitches, caravans, camping cars, chalets and mobile homes for hire. A playground and brasserie are on site.

€

A kid enjoying a splash down the water slide at Camping Les Breuils, Verdun

Price Guide
The following price ranges are based on one night's accommodation in high season for a family of four, inclusive of service charges and any additional taxes.
€ Under €100 €€ €100–200 €€€ over €200

Key to symbols *see back cover flap*

Champagne

The rich, undulating landscape patchworked with vineyards is a reminder of this area's most famous product. Its stature as a prosperous trading hub in medieval times is reflected in the Reims Cathedral. Further north are the forested Ardennes and borderlands that have been the scene of many historic disputes, to which the Château Fort de Sedan bears witness.

Château Fort de Sedan
p64

Reims Cathedral
p60

Below *A typical village near Épernay surrounded by vineyards*

① Reims Cathedral
Where kings were crowned

The Cathédrale Notre-Dame at Reims was built to impress – for this was the place where the French kings were crowned. The coronation tradition goes back to AD 498, when Clovis, king of the Franks, was baptized as a Christian on this site at the age of 30. The classic Gothic structure was begun in 1211 and completed over the century that followed. Coronation ceremonies continued to take place here till 1825. Above its entrance is a frothy mass of sculpture; inside are soaring spaces.

Jeanne d'Arc A statue of Joan of Arc in armour made by Prosper d'Epinay in 1902 stands in the apse.

Key Sights

Great Rose Window The 13th-century stained-glass window with the Virgin Mary, 12 apostles, musical angels, kings and prophets looks spectacular at sunset.

South transept

Flying buttresses High arches placed at the eastern end of the cathedral lend support to the building. This was done so that the walls around the altar could be filled with more stained glass.

Jeanne d'Arc

West façade

The Nave

Smiling angel

Chagall Window The stained-glass windows in the axial chapel behind the high altar were designed by the Russian-born artist Marc Chagall. They were installed in 1974.

The Nave The highest ceiling in Europe when it was built, this section rises to a height of nearly 38 m (125 ft).

Colossal scale The cathedral covers an area of 4,800 sq m (51,688 sq ft) – nearly the size of a soccer pitch. The exterior is nearly 149 m (489 ft) long.

Smiling angel Above the left doorway is the most famous of the angels that has given the cathedral its nickname "la cathédrale des anges".

West façade This section looks completely encrusted with stone carvings and sculptures. Try to spot the recent additions in metal, featuring gargoyles of three monstrous heads – a laughing bull, a rhino and a hound with chicken legs.

Prices given are for a family of four

The Lowdown

🌐 **Map reference** 5 B4
Address 51100 (Marne). Pl du Cardinal Luçon; 03 26 47 55 34; www.cathedrale-reims.com

🚗 **Train** TGV from Paris to Reims, then bus or tram from station

ℹ️ **Visitor information** 2 Rue Guillaume de Machault, 51100; 03 26 77 45 00; www.reims-tourisme.com

🕑 **Open** 7:30am–7:30pm daily

💲 **Price** Free

👪 **Skipping the queue** Go at the beginning or end of the day to avoid crowds.

🚩 **Guided tours** Audio guides of the main historical sites in English and other languages. Pick them up at the visitor information office next door.

👫 **Age range** 3 plus

⏲️ **Allow** 30–45 mins

☕ **Café** In the Palais du Tau next door (summer only)

🚻 **Toilets** Beside the visitor information office

Good family value?
The cathedral's high point is its sheer magnitude. On a bright day, the stained glass lights up the interior like a kaleidoscope.

Letting off steam

Walk around the pedestrianized streets northwest of the cathedral. There is a grand fairground **carousel** on Rue Condorcet. For open spaces, visit the **Parc Naturel Régional de la Montagne de Reims** (www.parc-montagnedereims.fr), 14 km (9 miles) south of Reims, a huge area of hills, woodland and vineyards.

Flying horses on the 1950s fairground carousel on Rue Condorcet

Eat and drink

Picnic: under €20; Snacks: €20–45; Real meal: €45–90; Family treat: over €90 (based on a family of four)

PICNIC Monoprix (34 Rue Jeanne d'Arc, 51100; 03 26 83 97 08) is an upmarket supermarket from where provisions can be picked up. Picnic in the Parc de la Patte d'Oie, the city centre's main park, nearby on Boulevard Leclerc.
SNACKS Crêperie Louise (15 Rue Marx-Dormoy, 51100; 03 26 78 00 61) is a beautiful little eatery where the old world meets the modern in a relaxed style. It serves salads, ice creams, coffee, *galettes* (savoury pancakes) and crêpes.
REAL MEAL Le Gaulois (2–4 Place Drouet d'Erlon, 51100; 03 26 47 35 76), a bar-brasserie-restaurant with a

A platter with desserts on display at the Café du Palais

sprawling pavement terrace, serves a great range of food, from salads and pizzas to elaborate dishes.
FAMILY TREAT Café du Palais (14 Pl Myron-Herrick, 51100; 03 26 47 52 54; www.cafedupalais.fr) has retained its ambience since the time it opened in 1930. This splendid café and restaurant, with an outdoor terrace, is the perfect location for a glass of the local wine – champagne.

Find out more

DIGITAL Kids aged 5 plus can browse www.historyforkids.org/learn/medieval/architecture/reims.htm to learn about the cathedral's history.

Shopping

The main shopping street is Rue Vesle, northwest of the cathedral. For individualistic shops, try the streets north of here, like Rue Condorcet and Rue Talleyrand. The latter has the city's biggest toy shop, **Le Royaume du Jouet** (7–9 Rue de Talleyrand, 51100; 03 26 03 80 18).

The art gallery at Palais du Tau, the archbishop's palace

Next stop...

A PALACE AND A CANAL Next to the cathedral is the **Palais du Tau** (palais-tau.monuments-nationaux.fr), the archbishop's palace, with its huge banqueting hall used by the kings of France after their coronation and a rich selection of costumes and treasures. To cool off, stroll along the Coulée Verte (a wide band of green), along the banks of the Vesle river and the adjacent Canal de l'Aisne à la Marne. The **AquaGlissConcept** (8 bis rue Gabriel Voisin, 51100; 33 06 67 45 13 00; www.aquaglissconcept.fr) offers canoeing and boat rides on the Vesle river. There are five municipal swimming pools in and around Reims (tinyurl.com/6c746s2).

② Épernay
Underground bubbles

A hub of champagne production, Épernay is not much to look at, but it is what goes on underground that makes it worth a visit. A number of major champagne *marques* (brands) such as **Moët et Chandon** have their headquarters here, with vast cellars chiselled out of the chalky hills and loaded with bottles. Tours explain the mysteries of champagne making – right down to how they get those bubbles in the bottle – by taking visitors to an underground world, where inverted

The Lowdown

- 🌐 **Map reference** 5 B5
  Address 51200 (Marne). Moët et Chandon: 20 Ave de Champagne; 03 26 51 20 20; *www.moet.com*. Mercier: 68–70 Ave de Champagne; *www.champagnemercier.fr*. De Castellane: 63 Ave de Champagne; *www.castel lane.com*
- 🚆 **Train** from Reims and Paris
- ℹ️ **Visitor information** 7 Ave de Champagne, 51200; *www.ot-epernay.fr*
- 🕐 **Open** Moët et Chandon: end-Mar–mid-Nov: daily; rest of the year: Mon–Fri. Mercier: mid-Mar–mid-Nov: daily. De Castellane: Apr–Dec: daily
- 🍴 **Eat and drink** *Snacks* Tout en Saveur (2 Rue du Général Leclerc, 51200; 03 26 32 14 13; www.tout ensaveur.fr) serves tasty submarine sandwiches. *Family treat* La Brasserie de la Banque (40 Rue du Général Leclerc, 51200; 03 26 59 50 50; www.brasserie-labanque.fr) offers a range of classic French dishes in a converted bank.

Wine barrels in the cellars of De Castellane, Épernay

bottles are turned every few days, a process called *remuage*. At **Mercier**, travel through some of its 18 km (11 miles) of cellars in a laser-guided electric train. **De Castellane** has a soaring tower; climb its 237 steps for spectacular views of the vineyards of Épernay and the Marne Valley.

Letting off steam

Kids can run around in the tree-shaded **Jardin de l'Hôtel de Ville** (7 bis Ave de Champagne, 51200), a central public park, in Épernay.

③ Troyes
Wild art and knitwear

The city centre of Troyes is said to be shaped like a champagne cork – appropriate for this former capital of the Champagne region. Troyes is a delightful historic city, with a largely pedestrianized old town, which has narrow alleys and is filled with multi-coloured half-timbered houses, *hôtels* (city mansions) and many churches. Do not miss the Ruelle des Chats, where houses are so close together that cats can supposedly jump from one house

The Lowdown

- 🌐 **Map reference** 5 B6
  Address 10000 (Aube). Musée d'Art Moderne: 14 Pl St-Pierre; 03 25 76 26 80. Musée de l'Outil et de la Pensée Ouvrière: 7 Rue de la Trinité; 03 25 73 28 26; *www.maison-de-l-outil.com*
- 🚆 **Train** from Paris to Reims, then bus 14 to Troyes
- ℹ️ **Visitor information** 16 Blvd Carnot, 10000; 03 25 82 62 70; *www.tourisme-troyes.com*
- 🕐 **Open** Musée d'Art Moderne: May–Sep: Tue–Sun; Oct–Apr: daily. Musée de l'Outil et de la Pensée Ouvrière: daily
- 🍴 **Eat and drink** *Snacks* Crêperie la Tourelle (9 Rue Champeaux, 10000; 03 25 73 22 40) serves *galettes* (savoury pancakes) or sweet crêpes. *Real meal* Café de la Paix (52 Rue du Général de Gaulle, 10000; 03 25 73 15 26) has *terrines* and also grilled meats.

to the other across the street. The Gothic Cathédrale St-Pierre-et-St-Paul, begun in the 13th century and built over the course of 400 years, has beautiful interior proportions, magically illuminated by stained glass – a speciality of the city. The **Musée d'Art Moderne**, next to the cathedral, contains an interesting mix of works – the Fauves, the Cubists and African art. The unusual **Musée de l'Outil et de la Pensée Ouvrière** displays 10,000 17th–19th-century tools and their related craftwork. Troyes is also famed as the "capital of knitwear", and has numerous clothing factory-outlet stores in the suburbs.

Letting off steam

Head for the **Jardin de Chevreuse** (Blvd Carnot, 10000) for a turn in its playground. The **Lac et Forêt d'Orient** (www.pnr-foret-orient.fr), 10-km (6-miles) east of Troyes, is a huge forest with nature reserves and well-indicated walks, along with artificial lakes, swimming beaches and watersports.

④ Chaource
See it, smell it, taste it!

A modest but pretty town with half-timbered houses, Chaource has an old outdoor laundry and a cast-iron covered market built in 1892.

Nativity scene in wood in the 12th-century Église St-Jean Baptiste, Chaource

Prices given are for a family of four

Half-timbered medieval houses in the old town of Troyes

But the town is best known for its eponymous soft and creamy cheese. The cheese used to be made on individual farms; visit the last surviving artisan producer at the **Fromagerie de Mussy**. There is a shop on site, tastings and a video film to watch. Go to the **Musée du Fromage**, which has a collection of historic cheese-making equipment.

Chaource is renowned for a remarkable sculpture: in its unusual 12th-century Église St-Jean Baptiste, the *Entombment of Christ* consists of 11 painted figures created in 1515 by the "Master of Chaource". The church also has a 16th-century nativity scene in sculpted wood.

The Lowdown

- 🌐 **Map reference** 9 B1
  Address 10210 (Aube).
  Fromagerie de Mussy: 30 Route de Maisons Lès Chaource; *www.fromageriedemussy.com*. Musée du Fromage: 17 Pl de l'Eglise; 03 25 40 10 67
- 🚌 **Bus** 6 from Troyes (*www.courriers delaube.fr*)
- ℹ️ **Visitor information**: 2 Pl de l'Echiquier, 10210; 03 25 40 97 22; *www.tourisme-en-chaourcois.com*
- 🕐 **Open** Fromagerie de Mussy: closed Wed & Sun. Musée du Fromage: closed Tue
- 🍽️ **Eat and drink** *Real meal* Les Routiers à Chaource (*1 Grande Rue, 10210; 03 25 40 12 81*) is an agreeable pizzeria. *Family treat* L'Auberge Sans Nom (*1 Rue des Fontaines, 10210; 03 25 42 46 74; www.aubergesansnom.fr*) serves not just proper meals, but also *tartines* (open sandwiches).

Letting off steam

Chaource is surrounded by the **Forêt d'Aumont** to the north and the **Forêt de Cussagny** to the south. Follow part of the 18-km (11-mile) marked path called the Circuit du Chaourçois to the west or south of Chaource.

⑤ Langres
Get ready for battle

Set on a rocky limestone spur, the little town of Langres has been a stronghold since Roman times and is almost entirely surrounded by medieval fortifications. These were erected to defend the borderlands between Champagne and Burgundy. There are breathtaking views in all directions, particularly splendid to the east over the Marne Valley and the Vosges mountains. Walk around the ramparts – a distance of 4 km (2 miles) – passing a series of towers and town gates. Or see the ramparts and the tightly packed streets of the town from the comfort of the Petit Train Touristique. The famous writer Denis Diderot, who was born here in 1713, went on to create the colossal *Encyclopédie*, one of the first modern encyclopaedias.

The Lowdown

- 🌐 **Map reference** 9 D1
  Address 52200 (Haute-Marne). Petit Train Touristique: 03 25 87 67 67; *www.tourisme-langres.com*
- 🚗 **Train** from Paris and intercity link from Reims
- ℹ️ **Visitor information** Pl Bel Air, 52200; 03 25 87 67 67; *www. tourisme-langres.com*
- 🍵 **Eat and drink** *Snacks* Le Kerimen (*9 Rue Jean Roussat, 52200; 03 25 84 58 06*) is a family-friendly restaurant that serves crêpes. *Real meal* Le Corsaire (*5 Rue de la Plage, 52200 Peigney; 03 25 88 76 48, www.le-corsaire. com*) has a terrace overlooking the Lac de Liez. It offers pizzas, pastas and substantial menus.

Letting off steam

Head for the Lac de la Liez, 5 km (3 miles) east of Langres, with views of the town, footpaths, swimming beaches in summer and canoes, electric boats and pedalos for hire. Or play in **Sensation Nature** (*sensation ature.com*), an adventure park 5 km (3 miles) south of Langres, with rope climbs and zip wires for kids 4 plus.

⑥ Château Fort de Sedan
Medieval mega-fortress

Perhaps the largest medieval castle in Europe, the Château Fort de Sedan is massive, with monstrously thick walls, cavernous halls, dripping passages, arrow slits and cannon ports. It was founded on the Meuse river in 1424 by the warlord Everard de la Marck and became the base of the princes of Sedan, who ruled over a territory that stood independent from France until 1642. Seasonal events, festivals, displays of jousting and falconry help to bring the castle alive.

Wax figures on display in the Château Fort de Sedan

Key Features

Bastion du Roy

Bastion des Gouverneur

Entrance

Bastion des Dames

⑤ **Le Tours Jumelles** Built in the 1420s, this massive gate was flanked by twin towers, which have since lost their cone-shaped tops. Inside, the slot for the portcullis can still be seen.

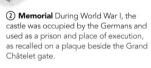

① **Mighty walls** The castle grew bigger and stronger over the centuries, to match the increasing power of cannons. Some 15th-century outer walls ended up 26 m (85 ft) thick.

② **Memorial** During World War I, the castle was occupied by the Germans and used as a prison and place of execution, as recalled on a plaque beside the Grand Châtelet gate.

③ **Hôtel le Château Fort** A wing of the old castle has been turned into a luxury hotel. The hotel's Restaurant Tour d'Auvergne recalls the family name of the princes of Sedan.

④ **Bastions** The pointed corner bastions, filled with earth and rubble, were built in the 1550s as a defence against the new cannons, which could destroy the older and weaker castle walls.

⑥ **Galerie des Princes** The once-luxurious apartments of the princes now house a small museum. Some artefacts recall the Battle of Sedan in 1870, which saw the defeat of Napoleon III in the Franco-Prussian War.

The Lowdown

🌐 **Map reference** 5 C3
Address 08200 (Ardennes). Cours Clos du Château, 08200 Sedan; www.chateau-fort-sedan.fr

🚗 **Train** TGV from Paris & Reims. **Bus** RDTA from Charleville-Mezières

ℹ **Visitor information** 6 Rue de la Rochefoucauld, 08208; 03 24 27 73 00; www.sedan.fr

🕐 **Open** Jul & Aug: 10am–6pm daily; Apr–Jun, Sep & school hols: 10am–noon & 1:30–5pm

daily; Oct–Mar: 10am–noon & 1:30–5pm Tue–Sun, closed Christmas & 1 Jan

💶 **Price** €26–36; under 6s free

🎟 **Skipping the queue** There is hardly any queue

🚩 **Guided tours** Audio tours available in English, French, Dutch and German

👫 **Age range** 4 plus. Note that there are several stone staircases and rough paths.

🏃 **Activities** The château offers a self-guided tour, using audio guides that can be loaded on to a portable phone. The tour starts from the castle courtyard.

⏱ **Allow** At least 1 hour and 30 mins

☕ **Café** A small café on site next to the shop

🛍 **Shop** La Boutique, close to the central courtyard, has all kinds of medieval-themed toys, games, souvenirs, books and figurines.

Prices given are for a family of four

Tree climbing in the charming Jardin Botanique

Letting off steam

There is plenty of open space both inside and outside the castle for kids to scamper about in. Down in the pretty, sandstone town is the lovely **Jardin Botanique** (Pl d'Alsace-Lorraine, 08200), a 10-minute walk away. Further south, next to the Meuse river, is an artificial lake, the **Lac de Sedan**, which has footpaths, a public swimming pool called Centre Aquatique de Sedan and also a swimming beach with lifeguards in July and August.

Eat and drink

Picnic: under €20; Snacks: €20–45; Real meal: €45–90; Family treat: over €90 (based on a family of four)

PICNIC Maison Jacquemart (10 Rue du Ménil, 08200; closed Sun & Mon) is a charcuterie-traiteur that stocks tasty snacks. The picturesque Jardin Botanique or the Lac de Sedan are good picnic spots.
SNACKS Crêperie du Château (10 Pl du Château, 08200; 03 24 22 08 49) is a pretty little gingham-decked

restaurant overlooking the castle's Bastion du Roy. The restaurant specializes in *galettes bretonnes* (savoury pancakes) and crêpes.
REAL MEAL Le St-Michel (3 Rue St-Michel, 08200; 03 24 29 04 61; www.le-saint-michel.fr) is an agreeable family-run hotel restaurant, popular with locals. The menus are reasonably priced and offer reliable standard dishes and local specialities. Spot the huge boar's head wearing a football scarf.
FAMILY TREAT Brasserie Artisanale du Château Fort (45 Promenoir des Prêtres, 08200; 03 24 53 13 52), is a jolly, traditional restaurant close to the castle's boutique. Decorated with retro posters and memorabilia, it serves a good range of typical brasserie dishes to suit all tastes.

Shopping

The best toy shop is in the castle. In Sedan, there is a small shopping hub between Rue du Ménil, Place de la Halle and Rue Gambetta.

The Horloge du Grand Marionette in Charleville-Mézières

Next stop...

CHARLEVILLE-MÉZIÈRES Located 13 km (8 miles) to the west of Sedan, capital of the Ardennes Department is also known as the "capital of marionette puppets" because of the **Institut International de la Marionette** (Pl Winston Churchill, 08000; www.marionnette.com), which holds temporary exhibitions. The Horloge du Grand Marionettiste, a giant animated clock, opens up as the hour strikes to play out scenes from a local legend here.

Where to Stay in Champagne

Champagne is proud of its bubbly traditions of hospitality, never far from the surface in this broad choice of *gîtes* and manor-house *chambres d'hôtes* – some of which are splendidly grand – and hotels that range between straight-down-the-middle reliable and agreeably quirky.

AGENCY
Tourisme Champagne-Ardenne
www.champagne-ardenne-tourism.co.uk
The website has links to the main self-catering accommodation agencies operating in the region.

Chaource
Map 9 B1

BED & BREAKFAST
Domaine Saint-Roch
42 Grande Rue, 10210 Prusy; 03 25 70 06 04; tinyurl.com/74slb2n
Located 12 km (7 km) southwest of Chaource, this is a group of farm buildings. There are two adjacent B&Bs, sleeping two to three, and a separate *gîte* sleeping four to five.
⌂ ⌂ P ◐   €€

Épernay
Map 5 B5

HOTEL
Hostellerie du Mont Aimé
51130 Bergères-les-Vertus; 03 26 52 21 31; tinyurl.com/3qfotgs
About 20 km (12 miles) south of Épernay, this comfortable Logis hotel-restaurant has family rooms for four. The restaurant offers a kids' menu.
⌂ P ◐   €€

Langres
Map 9 D1

HOTEL
Hôtel du Cheval Blanc
4 Rue de l'Estres, 52200; 03 25 87 07 00; www.hotel-langres.com
Recently renovated, it occupies a former abbey, parts of which date

Farm buildings around the swimming pool at Domaine Saint-Roch, Chaource

Key to symbols *see back cover flap*

from the 12th century. Several rooms have original stone features and are subtly styled. Restaurant on site.
⌂ P   €€

Reims
Map 5 B4

HOTELS
Hôtel Azur
7–9 Rue des Écrevées, 51100; 03 26 47 43 39; www.hotel-azur-reims.com
This friendly little hotel is close to the Place Drouet d'Erlon and is a short walk across the city centre from the cathedral. Rooms are brightly decorated, simple and modern.
⌂ P   €

Hôtel Crystal
86 Pl Drouet d'Erlon, 51100; 03 26 88 44 44; www.hotel-crystal.fr
An elegant 1920s Neo-Classical mansion with a delightful courtyard garden, this hotel is located in the thick of Reims' most popular public square. The rooms are comfortable. Underground car park nearby.
⌂   €

SELF-CATERING
Manoir de Maffrécourt Map 5 C5
51800 Maffrecourt; 02 53 44 20 52; www.champagne-gites.com
A lovely and enterprising manor-house *gîte* about 50 km (31 miles) east of Reims, it offers an apartment sleeping six, a cottage sleeping two to four, a fully-equipped "Sanglier Super Tent" sleeping up to four and facilities for "rustic camping". Home-cooked meals available.
⌂ ⌂ P ◐   €€

Sedan
Map 5 C3

HOTELS
Le Saint Michel
3 Rue St-Michel, 08200; 03 24 29 04 61; www.le-saint-michel.fr
A welcoming family-run Logis hotel near the castle, with modern and well-equipped rooms. The restaurant is popular with locals.
P ✳   €€

Simple but elegant room in the friendly Hôtel Azur, Reims

Hôtel Le Château Fort
08200 Portes des Princes; 03 24 26 11 00; www.hotelfp-sedan.com
This sleek, modern hotel within the Château Fort de Sedan has 54 rooms decorated in modern-antique style. Family rooms sleep four to five. Free visitor passes to the castle available.
⌂ P   €€€

CAMPING
Camping de Douzy
Map 5 D3
Base de loisirs, 08140 Douzy; 03 24 26 31 19; www.camping-douzy.com
About 3 km (2 miles) east of Sedan, this three-star camping site has 125 pitches, caravans, camping cars and five fully equipped chalets for rent. It offers lake swimming, fishing, a playground and a family restaurant.
P ◐   €

Troyes
Map 5 B6

HOTEL
Les Comtes de Champagne
54/56 Rue de la Monnaie, 10000; 03 25 73 11 70; tinyurl.com/6s3hbvw
This welcoming, centrally located two-star hotel has a quirky set of four 16th-century half-timbered mansions. Some family rooms and suites sleep up to six and have kitchenettes.
⌂ ⌂ P   €€

Price Guide
The following price ranges are based on one night's accommodation in high season for a family of four, inclusive of service charges and any additional taxes.
€ Under €100 €€ €100–200 €€€ over €200

Le Nord and Picardy

Magnificent Nausicaá brings year-round interest to the Côte d'Opale, where a rugged line of cliffs, sand beaches and marshy bays face the Channel. Lille, Arras and Amiens display the prosperity of medieval times, and the Somme reveals memories of World War I. The grand Château at Chantilly and Parc Astérix provide two more attractions.

Below The central atrium of the impressive and engaging sealife centre, Nausicaá

Nausicaá
p68

Parc Astérix
p74

① Nausicaá, Boulogne-sur-Mer
Explore beneath the waves – on land

With an inspired architectural design, Nausicaá is full of drama, but also delivers educational information underpinned by a strong ecological message. Get up close with scary sharks, dance with a sea lion or stroke a skate in one of the largest sea-life centres in Europe. Walk through darkened passageways, resonating with evocative sounds, to travel around the underwater world, from the ocean depths to the lakes of Africa, visiting a collection of 35,000 living creatures.

Key Features

Entrance   Entrance

Upper Floor The Nourishing Sea and Our Planet, Our Home

Entrance Level The World of the Sea and Man's Ocean

First Lower Level Managing Life's Diversity and Tropical Lagoon Village

Second Lower Level Managing Life's Diversity and Tropical Lagoon Village

Annexe Cap au Sud

③ **Cap au Sud** Imagine being on board a ship on a mission across the Atlantic with Jean-Michel Cousteau in this part of Nausicaá. The expedition ends with a 10-minute 4D film about saving the planet.

④ **Coral lagoon** View the wave-effect coral reef from above, then go downstairs to see 3,100 colourful species of fish and some sharks as well.

⑤ **Reptiles** Meet the two giant Aldabra tortoises from the Seychelles in the Tropical Lagoon Village section and caimans in the Submerged Tropical Forest section.

⑥ **Giant seaweed** The Californian tank has a forest of kelp, with smooth-hound sharks and bright Garibaldi damsel-fish weaving in and out.

① **Fishing business** A section of a large fishing trawler, with screen projections showing it being buffeted by high seas, forms the hub of this section devoted to the fishing industry.

② **Touch Pool** Stroke a pollack, cod, dogfish, stingray and turbot swimming at eye level in this aquarium. The stingrays, in particular, seem to enjoy it – and do not sting.

⑦ **Sea lions** Animal trainers demonstrate the amazing intelligence and agility of sea lions by getting them to mirror movements and read signs through a glass wall in the Sea Lion Reserve.

The Lowdown

🌐 **Map reference** 4 F1
Address 62000 (Pas de Calais) Blvd Ste-Beuve, 62203 Boulogne-sur-Mer; 03 21 30 99 99

🚗 **Train** TGV from Paris to Calais-Fréthun, then line 1 from town centre to Nausicaá

ℹ️ **Visitor information** Parvis de Nausicaá, 62203; 03 21 10 88 10; www.tourisme-boulogne surmer.com

🕐 **Open** Jul–Aug: 9:30am–7:30pm daily; Sep–Jun: 9:30am–6:30pm daily; closed 25 Dec, 1 Jan am & last three weeks in Jan

💶 **Price** €50–60; under 3s free. Students and concessions €12. Group ticket holders get discount at shops and snack bars.

👫 **Skipping the queue** Buy a ticket two hours before closing time, when the aquarium is less busy. Use the ticket until midday the following day. The NausicaaPass (www.nausicaa.fr) can be bought online to avoid queues and for discount on entry fees.

🚩 **Guided tours** Audio guides available in French, English

and Dutch. Limited places for "Behind the Scenes" guided tours (10am & 3pm); book in advance

👫 **Age range** All ages

🏃 **Activities** Look out for the daily schedule of presentations and activities, such as feeding the sea lions and feeding the fish of the Tropical Lagoon Village section.

⏱️ **Allow** At least 3 hours. Ticket holders can leave the building and return any time during the day.

Prices given are for a family of four

Rides and acitivities for kids at the beach next to Nausicaá

Letting off steam

Visit the superb sandy **beach** next door to Nausicaá; it has a broad promenade running along the back. Boulogne is located in the middle of the long stretch of coast called the **Côte d'Opale**. Just north of the city is **Wimereux**, with excellent beaches.

Eat and drink

Picnic: under €20; Snacks: €20–45; Real meal: €45–90; Family treat: over €90 (based on a family of four)

PICNIC Bourgeois Traiteur *(1 Grande Rue, 62203; 03 21 31 53 57; closed Mon)* has delicious prepared dishes and snacks. Stock up with picnic supplies on offer at the excellent food market *(8:30am–noon Wed & Sat)* at Place Dalton. Picnic at the small, tree-shaded park nearby or on the beach next to Nausicaá.

SNACKS Au Ch'ti Casse Croûte *(208 Rue National, 62200; 03 21 80 85 79)* serves snacks such as mussels and chips, kebabs, hamburgers.

REAL MEAL Chez Jules *(8 Pl Dalton, 62203; 03 21 31 54 12; www.chez-jules.fr)* is a brasserie, restaurant and pizzeria, with a wood-fired oven.

Café The Tropical Lagoon Bar and Au Bistrot du Port on site

Shop The on-site shop, close to the main entrance, sells a variety of aquatic-themed toys, posters, books, ornaments and clothes.

Toilets Near the entrance and also near the Tropical Lagoon Bar.

Good family value?
Educating and entertaining, Nausicaá appeals to all ages and makes for a fine family day out.

There is something for everyone here, including seafood and *plateaux de fruits de mer* (seafood platter). **FAMILY TREAT Restaurant de Nausicaá** *(on site; 03 21 33 24 24; till 10pm Tue–Sun)* offers views over the beach and sea. It serves mainly seafood. There is a tasting bar attached to it for lighter meals of oysters and seafood dishes.

Shopping

In Boulogne, the small Centre Ville area has a number of appealing shops such as the delightful kids' clothes chain **Sergent-Major** *(7/9 Rue Thiers, 62203; 03 21 31 56 45; www.sergent-major.com)*.

Find out more

DIGITAL Check out the kids' section on *www.nausicaa.co.uk/children. html* for printable colouring pages and animal cards. The Ocean Files section on *www.nausicaa.co.uk/ ocean-files.html* has illustrated articles on sharks, whales and other creatures of the deep, with links and news posts.

Towering stone walls surrounding the Haute Ville, Boulogne

Next stop...

BOULOGNE-SUR-MER Set above the city centre, the old town area of Boulogne, called Haute Ville, is a short walk from the city centre. The old city gates lead into an enclave that has changed little since the 18th and 19th centuries. Surrounded by medieval walls, it is tightly packed with houses, shops and restaurants. Walk around the walls and visit the **Château-Musée** *(Rue de Bernet, 62200; 03 21 10 02 22)*. Set in a medieval castle, this museum has an intriguing collection of historical curiosities on display.

Artistic glassware on display at Arc International, Arques near St-Omer

② St-Omer
Glass and rockets

An attractive town, St-Omer boasts the Gothic Cathédrale Notre-Dame, with 17th- and 18th-century streets clustering around it. The town makes an enjoyable base for visiting nearby sites. The **Ascenseur à Bateaux**, east of St-Omer, is a boat lift, built in the 1880s, on the Canal de Neuffossé. Though no longer used, a museum shows how it worked. Southeast of St-Omer, Arques has the famous glass factory **Arc International**, a source of Luminarc, Pyrex and Crystal d'Arques glassware. Located 5 km (3 miles) south of St-Omer is **La Coupole**, a World War II facility built by the Germans to fire V2 rockets

The Lowdown

🌐 **Map reference** 4 G1
Address 62500 (Nord-Pas-de-Calais). Ascenseur à Bateaux: Rue Denis Papin, 62510; 03 21 88 59 00. Arc International: Zone Industrielle, RN 43, 62510; 03 21 12 74 74; www.arc-intl.com. La Coupole: Rue de Mont-à-Car, D210, 62570 Helfaut; www.la coupole-france.com. Maison du Papier: Rue Bernard Chochoy, 62380; 03 21 95 45 25

� **Train** from Boulogne and Lille

ℹ **Visitor information** 4 Rue du Lion d'Or, 62500; 03 21 98 08 51; www.tourisme-saintomer.com

🕐 **Open** Ascenseur à Bateaux: Apr–Sep: daily. Arc International: Mon–Sat. La Coupole: daily. Maison du Papier: Apr–Aug: Tue–Fri (Jul & Aug: also Sat & Sun)

🍴 **Eat and drink** *Picnic* Auchan Rives de l'Aa (*2 Ave des Frais Fonds, 62219 Longuenesse; 03 21 98 78 00*) is a mega-supermarket just to the south of St-Omer. *Real meal* Chez Tante Fauvette (*10 Rue Ste Croix, 62500; 03 21 11 26 08; cheztantefauvette.com*) serves country kitchen-style meals and also authentic regional dishes.

Prices given are for a family of four

on London in 1943. A museum provides a story of rockets from that time to the space exploration era. The **Maison du Papier** in Esquerdes, southwest of St-Omer, a papermaking centre since the 15th century, shows how paper was traditionally made. It offers hands-on activities for kids.

Letting off steam

The Marais Audomarois, the marshes to the east of St-Omer, are a rare area of farmed wetlands crisscrossed by narrow canals. **Isnor** (*www.isnor.fr*) runs open-topped boat trips from Clairmarais, to the east of the town.

③ Lille
Brand new, old and prehistoric

The capital of French Flanders, Lille is one of France's biggest cities. Vieux Lille, its historic centre, has winding streets threading out from a cluster of three squares and is an excellent place to explore on foot. By contrast, "Euralille" located 2 km (1 mile) to the east, is an ultramodern development with a number of striking pieces of architecture and a mega shopping mall. Go to the **Palais des Beaux-Arts**, which has a great collection of paintings, notably of Flemish art. Visit the **Musée d'-Histoire Naturelle et de Géologie**, a wonderland of animals, shells and dinosaur models. Climb up the belfry of the **Hôtel de Ville** for fine views.

Letting off steam

The **Citadelle de Lille** (*59800 Esquermes; 08 91 56 20 04*) is a star-shaped fortress – typical of military engineer Vauban. Although still used as a military base, it is ringed by the Bois de Boulogne parkland, gardens and a playground.

The Lowdown

🌐 **Map reference** 4 H1
Address 59000 (Nord). Palais des Beaux-Arts: Pl de la République; 03 20 06 78 00; www.pba-lille.fr. Musée d'Histoire Naturelle et de Géologie: 19 Rue de Bruxelles; 03 28 55 30 80; www.mairie-lille.fr. Hôtel de Ville: Pl des Héros; 03 20 49 50 00

� **Train** TGV from Paris

ℹ **Visitor information** Pl Rihour, 59000; 03 33 59 57 94 00; www.lilletourism.com

🕐 **Open** Palais des Beaux-Arts: closed Tue. Musée d'Histoire Naturelle et de Géologie: closed Tue & Sat. Hôtel de Ville: Tue–Sun

🍴 **Eat and drink** *Snacks* Paul (*6 Pl de Strasbourg, 59000; 03 20 57 26 29*) is a chain of international bakeries and *salons de thé* since 1953. *Real meal* La Pâte Brisée (*63–65 Rue de la Monnaie, 59000; 03 20 74 29 00; www.lapatebri see.fr*) specializes in quiches and tarts and includes a kids' menu.

④ Arras
Beneath the streets

A grand little city, Arras is centered around its two main squares – the Grand'Place and the Place des Héros. Next to the cathedral, the Abbaye de St-Vaast houses the admirable **Musée des Beaux-Arts**, with beautiful paintings, tapestries and especially fine medieval carvings. Much of the city has been rebuilt in original style since its widespread destruction in World War I. *Les Boves*, a network of underground passages that spread beneath the city, was cut out from quarry stone in the 9th century and is a must-see. Go to the underground **Carrière**

Ferris wheel in the Grand'Place in the heart of Lille

Splendid view of the city's charming buildings and cathedral, Arras

The Lowdown

🌐 **Map reference** 4 H2
Address 62000 (Pas-de-Calais). Musée des Beaux-Arts: 22 Rue Paul Doumer; 03 21 71 26 43. Carrière Wellington: Rue Delétoile; 03 21 51 26 95; www.carriere-wellington.com Hôtel de Ville: Pl des Héros; 03 21 51 26 95

🚗 **Train** from Boulogne, Paris & Lille

ℹ️ **Visitor information** Hôtel de Ville, Pl des Héros, 62000; 03 21 51 26 95; www.ot-arras.fr

🕐 **Open** Musée des Beaux-Arts: closed Tue. Carrière Wellington: late Jan–Dec: daily. Hôtel de Ville: daily

🍽️ **Eat and drink** *Real meal* Le Petit Rat Porteur (11 Rue de la Taillerie, 62000; 03 21 51 29 70; www.le petitratporteur.fr) serves reasonably priced regional food, including a kids' menu. *Family treat* La Cave des Saveurs (36 Grand'Place, 62000; 03 21 59 75 24; lacavedes saveurs.free.fr) is a family-run restaurant with excellent food.

Wellington, which sheltered 24,000 Allied soldiers as they prepared for the Battle of Arras in April 1917, and its memorial museum. Climb the belfry of the **Hôtel de Ville** for a bird's-eye view of the city.

Letting off steam

Zip off to the **Jardin des Allées** (Blvd Crespel, 62000; 03 21 51 26 95), a park with walkways and playgrounds for kids.

⑤ Montreuil-sur-Mer

But don't bring swimming costumes

Although it is called sur-Mer, literally "on sea", Montreuil is actually 15 km (9 miles) inland. This hilltop town once overlooked a busy port on the

estuary of the Canche river – a fortified royal town with a castle and a meeting place of kings. But, the estuary silted up in the late Middle Ages and the sea retreated. The key attraction is its ramparts, with views out over the nearby countryside and to the coast. Visit the old fortress and former royal castle called the **Citadelle**. The flower-bedecked streets of the town, lined with 17th- and 18th-century buildings, make it a nice place to wander. Seek out the cobbled Rue du Clape-en-bas. Victor Hugo made Montreuil the setting for the first part of his novel *Les Misérables*. It is the subject of a *son et lumière* with hundreds of local actors at the Citadelle.

Letting off steam

Scamper about the ramparts of Montreuil or beaches of Le Touquet, located 18 km (11 miles) west of the town. On the seafront, to the northwest is **Aqualud** (www.aqualud. com), a giant pool with indoor and outdoor pools, shoots and tubes.

The quaint, flower-decked town of Montreuil-sur-Mer

The Lowdown

🌐 **Map reference** 4 F2
Address 62170 (Pas-de-Calais). Citadelle: Rue Carnot; 03 21 06 10 83

🚗 **Train** from Arras and Boulogne

ℹ️ **Visitor information** 21 Rue Carnot, 62170; 03 21 06 04 27; www.tourisme-montreuillois.com

🕐 **Open** Citadelle: Wed–Mon

🍽️ **Eat and drink** *Picnic* Le Cafe Victor Hugo (3 Place Gambetta, 67170 Montreuil; 03 21 06 01 74) sells sandwiches for a picnic. Picnic on the ramparts. *Family treat* Les Hauts de Montreuil (19–23 Rue Pierre Ledent, 62170; 03 21 81 95 92; tinyurl.com/3onmul6) offers tasty regional food and a menu for kids.

⑥ Baie de Somme
Birds, boats, beaches, bikes and seals

The Somme river is channelled into a canal at Abbeville, to make the last 15 km (9 miles) of its journey to the sea. It broadens out into a wide and beautiful estuary called the Baie de Somme, edged by salt marshes, beaches and nature reserves, with the easygoing fishing ports of Le Crotoy to the north and St-Valery-sur-Somme to the south. The upper town of St-Valery retains most of its medieval fortifications. William the Conqueror set out to invade England from here in August 1066. The **Parc du Marquenterre**, north of the bay, is a huge bird sanctuary, with many species of birds, including cranes, herons and storks. Rent kayaks, or take a guided trip in large Polynesian-style pirogues from the Quai Jeanne d'Arc in St-Valery to see seals at close quarters in the estuary. In summer, the historic steam trains of the **Chemin de Fer de la Baie de Somme** run between Le Crotoy and St-Valery, with a diesel train link 12 km (7 miles) to Cayeux-sur-Mer.

Cyclists approaching St-Valery on the cycling path running around the Somme Estuary

The Lowdown

- 🌐 **Map reference** 4 F3
  Address 80230 (Somme). Parc du Marquenterre: 25 bis Chemin des Garennes, 80120; 03 22 25 68 99, *www.marcanterra. fr*. Chemin de Fer de la Baie de Somme: Ave Gare, 80550 Le Crotoy; 03 22 26 96 96; *www. chemin-fer-baie-somme.asso.fr*
- 🚗 **Car** from Abberville
- ℹ️ **Visitor information** St-Valery: 2 Pl Guillaume le Conquérant, 80230; 03 22 60 93 50. Le Crotoy: 1 Rue Carnot, 80550; 03 22 27 05 25; *www.visit-somme.com*
- 🕐 **Open** Parc du Marquenterre: timings vary throughout the year. Chemin de Fer de la Baie de Somme: Apr–Oct (trains depart late morning)
- ☕ **Eat and drink** *Snacks* Les Galettes de Tante Olympe (*36 Rue de la Ferté, 80230 St-Valery; 03 22 60 42 59*) serves *galettes* (savoury pancakes) and crêpes, with a lovely bay view. *Family treat* Chez Mado (*6 Quai Léonard, 80550 Le Crotoy; 03 22 27 81 22; www.chezmado. com*) serves good seafood and offers great bay views.
- 🎊 **Festival** Fête de la Mer, sea festival with traditional costumes and parades in St-Valery (Aug)

Take cover

Go to the **Ecomusée Picarvie** (*5 Quai de Romerel, 80230 St-Valery; 03 22 02 69 49*) that reconstructs the local life and crafts of historic Picardy.

⑦ Grottes-Refuges de Naours
Explore an underground city

The extensive network of *muches* (cave-refuges) dug out of limestone beneath the town of Naours forms an underground city, all some 33 m (100 ft) below the surface. With 2 km (1 mile) of subterranean streets, public squares, as well as 300 rooms, there was enough space to shelter 2,600 people – complete with wells, bakeries and chapels, as well as stalls for their cattle and horses. The first caves were dug as quarries in Roman times, nearly 2,000 years ago. The caves were used by the Nazis as military headquarters in World War II. Be sure to dress warmly.

Letting off steam

Run about in the big wooded park above the caves, which has two windmills on top of the hill, a watermill, a playground, as well as animals such as peacocks and deer.

Splendid caribou statue at the Parc-Mémorial de Beaumont Hamel, Somme

The Lowdown

- 🌐 **Map reference** 4 G3
  Address 80260 (Somme).
- 🚗 **Car** from Amiens to Naours
- ℹ️ **Visitor information** 5 Rue des Carrières, 80260; 03 22 93 71 78; *www.grottesdenaours.com*
- 🕐 **Open** Feb–mid-Dec: daily; (45-min audio guides available)
- 💲 **Price** €36–46; under 4s free
- ☕ **Eat and drink** *Picnic* Carrefour Market (*22 Rue General Leclerc, 80000 Amiens; 03 22 91 07 38*) stocks supplies. Picnic in the park attached to the caves. *Snacks* Le Restaurant de la Cite Souterraine (*on site; May–Jun: Sat & Sun only; Jul & Aug: open daily*) serves savoury pancakes, quiches and salads.

⑧ Battlefields of the Somme
Memories of war

One of the most bitterly contested areas of the front in World War I was the Somme, east of Albert; some 20,000 British troops died on the first day of the Battle of the Somme on 1 July 1916, and between then and November around a million more men died in the fighting on both sides. Visit the trenches of the **Parc-Mémorial de Beaumont Hamel**, devoted to the Royal Newfoundland Regiment. At La Boisselle, the Lochnagar Crater made by a British mine bomb displays the power of the munitions used. The Memorial at Thiepval, to more than 72,000 missing British soldiers, dwarfs neat ranks of 600 British and French graves. The **Historial de la Grande Guerre**, a museum set in the château at Péronne, gives a full and moving account of the war through exhibits, posters and films.

The Lowdown

- 🌐 **Map reference** 4 G3 & 4 H3
  Address 80300, 80200 (Somme).
  Parc-Mémorial de Beaumont
  Hamel: D55, 62580; 03 21 50 68
  68. Historial de la Grande Guerre:
  Château de Péronne, 80201; 03
  22 83 14 18; www.historial.org
- 🚗 **Car** from Amiens to the
  battlefields
- ℹ️ **Visitor information** Albert: 9 Rue
  Gambetta, 80300; 03 22 75 16 42.
  Péronne: 16 Pl André Audinot,
  80200; 03 22 84 42 38; www.
  visit-somme.com
- 🕑 **Open** Parc-Mémorial de
  Beaumont Hamel: year round.
  Historial de la Grande Guerre:
  daily, closed mid-Dec–mid-Jan
- 🍴 **Eat and drink** Picnic Intermarché
  (Rue 11 Novermbre, 80300
  Albert; 03 22 75 21 21) is a
  convenient one-stop source of
  supplies. Real meal Le Bistrot
  d'Antoine (8 Pl André Audinot,
  80200 Péronne; 03 22 85 84 46;
  www.bistrot-antoine.fr) offers
  regional cookery and a kids menu.

Letting off steam

The Somme river provides a tranquil
setting for walks, especially along
the series of marshland pools called
Les Étangs de la Haute Somme near
Péronne. Take a trip on a historic
stream or diesel train: in summer, **Le
P'tit Train de la Haute Somme** (www.
appeva.perso.neuf.fr) runs along the
Somme river to the south of Albert.

⑨ Amiens
Soaring cathedral and floating gardens

The capital of the historic province
of Picardy, located on the Somme
river, Amiens boasts the Cathédrale
Notre-Dame, the largest Gothic
cathedral in France. Built between
the 13th and 15th centuries, it stuns
with masses of statues and relief
sculptures; the soaring nave is the
highest in France. The **Musée de
Picardie** has an art and archaeology
collection. Visit the **Maison de Jules
Verne**, home of the great pioneer
science-fiction and adventure-book
writer, who wrote the famous Around
the World in Eighty Days. A rare
attraction is the Hortillonages, an
area of cultivated marshlands
threaded by canals; boat trips run
through the little "floating" market
gardens and orchards.

Letting off steam

The **Parc St-Pierre**, a 10-minute walk
from the cathedral across a bridge
over the Somme, has riverside walks,
a lake, and climbing frame: it is a
good place to picnic.

Sculpture on the main portico of
Cathédrale Notre-Dame, Amiens

The Lowdown

- 🌐 **Map reference** 4 G3
  Address 80000 (Somme).
  Musée de la Picardie: 48 Rue
  de la République; 03 22 97 14
  00; tinyurl.com/68hykm5. Maison
  de Jules Verne: 2 Rue Charles
  Dubois; 03 22 45 45 75; www.
  jules-verve.net
- 🚗 **Train** from Paris, Calais, Boulogne
  and Lille
- ℹ️ **Visitor information** 40 Parvis Notre
  Dame, 80000; 03 22 71 60 50;
  www.amiens-tourisme.com
- 🕑 **Open** Musée de Picardie: Tue &
  Fri–Sat (till 9pm Thu). Maison de
  Jules Verne: mid-Apr–mid-Oct:
  daily; rest of the year: closed Tue
- 🍴 **Eat and drink** Real meal Le 7ème
  Art (7 Blvd de Belfort, 80000; 03
  22 67 17 17) is a fun place, with
  a broad menu and modern pizzas
  on offer. Family treat Au relais des
  Orfèvres (14 Rue des Orfèvres; 03
  22 92 36 01; www.restaurant-relais-
  orfevres.fr), in the heart of the old
  town, serves traditional dishes by
  chef Jean-Michel Descloux.
- 🎪 **Festival** Fête au Bord de l'Eau,
  a medieval festival in the historic
  St-Leu quarter (Sep)

⑩ Parc Astérix

Greedy Gauls, rotten Romans and roller coasters

By 50 BC, Julius Caesar had conquered most of Gaul, now France, except for a tiny unnamed village situated in the province of Armorica. Parc Astérix is centred around this legendary village, which Asterix the Gaul and his sidekick Obelix famously defended from the Roman invaders. The park, which has lots of charm and was approved by Asterix's creator, Albert Uderzo, has exhilarating rides, a calm cruise through the village and, of course, characters to meet and greet.

Figure of a Roman soldier in Parc Astérix

Key Features

① **Menhir Express** Get wet on this spectacular water ride while hurtling down the 13-m (43-ft) slide in one of Obelix's standing stones.

② **Trace du Hourra** Shoot along a bobsleigh. Run, slide, glide, swirl and shout hurray while plunging downwards.

③ **Goudurix** Twirl upside down seven times at a speed of 75 km (47 miles) per hour on this thrill-seeking roller coaster.

⑤ **Transdémonium** Step inside the dragon's mouth and into the medieval castle. Ride past the skeletons, monsters and phantoms on a ghost train.

- Entrance
- Roman City
- Roman Circus
- Ronde des Rondins
- Gaulish Village
- Poseidon Theatre
- Parking area
- Forest of the Druids

④ **Dancing dolphins** Watch these lively creatures in a superb magical show that will enchant kids.

⑥ **Oxygénarium** Take a deep breath before plunging 195 m (640 ft) in this giant water slide.

⑦ **Tonnère de Zeus** Ride the biggest, gravity-defying wooden roller coaster in Europe, which whizzes along at 80 km (50 miles) per hour to the summit of Mount Olympus.

Letting off steam

To take a break from the rides, run around the Gaulish village to spot Obelix and the others, or let loose in the **Forest of the Druids** playground nearby; walk in the wise old druid Getafix's footsteps through the menhirs across moving marshes, located next to the **Ronde des Rondins**, a mini roller coaster that is suitable for younger members of the family. When the park opens for Christmas holidays, there is plenty of entertainment to look out for, including a lovely ice-skating rink.

Prices given are for a family of four

Eat and drink

Picnic: under €25; Snacks: €25–45; Real meal: €45–90; Family treat: over €90 (based on a family of four)

PICNIC Buy picnic ingredients at Leclerc in Paris to keep costs down. Picnic by the lake.

SNACKS Food kiosks and cafés are scattered across the park.

REAL MEAL Aux Fastes de Rome is a fast food outlet in the Roman city, with a pleasant terrace. **Le Cirque** is the best bet for a good hot meal. It also has an indoor play area for kids near the Oxygénarium.

FAMILY TREAT Arcimboldo, located near the exit of the Gaulish village, is decorated with a mountain of plastic fruits and vegetables but has classic dishes on the menu.

Fun façade and entrance to the park's popular restaurant, Arcimboldo

The Lowdown

🌐 **Map reference** 4 G5
Address 60000 (Oise).
60128 Plailly; 08 26 30 10 40;
www.parcasterix.fr

🚗 **Train** RER B3 from Paris to
Aéroport Charles de Gaulle,
from where a shuttle bus leaves
every 30 mins, 9:30am–6:30pm.
Joint train and entry tickets are
available. **Bus** Direct shuttle
bus from Paris (€70–80 return)

🕐 **Open** Apr–Aug & some winter
school hols: 10am–6pm Mon–
Fri, 9:30am–6pm Sat & Sun;
Sep–Oct: 10am–6pm Sat
& Sun; late night opening for
Gaulish nights in Jul & Aug.
Check website for timings.

💲 **Price** €140–150; under 3s free.
Check website for special offers.

👪 **Skipping the queue** Avoid
Sunday as it gets too crowded.

👫 **Age range** 7 plus

⏱ **Allow** A day

🚻 **Toilets** On the left by
the entrance, on the left of
the village and by the circus
big top

Good family value?
Kids have to love the stories of
Asterix to get the best out of the
trip. Cut costs by bringing a picnic.

A boat tour through the Gaulish village at Parc Astérix

Shopping

There is no end to souvenirs with
Asterix, Obelix and Dogmatix on
towels, glasses, T-shirts, key rings
and refrigerator magnets. The park
offers a good selection of the books
and films in English. *Asterix and the
Golden Sickle*, the second volume
of the famous comic book series,
is set in Lutetia, now Paris.

Find out more

DIGITAL The magical web potion
can be taken at *www.asterix.com*.
FILM There are as many as 11 films
made on this popular comic strip.
The Twelve Tasks of Asterix (1976)
is a unique cartoon as it is not based
on an existing comic book. The
Romans almost win in *Asterix and
the Big Fight* (1989). Gerald
Depardieu is brilliant as Obelix in
Asterix and Obelix (1999), *Asterix*

and Obelix: Mission Cleopatra
(2002) and *Asterix and the Olympic
Games* (2008).

Take cover

There are shows over weekends
and in high season at the Poseidon
Theatre and the Roman Circus.

Next stop...

FORÊT D'ERMENONVILLE Be
Getafix and Dogmatix and gather up
leaves in the Forêt d'Ermenonville.
To get there, take the A1 to the city
of Senlis, 10 km (6 miles) north of
the theme park, then the D330A
east for 4 km (2 miles) and south
on the N330 through the forest.
Inhabited by wild boar, deer, hares,
roe deer and rabbits, the huge
forest has hiking trails and is also
suited for leisurely walks.

The real Asterix

In 52 BC, Gaulish warrior chief
Vercingetorix united the Gauls
and led a revolt against the
Romans. He was defeated in
the Battle of Alésia, which took
place in the village of Alise-Ste-
Reine in Burgundy. He was held
prisoner for five years until he
was paraded through the streets
of Rome by the
triumphant Caesar
and then executed.
There is a huge
statue of him on
the hilltop where
he fought till the
end, and a Métro
station in Paris
is named after
the battle.

Horse-riding through the lovely Forêt de Chantilly

⑪ Chantilly
Fabulous château and horses

This town is famous for four things: its Neo-Renaissance château, horse-racing, Chantilly cream and Chantilly lace. It has been the capital of French horse-racing since 1834, with an aristocratic history closely linked to the Château de Chantilly, and is still a centre for breeding and training. The château is actually two connected châteaux – the Grand Château and the Petit Château – all but surrounded by water. The Grand Château now houses the **Musée Condé**, filled with top-ranking paintings. The Petit Château's sumptuous apartments house a library containing the 15th-century *Les Très Riches Heures du*

The Lowdown

- 🌐 **Map reference** 4 G4
  Address 60500 (Oise). Musée Condé: Château de Chantilly; 03 44 62 62 62; www.chateaudechantilly.com. Musée Vivant du Cheval: 7 Rue Connétable; 03 44 57 75 51; www.museevivantducheval.fr
- 🚗 **Train** from Paris; RER from Châtelet Les Halles, Paris
- ℹ **Visitor information** 60 Ave du Maréchal Joffre, 60500; 03 44 67 37 37 37; www.chantilly-tourisme.com
- ◷ **Open** Musée Condé & Musée Vivant du Cheval: Wed–Mon
- 🍽 **Eat and drink** *Snacks* Le Hameau (03 44 57 46 21), the model village in the park, offers modest fare and food to take away. *Real meal* La Capitainerie (03 44 57 15 89) serves meals in the original kitchens of the château.
- 🎪 **Festival** Prix du Jockey Club, the main flat-racing meeting (Jun)

Duc de Berry, one of the world's greatest illuminated manuscripts. Outside, the stables, known as the Grandes Écuries, were built in 1719, with room for 240 horses and 500 dogs. They house the **Musée Vivant du Cheval**, which has a collection of 30 horse breeds and presents riding performances three times a day.

Letting off steam

The château is surrounded by a vast, beautiful park, laid out with water features in the late-17th century by the great landscape designer Le Nôtre. Le Petit Train tours the park and rowing boats can be hired at weekends. The huge **Forêt de Chantilly**, adjoining the city, has woodland paths.

⑫ Compiègne
Kings, emperors and a dictator

This is where Joan of Arc was captured in 1430 by the Burgundians and sold to the English. The city boasts the famous **Château de Compiègne**, which was built for Louis XV in the 18th century. It went on to become the favourite residence of Napoleon III. It now houses the Musée du Second Empire about the Napoleon III era (1852–70). The château also has the Musée de la Voiture, a collection of old carriages, bicycles and vintage cars. In the town centre, beside the 16th-century Hôtel de Ville, the **Musée de la Figurine Historique** has 100,000 model figurines in diorama settings.

About 5 km (3 miles) east of the city is the the Clairière de l'Armistice, a forest clearing where the Armistice ending World War I was signed in 1918, in a train carriage. The **Musée de l'Armistice** marks the site with a carriage of the same era. This is also where Hitler chose to sign the French surrender in 1940 (see p52).

The Lowdown

- 🌐 **Map reference** 4 H4
  Address 60200 (Oise). Château de Compiègne: Pl du Général de Gaulle; 03 44 38 47 02; www.musee-chateau-compiegne.fr. Musée de la Figurine Historique: 28 Pl de l'Hôtel de Ville; 03 44 40 72 55; www.musee-figurine.fr. Musée de l'Armistice: Route de Soissons; 03 44 85 14 18
- 🚗 **Train** from Paris and Amiens
- ℹ **Visitor information** Pl de l'Hôtel de Ville, 60200; 03 44 40 01 00; www.compiegne-tourisme.fr
- ◷ **Open** Château de Compiègne: Wed–Mon. Musée de la Figurine Historique: closed Mon. Musée de l'Armistice: daily; winter: closed Tue
- 🍽 **Eat and drink** *Real meal* Le Vivenel (30 Rue Vivenel, 60200, 03 44 86 10 15) offers a delicious range of dishes from the French West Indies, such as stuffed crab, creole sausages and spicy colombo stews. *Family treat* Le Bouchon (4 Rue Austerlitz, 60200; 03 44 20 02 03; www.le-bouchon.com) serves excellent traditional local cuisine in an ancient building with a summer terrace; includes kids' menu.

Above The beautiful Petit Parc of the Château de Compiègne
Below The Petit Château, Chantilly

Letting off steam

Kids can run about in the acres of parkland surrounding the Château de Compiègne, known as the **Petit Parc**, to distinguish it from the Grand Parc southeast of the city. East of the town is the old hunting forest of the **Fôret de Compiègne**, ideal for walks and picnics.

⑬ Château de Pierrefonds

A fairy-tale château

This 14th-century château was falling into ruins until 1857, when it was restored and transformed by Eugène Viollet-le-Duc, the master of French Neo-Gothic design, to create a medieval fantasy castle for Napoleon III. The outside is a decently accurate reproduction of a working military fortress. But work petered out when Napoleon III's reign ended and the planned sumptuous interior was never completed. Still, it remains a fun place to explore through its vast halls, towers, walkways and staircases.

The Lowdown

- 🌐 **Map reference** 4 H4
- **Address** 60350 (Oise). Rue Viollet-le-Duc; 03 44 42 72 72; www.pierrefonds.monuments-nationaux.fr
- 🚗 **Train** from Compiègne, then bus 27 (best reached by car)
- ℹ️ **Visitor information** Pl de l'Hôtel de Ville, 60350; 03 44 42 81 44; www.pierrefonds-tourisme.net
- 🕐 **Open** May–Aug: daily; Sep–Apr Tue–Sun
- 💶 **Price** €14–24; under 18s free
- 🍴 **Eat and drink** Snacks Ouradou Crêperie (8 Rue du Beaudon, 60350; 03 44 42 86 62) serves light meals. Real meal Le Commerce (11 Hôtel de Ville, 60350; 03 44 42 80 66) has a fuller menu, including seafood and pizzas.

Letting off steam

Just to the northwest of Pierrefonds is the Fôret de Compiègne. Walks begin at a number of points off the D973 and D85.

⑭ Laon

Cable car to an ancient capital

Once the capital of Frankish France, the old town of Laon, called the Ville-Haute, is set on a dramatic

The Lowdown

- 🌐 **Map reference** 5 B4
- **Address** 02000 (Aisne). Cathédrale de Notre-Dame: 8 Rue Cloître; 03 23 20 26 54
- 🚗 **Train** from Paris, Amiens & Reims
- ℹ️ **Visitor information** Hôtel Dieu, Pl du Parvis Gautier de Mortagne, 02000; 03 23 20 28 62; www.tourisme-paysdelaon.com
- 🍴 **Eat and drink** Real meal L'Estaminet St-Jean (23 Rue St Jean, 02000; 03 23 23 04 89; www.estaminetsaintjean.com), modelled on an old-style tavern, specializes in Picard cuisine and offers reasonably priced set menus. Family treat Le Péché Mignon (53 Rue Chatelaine, 02000; 03 23 21 16 14) serves traditional French cooking, and has a kids' menu.

ridge. Leave your car in the Ville-Basse (lower town) and take the Poma, an automated cable car, that climbs up to the Hôtel de Ville in the old town. The **Cathédrale de Notre-Dame**, one of the oldest in France, is impressive above all for the immense space beneath the vaults of its soaring nave, lit up by stained glass. Walking tours lead around the medieval streets. Walk right round the 16th-century Citadelle for great views. Starting from the cathedral, a Petit Train Touristique chugs its way around the medieval town.

Letting off steam

Head for **Le Dôme** (74 Ave Charles de Gaulle, 02000; 03 23 23 94 00; ledome-equalia.fr), a swimming pool and ice-skating complex. The **Forêt de St-Gobain** (evasion-aisne.com), to the west of Laon, is a hunting forest, with cycle paths and walking routes.

The Poma cable car ascending to Laon's old town

Where to Stay in Le Nord and Picardy

The salt breezes and silver marine light bring sparkle to the coastal accommodation, much of which seems designed to evoke the relaxed, sun-filled seaside holidays of childhood. Inland, hotels provide useful base camps from which to explore towns and cities on foot.

AGENCIES

Pour les Vacances
www.pour-les-vacances.com
This French company has a good range of cottages and farmhouses across the region, as well as B&Bs.

Belvilla
www.belvilla.fr
This well-established Dutch company represents numerous properties of all ages and sizes in Le Nord and Picardy.

Foliage-covered façade of Hôtel-Restaurant L'Escale, near Calais

Amiens
Map 4 G3

HOTEL
Hôtel Prieuré
17–6 Rue Porion, 80000; 03 22 71 16 71; www.hotel-prieure-amiens.com
Right by Amiens' cathedral, this is a converted 18th-century ecclesiastical building. Each of the 23 rooms in this modern hotel are different, with some beneath the exposed beams of the attic eaves.

€€

Arras
Map 4 H2

HOTEL
Ibis Arras Centre Les Places
11 Rue de Justice, Pl Ipswich, 62000; 03 21 23 61 61; www.accorhotels.com
This is a modern, comfortable, mid-range hotel in the Accor Group chain. It has an excellent location – close to the city's two main squares. Rooms sleep up to three. Interconnecting rooms for large families are available.

P €

BED & BREAKFAST
Le Clos Grincourt
18 Rue du Château, 62161 Duisans; 03 21 48 68 33; tinyurl.com/3kxnaba
Located 7 km (4 miles) northwest of Arras, this is a Neo-Classical 19th-century manor. The first floor has a two-room interconnecting *suite familiale* for four to five people, plus a separate double bedroom.

P €€

Boulogne-sur-Mer
Map 4 F1

HOTEL
Hôtel Faidherbe
12 Rue Faidherbe, 62200; 03 21 31 60 93; www.hotelfaidherbe.fr
A family-run hotel close to the city centre, the rooms, all individually styled and named, are somewhat basic, but there is a friendly welcome. Nausicaá is a 20-minute walk.

€€

Calais
Map 4 F1

HOTEL
Hôtel-Restaurant L'Escale
Rue de la Mer, 62179 Escalles; 03 81 85 25 20; www.hotel-lescale.com
This hotel, 11 km (7 miles) from Cap Blanc Nez, has simple, well-presented rooms. Family rooms sleep four to five. Playground and games court for kids available; restaurant on site.

P €

BED & BREAKFAST
La Grand'Maison
Hameau de la Haute-Escalles, 62179 Escalles; 03 21 85 27 75; lagrandmaison.chez-alice.fr
Located 10 km (6 miles) northeast of Calais, this modernized 17th-century courtyard farmhouse has rooms done in an antique-rustic style. Donkey rides and play equipment entertain.

P €€

Chantilly
Map 4 G4

HOTEL
Hôtel La Nonette
Pl de la Gare, 60560 Orry-la-Ville; 03 44 58 98 76; www.hotel-lanonette-oise.com
Located about 10 km (4 miles) from Chantilly and Parc Astérix, this is an attractive 29-room Logis hotel. The rooms are smart and comfortable. Restaurant options in Orry-la-Ville.

P €

Compiègne
Map 4 H4

CAMPING
La Croix du Vieux Pont
02290 Berny-Rivière; 03 23 55 50 02; www.la-croix-du-vieux-pont.com
A four-star camp site and holiday park on the Aisne river, 20 km (12 miles) east of Compiègne, it has pitches and chalet-style *gîtes*. There is an artificial lake and a restaurant on site.

P €

A handsomely decorated room with a baby cot in La Grand'Maison, near Calais

Le Crotoy
Map 4 F2

HOTEL
Les Tourelles
2–4 Rue Pierre Guerlain, 80550; 03 22 27 16 33; www.lestourelles.com
Right beside the Baie de Somme, this two-star eco-friendly hotel has a quirky decor: turreted exterior and a sun-bleached interior. Attractive restaurant; garden terrace in summer.
🛏️ €€

BED & BREAKFAST
La Villa en Baye
16 Rue du Moulin, 80120; 03 22 25 19 54; www.lavillaenbaie.com
This grand early 19th-century villa, 5 km (3 miles) from Le Crotoy, offers three *suites familiale* and *gîtes*. Dinner is available on reservation. Beaches at Le Crotoy and Fort-Mahon are 10 km (6 miles) away from the property.
🛏️ 🏠 P €€

CAMPING
Camping Le Champ Neuf
8 Rue du Champ Neuf, 80120 St-Quentin-en-Tourmont; 03 22 25 07 94; www.camping-lechampneuf.com
Located near Parc du Marquenterre and beaches of Le Crotoy and Fort-Mahon, this site has mobile homes, tents, caravans and camper vans. Playground, bike hire and bar on site.
P 🏊 €

Laon
Map 5 B4

HOTEL
Hôtel-Restaurant de la Bannière de France
11 Rue Franklin-Roosevelt, 02000; 03 23 23 21 44; tinyurl.com/6q639dy
An old coaching inn dating from 1685, this three-star hotel has a charmingly dated feel. Rooms are comfortable; some sleep four. Good range of set menus at the restaurant.
🛏️ P €€

Lille
Map 4 H1

HOTELS
Hôtel de la Paix
46 bis, Rue de Paris, 59800; 03 20 54 63 93; www.hotel-la-paix.com
This two-star hotel is close to the pedestranized centre. It has an Art-Nouveau-style café and rooms hung with replicas of 20th-century art. Free for kids under 14 sharing with parents.
🛏️ P €€

L'Hermitage Gantois
224 Rue de Paris, 59000; 03 20 85 30 30; www.hotelhermitagegantois.com
Formerly a 15th-century hospital, this five-star hotel near the Grand'Place has 72 sumptuous rooms. Restaurant in the former chapel; the *Estaminet* (tavern) serves modest but pricey fare.
🛏️ ❄️ €€€

SELF-CATERING
Citadines City Centre Lille
Ave Willy Brandt, 59777 Euralille; 03 28 36 75 00; www.citadines.com
This is a branch of the reliable Citadines chain, which specializes in apart'hotels. Modern, well-equipped, short-stay studio apartments, with a bedroom, living room and kitchen.
🛏️ 🏠 P €€

Montreuil-sur-Mer
Map 4 F2

HOTEL
Coq Hôtel
2 Pl de la Poissonerie, 62170; 03 21 86 64 67; www.coqhotel.fr
This recently renovated 19th-century townhouse makes a perfect base to explore the pretty town. Rooms are well-decorated. The Cocquempot restaurant offers good dining.
🛏️ P €€

Al fresco tables at the Hôtel des Trois Hiboux in Parc Astérix

Parc Astérix
Map 4 G5

HOTEL
Hôtel des Trois Hiboux
Parc Astérix, 60128 Plailly; 08 26 30 10 40; www.parcasterix.fr
Built like a giant woodland cabin in a tranquil forested area, this three-star hotel within Parc Astérix has spacious family rooms. There is

a child-friendly restaurant on site. Accommodation includes the entrance price to Parc Astérix.
🛏️ P €€€

Pierrefonds
Map 4 H4

HOTEL
Hôtel Beaudon
10 Rue du Beaudon, 60350; 03 44 42 80 18; www.hotel-pierrefonds.com
A two-star hotel overlooking a lake and Château de Pierrefonds, its 21 rooms are simply furnished. Family rooms sleep four. There is a pleasant restaurant and free parking nearby.
🛏️ €€

St-Omer
Map 4 G1

HOTEL
Saint Louis
25 Rue d'Arras, 62500; 03 21 38 35 21; en.hotel-saintlouis.com
This 18th-century coaching inn, in the city centre, has been modernized and extended around a courtyard garden. The rooms, sleeping up to four, are elegant. Le Flaubert restaurant specializes in local dishes.
🛏️ P €€

St-Valery-sur-Somme
Map 4 F2

HOTEL
Hôtel Picardia
41 Quai du Rommerel, 80230; 03 22 60 32 30; www.picardia.fr
A fine 19th-century mansion close to the seafront, it offers 18 airy rooms, with split-level family rooms sleeping up to six. An independent studio flat, with a kitchen, available by the week.
🛏️ P €€

BED & BREAKFAST
Chambres d'Hôtes à la Ferme
1 Rue Violette Szabo, 80860 Noyelles-sur-Mer; 03 22 23 40 96; www.chambresalaferme.com
A beautifully presented lodging in a 19th-century dairy farm, this offers four rooms with en-suite bathrooms. Microwave oven and fridge available.
🛏️ 🏠 P €

Price Guide
The following price ranges are based on one night's accommodation in high season for a family of four, inclusive of service charges and any additional taxes.
€ Under €100 €€ €100–200 €€€ over €200

Key to symbols *see back cover flap*

Paris
and Île de France

A mix of rich culture, delectable cuisine and child-friendly activities makes this area, which includes the French capital, perfect for a family holiday. Bask in the splendour of the palace at Versailles, then meet Mickey Mouse at Disneyland. In summer, unwind in Paris's parks or in Fontainebleau's forest; in winter, marvel at the city's Christmas lights; and, in autumn, take a stroll around the Île St-Louis at sunset.

Highlights

Notre-Dame
Visit this Gothic cathedral, which stands majestically on the Île de la Cité, the boat-shaped island on the Seine (see pp90–91).

Jardin du Luxembourg
Spend an afternoon in these vast gardens, a children's paradise. Sail wooden boats, catch a colourful puppet show and ride on the pretty belle époque carousel (see p93).

Musée du Louvre
Meet mummies, including those of fish, and smile at the Mona Lisa at the stunning Musée du Louvre (see pp98–9).

Eiffel Tower
Whizz up this towering structure and see the city of lights spread out like a wonderland at your feet. It is as magical at night as it is in the day (see pp104–5).

Château de Versailles
Spend a weekend exploring Louis XIV's sumptuous palace and stroll through the magnificent gardens. In summer, watch the Saturday night fireworks (see pp124–7).

Disneyland Resort Paris
Meet Mickey and Goofy, ride a runaway train, be Pocahontas or fly with Peter Pan in this magical park (see pp130–33).

Left The Pyramide du Louvre, the strikingly modern main entrance to the Musée du Louvre
Above left Sailing a wooden boat in the Jardin du Luxembourg

The Best of
Paris and Île de France

Families are spoilt for choice here. Paris is bursting with culture and historic monuments, but is also full of amazing cake shops and cafés, merry-go-rounds and marionettes. The French capital is surprisingly relaxing and its beauty is evident along the banks of the Seine and in its pretty parks. Île de France has the glamour of Versailles and the fun of Disneyland on offer, as well as scenic countryside and wild forests.

In a week

Start off exploring the many attractions along the streets of Île de la Cité, among them **Notre-Dame** (see pp90–91), the **Conciergerie** (see p92) and **Sainte-Chapelle** (see p92). Spend a day climbing the **Arc de Triomphe** (see pp106–110) or letting off steam in the **Jardin des Tuileries** (see p99) before exploring the world's biggest museum, the **Musée du Louvre** (see pp98–9). After all that culture, it is time for some crazy fun. Catch the RER to **Disneyland Resort Paris** (see pp130–33) and take the kids on some wild rides.

History buffs should visit Napoleon's tomb in **Les Invalides** (see p112), spend an afternoon in the lovely **Jardin du Luxembourg** (see p93), then go to the top of the **Tour Montparnasse** (see p111) to see the sunset. Take a day out to discover the majesty of the **Château de Versailles** (see pp124–7). And before leaving the city, do what everyone is dying to do – shoot to the top of the **Eiffel Tower** (see pp104–5).

Left Space to run around at the Château de Versailles
Below The magnificent Notre-Dame on the Île de la Cité

Candy-coloured paintings on the gilded ceiling of the main foyer of the Opéra Garnier

On a budget

Rent affordable self-catering accommodation in the countryside to the south of Paris. There is no fee for exploring the wild forests around **Fontainebleau** (see p129) and **Rambouillet** (see pp128–9), and the stunning gardens at the **Château de Versailles**. Use the RER to take day trips to Paris. Carry a picnic basket as the city is full of inexpensive bakeries and street markets that sell top-class food at reasonable prices.

There is no charge to enter **Notre-Dame**. Look for museums that allow free entry on any specific day, such as the **Musée du Louvre**, which offers free access to everyone on the first Sunday of the month. Considering the vast collection on show here, it is a bargain even on other days. End the day with a nice picnic in the **Jardins du Trocadéro** (see p106), and watch the **Eiffel Tower** begin to sparkle as night falls.

Culture vultures

There is no need to worry about bored kids in cultural places. Nearly all museums in Paris and Île de France have fun workshops and activity programmes especially for kids. Admire some of the world's most famous paintings in the impressive **Musée d'Orsay** (see pp110–11) before exploring buildings, parks and train stations. For mini ballerinas and avid theatre enthusiasts, a trip to the **Opéra Garnier** (see pp100–110) is an absolute must. Twirl down the staircase, and if the pocket allows, catch a show. There is plenty too for musical kids, with many concerts and plays aimed to engage them.

Relive the grandeur and richness of France's kings at two of the most magnificent châteaux in the nation: the glittering halls and rooms at the **Château de Versailles** are awe-inspiring, as is **Fontainebleau**, with its famous staircase and its striking gallery and garden. Paris also has some excellent Roman remains and the **Musée du Louvre** features one of the best Egyptology collections in the world.

Foody families

Colourful street markets abound all over Île de France and in Paris. And with numerous delis and bakeries selling delicious savouries and sweets, the city is also a picnicker's paradise. Treat children to an ice cream at the legendary **Berthillon** (see p92) on **Île St-Louis** (see p91). Do not miss the Sunday brunch and then a magic show in **Metamorphosis** (see p91). Eat yummy multi-coloured macaroons for tea at **Ladurée** (see p113), and satisfy a sweet tooth at **A La Mère de la Famille** (see p101).

Summer crowds enjoying the sun on the lawns of the Champ-de-Mars, beneath the Eiffel Tower

Paris and Île de France

Paris is a compact city and many of the main sights are within easy walking distance of each other. A small, folding push-chair is useful with smaller children. Métro and bus systems are excellent. The Métro serves the city, with 14 lines identified by number. The Île de France can be accessed by the RER, a regional train service, which has five lines identified by letters, and the main train network, the SNCF. The simplest way to get to Disneyland Resort Paris and Versailles is to take the RER. A car is not needed in Paris but is necessary for exploring the countryside to the south.

Puppet show in progress at the Marionettes du Champ-de-Mars, Paris

Places of interest

- **PARIS** *(see pp87–122)*
- **ÎLE DE FRANCE**
  1. Château de Versailles
  2. Château de Malmaison
  3. Le Parc Zoologique de Thoiry
  4. Rambouillet
  5. Fontainebleau
  6. Disneyland Resort Paris

Family enjoying a walk through peaceful countryside near the Château de Versailles

View of the Château de Fontainebleau rising above the neat garden

Exploring Paris by cruising on the Seine river

The Lowdown

🚗 **Getting there and around**
Air *(see p86)*. **Riverboat** www. batobus.com & www.bateaux-mouches.fr. **Train** Eurostar links London and Paris and the TGV connects major French cities with the capital. RER links the airports to the city centre as do the airport bus services *(see p86)*. *Autoroutes* (motorways) converge on Paris from every direction. **Bike** Self-service bike scheme Velib' is only for use by children over 14. **Métro, Bus, RER** Buy a carnet of tickets at any metro station for use on the metro, buses and the RER. Kids over 10 pay adult fare; under 3s travel free; (www.ratp.com). **Car** Avis: 01 42 66 67 68 (www. locationvoitureavis.fr). Hertz: 01 47 03 49 12 (www.hertz.fr)

🛒 **Supermarkets** The main chains are Monoprix (www.monoprix. fr); Franprix (www.franprix.fr) and Carrefour (www.carrefour.fr). **Markets** There are excellent markets on Rue Mouffetard, 75005; Avé Président Wilson, 75016 & Blvd Raspail, 75006. There are flea markets at St-Ouen and Porte des Vanves and a stamp market on the Champs-Elysées. For a full list of markets see www.parisinfo.com.

🎪 **Festivals** Foire du Trône, funfair in the Bois de Vincennes (Mar–May). Grandes Concerts de Versailles, open-air concerts and firework displays in the gardens (Apr–Jul). Les Grandes Eaux Musicales, Château de Versailles (Apr–Oct: Sat & Sun & some public hols). *Son et lumière* by the Versailles lake (Jun–Aug); Paris-Plages, a temporary beach along the Right Bank of the Seine (Jul & Aug). Bastille Day, military parade and fireworks by the Eiffel Tower (Jul 14). Christmas markets and ice-skating rinks in front of the Hôtel de Ville and the Tour Montparnasse (Dec & Jan)

🕐 **Opening hours** Shops are usually open 10am–7pm Monday to Saturday. Monoprix on Ave des Champs-Elysées is open till midnight Monday to Saturday. Local shops: closed Mon; many shops and restaurants close in Aug

➕ **Pharmacies** 24-hour pharmacy: Pharmacie Dhery, 84 Ave des Champs-Elysées, 75008; 01 45 62 02 41. See www. pharmaciesdegarde.com for a list of 24-hour pharmacies.

🚻 **Toilets** Although there are few decent public toilets in Paris, there are luxury public toilets in the Carrousel du Louvre, on the Champs-Elysées and in the Printemps department store (www.pointwc.com). Otherwise take a café pit stop.

Paris

0 km 1
0 miles 1

MONTMARTRE
LA VILLETTE
Sacré-Coeur *p114*
OPÉRA
CHAILLOT
Musée du Louvre *p96*
THE MARAIS
Musée d'Orsay *p108*
Eiffel Tower *p102*
INVALIDES
Notre-Dame *p88*
QUARTIER LATIN
La Seine
MONTPARNASSE

0 km 10
0 miles 10

Saint-Soupplets
St-Mesmes
Meaux
N3
risis
Claye-Souilly
Mareuil-lès-Meaux
La Ferté-sous-Jouarre
Disneyland Resort Paris
lès
Coutevroult
Collégien
Crécy-la-Chapelle
Villeneuve-le-Comte
Coulommiers
ault-bault
Tournan-en-Brie
Fontenay-Trésigny
Pézarches
Comte-ert
Vaudoy-en-Brie
N4
ry-Grégy-r-Yerre
D319
Guignes
Mormant
Chenoise
Villiers-Saint-Georges
ermain-Laxis
La Chapelle-Gauthier
D619
Nangis
Provins
Melun
Le Châtelet-en-Brie
Longueville
La Seine
ailly-en-Bière
Pamfou
Fontainebleau
Montereau-Faut-Yonne
Bray-sur-Seine
Yonne
Nemours
Lorrez-le-Bocage
Loing

Paris and Île de France Airports

Paris is a vital airport hub and direct flights from around the world serve the two main international airports: Roissy Charles-de-Gaulle and Orly. From the UK, British Airways, British Midland and bmibaby fly regularly to Paris. From the US, American, Continental, and United offer regular flights. Air Canada also runs direct flights, as does Qantas from Australia and New Zealand. Budget airlines and charter flights arrive at Beauvais Tillé.

The Orlyval train connecting Orly Airport to the metro system

Roissy Charles-de-Gaulle

Most international flights arrive at **Roissy Charles-de-Gaulle (CDG)**, 30 km (19 miles) northeast of Paris. It has three terminals, two of which – T1 and T2 – are linked by a driverless train. Negotiating the terminals involves walking long distances – important to remember if travelling with younger kids. It is poorly signposted as well, so always ask if not sure where to go. The best option for travelling into the city will depend on which part of Paris is your destination. The **RER** line B is the fastest run to the city centre (about 40 minutes). It stops at

Gare du Nord, Châtelet-Les Halles, Luxembourg and St-Michel. Trains run every 15 minutes from 4:58am to 11:58pm. **Air France buses** also run daily every 15 minutes from 6am–11pm from both terminals with links to Métro Etoile (40 minutes) and from 6am to 10:30pm to Gare de Lyon and Gare Montparnasse. The **RATP Roissybus** runs daily every 15–20 minutes from 5:45am to 11pm to Opéra Garnier, and is the easiest option if you are travelling to the Grands Boulevards area. A taxi from CDG to central Paris from the airport takes 30–60 minutes, and costs over €60, with a minibus for a large family up to €100. The **VEA** bus, which can be booked online, offers direct links to Disneyland Resort Paris.

Orly

Domestic and some international flights arrive at **Orly (ORY)**, 18 km (11 miles) south of the city. The airport, which has two terminals, is smaller and easier to negotiate than CDG, but can still involve a lot of walking. Air France buses depart every 30 minutes from 6am to 11:40pm and stop at Invalides and Montparnasse. The **Orlybus** runs to Denfert-Rochereau (lines 4, 6) and the RER (line B) every 20 minutes from 6am to11:50pm Mon–Fri, and

until 12:50am on weekends. The journey takes around 30 minutes. **Orlyval** is an automatic metro link to both the Orly terminals, and connects to the RER line B at Métro Antony. Taxis to the city centre take about 45 minutes – expect to pay €40 or more. The VEA bus links direct to Disneyland Resort Paris.

Paris airports have good facilities for families, including free play areas, Playstations, baby-changing areas and buggy loan. Look out for Gus, the airport mascot, who wanders about the terminals, giving colouring books and pencils during holidays.

Beauvais Tillé

Beauvais Tillé airport, situated 70 km (44 miles) north of Paris, is used by charter and some budget carriers like Ryanair. Trains depart for Gard du Nord, and the VEA bus to Disneyland Resort Paris also services the airport. The **shuttle bus** service is expensive: about €80 for a family. Buses depart for Porte Maillot 15–30 minutes after each arrival, and leave Porte Maillot for the airport 3 hours 15 minutes before each departure.

The Lowdown

Air France buses 08 92 35 08 20; *www.lescars-airfrance.com*

Airport information 39 50 (within France only); +33 170 36 39 50 (from outside France); *www.aeroportsdeparis.fr*

Orlyval 32 46 (within France only); *www.orlyval.com; www.ratp.fr*

Paris Airports Service A minibus service; 01 55 98 10 80; *www.paris airportservice.com*

RATP Roissy/Orlybus 32 46 (within France only); 08 92 68 41 14; *www.ratp.fr*

RER trains 32 46 (within France); *www.ratp.fr; www.transillien.com*

Shuttle bus Door-to-door service; 08 25 09 20 92; *www.parisshuttle.fr*

VEA *www.vea.fr*

Travellers waiting at the gates of Roissy Charles-de-Gaulle Airport

Paris

Paris is a wonderful city to visit with children of any age. The world-famous museums put on plenty of activities to attract even the youngest visitor. Afterwards, join local families in one of the city's parks, sample scrumptious pastries at a *pâtisserie*, take a boat trip on the Seine or climb the Eiffel Tower; the ingredients of a great family holiday are all here.

Below *Old-fashioned carousel with wooden horses in front of the Eiffel Tower*

Sacré-Coeur
p116

Musée
du Louvre
p98

Eiffel Tower
p104

Musée
d'Orsay
p110

Notre-
Dame
p90

Notre-Dame and around

Walking is a pleasure along the streets of the Île de la Cité, Île St-Louis, the Quartier Latin and the quaint yet fashionable neighbourhood of the Marais. A gentle stroll while taking in the fantastic views can be enjoyed at any time of the day, but some parts of the area are particularly lovely in the evening when most of the tourists have left. Bring a pushchair for small children, as exploring the sights can get tiring; the many scenic parks serve as pleasant stops for a relaxing break. On Sundays and public holidays, the Voie Georges Pompidou on the Seine's Right Bank is closed to traffic and becomes a haven for rollerbladers and cyclists.

Places of interest

SIGHTS
1. Notre-Dame
2. Conciergerie
3. Sainte-Chapelle
4. Quartier Latin
5. Panthéon
6. Place des Vosges
7. Rue des Rosiers
8. Musée Picasso
9. Centre Pompidou

EAT AND DRINK
1. Calixte
2. Café la Bûcherie
3. Pizza Marzano
4. Metamorphosis
5. Berthillon
6. Chez Clément
7. Franprix
8. Au Bougnat
9. Breakfast in America (17 Rue des Ecoles, 75005)
10. L Zyriab
11. Thé Cool
12. Le Comptoir du Panthéon
13. Au Levain de Marais
14. Carette des Vosges
15. Florence Kahn
16. Breakfast in America (4 Rue Malher, 75004)
17. Boulangerie Malineau
18. Merci
19. Le Hangar
See also Centre Pompidou (p95)

SHOPPING
1. Shakespeare & Company

WHERE TO STAY
1. Appartement d'hôtes Folie Méricourt
2. Bonne Nuit Paris
3. Citadines St-Germain-des-Prés
4. Hôtel Britannique
5. Hotel Ibis Bastille Opéra
6. Hôtel du Jeu de Paume
7. Hôtel Résidence Henri IV
8. Le Pavillon de la Reine
9. Résidence Le Petit Châtelet
10. Résidence Le Prince Regent

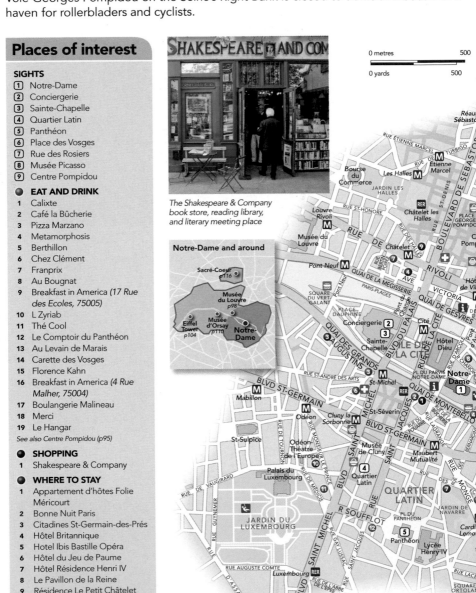

The Shakespeare & Company book store, reading library, and literary meeting place

0 metres 500
0 yards 500

The glassed-in escalator of the Centre Pompidou overlooking Place Georges Pompidou

Façade of the Gothic masterpiece, Notre-Dame

The Lowdown

🚗 **Métro** Cité or St-Michel & St-Sulpice or Les Halles, line 4; Sully Morland, Jussieu & Châtelet, line 7; Maubert Mutualité, line 10; Bastille, lines 1 & 8 or Rambuteau, line 11. **RER** St-Michel, lines B & C; Gare d'Austerlitz, line C or Châtelet les Halles, lines A, B & D. **Bus** 21, 24, 38, 47, 67, 76, 85, 86, 87, & 96. **River boat** Quai de Montebello

ℹ **Visitor Information** Kiosks: Pl du Parvis-Notre-Dame, 75004; end-May–mid-Oct: 10am–7pm daily. Pl de l'Hôtel de Ville, near Rue de Rivoli, 75004; Jul & Aug: 10am–6pm daily

🍴 **Supermarkets** Monop', 35 Blvd, St-Michel, 75005 & 135 Rue St-Martin, 75004. Monoprix, 71 Rue St-Antoine, 75004 & 24 Blvd St-Michel, 75006. Franprix, 87 Rue de la Verrerie, 75004
Markets Marché aux Fleurs et Oiseaux (Flower and Bird Market): Pl Louis Lepine, 75004; Flowers: 8am–7pm Sun; Birds: 8am–7:30pm Mon–Sat

🎪 **Festivals** Fête du Pain: bread festival; www.fetedupain.com (May). La Course des Garçons de Café, Hôtel de Ville: waiters race around the city balancing heavy trays; www.waitersrace. com (late-Jun/early-Jul). Paris-Plages: artificial beaches on the Seine's Right Bank during summer; www.parisplages.fr (Jul & Aug, see p91). Christmas crèche, Notre-Dame (Dec & Jan). Ice-skating rink, Pl de l'Hôtel de Ville (mid-Dec–Feb)

➕ **Pharmacy** Pharmacie des Halles, 10 Blvd de Sébastopol, 75001; 01 42 72 03 23; open till midnight Mon–Sat, till 10pm Sun. Pharmacy Bader, 12 Blvd St-Michel, 75005; 01 43 26 92 66; 9am–9pm Mon–Sat, 11am–9pm Sun

🛝 **Nearest playgrounds** Square Jean XXIII, Pl du Parvis-Notre-Dame, 75004; dawn–dusk daily (see p91). Jardin du Luxembourg, Blvd St-Michel, 75006; dawn–dusk daily (see p93). Jardin des Plantes, 54 Rue Cuiver, 75005; dawn–dusk daily (see p93). Jardin de l'Hotel Salé, 101 Rue Coutures St-Gervais, 75003; dawn–dusk daily (see p95).

① Notre-Dame
History, hunchbacks and gargoyles

Home to Victor Hugo's hunchback, Quasimodo, Notre-Dame is over 800 years old, and built on the site of a Roman temple. The cathedral, covered with swooping buttresses and funny-faced gargoyles, took over a century to complete, and can accommodate 6,000 people. Many dramatic events in French history occurred here. In the Revolution, it was looted and made into a wine warehouse. In 1804, Napoleon crowned himself emperor here, instead of waiting for the pope.

Stained-glass rose window, Notre-Dame

Key Features

Biblical characters The façade, covered in easily recognizable biblical characters, was known as the poor man's Bible. Most Parisians could not read when the cathedral was built.

The spire This was added by the architect Viollet-le-Duc in the 19th century, and soars to a height of 90 m (295 ft).

Rose windows Their colours are magnificent on a sunny day. Louis IX gifted the southern window.

Crown of Thorns Viollet-le-Duc designed the gilded, diamond-encrusted shrine that holds this and other famous relics on display in the Treasury.

Gothic masterpiece Finished in 1330, the cathedral is 130 m (430 ft) tall, and features flying buttresses, a large transept and 69-m (228-ft) high towers.

Gargoyles and chimeras Glare back at these creatures sitting hunched up on the façade and up in the tower.

Chancel screen Located in the centre of the church, the chancel screen tells the story of the life of Jesus like a medieval comic strip.

The Lowdown

🌐 **Map reference** 25 A6
Address 6 Pl du Parvis-Notre-Dame, Pl Jean-Paul II, 75004; 01 42 34 56 10; www.notredame deparis.fr. Towers: 01 53 40 60 80 & 01 53 10 07 00; www. notre-dame-de-paris. monuments-nationaux.fr

🚗 **Métro** Cité or St-Michel, line 4 or Châtelet, lines 1, 4 & 14. **RER** St-Michel, lines B & C. **Bus** 21, 24, 27, 38, 47, 85 & 96. **River boat** Quai de Montebello

🕐 **Open** Cathedral: 8am–6:45pm, till 7:15pm Sat & Sun. Treasury: 9.30am–6pm, from 1:30pm Sun. Towers: Apr–Sep: 10am–6:30pm

daily; Jul & Aug: 10am–6:30pm Mon–Fri, 10am–11pm Sat & Sun; Oct–Mar: 10am–5:30pm. For access to the towers, climb the 387 steps from Rue du Cloître.

💶 **Price** Cathedral: free. Towers: €16–26; under 18s & EU citizens under 26 free. Treasury: €6–16

👪 **Skipping the queue** Paris Museum Pass (www.parisinfo.com) accepted. To avoid long queues for the towers, visit in the evening when there are fewer people, or early in the day before the crowds arrive.

🚩 **Guided tours** In English at 2pm Wed & Thu & at 2:30pm Sat. English audio guide €5

👫 **Age range** 3 plus; under 12s to be accompanied by adults

🎭 **Activities** Magic shows in Metamorphosis; 01 43 54 08 08

⏱ **Allow** 2–3 hours

♿ **Wheelchair access** Limited

🚻 **Toilets** By the cathedral exit

Good family value?
Entry to the cathedral itself is free. So no entry fee has been wasted if the kids cannot bear more than a quick look inside. Children enjoy climbing up the towers, and everyone loves the view.

Letting off steam

Twirl around the square in front of the cathedral like Esmerelda, the gypsy dancer in Victor Hugo's novel *Notre Dame de Paris* (1831), and stroll along the quayside. **Square Jean XXIII**, behind Notre-Dame, is a park with a sandpit. In summer, head for the **Paris-Plages** on the Right Bank, where the main road along the river is transformed into beaches with real sand, water fountains and activities. In winter, go skating at the **Place de l'Hôtel de Ville** on the Right Bank.

Square Jean XXIII with Notre-Dame in the background

Eat and drink

Picnic: under €25; Snacks: €25–45; Real Meal: €45–90; Family treat: over €90 (based on a family of four)

PICNIC Calixte (64 Rue St-Louis-en-l'Île, 75004) sells luxury picnic supplies, which can be enjoyed in the park alongside the cathedral.
SNACKS Café la Bûcherie (41 Rue de la Bûcherie, 75005; 01 43 54 24 52; open daily) is a great spot to unwind with a drink and nibbles, and has splendid views of Notre-Dame.
REAL MEAL Pizza Marzano (2 Pl St-Michel, 75006; 01 44 07 32 27), part of the ever reliable and tasty Pizza Express family, is a safe bet in a section of the city that can be a tourist trap.
FAMILY TREAT Metamorphosis (Quai de Montebello, 75005; 01 43 54 08 08; www.metamorphosis-spectacle.fr; Apr–Sep: 7:30pm Tue–Sat & 12:30pm Sun) serves dishes such as chicken breast in mushroom sauce, curried lamb and chocolate cake. It is the best place to watch magic tricks over dinner, and also for Sunday brunch.

Shopping

Flick through English books in **Shakespeare & Company** (37 Rue de la Bûcherie, 75005), and in the green boxes of the Bouquinistes, who have been selling books on the Seine's banks since the 16th century. After the Revolution, they peddled entire libraries that had been seized from noble families.

Find out more

DIGITAL The cathedral website www.notredamedeparis.fr/-Children-s-site has a kids' section. Watch the video *General de Gaulle at Notre Dame on 26 August 1944* on tinyurl.com/3jyujw5 and *King Babar hunting Father Christmas in Paris* in the Babar Christmas Special on tinyurl.com/3v7gvto. Discover Roman Paris on www.paris.culture.fr/en/
FILM Disney's *Hunchback of Notre Dame* (1996) will show kids how the cathedral dominated medieval Paris.

Next stop...

ÎLE ST-LOUIS This tranquil village in the heart of Paris was known as Île des Vaches, after the cows that grazed here. It was only in 1614 that the 13-year-old Louis XIII was persuaded that building stylish town houses here would be a good idea. But thanks to its narrow streets, Île St-Louis retains its village-like feel even now. Lined with historic houses, it is a fun place to walk and peruse the shops. Look out for the dragons on No. 51 and No. 54, once a real tennis court, on Rue St-Louis-en-l'Île. The street is a foody paradise, so there is a lot of grazing going on still.

Street musicians on the Pont de Sully, on the eastern end of Île St-Louis

View of the Conciergerie with the Pont au Change in the foreground

② Conciergerie
Fairy-tale towers fit for a torturer

A haunting symbol of the Revolution of 1789, the Conciergerie is the oldest remaining part of a royal palace built around 1300 by Philippe le Bel (Philip the Fair). After Charles V moved to the Louvre, it became a prison with a grim reputation. In 1793, the Revolutionary Tribunal condemned thousands to death here during the Reign of Terror. Prominent inmates, including Marie Antoinette, spent their final night here before being taken to the guillotine.

Visit the Salle de Toilette, where inmates were stripped of their belongings and had their heads shaved; wander into the so called Rue de Paris where the poorest

The Lowdown

🌐 **Map reference** 24 G5
Address 2 Blvd du Palais, 75001; www.conciergerie.monuments-nationaux.fr/en

🚗 **Métro** Cité or St-Michel, line 4. **RER** St-Michel, lines B & C. **Bus** 21, 24, 27, 38, 58, 81 & 85. **River boat** Quai de Montebello

🕐 **Open** 9:30am–6pm daily; Nov–Feb: 9am–5pm; closed 1 Jan, 1 May & 25 Dec

💶 **Price** €14–24; under 18s & EU citizens under 26 free

👪 **Skipping the queue** Paris Museum Pass accepted

👉 **Guided tours** Tours in English. (book ahead); 01 44 54 19 30

👫 **Age range** 8 plus

⏱ **Allow** 1–2 hours

♿ **Wheelchair access** Limited

🍴 **Eat and drink** *Snacks* Berthillon (31 Rue St-Louis-en-l'Île, 75004; 01 43 54 31 61; www.berthillon.fr) is famed for its marvellous ice cream. *Real Meal* Chez Clément (Pl St-André des Arts, 75006; 01 56 81 32 00; www.chezclement. com; open daily) has kids' menus.

👫 **Toilets** In one of the towers

Prices given are for a family of four

---

prisoners slept in tiny cells, and be awed by the Salle des Gens d'Armes, Europe's largest surviving medieval hall. The Conciergerie remained a prison until 1914.

Letting off steam

After a walk through the past, enjoy playing *boules* (a game played with metal balls) in **Place Dauphine** (enter by *Rue Henri-Robert, 75001*) built by Henri IV to honour his son and heir, Louis. In summer, children can build sandcastles on the **Paris-Plages on the Right Bank** (see p91).

③ Sainte-Chapelle
Psychedelic heaven

The only French king to be made a saint, Louis IX was a keen collector of relics. He built the breathtakingly beautiful Sainte-Chapelle in 1239 for his prize acquisitions, including the Crown of Thorns and a fragment of Christ's Cross. Built in just 10 years, this architectural marvel also served to express the king's absolute power.

The Flamboyant-Gothic-style chapel has some of the finest medieval stained-glass windows in the world. The 15 giant windows tell the stories of the Bible in a cartoon strip that soars to the star-studded roof. The 33-m (108-ft) high spire seems to point to heaven, while the rose window ominously depicts the Day of Judgement.

Letting off steam

The **Square du Vert-Galant**, at the tip of the Île de la Cité, is an ideal place for a picnic. This is the point from where the Vedettes du Pont Neuf pleasure boats depart.

Stunning stained-glass windows in Sainte-Chapelle showing scenes from the Bible

---

The Lowdown

🌐 **Map reference** 24 G5
Address 6 Blvd du Palais, 75001; 01 53 40 60 80; www.sainte-chapelle.monuments-nationaux.fr/en

🚗 **Métro** Cité or St-Michel, line 4. **RER** St-Michel, lines B & C. **Bus** 27, 38, 85 & 96

🕐 **Open** 9:30am–6pm Mon–Fri; Nov–Feb: till 5pm; 15 May–15 Sep: till 9pm to see the chapel lit by the setting sun; closed 1 Jan, 1 May & 25 Dec

💶 **Price** €16–26; under 18s & EU citizens under 26 free

👪 **Skipping the queue** Buy joint tickets with Conciergerie: €11 per person; Paris Museum Pass accepted

👉 **Guided tours** Tours in English can be arranged three weeks in advance; 01 44 54 19 33

👫 **Age range** 8 plus

⏱ **Allow** 30–45 mins

♿ **Wheelchair access** Limited

🍴 **Eat and drink** *Picnic* Franprix (16 Rue Bertin Poirée, 75001; Mon–Sat) is the best place to buy supplies. Picnic in Square du Vert-Galant. *Real meal* Au Bougnat (26 Rue Chanoinesse, 75004; 01 43 54 50 74; www. aubougnat.com; open daily) is a bar-restaurant that serves excellent ravioli and duck.

👫 **Toilets** By the entrance, in the courtyard

④ Quartier Latin
Downtown Lutetia

Since the Middle Ages, this ancient part of the city has been associated with scholarly learning; its university, Sorbonne, was founded in 1257. The students often studied outdoors on straw laid down in Rue de Fouarre (Straw Street). For centuries, it was obligatory for all the inhabitants to speak only Latin, and the area came to be known as the Latin Quarter.

The area is a wonderful maze of cobbled streets and narrow passages. Among them sits the **Musée de Cluny**, which features some stunning medieval art. Stroll down the Gallery of Kings and see 21 of the 28 decapitated stone heads of the Kings of Judah. There are also Gallo-Roman artefacts, such as shields and jewellery, as well as stained-glass windows from Sainte-Chapelle. Of particular interest to kids are the remains of the large Thermes de Cluny Roman baths, dating back to AD 200.

Stone heads of the Kings of Judah in the Musée de Cluny, Quartier Latin

The Lowdown

🌐 **Map reference** 28 G1
Address 75005. Musée de Cluny: 6, Pl Paul-Painlevé, 75005; *www. musee-moyenage.fr*

🚗 **Métro** Cluny-La-Sorbonne, line 10; St-Michel, line 4; Maubert Mutualité, line 10 or Odéon, lines 4 & 10. **RER** St-Michel, line C. **Bus** 24, 47, 63, 86 & 87

🕐 **Open** Musée de Cluny: 9:15am–5:45pm; closed Tue, 1 Jan, 1 May & 25 Dec

💶 **Price** Musée de Cluny: €16–26; under 18s & EU citizens under 26 free

👫 **Age range** Musée de Cluny: 8 plus

⏱ **Allow** 2 hours

🍴 **Eat and drink** *Snacks* Breakfast in America (17 Rue des Ecoles, 75005; 01 43 54 50 28), a diner, is popular with local families and students. *Real meal* L Zyriab (1 Rue des Fossées-St-Bernard, 75005; 01 40 51 38 38; www. noura.com), located on the roof of the Institut du Monde Arabe, offers stunning views and is best for afternoon tea or a meal.

👫 **Toilets** Sanisette, 123 Rue St-Jacques, 75005 & in the Musée de Cluny.

Letting off steam

There are many activities on offer at the botanical garden, **Jardin des Plantes** (54 Rue Cuvier, 75005). Enjoy leafy walks under trees that are hundreds of years old, or stroll through greenhouses filled with exotic flowers. There is also a small zoo and a maze.

⑤ Panthéon

Panoramas and famous tombs

The sheer size of the Panthéon is stunning. This Roman-looking temple was commissioned to be built as a church by Louis XV in 1757. However, money for the grandiose project soon ran out, as France teetered on the brink of bankruptcy. By the time it was finished, the Revolution was in full swing and churches were out of

fashion. It was rededicated as a temple of reason, then became the secular resting place of famous people such as Victor Hugo, Emile Zola, Alexander Dumas and Marie Curie. The Panthéon's 85-m (278-ft) high dome has a magnificent ceiling. Climb up for fantastic views of Paris.

Letting off steam

Head straight down the hill to the **Jardin du Luxembourg** (Blvd St-Michel, 75006), one of Paris' prettiest parks. Kids are sure to love the merry-go-round; puppet shows at Théâtre des Marionnettes de Paris also enthrall. The octagonal lake in front of the palace is the best place to watch ducks swimming or to rent wooden boats to sail.

A model of the Statue of Liberty in the lovely Jardin du Luxembourg

The Lowdown

🌐 **Map reference** 28 H2
Address Pl du Panthéon, 75005; *www.pantheon.monuments-nationaux.fr*

🚗 **Métro** Maubert Mutualité or Cardinal Lemoine, line 10. **RER** Luxembourg, line B. **Bus** 21, 27, 38, 82, 84, 85 & 89

🕐 **Open** Apr–Sep: 10am–6:30pm daily; Oct–Mar: 10am–6pm daily, closed 1 May, 25 Dec & 1 Jan

💶 **Price** €16–26; under 18s & EU citizens under 26 free

🎫 **Guided tours** In English upon reservation: 01 44 54 19 30. Access to the dome at regular intervals during the day, by guided tour only

👫 **Age range** 10 plus

⏱ **Allow** 2 hours

🍴 **Eat and drink** *Snacks* Thé Cool (13 Rue Médicis, 75005; 01 43 25 21 81; open daily) is a good spot for a Sunday brunch. *Family Treat* Le Comptoir du Panthéon (5 Rue Soufflot, 75005; 01 43 54 75 36; bar closed Sun; restaurant open daily) just scrapes into the top price band with food to match other more expensive venues.

👫 **Toilets** By the entrance

⑥ Place des Vosges

All for one and one for all!

Bring a cape and a sword – this is Three Musketeers country. One of the world's most beautiful squares, Place des Vosges in the Marais area, is surrounded by matching rose-coloured houses with slate roofs and atmospheric arcades. At its heart is a lovely park that little children will enjoy. Built in 1605 by the dashing but smelly Henri IV, the square was once called Place Royal, and Cardinal Richelieu, the bad guy in Dumas' classic novel, lived at No. 21.

Perfectly symmetrical, the square is bordered by 36 identical houses, nine on each side. Of these, only 24 were built of brick; the others were finished with plaster to speed up the building schedule. Victor Hugo lived in **Maison de Victor Hugo** at No. 6 with his four children. He wrote part of his classic Les Misérables here. Dip into his house to see his belongings.

Take Cover

Le Double Fond (1 Pl du Marché Ste-Catherine, 75004; 01 44 71 40 20; www.doublefond.com) is a café that features a magic show.

The Lowdown

- 🌐 **Map reference** 25 D5
  Address 75003 & 75004; Maison de Victor Hugo: 6 Pl des Vosges, 75004; 01 42 72 10 16; www.maisonsvictorhugo.paris.fr
- 🚗 **Métro** Bastille, lines 1, 5 & 8; St-Paul, line 1 or Chemin Vert, line 8. **Bus** 20, 29, 65, 69 & 96
- 🕐 **Open** Maison de Victor Hugo: 10am–6pm, closed Mon & public hols
- 💶 **Price** Maison de Victor Hugo: free
- 🗣 **Guided tours** Audio guide in English at Maison de Victor Hugo
- 👫 **Age range** Maison de Victor Hugo: 8 plus
- ⏱ **Allow** 45–90 mins
- ☕ **Eat and drink** Picnic Au Levain de Marais (32 Rue de Turenne, 75003; closed Sun & Mon) sells particularly good brioche and tasty picnic savouries. Picnic in the Place des Vosges. Family treat Carette des Vosges (25 Pl des Vosges, 75003; 01 48 87 94 07) is a popular brunch spot. There is also a takeaway service at the counter.
- 🚻 **Toilets** In Maison de Victor Hugo

Above The tree-lined Place des Vosges, surrounded by symmetrical façades
Below Colourful interiors of the Maison de Victor Hugo

⑦ Rue des Rosiers

Falafels, bagels and poppy seed cake

There is nothing nicer on a sunny Sunday afternoon than a stroll down Rue des Rosiers, the hub of Paris's traditional Jewish quarter. Kids love it, as it is all about eating. The street is lined with bakeries selling bagels and cakes from Eastern Europe, and restaurants serving great Jewish fare, as well as shops full of candlesticks and other Jewish artefacts and antiques. At the end of the 19th century, Ashkenazi Jews from Eastern Europe fled the Russian Empire, and settled in the run-down, ramshackle area around Rue des

The Lowdown

- 🌐 **Map reference** 25 C5
  Address 75004
- 🚗 **Métro** St-Paul, line 1. **Bus** 67, 69, 76 & 96
- ☕ **Eat and drink** Picnic Florence Kahn (19 Rue des Rosiers, 75004; http:florence-kahn.fr), a deli, sells gefilte (stuffed) fish and pletzels (onion and poppy seed covered flat bread), and vatrushka, a cheese cake. Real Meal Breakfast in America (4 Rue Malher, 75004; www.breakfast-in-america.com) is a burger bar serving burgers and fries and all-day breakfasts with bacon and pancakes.
- 🚻 **Toilets** No

Rosiers. In the 1950s and 1960s, Jews from North Africa joined them, bringing a different cuisine of falafels, hummus and tabbouleh, giving the place a deliciously cosmopolitan flavour. The street is immortalized in the hilarious, cult French comedy, The Mad Adventures of Rabbi Jacob (1973).

Take cover
Le Musée de la Magie (11 Rue St-Paul, 75004; www.museedelamagie.com) is a subterranean 16th-century vault full of curios, optical illusions, games and magic tricks.

⑧ Musée Picasso

Sculptures and ceramics

The dominant artist of the 20th century, Pablo Picasso was one of the greatest creative geniuses of all time. Born in Málaga, he lived and studied in Barcelona, Spain, before moving to France, where he spent most of his life. This collection of his work is the world's finest, and was inherited by the state in lieu of the $50m in death duties owed by his family. The collection is housed in the Hôtel Salé. The airy museum spans his lifetime, and covers paintings, sculpture, textiles and ceramics. The museum is closed for renovation but Picasso enthusiasts can visit the Musée National d'Art Moderne in Centre Pompidou and other museums.

A popular Jewish bakery selling falafels and other savouries in Rue des Rosiers

The Lowdown

🌐 **Map reference** 25 D4
Address Hôtel Salé, 5 Rue de
Thorigny, 75003; www.musee-
picasso.fr

🚇 **Métro** St-Paul, line 1 & Chemin
Vert, line 8. **Bus** 29, 96, 69 & 75

🕐 **Open** To reopen in Spring 2013

🚹 **Age range** 3 plus

🕐 **Allow** 1–2 hours

🍴 **Eat and drink** Picnic Boulangerie
Malineau (18 Rue Vieille du
Temple, 75004; 01 42 76 94 88;
closed Sun) sells a delicious pain
au chocolat framboise (chocolate
raspberry bread) and an equally
scrummy pain au chocolat banane
(chocolate banana bread). Have a
picnic in Place des Vosges. Snacks
Merci (111 Blvd Beaumarchais,
75003; 01 42 77 78 92; closed
Sun) is a concept store; inside it
is the Used-Book Café, which
serves grilled cheese, soups,
salads and cakes.

Letting off steam

The **Jardin de l'Hôtel Salé** (101 Rue
Coutures St-Gervais, 75003) has a
playground and ping-pong tables.
There is also a merry-go-round at
Métro St-Paul, which is a convenient
treat at the end of a day out.

⑨ Centre Pompidou
Cubes, views and tubes

President Pompidou of France, who
was in office from 1969–74, himself
chose the winning entry by Richard
Rogers and Renzo Piano for the
Centre Pompidou, often just
referred to as Beaubourg. It is a
crazy glass building turned inside
out with its air-conditioning shafts,
escalators and pipes on the outside.
Inside is the Musée National d'Art
Moderne, which exhibits cutting-
edge modern art that is always on
the move; its 65,000 pieces rotate
constantly. La Galerie des Enfants
makes art and design accessible to
kids as young as two. Children will
love the views of Paris from the
building's panoramic terrace.

Letting off steam

The big pedestrianized piazza, **Place
Georges Pompidou**, in front of
the museum, is buzzing with street
entertainers. Around the corner, the
colourful Stravinsky Fountain is like
a giant musical box.

Street entertainer on a unicycle in front
of the Centre Pompidou

The Lowdown

🌐 **Map reference** 25 B4
Address Pl Georges Pompidou,
75004; www.centrepompidou.fr

🚇 **Métro** Rambuteau, line 11 & Hôtel
de Ville, line 1. **RER** Châtelet–Les
Halles, lines A, B & D. **Bus** 21, 29,
38, 47, 58, 69, 70, 72, 74, 75, 81,
85 & 96

🕐 **Open** 11am–9pm Wed–Mon

💶 **Prices** Exhibitions, museums and
panoramic viewing point: €20–
36 or €24–42 depending on the
season; under 18s & EU citizens
under 26 free. Panoramic viewing
point only: €6–16; under 26s free.
Écran des Enfants, inside Galerie
des Enfants: €11–21

🎟 **Skipping the queue** Paris Museum
Pass accepted. Free entry every first
Sun of the month. Tickets for adults
can be bought online or at the
automatic machines. Older kids have
to show their IDs to get free tickets.

📣 **Guided tours** Audio guides in
English. Tours in French at 3:30pm
every Sat & 4pm every Sun. The
bookshop sells My Little
Pompidou, a children's guide

🚹 **Age range** 2 plus

👥 **Activities** Workshops on Wed &
Sat. Family activities on Sun &
during school hols. Films at Écran
des Enfants, occasionally in English

🕐 **Allow** 1–2 hours

🍴 **Eat and drink** Real meal Le Hangar
(12 Impasse Berthaud, 75003; 01 42
74 55 44; closed Sun) is a traditional
bistro. Family treat Georges (on
site; 01 44 78 47 99; closed Tue)
serves mostly French dishes

🚻 **Toilets** At several locations

Picnic under €25; Snacks €25–45; Real meal €45–90; Family treat over €90 (based on a family of four)

Musée du Louvre and around

The biggest museum in the world, the Musée du Louvre dazzles through the sheer scale and brilliance of its art collections. This bustling heart of Paris is also home to two pretty parks: Jardin des Tuileries and Jardin du Palais Royal. Both are ideal for a break or picnic. Traffic is heavy during rush hours, so pick a Sunday morning or a public holiday for a walk, or cut across the Jardin des Tuileries to Place de la Concorde and Place Vendôme to avoid traffic.

0 metres   400
0 yards   400

Musée du Louvre and around

Sacré-Coeur p116

Eiffel Tower p104

Musée du Louvre

Musée d'Orsay p110

Notre-Dame p90

The Lowdown

🚗 **Metro** Concorde, lines 1, 8 & 12; Tuileries, line 1; Bourse, line 3; Palais Royal–Musée-du-Louvre, lines 1 & 7; Opéra, lines 3, 7 & 8 or Grands Boulevards & Richelieu-Drouot, lines 8 & 9. **RER** Musée d'Orsay, line C; Auber, line A. **Bus** 20, 21, 22, 27, 29, 39, 42, 48, 53, 66, 67, 68, 69, 72, 74, 81, 85 & 95. **River Boat** Quai du Louvre

ℹ️ **Visitor information** 25 Rue des Pyramides, 75001; summer: 9am–9pm Mon–Sat; winter: 10am–7pm Mon–Sat; year round: 11am–7pm Sun & public hols. Carrousel du Louvre, 99 Rue de Rivoli, 75001; 10am–6pm daily

🍴 **Supermarkets** Mon'op, 9 Blvd de la Madeleine, 75001. Franprix, 9 Rue du Mail, 75001 & 20 Pl Marché St-Honoré, 75001 **Markets** Marché St-Honoré, Pl du Marché St-Honoré, 75001; 12:30–8:30pm Wed & 7am–3pm Sun

🎡 **Festivals** Fêtes des Tuileries funfair (Jul & Aug). Paris-Plages (Jul & Aug, see p91)

➕ **Pharmacy** Pharmacy des Petits-Champs, 21 Rue des Petits-Champs, 75002; 01 42 96 97 20; 8am–8:30pm Mon–Fri, 9:30am–8pm Sat

🛝 **Nearest playgrounds** Jardin des Tuileries, Rue de Rivoli, 75001 (see p99). Square de Montholon, 80 Rue Lafayette, 75009 (see p101)

🚻 **Toilets** Point WC: Carrousel du Louvre; Printemps, 64 Blvd Haussmann, 75009

The well-manicured lawns of the Jardin du Palais Royal

The stunning interiors of the historic waxworks museum, the Musée Grévin

The Musée du Louvre lit up at night

The Vendôme Column in Place Vendôme

Places of interest

SIGHTS
1. Musée du Louvre
2. Place de la Concorde
3. Place Vendôme
4. Opéra Garnier
5. Musée Grévin

● **EAT AND DRINK**
1. Paul
2. Mira
3. Café Marly
4. Water Bar
5. Ladurée
6. Les Ambassadeurs
7. Le Zinc d'Honoré
8. Le Soufflé
9. Monoprix
10. Chez Clément
11. A La Mère de la Famille
12. Le Bouillon Chartier

● **SHOPPING**
1. Virgin Megastore
2. Nature et Découvertes
3. W H Smith
See also Musée du Louvre (p99)

● **WHERE TO STAY**
1. Hôtel du Louvre
2. Le Bristol
3. Le Burgundy
4. Résidhome Paris-Opéra
5. The Westin

① Musée du Louvre
Mummies, mysterious ladies and medieval moats

Fascinating and beyond famous, the Musée du Louvre houses a stunning selection of art from the Middle Ages to 1848, as well as one of the biggest collections of ancient Egyptian treasures in the world. In all there are 35,000 things to see. In over 800 years, the Louvre has metamorphosed from fortress to palace, stable, granary and, after Louis XIV moved the court to Versailles in 1678, squatters' home. In 1793, after the Revolution, it opened as a museum of royal treasures.

Key Features

■ **Second Floor** French and Dutch paintings

■ **First Floor** French and Italian paintings, Decorative and Islamic art

■ **Ground Floor** French and Italian sculpture; Egyptian, Greek and Near Eastern antiquities

■ **Lower Ground Floor** French and Italian sculpture, and Islamic art

Richelieu Wing

Denon Wing

Sully Wing

Main Entrance

⑥ **Winged Victory of Samothrace** The more natural style typical of the Hellenistic period is obvious in this very famous ancient Greek statue.

⑦ **The Galerie d'Apollon** Looking like a jewel box, this gallery holds the crown jewels, including Empress Eugenie's crown, which had 2,490 diamonds.

⑧ **The Coronation of Napoleon** Jacques-Louis David painted this piece of propaganda in 1807. Napoleon's family is shown, including his mother, who was not even present for the ceremony.

① **Mona Lisa** Da Vinci never revealed the identity of the mysterious lady in this famous painting, which has hung both on Louis XIV's and Napoleon's bedroom walls.

② **Arc de Triomphe du Carrousel** This triumphal arch was built to celebrate Napoleon's victories in 1805. Its marble columns are adorned with statue of soldiers of the Grande Armée.

③ **Medieval moat** The sheer size of the twin towers and the drawbridge in the moat will impress the kids and give them a taste of the vast fortified castle that stood there.

④ **Marly Horses** These dramatic statues once stood in the garden of Louis XIV's Château de Marly, but were later shifted to the Place de la Concorde.

⑤ **The Giant Sphinx** A mythical monster guards the museum's amazing collection of ancient Egyptian treasures.

Prices given are for a family of four

The Lowdown

🌐 **Map reference** 24 F4
Address 75001; 01 40 20 50 50; www.louvre.fr

🚗 **Métro** Palais-Royal–Musée-du-Louvre, lines 1 & 7. **Bus** 21, 24, 27, 39, 48, 68, 69, 72, 81 & 95. **River boat** Louvre–Quai du Louvre

🕐 **Open** 9am–6pm, till 10pm Wed & Fri; closed Tue, 1 Jan, 1 May & 25 Dec

💶 **Price** €9–19; under 18s & EU citizens under 26 free. €6 after 6pm on Wed & Fri; free entry on first Sun of the month & 14 Jul

👥 **Skipping the queue** Paris Museum Pass accepted. Buy tickets in advance online, through TicketWeb, FNAC, Virgin Megastores or from the automated machines in the Carrousel du Louvre. Tickets are valid for the entire day. Queues are shorter at the entrance by the Arc de Triomphe du Carrousel and at the Porte de Lions by the Seine; entry from 99 Rue de Rivoli is only for tickets bought in advance. If you have a pushchair, walk to the front of the queue and the staff will let you through.

Letting off steam

On the doorstep of the Louvre is one of Paris's oldest and loveliest parks, the **Jardin des Tuileries** *(Rue de Rivoli, 75001).* Sail wooden boats or play in the playground. As tickets to the Louvre are valid all day, it is a good idea to treat it as a number of different museums, and take a long midday break at the park, if tired.

Children playing in the playground in Jardin des Tuileries

Eat and drink

Picnic: under €25; Snacks: €25–45; Real meal: €45–90; Family treat: over €90 (based on a family of four)

PICNIC Paul *(Passage Lemonnier, Jardin du Carrousel, 75001; 01 49 27 99 55; www.paul.fr; open daily),* a bakery chain, serves sandwiches. Opt for a picnic on the grass nearby or in the museum's Cour Carrée.
SNACKS Mira *(Carrousel du Louvre; 01 55 35 12 60; open daily)* is a self-service Spanish tapas bar, which also serves a tasty paella.
REAL MEAL Café Marly *(Richelieu Wing; 01 49 26 06 60; open daily)* offers stunning views of the Louvre, pasta and sandwiches.
FAMILY TREAT Water Bar *(213 Rue St-Honoré, 75001; 01 55 35 33 90; open daily)* in the trendy concept

store Colette, sells bottled water from around the world and bites to eat. Enjoy lunch or tea.

Find out more

DIGITAL The Louvre website is child-friendly. Simply click on the cartoon figure of the first director, Dominique Vivant Denon, or the trap door that leads to his office. The museum shops sell two good CD ROMs, *The Louvre, Art for Kids* and *One Minute at the Museum.*
FILM The museum has excellent films for children. Enjoy watching *The Amazing Museum,* which is sold in the shop. Looney Tunes' *Louvre Come Back to Me* (1962) is a bit more light-hearted.

Shopping

The underground Carrousel du Louvre is full of shops, including the **Virgin Megastore** *(99 Rue de Rivoli, 75004),* **Nature et Découvertes** *(174 Rue de Rivoli, 75004),* a branch of the scientific toy shop, and many shops full of knick knacks.
W H Smith *(248, Rue de Rivoli, 75001; www.whsmith.fr)* has the best collection of English-language books for children in Paris.

Next stop...

JARDIN DU PALAIS ROYAL After a trip to the Musée du Louvre, everyone needs some time to relax. In summer, the gardens at the Palais Royal, once home of the all-powerful Cardinal Richelieu, are a lovely place to take a shady stroll or unwind over a drink.

 Guided tours For adults in English: €5–15. For children in French during school hols, Mon, Tue, Thu & Fri; 01 40 20 51 77. Download themed tours; audio guide €5. The bookshop sells a variety of useful guides for children and families.

 Age range 5 plus

Activities Workshops, films and talks for children and families in French. Take a walk after dark in the Cour Carrée, which is magical.

Allow At least 2–3 hours

Wheelchair access Limited

Shops The subterranean Carrousel du Louvre is a great place to browse the shops.

Toilets In the lobby, on all floors, and at the Point WC in the Carrousel du Louvre.

Good family value?
Considering the amount on show in what is one of the world's most important museums, it is a bargain. Plan the trip in advance using the children's website.

The Fountain of River Commerce and Navigation in Place de la Concorde

② Place de la Concorde

Revolutionary guillotine and an Egyptian obelisk

The Place de la Concorde provides great views of the Champs-Elysées, north to La Madeleine, east to the Louvre and south across the river to the Assemblée Nationale. It is truly magical after dark. Laid out in 1757, and named Place Louis XV, it was the main location for the guillotine during the Revolution. In 1792, the square literally ran with blood as thousands, including Louis XVI and Marie-Antoinette, were all executed here. Later, after the horrors of the Revolution, it was named "concorde" or "harmony" in the hope of peaceful times ahead.

On the square's northwestern corner is one of the most luxurious hotels in the city, Hôtel Crillon. The identical, imposing building located on the northeastern side is the Navy Ministry. The obelisk in the middle of the square was made 3,200 years ago, and is the oldest monument in

Paris. At one time, it stood in the Temple of Ramses in Luxor, but was given to the French people by the Pasha of Egypt in 1829. In exchange for this gift, the pasha received a clock that never worked.

Take cover
La Madeleine *(Pl de la Madeline, 75008)* is a church dedicated to Mary Magdalene. Although work began on it in 1764, it was only consecrated in 1845. Its design was ordered by Napoleon who wanted a Roman-style temple honouring his army, which is why it has no bell and does not face towards Jerusalem like most other churches.

③ Place Vendôme

Paris's chicest square

Built in 1699 to reflect the glory of the statue of Louis XIV placed in the centre, the square failed to impress the revolutionaries who melted the statue to make canons. In 1806, a huge column made out of captured enemy canons was erected, showing the exploits of Napoleon's army in a spiral comic strip around the edge. Although it was torn down in 1871 by revolutionaries again, a copy of the column now stands in its place.

The square is simply beautiful at night, and has also witnessed some famous events, such as the marriage of Napoleon to Josephine at No. 3. The Ritz hotel at No. 15 has a long list of illustrious guests including Ernest Hemingway, Edward VII, Charlie Chaplin and Princess Diana.

Letting off steam
Nearby is the **Jardin des Tuileries** *(see p99)* with a popular playground. Let the kids be mini-Parisians and sail wooden boats on the lake.

Elegant buildings on Place Vendôme, housing exclusive shops

The Lowdown

🌐 **Map reference** 24 E2
Address 75001

🚌 **Métro** Tuileries, line 1. **Bus** 67, 74, 81 & 85

🧍 **Age range** All ages

🍽 **Eat and drink** *Picnic* Le Zinc d'Honoré *(36 Pl du Marché St-Honoré, 75001; open daily)* serves steak with potato gratin or fries. *Real meal* Le Soufflé *(36 Rue du Mont Thabor, 75001; 01 42 60 27 19)* serves sweet and savoury soufflés.

🚻 **Toilets** No

④ Opéra Garnier

Phantoms and chandeliers

Decorated like a giant birthday cake, the Opéra National de Paris Garnier or Palais Garnier, was designed by Charles Garnier in 1861. Its opulent splendour and red velvet boxes exude the sensuous and slightly sinister atmosphere of a short story by writer Guy de Maupassant. The red and gold auditorium is lit by a gigantic crystal chandelier. In 1896, it fell down and crushed the audience below. This event, as well as the

The Lowdown

🌐 **Map reference** 18 E6
Address 1 Pl de l'Opéra, 75009; www.operadeparis.fr

🚌 **Métro** Opéra, lines 3, 7 & 8. **RER** Auber, line A. **Bus** 21, 22, 27, 29, 42, 53, 66, 68, 81 & 95

🕐 **Open** 10am–5pm daily; Jul–Sep: till 6pm; matinee days: till 1pm; closed 1 Jan, 1 May & 25 Dec

💶 **Price** €28–38; under 10s free. Entry tickets offer a reduction to the Musée d'Orsay, valid for a week after the visit

🚩 **Guided tours** In English at 11:30am daily; 2:30pm on Wed, Sat & Sun in Jul & Aug & school hols; €36 for a family; 1 hour 30 mins

🧍 **Age range** 5 plus

♿ **Wheelchair access** Yes

🎨 **Activities** Family workshops in French; 01 40 01 19 88.

⏱ **Allow** 45 mins

🍽 **Eat and drink** *Picnic* Monoprix *(21 Ave de l'Opéra, 75009)* is a great stop to pick up supplies for a picnic in the Jardin du Palais Royal. *Real meal* Chez Clément *(17 Blvd des Capucines, 75002; 01 53 43 82 00; www.chezclement. com)* serves tasty meals and is child friendly.

🚻 **Toilets** On all levels

The Lowdown

🌐 **Map reference** 23 C2
Address 75008

🚌 **Métro** Concorde, lines 1 & 8. **Bus** 24, 42, 52, 72, 73, 84, & 94

🎡 **Activities** Giant Ferris wheel from Nov–Jan. Summer funfair in the Jardin des Tuileries

🍽 **Eat and drink** *Real meal* Ladurée *(16 Rue Royale, 75008; closed Sun)*, which opened in 1862, is a luxury tearoom. *Family treat* Les Ambassadeurs *(10 Pl de la Concorde, 75008; 01 44 71 16 16; open daily)*, is the Hôtel Crillon's fairy-tale restaurant, where families go for lunch.

🚻 **Toilets** At the entrance to the Jardin des Tuileries

The statues, fountains and trim hedges of the Jardin du Palais Royal on a sunny day

building's underground lake and vast cellars, inspired Gaston Leroux's novel *Phantom of the Opera*. There is a shop too, so bring the piggy bank.

Letting off steam

Walk down to the lovely gardens at the **Palais Royal** *(Pl de Palais Royal, 75001)* situated at the end of Avenue de l'Opéra. The present garden is smaller than the original one laid out for Cardinal Richelieu in the 1630s.

5 Musée Grévin

Great events and ghoulish murders

This is the best place for spotting celebrities captured in wax – kings and queens, pop stars and footballers. Comparisons with London's Madame Tussauds are inevitable, but Grévin is less gruesome and more authentic. Mingle with celebrities in the stunning Le Théâtre Tout-Paris. Step back in time in the Histoire de France, which features numerous

historical scenes, among them a gory portrayal of the Revolution, and depictions of the big events of the 20th century. But what steals the show is the museum's splendid Baroque building, home to the original light and sound show from the 1900 Universal Exhibition.

Letting off steam

A 10-minute walk to the northeast is the **Square de Montholon** *(80 Rue Lafayette, 75009)*. The pretty park here has a playground and some ping-pong tables.

Opéra Garnier, symbolizing the opulence of the Second Empire

KIDS' CORNER

Look out for...

1 The old barometer on the corner of Rue Duphot and Rue St-Honoré, not far from Place Vendôme.
2 An axe, a helmet and a lion on the base of the Vendôme Column.
3 The eight ladies in Place de la Concorde. Each one represents a French city.
4 Buzzing bees. 450,000 of them live on the roof of Opéra Garnier.

CARTOON CAPER

The first animated film was shown at the Musée Grévin in 1894 by Charles Émile Reynaud. He died penniless after the audiences deserted him preferring to watch real movies rather than animation. Despondent, he threw most of his work into the Seine before he died.

Mr Meyer's model

Waxwork museums were the celebrity magazines of their day as photos were still a novelty and TV was yet to be invented. In 1882, a trip to theatre designer Alfred Grévin's new museum was the only way to get a good look at the people who were hitting the headlines in the new mass-circulation newspapers that were taking Paris by storm. Look out for Grévin's friend, journalist Arthur Meyer, who cleverly came up with the whole idea – he is portrayed sleeping over a copy of his own newspaper!

The Lowdown

🌐 **Map reference** 18 G6
Address 10 Blvd Montmartre, 75009; www.grevin.com

🚗 **Métro** Grands Boulevards & Richelieu-Drouot, lines 8 & 9; Bourse, line 3. **Bus** 20, 39, 48, 67, 74 & 85

🕐 **Open** 10am–6:30pm, till 7pm Sat, Sun, public & school hols; from 9am autumn & Christmas school hols; closed for five days after Christmas

💰 **Price** €68–78; under 6s free

🎟 **Skipping the queue** Paris Museum Pass accepted. Buy tickets in advance, or go at lunchtime.

👣 **Guided tours** Tours in French at 2.30pm Wed, Sat & Sun, except during school hols; €18 per child; 01 47 70 83 97

👫 **Age range** 6 plus.

⏱ **Allow** 1 hour 30 mins

♿ **Wheelchair access** Yes

☕ **Café** Café Grévin, next to the museum
Eat and drink *Picnic* A La Mère de la Famille *(35 Rue du Faubourg Montmartre, 75009)* opened in 1761 and sells everything to satisfy a sweet tooth. Walk over to the Square de Montholon for a picnic.
Real meal Le Bouillon Chartier *(7 Rue du Faubourg Montmartre, 75009; 01 47 70 86 29; www. restaurant-chartier.com; open daily)* is a classic French bistro, with waiters dressed in white aprons.

👫 **Toilets** At several locations

Picnic under €25; Snacks €25–45; Real meal €45–90; Family treat over €90 (based on a family of four)

Eiffel Tower and around

From the moment most kids arrive in Paris, they want to get to the top of the Eiffel Tower. In summer, be prepared for big crowds. Across the river on the Right Bank, the area known as the Trocadéro is crammed with museums that are a good option on a rainy day. The grand Avenue des Champs-Elysées, leading up to the Arc de Triomphe, is perfect for strolling. Exploring this area requires a lot of walking; the best way to get around is by bus. On Sundays and public holidays, Quai Branly is closed to traffic, and is a fun place to Rollerblade or take a family stroll.

Places of interest

SIGHTS
1. Eiffel Tower
2. Palais de Chaillot
3. Arc de Triomphe
4. Avenue des Champs-Elysées

EAT AND DRINK
1. Boulangerie Secco
2. Thé aux 3 Cerises
3. 58 Tour Eiffel
4. Le Jules Verne
5. Café Carlu
6. Ozu
7. Ladurée
8. Drugstore Publicis
9. Dalloyau
10. 114 Faubourg

WHERE TO STAY
1. Adagio Paris Tour Eiffel
2. Citadines Trocadéro
3. Four Seasons George V
4. Hilton Arc de Triomphe
5. Jays
6. Novotel Eiffel Tower
7. Plaza Athenée

Eiffel Tower and around

Bronze statues atop the pillars on Pont Alexandre III

People under the Eiffel Tower splendidly lit up at night

0 metres   500

0 yards   500

The Eiffel Tower with the Champ-de-Mars in the foreground

A view of the Trocadéro from the Eiffel Tower

Marionettes du Champ-de-Mars

Triumph of Napoleon relief on the Arc de Triomphe's base

The Lowdown

🚇 **Metro** Bir Hakeim, line 6; Charles de Gaulle-Etoile, lines 1, 2, & 6 or Trocadéro, lines 6 & 9. **RER** Champ-de-Mars–Tour Eiffel, line C or Pont de l'Alma, line C. Charles de Gaulle-Etoile, line C. **Bus** 22, 30, 32, 42, 63, 72, 73, 80, 82 & 93. **River boat** Quai de la Bourdannais

ℹ️ **Visitor information** Kiosk at the corner of Ave des Champs-Elysées & Ave de Marigny, 75008; mid-Apr–mid-Oct: 9am–7pm; closed 14 Jul

🛒 **Supermarkets** Franprix, 107 Ave La Bourdonnais, 75007 & 155 Ave de Suffren, 75015. Monoprix, 52 Ave des Champs-Elysées, 75008 & 18 Rue de Passy, 75016
Markets Marché Président Wilson, Ave du Président Wilson, 75016; 7am–2:30pm Wed & Sat

🎪 **Festivals** Famillathlon: family sports day in the Champ-de-

Mars; www.famillathon.org (Sep). Ice-skating at the Eiffel Tower (mid-Dec–end-Jan). Paris Marathon (Apr). La Defilé, a huge military parade (14 Jul). Tour de France; www.letour.fr Armistice (11 Nov).

➕ **Pharmacy** Pharmacie de la Tour Eiffel, 24 Rue de Monttesseuy, 75007; 8am–8pm Mon–Sat

🎨 **Nearest playgrounds** There is a large playground with a sandpit at the southern end of the Champ-de-Mars, 75007; dawn–dusk daily (see p105). Jardins du Trocadéro, 75016; dawn–dusk daily (see 106). Parc Monceau, Blvd de Courcelles, 75008; 7am–10pm daily (see p107). Jardin de Champs-Elysées, 75008; dawn–dusk daily (see p107)

🚻 **Toilets** Point WC, 26 Ave des Champs-Elysées, 75008; baby changing facilities €2

① Eiffel Tower
The iron lady of Paris

There is something irresistible about the Meccano-style star of the Paris skyline. It is a magnet for children, whose main ambition is to get to the top as fast as possible. In 1886, a competition was held to build a tower at the gates of the Universal Exhibition of 1889, to commemorate 100 years since the Revolution. Gustave Eiffel emerged as the winner from among 700 entries, which included a giant watering can and an enormous guillotine. Far from an instant hit, the Eiffel Tower (Tour Eiffel) was lucky not to be torn down later.

Colourful souvenirs of the Eiffel Tower

The Lowdown

🌐 **Map reference** 22 E3
Address Champ-de-Mars, 75007; 08 92 70 12 39; *www.tour-eiffel.fr*

🚗 **Métro** Bir Hakeim, line 6 or Trocadéro, lines 6 & 9. **RER** Champs-de-Mars–Tour Eiffel, line C. **Bus** 42, 69, 82 & 87. **River boat** Quai de la Bourdonnais

🕐 **Open** 9:30am–11pm; mid-Jun–Aug: 9am–midnight; Easter weekend: to midnight

€ **Price** Summit: €45–50; first & second levels: lift €25–30; stairs: €16–17; under-4s free

👬 **Skipping the queue** The queues are shorter at night. Buy tickets online.

📣 **Guided tours** Download guides and iPhone apps from *www.eiffel-tower.com*.

👫 **Age range** All ages, but small children may find the summit frightening.

🤸 **Activities** Send a postcard from the post office on the first level. Download kids' quiz book from *www. eiffel-tower.com*.

⏱ **Allow** 1 hour 30 mins, or 3 hours in high season

♿ **Wheelchair access** Yes, but first and second levels only

☕ **Café** On first and second levels

🚻 **Toilets** By the east pillar and on the first and second levels

Good family value?
It may be pricey, but the kids will love it. It is best to visit the tower at the end of a trip to Paris so that children can spot from above the sights they have visited.

Key Features

Viewing gallery On a clear day, it is possible to see Chartres Cathedral, 80 km (50 miles) away.

Bust of Eiffel Eiffel was sculpted by Antoine Bourdelle in 1929, and the bust was placed below the tower in his memory.

Double-decker lifts These vintage lifts ply their way up and down the tower.

Eiffel's staircase See a piece of the original staircase that was taken down in 1983 to make way for new lifts. Gustave Eiffel would walk up to the top to his office.

Cineiffel Watch the crazy and daring stunts inspired by the tower in this museum, as well as footage of the famous people who have visited the tower, among them Adolf Hitler, who wanted to blow it up.

Third level The viewing gallery is 276 m (906 ft) above the ground. Mr Eiffel had an office here.

Sparkling Eiffel Every evening since the millennium, a 200,000-watt lighting system makes the Eiffel Tower sparkle for 5 minutes every hour, on the hour, till midnight.

Crisscross girders The complex pattern of the girders helps to stabilize the tower on windy days. The metal parts can expand up to 12 cm (5 inch) on hot days.

Second level At 115 m (376 ft), this level is separated from the first by 359 steps, or a few minutes in the lift.

First level At a height of 57 m (187 ft), this level can be reached by lift or by 360 steps.

Bust of Eiffel

The Eiffel Tower soaring above a playground on Champ-de-Mars

Letting off steam

The adjoining **Champ-de-Mars**, with its sweeping pathways, is perfect for riding a bike or kicking a ball about. Watch a puppet show at the Marionettes du Champ-de-Mars theatre in the northeastern side of the park; this is fun even if the kids do not speak a word of French.

Eat and drink

Picnic: under €25; Snacks: €25–45; Real meal: €45–90; Family treat: over €90 (based on a family of four)

PICNIC Boulangerie Secco *(20 Rue Jean Nicot, 75007; closed Sun & Mon)* is famous for its seasonal selection of pastries. Picnic in the Champ-de-Mars.

SNACKS Thé aux 3 Cerises *(47 Ave de Suffren, 75007; 01 42 73 92 97; 12–6pm Tue–Fri, till 7pm Sat & Sun)* is ideal for a cup of tea. Kids can enjoy a delicious hot chocolate with whipped cream.

REAL MEAL 58 Tour Eiffel *(08 25 56 66 62; www.restaurants-toureiffel.com; 11:30am–5:30pm & 6:30–11:30pm daily)* is located on the first floor. Lunch is the best option, when the menu is lighter and prices more competitive.

Contemporary decor at 58 Tour Eiffel, the first-floor restaurant

FAMILY TREAT Le Jules Verne *(01 45 55 61 44; www.lejulesverne-paris.com; 12:30–1:30pm & 7–9:30pm daily)*, on the tower's second floor, is perfect for a special meal. It has stunning panoramic views, and is in the hands of Michelin-starred chef Alain Ducasse.

Find out more

DIGITAL On tinyurl.com/2g5beua, watch daredevil French inline skater Taïg Khris set the world record for the highest rollerskate jump, at 40 m (131 ft), from the first floor of the Eiffel Tower in 2010. Find out about more towers on www.great-towers.com and play games with the Eiffel Tower on www.tour-eiffel.fr. **FILM** Check out James Bond in action on the tower in *A View to Kill* (1985), Chuckie and his friends in *Rugrats in Paris* (1996) and the cartoon heroes in *Looney Tunes Back in Action* (2003). It appears in *Zazie dans le Métro* (1960), *The Aristocats* (1970) and *Ratatouille* (2007). Ludwig Bemelmans' heroine Madeline lives in a leafy street nearby in *Madeline* (1998).

Shopping

The only thing to buy next to the Eiffel Tower is a model of it. The original models were made of scrap metal from the tower, but now they come in all colours and materials.

Next stop...

NOTRE-DAME Take a river cruise from the Eiffel Tower past various famous sights, ending up at the other ultimate Parisian symbol, Notre-Dame *(see pp90–91)*.

② Palais de Chaillot

Fishy films and model boats

From humble beginnings as a pastoral village, this part of Paris is now dominated by the monumental Palais de Chaillot, universally known by the locals as the Trocadéro. It is the best place from which to gaze at the Eiffel Tower, but also somewhere to take a crash course in architecture, French maritime heritage and the history of humankind, by visiting its museums.

The **Musée de l'Homme** houses one of the world's best prehistoric collections, while the **Musée de la Marine** is a must for fans of blistering barnacles and model boats. The palace's east wing houses the **Cité de l'Architecture et du Patrimoine**, featuring France's most famous buildings in miniature. That done, relax at **Cinéaqua**, touring its aquarium or taking in a film.

The Lowdown

- 🌐 **Map reference** 21 D1
  Address 17 Pl du Trocadéro, 75016. Musée de l'Homme: reopens during 2012. Musée de la Marine: www.musee-marine.fr. Cité de l'Architecture: www.citechaillot.fr. Cinéaqua: www.cineaqua.com

- 🚗 **Métro** Trocadéro, lines 6 & 9. **RER** Champ-de-Mars–Tour Eiffel, line C. **Bus** 22, 30, 32, 63, 72 & 82. **River boat** Quai de la Bourdonnais

- 🕐 **Open** Musée de la Marine: 10am–6pm, till 9pm Fri & till 7pm Sat & Sun. Cité de l'Architecture et du Patrimoine: 11am–7pm, till 9pm Thu. Museums are closed Tue, 1 Jan, 1 May & 25 Dec. Cinéaqua: 10am–6pm, till 7pm Sat & Sun

- 💰 **Price** Musée de la Marine: €14–24; under 18s & EU citizens under 26 free. Cité de l'Architecture et du Patrimoine: €16–26; under 18s and EU citizens under 26 free. Cinéaqua: €70–80; under 3s free

- 🍴 **Eat and drink** Snacks Café Carlu (Cité de l'Architecture) is a self-service eatery with views of the Eiffel Tower. Real Meal Ozu (Cinéaqua, 5 Ave Albert de Mun; www.ozurestaurants.com; Tue–Sat eve & Wed–Sun lunch) is a good place for Japanese tempura and sushi. One of its walls is part of the Cinéaqua's giant fish tank.

- 🚻 **Toilets** At several locations

View of the Arc de Triomphe from Avenue Marceau

Letting off steam

The **Jardins du Trocadéro** run down to the Seine alongside Paris's most fantastic fountain. The gardens also have a vintage merry-go-round and a playground. On weekends, street performers dance on the esplanade.

③ Arc de Triomphe

Generals and French history

After defeating the Austrian and Russian troops at the Battle of Austerlitz in 1805, Napoleon commissioned a triumphal arch in the Roman style. However, no sooner were the foundations for the arch laid, than his empire began to collapse. The arch was finally completed in 1836. Four years later, Napoleon's remains passed under it, on the way to his final resting place at Les Invalides. Since then, both occupying armies and liberating troops have marched through it.

Known for having witnessed the best as well as the worst moments in the nation's history, this monument celebrates France's military heroes; the names of generals who served in Napoleon's army are engraved here, and the names of those who died on the battlefield are underlined. A relief on the left base celebrates the Treaty of Vienna peace agreement of 1810, a symbol of Napoleon's triumph. A great place to get a feel for French history, the Arc de Triomphe is also possibly one of the best spots in Paris to enjoy fine views, especially at sunset.

Tropical fish at the state-of-the-art aquarium in Cinéaqua, Palais de Chaillot

The Lowdown

- 🌐 **Map reference** 16 E4
  Address Pl Charles de Gaulle, 75008; www.monuments-nationaux.fr

- 🚗 **Métro** Charles de Gaulle-Etoile, lines 1, 2 & 6. **RER** Charles de Gaulle-Etoile, line A. **Bus** 22, 30, 31, 52, 73 & 92

- 🕐 **Open** Apr–Sep: 10am–11pm; Oct–Mar: 10am–10:30pm; closed 1 Jan, 1 Apr, 8 May am, 14 Jul am, 11 Nov am & 25 Dec

- 💰 **Price** €18–28; under 18s & EU citizens under 26 free

- 👫 **Age range** All ages

- 🎖 **Activities** Ceremony to relight the eternal flame: 6.30pm daily. Annual military parade: 14 Jul

- ⏱ **Allow** 1 hour

- ♿ **Wheelchair access** Yes, but limited. No access to the roof/views

- 🍴 **Eat and drink** Snacks Ladurée (75 Champs-Elysées, 75008; open until midnight) serves macaroons in its belle époque tea rooms. Family treat Drugstore Publicis (133 Champs Elysées, 75008; www.publicisdrugstore.com; open daily) is famous for its giant club sandwiches.

- 🚻 **Toilets** In Drugstore Publicis nearby

Letting off steam

Opt for a short ride on bus No. 30 or take an easy walk to **Parc Monceau** (Blvd de Courcelles, 75008), a great place for kids to run around. Created in 1769, this English-style garden has curving paths and some monuments. Look out for an Egyptian pyramid and Paris's biggest tree, an Oriental plane, whose trunk measures a whopping 7m (23 ft) round.

④ Avenue des Champs-Elysées

Stroll along in style

Running southeast from the grand Arc de Triomphe, the lively Champs-Elysées is one of the most famous avenues in the world. Although this is where the exclusive designer shops cluster, it also offers some regular shopping, especially on a Sunday. Further down, towards the Seine, are two galleries, the Grand and the Petit Palais, which were built for the Universal Exhibition of 1900. Check out the permanent art exhibition at the latter. From here, a few steps lead to the prettiest bridge in Paris, the glittering Pont Alexandre III. Double back and cross the Jardin de Champs-Elysées to take a quick look at the Palais de l'Elysées, which is and has been the official residence of the French President since 1873.

Letting off steam

Paris's oldest puppet theatre, **Théâtre Guignol** (Rond Point de Champs-Elysées, 75008; 01 42 45 38 30; www.theatreguinol.fr; 3pm, 4pm & 5pm Wed, Sat, Sun & school hols), in the Jardin de Champs-Elysées has been entertaining children since

A puppet show in progress at the Théâtre Guignol in the Jardin de Champs-Elysées

1818. The colourful marionettes are a treat for kids even if they do not follow the language. Be sure to catch another Paris institution in the park's northern corner, and start a stamp collection at the **Marché aux Timbres** (Ave Gabriel, 75008; open Thu, Sat & Sun and on public hols).

The Lowdown

- 🌐 **Map reference** 16 G5 **Address** 75008
- 🚗 **Métro** Charles de Gaulle-Etoile, lines 1, 2 & 6 or Champs-Elysées–Clémenceau, lines 1 & 13. **RER** Charles de Gaulle-Etoile, line A. **Bus** 28, 42, 72, 73, 83, & 93
- 🕐 **Allow** 1 hour 30 mins
- 🍴 **Eat and drink** *Picnic* Dalloyau (101 Rue du Faubourg St-Honoré, 75008) serves tasty macaroons and other delicacies. Their invention, the famous l'Opéra cake, is a must-try. Picnic in the Jardin des Champs-Elysées. *Family treat* 114 Faubourg (01 53 43 43 00; www.lebristolparis.com; open daily), Hôtel Bristol's restaurant serves waffles with smoked salmon.
- 🚻 **Toilets** No

Pont Alexandre III, connecting the Left Bank to the Grand Palais

Picnic under €25; **Snacks** €25–45; **Real meal** €45–90; **Family treat** over €90 (based on a family of four)

Musée d'Orsay and around

Children love the bright colours and the liveliness depicted in the Impressionist paintings in the Musée d'Orsay, and young military historians will discover one of the best collections of guns, flags and armour at the Invalides. This area is a good rainy-day option as the sights are all indoors and there are several shops and cafés along the Left Bank. The sights are spread over a large area, so best explored by river boat, RER or bus. Alternatively, take a taxi to travel between the museums and St-Germain.

Musée d'Orsay and around

Sacré-Coeur p116

Eiffel Tower p104

Musée du Louvre p98

Musée d'Orsay

Notre-Dame p90

Kids playing football in the gardens in front of Les Invalides

The Lowdown

🚗 **Métro** Solferino, line 12; Invalides, lines 8 & 13; La Tour-Maubourg, line 8; Varenne or St-François Xavier, line 13; St-Germain-des-Prés, line 4. **RER** Invalides & Musée d'Orsay, line C. **Bus** 24, 63, 68, 69, 73, 83, 84 & 94

ℹ️ **Visitor information** Carrousel du Louvre, 99 Rue de Rivoli, 75001; 10am–6pm daily.

🍲 **Supermarkets** Ed, 84 Rue St-Dominique, 75007. Monoprix, 50 Rue de Rennes, 75006 & 35 Rue du Bac, 75007
Markets Marché St-Germain

(covered market), 4/6 Rue Lobineau, 75006; 8:30am–1pm & 4–8pm Tue–Sat, 8:30am–1:30pm Sat & 8am–1:30pm Sun

🎪 **Festivals** Christmas village, Pl St-Germain-des-Prés, 75006

➕ **Pharmacies** Pharmacie St-Germain-des-Prés, 45 Rue Bonaparte, 75006; 01 43 26 52 92; 9am–midnight daily. Pharmacie des Invalides, 25 Blvd de la Tour Maubourg, 75007; 01 47 05 43 77; 8am–8pm Mon–Fri, 9am–8pm Sat, closed Sun

🛝 **Nearest playgrounds** Jardin des Tuileries, Rue de Rivoli, 75001; dawn–dusk daily (see p99). Ave de Breteuil, south of Les Invalides, 75007; dawn–dusk daily (see p112). Champ-de-Mars, 75007; dawn–dusk daily (see p105). Jardin Catherine Labouré, 33 Rue de Babylone, 75007; dawn–dusk daily (see p112). Square Félix Desruelles, 168 Blvd St-Germain, 75006; dawn–dusk daily (see p113).

Paris from the 56th floor of Tour Montparnasse

A view of the Musée d'Orsay across the Seine

Elegant Art Deco tiles in Brasserie Lipp, one of St-Germain's cafés

Places of interest

SIGHTS
1. Musée d'Orsay
2. Les Invalides
3. Musée Rodin
4. St-Germain-des-Prés
5. Cafés of St-Germain-des-Prés

🔴 **EAT AND DRINK**
1. Debauve & Gallais
2. Kayser
3. Eggs & Co
4. Le Télégraphe

5. Les Cocottes de Christian Constant
6. Bellota-Bellota
7. Besnier Père et Fils
8. Le Bon Marché
9. Grom
10. Ladurée
11. Le Bonaparte
12. Café de Flore

🔴 **SHOPPING**
1. Stock Bonpoint
2. Six Pieds Trois Puces
See also Musée d'Orsay (p111)

① Musée d'Orsay
All aboard for world-class art

Home to some of the most famous Impressionist paintings in the world, the light and airy Musée d'Orsay used to be a steam train station, but it had to close when its platforms became too short for modern trains. The giant station clock is still here, and the halls are still bustling, but now with art lovers of all ages who flock here to see the amazing collection of paintings, artistic oddities and intriguing Art Nouveau objects. Kids as young as three come here on school trips, jumping on the glass floor that covers a scale model of the Opéra quarter.

Clock in the main hall

Key Artists

① **François Pompon** Get nose to nose with the *Ours Blanc*, a huge polar bear sculpted in 1922.

② **Georges Seurat and Paul Signac** These artists were the pioneers of the Pointillist style, using tiny dots of colour that blend together to form an image when viewed from a distance. See Seurat's *Le Cirque* (The Circus) and Signac's *Femmes au Puits* (Women at the Well).

③ **Van Gogh** *Bedroom at Arles* was one of Van Gogh's favourite paintings. He also painted more than 40 self-portraits. Spot one hanging over the bed in the painting.

④ **Henry Matisse** In 1905, critics were shocked by the works of Matisse and his friends, which used bright, clashing colours, and called the artists *fauves* (wild beasts), from which Fauvism took its name. Look out for Matisse's *Luxe, Calme et Volupté*.

⑤ **Honoré Daumier** *The Washerwoman* by Daumier depicts one of the many women who would spend their days washing laundry in the Seine, a child in tow.

■ **Le Pavillon Amont** Art from European schools, Rodin

■ **Upper Floor** Impressionism and Post-Impressionism

■ **Middle Floor** Art Nouveau Symbolist and other decorative art and sculptures from the late 19th century

■ **Ground Floor** Pre- and early-Impressionist paintings, mid-19th-century sculpture

⑥ **Pierre-Auguste Renoir** Poor and excluded from the official art world, painters such as Renoir spent a lot of time in working-class bars and cafés, painting real people. Look out for his *Dancing at the Moulin de la Galette*.

Letting off steam

Head across the river to the **Jardin des Tuileries** (see p99) to sail wooden boats on the lake. There is also a nice free playground here.

Musée d'Orsay, housed in a converted iron-and-glass railway station

Prices given are for a family of four

Eat and drink

Picnic: under €25; Snacks: €25–45; Real meal: €45–90; Family treat: over €90 (based on a family of four)

PICNIC Debauve & Gallais (30 Rue des Sts-Pères, 75007; www. debauve-et-gallais.com; closed Sun), Paris's oldest chocolate shop, at one time prepared chocolate delicacies for Marie Antoinette.
SNACKS Kayser (18 Rue du Bac, 75007), a popular bakery, has sandwiches to take away, and a café serving risotto, salads and tartines (open sandwiches).
REAL MEAL Eggs & Co (11 Rue Bernard Palissy; 01 45 44 02 52) offers eggs in all shapes and sizes.

FAMILY TREAT Le Télégraphe (41 Rue de Lille, 75007; 01 58 62 10 08; www.restaurantletelegraphe. com) serves a very good luxury brunch. The restaurant is housed in an Art Nouveau post office and has a terrace.

Shopping

Stock Bonpoint (42 Rue de l'Université, 75007; www.bonpoint. com) has great reductions for kids on previous season's clothes. **Six Pieds Trois Pouces** (223 Blvd St-Germain, 75007; www.sixpieds troispouces.com) sells stylish and trendy children's shoes.

The Lowdown

🌐 **Map reference** 23 D4
Address 1 Rue de la Légion d'Honneur, 75007; 01 40 49 49 78; www.musee-orsay.fr/en

🚗 **Métro** Solférino, line 12. **RER** Musée d'Orsay, line C. **Bus** 24, 63, 68, 69, 73, 83, 84 & 94

🕐 **Open** 9:30am–6pm, till 9:45pm Thu, closed Mon & public hols

€ **Price** €16–26; under 18s & EU citizens under 26 free

👪 **Skipping the queue** Paris Museum Pass accepted. Joint ticket with Musée Rodin & l'Orangerie; family ticket is €24. Avoid Tue when the museum is one of the few in the city that is open. Buy tickets online in advance.

☞ **Guided tours** For adults in English; for families and kids in French. Audio guide available. The bookshop offers children's guides, *My Little Orsay* and *A Trip to the Orsay Museum*.

👫 **Age range** 3 plus

Activities Workshops & activities for children in French; 01 40 49 47 50. Lovely colouring books for budding artists are available in the museum shop.

⏱ **Allow** At least 2 hours

♿ **Wheelchair access** Yes

☕ **Café** On the ground floor; the restaurant on the middle floor has good views of the clock.

🛍 **Shop** The museum bookshop in the entrance hall has a special kids' section.

👫 **Toilets** On the ground floor

Good family value?
The museum is very child-friendly. Introduce kids to the lives and pictures of the artists displayed here. The ticket also gives a reduced rate at the Palais Garnier and the Opera house for a week after the visit.

⑧ Edgar Degas Interested in movement, Degas focused much of his work around two very diverse subjects – racehorses and dancers, the latter beautifully observed in his painting, *The Ballet Class*.

⑦ Claude Monet The Impressionists wanted to catch the moment. Monet was fascinated by how light changed at different times of the year, especially when it snowed. *The Cart* is one of the many works on show by the artist in the museum.

Find out more
DIGITAL Download colouring pages from *www.nowyouknowabout.com* and watch a BBC mini series about the history of Impressionism on *tinyurl.com/3jwqsz3*.
FILM *Now You Know About Artists* (2006), a documentary film for kids is based on the great painters. *Degas and the Dancer* (1998) is the story behind the famous statuette.

Next stop...
TOUR MONTPARNASSE At 210 m (688 ft), this is one of the tallest skyscrapers in France (*Rue de l'Arrivée 75015; 01 45 38 53 16;*

www.tourmontparnasse56.com). Take the Métro from Solférino to Montparnasse Bienvenüe (line 12) for views of Paris from the rooftop terrace. See the lights come on at the Eiffel Tower – or watch planes taking off at Orly airport from the deck.

View of Paris from the dizzying heights of Tour Montparnasse

② Les Invalides
A dome, guns and generals

Louis XIV built the Hôtel des Invalides in 1671–76, for the thousands of soldiers who were wounded and disabled in his endless campaigns. At its centre rises the glittering dome of the Eglise du Dôme, the final resting place of Napoleon Bonaparte. More about him, as well as wars and weapons from medieval times to World War II, can be found in the museums surrounding the church. One of the best collections of military history in the world, it is a must for toy soldier enthusiasts – the complex is home to the Musée de l'Armée and the Musée de l'Ordre de la Libération.

Letting off steam

Kids can run on the lawns in front of Hôtel des Invalides or in the playground on Avenue de Breteuil. The nearby **Champ-de-Mars** *(see p105)* is another lovely park, just a 10-minute walk away.

Children's playground on Avenue de Breteuil, south of Les Invalides' golden dome

The Lowdown

🌐 **Map** 23 A5
Address 129 Rue de Grenelle, 75007; www.invalides.org

🚇 **Métro** Invalides, lines 8 & 13; La Tour-Maubourg, line 8; Varenne or St-François Xavier, line 13. **RER** Invalides, line C. **Bus** 28, 63, 69, 80, 82, 83, 87, 92 & 93

🕐 **Open** Apr–Sep: 10am–6pm, till 9pm Tue; Oct–Mar: till 5pm; closed first Mon of the month & 1 Jan, 1 May, 1 Nov & 25 Dec

💶 **Price** €18–28; under 18s & EU citizens under 26 free. €14–24 on Tue eve & after 5pm on other days; free on 14 Jul

🎫 **Skipping the queue** Paris Museum Pass accepted

👉 **Guided tours**: Multimedia guides for adults and children; tours in English for children

👫 **Age range** 7 plus

🎨 **Activities** Kids' workshops and activities; 01 44 42 51 73

⏱ **Allow** 2–3 hours

♿ **Wheelchair access** Yes, for the Musée de l'Armée

🍴 **Eat and drink** *Real meal* Les Cocottes of Christian Constant *(139 Rue St-Dominique, 75007; 01 47 53 73 34; closed Sun)* whips up good-value gourmet food in a relaxed diner-style setting. *Family treat* Bellota-Bellota *(18 Rue Jean Nicot, 75007; 01 53 59 96 96; open daily)* specializes in Spanish food.

🚻 **Toilets** Near the ticket office

③ Musée Rodin
People in bronze and plaster

Home to beautiful masterpieces by the greatest French sculptor of the 19th century, Auguste Rodin, this museum, set amidst a vast garden, is one of the most peaceful places in the city. There is nothing nicer than strolling around the garden with an ice cream in hand, admiring some of the world's most famous sculptures – *The Kiss*, *The Thinker*,

The Thinker by Rodin, one of the many well-known sculptures in the Musée Rodin

The Lowdown

🌐 **Map** 23 B5
Address 77 Rue de Varenne, 75007; www.musee-rodin.fr

🚇 **Métro** Varenne, line 13. **RER** Invalides, line C. **Bus** 69, 82, 87 & 92

🕐 **Open** 10am–5:45pm, closed Mon, 1 Jan, 1 May & 25 Dec. On the second Sun in May, the gardens are lit by torchlight.

💶 **Price** Family ticket: €10. €6 per person; under 18s & EU citizens under 26 free. Garden: €1

🎫 **Skipping the queue** Paris Museum Pass accepted. Combined ticket for use on the same day with Musée d'Orsay: €12. Buy tickets online.

👫 **Guided tours** For children Wed & school hols: 2:30pm for children

The Burghers of Calais and *The Gates of Hell*. Works spanning Rodin's whole career are presented in a chronological order. A room devoted to works by Rodin's lover Camille Claudel is also here.

Letting off steam

The garden at the Musée Rodin has the best sculptures. Bring a spade and bucket and create your own sculptures in the sandpit. The **Jardin Catherine Labouré** *(33 Rue de Babylone, 75007)*, a 10-minute walk from the museum, has a little playground.

④ St-Germain-des-Prés
The oldest church in Paris

The church of St-Germain-des-Prés once stood at the centre of a large abbey, founded in the 6th century by Childebert I, the son of Clovis,

between 6–12, €6; 10:30am for under 6s

👫 **Age range** 5 plus

⏱ **Allow** 1–2 hours

♿ **Wheelchair access** Limited

🍴 **Eat and drink** *Picnic* Besnier Père et Fils *(40 Rue de Bourgogne, 75007; closed Sat & Sun)* sells excellent *brioche* (sweet French bread). Picnic in the lawns of the Invalides. *Snacks* Le Bon Marché *(24 Rue des Sevres, 75007)*, the oldest department store in Paris, has a great food hall, La Grande Epicerie de Paris *(www.lagrandeepicerie.fr)*.

🚻 **Toilets** In the garden café

The Lowdown

🌐 **Map** 24 E6
Address 3 Pl St-Germain-des-Prés, 75006; www.eglise-sgp.org

🚇 **Métro** St-Germain-des-Prés, line 4. **Bus** 39, 95 70, 63 & 86

🕐 **Open** 8am–7:45pm Mon–Sat, 9am–8pm Sun

ⓢ **Price** Free

♿ **Wheelchair access** Yes

🍽 **Eat and drink** Picnic Grom (81 Rue de Seine, 75006) serves excellent ice cream, or buy a sandwich to eat in the square in front of the church, or bring to Jardin du Luxembourg. Snacks Ladurée (21 Rue Bonaparte, 75006; 01 44 07 64 87) serves the best macaroons in the city.

🚻 **Toilets** Sanisette, 186 Blvd St-Germain, 75006

King of the Franks. Initially not even inside the city walls, the abbey became an important centre of intellectual life for the French Catholic church, and also the burial place for France's kings before the founding of the basilica of St-Denis. The church originally had three towers, but the two on the eastern side were badly damaged in the Revolution. Among the notables buried inside are John Casimir, king of Poland, and the father of modern philosophy, René Descartes. Look out for a statue of the Egyptian goddess Isis at the entrance – a bit surprising in a church.

Letting off steam

There is a small playground with a sandpit on **Square Félix Desruelles** (168 Blvd St-Germain, 75006), to the south of the church. The nearby Pont des Arts footbridge is perfect

Tower of St-Germain-des-Prés, with one of the oldest belfries in France

for a picnic. The covered market, Marché St-Germain, also houses a swimming pool, **Piscine St-Germain** (12 Rue Lobineau, 75006; 01 56 81 25 40), but be aware that swimming hats are obligatory.

⑤ Cafés of St-Germain-des-Prés
Coffee for culture vultures

The café is a vital part of Parisian life and people of all ages come here for conversation, discussion and gossip over a coffee, apéritif or citron pressé; it is a great place to introduce kids to Parisian culture.

In the mid-20th century, St-Germain was a buzzing place where American authors and jazz musicians mingled with local artists, writers and philosophers. Ernest Hemingway, Bud Powell, Pablo Picasso, Alfred Camus, Jean-Paul Sartre and Simone de Beauvoir all quenched their thirst in the cafés that cluster around the belfry of St-Germain-des-Prés. The most famous ones are Café de Flore; Les Deux Magots, which takes its name from the two wooden statues of Chinese merchants inside; and the Brasserie Lipp, a distinguished restaurant-brasserie.

Letting off steam

Walk down Rue Bonaparte to the **Jardin du Luxembourg** (see p93), one of the best parks in town, for a real Parisian experience.

The Lowdown

🌐 **Map** 24 E6
Address Brasserie Lipp: 151 Blvd St-Germain, 75006. Les Deux Magots: 6 Pl St-Germain, 75006. Café de Flore (see below)

🚇 **Métro** St-Germain-des-Prés, line 4. **Bus** 63 & 95

ⓢ **Price** All the cafés are expensive.

🧑‍🤝‍🧑 **Age range** All ages

♿ **Wheelchair access** Limited

🍽 **Eat and drink** Snacks Le Bonaparte (42 Rue Bonaparte, 75006; 01 43 26 42 81) serves drinks with a sandwich or salad on its terrace. Family treat Café de Flore (172 Blvd St-Germain, 75006; 01 45 49 31 29; www.cafe-de-flore.com) serves quiches, sandwiches, omelettes and onion soup. The café still has a literary clientele.

🚻 **Toilets** In the cafés

Sacré-Coeur and around

Children may be drawn to the meringue-like domes of the sparkly white Basilica of Sacré-Coeur. The easiest way to get to the heart of things is to take the little tourist train or the funicular; climbing the steps can be tiring. Walk back down Rue Lepic for a real Montmartre experience. On Sundays, traffic is restricted on Rue des Martyrs and across Montmartre, adding to the village-like feel. To the east of Montmartre is the creatively designed, very modern Parc de la Villette, which houses a fantastic science museum – a huge attraction for families.

Entrance to the Art Nouveau Métro Abbesses, the nearest station to Montmartre

The Lowdown

🚐 **Metro** Abbesses, line 12; Anvers, line 2; Pigalle, lines 2 &12; Porte de la Villette, line 7. **Bus** 30, 31, 80, 81 & 95 & Montmartrobus 64. Parc de la Villette: PC2, PC3, 75, 139, 150, 152 & 249 **Train** Le Petit train de Montmartre from Pl Pigalle; Funiculaire de Montmartre from Square Louise Michel; Montmartrain (tourist train) from Pl Pigalle

ℹ️ **Visitor information** Pl du Tertre, 75018; 10am–6pm daily. Gare du Nord, 18 Rue de Dunkerque, 75010; 8am–6pm daily, closed 1 Jan, 1 May & 25 Dec

🍴 **Supermarkets** Carrefour, 17 Rue Clignancourt, 75018 & 63 Blvd de Rochechouart, 75009. Monoprix, 52 Rue Fontaine, 75009. Mon'op, 200 Ave Jean Jaurès, 75019
Markets Marché Place d'Anvers (produce market), 75009; 3–8:30pm Fri. Marché Jean Jaurès, 75019; 7am–2:30pm Tue & Thu, till 3pm Sun

🎉 **Festivals** Lavagem do Sacré-Coeur: a religious procession by the city's Brazilians (early-Jul). Fête des Vendanges: grape harvest in Montmartre Vineyard; www.fetedesvendangesdemontmartre.com (Oct). Christmas creche, Sacré-Coeur basilica (Dec). Open-air film festival, Cinema en Plein Air, Parc de la Villette (Jul & Aug).

➕ **Pharmacy** Pharmacie Centrale de Montmartre, 42 Ave Junot, 75018; 01 46 06 79 40; 2pm–8pm Mon, 9am–8pm Tue–Sat; closed Sun

🐾 **Nearest playgrounds** Parc de la Turlure, Rue de la Bonne, 75018; dawn–dusk daily *(see p116)*. Square Louise Michel, 75018, between Pl St-Pierre and Sacré-Coeur; dawn–dusk daily *(see p116)*. Parc de la Villette, 211 Ave Jean Jaurès, 75019; 01 40 03 75 75; dawn–dusk daily *(see pp118–19)*

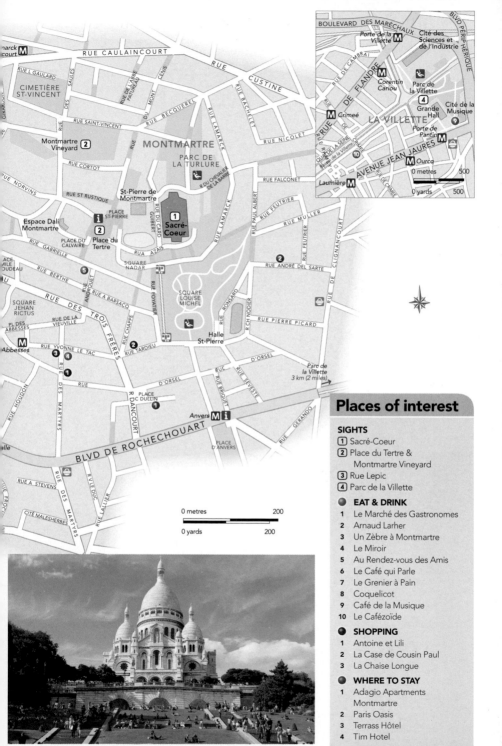

RUE CAULAINCOURT

CIMETIÈRE
ST-VINCENT

RUE SAINT-VINCENT

Montmartre
Vineyard 2

MONTMARTRE

PARC DE
LA TURLURE

RUE CORTOT

RUE NORVINS

RUE ST RUSTIQUE

St-Pierre de
Montmartre

Espace Dali
Montmartre

PLACE
ST-PIERRE

1 Sacré-
Coeur

PLACE DU
CALVAIRE

Place du
Tertre

RUE GABRIELLE

RUA ATAIS

SQUARE
NADAR

RUE BERTHE

5

SQUARE
JEHAN
RICTUS

RUE DES

TROIS FRERES

SQUARE
LOUISE
MICHEL

PL DES
ABBESSES

RUE DE LA
VIEUVILLE

M
Abbesses

RUE YVONNE LE TAC

2

3 4

1

Halle
St-Pierre

RUE

D'ORSEL

BLVD DE ROCHECHOUART

PLACE
D'ANVERS

Anvers M i

BOULEVARD DES MARÉCHAUX

Porte de la M
Villette

Cité des
Sciences et
de l'Industrie

Corentin
Cariou

Parc de
la Villette

M Grimeé

4

Grande
Hall

Cité de la
Musique

9

LA VILLETTE

Porte de
Pantin

M

AVENUE JEAN JAURÈS

M Ourcq

Laumière M

0 metres   500

0 yards   500

RUE ANDRÉ DEL SARTE

RUE PIERRE PICARD

Parc de
la Villette
3 km (2 miles)

0 metres   200

0 yards   200

View of Sacré-Coeur from Square Louise Michel

Places of interest

SIGHTS
1. Sacré-Coeur
2. Place du Tertre &
   Montmartre Vineyard
3. Rue Lepic
4. Parc de la Villette

● **EAT & DRINK**
1. Le Marché des Gastronomes
2. Arnaud Larher
3. Un Zèbre à Montmartre
4. Le Miroir
5. Au Rendez-vous des Amis
6. Le Café qui Parle
7. Le Grenier à Pain
8. Coquelicot
9. Café de la Musique
10. Le Cafézoïde

● **SHOPPING**
1. Antoine et Lili
2. La Case de Cousin Paul
3. La Chaise Longue

● **WHERE TO STAY**
1. Adagio Apartments
   Montmartre
2. Paris Oasis
3. Terrass Hôtel
4. Tim Hotel

① Sacré-Coeur
A big white meringue

Perched on the highest point in Paris, Sacré-Coeur reaches almost as high in the sky as the Eiffel Tower. Paris lies at its feet, and kids will love the view from above. Built as a penance to expiate the sins of France in 1873, it was intended to symbolize the restoration of conservative, Catholic values. Hence many of the Neo-Byzantine design elements incorporate nationalist themes. It is also seen as a symbol of the repression of the Paris Commune uprising of 1871, which both started and came to a bloody climax here.

Stained-glass rose window, Sacré-Coeur

Key Features

Great Mosaic of Christ This glittering mosaic, dominating the chancel vault, is one of the largest in the world, and represents France's devotion to the Sacred Heart.

Bronze doors Beautifully decorated with relief sculptures, the doors in the portico entrance illustrate the story of the life of Jesus.

Belltower Added in 1904, the belltower is home to a 19-ton (19-tonne) Savoyarde bell. It is one of the heaviest bells in existence.

Spiral staircase

Stained-glass gallery

Tall dome There are incredible views of Paris and beyond from the tip of the 129-m (423-ft) high dome, especially stunning at sunset.

Statue of Christ This statue is symbolically placed in a niche over the main entrance above the two bronze saints.

Joan of Arc

Portico

Crypt vaults

King St-Louis IX

Main entrance

Letting off steam

In Montmartre, kids are spoilt for choice. The pretty gardens of **Square Willette** slope down in front of Sacré-Coeur, and there is a carousel at the bottom of the hill. There is also **Square Louise Michel** between Place St-Pierre and the Sacré-Coeur. Behind the church is the **Parc de la Turlure**, where the Turlure windmill once stood. It is a peaceful place for a picnic.

Prices given are for a family of four

Eat and drink

Picnic: under €25; Snacks: €25–45; Real meal: €45–90; Family treat: over €90 (based on a family of four)

PICNIC Le Marché des Gastronomes (9 Pl Pigalle, 75009; 01 80 06 85 56) sells fresh dairy products and meat, as well as cheese, wine, vegetables, soups, jams, chocolates and luxury foodstuff, all perfect to bring along to Parc de la Turlure for a picnic.

SNACKS Arnaud Larher (53 Rue Caulaincourt, 75018; www. arnaud-larher.com; closed Sun & Mon) is one of the few prize-winning chocolatiers to make delicious milk chocolates.

REAL MEAL Un Zèbre à Montmartre (38 Rue Lepic, 75018; 01 42 23 97 80) is a friendly, laid-back little restaurant, which serves an excellent chocolate mousse.

The Lowdown

 Map reference 18 G2
Address 35 Rue du Chevalier de la Barre, 75018; 01 53 41 89 00; www.sacre-coeur-montmartre.com

Métro Abbesses, line 12; Anvers, line 2; Pigalle, lines 2 & 12. Catch the funicular, using the same tickets, or the tourist train (www.promotrain.fr), from Pl Pigalle. **Bus** 30, 31, 80 & 85

Open 6am–10:30pm daily. Dome: 9am–7pm; winter: till 6pm. Crypt: opening times vary

Price Basilica: free. Crypt & dome: €20–30

Skipping the queue Sacré-Coeur is a very busy place, but is less crowded in the evening, when the basilica is at its most magnificent and romantic.

Guided tours No

 Age range All ages

Allow 30 mins–1 hour

Wheelchair access Limited

Café No

 Toilets By the exit

Good family value?
Montmartre's charms are for free and the view from the basilica's steps is almost as good as from the top of the dome. Inside the basilica, silence is the rule.

FAMILY TREAT Le Miroir (94 Rue des Martyrs, 75018; 01 46 06 50 73; closed Mon, Sun lunch & Aug), a casual bistro, serves delicious duck with wild mushrooms and little pots de crème vanille (pots of vanilla cream).

Shopping

Montmartre has lots of interesting shops selling original gift items, homewares and clothes. Do not miss the outfits and accessories at **Antoine et Lili** (90 Rue des Martyrs, 75018; www.antoineetlili.com) or the garlands of fancy lights (choose your own colour combination) in **La Case de Cousin Paul** (4 Rue Tardieu, 75018; lacasedecousinpaul.com). **La Chaise Longue** (91 Rue des Martyrs, 75018; www.lachaiselongue.fr) is also a fun place to browse around for home decor items.

The Moulin Rouge cabaret with its red windmill, a symbol of fin-de-siècle Paris

Find out more

DIGITAL Watch rock band U2's music video Two Hearts Beat as One, shot in front of the basilica and around Montmartre, at tinyurl.com/b8epuk.

FILM Moulin Rouge (2001) is a romantic musical with Nicole Kidman. Most films set here reflect life's grittier side and are better for older kids. Louis Feuillade's Fantômas films (1913–14), set in and around Place Pigalle, depict the criminal exploits of a slick but dastardly villain. Watch a clip at tinyurl.com/3naqnu3.

Next stop...

A CABARET AND A CEMETERY
One of the world's most famous cabarets, the **Moulin Rouge** (82 Blvd de Clichy, 75018; 01 53 09 82 82; www.moulinrouge.fr) was built in 1885 and is topped off with a red windmill. Its name is synonymous with the high-kicking dance, the cancan, and was made famous in Henri de Toulouse-Lautrec's drawings and posters. The building is worth a look from the outside, and if families fancy a show, 6–12 year olds can get in to matinees half-price on two Sundays a month. The tourist train that leaves from Place Pigalle passes right in front and heads up to Sacré-Coeur.

Close by, the **Cimetière de Montmartre** (20 Ave Rachel, 75018), built in the hollow of an old quarry, is also the final resting place of Louise Weber, or "La Goulou", the cancan dancer painted by Toulouse-Lautrec.

Strollers in the Montmartre Vineyard, a peaceful corner behind Place du Tertre

② Place du Tertre & Montmartre Vineyard

The roof of Paris

"Tertre" means a little hill and, at 130 m (430 ft), this square is one of the highest spots in Paris. It was once the site of a gallows but, in the 19th century, artists began to sell their work here. It is still full of painters peddling their wares. To visit Montmartre without going for a wander in the quieter, narrow cobbled streets behind Place du Tertre is to miss out on the spirit of the area. The Montmartre Vineyard on Rue St-Vincent is one such peaceful corner, and is all that is left of the acres of vineyards that once grew on the hill. It is particularly

The Lowdown

- 🌐 **Map reference** 18 G2 & 18 G1
  Address 75018
- 🚇 **Métro** Abbesses, line 12. **Bus** Monmartrobus 64 runs from Pl Pigalle to the top of Montmartre
- 🕐 **Open** Montmartre Vineyard: not open to the public
- 👥 **Skipping the queue** Pl du Tertre is very popular with visitors, so go in the evening or the early morning when it is less crowded.
- 👫 **Age range** All ages
- ⏱ **Allow** 1 hour
- ☕ **Eat and drink** *Snacks* Au Rendez-vous des Amis (*23 Rue Gabrielle, 75018*), a cosy café-bar, is a good stop for a drink. *Real meal* Le Café qui Parle (*24 Rue Caulaincourt, 75018; 01 46 06 06 88; 11am–5pm; no reservations, so arrive early*) is great for brunch on Sat, Sun & public hols.
- 🚻 **Toilets** No

lovely in autumn, and can be viewed through the surrounding fence. Pull away the tourist veneer and Montmartre has a lot of character and a strong local community, which celebrates the wine harvest in style every October.

Take cover
Espace Dalí Montmartre (*11 Rue Poulbot, 75018; 01 42 64 40 10; www.daliparis.com*) is the only place to get a look at some famous works of art in the area, and although it is a bit commercial, it is a fun place to visit with kids. The museum has an exciting collection of sculptures and other objects by the Spanish Surrealist artist, Salvador Dalí (1904–89). Children will find his dreamlike models of melting watches, a table with human feet and crazy sculptures intriguing.

③ Rue Lepic

Montmartre from top to bottom

The best way to see Montmartre with children is to take the little tourist train from Place Pigalle and then to walk back down Rue Lepic, a great place to shop and eat, ending in Rue des Abesses. At the top of the street, there are two windmills that once milled flour. In 1870, they were converted into a dance hall and restaurant, and are immortalized in the painting *Dance at the Moulin de la Galette* by Pierre-Auguste Renoir. The artist Vincent van Gogh and his brother Theo once lived at No. 54. Just behind Place des Abbesses is the

Children's clothes and accessories on display in a shop on Rue Lepic

The Lowdown

- 🌐 **Map reference** 18 E2
  Address Rue Lepic, 75018
- 🚇 **Métro** Abbesses, line 12. **Bus** 54, 80 & Montmartrobus 64
- 👫 **Age range** All ages
- ⏱ **Allow** 30 mins–1 hour
- ☕ **Eat and drink** *Picnic* Le Grenier à Pain (*38 Rue Abbesses, 75018*), President Sarkozy's favourite bakers, sell tasty cakes and sandwiches. They won the 2010 Golden Bagette award. Head to the gardens in front of Sacré-Coeur, or walk up to Rue Lepic to Square Suzanne Buisson, which is popular with local families. *Real meal* Coquelicot (*24 Rue des Abbesses, 75018; 01 46 06 18 77; open daily*) offers boiled and poached eggs in brioche, has a good selection of takeaway food and a scrummy sweet counter.
- 🚻 **Toilets** No

pretty Place Emile Goudeau, where Pablo Picasso painted the ground-breaking Cubist picture, *Les Demoiselles d'Avignon*, in 1907. Head home from the Métro Abbesses. Built in 1912, it is one of the prettiest, and has one of the only three original Hector Guimard-designed Art Nouveau glass entrances left in Paris. It is also the deepest station in the city.

Letting off steam
There is a tiny square, **Square Jehan Rictus**, close to Place des Abbesses, which is known for its "*mur des je t'aime*" (wall of love).

④ Parc de la Villette

Museums, themed gardens and canal boats

In the northeastern corner of Paris, the old slaughterhouses and livestock market have been transformed into a wonderfully whacky park that runs along Canal de l'Ourcq. Full of playgrounds for kids, the complex also houses a concert hall, music centre and exhibition pavilion. The main attraction for families is the futuristic **Cité des Sciences et de l'Industrie**, Europe's biggest science museum – it houses the thematic Cité des Enfants. Here children aged 2–12 can pretend to be TV presenters,

Helicopter in the Cité des Sciences et de l'Industrie museum, Parc de la Villette

weather forecasters or robot designers. Fly over the surface of Mars in the Planetarium, or travel through the human body in the Explora exhibit.

Climb aboard and discover marine life through the radar screens and periscopes in the L'Argonaute, a submarine from the 1930s. The park also boasts **La Géode** – the giant hemispherical screen, and **La Cinaxe**, a moving movie theatre with virtual-reality technology. The **Cité de la Musique** has a museum with a vast collection covering the history of music since the Renaissance. The Grande Hall, once a cattle market, when La Villette was a huge abattoir, now hosts temporary exhibitions.

Letting off steam
In front of the Cité des Sciences et de l'Industrie museum there are 10 different themed gardens, among them the garden of mirrors, mists and acrobatics. There are lots of activities for kids over the weekend.

La Géode, the giant movie screen in the Parc de la Villette

Watch a show on the canal boat, *Antipode (55 Quai de la Seine, 75019; 01 42 03 39 07; www. abricadabra.fr; open daily but timings vary).*

The Lowdown

- 🌐 **Map reference** *(see inset p115)*
  Address Parc de la Villette: 211 Ave Jean Jaurès, 75019; 01 40 03 75 75; www.lavillette.com.
- 🚗 **Métro** Porte de la Villette, line 7 for Cité des Sciences; Porte de Pantin, line 5 for Cité de la Musique. **Bus** PC2, PC3, 75, 139, 150, 152 & 249
- 🕐 **Open** Parc de la Villette: daily. Cité des Sciences et de l'Industrie: 9am–6pm, till 7pm Sun, closed Mon. La Géode: 10:30am–8:30pm, closed public hols. Cité de la Musique: noon–6pm, 10am–6pm Sun, closed Mon
- 💲 **Price** Parc de la Villette: Free. Cité des Sciences: Explora: €28–38. Cité des Enfants: €12–22. La Géode: €21–31. Joint ticket: €63–73; €3 additional for the Planetarium & €4.80 for La Cinaxe. Family ticket: €64–74. Cité de la Musique: €16–26
- 🏛 **Skipping the queue** Paris Museum Pass accepted.
- 🚩 **Guided tours** Guided tours in French. Shows in the Planetarium in English and French.
- 👫 **Age range** All ages
- ⏱ **Allow** 1 day
- 🍴 **Eat and drink** *Picnic* Café de la Musique *(34 Rue Yves Toudic, 75010)* sells savoury tarts and pastrys. Picnic in the Parc de la Villette. *Snacks* Le Cafézoide *(92 Quai de la Loire, 75019; 01 42 38 26 37;* www.cafezoide.asso.fr*)* is a café where kids can play games, see concerts, or join a workshop.
- 👫 **Toilets** At several locations

Picnic under €25; **Snacks** €25–45; **Real meal** €45–90; **Family treat** over €90 (based on a family of four)

Where to Stay in Paris

Hotels tend to cluster by type in Paris. Most of the deluxe hotels, among them some of the most family-friendly in Europe, are to be found around the Champs-Elysées and the Tuileries, while boutique hotels, which have fewer family facilities, are more numerous on the Left Bank and in Montmartre.

AGENCIES

RentApart
www.rentapart.com
The most upmarket of the rental agencies. Rates begin at around €100 per night for a one-bedroom apartment.

A Haven in Paris
www.haveninparis.com
A boutique vacation rental agency, which offers luxury apartments and villa rentals across Paris.

Elegant façade of the hotel Le Pavillon de la Reine, Place des Vosges

Notre-Dame and around

HOTELS

Hotel Ibis Bastille Opéra
Map 26 F5
15 Rue Breguet, 75011; 01 49 29 20 20; www.ibishotel.com;
Métro: Bastille or Breguet-Sabin
This no-frills hotel has air-conditioned interconnecting rooms that are cheaper at weekends and if booked online. The bonus for families is a great price for the location.
🍴 P   €

The Five
Map 29 A5
3 Rue Flatters, 75005; 01 43 31 74 21; www.thefivehotel.com;
Métro: Gobelins
With floating mattresses and a Jacuzzi on the terrace of the suite, this hotel is about statement – from the red leather lifts to the customized room fragrance and the star-studded ceilings. The designer rooms for up to four are excellent value.
                                €€

Hôtel Britannique
Map 24 H5
20 Ave Victoria, 75001; 01 42 33 74 59; www.hotel-britannique.fr;
Métro: Châtelet
Located near the main sights on the Île de la Cité, close to the Tour St-Jacques, this three-star hotel oozes Grand Tour charm. There is a warm welcome for kids and a hearty breakfast. The suite for four is good value and the hotel is air conditioned.
                                €€

Hôtel Résidence Henri IV
Map 28 H2
50 Rue des Bernardins, 75005; 01 44 41 31 81; www.residencehenri4.com;
Métro: St-Michel
This hotel is located in the heart of the Quartier Latin, opposite a pretty playground and near the Panthéon. All rooms have kitchenettes, and some interconnect, so that a family can take over an entire floor. The hotel attracts a lot of guests with very small children who settle down early.
🛏   €€

Hôtel du Jeu de Paume
Map 25 C6
54 Rue St-Louis en l'Île, 75004; 01 43 26 14 18; www.jeudepaumehotel.com; *Métro: Pont Marie*
A discreet courtyard entrance leads to a magical, unique 17th-century timbered building, once a tennis court. The Labrador greets guests at the door and sets the tone for this homely but chic hotel. For the upper price band, it is good value.
🐾   €€€

Le Pavillon de la Reine
Map 25 D5
28 Pl des Vosges, 75003; 01 40 29 19 19; www.pavillon-de-la-reine;
Métro: Bastille or St-Paul
This has suites for families of four and, although there is no restaurant, the café Carette des Vosges, on the doorstep, more than compensates for this. Air conditioning and spa, and babysitting can be provided.
P   €€€

BED & BREAKFAST

Appartement d'hôtes Folie Méricourt
Map 26 F3
20 Rue de la Folie Méricourt, 75011; 01 77 15 69 54; www.appartement-hotes-folie-mericourt.com; *Métro: St-Ambroise*
This B&B, in a self-contained apartment for four to six people, offers breakfast and the option of dinner. Cots are available. There are similar apartments near Oberkampf and République, if this is booked.
🍳   €

Bonne Nuit Paris
Map 25 D3
63 Rue Charlot, 75003; 01 42 71 83 56; www.bonne-nuit-paris.com;
Métro: République or Temple
Built in 1609, this restored house is full of old beams and modern comforts. The owners serve home-made jams and their own honey for breakfast. Their daughter, a history graduate, offers personalized guided tours of the city. A baby crib and child's folding bed are available.
                                €€

SELF-CATERING

Résidence Le Petit Châtelet
Map 25 A4
9 Rue St-Denis, 75001; 01 42 33 32 31; www.lepetitchatelet.com;
Métro: Châtelet
Housed in a charming old-fashioned house in the heart of historic Paris, these apartments for four to six people have air conditioning. Those on the top floors have balconies but the downside is that there is no lift and it can be a little noisy at night.
🛏   €

Interior of a self-catering apartment in Résidence le Petit Châtelet

Citadines St-Germain-des-Prés
Map 24 G5

53 Quai des Grands Augustins, 75006; 01 44 07 70 00; www. citadines.com; Métro: St-Michel

These self-catering apartments are in a magnificent location opposite the Île de la Cité, close to several main sights. The apartments are air conditioned and have kitchenettes. A babysitting service is provided, and breakfast is optional.

🛏 P   €€

Résidence Le Prince Regent
Map 28 G1

28 Rue Monsieur le Prince, 75006; 01 56 24 19 21; http:// leprinceregent.com; Métro: Odéon

A great option for families staying for more than just a few nights, these air-conditioned apartments for up to six people have fully fitted kitchens.

🛏   €€

Musée du Louvre and around

HOTELS

Le Bristol
Map 17 B6

112 Rue du Faubourg St-Honoré, 75008; 01 53 43 43 25; www. lebristolparis.com; Métro: Miromesnil

One of the city's best luxury hotels for families, this is a place where kids can relax. The rooms are big and there are many interconnecting suites – two with roof terraces. There is a gourmet restaurant, the 114, and a special Japanese breakfast. Kids love the penthouse swimming pool.

🐾 🍽 P   €€€

Le Burgundy
Map 23 D2

6 Rue Duphot 75001; 01 42 60 34 12; www.leburgundy.com; Métro: Madeleine

Le Burgundy offers family-friendly luxury all round. A light and airy hotel with a welcome pack and teddy bears for kids, its duplex rooms are excellent for families. The location within walking distance of several main sights. There is a swimming pool and a babysitting service.

🍽   €€€

Hôtel du Louvre
Map 24 F3

Pl André Malraux, 75001; 01 44 58 38 38; www.hoteldulouvre.com; Métro: Palais Royal–Musée du Louvre

Built in 1887, this hotel is just across the road from the Musée du Louvre. The double rooms, misleadingly

Tables laid out in the pretty garden of the one of Paris's finest hotels, Le Bristol

called suites, have room for an extra bed and cot. There are six actual suites, one of which hosted actress Angelina Jolie's sizeable family.

🍽 P   €€€

The Westin
Map 23 D2

3 Rue de Castiglione, 75001; 01 44 77 11 11; www.westin.com; Métro: Tuileries

This rather grand, family-friendly four-star hotel is right opposite the Jardin des Tuileries. The rooms are large but the smaller attic rooms have the most charm. Cots and highchairs are provided.

🐾 🍽   €€€

SELF-CATERING

Résidhome Paris-Opéra
Map 17 D5

30 Rue Joubert, 75009; 01 56 35 00 35; www.residhome.com; Métro: Havre Caumartin

This hotel has modern, air-conditioned apartments, some of which are duplexes for up to six people. There are wooden floors. Facilities for babies include babysitting. Though cleaned weekly, additional cleaning is available.

🛏 P   €€

Eiffel Tower and around

HOTELS

Novotel Eiffel Tower
Map 21 C5

61 Quai de Grenelle, 75015; 01 40 58 20 00; www.novotel.com; Métro: Dupliex or Bir Hakeim

The family-friendly Novotel chain has a good location 10 minutes from the Eiffel Tower. There is a playroom, pool and Japanese restaurant. It is a great value location for families with 50 per cent reduction on a second room.

🍽 P   €

Four Seasons George V
Map 16 F5

31 Ave George V, 75008; 01 49 52 70 00; www.fourseasons.com/paris; Métro: Georges V

This traditional deluxe hotel has a fantastic array of children's activities, which include whizzing up some madeleines in the kitchen with the pastry chef and special kids' tours of Paris. Kids have their own Bulgari soap set and are greeted by balloons and a chocolate Eiffel Tower. A babysitting service is provided.

🐾 🍽 P   €€€

Hilton Arc de Triomphe
Map 16 G3

51–57 Rue de Courcelles, 75008; 01 58 36 67 00; www.hilton.com; Métro: Courcelles

This modern hotel, inspired by the great ocean liners, has good-sized rooms. The location is excellent, just a stone's throw from the Champs-Elysées and by the golden gates of the Parc Monceau. The 59 suites are the best option for families and the executive lounge has all-day refreshments. A babysitting service is provided.

🐾 🍽 P   €€€

Plaza Athenée
Map 16 G6

25 Ave Montaigne, 75008; 01 53 67 66 65; www.plaza-athenee-paris.fr; Métro: Franklin D Roosevelt

This world-famous hotel bends over backwards to welcome families. There is free bike hire, with picnics supplied, a private river boat and in winter, an ice rink. The hotel has an incredible range of huge suites.

🐾 🍽 P   €€€

Beautiful belle époque exterior of the Westin

Price Guide
The following price ranges are based on one night's accommodation in high season for a family of four, inclusive of service charges and any additional taxes.

€ Under €200 €€ €200–500 €€€ over €500

Key to symbols *see back cover flap*

Radio taxi dropping off passenger in front of the handsome 19th-century Terrass Hôtel

SELF-CATERING
Adagio Paris Tour Eiffel
Map 21 C5

14 Rue du Théâtre, 75015; 01 45 71 88 88; www.adagio-city.com; Métro: Dupleix

This hotel offers unbeatable value apartments for up to six people, each with a kitchenette and microwave, in a high-rise with great views. There is a laundry room and a pool. It is a ten-minute walk to the Eiffel Tower.

 P €

Citadines Trocadéro
Map 15 C6

29 bis Rue St-Didier 75116; 01 56 90 70 00; Métro: Victor Hugo

A short walk from the Trocadéro museums and gardens, the location of these air-conditioned apartments is great for families, accommodating up to six people. The apartments have kitchenettes with a grill and microwave. Babysitting and breakfast are provided.

 P €€

Jays
Map 15 D5

6 Rue Copernic, 75016; 01 47 04 16 16; www.jays-paris.com; Métro: Victor Hugo

The draw for families is the beautiful spacious apartments, in a great location close to the Trocadéro and the Arc de Triomphe. Families with children are welcome. Daily cleaning and breakfast are provided.

 P €€€

Musée d'Orsay and around
HOTELS
Hôtel Aviatic
Map 27 C2

105 Rue de Vaugirard, 75006; 01 53 63 25 50; www.aviatic.fr; Métro: Montparnasse Bienvenüe

This friendly boutique hotel is close to the Invalides and the Jardin du

Luxembourg. Rooms are in tones of chocolate, berry and cream. You can ask for triple rooms, or for a baby cot. There is also one communicating room that sleeps up to four. Staff is happy to pack guests a picnic.

€€

Pullmann Montparnasse
Map 27 C4

19 Rue du Commandant René Mouchotte, 75014; 01 44 36 44 36; www.pullmanhotels.com; Métro: Gaité

The hotel has good-sized modern family rooms with two double beds for three or four people. There is entertainment for children at Sunday brunch. There are excellent deals if booked online in advance. There is a babysitting service.

P €€

Sacré-Coeur and around
HOTELS
Ibis Berthier Porte de Clichy
Map 17 C1

163 bis Ave de Clichy, 75017; 01 40 25 26 00; www.accor.com; Métro: Porte de Clichy or Brochant

This is an excellent-value chain hotel with family and interconnecting rooms, some of which have views of the Eiffel Tower. The draw for families besides the price, is the location opposite a modern park on the edge of the Batignolles district, which has another, more traditional park and restaurants.

 P €

Tim Hotel
Map 18 F2

11 Rue Ravignan, 75018; 01 42 55 74 79; www.timhotel.com; Métro: Abbesses

A picturesque hotel, it is located in a pedestrianized square not far from Sacré-Coeur. The rooms are tiny

and basic, but outstanding value given the location. For families there are rooms for three and a suite for five with a great view.

€

Terrass Hôtel
Map 18 E2

12 Rue Joseph de Maistre, 75018; 01 46 06 72 85; www.terrass-hotel. com; Métro: Blanche

This four-star is in a building with a stunning seventh-floor terrace. It has big, airy suites and junior suites that are ideal for families. Many have balconies with amazing views and one of the suites has an interactive touch-screen table and floating bed that will delight older kids.

 €€

BED & BREAKFAST
Manoir de Beauregard

43 Rue des Lilas, 75019; 01 42 03 10 20; www.manoir-de-beauregard-paris.com; Métro: Pré St-Gervais

In summer, breakfast with home-made jam is served in the garden of this country house-style B&B east of Parc des Buttes-Chaumont. The decor is traditional French and there is a family room for four people. The minimum booking is for two nights.

 P €€

SELF-CATERING
Adagio Apartments Montmartre
Map 18 G3

10 Pl Charles Dullin, 75018; 01 42 57 14 55; www.adagio-city.com/montmartre; Métro: Pigalle

The big draw for families is the good location, just moments from Sacré-Coeur in an area packed with restaurants and delis. There are fully modern air-conditioned apartments for up to six people, each with a kitchenette and a microwave. Kids will love the small, pretty garden. Cots are available and there is a laundry room.

  P €€

Paris Oasis
Map 18 H2

14 Rue André del Sarte, 75018; 01 42 55 95 16; www.paris-oasis.com; Métro: Anvers

These family-sized top-floor apartments are well maintained. Kids will love the indoor pool and the garden. There is a minimum stay of three nights but it is excellent value for the location. Guests can use the washing machine. Breakfast is not provided.

 €€

Île de France

The Périphérique, the urban motorway that runs around Paris, divides the city from the suburbs. Beyond the suburban sprawl, Île de France has pretty, rural countryside, the very essence of provincial France. The area is great for a family holiday combined with day trips to Paris and Disneyland. The major sights can be reached by public transport from Paris.

Below *A fountain adorned with statues in the formal gardens of Château de Versailles*

Château de
Versailles
p124

Disneyland
Resort Paris
p130

① Château de Versailles

Playground of the Sun King and his shepherdess queen

A stunning palace with fabulous gardens, Versailles is a great place for a day trip, or even a weekend, as there is so much to see and do. All that stood here before 1661 was an old royal hunting lodge, but Louis XIV converted it into Europe's largest palace (see pp126–7). The gardens were just as important to him, and his gardener, André Le Nôtre, spent 40 years flattening hills and draining marshes to make them perfect. Truly special, they are full of fountains and home to two smaller palaces, the Grand and Petit Trianons.

Key Features of the Gardens

① **Orangerie** Louis XIV loved oranges, which were a delicacy, and built this huge garden so he could grow his own.

Main Entrance

④ **Potager du Roi**
1 km (½ mile)

Palace (see pp126–7)

Children's Island

**Hameau de
la Reine** ⑥
2 km (1 mile)

② **Fountains** Ranging from bombastic multi-tiered creations to calm mirrors, fountains abound here. Find the one with a writhing dragon, or where the sun god Apollo is having a bath.

③ **Grand Canal** Louis XIV held extravagant boating parties here. He also kept gondolas, a gift from the Republic of Venice, at the head of the canal in a building known as "Little Venice".

The Lowdown

Address 78008 (Yvelines) Pl d'Armes, Versailles (21 km/13 miles southwest of Paris); 01 30 83 78 00; www.chateauversailles.fr

RER Line C from central Paris to Versailles Rive Gauche; trains depart every 15 mins. **Train** SNCF Montparnasse to Versailles Chantiers or St-Lazare to Versailles Rive Droite, both a 20-minute walk from the palace. **Car** A13, exit 2. **Taxi** By the train stations; 01 39 50 50 00 or 01 39 51 04 04 **Getting around** A mini-train runs from the château to the Trianon palaces & Hameau de Marie Antoinette, 20 minutes on foot,

(family ticket €23–33); electric cars €30 per hour; the best option is to hire a bike at the entrance to the park; €6.50 per hour

ℹ **Visitor information** 2 bis Ave de Paris, 78000; 01 39 24 88 88; www.versailles-tourisme.com; Apr–Sep: 9am–7pm Tue–Sun, 10am–6pm Mon; Oct–Mar: 9am–6pm Tue–Sat, 11am–5pm Sun–Mon

🕐 **Open** Gardens: 7am–5:30pm daily; summer: till 8:30pm; closed Mon & public hols. Palace: 9am–5:30pm daily; winter: till 6:30pm; summer: closed Mon & public hols. Potager du Roi: Mar–Oct: 10am–6pm Tue–Sun

Price €56–66; under 18s and EU citizens under 26 free. Trianon palaces: €32–42. Gardens: free. Passport to all sights: €62–72. Grandes Eaux Musicales & Jardins Musicaux; special sessions when all the fountains are turned on, with music and, at night, fireworks: €90–100

Skipping the queue Buy tickets online or at www.fnac.com. Paris Museum Pass accepted. Entrance C with a passport ticket is often faster. Joint RER tickets are sold at the stations. The palace is busiest on Tue & Sun. Book in advance for concerts and firework shows.

④ **Potager du Roi** Louis XIV loved food, especially melons, figs, peas and asparagus. The king's vegetable garden, Potager du Roi, outside the main gardens, in front and to the left of the entrance to the palace, is a fun place to explore with kids in the summer and autumn months.

⑤ **Petit Trianon** This small château was given to Marie Antoinette by her husband, Louis XVI, when she was 18 years old. It is a magical miniature palace.

⑥ **Hameau de la Reine** About 2 km (1 mile) from the main palace is a thatched village, the Hameau de La Reine. This was Marie Antionette's dream world, with a ballroom disguised as a barn and a large billiard room.

⑦ **Grand Trianon** On summer evenings, Louis XIV would hold parties at this small palace. Only the ladies of the court were invited.

KIDS' CORNER

Look out for...

1 Apollo. Why are statues and paintings of the Greek sun god all over the palace?

2 Statues representing the rivers of France around the Water Parterre. Can you name any of them?

3 Golden babies sit on the Children's Island near the garden. How many are there?

....

Answers at the bottom of the page.

Where's the queen?

Marie Antoinette spent too much time hiding away at the Petit Trianon. It set tongues wagging, alienated the court and added to her reputation for being an airhead. She alone held the key, which was decorated with 531 diamonds, to her palace.

A FRIVOLOUS QUEEN

While Marie Antoinette tied blue bows around the necks of her sheep, French peasants starved to death. A volcanic eruption in Iceland led to poor harvests and cold winters, but the queen got the blame.

Flying sheep

Plenty of scientific discoveries were made at Versailles. Louis XIV brought the best scientific minds to the palace and founded an Académie des Sciences here in 1666. He also had a rhinoceros brought all the way from India to put in his personal zoo. Later, there was an electricity demonstration in the Hall of Mirrors and in 1783 the first hot-air balloon took to the air. The passengers were a rooster, a duck and a sheep called *Mont au Ciel*, or "Up to the Sky".

....

Answers: 1 Louis XIV, who was known as the Sun King, identified with him. **2** The Marne, the Loire and the Rhône among others **3** Six.

Guided tours Audio guide for kids over 8 years old. The palace shop sells a useful children's guide *My Little Versailles*. Tours in English €18–28; check website for themes and times. Download podcasts from *www.chateauversailles.fr*

👶 **Age range** 5 plus for château

Activities Children's workshops in French. *Son et lumière*, History Galleries; 01 30 83 78 00; Oct–Jun for school groups; during school hols & Jul during summer hols for families. Farm workshop at the Petit Trianon

⏱ **Allow** 2–3 hours

♿ **Wheelchair access** Yes

☕ **Café** Grand Café d'Orléans, just outside the palace, and several restaurants along the canal

🛍 **Shop** Children's books in English available at the palace shop near the main entrance

🚻 **Toilets** Cour Royale, Hameau de Marie Antoinette, La Petite Venise & the Buvette du Dauphin for baby-changing facilities

Good family value?
Excellent value especially if visitors get around on foot. Although it can be tiring, the sheer diversity of things to see makes boredom impossible.

① Château de Versailles continued ▶

Château de Versailles, continued
700 rooms, 67 staircases and 2,153 windows

After Louis XIV moved into his splendid new palace, he made most French aristocrats come and spend time at his court. Around 6,000 people lived in the palace at any one time, often in cold and dingy apartments, but near the centre of power and favours. It symbolized all that was wrong with the Ancien Régime and only just escaped being destroyed in the Revolution. Head for the Hall of Mirrors, passing through the first floor rooms, and then head for the park.

Queen's bedroom

Key Features of the Palace

King's Bedroom This room was strategically located on the axis of the sun's journey across the sky, affirming that Louis XIV was at the centre of the world.

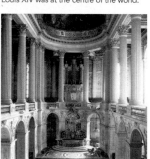

Chapelle Royale Louis XIV attended mass here every morning. The first floor was reserved for the royal family and the ground floor for the court.

Queen's Bedroom Courtiers crowded around in this room to watch the birth of royal children and make sure that the new heir was actually the queen's child.

Place d'Armes Louis XIV reviewed his troops in the square in front of the château. A warrior king, he had a large army and fought numerous battles.

Hall of Mirrors

King's Bedroom

Entrance

Entrance

Chapelle Royale

Hall of Mirrors The peace treaty after the end of World War I was signed in this sparkling hall in June 1919.

Eat and drink

Picnic: under €25; Snacks: €25–45; Real meal: €45–90; Family treat: over €90 (based on a family of four)

PICNIC Guinon (*60 Rue de Paroisse, 78000; 01 39 50 01 84; closed Mon*) is the place to shop for a picnic in the town of Versailles. This bakery has been cooking up delicious food since 1802. Picnic in the gardens.
SNACKS Angelina (*Pavillon d'Orleans, Château de Versailles 78000*), located in the château, is perfect for a teatime treat. Eat macaroons and drink its famous

Prices given are for a family of four

hot chocolate. There are also many cafés and ice-cream stalls in and around the château and gardens.
REAL MEAL La Flottille (*Parc du Château de Versailles; 01 39 51 41 58; www.laflottille.fr*), situated in the gardens, has a pretty 19th-century terrace and serves classic French dishes as well as lighter snacks.
FAMILY TREAT Trianon Palace (*1 Blvd de la Reine, 78000; 01 30 84 50 00; www.trianonpalace.fr*), located outside the gardens, is a luxurious hotel with a restaurant run by British chef Gordon Ramsay. Sunday brunch

Angelina, a great tea-time spot inside the palace

Shopping at the fruit and vegetable shop in the Potager du Roi

at the hotel is a family affair, served on the terrace overlooking the park in summer. In winter, it is in the room where President Clemenceau once dictated the terms of the 1919 peace agreement to the German delegates. The hotel is especially good around Christmas, when there are cookery courses for children, a Christmas market and an ice rink here.

Find out more

DIGITAL At *tinyurl.com/239gsg8* watch *Marie Antoinette, The Last Queen of France*, a drama-documentary that sheds a different light on the accepted story of a frivolous, self-indulgent queen who alienated France. Two historical video games, *Versailles Mysteries* and *Marie Antoinette and the War of Independence*, can be found at *www.nemopolis.net*.
FILM Older children will enjoy watching *Marie Antoinette* (2006), directed by Sofia Coppola and starring Kirsten Dunst, which gives a Hollywood view of life at Versailles, while *Versailles: Le Rêve d'un Roi* (2007) is a colourful French drama about Louis XIV.

Shopping

There are plenty of designer shops selling children's clothes in the town of Versailles but they are a bit stuffy and prim. Pick up some unusual vegetables at the **Potager du Roi** *(see p125)*, the former palace kitchen garden where, in the 18th century, they grew new and exotic fruits from the overseas colonies.

Next stop...

FRANCE MINIATURE Laid out on a piece of land shaped like the map of France, this miniature landscape *(Blvd André Malraux, Elancourt, 78990; 01 30 16 16 30; www.franceminiature.com)* is crisscrossed by rivers, train tracks and engines. An outdoor theme park, it has scale models of major French landmarks and monuments. Look out for the Alps; the Autoroute de Soleil, which runs south to the Mediterranean; the amphitheatre at Arles; and St-Tropez with film stars' yachts bobbing in the bay. Feel like a giant beside a mini version of the famous Eiffel Tower. Kids can drive electric cars around a cartoon town in **Ronde des Zotos**.

Examining the small-scale wonders at France Miniature

Lion on the roof of the glass tunnel in the thrilling Parc Zoologique

② Château de Malmaison

An emperor's new house

Napoleon's first wife, the charming Joséphine de Beauharnais, bought Malmaison in 1799 when Napoleon was campaigning in Egypt. She spent a small fortune transforming the house and the gardens. There was soon a heated orangerie with 300 pineapple plants, perhaps to evoke her native Caribbean island of Martinique, and a garden full of llamas, ostriches and zebras.

Napoleon was at his happiest in this small and cosy house and during the early part of his reign, he took

The Lowdown

- 🌐 **Address** 92000 (Hauts-de-Seine) Ave du Château de Malmaison, Rueil-Malmaison (12 km/7 miles northwest of Paris along RN13); 01 41 29 05 55; www.chateau-malmaison.fr
- 🚗 **RER** La Défense, line A, then bus 258 to stop Le Château
- 🕐 **Open** 10am–12:30pm & 1:30–5:15pm; till 5:45pm Sat & Sun; summer: till 5:45pm; Apr–Sep: till 6:15pm Sat & Sun; closed Tue & public hols
- 💰 **Price** €12–22; under 18s and EU citizens under 26 free
- 🚩 **Guided tours** Book in advance for kids' activities and family tours.
- 👫 **Age range** 8 plus
- 🎨 **Activities** Workshops in French
- ⏲ **Allow** 2 hours
- ☕ **Eat and drink** *Picnic* Au Pain du Cardinal (3 Pl Richelieu, 92500) is a good boulangerie for bread and cakes. Picnic in the park. *Family treat* Les Ecuries de Richelieu (21 Rue du Docteur Zamenhof, 92501; 01 47 08 63 54; open daily) serves classic French food.
- 🚻 **Toilets** Near the entrance

Prices given are for a family of four

many of his most important decisions here. After they separated, Joséphine continued to live here until her death in 1814. Napoleon came back to spend several days here after his defeat at Waterloo, before departing into exile on the island of St Helena.

There is a fascinating collection of swords in the house. Also on display are the cups from which Napoleon drank his coffee.

Letting off steam

South of the château, the forrested grounds include a 15-minute walk to **Etang de St-Cucufa** (www.marie-rueilmalmaison.fr), a small lake.

③ Le Parc Zoologique de Thoiry

Animal magic

Kids will love the drive through this safari park, one of Europe's finest, full of elephants, hippos and bears. There is also a zoo, which can be visited on foot. Here kids can watch lions from glass tunnels, and get face-to-face with a tiger. Among other inhabitants are lemurs and even Komodo dragons. The park also has rare plants, and there is a maze with a few raised bridges from which to plan a route to the middle, or spot lost kids. It makes for a great day out.

Take cover

Visit the **Château de Thoiry** (01 34 87 52 25) in the park, which includes the Salon Blanc, where everything, including the piano, is white. The château is uniquely positioned so that during the summer and winter solstices, the sun's rays form a "bridge of light" in the main hall that lights up the building like a lantern.

Geese on the lush lawns of the Château de Rambouillet

The Lowdown

- 🌐 **Address** 78770 (Yvelines) Rue du Pavillion de Montreuil, Thoiry (40 km/25 miles west of Paris); 01 34 87 40 67; www.thoiry.net
- 🚗 **Car** Take the A13, then follow D76 & D11. The nearest train station is over 6 km (4 miles) away.
- 🕐 **Open** Late-Feb–early-Apr, Sep–mid-Nov: 10am–5pm daily (till 6pm late-Apr–Aug, Sat & Sun and during school hols); closed mid-Dec–early-Feb
- 💰 **Price** €52–62; under 3s free
- 🚩 **Guided tours** Tours in English for the château by a guide in period costume; www.parisvision.com
- 👫 **Age range** All ages
- ⏲ **Allow** A day
- ☕ **Eat and drink** *Picnic* Migros (Centre Commercial Val Thoiry, 01710) is best for supplies. Picnic in the zoo. *Snacks* There are kiosks selling snacks in the park.
- 🚻 **Toilets** At several locations

④ Rambouillet

Lambs, trains and trees

Rambouillet is a lovely, classic French town situated on the edge of the Forêt de Rambouillet, an enchanting forest full of birds of prey, deer and wild boar. It is dominated by the **Château de Rambouillet**, the official summer residence of France's President, which has fairy-tale towers, as well as a Queen's Dairy, where Marie Antoinette used to play at being a milkmaid. Napoleon spent his last night in France here, on 30 June 1815.

For kids, the highlight of the trip is bottle-feeding the lambs during the lambing season at the **Bergerie Nationale**, the national sheep farm, founded in 1784. Do not miss the **Musée Rambolitrain**, which has 4,000 miniature train models.

Letting off steam

Climb trees or get up close to the birds at Odyssée Verte, the forest park at **Espace Rambouillet** (3 Rue de Groussay, 78120 Rambouillet; 01 34 83 05 00; www.espacerambouillet.onf.fr), which features 19 bridges and 18 platforms. Take a walk and enjoy rock climbing by the Abbaye des Vaux-de-Cernay, a ruined abbey in the stone quarries located near Forêt de Rambouillet. There is also an ice-skating rink in Place Félix Faure in winter.

Galerie François I in the palace of Fontainebleau

palace by François I, who discovered this style while campaigning in Italy. Later kings, queens and mistresses left their mark too and it was one of Napoleon's favourite residences. Much quieter and more intimate than Versailles, Fontainebleau is surrounded by a fairy-tale forest with villages and winding paths, and beautiful gardens. A 1200-m (3,937-ft) long canal runs through the wooded park.

The Lowdown

- **Address** 78120 (Yvelines) Château de Rambouillet (55 km/ 34 miles southwest of Paris); *www.rambouillet-tourisme. fr.* Bergerie Nationale: Parc du Château, 78120. Musée Rambolitrain: 4 Pl Jeanne d'Arc, 78120; *www.rambolitrain.com*
- **Train** Gare Montparnasse to Rambouillet. **Car** A13, then A12, then N10
- **i Visitor information** Pl de la Libération, 78120; 01 34 83 21 21
- **Open** Château de Rambouillet: 10am–noon & 2–5pm; summer: till 6pm; closed Tue, public hols & when the President is in residence. Bergerie Nationale: 2–5pm Wed–Sun & public hols, daily in school hols; winter: Sat & Sun only. Musée Rambolitrain: 10am–noon & 2–5:30pm Wed–Sun
- **Price** Château de Rambouillet: €14–24; under 18s free. Bergerie Nationale: €15–25. Musée Rambolitrain: €12–22
- **Activities** Children's workshops during the school hols at the château & the Musée Rambolitrain
- **Allow** At least half a day
- **Eat and drink** Picnic Pâtisserie de Château Paquet (6 Rue Général de Gaulle, 78120) sells sweet and savoury snacks. Picnic in the forest. *Real meal* Villabate (15 Ave du Maréchal Leclerc, 78120) serves good pizza.
- **Toilets** In the château & museum

⑤ Fontainebleau

Tranquil forests and formal gardens

The royal château at Fontainebleau was little more than a hunting lodge when, in the early 16th century, it was transformed into a Renaissance

Letting off steam

Run along the paths around the Grand Canal and play in the gardens. Row across the lake in a boat or ride in a horse-drawn carriage through the grounds. Stop at the playground at the nearby **Musée Napoleon d'Art et d'Histoire Militaire** (88 Rue St-Honore, 77300 Fontainebleau).

The Lowdown

- **Address** 77300 (Seine-et-Marne) Fontainebleau (69 km/43 miles south of Paris); 01 60 71 50 60; *www.musee-chateau-fontainebleau.fr*
- **Train** Gare de Lyon to Gare de Fontainebleau-Avon, then bus A to the château. **Bus** Shuttle bus by Parivision (*www.parisvision. com*) **Car** A6 direction Lyon, exit Fontainebleau
- **Open** Château: Oct–Mar: 9:30am–5pm Wed–Mon; Apr–Sep: 9:30am–6pm Wed–Mon. Gardens: Mar, Apr & Oct: 9am–6pm daily; Nov–Feb: 9am–5pm daily; May–Sep: 9am–7pm daily
- **Price** Château: €20–30; under 18s free for main apartments; garden free
- **Guided tours** Audio guide: €1 per person; kids' audio guide in French
- **Age range** All ages
- **Activities** Workshops for children in French.
- **Allow** 1 hour 30 mins
- **Wheelchair access** Yes, for the château
- **Eat and drink** Snacks Le Grand Café, (33 Pl Napoleon Bonaparte, 77300) is a good place for a drink. *Real meal* Pizza Pazza (1 Rue Bouchers, 77300; 01 60 72 05 61), a pizzeria, serves small versions of any pizza for kids.
- **Toilets** At several locations

Picnic under €25; **Snacks** €25–45; **Real meal** €45–90; **Family treat** over €90 (based on a family of four)

⑥ Disneyland Resort Paris
Mickey's kingdom

There is hardly a kid on the planet who would turn down a trip to Disneyland, so it is not surprising that Disneyland Resort Paris is the most visited theme park in Europe. In fact it comprises two theme parks – Disneyland and Walt Disney Studios. Here, children can meet their favourite cartoon characters and take a spin on some of the best rides on the continent. In addition, there is the Disney Village, which has restaurants, shops and the Buffalo Bill Wild West Show. The main Disneyland Park is divided into five different lands, linked by the 19th-century-style shopping street, Main Street, USA.

Mickey in Buffalo Bill Wild West Show, Disney Village

Key Features

① **Main Street, USA** Based on Disney's home town of Marceline, Missouri, this fantasy land is full of shops and restaurants. The magical Disney parade takes place here every afternoon, making it a good place to finish the day.

② **Disneyland Railroad** Walt Disney was a great train enthusiast and had his own miniature steam train in his garden. The railroad here runs along the perimeter of the park and stops in Main Street, USA; Frontierland; Fantasyland and Discoveryland.

③ **Adventureland** Enjoy the wild rides and exciting animatronics, be Peter Pan and battle the pirates here. Take a perilous jungle ride with Indiana Jones, then play Swiss Family Robinson up in the trees.

Walt Disney Studios

Entrance

Disney Village

④ **Frontierland** Visit the haunted house, ride on a paddle steamer and get the adrenalin going on the thrilling roller coaster, Big Thunder Mountain, in this homage to America's Wild West. Phantom Manor is a ghost ride with excellent special effects.

⑤ **Sleeping Beauty's Castle** Step into the pink fairy-tale castle, which features a dragon in its dungeon and stained-glass windows showing popular characters.

Prices given are for a family of four

⑥ **Discoveryland** With a futuristic theme, this is the place to set off on an intergalactic adventure. It includes Buzz Lightyear Laser Blast, an interactive ride, and is the most interesting part of the park for older kids.

⑦ **Fantasyland** Make this the first stop – it is where the true Disney magic is found. All the classic characters are here to be greeted. It is the perfect part of the park for younger kids, with fairy tales such as Snow White and the Seven Dwarfs brought to life.

Top 10 Rides

1. PHANTOM MANOR
Ghoulish laughter and ghostly apparitions provide scary company on this classic ghost train ride in Frontierland. The graveyard scenes are a little scary for very small children.

2. BIG THUNDER MOUNTAIN
Enjoy discovering an abandoned mine aboard a runaway train that cranks and creaks in the most ominous way before plunging at high speed into the darkness. One of the park's most popular attractions, it is in Frontierland.

3. PINOCCHIO'S FANTASTIC JOURNEY
Set in Fantasyland, this ride revisits the second full-length feature film made by Disney, as the little wooden puppet struggles to become a real boy.

4. IT'S A SMALL WORLD
In Fantasyland, this is the best ride in the park for smaller children. Take the kids on a musical tour of the world, watching out for the monkeys swinging overhead.

5. SNOW WHITE AND THE SEVEN DWARFS
Travel through the forest past the wicked witch and then watch Snow White being rescued by her prince in Fantasyland. This ride is quite scary for very young children.

6. PETER PAN'S FLIGHT
Located in Fantasyland, this is perhaps the most magical ride in the park. Jump aboard a pirate ship and fly across London at night, all the way to Neverland.

7. PIRATES OF THE CARIBBEAN
Watch pirates attack a Spanish fort from a river boat on this great boat ride in Adventureland.

8. INDIANA JONES AND THE TEMPLE OF PERIL
Rattle on a roller coaster through a jungle full of exotic ruins on this perilous ride in Adventureland.

9. SPACE MOUNTAIN: MISSION 2
Blast off into space and travel to the edge of the universe on the biggest thrill ride in Discoveryland. Not for the faint-hearted, and only for those over 1.32 m (4 ft).

10. BUZZ LIGHTYEAR LASER BLAST
Head to Discoveryland for this exciting, interactive game – ride in laser-armed star cruisers and help Buzz save the universe.

⑥ Disneyland Resort Paris continued ▶

Disneyland Resort Paris, continued

Letting off steam

There are two playgrounds in the park: the Pocahontas Indian Village in Frontierland and the Plage des Pirates in Adventureland.

Eat and drink

Picnic: under €25; Snacks: €25–45; Real meal: €45–90; Family treat: over €90 (based on a family of four)

PICNIC Even though picnics are not allowed in the park, no one is going to stop kids from eating so carry snacks and water. The money-saving option is to buy biscuits from the souvenir shops. There is a designated picnic area outside the entrance too.

SNACKS Casey's Corner *(Main Street, USA)* serves hot dogs. Eat a waffle from one of the stands that are scattered all over the park.

REAL MEAL Rainforest Café *(Disney Village; 01 60 30 40 50)* is where visitors can experience eating in a jungle, complete with a tropical rainstorm every 30 minutes.

FAMILY TREAT Auberge de Cendrillion *(Fantasyland; 01 60 30 40 50)* is the best – and the most expensive – restaurant in the park. Classic French dishes are on offer, but the main draw for kids is the chance to spend quality time with Cinderella and her mice, along with other Disney princesses and princes.

Find out more

DIGITAL Go to www.disney.go.com, www.disney.co.uk/playhouse-disney or www.hiddenmickeys.org for Disney-themed fun and games.
FILM Watch DVDs of the cartoons with a French feel such as *Aristocats* (1970), *Beauty and the Beast* (1991), *Sleeping Beauty* (1959), *Cinderella* (1950), *The Hunchback of Notre-Dame* (1996) and *Ratatouille* (2007).

Shopping

The **Disney Village**, just outside the park, is full of shops and restaurants, which stay open after the park has closed so there is no need to rush to shop in the park itself. Purchases made in the park before 3pm can be delivered to hotels or to the Disney Village for collection at the end of the day. Souvenirs are expensive, so choose the bigger shops where there is more choice among the cheaper

A meal in the jungle at the tropical-themed Rainforest Café

The Lowdown

🌐 **Address** 77705 (Seine-et-Marne) Marne-la-Vallée, (32 km/20 miles east of Paris); www.disneyland paris.com

🚗 **Train** RER A to Marne la Vallée, just outside the park, takes 45 mins from Paris; trains run every 15 mins; joint RER & entry ticket available. Direct Eurostar from London St Pancras; www.eurostar. com. **Bus** Airport buses from Charles-de-Gaulle & Orly airports every 30 mins; www.vea.fr. **Car** A4, exit 14; parking €15

ℹ️ **Visitor information** City Hall, Main Street, USA. Studio Services, Walt Disney Studios, Pl des Frères Lumière. Lost & found: Kids who get lost in the park are taken to Coin Bébé by the Plaza Gardens Restaurant, Main Street, USA. Lost property is taken to City Hall, Main Street, USA.

➕ **First-aid centre** In the park by the Plaza Gardens Restaurant, Main Street, USA

🕐 **Open** 10am–8pm Mon–Fri, 10am–10pm Sat & Sun; check the website before visiting as there are different hours for the main park and Walt Disney Studios. Times may also vary according to season. Disney Village is open all day until very late at night.

💲 **Price** One-day one-park pass for main park only: €206–216; under 3s free; Hopper pass, or day pass, for both parks: €258–68; under 3s free. Tickets are cheaper if bought online; 2–3 & 4-day Hopper passes available. Look out for promotions, especially in Jan–Mar when ticket price covers admission to all parks. See the website for promotions on hotel packages; there are often good deals for families but they change seasonally. Disney Village: free

👫 **Skipping the queue** There can be long queues both to get into the parks and for individual rides – up to an hour in high season. To avoid entrance queues, arrive at least 30 mins before the park opens, or book in advance online, by phone, through a travel agent, on Channel ferries, at Eurostar terminals, at Disney Stores or at RATP Métro stations. Avoid Sundays and, if possible, peak holiday seasons. Once inside, the **Fastpass** system allows visitors to pre-book for some rides without queueing: insert the park ticket into the Fastpass machine at a ride entrance to get a Fastpass ticket with a time slot, and return at the allotted time. However, each person can only hold one Fastpass ticket at a time and many rides are fully booked by noon. The **VIP Fastpass** offered by some Disney hotels gives instant access to some rides, and the **Hôtel Disneyland Fastpass** gives timed entry to a choice of attractions for guests. Disney hotel guests can enter the park at 8am in high season.

Prices given are for a family of four

Colourful entrance to the Disney Store in the Disney Village

The fantasy-castle architecture of the Disneyland Hotel

options. The **Liberty Arcade** *(City Hall)* shop is a good option. Buy books, stationery, videos, posters and CDs at the cosy **Storybook Store** *(Main Street, USA)*. **La Boutique du Château** *(Fantasyland)* is a year-round Christmas-themed shop. Shop here for Christmas cards and holiday decorations. Kids will enjoy spending hours in the big **Disney Store** *(Disney Village)* and browsing through the collection of merchandise, including clothes and toys. If the plan is to stay overnight, it might be better to pay a visit to the souvenir shops the next morning, when nobody is overtired.

Staying over

The best way to relax is to stay overnight at one of the on-site hotels, which are also in Disney Village. For children the bonus is that at the end of the day, when the park is empty, it is possible to have several turns on some of the rides. The hotels closest to the park are the most expensive. The most luxurious hotel is the **Hôtel Disneyland** *(see p134)*. The main attraction here is a view of the fairy-tale castle down Main Street, USA, and the copious breakfast with Disney characters. Kids will love **Hôtel Cheyenne** *(see p134)*, which looks like a Wild West movie set. Some hotels also have indoor and outdoor pools. Watch out for seasonal package deals available for families on the official website.

Next stop...

WALT DISNEY STUDIOS Under-10s will be exhausted by a day out at Disneyland Park, so do not plan anything for the first evening. On day two head over to **Walt Disney Studios**, the smaller theme park, next to the Disneyland Park. This is the place to discover the world of the movies and find out how films are made, especially animated cartoons in the Toon Studio. The central feature of Front Lot, just inside the giant studio gates, is a fountain in the shape of Mickey. The big attraction is Toy Story Playland with rides such as the Toy Soldiers Parachute Drop and the Slinky Dog Zigzag. Do not miss the Studio Tram tour, which travels through an earthquake in an oilfield and on to the destroyed city of London. The Twilight Zone Tower of Terror is a white-knuckle ride, good for older children.

Baby Switch allows parents to take turns holding the baby while the other one rides, without going to the back of the queue.

Queue fatigue busters An information board in the Central Plaza lists queueing times. Some attractions in Adventureland rarely get busy: Les Cabanes des Robinson, Adventure Isle, Le Passage Enchanté d'Aladdin and Sleeping Beauty's Castle in Fantasyland. In bad weather, rides may be closed, if so take cover in the Liberty and Discovery arcades.

Guided tours Enquire at City Hall; €30–40; under 3s free

Age range All ages

Activities Disney Parade, 5pm daily; check website or central notice board by the Plaza Gardens Restaurant, Main Street, USA. Get an entertainment programme from City Hall; the Lion King show is especially good for families.

⏱ **Allow** A full day, or two days for both parks. If staying in a Disneyland hotel, arrive the night before to meet the Disney characters at breakfast.

☕ **Café** There are food kiosks and cafés across the park and a baby change with microwaves by the Plaza Gardens Restaurant, Main Street, USA.

🚻 **Toilets** Across the park. Baby-changing facilities by the Plaza Gardens Restaurant in the Central Plaza, Main Street, USA

Good family value?
Disneyland Paris is very expensive, and it is not everybody's cup of tea. Some visitors feel it has not stood the test of time well and is getting a little shabby, but most kids love it. It is well worth seeking out special promotions and planning your visit carefully to make the most of it.

Entrance to the all-action Walt Disney Studios park

Picnic under €25; **Snacks** €25–45; **Real meal** €45–90; **Family treat** over €90 (based on a family of four)

Where to Stay in Île de France

You will find hotels aplenty across Île de France, especially in Fontainebleau and Versailles, but you could take things at a slower pace by hiring a *gîte* or farmhouse (with a garden for the kids to run around in). There are also many camp sites around Paris. Whatever you choose, there are great deals to be had.

AGENCIES

Clé Vacances
www.clevacances-paris-idf.com/
This agency lists quality houses, apartments and B&Bs in Île de France, all certified by France's tourism board.

Gîtes Île-de-France
www.gitesiledefrance.com/
Part of Gîtes de France, this site lists over 280 *gîtes* available to rent in the area surrounding Paris.

Auvers-sur-Oise   Map 4 G5

SELF-CATERING
Le Relais du Porche
Pl de la Mairie, 95430 Auvers-sur-Oise; 01 30 36 16 50/06 81 31 30 86; www.relaisduporche.com
A range of self-catering apartments in the village immortalized by Van Gogh, this place is great for a short break. The owners also run a family-friendly restaurant in the main square.
🍴 P   €€

Disneyland Resort Paris   Map 4 H5

HOTELS
Hôtel Cheyenne
Disneyland Resort Paris BP 112, Marne-la-Vallée Chessy, 77777 Seine-et-Marne; www.hotels. disneylandparis.co.uk
Take a trip to the Wild West in this clapboard hotel that will delight the kids. Up to four people can stay in a room, which has bunk beds for kids.

Typically French façade of the Hôtel des Londres, Fontainebleau

There is a self-service restaurant, kids' corner and outdoor play area. Book online for the best deals.
🍴 IOI   €€

Hôtel Disneyland
Disneyland Resort Paris BP 112, Marne-la-Vallée Chessy, 77777 Seine-et-Marne; www.hotels. disneylandparis.co.uk
Rooms can accommodate up to four people, and the big draw is the amazing buffet breakfast with Disney characters. Kids like the swimming pool and the Snow White and Seven Dwarfs mirror in the bathroom. Book online for the best deals.
IOI   €€€

BED & BREAKFAST
Le Logis de La Voulzie   Map 5 A6
16 Rue Aristide Briand, 77160 Provins; 06 14 02 25 10; www.en. logisdelavoulzie.com
This B&B is located in the historic town of Provins, which is classified as a UNESCO World Heritage Site. There are four large bedrooms, with extra beds to convert the doubles into family rooms. Guests can use the kitchen and the charming, leafy garden. It is just 30 minutes from Disneyland Resort Paris.
🚫 🐾 🍴 P   €

Le Moulin de St-Martin
7 Rue de St-Martin, 77580 Crécy-la-Chapelle; 01 64 63 69 90; www. chambresdhotes.org.
Housed in an old mill, this B&B is just a 20-minute drive from Disneyland Resort Paris. There are two bedrooms with an extra bed, and a garden.
P   €€

Fontainebleau   Map 4 H6

HOTELS
Novotel Ury   Map 4 G6
Route Nationale 152, 77760 Ury; 01 60 71 24 24; www.novotel.com
This hotel is located on the edge of a pretty village close to Fontainebleau. Kids can stay free in their parents'

room and there is a 50 per cent discount on the second room. There is a pool, a tennis court and bike hire.
🐾 IOI P   €

Hôtel Aigle Noir
27 Pl Napoleon Bonaparte, 77300 Fontainebleau; 01 60 74 60 00; www.hotelaiglenoir.com
Set in a 17th-century manor close to the château, this lovely hotel has excellent service. Its interconnecting rooms are ideal for families. Highchairs and cots are available.
P   €€

Hôtel des Londres
1 Pl Général de Gaulle, 77300 Fontainebleau; 01 64 22 20 21; www.hoteldelondres.com
This family-run hotel offers spacious rooms for three, as well as suites. Some rooms have a fabulous view of the château. The hotel is located in a peaceful setting close to the town centre. It is closed for Christmas and two weeks in August.
🐾 P   €€

BED & BREAKFAST
Le Clos du Tertre
6 Chemin des Vallées, 77760 La Chapelle la Reine, near Fontainebleau; 01 64 24 37 80; www.leclosdutertre.com
This friendly B&B has a home away from home atmosphere. There is a kitchen corner for guests. It is a good option for those who plan to stay overnight to see Vaux-le-Vicomte by candlelight. Disneyland Resort Paris is just a short drive away.
🚫 🐾 🍴 P   €

Maffliers   Map 4 G5

HOTEL
Novotel Château de Maffliers
Allées des Marroniers, 95560 Maffliers; 01 34 08 35 35; www.novotel.com
This Novotel hotel provides modern accommodation in the grounds of a

19th-century château, north of Roissy Charles-de-Gaulle airport. In addition to the family-friendly facilities, there are tennis courts and close by, horse-riding for kids.

P   €

Provins   Map 5 A6

BED & BREAKFAST
Le Clos de Provins
4 Rue des Jacobins, Ville Haute, 77160 Provins; 06 85 80 86 45; www.lesclosdeprovins.com
Children get a warm welcome at this B&B, near the historic town centre. The family suite has room for four; under 3s stay for free. The garden has swings and a sandpit. The breakfast is excellent.

P   €€

La Maison Stella Cadente
Rue Maximilien Michelin, 77160 Provins; 01 60 67 40 23; www.stella-cadente.com
A luxurious wonderland, all the rooms are themed on fairy tales in this beautiful, 19th-century villa with a huge garden. A ping-pong table is available for children.

🛁   €€€

Rambouillet   Map 4 F5

HOTEL
Relays du Château Mercure Rambouillet
1 Pl de la Libération, 78120 Rambouillet; 01 34 57 30 00; www.mercure.com
This three-star hotel, now part of the Accor group, is opposite the château in Rambouillet. There is room for one extra bed in a double room, and a 50 per cent reduction on a second room. Cots are available.

🍴 P   €

Rolleboise   Map 4 F5

HOTEL
Hôtel Domaine de la Corniche
5 Route de la Corniche, 78270 Rolleboise; 01 30 92 20 00; www.domainedelacorniche.com
This hotel offers stunning views across the Seine and has a great restaurant – meals are served on the terrace in summer. Close to Giverny, the area is ideal for a short break.

🍴 P   €€

Spacious deluxe room at the Hôtel Trianon Palace

Versailles   Map 4 G5

HOTELS
Novotel Château de Versailles
4 Blvd St-Antoine, 78150 Le Chesnay; 01 39 54 96 96; www.novotel.com/1022
This offers classic Novotel family-friendly facilities, just 5 minutes' walk from the palace. Under-16s can stay free in their parents' room and there is a late check out on Sundays. There is a 50 per cent discount on a second room, and a children's play area.

🍴 P   €

Hôtel des Roys
14 Ave de Paris, 78000 Versailles; 01 39 50 56 00; www.hotel-roys-versailles.com
Located just 5 minutes' walk from the palace, the hotel is close to the RER, shops and restaurants. It is a good option if looking for something that is not a chain hotel, in Versailles.

P   €€

Hôtel Trianon Palace
1 Blvd de la Reine, 78000 Versailles; 01 30 84 51 20; www.trianonpalace.com
This is one of the most serene hotels in the region. The rooms are spacious and some have park views. The Gordon Ramsay bistro, La Veranda, has a kids' menu and serves a Sunday

brunch. The hotel also has an indoor pool and spa, and two tennis courts. There is a skating rink on Christmas.

🍴 P   €€€

BED & BREAKFAST
L'Orangeraie
7 Rue Hardy, 78000 Versailles; 01 39 53 26 78; www.versailles-orangeraie.com
Located just 5 minutes from the RER and the château, in an attractive part of Versailles town, this B&B has an enclosed garden and a family room with a kitchenette and garden access. There is an extra charge for use of a folding bed and the kitchenette.

🍽 🛏 P   €

Villa Versailles
6 Rue Borgnis Desbordes, 78000 Versailles; 06 14 86 90 46; www.villa-versailles.com
Located near the château, this little house in a pretty garden serves as a B&B. There is a double room upstairs and a sofa cum bed downstairs. Lunch and dinner can be provided, but at an extra charge.

🛏   €€€

CAMPING
Huttopia Versailles
31 Rue Berthelot; 01 39 51 23 61; www.huttopia.com
The camp site is a short walk from the Palace of Versailles, and a 30-minute train ride from Paris to the nearby Porchefontaine RER station. It has cabins and wooden caravans, and a kids' club. There is another Huttopia at Rambouillet.

🍴 P   €

Price Guide
The following price ranges are based on one night's accommodation in high season for a family of four, inclusive of service charges and any additional taxes.
€ Under €200 €€ €200–500 €€€ over €500

Deckchairs along the picturesque pool area of the L'Orangeraie, Versailles

Key to symbols *see back cover flap*

Western France

Western France is a region of majestic rivers, splendid coastlines and sumptuous gardens. Beach resorts and fishing ports line the coast, while the Loire Valley is famed for its Renaissance châteaux and gardens, built by kings and queens. William the Conqueror, Richard the Lionheart, Joan of Arc, Leonardo da Vinci and Claude Monet are a few figures who have left their mark on the area's rich array of historic towns.

Highlights

Mont-St-Michel
Follow the footsteps of medieval pilgrims to this stunning granite abbey, surrounded by the sea during high tides (see pp152–3).

Château Royal de Blois
Visit one of the Loire Valley's most beautiful châteaux and the fascinating Maison de la Magie Robert-Houdin nearby (see pp184–5).

Les Machines de l'Île, Nantes
Ride the extraordinary mechanical elephant and watch the latest fantastic machines being built in the grand galleries of this workshop (see pp174–5).

The D-Day Beaches
Relive the biggest one-day invasion in history at the landing beaches and evocative museums and memorials. Take a look at the Bayeux Tapestry, which depicts the Norman Conquest of 1066 (see pp148–9).

Océanopolis, Brest
Travel through polar, temperate and tropical climates inhabited by marine animals (see pp162–3).

Chartres Cathedral
Marvel at this Gothic masterpiece in near perfect condition, with its impressive stained glass and sculpture (see pp188–9).

Left Crystal-clear ocean water lapping against the crags and rocks of Brittany's coast
Above left A petit train outside Chartres Cathedral, the greatest Gothic cathedral in Europe

The Best of
Western France

With a remarkably varied coastline and mild climate, Western France is not just celebrated for its beaches and seafaring traditions, but also for its spectacular Gothic cathedrals, Renaissance châteaux and gardens. There are no end of things to see and do: combine historical sights and dazzling art and architecture with picnics and afternoons by the sea.

Hungry for history

Children are fascinated by the medieval island abbey of **Mont-St-Michel** (see pp152–3) and the soaring Gothic majesty of the **Chartres Cathedral** (see pp188–9) and the stories of the Norman Conquest depicted on the **Bayeux Tapestry** (see p149) that can be read like a cartoon strip. Along the Loire river, the **Château Royal de Blois** (see pp184–5) relates stories of kings and assassins, while the **Château de Chenonceau** (see p183) offers the thrill of canoeing right under its majestic arches. In **Rouen** (see pp144–5) visit the Cathédrale Notre-Dame and the excellent Impressionist works in its Musée des Beaux Arts. For towns filled with art and history, head for **Angers** (see pp178–9), **Bourges** (see pp186–7), **Le Mans** (see p179), **Saumur** (see p178) and **Chinon** (see p182). Fans of Asterix will not want to miss the megalithic sites around **Carnac** (see pp166–7),

while the fascinating spectacles and Cinéscénie at **Grand Parc Puy du Fou** (see p177) make history fun for even the youngest child.

The great outdoors

Seaside marvels hold pride of place – from the dramatic cliff arch of **Étretat** (see p147) to the wide sands of **St-Jean-de-Monts** (see p177), where older kids can learn to sand-yacht. In Finisterre, take a boat out to **Île d'Ouessant** (see p163), populated by the world's smallest sheep. Renowned as the "Garden of France", the Loire Valley boasts the **Château de Villandry** (see p181) with spectacular gardens. The **Terra Botanica** (see p179), a botanical theme park in Angers, is superb for whetting kids' appetites for the plant world. Everyone loves Monet's house and gardens at **Giverny** (see p146). In Brittany, follow the trail of Merlin in the **Forêt de Brocéliande** (see p160).

Below The fabulous mechanical elephant at Les Machines de l'Île, Nantes

Above *Mont-St-Michel towering over the marshes*
Middle *A medieval combat with knights on horses at the Grand Parc Puy du Fou* **Bottom** *A Japanese-style bridge and lily ponds at the Fondation Claude Monet, Giverny*

In a week

Start with **Chartres Cathedral** before spending a couple of days around **Tours** *(see pp180–81)*, visiting the Loire châteaux. Children may especially like the **Château de Clos Lucé** *(see p186)* at Amboise, where there are models of Leonardo da Vinci's inventions; the **Château de la Ferté** *(see p187)*, with its many fun activities; or the **Château de Cheverny** *(see p185)* – "Tintin's Château". Follow this with two days by the beach in the beautiful corsair port of **St-Malo** *(see p161)*. Stop for a day at **Mont-St-Michel** to visit the famous abbey in the bay before heading on to Bayeux, a great base for visiting the **D-Day Beaches** *(see pp148–9)* and its famous tapestry.

By season

By late spring, the gardens in Western France are in full glory – visit **Giverny** when the irises are in bloom. It is also a lovely time to explore arty destinations such as Gauguin's **Pont-Aven** *(see pp168–9)* and **Honfleur** *(see p147)*, with its museum of the Impressionists and the Maisons Satie, an offbeat look at composer Erik Satie.

In summer, there are moving commemorations on the **D-Day Beaches**, and the historical spectacles at the **Grand Parc Puy du Fou** are in full flow. A stroll on the mechanical elephant at **Les Machines de l'Île** *(see pp174–5)*, in Nantes, also makes for a fine outing.

Autumn is a time of apple and grape harvests, rich colours and the light beloved by artists in the **Suisse Normande** *(see p151)*.

Winter is a great time to visit the cities and museums for a dose of culture, such as the **Mémorial de Caen** *(see p150)*, **Océanopolis** *(see pp162–3)* in Brest or the museums in **Bourges**.

Western France

The west is France's maritime region *par excellence*, flanked by the English Channel and the Atlantic Ocean, and where two of the country's biggest rivers – the Loire and the Seine – meet the sea. The area offers every imaginable coastal feature, from cliff to cove to salt marsh to beach and a smattering of fascinating islands. Inland are forests, apple orchards, vineyards and gardens. While there are no mountains, there are rolling hills, known as the Suisse Normande, south of Caen. Road and rail networks are excellent.

Places of interest

⬤ NORMANDY
1 Rouen
2 Giverny
3 Dieppe
4 Le Havre
5 Honfleur
6 The D-Day Beaches
7 Cherbourg
8 Caen
9 St-Pierre-sur-Dives
10 Falaise
11 Mont-St-Michel
12 Granville
13 Coutances
14 Villedieu-les-Poêles
15 Mortain

⬤ BRITTANY
1 Rennes
2 Forêt de Brocéliande
3 Dinan
4 St-Malo
5 Océanopolis, Brest
6 Roscoff and the Pays du Léon
7 Paimpol
8 Douarnenez
9 Standing Stones of Carnac
10 Vannes
11 Lorient
12 Pont-Aven
13 Quimper

⬤ THE LOIRE VALLEY
1 Les Machines de l'Île, Nantes
2 St-Nazaire
3 Batz-sur-Mer
4 Les Sables d'Olonne
5 Grand Parc Puy du Fou
6 Abbaye Royale de Fontevraud
7 Saumur
8 Angers
9 Le Mans
10 Tours
11 Chinon
12 Château d'Ussé
13 Château de Chenonceau
14 Château Royal de Blois
15 Château d'Amboise
16 Bourges
17 Orléans
18 Chartres Cathedral

Impressive cluster of megalithic standing stones at Carnac

Map of Western France showing locations including Le Tréport, Varengeville-sur-Mer, St-Valery-en-Caux, Dieppe, Fécamp, Neufchâtel-en-Bray, Étretat, Tôtes, Harfleur, Bolbec, Yvetot, Cléres, Le Havre, Rouen, Honfleur, Deauville, Elbeuf, Les Andelys, Ouistreham, Caen, Lisieux, HAUTE NORMANDIE, St-Pierre-sur-Dives, Bernay, Vernon, Giverny, Evreux, Falaise, Vimoutiers, BASSE NORMANDIE, L'Aigle, Sées, Verneuil-sur-Avre, Dreux, Alençon, Mortagne-au-Perche, Chartres Cathedral, Nogent-le-Rotrou, La Ferté-Bernard, Pithiviers, Châteaudun, Artenay, Le Mans, St-Calais, Montargis, Ecommoy, Meung-sur-Loire, Orléans, Châteauneuf-sur-Loire, La Flèche, Château-du-Loir, Beaugency, La Ferté-St-Aubin, Gien, Château Royal de Blois, Chambord, Briare, Château-Renault, Château d'Amboise, Cheverny, CENTRE, Longué, Tours, Château de Chenonceau, Romorantin-Lanthenay, Cosne-Cours-sur-loire, Château d'Ussé, Azay-le-Rideau, Valençay, Vierzon, La Charité, Abbaye Royale de Fontevraud, Chinon, Loches, Ste-Maure-de-Touraine, Châtillon-sur-Indre, Issoudun, Salbris, St-Florent-sur-Cher, Bourges, Châteauroux, Le Blanc, St-Amand-Mont-Rond, Argenton-sur-Creuse, La Châtre

Magnificent façade of the Château d'Ussé, Rigny-Useé

0 km   50

0 miles   50

The Lowdown

Getting there and around
Air (see p142). **Ferry** from the UK or Ireland, linking Newhaven to Dieppe; Poole, Portsmouth and Rosslare to Cherbourg; Portsmouth, Poole and Weymouth to St-Malo; Portsmouth to Le Havre & Caen, and Plymouth, Cork & Rosslare to Roscoff. **Train** High-speed TGV trains from Paris, with links to Rouen and Le Havre, Le Mans, Rennes, Quimper and Brest, as well as Angers, Saumur, Tours, Nantes and the coast. Slower-speed trains run from Paris to Caen and northwest Normandy. TER regional trains link many towns in Normandy, Brittany, the Loire and Centre-Val de Loire; www.ter-sncf.com (in French only) lists links to the regional networks. **Bus** Buses provide links in tourist areas around Mont-St-Michel and the D-Day Beaches. Major cities have excellent urban transport: buses (www.tcar.fr) in Rouen; métro and buses (www.star.fr) in Rennes; buses and tramways (www.tan.fr) in Nantes; buses (www.filbleu.fr) in Tours, and buses and trams (www.reseau-tao.fr) in Orléans. **Car** Avis (www.avis.fr) has branches in most towns.

Supermarkets Essentials can be bought from branches of Intermarché, Carrefour, Super U, Monoprix and Leclerc. **Markets** Most cities have a covered market, usually open Tue–Sun. A list of markets is available from the local tourist and *Département* offices.

Opening hours Many shops are closed on Monday, but open on Sunday morning.

Pharmacies There is at least one pharmacy, identified by a green cross outside, in each town and many villages. A list in the window will give details of the nearest *pharmacie de garde* open outside normal hours (on Sundays and at night). They are also listed in local newspapers and on www.pharmaciesdegarde.com.

Toilets Towns have municipal public toilets, but do carry a supply of emergency toilet paper. Cities have pay or free street toilets that automatically clean themselves.

Spectacular cliffs lining the pebbly beach at Étretat

Western France Regional Airports

Brest and Nantes are the busiest airports in Western France, both linked to cities around Europe and France. Some of the smaller airports rely on low-cost flights from the UK and Ireland. For families travelling to France from outside of Europe, Paris (see p86) will be the hub. While Normandy and the Loire Valley are easy to reach from there by train, Brittany is a bit further – a connecting flight might be worth it.

Deauville

Just 5 km (3 miles) east of Deauville, this is a small airport, only offering chartered flights with package holidays. The airport is easy to get around. There is a restaurant.

Rennes-St Jacques

Located 8 km (5 miles) southwest of Rennes, just off the rocade (bypass), this airport is used by Air France, Flybe, Chalair and Aer Lingus. Bus 57 (€1.20), which goes to the city centre, has a stop near the airport. Families with a lot to carry may want to take a taxi (€20). The airport services are easy to locate. There is a restaurant and a café.

Dinard-Pleurtuit-St Malo

The airport is situated 5 km (3 miles) southeast of Dinard on the D64 and 13 km (8 miles) from St-Malo. Ryanair and Aurigny fly here. There are no shuttle buses, but taxis (€13 for Dinard; €25–30 for St-Malo) and car hire are available at the airport. The airport is small and easy to get around. There is a restaurant. The nearest hotel is the Kyriad Saint-Malo Dinard (02 99 56 09 26; www.kyriadsaintmalo.fr), with family rooms.

Brest-Bretagne

In Guipavas, 10 km (6 miles) northwest of Brest, just off the E50, Brest-Bretagne is served by Air France, Chalair, (to Paris and Lyon), Flybe, Jetair and Ryanair. Shuttle buses (€4.60) link the

A plane preparing for a flight at the Deauville airport

airport to the centre of Brest and the train station. It is a small airport and is easy to get around. There is a restaurant and sandwich/crêperie/bar. Hôtel Oceania Brest Aéroport (02 98 02 32 83; www.oceania hotels.com) is pleasant and closest to the airport.

Lorient-Bretagne Sud

This airport is located 10 km (6 miles) west of Lorient on the D163 and is served by Air France and Aer Arann. It is linked to Lorient's city centre by taxi or hire car only. It is a small airport, closes at night and easy to get around. There is no restaurant. The closest hotel is the expensive Domaine de Kerbastic (Route de Locmaria, 56520 Guidel; 02 97 65 98 01). There are several other accommodation options in Lorient.

Nantes Atlantique

Nantes Atlantique is 10 km (6 miles) southwest of Nantes, just off the péripherique (ring road) that encircles the city. It is served by

Air France, Ryanair, Iberia, easyJet, Air Austral, Jet4u, Royal Air Maroc, Tunisair, Vueling, Eastern Airways and Flybe. An airport shuttle (€7) runs every 30 minutes (every hour on Sunday) from the train station and Nantes centre, where the city's three tram lines meet. Although this is one of the biggest airports in the west, it is easy to get around. There is a brasserie and several cafés/snack bars. The Hôtel Escale Oceania Nantes Airport (02 40 32 14 14; www.oceaniahotels.com), close to the airport, has family rooms.

Angers Loire

Only Airvalle flights fly to the small Angers Loire in Marcé, 27 km (17 miles) east of Angers, just off the A11. There is no public transport, just taxis. It is easy to get around and has a snack bar.

Tours Val de Loire

The airport is 6 km (4 miles) north of Tours, just off the A10. It is used by Ryanair flights. Alphacar shuttles (€5) go from the airport to Tours train station and depart from there two hours before each flight. The airport is small and easy to get around. There is a restaurant.

The Lowdown

Angers Loire 02 41 33 50 20; www.angersloireaeroport.fr

Brest-Bretagne 02 98 32 86 00; www.brest.aeroport.fr

Deauville 02 31 65 65 65; www.deauville.aeroport.fr

Dinard-Pleurtuit-St-Malo 02 99 46 18 46; www.dinard.aeroport.fr

Lorient-Bretagne Sud 02 97 87 21 50; www.lorient.aeroport.fr

Nantes Atlantique 02 40 84 80 00; www.nantes.aeroport.fr

Rennes-St Jacques 02 99 29 60 00; www.rennes.aeroport.fr

Tours Val de Loire 02 47 49 37 00; www.tours.aeroport.fr

The arrival terminal of Nantes Atlantique airport bustling with travellers

Normandy

Named for the Norsemen, or Vikings, who landed here in the 9th century, Normandy is situated on the English Channel, which has shaped much of its history. The D-Day Beaches evoke World War II, but there are also handsome old resorts such as Honfleur and Deauville and inland pastoral landscapes. To the west is the fantastic medieval abbey of Mont-St-Michel.

Below Looking across the Old Harbour to the "skyscrapers" of Quai Ste-Catherine, Honfleur

The D-Day
Beaches
p148

Rouen
p144

Mont-St-Michel
p152

① Rouen
Monet's cathedral

Rouen was badly damaged during World War II: first in 1940, then before and after the D-Day landings. Despite major postwar rebuilding, the city's medieval core of half-timbered houses is very evocative, with its Gothic cathedral as the centrepiece. During the Hundred Years' War, Rouen was the seat of the English occupation, and Joan of Arc was burnt at the stake here, while in the 19th century the city played a crucial role in the Impressionist movement.

The Cathédrale Notre-Dame

Key Sights

① **Pont Gustave-Flaubert**
Finished in 2008, this is the world's highest drawbridge, allowing ocean vessels to sail up the Seine to Rouen's port.

② **Place du Vieux-Marché**
Joan of Arc was burnt here in 1431. A statue of her stands in the square, along with the strikingly modern Église de Jeanne d'Arc.

③ **Palais de Justice** Begun in 1499, the façade of this former seat of Normandy's parliament rises into a forest of pointy pinnacles.

④ **Gros Horloge** A landmark Renaissance tower, it has a 16th-century astronomic clock, with workings from 1389. Now a city museum, its top floor offers stunning views of the cathedral.

⑤ **Musée des Beaux Arts**
Along with one of Monet's cathedral paintings, this museum displays other Impressionists and works by Surrealist Marcel Duchamp.

⑥ **Musée d'Histoire Naturelle** This museum's displays range from butterflies to Samurai armour.

⑦ **Abbatiale St-Ouen**
Founded in 750 to house the relics of Rouen's bishop, this Gothic church measures a massive 137 m (450 ft) in length. It has a magnificent organ in a Baroque loft from 1630.

⑧ **Cathédrale Notre-Dame** The cathedral has a unique 16th-century "Butter Tower", which was paid for by the locals in exchange for the right to eat butter during Lent.

The Lowdown

🌐 **Map reference** 4 E4
Address 76000 (Seine-Maritime). Gros Horloge: Rue du Gros Horloge. Musée des Beaux Arts: Esplanade Marcel Duchamp; *www.rouen-musees.com*. Musée d'Histoire Naturelle: 198 Rue Beauvoisine. Abbatiale St-Ouen: Pl du Général de Gaulle. Cathédrale Notre-Dame: 3 Rue St-Romain; *www.cathedrale-rouen.net*

🚗 **Train** from Paris

ℹ️ **Visitor information** 25 Pl de la Cathédrale; 02 32 08 32 40; *www.rouenvalleeseine.com*

🕐 **Open** Gros Horloge: Apr–Oct: 10am–1pm & 2–7pm Tue–Sun; Nov–Mar: 2–6pm Tue–Sun. Musée des Beaux Arts: 10am–6pm Wed–Mon. Musée d'Histoire Naturelle: 2–5:30pm Tue–Sun. Abbatiale St-Ouen: 10am–12:30pm & 2–5:30pm Tue–Thu, Sat & Sun (till 6pm Apr–Oct). Cathédrale Notre-Dame: Apr–Oct: 2–6pm Mon, 9am–7pm Tue–Sat, 8am–6pm Sun; Nov–Mar: 8am–6pm Sun, 2–6pm Mon, 9am–noon & 2–6pm Tue–Sat

€ **Prices** Gros Horloge: €36–46; under 6s free. Musée des Beaux Arts: €20–30; EU residents

under 26 free. Musée d'Histoire Naturelle: €12–22; under 18s free

👥 **Skipping the queue** Buy a €10 City Pass online (*www.monpassen liberte.com*); it offers discounts to 200 hotels, restaurants and attractions listed on the website.

🗯 **Guided tours** Contact the tourist office for details.

👫 **Age range** All ages

🏃 **Activities** Take the "Walk of the Impressionists" (map available at tourist office) to check out copies of paintings displayed at the sites where they were painted. On summer evenings,

Prices given are for a family of four

Letting off steam

There are fenced playgrounds in the charming **Jardins de l'Hôtel de Ville** (Rue des Faulx, 76000; 02 32 08 32 40). Race around the indoor track at **Rouen Espace Karting** (149–169 Chemin du Croisset, 76000; 02 32 12 34 05; www.rouen-espace-karting.fr). Go swimming or ice-skating at the indoor and outdoor pools at the **Centre Sportif Dr Duchêne** (Île Lacroix, 76000; 02 35 07 94 70). Ring ahead for hours and availability for karting and ice-skating.

Outside terrace of Brasserie Paul near the Cathédrale Notre-Dame

Eat and drink

Picnic: under €20; Snacks: €20–45; Real meal: €45–90; Family treat: over €90 (based on a family of four)

PICNIC Les Halles (Pl du Vieux Marché, 76000) stocks great goodies for picnics. Square André Maurois in the centre of the city is a good place for a picnic.

head for the sound and light show at the Cathédrale Notre-Dame.

⏱ **Allow** A day

🎪 **Festivals** Les Hivernales des Cuivres, brass and vocal concerts (Jan–Mar). Foire St-Romain, one of the biggest fun fairs in France (mid-Oct–mid-Nov)

Good family value?
Rouen makes for an affordable day out for culture and history, even if a lot in the city is not specifically oriented to kids.

SNACKS Dame Cakes (70 Rue de St-Romain, 76000; 02 35 07 49 31) is a tea room that serves tasty hot chocolates and cakes.
REAL MEAL Brasserie Paul (1 Pl de la Cathédrale, 76000; 02 35 71 86 07; www.brasserie-paul.com) is the oldest brasserie in Rouen, specializing in free-range chicken, varieties of cheese and tarte tatin (apple pie).
FAMILY TREAT Gill Côté Bistro (14 Pl du Vieux Marché, 76000; 02 35 89 88 72; www.gill.fr) is a laid-back bistro run by a Michelin-starred chef, serving savoury tarts in flaky pastry and dishes such as chicken with apples in Calvados sauce.

Shopping

Head for **La Chocolatière** (18 Rue Guillaume-le-Conquérant, 76000; 02 35 71 00 79), one of the most famous chocolate-makers in France, housed in a sleek red shop. Visit **Patrick Chasset** (12 Rue de la Croix-de-Fer, 76000; 02 35 70 59 97), an antique shop that specializes in 18th- and 19th-century toys.

Find out more

DIGITAL Read a kids-oriented article about Impressionism on artsmarts 4kids.blogspot.com/2007/09/impressionism.html.
FILM Over 20 films have featured Joan of Arc. The first film, Jeanne d'Arc, was also one of the earliest films ever to be released in 1895.

Artistically sculpted topiaries engage in a fight in the garden of Château Gaillard

Next stop...

CHÂTEAU GAILLARD Located 32 km (19 miles) to the south, is Les Andelys (train to Vernon, then taxi), site of the fabulous ruins of Château Gaillard (lesandelys.com/chateau-gaillard). It was designed and built in one single year, 1198, at a huge cost by Richard the Lionheart, then Duke of Normandy and King of England.

② Giverny
Monet's paradise garden

In 1883, Impressionist painter Claude Monet moved to a lovely house in the small village of Giverny. He spent much of the rest of his life painting the lily pond and gardens, which he designed to create a riot of shapes and colours. Known as the **Fondation Claude Monet**, the gardens and the house, with its delightful yellow and blue kitchen and scores of Japanese prints, have been carefully preserved as they were in the artist's lifetime. Few historic houses can match its simple beauty or popularity. Nearby, the **Musée des Impressionismes** hosts temporary expositions sometimes featuring top Impressionist works, either general collections or devoted to certain artists – many with a connection to Normandy.

The Lowdown

- 🌐 **Map reference** 4 F5
  Address 27620 (Eure). Fondation Claude Monet: 84 Rue Claude Monet; 02 32 51 28 21; *www.fondation-monet.fr*. Musée des Impressionismes: 99 Rue Claude Monet; 02 32 51 94 65; *www.museedesimpressionnismes giverny.com*
- 🚗 **Train** from Rouen or Paris to Vernon, then shuttle bus
- ℹ️ **Visitor information** 36 Rue Carnot, 27620; 02 32 54 48 05; *www.vernon-visite.org*
- 🕐 **Open** Fondation Claude Monet & Musée des Impressionismes: Apr–Oct: daily (arrive before 10am to avoid queues)
- 🍽️ **Eat and drink** *Real meal* Hôtel Baudy (*81 Rue Claude Monet, 27620; 02 32 21 10 03; Apr–Oct*), is where American and French Impressionists once stayed; kids' menu and lovely gardens open to the public. *Family treat* L'Esquisse Gourmande (*73 Bis Rue Claude Monet, 27620; 02 32 51 86 95; www.lesquissegourmande. fr*) serves delicious grilled salmon and camembert crumble.
- 🎏 **Festival** Festival de Giverny, French pop jazz and rock (Sep)

Letting off steam

Play in the gardens of **Hôtel Baudy**. Or hop on to an old fashioned train on the **CFVE** (*www.cfve.org*) for a ride through the pretty Eure valley. The ride starts in Pacy-sur-Eure,

Boats lining the jetties in Dieppe's busy marina

which is located 18 km (11 miles) southwest of Giverny. Rides are available mostly in June.

③ Dieppe
The ivory port

Named as *djepp* (deep) by the Vikings, Dieppe's port was always a prize. The town had a famous map-making school in the 15th century and sent explorers and corsairs to the New World, reminders of which appear across the town. In **Église St-Jacques**, a 16th-century frieze in the treasury depicts indigenous life in America, Africa and the Indian Ocean. Dieppe was the main ivory client in the Côte d'Ivoire: the 15th-century **Château Musée** shows a collection of sculpted ivories, ship models, maps and Impressionist paintings. Films, reconstructions and models at **L'Estran-La Cité de la Mer** explain the practical aspects of boat building, fishing, marine biology and more. It also has an aquarium of sea creatures from Dieppe's waters.

The Lowdown

- 🌐 **Map reference** 4 E3
  Address 76200 (Seine-Maritime). Église St-Jacques: Pl St-Jacques, 76200; 02 35 84 21 65. Château Musée: Rue de Chastes (on the west cliff); 02 35 06 61 99. L'Estran-La Cité de la Mer: 37 Rue de l'Asile Thomas; 02 35 06 93 20; *www.estrancitedelamer.fr*
- 🚗 **Train** from Rouen and Paris
- ℹ️ **Visitor information** Pont Jehan Ango, 76200; 02 32 14 40 60; *www.dieppetourisme.com*
- 🕐 **Open** Château Musée: daily; Oct–May: closed Tue. L'Estran-La Cité de la Mer: daily
- 🍽️ **Eat and drink** *Real meal* Le Calvados (*19 Rue Lemoyne, 76200; 02 35 84 20 11; closed Sun*) offers home-style Normandy cooking. *Family treat* La Victoire 2 (*2–4 Grande Rue du Pollet, 76200; 02 35 84 15 92*) serves excellent fresh seafood.
- 🎏 **Festival** Festival International de Cerfs-Volants, the biggest kite flying festival in the world (Sep)

Letting off steam

Head to Dieppe's beach. Or take bus 61 west to Varengeville-sur-Mer to visit the classic gardens of **Parc du Bois-des-Moutiers** (*www.bois desmoutiers.com*), designed by Sir Edwin Lutyens. It is the the only Arts and Crafts mansion outside of Britain. Go to the **Manoir d'Ango** (*www. manoirdango.fr*), home of 16th-century pirate Jean Ango.

④ Le Havre
Comeback city

Founded at the mouth of the Seine, in the 16th century by François I, the busy port of Le Havre suffered major

The exquisite lily pond at the Fondation Claude Monet, Giverny

destruction during World War II. In the 1960s, the city centre was rebuilt in concrete and glass by famous architect Auguste Perret – buildings designated as a World Heritage Site in 2005. His students designed the ship-shaped **Musée Malraux**, home to the second-best collection of Impressionist art in France, after Paris's Musée d'Orsay. Take the LER commuter train to Montvilliers to visit the **Abbaye de Montivilliers**, founded in the 7th century, ruined during the French Revolution, and now an interactive museum on the history of Normandy.

Personnages sur la plage de Trouville by Boudin, Musée Eugène Boudin

Letting off steam

Take bus 24 north to the beaches of Étretat – with walks along Normandy's most spectacular cliffs. The same bus goes to Fécamp, home to **Woody Park** (www.woody-park.com). Kids can take part in a tree-top adventure course, play treasure hunt and paintball, or go sea kayaking.

The Lowdown

- **Map reference** 3 D4
  Address 76200 (Seine-Maritime). Musée Malraux: 2 Blvd Clémenceau, 76600; 02 35 19 62 62. Abbaye de Montivilliers: Jardin de l'Abbaye, 76290; 02 35 30 96 66; www.abbaye-montivilliers.fr
- **Train** from Rouen
- **Visitor information** 186 Blvd Clemenceau, 76600; 02 32 74 04 04; www.lehavretourisme.com
- **Open** Musée Malraux: daily. Abbaye de Montivilliers: Oct–Mar: closed Mon
- **Eat and drink** Real meal Le Diplodocus (21 Rue du Maréchal Galliéni, 76600; 02 35 21 32 31; www.lediplodocus.com; closed Mon dinner, Sat lunch & Sun) serves succulent meats. Family treat L'Orchidée (41 Rue du Général Faidherbe, 76600; 02 35 21 32 42; www.restaurant-orchidee. com) prepares delicious seafood.
- **Festival** Les Z'estival, summer festival with music & theatre (Jul)

⑤ Honfleur
The perfect little harbour

The Pont de Normandie crosses the Seine estuary to Honfleur, Normandy's most engaging port. It has a tiny inner harbour lined by unique 17th-century "skyscrapers" and ringed by restaurant terraces. One of the several landmarks in town is the 15th-century church of Ste-Catherine, built entirely of wood. The **Musée Eugène Boudin** has works by the Honfleur-born pre-Impressionist artist and teacher and friend of Monet, Eugène Boudin (1824–98). The **Maisons Satie**, in the birthplace of avant-garde composer Erik Satie (1866–1925), is an off-beat "museum" that uses sound, light and modern technology to present his music in many fun, imaginative ways.

The Lowdown

- **Map reference** 3 D4
  Address 14600 (Calvados). Musée Eugène Boudin: Rue de l'Homme de Bois; 02 31 89 54 00; www.musees-honfleur.fr. Maisons Satie: 88 Rue Haute; 02 31 89 11 11; www.musees-honfleur.fr
- **Train** to Deauville or Le Havre, then bus 20
- **Visitor information** Quai Lepaulmier, 14600; 02 31 89 23 30; www.ot-honfleur.fr
- **Open** Musée Eugène Boudin: closed Tue. Maisons Satie: Wed–Mon; closed Jan–mid-Feb
- **Eat and drink** Real meal La Cidrerie (26 Pl Hamelin, 14600; 02 31 89 59 85; Oct–Apr: closed Tue & Wed) serves stuffed crêpes. Family treat La Lieutenance (12 Pl Ste-Catherine, 14600; 02 31 89 07 52; www.restaurant-honfleur. com; Wed–Sun) cooks delicious French classics.
- **Festival** Fête des Marins, parade of boats adorned with paper flowers (Jun)

Letting off steam

Honfleur's beach is safe for kids, but has dismal views of Le Havre. Take bus 20 west to the beaches in chic Deauville, the favourite of film stars, with its seaside villas or the slightly more down-to-earth Trouville-sur-Mer with the **Natur Aquarium** (www. deauville.org). At Trouville, kids aged 6 plus can learn to surf at **North Shore** (72 Rue Bains, 14360 Trouville-sur-Mer; 02 31 87 28 98).

⑥ The D-Day Beaches

Operation Overlord: the biggest invasion in history

The Normandy landings on 6 June 1944 were an undertaking that involved over a year of planning and secrecy. Supported by 5,000 ships and 13,000 aircraft, 160,000 Allied soldiers landed on this 80-km (50-mile) stretch of coast, and gained a foothold against the defences of the Germans' Atlantic Wall. Though the landings were a turning point in the battle for the western front, they were only the start of the Battle of Normandy.

Cemetery near Omaha beach

Key Sights

0 km   10

0 miles   10

① **Musée Airborne** This museum in Ste-Mère-Église honours the American 82nd and 101st Airborne Divisions who parachuted into the town on D-Day, during which Private John Steele's parachute got entangled in the church tower.

② **Omaha Beach** The Americans faced the fiercest fighting here. Rangers scaled and captured the battle-scarred Pointe du Hoc. Nearby is the huge US military cemetery.

③ **Arromanches-les-Bains** The ruins of the prefabricated "Mulberry" harbour, Port Artificiel, can be seen here. Head for the Musée du Débarquement and Arromanches 360, a circular cinema room with nine screens.

④ **Centre Juno Beach** Canadian troops landed on this beach. The museum honours all 45,000 Canadians who died in World War II.

⑤ **Mémorial Pégasus** This museum focuses on a unit of the British 6th Airborne Division, sent in by gliders to surprise the Germans and take the bridge code-named Pegasus.

⑥ **Grand Bunker-Musée du Mur-de-l'Atlantique** This tower has exhibits on the 2,000 German fortifications built by 300,000 men. It also covers some of German Field Marshall Rommel's clever but fortunately unused ideas.

⑦ **Batterie Merville** Overlooking Sword Beach, a museum evokes how this German stronghold was captured by the British 9th Battalion, the Parachute Regiment, with only 150 of the planned 750 troops.

The Lowdown

🌐 **Map reference** 3 C4
Address 14000 & 50000 (Calvados & Manche). Musée Airborne: 14 Rue Eisenhower, 50480 Ste-Mère; www.musee-airborne.com. Musée du Débarquement: Pl du 6 Juin, 14117 Arromanches-les-Bains; www.musee-debarquement.fr. Arromanches 360: Chemin de Calvaire, 14117 Arromanches-les-Bains; www.arromanches360.com. Centre Juno Beach: Voie des Français-Libres, 14470 Courseulles-sur-Mer; www.juno beach.org. Mémorial Pégasus: Ave du Major Howard, 14860 Ranville; www.memorial-pegasus.org. Grand Bunker-Musée du

Mur-de-l'Atlantique: Ave 6 Juin, 14150 Ouistreham; www.musee-grand-bunker.com. Batterie Merville: Pl du 9ème Bataillon, 14810 Merville Franceville; www.batterie-merville.com

🚌 **Bus** Verts (www.busverts.fr) links sights to both Caen (buses 1 & 3) and Bayeux (buses 70 & 74). A special daily D-Day bus runs along the coast in Jul and Aug.

ℹ️ **Visitor information** Pont St-Jean, 14400 Bayeux; 02 31 51 28 28. www.bessin-normandie.com provides information about the D-Day beaches.

🕐 **Open** Musée Airborne and Mémorial Pégasus: closed Dec & Jan. Musée du Débarquement, Arromanches 360, Centre Juno Beach and Grand Bunker-Musée du Mur-de-l'Atlantique: closed Jan. Batterie Merville: 15 Mar–15 Nov (book in advance)

💰 **Prices** Musée Airborne €22–32; under 6s free. Musée du Débarquement: €24–34. Arromanches 360: €16; under 10s free. Centre Juno Beach: €23–33; under 8s free. Mémorial Pégasus: €21–31. Grand Bunker-Musée du Mur-de-l'Atlantique €24–34; under 6s free. Batterie Merville: €20–30; under 6s free

Prices given are for a family of four

Letting off steam

Kick up sand on the Plage de Riva Bella in Ouistreham. If it rains, take bus 11 or 23 to the indoor **Ouga Park** *(www.ougapark.fr)*, located 5 minutes south of Caen, with bouncy castles, electric karts, art workshops, laser games, bowling and magic golf.

Beach huts at Riva Bella beach in Ouistreham

Eat and drink

Picnic: under €20; Snacks: €20–45; Real meal: €45–90; Family treat: over €90 (based on a family of four)

PICNIC Carrefour *(Route de Vaux-sur-Aure, 14400 Bayeux; 02 31 92 06 62)* stocks provisions for picnics on Omaha Beach.
SNACKS Café Gondrée *(12 Ave Commandant Kieffer, 14970 Bénouville; 02 31 44 62 25)*, near the Pegasus Bridge, was the first house to be liberated on D-Day. Today, it offers light snacks and hosts a small exhibition.
REAL MEAL La Sapinère *(100 Rue de la 2ème Infanterie US, 14710 St-Laurent-sur-Mer; 02 31 92 71 72; www.la-sapiniere.fr; closed Nov–early-Mar)*, surrounded by lawns, is an informal restaurant by Omaha Beach that serves *moules-frites*

👥 **Skipping the queue** A Normandie Pass *(www.normandiepass.com)*, available at the D-Day sights, offers discounts on other sights.
👆 **Guided tours** Contact the tourist office for details.
👫 **Age range** 7 plus
⏱ **Allow** At least a day
🚻 **Toilets** In the museums
🎵 **Festival** Festival d'Arromanches, a festival of classical music (Jul)

Good family value?
A fantastic and moving educational experience for children, along with fun at the beaches.

(mussels and french fries), salads, sandwiches and also excellent dessert waffles.
FAMILY TREAT Le Lion d'Or *(71 Rue St-Jean, 14400 Bayeux; 02 31 92 06 90; www.liondor-bayeux.fr; closed Mon, Tue & Sat lunch)* is a long established, kid-friendly gourmet restaurant that serves velvety chestnut soup and plaice rolled in sesame seeds.

Find out more

DIGITAL Go to *www.britannica.com/dday* and *www.army.mil/d-day/* for photos and videos of D-Day. Play a strategy game based on the event on *www.schoolshistory.org.uk/dday.htm*.
FILM Watch *The Longest Day* (1962), about Operation Overlord's build-up and D-Day from the perspective of the Allies, the Germans and the French Resistance.

The spectacular Gothic Cathédrale Notre-Dame in Bayeux

Next stop...

BAYEUX The first city to be liberated in France during World War II, Bayeux boasts the **Cathédrale Notre-Dame** *(6 Rue du Bienvenu, 14400; 02 31 92 01 85)*, but above all the Bayeux Tapestry – commissioned for the cathedral's inauguration in 1077. The 70-m (230-ft) embroidered "comic strip" tells the story of the Battle of Hastings, and is now in the **Musée de la Tapisserie** *(www.tapisserie-bayeux.fr)*. The **Musée-mémorial de la Bataille de Normandie** *(www.mairie-bayeux.fr)* exhibits memorabilia that recounts the harrowing battles after D-Day.

KIDS' CORNER

In the museums, find out...
1 The French call D-Day "Jour J". Both the initials stand for the same word. What is it?
2 How many "Mulberries" were there?
3 How did paratroopers surprise the Germans the night before the D-Day invasion?
4 When the rangers scaled Pointe du Hoc, what did they find there?
....
Answers at the bottom of the page.

FEARSOME BATTLE
The Battle of Normandy lasted until the end of August 1944, costing 425,000 Allied and German casualties. An estimated 15–20,000 French civilians were killed as well.

Napping on D-Day
In the months that led up to D-Day, the Allies' strength in the air stopped the Germans from conducting surveillance flights that would have revealed the massive build-up around Portsmouth, on the south coast of England. Some German pilots were "allowed" to fly over the easterly county of Kent and its coast, where they photographed dummy landings, inflatable tanks and planes. The Germans, who thought that the landings would happen further north around Calais, were caught napping on D-Day.

....
just inland and damaged them. bombed, but the rangers found them moved the real guns, fearing they'd be guns were fakes! The Germans had which made no noise. 4 The six field in a storm. 3 They jumped out of gliders the one for Omaha Beach was wrecked of Two, but beginning of an operation. 2 Two, but was a common military term for the Answers: 1 It stands for "day", and

⑦ Cherbourg
A Viking ship and a submarine

Set on the tip of the rugged granite Cotentin peninsula, Cherbourg has the world's largest artificial port. See it in its entirety from the lofty Fort du Roule, which now houses the **Musée de la Libération**, dedicated to the Battle of Cherbourg in 1944.

Cherbourg was a big trans-atlantic port in the 19th and 20th centuries, but has converted its massive Art Deco port of 1933 into the **Cité de la Mer**, a museum filled with good interactive exhibits on the oceans and their exploration throughout history. Visit the 11-m (36-ft) high aquarium, which is filled with over 1,000 tropical fish or explore France's first nuclear submarine *Redoutable*, the largest in the world that is open for visits. Also, have a look at the *Dreknor*, a replica of a 9th-century Viking ship at the Quai de Caligny and the botanical gardens in Parc Emmanuel Liais, where the displays of the **Musée d'Histoire Naturelle** remain as they were in 1910.

The colourful and traditional Monday market in St-Pierre-sur-Dives

Letting off steam

Take an hour-long cruise around Cherbourg's harbour aboard the *Port Liberté (02 33 78 19 29; mid-July–Aug)*, departing from either the Cité de la Mer or Pont Tournant.

⑧ Caen
A city of war and peace

Caen was a simple village in 1060 when Duke William of Normandy built the Château de Caen. Today, the château houses the **Musée de Normandie**, which displays exhibits focusing on the Gallo-Romans and Merovingians, as well as lace and cider and the **Musée des Beaux Arts** with some fine Old Master paintings, including Perugino's *Marriage of the Virgin*, French 19th-century art and temporary exhibitions. William lies buried in the **Abbaye aux Hommes**, which he built in 1067. It is attached to the Église St-Etienne. His wife Matilda lies in the more graceful **Abbaye aux Dames**, built in 1066.

Much of Caen was ruined during the Battle of Normandy in 1944. The massive multimedia **Mémorial de Caen** is one of Normandy's main sights vividly retelling the story of the D-Day campaign and other defining moments of the 20th century.

Letting off steam

Play in the Parc du Château, housed within the château's walls. It has the biggest playground in the city centre, and loads of car-free running room.

Underwater exploration vessel in the Cité de la Mer, Cherbourg

The Lowdown

🌐 **Map reference** 3 B3
Address 50100 (Manche). Musée de la Libération: Fort du Roule; 02 33 20 14 12; *www.ville-cherbourg.fr*. Cité de la Mer: Gare Maritime Transatlantique; 02 33 20 26 26; *www.citedelamer.com*. Musée d'Histoire Naturelle: 19 Rue Bonhome; 02 33 53 51 61

🚆 **Train** from Caen

ℹ **Visitor information** 2 Quai Alexandre III, 50100; 02 33 93 52 02; *www.cherbourgtourisme.fr*

🕐 **Open** Musée de la Libération & Musée d'Histoire Naturelle: Oct–Apr: Tue–Sun pm; May–Sep: Tue–Sat & Sun pm; closed Mon & Sun am. Cité de la Mer: year round (Nov: closed Mon)

🍽 **Eat and drink** *Snacks* Rapid Pizza *(31 Rue au Blé, 50100; 02 33 53 30 44)* is a good bet for pizza, salads and Ben & Jerry's ice creams. *Real meal* Les Tonnelles *(24 Rue de l'Union, 50100; 02 33 08 09 25; www.les-tonnelles.com; closed Mon dinner & Sun)* serves such things as stuffed mussels, pizzas and pastas.

🎪 **Festivals** Le Mois des Jardins, city garden tours (mid-Apr–mid-May). Festival of children's books (May)

The Lowdown

🌐 **Map reference** 3 D4
Address 14000 (Calvados). Musée de Normandie: Esplanade du Château; 02 31 30 47 60; *www.ville-caen.fr/mdn*. Musée des Beaux Arts: Esplanade du Château; 02 31 30 47 70; *www.mba.caen.fr*. Abbaye aux Hommes: Esplanade Jean-Marie Louvel; 02 31 30 42 81. Abbaye aux Dames: Pl de la Reine-Mathilde; 02 31 06 98 98; *www.abbayeauxdames.org*. Mémorial de Caen: Esplanade Général Eisenhower, 14050; 02 31 06 06 45; *www.memorial-caen.fr*

🚆 **Train** from Paris

ℹ **Visitor information** Pl St Pierre, 14000; 02 31 27 14 14; *www.tourisme.caen.fr*

🕐 **Open** Musée de Normandie: Oct–May: Wed–Mon; Jun–Sep: daily. Musée des Beaux Arts: Wed–Mon. Abbaye aux Hommes: 9:30am, 11am, 2:30pm & 4pm. Abbaye aux Dames: 2:30–4pm daily. Mémorial de Caen: Feb–Oct: daily; Nov–Dec: Tue–Sun

🍽 **Eat and drink** *Snacks* Boulangerie Paul *(14 Blvd Yves Guillou, 14000; 02 31 23 76 45)* is good for sandwiches and cakes. *Real meal* Maître Corbeau *(8 Rue Buquet, 14000; 02 31 93 93 00; www.maitre-corbeau.com; closed lunch Sat & Mon, Sun)* is a cheerful restaurant that specializes in delicious fondues and also chocolate desserts.

⑨ St-Pierre-sur-Dives

Tiny furniture and fountains

The attractive market town of St-Pierre-sur-Dives has a medieval market hall and ornate Renaissance choir stalls in an abbey church that celebrated its 1,000th birthday in 2011. Just 6 km (4 miles) south of the centre is the elegant 17th-century **Château de Vendeuvre**. It has a great collection of miniature furniture, gardens with fountains and a maze.

Letting off steam

Go for a swim in St-Pierre's outdoor pool (Rue des Sports, 14170; 02 31 20 74 99; www.otourisme.com). Take a taxi 10 km (6 miles) north to Mézidon-Canon to visit the 18th-century **Château de Canon** (tinyurl.com/3l9mx9p), with a stunning well-preserved English-French garden.

The Lowdown

◉ **Map reference** 3 D5
  Address 14170 (Calvados). Château de Vendeuvre: Route de Falaise; 02 31 40 93 83; www.vendeuvre.com

🚃 **Train** TER from Caen

ℹ **Visitor information** Rue St-Benoît, 14170; 02 31 20 97 90; www.mairie-saint-pierre-sur-dives.fr

🕓 **Open** Château de Vendeuvre: Apr–Sep: daily; Oct: Sun & hols

🍴 **Eat and drink** Snacks Le Baladin (134 Rue de Falaise, 14170; 02 31 20 39 63; closed Wed dinner & Thu) offers delicious crêpes. Real meal Auberge de la Dives (27 Blvd Collas, 14170; 02 31 20 50 50; closed Mon dinner & Tue) serves traditional Norman cuisine.

⑩ Falaise

William the Conqueror's hometown

In 1024, William the Conqueror was born in Falaise's castle, today known as the **Château Guillaume-le-Conquérant**, where his colourful life is covered in a non-stop audio-visual presentation.

The castle had to be extensively restored after the fierce battle here in August 1944: Hitler had hoped to bottle the Allies up in Normandy at the Falaise Gap, but it was the German Army that got trapped in

William's statue at the entrance to Château Guillaume-le-Conquérant

the "Cauldron of Death" between Falaise, Mortain and Argentan. On a lighter side, there is the **Musée André Lemaitre** dedicated to the artist born in Falaise in 1909; the **Musée des Automates** where 300 automatons bring Old Paris to life and the **Chapelle St-Vigor**, made into a magical work of art in the 1990s by a Japanese artist Kyoji Takubo.

Letting off steam

The castle has plenty of open space. Take a taxi west to **Pont d'Ouilly** (pontdouilly-loisirs.com) in scenic Suisse Normande to canoe on the Orne river.

The Lowdown

◉ **Map reference** 3 D5
  Address 14700 (Calvados). Château Guillaume-le-Conquérant: Rue de la Roche; 02 31 41 61 44. Musée André Lemaitre: Blvd de la Liberation; 02 31 90 02 43; www.musee-andre-lemaitre.fr. Musée des Automates: Blvd de la Liberation; 02 31 90 02 43; www.automates-avenue.fr. Chapelle St-Vigor: 14700 St-Martin-de-Mieux

🚌 **Bus** 35 from Caen

ℹ **Visitor information** Blvd de la Libération, 14700; 02 31 90 17 26; www.falaise-tourisme.com

🕓 **Open** Château Guillaume-le-Conquérant: mid-Feb–Dec: daily. Musée André Lemaitre & Musée des Automates: Apr–Sep & Dec: daily; other times Sat, Sun & French school hols. Chapelle St-Vigor: late-Jul–mid-Sep: 2:30–6pm daily closed Mon

🍴 **Eat and drink** Real meal Le Jardin (7/9 Rue du 9ème arrondissement de Paris; 02 31 90 20 74; closed Sun and Mon dinner & Wed) serves classic dishes. Family Treat La Fine Fourchette (2 Rue Georges Clemenceau, 14700; 02 31 90 08 59; closed Tue dinner & Feb) offers a gourmet treat with a kids' and vegetarian menu.

⑪ Mont-St-Michel
The rock of the Archangel

Rising like an enchanted island out of the sea and coastal plain, Mont-St-Michel is the icon of Western France, encircled by mighty ramparts and surrounded by a bay subject to the strongest tides in Europe. Founded in 708 as a small oratory, it developed into a great centre of medieval learning after monks began to build an abbey on the Mont's granite pinnacle in the early 11th century. It was used as a prison after the French Revolution until 1863; in 1969 it became a functioning abbey again.

Statue of St Michel

Key Features

Grand Rue *Miquelots* (pilgrims) were the first to travel along this road to the abbey, now lined with shops and restaurants.

Abbey church Begun in 1017, the abbey has two crypts, a Romanesque nave and a Flamboyant-Gothic choir.

The spire A gilded St Michel wields his mighty sword on top of the spire.

La Merveille Nicknamed "The Miracle", this three-storey abbey complex, built over 16 years (1211–28), is a medieval feat of engineering.

Refectory The full-length windows in the dining hall let in plenty of light without providing distracting views.

Terrace

Baie du Mont-St-Michel This bay is famous for the strongest tides in Europe, varying in height by 15 m (49 ft) in six hours.

Refectory

Cloisters

Ramparts

Entrance

Cloisters The graceful 137 double columns in the 13th-century cloister are a complete contrast to the compact walls of the abbey.

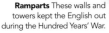

Ramparts These walls and towers kept the English out during the Hundred Years' War.

The Lowdown

🌐 **Map reference** 3 B5
Address 50170 (Manche). Abbaye de Mont-St-Michel: Mont-St-Michel; *mont-saint-michelmonumentsnationaux.fr*

🚗 **Train** from Paris, then a Keolis Emeraude bus (*www.destination-montsaintmichel.com*) that meets TGVs from Paris in Rennes or Dol-de-Bretagne. There are also two buses (No. 17) a day from St-Malo to Pontorson, coinciding with bus 6 (*www.mobi50.com*) to Mont St-Michel. A new bridge connecting the Mont to the mainland is due in 2014.

A train-bus-bike transport scheme has been set up between Granville and St-Malo called Ligne Baie (*www.lignebaie.fr*). It offers day passes and discounts.

ℹ️ **Visitor information** Blvd de l'Avancée, at the entrance to the Mont, 50170; 02 33 60 14 30; *www.ot-montsaintmichel.com*

🕐 **Open** Abbaye de Mont-St-Michel: May–Aug: 9am–7pm; Sep–Apr: 9:30am–6pm; Jul & Aug: evening visits with sound and light effects from 7–11:30pm. Ticket desks close an hour before closing time.

💶 **Prices** Day or night tours: €18–28; under 18s and EU members under 26 free. Combined day and night tickets (used the same day): €28–38

👥 **Skipping the queue** The Mont can be crowded in Jul–Aug. Pick up abbey tickets from the tourist office to avoid the queue.

🚩 **Guided tours** There are 75-min guided tours available in English and French year round within the abbey; ring ahead for timings. Multilingual audio guides are also available at an extra charge.

Prices given are for a family of four

Letting off steam

Take a taxi or drive to the nearby village of Beauvoir, 6 km (4 miles) from the Mont, to visit **Alligator Bay** (www.alligator-bay.com). A reptilian delight, this animal park has Europe's largest collection of alligators and crocodiles, as well as a dragon maze and a tortoise farm.

An iguana resting on a branch in Alligator Bay, Beauvoir

Eat and drink

Picnic: under €20; Snacks: €20–45; Real meal: €45–90; Family treat: over €90 (based on a family of four)

PICNIC Le Jardin d'Anouck (*Le Bas Pays, 50170 Beauvoir; 02 33 58 46 79*) makes up picnic baskets for adults and kids and has a free picnic area, which is a five-minute drive from the bridge.

SNACKS Crêperie La Cloche (*on the Mont; 02 33 60 15 65; year-round*) is a good stopover for sweet crêpes or savoury *galettes*, salads and ice creams.

REAL MEAL Les Pieds dans le Plat (*1 bis Pl St Gervais, 50300 Avranches; 02 33 68 31 60; www. les-pieds-dans-le-plat.fr; closed Wed & Sun dinner*), located near Le Scriptorial, is different from the restaurants on or near the Mont that rely on passing trade and tend to

🚻 **Age range** 5 or 6 plus; the abbey's steep steps and crowds can be daunting for young kids.

⏱ **Allow** At least a day

☕ **Cafés** Many on or near the Mont, but expensive

🚻 **Toilets** Inside the abbey

🎉 **Festival** Fête de St-Michel (Sep)

Good family value?

Mont-St-Michel is not only an architectural masterpiece, but many kids love it because it reminds them of Harry Potter's Hogwarts.

be pricey. It serves pork braised in cider, seafood and warm *moelleux au chocolat* (chocolate pudding).

FAMILY TREAT La Ferme Saint Michel (*Le Bas Pays, 50170 Beauvoir; 02 33 58 46 79; www.restaurant-ferme-saint-michel.com*) is a welcoming farmhouse restaurant, 2 km (1 mile) from the Mont. It specializes in traditional *agneau de pré-salé* (lamb raised on the coastal salt-marsh meadows) cooked on a wood fire; there is a kids' menu too. It also runs Le Jardin d'Annouck.

Find out more

FILM The grand finale of the film *The Elusive Pimpernel* (1950), in which David Niven played the Pimpernel, was shot in Mont-St-Michel.

Take cover

Visit **Archeoscope** (*www.au-mont-saint-michel.com*) on the Mont for a multimedia presentation on the history of the abbey. Alternatively, stop off at the **Projet Mont-Saint-Michel** (*www.projetmontsaint michel.fr*) pavilion by the causeway on the mainland to learn about the plans to return the rapidly silting bay to its original state.

Visitors looking at the scriptures in Le Scriptorial, Avranches

Next stop...

AVRANCHES Drive to the town of Avranches, 25 km (15 miles) from the Mont, to see the masterpieces produced by Mont-St-Michel's scribes in **Le Scriptorial** (*www. scriptorial.fr*). When the abbey was converted into a prison in 1791, its library, including 203 medieval manuscripts, was sent here for safekeeping. Multimedia displays show how the monks copied and illuminated the texts, in a tour guided by a virtual Titivillus, the patron demon of scribes in the Middle Ages. The hotel **Jardin des Plantes** (*10 Pl Carnot, 50300; 02 33 58 03 68*) offers the best views of the Mont.

⑫ Granville
Fashion and beach life

Like many Normandy ports, Granville has worn many hats – as a fishing, oyster and corsair (privateer) port, as well as port for the Channel Islands, before it found its more recent niche as a beach resort. In the haute ville (upper town), where successful 16th-century corsairs built their granite mansions along Rue St-Jean, the **Musée du Vieux Granville** tells the history of the town, while the **Musée d'Art Moderne Richard Anacréon** displays a collection of paintings and early 20th-century original editions of books. In lower Granville, the Villa Les Rhumbs, which was the childhood holiday home of fashion designer Christian Dior, is now the **Musée et Jardin Christian Dior**, with frequently changing exhibitions on his haute couture styles. Its garden is full of scents that inspired his perfumes.

Letting off steam

Hit Granville's beach and visit its wonder-filled **Roc des Harmonies** (www.aquarium-du-roc.com), with an aquarium, insect and butterfly

One of the nine gardens in Jardins d'Argences, near Coutances

zoo, the Palace of Minerals and an array of miniature famous buildings, as well as other objects made out of seashells.

⑬ Coutances
Gardens of rare delight

The old capital of the Cotentin peninsula, Coutances is a lively little city, in spite of being devastated in the Battle of Normandy. Miraculously, the bombs missed its architectural jewel: the **Cathédrale Notre-Dame**, a church first mentioned in 1056 and rebuilt in Gothic style in 1494, with twin towers that resemble rockets, a massive octagonal tower crowning the crossing and a splendid apse. The church has some of its original stained glass, including a window depicting the Last Judgement. The romantic **Jardin des Plantes**, bequeathed to the city in 1850, is a delight, with terraces, rare trees and a labyrinth.

Just south of Coutances, the award-winning **Jardins d'Argences** feature nine gardens surrounding a beautiful 17th-century manor.

Letting off steam

Besides playing in Coutances' gardens, zip off to the sandy beach at Agon-Coutainville, located 11 km (7 miles) northwest of the city.

The Lowdown

🌐 **Map reference** 3 B5
Address 50200 (Manche). Cathédrale Notre-Dame: 1 Rue du Puits Notre Dame; 02 33 45 00 41. Jardin des Plantes: Rue Quesnel-Morinière; 02 33 19 08 10. Jardins d'Argences: Saussey; www.jardins-argences.com

🚗 **Train** from Pontorson, Granville and Caen

ℹ️ **Visitor information** Pl Georges Leclerc, 50200; 02 33 19 08 10; www.tourisme-coutances.fr

🕐 **Open** Jardin des Plantes: daily. Jardins d'Argences: May–10 Oct: daily pm

🍴 **Eat and drink** Picnic Carrefour Market (6 Rue Planche Maurice, 50200; 02 33 19 16 16) stocks supplies for picnics. Picnic at the Jardin des Plantes. Real meal Le Don Camillo (4 Rue d'Harcourt, 50200; 02 33 45 00 67; closed Sun out of season) features an array of thin-crust pizzas and other kid-friendly Italian dishes.

⑭ Villedieu-les-Poêles
Copper pans and 20-ton bells

Inland from Granville, Villedieu-les-Poêles, "God's City of the Copper Pans", is a lovely town that, unlike many in Normandy, escaped damage during World War II. Its people have been uniquely skilled in working metals and making lace since the early Middle Ages, and it has several museums to show off this expertise. The **Musée de la Poêlerie**, dedicated to copper pans, shares a handsome medieval workshop with the **Maison de la Dentellière**, which focuses on traditional lace-making. The **Musée du Meuble Normand** has a fine collection of furniture from across

The Lowdown

🌐 **Map reference** 3 B5.
Address 50400 (Manche). Musée du Vieux Granville: 2 Rue Lecarpentier. Musée d'Art Moderne Richard Anacréon: Pl de l'Isthme; www.ville-granville. fr. Musée et Jardin Christian Dior: Prom du Plat-Gousset; www. musee-dior-granville.com

🚗 **Train** from Pontorson, Cherbourg or Argentan. **Bus** from Mont-St-Michel

ℹ️ **Visitor information** 4 Cours Jonville, 50400; 02 33 91 30 03; www.ville-granville.fr

🕐 **Open** Musée du Vieux Granville: Oct–Mar: Wed & Sat–Sun; Apr–Sep: closed Tue; closed Jan. Musée d'Art Moderne Richard Anacréon: Jun–Sep: closed Mon; mid-Feb–May & Oct–Nov: closed Mon & Tue; closed Dec–mid-Feb. Musée et Jardin Christian Dior: mid-May–late Sep: daily

🍴 **Eat and drink** Real meal Le Cosy (Rue Paul Poirier, 50400; 02 33 91 98 28; closed Sun & Mon), serves simple dishes and frites (chips). Family treat La Citadelle (34 Rue du Port, 50400; 02 33 50 34 10; www.restaurant-la-citadelle.com) offers mouth-watering fish soup and seafood platters.

Splashing in the waves on Granville beach during summer

Normandy, dating from the 15th century. But the best of all is the tour of **La Fonderie des Cloches Cornille-Havard**, a bell foundry practically unchanged since 1865 – come on a weekday to watch bellmakers at work.

Letting off steam

Go to **Piscine arc-en-ciel** (*Rue du 8 Mai, 50800; www.piscine-villedieu. com*), a covered pool. A short drive, 8 km (5 miles) west of Villedieu, is the **Parc Zoologique de Champrépus** (*zoo-champrepus.com*), devoted to preserving endangered species from around the world. There is a petting zoo and playgrounds for kids.

The Lowdown

- 🌐 **Map reference** 3 B5
  Address 50800 (Manche). Musée de la Poêlerie & Maison de la Dentellière: 25 Rue du Général Huard & Musée du Meuble Normand: 9 Rue du Reculé; *www.museesville dieu.sitew.com*. La Fonderie des Cloches Cornille-Havard: Rue du Pont-Chignon; *www.cornille-havard.com*

- 🚂 **Train** from Granville or Argentan

- ℹ️ **Visitor information** 8 Pl des Costils, 50800; 02 33 61 05 69; *www.ot-villedieu.fr*

- 🕐 **Open** Musée de la Poêlerie, Maison de la Dentellière & Musée du Meuble Normand: Apr–15 Nov: closed Mon am & Sun. La Fonderie des Cloches Cornille-Havard: mid-Feb–11 Nov: Tue–Sat; mid-Jul–Aug: daily

- 🍽️ **Eat and drink** *Real meal* La Cuisine de Léonie (*6 Pl des Chevaliers de Malte, 50800; 02 33 61 07 94*) is a good place for *galettes* (savoury pancakes) and crêpes. *Family treat* A la Table Ronde (*8 Rue des Cohues, 50800; 02 33 61 99 27*) is an eatery that serves grilled meats and seafood classics.

- 🎭 **Festival** Festival du Film d'Animation (late-Oct)

⑮ Mortain

The model for the Holy Grail

Although off the beaten track east of Mont-St-Michel, Mortain was in the centre of a vicious battle on 2 August 1944, when the German Panzers launched a counterattack against the American 30th Infantry Division. A memorial by the hilltop Chapelle St-Michel honours the 700 American soldiers who were cut off and surrounded but held out for a

A bellmaker at work in the Fonderie des Cloches Cornille, Villedieu-les-Poêles

week – only 300 survived. In the centre of town, visit the **Église de St-Evroult**, founded in 1082 and rebuilt in the 13th century. Inside the church are amusing choir stalls (lift the seats to see the figures carved beneath them in the 15th and 16th centuries) and a unique treasure – the 7th-century chrismal, a copper clad box made in Ireland, decorated with angels and 38 runes. It is said to have been made to carry the communion wafers used in Mass during the conversion of Britain and Ireland to Christianity. Some say poet Christian de Troyes had this object in mind when he wrote his Arthurian romances about the Holy Grail.

Letting off steam

Take a walk – follow the signs from Mortain to Villedieu-Sourdeval to the Cistercian Abbaye Blanche. Just ahead, in a lush setting, is the Grande Cascade – at 20 m (66 ft) it is the highest waterfall in Western France.

The Lowdown

- 🌐 **Map reference** 3 C5
  Address 50140 (Manche). Église de St-Evroult: Grande Rue; 02 33 59 19 74

- 🚂 **Train** from Granville to Vire, then bus 120

- ℹ️ **Visitor information** Rue du Bourgloplin, 50140; 02 33 59 19 74; *www.mortain-tourisme.fr*

- 🍽️ **Eat and drink** *Real meal* Au Bon Vent (*64 Rue du Rocher, 50140; 02 33 59 00 68*) offers a buffet of starters and choice of no-fuss mains. *Family treat* La Table de Saint Vital (*Pl des Arcades, 50140; 02 33 59 00 05; www.hoteldela poste.fr*) features Norman cuisine, including unusual dishes such as crème brulée au camembert.

Picnic under €20; **Snacks** €20–45; **Real meal** €45–90; **Family treat** over €90 (based on a family of four)

Where to Stay in Normandy

A summer holiday destination since the early 19th century, Normandy has an excellent range of places to stay, from stone farmhouses and grand old seafront hotels to simple rural cottages and family-oriented camp sites near the beaches.

AGENCY
Discover Normandy
www.discover-normandy.info
This agency offers over 120 self-catering properties throughout Normandy for all budgets, from cosy thatched cottages to villas with pools.

The D-Day Beaches
Map 3 D4

HOTELS
Hotel des Quatrans
17 Rue Gémaire, 14000 Caen; 02 31 86 25 57; www.hotel-des-quatrans.com
In Caen's city centre, this is a pleasant hotel convenient for visiting the Château de Caen and the D-Day Beaches. Rooms are comfortable and equipped with Wi-Fi and satellite TV. Excellent restaurant on site.
 P €

Hotel Churchill
14–16 Rue St-Jean, 14400 Bayeux; 02 31 21 31 80; www.hotel-churchill.fr
A 10-minute drive from the D-Day Beaches, rooms are cosy and come with Wi-Fi and satellite TV. Day trips to Mont-St-Michel can be organized.
€€

Hôtel d'Argouges
21 Rue St-Patrice, 14400 Bayeux; 02 31 92 88 86; www.hotel-dargouges.com
A lovely, ivy-covered 18th-century mansion with a flower-filled garden,

Hotel d'Argouges in Bayeux, near the D-Day Beaches

it offers bedrooms with mod cons such as Wi-Fi and satellite TV. It also has two beautiful apartments to rent.
P €€€

CAMPING
Camping Port'land
Chemin du Castel, 14520 Port en Bessin Huppain; 02 31 51 07 06; www.camping-portland.com
Located next to the D-Day Beaches, this camp ground has simple pitches and luxurious three-bedroom mobile homes. Games, sport grounds and organized activities for ages 5–12.
P €–€€

Un Lit au Pré
52800 Louvières; 01 41 31 08 00; www.unlitaupre.fr
This organization offers an old-fashioned and authentic farmstay experience, for a weekend or a week in luxury tents on select farms. This includes La Ferme de la Folivraie, an organic dairy farm by Omaha Beach.
P €€

Honfleur
Map 3 D4

CAMPING
La Briquerie
14600 Equemauville; 02 31 89 28 32; www.campinglabriquerie.com
Located just south of Honfleur and its beaches, this well-equipped camp site has mobile homes and chalets to rent plus mini-golf, bouncy castle and a games room. Free Wi-Fi.
P €

Mont-St-Michel
Map 3 B5

HOTELS
Le Relais du Roy
Route du Mont-St-Michel, 50170; 02 33 60 14 25; www.le-relais-du-roy.com
Just opposite Mont-St-Michel on the mainland, this cheerful hotel boasts 15th-century fireplaces in its public rooms. The pretty pastel guest rooms are Wi-Fi-equipped. Good restaurant; offers a kids' menu.
P €€

Auberge St-Pierre
Grande Rue, 50170; 02 33 60 14 03; www.auberge-saint-pierre.fr
This handsome stone building on the mont itself makes for a superb base to visit the abbey in the morning, before the crowds arrive. There is a restaurant and a private terrace; baby kits, cots and highchairs available.
€€€

CAMPING
Camping Haliotis
Map 3 B6
Chemin des Soupirs, 50170 Pontorson; 02 33 68 11 59; tinyurl.com/3owj6cn
This attractive camp site, 10 km (6 miles) from Mont-St-Michel, has spacious pitches and three-bedroom mobile homes. Playgrounds on site.
P €

The dining room in Auberge St-Pierre, Mont-St-Michel

Rouen
Map 4 E4

HOTEL
Hotel Ermitage Bouquet
58 Rue Bouquet, 76000; 02 32 12 30 40; www.hotel-ermitagebouquet.com
A 10-minute walk from the historic city centre, this modernized 19th-century hotel has rooms that come with flat-screen TVs and free Wi-Fi. Helpful English-speaking staff; baby cots and highchairs available.
P €€

Price Guide
The following price ranges are based on one night's accommodation in high season for a family of four, inclusive of service charges and any additional taxes.
€ Under €100 €€ €100–200 €€€ over €200

Brittany

Stretching far into the Atlantic, Brittany's jagged coastline is an exciting mix of coves, islets and some of France's prettiest beaches. The region's Celtic culture, music and language, as well as its mighty megalithic mounuments, lend a mystic allure, while its atmospheric ports and Brest's great Océanopolis aquarium tell of its close links to the sea.

Below *View over the beach from the ramparts of St-Malo*

Océanopolis, Brest
p162

Rennes
p158

Standing Stones
of Carnac
p166

① Rennes
Britanny's young and vibrant capital

Although named after the local Celtic tribe, Rennes only started making a name for itself in 1356–7, when the great Breton knight Bertrand du Guesclin defended it from the English in the Hundred Years' War. Made the capital of Brittany in 1551, when the region became part of France, Rennes is one of the country's fastest-growing cities, with 60,000 university students, the Champs Libres cultural centre, a modern Métro and a lively calendar of music events.

Half-timbered house, Rennes

Key Sights

Champs Libres The complex houses the Musée de Bretagne, which covers Brittany's ancient and modern history, and L'Espace des Sciences, Rennes' high-tech science museum that has Merlin's laboratory, a 3D Planetarium and other exhibits.

Parlement de Bretagne The 17th-century regional parliament is a fine example of French Classical style, its Grand Chamber oozing splendour.

Hôtel de Ville Built in 1720 by Jacques Gabriel, the town hall has a distinct bulb-topped belfry, an elaborate grand stair and a wedding hall.

Musée des Beaux Arts
Objects from ancient Egypt share space with paintings by Veronese, the Pont-Aven School and Picasso.

Cathédrale St-Pierre Gradually rebuilt after its Gothic façade collapsed in 1490, this cathedral has a beautiful 16th-century altarpiece of the Nativity.

Musée des Beaux Arts 500 m (450 yards)

Champs Libres, 900 m (800 yards)

Timber-framed houses The house at No. 22 Rue du Chapitre has some sculpted carvings from 1580.

Place des Lices Knights once jousted in the city's most picturesque square, lined with 17th-century houses. On Saturdays it hosts one of the largest markets in France.

The Lowdown

 Map reference 7 B1
Address 35000 (Ille-et-Vilaine). Musée des Beaux Arts: 20 Quai Emile Zola; www.mbar.org. Cathédrale St-Pierre: Rue de la Monnaie; 02 99 78 48 80. Musée de Bretagne & L'Espace des Sciences: 10 Cours des Alliés; www.musee-bretagne.fr. Parlement de Bretagne: Rue Nationale; 02 99 67 11 66

🚆 **Train** from Paris

ℹ️ **Visitor information** 11 Rue St-Yves, 35000; 02 99 67 11 11; www.tourisme-rennes.com

🕐 **Open** Musée des Beaux Arts: 10am–6pm Tue, 10am–noon & 2–6pm Wed–Sun, closed hols. Musée de Bretagne & L'Espace des Sciences: Sep–Jun: noon–9pm Tue, noon–7pm Wed–Fri and 2–7pm Sat & Sun; Jul–Aug: 1–7pm Tue–Fri, 2–7pm Sat & Sun; closed hols. Parlement de Bretagne: book a guided tour

💶 **Prices** Musée des Beaux Arts: €14–24; under 18s free. Musée de Bretagne & L'Espace des Sciences: €28–38; under 8s free. Parlement de Bretagne: €22–33; under 7s free

👪 **Skipping the queue** Rennes Metropole City Pass – check tourist office website for details

🚩 **Guided tours** Reserve on the tourist office website.

👫 **Age range** 5 plus

👨‍👦 **Activities** See Rennes from the Canal d'Ille-et-Rance and the Vilaine river on an electric canal boat (www.urbavag.com).

⏱️ **Allow** A day

Good family value?
Rennes can be fun, but the place has much more to offer teenagers than younger kids.

Letting off steam

Kids can splash around in the indoor pool at the **Jardin St-Georges** (*2 Rue Gambetta, 35000*). The Parc du Thabor, east of the Parlement de Bretagne, is the city's largest park, with botanical gardens, caves and a duck-filled lake.

Scrumptious fresh oysters served with lemon wedges at a restaurant in Rennes

Eat and drink

Picnic: under €20; Snacks: €20–45; Real meal: €45–90; Family treat: over €90 (based on a family of four)

PICNIC Halles Martenot (*Pl des Lices, 35200*) is a good place to pick up supplies. Picnic at the Jardin St-Georges by the Palais St-Georges on Rue Gambetta.
SNACKS Miam & Caetera (*5 Pl Bretagne, 35200; 02 99 30 46 43; closed Sun*) offers delicious gourmet sandwiches and soups made with organic ingredients, as well as other goodies to eat in or take away.
REAL MEAL Le Comptoir des Halles (*17 Rue Jules Simon, 35200; 02 99 78 20 07; www.lecomptoir deshalles.com*) is an affordable seafood restaurant that also serves meat dishes. It has a kids' menu.
FAMILY TREAT La Fontaine aux Perles (*96 Rue de la Poterie, 35200; 02 99 53 90 90; www.lafontaineaux perles.com; closed Sun dinner & Mon*) is Rennes' gourmet temple

with a lovely wooded garden. Dishes such as seafood risotto and a fillet of beef with *cèpes* (wild mushrooms) are available; children are welcome.

Shopping

Visit **Flic en Flac** (*19 Rue Penhoët, 35000; 02 99 79 30 49*), which is full of toys. **Durand** (*5 Quai Chateaubriand, 35000; 02 99 78 10 00; www.durandchocolatier.fr*) makes Rennes' top chocolates. In **Même Pas Peur du Loup** (*49 Rue Vasselot, 35000; 02 99 78 39 75; www.memepaspeurduloup.fr*), there are toys, accessories, angel wings and princess dresses.

Find out more

DIGITAL There is an excellent, easy-to-understand online account of the Hundred Years' War at *www. theotherside.co.uk/tm-heritage/ background/100yearswar.htm*. The website chronicles a detailed timeline of the various wars fought between the English and the French.

Next stop...

LA ROCHE-AUX-FÉES Head 32 km (20 miles) south to La Roche-aux-Fées (*www.cc-rocheauxfees.fr*), one of the best preserved and biggest passage graves in France. According to legend, it was erected by fairies in one night to prove their existence; according to archaeologists, it dates from around 3,000 BC. It measures 20 m (64 ft) and is tall enough to walk through; the stones were transported from the Theil-de-Bretagne forest, 4 km (2 miles) away from La Roche-aux-Fées. The heaviest stone weighs 45 tons (50 tonnes). On the winter solstice (21 December), the first rays of the sun illuminate the entrance.

The prehistoric stone tombs of La Roche-aux-Fées, Esse

② Forêt de Brocéliande

The Lady of the Lake's realm

The Brocéliande, the last remnant of Brittany's primeval forest, is steeped in Arthurian legends. Start at Paimpont, where the visitor centre provides free maps of places associated with Arthur, Merlin and the Knights of the Round Table, as well as guides to walks. To the north, near Concoret, is the lakeside **Château de Comper**, where the Lady of the Lake is said to have given Arthur his sword, Excalibur. Today, the castle hosts the Centre de l'Imaginaire Arthurien, presenting exhibitions on the Arthurian legends.

At the village of Tréhorenteuc, 11 km (7 miles) southwest of Concoret, the *Chapelle du Graal* ("Chapel of the Grail") is renowned for its mix of Christian and pagan symbolism; it is near the beginning of a 4-km (3-mile) trail into the *Val-sans-Retour* (Valley of No Return – pick up a map at the Tréhorenteuc tourist office) where Morgan le Fay's spell trapped faithless knights. A map points to sights in Brocéliande – a 1,000-year-old oak tree called the Chêne à Guillotin and a beautiful spring, the Fontaine de Barenton

Rushing streams running through the Forêt de Brocéliande

in the hamlet of La Folle-Pensée where Merlin the magician left a spell to cure madness.

Letting off steam

Head to the **Jardins de Brocéliande** (*www.jardinsdebroceliande.fr*; early-Apr–late-Oct), 26 km (16 miles) east of Paimpont. It offers a wide range of family activities and games, including some based on Arthurian legends.

③ Dinan

Walls and a hero's heart

Walled Dinan is one of Brittany's prettiest towns, where cobbled streets lined with timbered houses are still defended by an impressive château of 1380, now the **Musée du Château**, the local history museum. It was the hometown of Bertrand du Guesclin, the "Eagle of Brittany" who in 1357 defeated Englishman Thomas de Cantorbery in combat; his statue in the Place du Guesclin marks the spot. Although Bertrand du Guesclin was buried with the kings of France in St-Denis in Paris, his heart is in the 12th-century Romanesque church of St-Sauveur, which has some curiously

carved capitals. Dinan's landmark is its 15th-century Tour de l'Horloge (clocktower). The **Musée du Rail** has a collection of model trains and the **Musée de la Veilleuse Théière** displays over 700 teapots from the 17th and 18th centuries.

Letting off steam

Run around **Jardin du Val Cocherel** (*02 96 87 69 76*) with its playground and picnic tables or take a cruise down the Rance river on the *Jaman IV* (*www.vedettejamaniv.com*).

A medieval bridge over the Rance river in old Dinan

Above Dinghy-sailing off the beaches of St-Malo
Below One of old Dinan's winding cobbled streets

④ St-Malo
The city of corsairs

Sheltered on its islet, picturesque St-Malo has a history filled with adventure, corsairs and explorers. At the entrance to the old city, the **Musée d'Histoire de St-Malo**, housed in the Château des Ducs de Bretagne, displays paintings, astrolabes, ships' models, scrimshaw, maps and other maritime artefacts. The **Musée du Long Cours Cap-**Hornier, inside the 30-m (100-ft) Tour Solidor, in the southern quarter of St-Servan, commemorates the history of sailing ships that rounded the dangerous Cape Horn in South America. The **Demeure de Corsaire**, one of the few mansions that escaped damage by Allied bombs in the World War II, was built by François-Auguste Magon, an 18th-century privateer and director of the French East India Company. The 12th-century Cathédrale St-Vincent had to be rebuilt after the war. A mosaic on the floor of the nave marks the spot where Jacques Cartier knelt to be blessed before setting off to claim Canada for France in 1534.

After his third and final voyage, Cartier retired to the Manoir de Limoëlou, located outside St-Malo on the Cancale Road. Today, it is known as the **Musée Jacques Cartier**. Older kids may enjoy here.

Letting off steam
St-Malo has a number of gorgeous beaches. The most sheltered is the Plage du Môle.

The Lowdown

Map reference 3 A5
Address 35400 (Ille-et-Vilaine). Musée d'Histoire de St-Malo: Pl Chateaubriand; www.ville-saint-malo.fr. Musée du Long Cours Cap-Hornier: Rue du Dick; www.ville-saint-malo.fr. Demeure de Corsaire: 5 Rue d'Asfeld; www.demeure-de-corsaire.com. Musée Jacques Cartier: Rue David MacDonald Stewart; 02 99 40 97 73; musee-jacques-cartier.com

Train from Rennes

Visitor information Esplanade St-Vincent, 35400; 08 25 13 52 00, www.saint-malo-tourisme.com

Open Musée d'Histoire de St-Malo & Musée du Long-Cours Cap-Hornier: Apr–Sep: daily; Oct–Mar: closed Mon. Demeure du Corsaire: Tue–Sun; closed Dec & Jan (guided tours during school hols). Musée Jacques Cartier: Jul–Aug: daily; Sep–Jun: closed Sun

Eat and drink *Real meal* Crêperie Margaux (*3 Pl Marché aux Légumes, 35400; 02 99 20 26 02; www.creperie-margaux.com; closed Jan*) serves crêpes and salads. *Family treat* Restaurant Gilles (*2 Rue de la Pie Qui Boit, 35400; 02 99 40 97 25; www.restaurant-gilles-saint-malo.com; closed Wed & Thu*) is a reliable place for seafood and meat dishes.

Festival Route du Rock, music festival (Feb & Aug)

Picnic under €20; **Snacks** €20–45; **Real meal** €45–90; **Family treat** €90 or more (based on a family of four)

⑤ Océanopolis, Brest
Shuffling penguins and dancing jellyfish

The city of Brest has always been closely linked to the ocean. A military port since the 17th century, it was flattened in a World War II siege but has now developed into an important centre for sea and polar research. This is reflected in its top attraction Océanopolis, a magnificent ocean discovery park housed in a futuristic complex. An amazing 10,000 marine animals belonging to 1,000 species live in aquariums arranged in different pavilions, each with its own climate.

Pavillon Biodiversité, Océanopolis

Key Features

① Aquarium des Méduses
This huge cylindrical aquarium contains *aurelia aurita* jellyfish that seem to dance a ballet in the current. Nearby tanks contain baby jellyfish polyps.

② Flaque de Démonstration
In an area that resembles a marine lab, visitors are invited to touch the scallops, starfish and sea urchins, or examine undersea flora and fauna through microscopes.

③ Serre Tropical Exotic hot weather trees, ferns and orchids collected in Guadaloupe make up this luxuriant Caribbean forest, with an aquarium full of fish from the Amazon.

④ Mur de Coraux Vivants
This tremendous 13-m (42-ft) tank evokes the world of Australia's Great Barrier Reef and the Indonesian archipelago, with 60 different colourful hard and soft corals.

⑤ Bassin des Requins
This aquarium re-creates a Polynesian atoll, populated by four kinds of shark and many other fish. A glass-walled diving platform allows visitors to descend into their midst.

⑥ La Manchotière King, Gentoo and Rockhopper penguins make up what is Europe's biggest penguin colony, frolicking in a sub-Arctic wonderland of water, snow and cliffs.

The Lowdown

🌐 **Map reference** 2 E3
Address 29200 (Finistère). Port de Plaisance du Moulin Blanc; 02 98 34 40 40; www.oceanopolis.com

🚗 **Train** from Rennes to Brest, then bus 15

ℹ **Visitor information** 8 Ave Georges Clemenceau, 29200; 02 98 44 24 96; www.brest-metropole-tourisme.fr

🕓 **Open** mid-Jan–mid-Apr & late-Aug–Sep: 10am–5pm Tue–Sun; mid-Apr–mid-Jul: 10am–6pm daily; mid-Jul–late-Aug: 9am–7pm daily; Oct–Dec: 10am–5pm

Tue–Sun; school hols: 10am–6pm; closed 25 Dec & 1–18 Jan. Last admn: 1 hour before closing

💶 **Prices** €56–66; under-3s free. There are discounts for families with three or more children.

👫 **Skipping the queue** Buy tickets online at the Brest tourist office or from any large FNAC, Géant Casino, Carrefour, Auchan, Leclerc or Virgin with a France Billets or Ticketnet counter. Arrive early to beat summer crowds.

👫 **Age range** All ages

👫 **Activities** Save used tickets for discounts on boat tours.

⏱ **Allow** 4–5 hours

☕ **Café** Inside Océanopolis

🚻 **Toilets** In every pavilion

🎭 **Festivals** Jour de la St-Patrick, with Breton and Irish musicians in Brest (Mar). Les Jeudis du Port, huge Thursday night street parties along the Quai de la Douane (mid-Jul & Aug)

Good family value?
A fascinating and educational day out for people of all ages filled with hands-on activities that should keep even the youngest tot amused.

Letting off steam

Have a swim at the Plage du Moulin-Blanc, a big sandy beach within walking distance of Océanopolis. Head north to Milizac, 13 km (8 miles) from Brest, to **La Récré des Trois Cures** (www.larecredes3cures.fr), with rides, a petting zoo, pirate ship and in summer, a water park to splash in.

Oscar with Ernie and Bernie in a still from the animated movie Shark Tale

Eat and drink

Picnic: under €20; Snacks: €20–45; Real meal: €45–90; Family treat: over €90 (based on a family of four)

PICNIC St-Louis (*Rue des Halles St-Louis, 29200*) and **St-Martin** (*4 Rue Massillon, 29200*) are covered markets in central Brest, great for picking up picnic supplies. Océanopolis has both an outdoor picnic area and playground, as well as a heated indoor picnic area.
SNACKS Atlantic Express, a self-service restaurant, and **Atoll** (*both on site*) offer ice creams, pastries, sandwiches and drinks to either eat in or take away. **Tour du Monde** (*Port de Plaisance du Moulin Blanc, 29200; www.tourdum.fr*) serves *moules et frites* (mussels and chips).
REAL MEAL Brasserie Vent d'Ouest (*on site*) serves a choice of seafood menus, including *moules marinières* (mussels with garlic and white wine) and a kids' menu.
FAMILY TREAT L'Imaginaire (*23 Rue Fautras, 29200; 02 98 43 30 13; www. imaginaire-restaurant.blogspot.com; closed Sun dinner, Wed dinner & Mon*) combines surprising ingredients to great acclaim; kids' menus too.

Shopping

Océanopolis has two boutiques; Les Comptoirs de Océanopolis and Le Monde de Jonas, which are full of fun and educational maritime gifts, books, toys and DVDs. Many locals do their Christmas shopping here.

Find out more

DIGITAL Play the new Facebook game Oceanopolis – *apps.facebook. com/oceanopolis/* – in which players have to survive on an island.
FILM Watch *Finding Nemo* (2003), the adventures of a clown fish, *Shark Tale* (2004) or *Happy Feet* (2006) and *Happy Feet 2* (2011), about a tap-dancing penguin.

Take cover

Visit the **Château de Brest** located near the Pont de Recouvrance. It occupies the same spot as a Roman fortress, first built to defend against barbarian attacks around AD 260. It has been refortified since, lastly by Louis XIV's great military engineer Vauban, who did a good job, as it was one of the few buildings in Brest to survive the bombs in 1945. Part of it now houses the **Musée de la Marine** (*www.musee-marine.fr*) dedicated to the history of the French Navy, with beautiful model ships, paintings and sculptures.

Phare du Créac'h, Île d'Ouessant's impressive lighthouse

Next stop...

ÎLE D'OUESSANT Make an unforgettable voyage to France's westernmost territory, but not without a return ticket and hotel reservations for overnight stays. Two and a half hours from Brest by boat (*www.pennarbed.fr*), this UNESCO biosphere reserve is home to birds and miniature sheep. Shuttles link the port to Lampaul, the Île d'Ouessant's capital. Enjoy violently beautiful cliffs, rocks and waves at the Pointe de Pern and visit the **Phare du Créac'h**, France's most powerful lighthouse and its adjacent museum.

⑥ Roscoff and the Pays du Léon

Pink onions and artichokes

Roscoff is the port of the Pays du Léon, a region blessed with such a warm micro-climate that it grows most of France's special pink onions, artichokes and cauliflowers. The **Maison des Johnnies et de l'Oignon Rosé** commemorates and explains the history of the pink Roscoff onion. Located high on a granite belvedere by the sea, the **Jardin Exotique de Roscoff** is filled with 3,500 colourful plants, mainly from the southern

The towering roofs and chimneys of the Château de Kerjean, St-Vougay

hemisphere. The town's charming historic centre is dominated by the granite **Église Notre-Dame-de-Croaz-Batz**, decorated with ships, cannons, dragons and mermaids in high relief. Its Renaissance belltower is unusual; some say it resembles a giant cactus.

Letting off steam

Head to the playground at the Quai d'Auxerre or take a 15-minute boat ride to the car-free Île de Batz. Explore its sandy beaches and the charming **Jardin Georges Delaselle** (www.jardin-georgesdelaselle.fr) planted in 1897. Drive or take a taxi to the village of St-Vougay, 21 km (13 miles) southwest of Roscoff, to the 16th-century **Château de Kerjean** (www.cdp29.fr/kerjeanle chateauenbref.html), with gardens and a treasure hunt.

⑦ Paimpol

A steam train by the sea

Paimpol is a pretty port where medieval pilgrims from Ireland, Cornwall and Scotland landed to begin the 1,520-km (946-mile)

walk to the shrine of Santiago de Compostela in northwest Spain. In those days, they were received at **L'Abbaye Maritime de Beauport**, founded in 1202; although partly ruined, the abbey is set in a large park on a wild stretch of the coast. In town, the **Musée de la Mer** recalls how local cod fishermen spent six months of the year in Iceland. Also pay a visit to the **Musée du Costume Breton**, which displays the local costumes and elaborate coifs.

From May to early September, take a ride on La Vapeur du Trieux, a steam train from Paimpol to Pontrieux. On Saturdays in July and August, there is a magician on board.

Letting off steam

Take a coastal walk along the GR34 towards Ploubazlanec. The coast west of Paimpol, known as Côte de Granit Rose, has fabulous beaches.

Visitors strolling in the gardens of L'Abbaye Maritime de Beauport

The Lowdown

🌐 **Map reference** 2 F2
Address 29680 (Finistère). Maison des Johnnies et de l'Oignon Rosé: 48 Rue Brizeux, 28680; 02 98 61 25 48. Jardin Exotique de Roscoff: Roc'h Hievec, 29682; 02 98 61 29 19; www.jardinexotiqueroscoff.com. Église Notre-Dame-de-Croaz-Batz: 10 Rue Albert de Mun, 29680

🚗 **Train** from Paris to Morlaix, then bus or local train

ℹ️ **Visitor information** Quai d'Auxerre, 29680; 02 98 61 12 13; www.roscoff-tourisme.com

🕐 **Open** Maison des Johnnies et de l'Oignon Rosé: mid-Jun–mid-Sep: 11am, 3pm & 5pm; mid-Sep–mid-Jun: 3pm Mon, Tue, Thu & Fri. Jardin Exotique de Roscoff: Mar–Nov: daily (Mar & Nov: pm)

☕ **Eat and drink** *Real meal* La Moussaillonne (38 Rue Amiral Réveillère, 29680; 02 98 69 70 50 www.lamoussaillonne.com; closed Mon) serves crêpes and pizza. *Family treat* L'Écume des Jours (Quai d'Auxerre, 29680; 02 98 69 70 50) offers some of Roscoff's best seafood and meat dishes.

🎪 **Festival** Festival Place aux Mômes, child-oriented events every Wed evening (Jul–Aug)

Artichokes and other fresh produce in the local market, Roscoff

Prices given are for a family of four

The Lowdown

🌐 **Map reference** 2 G2
Address 22500 (Côtes-d'Armour). L'Abbaye Maritime de Beauport: Chemin de l'Abbaye; 02 96 55 18 58; www.abbaye-beauport.com. Musée de la Mer: Rue de Labenne; www.museemerpaimpol.com. Musée du Costume Breton: Rue Raymond Pellier; 02 96 22 02 19

🚗 **Train** from Brest or Rennes to St-Brieuc, then bus to Paimpol. TER from Guingamp to Paimpol

ℹ️ **Visitor information** Pl de la République, 22500; 02 96 20 83 16; www.paimpol-goelo.com

🕐 **Open** L'Abbaye Maritime de Beauport: daily. Musée de la Mer: mid-Apr–mid-Jun & 1–15 Sep: daily pm; mid-Jun–Aug: daily. Musée du Costume Breton: early-Jul–early-Sep: Tue–Sun

☕ **Eat and drink** *Snacks* La Fournée Gallien Gérard (2 Ave Géneralé de Gaulle, 22500; 02 96 20 84 25; closed Mon) is a good place to pick up sandwiches, ice creams and pastries for a picnic. *Real meal* Restaurant du Port (Quai Morand, 22500; www.paimpol-restaurant-du-port.com) has a terrace to watch the boats while feasting on seafood.

One of the pink-sand beaches of the Côte de Granit Rose, Paimpol

Paimpol's La Tossen beach has lifeguards in season. Kids aged 4 plus can have their first sailing lesson at the **Base de Poulafret** *(www.pole-nautique-paimpol.com)*.

⑧ Douarnenez
The kingdom of sardines

South of Brest, the bustling sardine port of Douarnenez is home to the excellent **Port-Musée**. Installed in a former sardine cannery, the museum is dedicated to sailing traditions throughout the world, with a collection of boats to explore the water at Port-Rhu. Find out more about sardines along the Chemin de la Sardine, a walk dotted with French and English plaques on the fishery's history, and at **Penn Sardin**, a specialist sardine shop full of fishy memorabilia. Douarnenez is also famous for *kouign amann*, a buttery flaky cake. Watch them being made at the **Biscuiterie de Douarnenez**.

Letting off steam

Hire a taxi or a private car to explore the beaches – the Plage des Dames and Plage des Sables Blancs in town, or take the pretty walk to the Site

Men building a boat using traditional methods, Port-Musée, Douarnenez

Naturel des Plomarc'h with a play area. Drive west to the Presqu'île de Crozon where kids of all ages can ride on donkeys on coastal paths from the **Asinerie de Kéraël** donkey stable *(www.oceane-crozon.net)* in Lanvéoc. Get lost in a giant wooden maze in Crozon's **Peninsula Le Labyrinthe** *(peninsulabyrinthe.com)*.

The Lowdown

- 🌐 **Map reference** 2 F3
  Address 29100 (Finistère). Port-Musée: Pl de l'Enfer; 02 98 92 65 20; www.port-musee.org. Penn Sardin: 7 Rue Le Breton; pennsardin.com. Biscuiterie de Douarnenez: 93 Ave de la Gare; 02 98 74 39 44

- 🚃 **Train** from Rennes and Vannes to Quimper, then bus

- ℹ **Visitor information** 1 Rue du Docteur Mével, 29172; www.douarnenez-tourisme.com

- 🕐 **Open** Port-Musée: Feb, Oct & school hols: Tue–Sun; Jul & Aug: daily. Penn Sardin: closed Tue & Sun. Biscuiterie de Douarnenez: 15 Jun–15 Sep: Wed & Fri

- 🍴 **Eat and drink** *Real meal* Au Régal *(25 Rue des Professeurs Curie, 29100; 02 98 75 53 93; Tue–Sun & school hols)* serves crêpes, soups and salads. *Family treat* Le Clos de Vallombreuse *(7 Rue d'Estienne d'Orves, 29100; 02 98 92 84 98; www.closvallombreuse.com)* serves creative cuisine with an excellent wine list. There is a petit gourmet menu for kids.

- 🎉 **Festivals** Carnaval des Gras, the weekend before Mardi Gras (Mar). Grande Fête des Bateaux, a huge gathering of boats, music and fun, once every two years (Jul). Festival du Cinéma (Aug)

The city that drowned

King Gradlon of Cournouaille built a beautiful city for his daughter Dahut in the bay of Douarnenez. Called Ys, the city had a gate, which could only be opened for ships at low tide. But Dahut fell in love with a handsome man who was a devil in disguise. He asked her to steal the key of the gates from Gradlon. She did at high tide, and the waves engulfed Ys. They say bells of Ys can still be heard on a quiet night.

Brittany's "Johnnies"

In Roscoff in the 1820s, a local had the idea of weaving his pink onions into plaits and taking them to England to sell. By the 1930s there were over 1,000 bicycle-riding onion sellers in England. They became known as "Onion Johnnies" because so many Bretons are named Jean, French for John.

Picnic under €20 **Snacks** €20–45 **Real meal** €45–90 **Family treat** over €90 (based on a family of four)

⑨ Standing Stones of Carnac
Obelix's playground

Situated on the Gulf of Morbihan, Carnac is France's Stonehenge, with the longest alignments of standing stones (menhirs) anywhere. There are some 3,000 in all, arranged in such straight lines people thought they were Roman legions turned into stone by Merlin the magician. Erected before Merlin or Obelix, between 5,000 and 3,000 BC, these World Heritage alignments make up only part of a vast concentration of megalithic sites, near some of Brittany's prettiest beaches.

Table des Marchand

Key Sights

③ Quadrilatère du Manio This rectangle of stones once surrounded a tumulus (burial mound). Nearby stands the 6-m (20-ft) Géant de Manio, Carnac's tallest menhir.

Erdeven
① Alignements de Kerzerho
Plouharnel
Quadrilatère du Manio ③
Kermario ④ Kerlescan
Saint-Pierre-Quiberon
Musée de Préhistoire ②
Carnac
Carnac-Plage
Alignements de Carnac
La Trinité-sur-Mer
St-Philibert
Larmor-Baden
Gavrinis ⑥
Mégaliths de Locmariaquer ⑤
Locmariaquer
Arzon
Petit-Mont ⑦

0 km   2
0 miles   2

⑤ Mégalithes de Locmariaquer The Menhir d'Er Grah, at 21 m (68 ft), is the largest Neolithic monolith in Morbihan. Nearby is a tumulus and the Table des Marchand (Merchants' Table) dolmen and cairn.

⑥ Gavrinis This is an islet with a cairn in which 23 of the 29 slabs lining its 14-m (46-ft) passage into a small burial chamber are decorated with swirling engravings resembling giant fingerprints.

⑦ Petit-Mont This 36 m (118 ft) cairn was built over a long period in concentric levels.

① Alignements de Kerzerho These alignments consist of 1,100 stones, running in ten rows, with the Géant de Kerzerho closing the west end.

② Musée de Préhistoire One of the largest collections of prehistoric finds, this museum's pottery and engravings trace the evolution of Neolithic construction and art.

④ Alignements de Carnac The menhirs, ranging in height from 0.6 m (2 ft) to 4 m (13 ft), are divided into Alignments de Ménac, Kermario and Kerlescan.

The Lowdown

🌐 **Map reference** 2 G4
Address 56342 (Morbihan). Alignements de Kerzerho: D781, en route to Erdevan. Musée de Préhistoire: 10 Pl de la Chapelle, 56342 Carnac; www.museede carnac.com. Alignements de Carnac: Maison des Mégalithes (interpretive centre), 56342 Le Ménec; www.carnac.monuments-nationaux.fr. Mégalithes de Locmariaquer: Route de Kerlogonan, 56740 Locmariaquer; 02 97 57 37 59. Gavrinis: Larmor-Baden dock, 56432; 02 97 57 19 38. Petit-Mont: 56432 Arzon; 06 03 95 90 78

🚗 **Train** from Rennes to Auray, then TIM bus 1 to Carnac. To go to Locmariaquer, change from TIM

bus 1 to 1 bis at the Chat Noir stop in St-Philibert. For Gavrinis, take TIM bus 1 to Auray, then bus 6 to Larmor-Baden, then boat. For Petit-Mont, take bus 7 from Vannes to Arzon, then walk

ℹ️ **Visitor information** 74 Ave des Druides, Carnac-Plage, 56432; 02 97 52 13 52; www.ot-carnac.fr. For the megalithic sites, see tinyurl.com/3bwsj3n

🕐 **Open** Alignements de Kerzerho: year round. Musée de Préhistoire: Apr–Jun & Sep: 10am–12:30pm & 2–6pm (Oct–Mar: till 5pm) Wed–Mon; Jul & Aug: 10am–6pm daily; closed most of Jan. Alignements de Carnac: May & Jun: 9am–6pm; Jul–Aug: 9am–7:30pm; Sep–Apr: 10–5pm. Petit-

Mont: Mar–Jun & Sep: 2:30–6:30pm: Thu–Tue; Jul–Aug: 11am–6:30pm: daily. Mégalithes de Locmariaquer: May–Jun: 10am–6pm (Jul–Aug: till 7pm), Sep–Apr: 10am–12:30pm & 2–5:15pm. Gavrinis: Apr–May: 2–6pm Mon–Fri, 10am–noon & 2–6pm Sat, Sun & hols; Jun–Sep: 10am–noon & 2–6pm daily; Oct: 2–6pm Wed–Mon (book ahead)

💶 **Prices** Alignements de Carnac: €12–22; under 18s free. Musée de Préhistoire: €15–25. Petit-Mont: €18–28; under 8s free. Mégalithes de Locmariaquer: €17–27; under 18s free. Gavrinis: €28–38 (boat trip & guided tour)

👫 **Skipping the queue** Pick up a Megalithic Pass: pay full price

Letting off steam

Hit Carnac's beaches or play in the **Parc Jeux Petit Delire** (*www.parc-jeux-petit-delire.com*) in the popular beach town of Ploemel, 9 km (6 miles) from Carnac. Take bus 1 to Quiberon on its peninsula to visit its rocky westerly Côte Sauvage. The east coast has kid-safe beaches such as **St-Pierre-Quiberon**.

Holidaymakers on one of Carnac's many sandy beaches

Eat and drink

Picnic: under €20; Snacks: €20–45; Real meal: €45–90; Family treat: over €90 (based on a family of four)

PICNIC Marché de Carnac (*Pl de la Chapelle, 56340; on Wed & Sun*) is an outdoor market held in the centre of Carnac. The Site Natural de Kervilhen (signposted between Carnac and La Trinité-sur-Mer) with sand dunes, ponds and trees is a good spot for a picnic. **SNACKS Chevillard** (*2 Rue du Tumulus, 56340; 02 97 52 05 56*) is a bakery that offers old-fashioned breads, pizzas, toasted sandwiches and delicious pastries.

for one of the five sites (Gavrinis, Locmariaquer, Carnac, Petit-Mont or Musée de Préhistoire) and save money on other sites

🗝 **Guided tours** Compulsory from Apr–Sep at the Alignements de Carnac

👫 **Age range** 4 plus

⏱ **Allow** An hour for Carnac and a day for all the megalithic sites

☕ **Café** Near the Maison des Mégalithes car park

🚻 **Toilets** In Maison des Mégalithes, Carnac

Good family value?
Kids have a natural affinity for dolmens and beautiful sandy beaches. Prices are kind, too.

REAL MEAL La Chaumière des Salines (*Ave de St-Colomban, 56340; 02 97 52 17 20; Apr–mid-Sep*) offers simple dishes that are likely to appeal to kids, such as crêpes and *raclettes*.
FAMILY TREAT Le Tumulus (*Chemin de Tumulus, 56342; 02 97 52 08 21; www.hotel-tumulus.com*) features well-prepared lobster and a kids' menu served with organic Carnac apple juice.

Shopping

Drop in to **Le Comptoir Florentin** (*8 Rue St-Cornely, 56340 Carnac*) and shop for Breton specialities such as biscuits, sea salt and cider.

Take cover

Take bus 1 that goes from Carnac to St-Pierre-Quiberon to visit the **Maison d'Armorine** (*www.maison-armorine.com*) where they make 49 different kinds of lollipops with all kinds of confectionery.

Fascinating iron sculptures at the Univers du Poète Ferrailleur, Lizio

Next stop…

BEACHES, INSECTS AND SCULPTURES There are more beaches east of Carnac along the beautifully indented coastline of the Gulf de Morbihan, especially around the Presqu'île de Rhys (site of Petit-Mont). Take a boat tour of the Gulf and its islands with **Navix** (*www.navix.fr*), departing from Auray, Vannes or Locmariaquer. Take a taxi inland to the village of Lizio to the **Insectarium** (*www.insectariumdelizio.fr*) and see up to 60 species of insects. Or head for the **Univers du Poète Ferrailleur** (*poeteferrailleur.com*), the realm of the delightfully mad inventor Robert Courday, who created over 80 animated iron sculptures on his farm.

The Moulin du Grand Poulguin restaurant, housed in a working mill, Pont-Aven

⑩ Vannes

Seahorses and butterflies

The lovely city of Vannes was hit by just one bomb in World War II, and it did not explode. The Morbihan department's finest artefacts are on display in the handsome interior of the splendid 15th-century Château Gaillard's **Musée de Préhistoire et d'Archéologie**. The medieval market houses the **Musée des Beaux Arts**, with Delacroix's *Christ on the Cross* and Breton paintings. Nearby looms the massive Cathédrale St-Pierre, first built in the 13th century and remodelled many times since.

A free summer shuttle bus goes to the Parc du Golfe, home to the **Aquarium du Golfe**, specializing in tropical fish, cuttlefish and seahorses; and the **Jardin des Papillons**, which is a greenhouse that houses exotic flora and butterflies.

Letting off steam

Take bus 7 to Questembert, just east of Vannes, and then a taxi to the **Parc Animalier et Botanique de Branféré**

(*www.branfere.com*), where animals roam free and birds perform aerial ballets, while kids can scamper on nets hanging from trees.

⑪ Lorient

Trawlers and sailing ships

France's second most important fishing port was founded by King Louis XIV to serve as the port of his Compagnie des Indes Orientales,

One of Vannes's two gateways, part of the old city wall

The Lowdown

🌐 **Map reference** 2 H4
Address 56000 (Morbihan). Musée de Préhistoire et d'Archéologie: 2 Rue Noé; 02 97 42 59 80; *www.mairie-vannes. fr*. Musée des Beaux Arts: Pl St-Pierre; 02 97 01 63 00; *www. mairie-vannes.fr*. Aquarium du Golfe: 21 Rue Daniel Girard; *www. aquarium-du-golfe.com*. Jardin des Papillons: Rue Daniel Girard; *www. jardinauxpapillons.com*

🚃 **Train** from Rennes. **Bus** from Carnac

ℹ️ **Visitor information** Quai Tabarly, 56000; 08 25 13 56 10; *www. tourisme-vannes.com*

🕐 **Open** Musée de Préhistoire et d'Archéologie: Jun–Sep: daily.

Musée des Beaux Arts: Jun–Sep: daily; Oct–May: daily pm. Aquarium du Golfe: daily (Oct–Mar pm only, except during school hols). Jardin des Papillons: Apr–Sep: daily

🍽️ **Eat and drink** *Real meal* Au Pont Vert (*40 Ave du Maréchal de Lattre de Tassigny, 56000; 02 97 40 80 13; Mon–Sat lunch only*) serves dishes based around market produce. *Family treat* Le Boudoir (*43 Rue de la Fontaine, 56000; 02 97 42 60 64; www.restaurantleboudoir.com*) offers gourmet children's menus.

🎪 **Festival** Fêtes Historiques de Vannes, parades and street theatre relive various periods of Vannes's history (Jul)

Prices given are for a family of four

The Lowdown

🌐 **Map reference** 2 G4
Address 56100 (Morbihan). La Thalassa: Quai de Rohan, 56100; *www.la-thalassa.fr*. La Cité de la Voile Eric Tabarly: Base des Sous-Marins, 56323 Keroman; *www.citevoile-tabarly.com*

🚃 **Train** from Paris, Vannes and Nantes

ℹ️ **Visitor information** Maison de la Mer, Quai de Rohan, 56100; 02 97 84 78 00; *www.lorient-tourisme.fr*

🕐 **Open** La Thalassa: May–Jun & Sep: closed Mon; Apr, Jul–Aug: daily and on All Saints holidays. La Cité de la Voile Eric Tabarly: daily during school hols, closed Mon other times & Jan

🍽️ **Eat and drink** *Real meal* L'Eveil des Sens (*11 Rue Fénelon, 56100; 02 97 84 05 79; closed Sun, Mon dinner & Sat lunch*) has home-style cooking. *Family treat* Le Neptune (*15 Ave de la Perrière, 56100; 02 97 37 04 56; www. restaurantleneptune.fr; closed Wed dinner and Sun*) serves delicious fish and seafood.

which also gave the town its name. Badly bombed in World War II, Lorient has since developed an array of maritime attractions, which starts off with a child-friendly tour of **La Thalassa**, an oceanographic research vessel. The colossal Base de Sous-Marins Keroman houses **La Cité de la Voile Eric Tabarly**, where families can learn about sailing, followed by an excursion in Lorient's bay (Apr–Sep if weather permits.)

Letting off steam

Play in the Jardin Jules Ferry located in Lorient's centre. Or take bus 50 to Pont-Scorff to visit **Odyssaum** (*www.odyssaum.fr*), which has a fresh-water aquarium by a salmon-filled river.

⑫ Pont-Aven

Crazy for art

Before 1886, the charming village of Pont-Aven was best known for its watermills, but that was before it found itself in the vanguard of French art, thanks to Paul Gauguin and a handful of like-minded artists who retreated here to work out a new theory they called Synthetism. Instead of just depicting a subject realistically, the artists painted their own emotional impression of it, in bold colours and with strong outlines. To learn more, visit the **Musée des Beaux Arts**, which houses works by members of the Pont-Aven school. As for the village, it remains a beacon for artists: the **Centre International d'Art Contemporaine**, founded in 1993, exhibits works by young artists from all over the world.

Letting off steam

Take a kayak trip with **360 Kayak Discovery** on the Aven river. Or head inland by taxi to Locunolé's **Village de Loisirs de Ty Nadan** (*www.tynadan-loisirs.fr*) with ponies, karting, tree acrobatics and paintball for kids aged 5 plus.

The Lowdown

⊕ **Map reference** 2 F4
Address 29930 (Finistère). Musée des Beaux Arts: Pl de l'Hôtel-de-Ville; 02 98 06 14 43; *www.museepontaven.fr*. Centre International d'Art Contemporaine: 10 Rue de la Belle Angèle; 02 98 09 10 45; *www.ciac-pa.com*

🚆 **Train** from Rennes or Vannes to Quimper, then bus

ℹ **Visitor information** 5 Pl Hôtel de Ville, 29930; *www.pontaven.com*

🕙 **Open** Musée des Beaux Arts: daily; closed Jan. Centre International d'Art Contemporaine: Mon–Fri.

🍽 **Eat and drink** *Real meal* Moulin du Grand Poulguin (*Quai Botrel, 29930; 02 98 06 02 67; moulin-pontaven.com; closed Nov*) serves crêpes, pizzas and brasserie-style dishes. *Family treat* Le Graal (*Prom Xavier Grall, 29930; 02 98 06 08 99; Jul–Aug: open daily; Sep–Jun: closed Tue dinner & Wed*) specializes in scallops.

🎉 **Festival** Festival des fleurs d'Ajonc, procession celebrating the Queen's arrival (Aug)

⑬ Quimper
Hand-painted pottery

Finistère's proud capital Quimper, or "Quimperon en Cornouaille" as it likes to be known, is where the legendary King Gradlon of Cornouaille relocated after his beautiful city of Ys, built for his unruly daughter Dahut, was drowned by waves (*see p165*). Gradlon's hermit friend Corentin became the city's first bishop and gave his name to the Gothic cathedral (the statue between its spires is Gradlon).

Traditional ceramics on display at a workshop in Quimper

Around it nestles a handsome art city, where the **Musée des Beaux Arts** has paintings by the Pont-Aven school and Breton Realist painters. The **Musée Départemental Breton** has artefacts showcasing 4,000 years of history as well as hand-painted faience, a traditional craft which is Quimper's speciality. Watch faience artists at work at **H.B. Henriot**.

Letting off steam

Take bus 16 to the beaches in the town of Bénodet, perhaps for a cruise with **Vedettes Odet** (*www.vedettes-odet.com*). Or take bus 14a to visit Concarneau's beaches (*www.tourismeconcarneau.fr*).

The Lowdown

⊕ **Map reference** 2 F3
Address 29000 (Finistère). Musée des Beaux Arts: 40 Pl St-Corentin; *www.musee-beauxarts.quimper.fr*. Musée Départemental Breton: 1 Rue du Roi-Gradlon; *www.museedepartementalbreton.fr*. H.B. Henriot: Rue Haute; *www.hb-henriot.com*

🚆 **Train** from Paris, Rennes & Vannes

ℹ **Visitor information** Pl de la Résistance, 29000; 02 98 53 04 05; *www.quimper-tourisme.com*

🕙 **Open** Musée des Beaux Arts: Jul–Aug: daily; Sep–Jun: closed Tue & Sun am. Musée Départemental Breton: daily; Oct–May: closed Sun am & Mon. H.B. Henriot: tours in English and French (book in advance)

🍽 **Eat and drink** *Real meal* Le Globe (*9 Blvd Amiral-Kerguelen, 29000; 02 98 95 09 10; closed Sat, Sun & Mon lunch*) serves dishes from around the world. *Family treat* Le Cosy (*2 Rue du Sallé, 29000; 02 98 95 23 65; www.lecosy-restaurant.fr; closed Tue & Sun lunch*) is a little restaurant that serves perfectly prepared fish and meat dishes, and also has a kids' menu.

Where to Stay in Brittany

A top holiday region, Brittany offers everything from cheap and cheerful camp grounds by the sea to upmarket boutique hotels and luxurious B&Bs. Most accommodation is concentrated near the coasts and air conditioning is rare – but with the region's ocean breezes it is rarely needed.

AGENCIES

Brittany Travel
www.brittany.co.uk
This company lists villas and cottages throughout the region, ranging from high end to budget prices, with a selection of lodging for people with reduced mobility.

Brittany Cottages
www.brittanycottages.com
This website features self-catering properties in all price ranges and also cottages with private pools.

Pretty garden outside a cottage near Rennes, listed on Brittany Cottages

Brest
Map 2 E2

HOTELS
Hotel Center
4 Blvd Léon Blum, 29200; 02 98 80 78 07; www.hotelcenter.com
This modern hotel, near the airport shuttle and city centre, is a good base for visiting Océanopolis and the beaches around the bay of Brest. Family rooms have mezzanines and are equipped with Wi-Fi and satellite TV. Restaurant on site.

 P €

Hôtel La Baie des Anges
350 Route de l'Aber Wrac'h, 29870 Landeda; 02 98 04 90 04; www.baie-des-anges.com
A 20-minute drive north of Brest, this fashionable hotel, housed in a 20th-century mansion, has superb sea views. There are family rooms, suites and apartments with kitchenettes. Kids are catered for with DVDs and comic books; babysitting is provided.

€€€

BED & BREAKFAST

Domaine de Moulin Mer
34 Route de Moulin Mer, 29460 Logonna-Daoulas; 02 98 07 24 45; www.domaine-moulin-mer.com
In a village 26 km (18 miles) south of Brest, where the sheltered coast enjoys a lush micro-climate, this 19th-century mansion is set in a garden of palms and mimosas and has been restored by its owner. Fitted with Wi-Fi, it has two suites that can be used as a family room sleeping four.

P €€

SELF-CATERING

Auberge de Kéringar
Lochrist, 29217 Le Conquet; 02 98 89 09 59; www.keringar.fr
Located 23 km (14 miles) west of Brest on the coast, this hotel offers three exceptional *gîtes* sleeping up to six, in thick-walled granite houses. The beach is a short walk away; the owners offer shuttles to the port for visits to Île d'Ouessant.

P €

CAMPING

Le Village Loisirs
29290 Milizac; 02 98 07 92 17; www.camping-village-loisirs-3cures.com
Linked to the La Récré des Trois Curés theme park, 8 km (5 miles) away, this small family camp ground has 50 pitches, bungalows, mobile homes and chalets. There are pedal boats, playgrounds, mini-golf and daily kids' activities in July and August.

 P €

Carnac
Map 2 G4

HOTELS
Auberge du Petit Matelot
Penthièvre Plage, 56510 St-Pierre-Quiberon; 02 97 52 31 21; www.auberge-du-petit-matelot.com
By a sandy beach midway down the beautiful Quiberon peninsula west of Carnac, this jolly little hotel has simple

rooms, with satellite TV. There is half-board arrangement with the adjacent restaurant, La Balise.

P €

Hotel Celtique
82 Ave des Druides, Carnac Plage, 56340; 02 97 52 14 15; www.hotel-celtique.com
Colourful Celtic designs decorate this modern hotel, a 2-minute walk from the beach and a short drive from the standing stones. Family rooms have beds for up to three kids on the mezzanine and are equipped with Wi-Fi and satellite TV; grown-ups can indulge in the spa.

P €€

L'Hippocampe
Route de Carnac, Kerhueno, 56340 Plouharnel; 02 97 52 39 51; www.hotel-hippocampe.fr
In green countryside, just 3 km (2 miles) northwest of Carnac's sandy beaches, this little family-run hotel enjoys a garden setting. The family room has a mezzanine and balcony, flat screen TV and Wi-Fi. The owners cultivate oysters – try them in the hotel restaurant.

P €€

BED & BREAKFAST
Ker Kristal
12 Kerguéarec, 56340; 02 97 56 73 57; www.kerkristal.com
Jocelyne et Jürgen Heiligtag's modern yet traditionally styled house is set in beautiful gardens. It offers

Lush trees shading the charming lake in Le Village Loisirs, Brest

a handsome two-bedroom family suite with satellite TV, a kitchenette and private garden terrace. Games and baby facilities are available.

 P €

SELF-CATERING
Erdeven Holidays
56410 Erdeven; 06 08 53 63 77; www.carnacgites.com
In Erdeven, 10 km (6 miles) west of Carnac, families can stay in the traditional, stone-built, 150-year-old Maison de Pêcheur, lovingly restored and comfortably furnished, with satellite TV. The house has fields on three sides and the garden has a barbecue and room for playing.

 P €€

CAMPING
Camping La Grande Metairie
Route des Alignements de Kermario, 56342 Kerlescan; 02 97 52 24 01; www.lagrandemetairie.com
Located near the standing stones, this long established camp ground offers pitches, mobile homes, tree houses and huts. A riding stable, tree-top adventure course and even a children's disco are on offer.

P ⊙ €

Concarneau Map 2 F4

HOTEL
Hôtel de France et d'Europe
9 Ave de la Gare, 29900; 02 98 97 00 64; www.hotel-france-europe.com
This century-old hotel, with a friendly staff, is just outside Concarneau's Ville Close, a 5-minute walk from the beach. The cheerfully decorated rooms have comfortable beds, Wi-Fi and double-glazed windows. See website for breakfast charges.

P €€

Côte de Granit Rose Map 2 G2

HOTEL
Le Manoir de St Michel Map 3 A5
38 Rue de la Carquois, 22240 Frehel; 02 96 41 48 87; www.fournel.de
Just west of Cap Frehel, overlooking the Plage de Sables-d'Or-des-Pins, this hotel in a 16th-century granite manor offers excellent value for money. The "cottages" sleep up to six; other delights include the superb breakfast, a fishing lake and lawns.

P €€

SELF-CATERING
Stereden Village des Gîtes
Route du Radôme, 22560 Pleumeur-Bodou; 02 96 91 80 57; www.stereden.com
This car-free village of basic chalet-gîtes, sleeping up to five, is only 2 km (1 mile) from the beaches. There are large play areas, barbecues, as well as bikes to hire. Short stays are available.

P €

CAMPING
Tourony
Route de Poul Palud, 22730 Trégastel; 02 96 23 86 61; www.camping-tourony.com
Overlooking the port of Ploumanac'h between Perros-Guirec and Trégastel, this camp site offers pitches, chalets and mobile homes sleeping up to six. Playgrounds on site and beaches are close by; bikes can be rented.

P €

Dinan Map 3 A6

HOTEL
Le Challonge
29 Pl Duguesclin, 22100; 02 96 87 16 30; www.hotel-dinan.fr
In the heart of Dinan, this hotel has spacious and cosy carpeted rooms, including two for families, with Wi-Fi, satellite TV and towel heaters. There is a brasserie-style restaurant. Pay street parking nearby.

  €€

BED & BREAKFAST
La Motte Beaumanoir
35720 Pleugueneuc-Plesder; 02 23 22 05 00; www.la-motte-beaumanoir.com
Located 15 km (9 miles) east of Dinan and midway between Rennes and St-Malo, this stately château is set in a park of woodlands, by a lake. Rooms are luxurious, with modern furnishings. Babysitting available.

P ⊙ €€€

Pont-Aven Map 2 F4

BED & BREAKFAST
Castel Braz
12 Rue du Bois d'Amour, 29930; 02 98 06 07 81; www.castelbraz.com
This handsome 19th-century white house with blue shutters on the banks of the Aven river has been artily transformed into a B&B by its owners.

Plush furnishings in the lobby of the Château de Kerminaouët, Pont-Aven

Equipped with Wi-Fi, each room has a theme. The impressive Asian and African suites sleep four.

P €€

Château de Kerminaouët
29910 Tregunc; 02 98 50 19 68; www.chambres-hotes-france-bretagne.fr
Located west of Pont-Aven, 5 km (3 miles) from the beaches, this B&B in a 19th-century castle is set in a huge park of lakes, woodlands and meadows. They also rent out a pair of gîtes.

P €€

CAMPING
Domaine de Kerlann
29930 Land Rosted; 05 56 07 90 17; www.siblu.fr
Spread around an indoor-outdoor water park, this camp ground has five playgrounds and free kids' clubs for all ages. There are pitches, motor homes and mobile homes to rent, spread out among the trees. Baby kits, sheets and towels can be hired.

P ⊙ €-€€

Presqu'île de Crozon Map 2 E3

BED & BREAKFAST
Kastell Dinn
29160 Kerlouantec; 02 98 27 26 40; www.gite-rando-bretagne.com
Just south of Crozon, on the Cap de la Chèvre, this B&B has four themed rooms, sleeping four – scarecrow, marine, beach and pullover – along with two rooms in and under old boats in the garden.

P €

Price Guide
The following price ranges are based on one night's accommodation in high season for a family of four, inclusive of service charges and any additional taxes.
€ Under €100 €€ €100–200 €€€ over €200

Key to symbols *see back cover flap*

CAMPING
Trez Rouz
Route de Camaret à Roscanvel, 29160 Camaret-sur-Mer; 02 98 27 93 96; www.trezrouz.com
This basic little camp ground is set just back from a sandy beach on Brittany's westernmost coast, amidst the splendid Parc Naturel Régional d'Armorique. Chalets and mobile homes can be hired for a minimum of four days. There is a playground too. Nearby, regular boat services to Brest makes it easy to visit Océanopolis.
P €

Stately exterior of the friendly Hôtel de l'Univers, St-Malo

Rennes
Map 7 B1
HOTEL
Le Victoria
35 Ave de Janvier, 35000; 02 99 31 69 11; www.hotel-levictoria.com
A stone's throw from the train station and within walking distance of the centre, this hotel's rooms are small, but comfortable, with Wi-Fi and satellite TV. The breakfast is good and there is a brasserie-style restaurant. The staff is friendly.
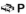 P €

BED & BREAKFAST
Symphonie des Sens
8 Rue du Chapître, 35000; 02 99 79 30 30; www.symphoniedessens.com
Located in the centre of historic Rennes, this is a two-bedroom flat on the third floor of a timbered house of 1651, sympathetically restored with designer fabrics and modern furniture. The family apartment has Internet access and TV. Breakfast is served in the apartment or out on the terrace.
P €€€

Key to Price Guide *see p171*

SELF-CATERING
Apart'City
Rennes Ouest
7 Rue Pierre-Joseph Colin, 35000; 02 99 02 61 61; www.appartcity.com
These modern, clean, functional self-catering apartments are just west of the centre and linked by bus 53 and 30. They also make an easy base for families exploring Brittany by car. Buffet breakfast available.
P €

Roscoff
Map 2 F2
HOTELS
Regina
1 Rue Ropartz Morvan, 29680; 02 98 61 23 55; www.hotel-regina.fr
Near the train station and the centre of Roscoff, this old, simple, but clean hotel offers good value for money. Rooms have satellite TV. There is no restaurant on site, but there are quite a few eateries, a walking away. The staff is helpful.
P €

Le Brittany
Blvd Ste-Barbe, 29681; 02 98 69 70 78; www.hotel-brittany.com
Housed in a 17th-century building, disassembled and rebuilt in Roscoff in 1974, this Relais & Châteaux hotel is a haven of peace in the busy port. The comfortable rooms have satellite TV and Wi-Fi; under 2s stay for free. Expect top service from the Chapalain family, who have been at the helm for years.
P €€€

St-Malo
Map 3 A5
HOTELS
Hôtel Le Nautilus
9 Rue de la Corne de Cerf, 35400; 02 99 40 42 27; www.lenautilus.com
This cheerful little hotel, housed in a listed granite building, has bright yellow and orange rooms equipped with Wi-Fi and satellite TV. The owners are helpful; the breakfast, with home-made bread, is delicious and good value for money.
P €

Aubade Hôtel
8 Pl Duguesclin, 35400; 02 99 40 47 11; www.aubade-hotel.com
Located close to the beach and a short walk to historic St-Malo, this boutique hotel, decorated in shades of mint and chocolate, is comfortable

and welcoming. Rooms have Wi-Fi and large flat-screen TVs. There is a library with books, comic books and DVDs about the area. Staff is helpful.
P €€

Hôtel de l'Univers
Pl Châteaubriand, 35400; 02 99 40 89 52; www.hotel-univers-saintmalo.com
Located opposite St-Malo's château, this friendly hotel, a former local yacht club, is linked to a famous bar packed full of memorabilia. Rooms have comfortable beds and there are countless restaurants nearby; the beach is just a stroll away.
€€

BED & BREAKFAST
Château Richeux
Map 3 B5
St Méloir des Ondes, 35350 Cancale; 02 99 89 64 76; www.maisons-de-bricourt.com
East of St-Malo, in the beach village of Cancale, this château is a lovely granite villa from the 1920s, set in a park, with splendid sea views. The beautiful rooms are furnished with antiques, while the ground floor has a magnificent restaurant, La Coquillage. They also offer four very comfortable self-catering *gîtes*.
P €€€

CAMPING
Domaine des Ormes
Map 3 B6
Epiniac, 35120 Dol de Bretagne; 02 99 73 53 00; www.lesormes.com
This huge, top-rated holiday resort is a half hour's drive from St-Malo. There are 800 pitches for campers and tree houses, apartment hotels, Russian dachas and thatched lodges. An 18-hole golf course, horse and pony riding, water park, playground and cultural events are also on offer.
P €–€€

Vannes
Map 2 G4
SELF-CATERING
Port dux Crouesty
D780, 56640 Arzon; 01 58 21 55 50; www.pv-holidays.com
Set around a pleasant port on the gulf of Morbihan, south of Vannes, these handsome family apartments are spread over four buildings in a pedestrian zone, just a short distance from Fogéo beach. There are kids' clubs, a sailing school and a thalassotherapy spa for grown-ups. Bike hire available.
P €€

The Loire Valley

For many, the broad green valley of the Loire is the real heart of France. The valley is known for its Renaissance châteaux – Amboise, Chambord and Blois among others – filled with history and culture. Between the châteaux are cities: Orléans and Chartres have great cathedrals, while Nantes offers maritime history and the futuristic Les Machines de l'Île.

Chartres Cathedral
p188

Tours
p180

Château
Royal
de Blois
p184

Les Machines
de l'Île
p174

Below *The magnificent central lantern tower of the Château de Chambord*

① Les Machines de l'Île, Nantes
The factory of imaginary machines

When the shipyards closed on the Île de Nantes in 1987, the vast industrial zone situated on the banks of the Loire seemed like a hole in the heart of Nantes – until two theatre experts, François Delarosières and Pierre Orefice, came up with a plan to re-use the workshops. Inspired by the sketches in Leonardo da Vinci's *Notebooks* and the imagination of Nantes native Jules Verne, the workshops were used to build things no one had seen before.

Key Features

Entrance

② **Le Grand Eléphant** The articulated 45-ton (40-tonne) 12-m (39-ft) tall wooden elephant takes visitors on a 40-minute stroll around the Île de Nantes.

④ **L'Atelier de la Machine** Prototypes such as Le Manège des Mondes Marins and L'Arbre de Hérons are brought to life in this workshop, using wood, custom metal pieces and state-of-the-art high-tech. The workers demonstrate their current projects.

⑤ **Terraces** Walk along terraces above the workshops to get an overview of ongoing projects. A film on the west terrace explains the stages of creating a machine from the drawing board to the finished product.

① **The buildings** Dating from around 1900, these enormous structures were built for the Chantiers de la Loire shipyards. They found a new life as home to all the prototypes of Les Machines de l'Île when they opened to the public in 2007.

③ **La Galerie des Machines** Scale models of current and future projects are displayed here, as well as completed, working sections of machines to ride.

⑥ **Le Centre Européen d'Essai en Vol** This is Europe's only simulated high-speed wind tunnel, designed to test the air worthiness of the machines. Some lucky visitors may be invited to experience it.

Letting off steam

Take a five-minute taxi ride to the town of Bouguenais, site of the **Labyrinth de Nantes-Bouguenais** (www.lelabyrinthe.fr). It is one of the world's biggest hedge mazes, specially designed for kids.

Eat and drink

Picnic: under €20; Snacks: €20–45; Real meal: €45–90; Family treat: over €90 (based on a family of four)

PICNIC Marché de Talensac *(Rue de Talensa, 44000 Nantes)* is a good place for supplies. Picnic at Le Parc du Crapa, on the eastern tip of Île de Nantes, with tables and playgrounds. **SNACKS Café de la Branche** *(on site)* offers drinks, cakes and snacks in the mid and high season; it is also a great place to see Le Grand Eléphant trumpet past.

Prices given are for a family of four

REAL MEAL Pirates! *(13 Blvd de Stalingrad, 44000 Nantes; 02 40 74 05 15; closed Sat lunch, Sun dinner & Mon)* serves traditional and French cuisine in a fun atmosphere. **FAMILY TREAT Le Manoir de la Regate** *(155 Route de Gachet, 44300 Nantes; 02 40 18 02 97; www. lesfreresperou.fr; closed Sun dinner)*

A children's maze at the Labyrinth de Nantes-Bouguenais, Bouguenais

is an elegant restaurant housed in a 19th-century mansion, offering a wide choice of Breton and Loire specialities, as well as a kids' menu.

Shopping

For a huge assortment of miniature cars, models and antique toys, go to **Au Petit Prince** *(5 Pl Port Communeau, 44000; 02 40 47 64 78)*. **Chocolat Gautier-Debotté** *(9 Rue de la Fosse, 44000; 02 40 48 23 19; www.gautier-debotte.com)* has lovely decorated chocolates.

Find out more

DIGITAL Play Around the World in 80 Days, a Game Boy Advance video game. Kids can also opt for Voyage, a computer game that is inspired by the works of Jules Verne.

The Lowdown

🌐 **Map reference** 7 B2
Address 44000 (Loire-Atlantique). Les Chantiers, Blvd Léon Bureau, 44200 Nantes; 08 10 12 12 25; www.lesmachines-nantes.fr

🚗 **Train** from Paris to Nantes, then Tramway 1

🕑 **Open** Mid-May–Jun: 10am–5pm Mon–Fri, 10am–6pm Sat–Sun; Jul–Aug: 10am–7pm daily; other times usually 2–6pm Tue–Sun (check website for variations in French school hols); closed Jan–early-Feb (ticket office closes an hour before). Le Grand Eléphant: Elephant rides at 2:45pm & 4:15pm; 3:30pm & 5pm Sat & Sun & school hols

💶 **Prices** €25–35; under 4s free. Le Grand Eléphant: €25–35; under 4s free (buy tickets at the entrance)

👥 **Skipping the queue** Go on a weekday, when it is less crowded and all the workers will be busy in the workshops.

🚠 **Guided tours** No

🚶 **Age range** 2 plus

🕐 **Allow** 3–4 hours

☕ **Café** on site (see p174)

🛍 **Shops** La Boutique des Machines (on site) stocks an array of imaginative gifts.

🚻 **Toilets** By the café

🎭 **Festivals** Carnaval des Nantes (Apr). Christmas events at La Galerie des Machines

Good family value?
Les Machines de l'île offers a unique experience and is inspiring fun for all ages.

Le Manège des Mondes Marins A giant squid, manta ray and lantern fish are among the wonderful, articulated creatures that circle in an aquatic ballet on the three levels of this amazing carousel. Its various elements are being currently worked on. It will open to the public in 2012.

L'Arbre de Hérons This hanging garden will feature rides under the wings of two giant herons when it is completed in 2015. A scale model is currently on display.

FILM There are dozens of films based on the stories of Jules Verne. Classic versions include *Around the World in 80 Days* (1956) with David Niven and Cantinflas; *20,000 Leagues Under the Sea* (1954) with James Mason and Kirk Douglas.

Next stop...

NANTES Visit Nantes' historic centre, clustered beneath the 15th-century **Château des Ducs de Bretagne** *(Rue du Château, 44000; 02 51 17 49 48; www.chateau-nantes.fr).* Its Renaissance core holds a fascinating multimedia museum of the city. The **Musée des Beaux-Arts** *(10 Rue Georges-Clemenceau, 44000; 02 51 17 45 00; www.museedesbeauxarts. nantes.fr)* has paintings and sculptures from each period of Western art – do not miss the life-sized ostrich.

The solid ramparts of the Château des Ducs de Bretagne, Nantes

An 18-m (59-ft) skeleton of a fin whale that got hit by a boat is in the **Musée d'Histoire Naturelle** *(Pl de la Monnaie, 44000; 02 40 41 55 00; www.museum.nantes.fr).* The **Musée Jules-Verne** *(3 Rue de l'Hermitage, 44000; 02 40 69 72 52; www.nantes. fr/julesverne)* is dedicated to the author's life and works, with 98 of his original manuscripts.

A field gun at the exterior of Le Grand Blockhaus-Musée de la Poche, Batz

② St-Nazaire
The city of ocean liners

Located on the Loire estuary, by its namesake landmark bridge and the magnificent beaches of the Côte d'Amour, with its pale golden sands, St-Nazaire remembers its history with guided audio tours of the submarine **Espadon** and also the **Escal'Atlantique**, a unique museum designed like an ocean liner. It evokes the glamour of great ships, including the last operating ocean liner, the *Queen Mary II*, built in St-Nazaire. The **Ecomusée de St-Nazaire** houses exhibits on the history of the port and estuary.

The Lowdown

🌐 **Map reference** 2 H5
Address 44600 (Loire-Atlantique). Escal'Atlantique & Espadon: Blvd de la Legion d'Honneur; 08 10 88 84 44. Ecomusée de St-Nazaire: Ave St-Hubert; 08 10 88 84 44

🚗 **Train** from Nantes and Paris

ℹ️ **Visitor information** Blvd de la Légion d'Honneur, Base Sous-marine Ville-Port, 44600; 02 40 22 40 65; www.saint-nazaire-tourisme.com. There is a central ticket office for all the sites next to the tourist office.

🕐 **Open** Espadon, Escal'Atlantique & Ecomusée de St-Nazaire: Apr–Sep: daily; Feb, Mar, Oct, Nov & Dec: closed Mon, Tue & school hols; closed Jan

🍴 **Eat and drink** *Real meal* Ar Blaz Mad (*23 Ave René Coty, 44600; 02 40 15 63 70; closed Sun & Mon*) is good for sandwiches, salads and tartines as well as fruit crumbles. *Family treat* La Grillandine (*20 Rue de la Trinité, 44600; 02 40 70 09 30*) serves succulent *entrecôtes* (rib steaks) and seafood dishes.

🎪 **Festival** Les Escales, a festival of world music (Aug)

Letting off steam
STRAN buses 40 or 45 go to Plage de Monsieur Hulot, 4 km (6 miles) west, in St-Marc-sur-Mer, where the classic French comedy, *Les Vacances de Monsieur Hulot* (1953) was filmed by Jacques Tati – his statue overlooks the beach. Further west, play on the sands of Côte d'Amour at La Baule or at Pornichet, which offers roller skating on the Boulevard des Océanides on Wednesdays.

③ Batz-sur-Mer
On the peninsula of salt

A pretty port with a Breton feel, Batz-sur-Mer boasts the 15th-century **Église St-Guénolé**. Climb its granite tower for a view of the Guérandaise peninsula. On the edge of town is **Le Grand Blockhaus-Musée de la Poche**, a German command post that was disguised as a hotel during World War II to deter bombs. Today, it is a museum that tells the story of the St-Nazaire "Pocket" and how it held out against the Allies for so long.

Visitors surrounded by marine life in Océarium, Le Croisic

The Lowdown

🌐 **Map reference** 2 H5
Address 44740 (Loire-Atlantique). Église St-Guénolé: Pl du Garnal; 02 40 23 92 36. Le Grand Blockhaus-Musée de la Poche: 12 Route du Dervin; www.grand-blockhaus.com. Musée des Marais Salants: 29 bis Rue Pasteur; www.cap-atlantique.fr/

🚗 **Train** from Nantes or St-Nazaire

ℹ️ **Visitor information** 25 Rue de la Plage, 44740; 02 40 23 92 36; www.ot-batzsurmer.fr

🕐 **Open** Tower of Église St-Guénolé: Apr–mid-Sept: daily. Le Grand

Since at least the 14th century, this area has been producing France's gourmet salt, *sel de Guérande*, a story told in the **Musée des Marais Salants**. Salt marshes surround the town of Guérande, just inland.

Letting off steam
There are beaches in Batz or take Bus E west to Le Croisic, France's prime pink prawn port. The **Océarium** in Le Croisic (*www.ocearium-croisic.fr*) has an aquarium and a marine tunnel.

④ Les Sables d'Olonne
France's most famous boat race

Once a cod fishing port, and a resort since the mid 19th-century, the seaside town of Les Sables is named for its superb long sandy beaches. It is the base for the prestigious round-the-world Vendée Globe, a sailing race that takes place every four years. It has a pretty 19th-century covered market and grand villas lining Le Remblai promenade.

The town's 17th-century abbey houses the **Musée de l'Abbaye Ste-Croix**, featuring whimsical, often humorous Art Brut works by Gaston Chaissac and Victor Brauner, which appeal to children, as well as a marine history section with ships' models. Situated by the fishing port, the **Muséum du Coquillage** showcases a stunning seashell collection. Tour Les Salines (*www.lessalines.fr*), the local salt marshes, by boat, canoe or on foot.

Letting off steam
Les Sables has a little **Zoo** (*www.zoo-des-sables.com*) dedicated to endangered species. Take bus 168

Blockhaus-Musée de la Poche: Apr–11 Nov: daily; Feb school hols. Musée des Marais Salants: Jun–Sep: daily; Oct–Nov: Mon–Fri

🍴 **Eat and drink** *Real meal* Derwin (*Baie du Derwin, 44740; 02 40 23 90 06; closed Tue*) serves both crêpes and seafood platters. *Family treat* Le Neptune (*11 Ave Port Val, Le Croisic; 02 40 23 02 59; www.restaurant-leneptune.fr*) is perfect for dining on Breton-style seafood with the kids.

🎪 **Festival** Les Celtiques de Guérande, five days of Celtic music and games (Aug)

A spectacular pirate show in progress, Grand Parc Puy du Fou

The Lowdown

🌐 **Map reference** 7 A4
Address 85100 (Vendée).
Musée de l'Abbaye Ste-Croix:
Rue de Verdun; 02 51 32 01 16;
www.lemasc.fr. Muséum du
Coquillage: 8 Rue du Maréchal
Leclerc; 02 51 23 50 00; www.
museum-du-coquillage.com

🚗 **Train** from Nantes

ℹ️ **Visitor information** 1 Prom Joffre,
85100; 02 51 96 85 85; gb.ot-
lessablesdolonne.fr

🕐 **Open** Musée de l'Abbaye Ste-
Croix: closed Mon. Muséum du
Coquillage: daily; Sep–Apr:
closed Sun am

🍴 **Eat and drink** *Snacks* Delis
House *(3 Rue de la Tour, 85100;
02 51 96 98 40; www.delishouse.
fr; open daily)* offers salads, pizzas
and desserts to eat on the spot
or take to the beach. *Real meal*
Don Rico *(6 Rue des Ecoliers,
85100; 02 51 32 79 46; closed
Wed, Sat & Sun lunch)* serves
excellent pizzas.

🎪 **Festival** Les Sables en Fête,
includes an international salsa
festival in early July (Jul & Aug)

to **St-Jean-de-Monts**, in the northern
Vendée, where kids 8 plus can learn
to sand-yacht at the **Base Nautique**
(www.saint-jean-de-monts.com).

⑤ Grand Parc Puy du Fou

Gladiators, vikings and musketeers

In 1977, the ruined 15th-century
castle of Guy de Puy du Fou was
made the centrepiece for a summer
night pageant called the Cinéscénie.
A torch-lit spectacle retracing the
history of a local family, from the
Middle Ages to World War II, it
featured a cast of 1,200 local
volunteers. It was so popular that, in
1989, the Grand Parc Puy du Fou was
created. It is the fourth most-visited
theme park in France – and without
a single ride. The park re-creates
historic settings and spectacles in
full costume: Viking attacks, sword-
fighting Musketeers, a show with
150 birds of prey and more.

Take cover

Head for Cholet, 20 km (12 miles)
north of Le Puy du Fou, to visit its
two unusual museums. The **Musée
du Textile** (www.museedutextile.com)
covers how Cholet once made its
famous red handkerchiefs and the
Musée des Metiers de la Chaussure
(www.museechaussure.fr) is devoted
to the local craft of shoe making
that still employs 10,000 workers.

The Lowdown

🌐 **Map reference** 7 C3
Address 85504 (Vendée).
BP 25, 85590 Les Epesses; 08 20
09 10 10; www.puydufou.com

🚗 **Train** to Angers, then shuttle bus

ℹ️ **Visitor information** 2 Grande-Rue
St-Blaise, 85500 Les Herbiers; 02
44 40 20 20; www.ot-lesherbiers.fr

🕐 **Open** mid-Apr–Sep: daily.
When reserving online, book
headphones for English
translations. An extra ticket is
required to see the Cinéscénie
on Fri and Sat nights. During
most French school hols,
admission includes evening
fireworks and water spectacle.

💲 **Price** €73–83

🍴 **Eat and drink** *Picnic* LeClerc
*(Rue des Chauvières, 85500 Les
Herbiers; 02 51 92 93 13)* stocks
supplies for picnics in the park's
picnic area. *Real meal* Halle
Renaissance *(on site; 08 20 09 10
10)* has a fixed price menu, which
includes a meaty salad, grilled
chicken and almond and pear tart.

Picnic under €20; **Snacks** €20–45; **Real meal** €45–90; **Family treat** over €90 (based on a family of four)

⑥ Abbaye Royale de Fontevraud

Richard the Lionheart lay here

In 1101, Robert d'Arbrissel founded the Abbaye Royale de Fontevraud and rather unusually created a monastery for men and women. The Plantagenets took special interest in it when Matilda d'Anjou, aunt of Henry II of England, became the abbess. With their donations, it soon became one of Europe's major abbeys, ruled by powerful abbesses. The tombs of Henry II and Eleanor of Aquitaine hold pride of place inside the church, along with those of their son Richard the Lionheart and daughter-in-law Isabelle d'Angoulême, although they are almost certainly empty, since the bodies were probably removed during the French Revolution. Visit the huge cloister, 16th-century paintings in the *Salle Capitulaire* and the impressive medieval kitchen, which is the oldest in France.

The fairy-tale turrets of the Château de Saumur

The Lowdown

- 🌐 **Map reference** 7 D3
  Address 49590 (Maine-et-Loire). Rue St Jean de L'Habit BP 14; 02 41 51 73 52; www. abbaye defontevraud.com/v3
- 🚌 **Bus** 1 from Saumur
- ℹ **Visitor information** Fontevraud l'Abbaye, Pl St-Michel, 49590; www.fontevraud-abbaye.fr
- 🕐 **Open** Daily; Oct–Apr closed Mon
- 🍽 **Eat and drink** *Real meal* L'Amuse Bouche (*512 Route de Montsoreau, 49400 Dampierre-sur-Loire; 02 41 67 79 63; closed Sun & Tue dinner and Wed*) serves delicate chestnut soup and great desserts. *Family treat* Le Plantagenêt (*7 Pl des Plantagenêts, 49400; 02 41 51 71 11; open daily*) offers fine cuisine; includes a kids' menu.

Letting off steam

There is plenty of room to run about at the abbey. Take a taxi 10 km (6 miles) west to the **Château de Brézé** (*www.chateaudebreze.com*) with the deepest moat in Europe and a spectacular underground labyrinth.

⑦ Saumur

Mushrooms and cavaliers

On the banks of the Loire river, Saumur basks beneath the pointy towers of the dramatic **Château de**

Saumur, founded by the counts of Blois in the 10th century to defend the Loire Valley from the Normans. Inside there are displays on its history and sculpture, while the gardens enjoy splendid views over the Loire river. St-Hilaire-St-Florent, a Saumur suburb, is famous for its tufa, a limestone formed over millions of years by mineral deposits left by the river. The stone itself was used to build castles; the cavities left are great for storing the local sparkling wine and mushroom farming. Since 1771, Saumur has been the seat of the **École Nationale d'Equitation**, the French Army's riding school, whose guided tours are offered along with occasional demonstrations of riding prowess. The **Musée des Blindés** focuses on more up-to-date methods of warfare; it is filled with historic tanks from around the world.

Letting off steam

In Saumur, take a ride on the Loire with the **Bateaux Nantais** (*www. bateaux-nantais.fr*), or take bus 23 to the town of Doué-la-Fontaine, where a former quarry shelters the **Bioparc Zoo de Doué** (*www.zoodoue.fr*).

Detail of the Tapisserie de l'Apocalypse *in the Château d'Angers*

The Lowdown

- 🌐 **Map reference** 7 D2
  Address 49400 (Maine-et-Loire). Château de Saumur: 6 Rue de Lorraine, 49400; 02 41 40 24 40. École Nationale d'Equitation: St-Hilaire-St-Florent, 49411; www. cadrenoir.fr. Musée des Blindés: 1043 Route de Fontevraud; 02 41 83 69 95; www.museedes blindes.fr
- 🚃 **Train** from Paris, Tours and Angers
- ℹ **Visitor information** Pl de la Bilange, 49400; 02 41 40 20 60; www.ot-saumur.fr
- 🕐 **Open** Château de Saumur: Apr–Sep: daily (currently closed for restoration; only some rooms can be visited). École Nationale d'Equitation: mid-Feb–early-Nov: closed Sun, Mon am and Sat pm. Musée des Blindés: daily
- 🍽 **Eat and drink** *Real meal* La Toscana (*44 Rue du Maréchal Leclerc, 49400; 02 41 51 04 14; closed Sun, and Mon & Tue dinner*) serves pizzas, salads and luscious desserts. *Family treat* Le Gambetta (*12 Rue Gambetta, 49400; 02 41 67 66 66; restaurant legambetta.com; closed Sun dinner, Mon & Wed*) has a special gourmet menu for under 10s.

⑧ Angers

The city of the Apocalypse

The capital of the powerful Counts d'Anjou, Angers has their formidable medieval **Château d'Angers**, built of the city's black schist. Inside, elegance prevails; look for the rare masterpiece commissioned by Count Louis I in 1375 – the 100-m (328-ft) *Tapisserie de l'Apocalypse*, illustrating scenes from the Bible's Book of the Apocalypse. Although cut up in the 18th century, 67 of the original 84

Prices given are for a family of four

The Lowdown

🌐 **Map reference** 7 C2
Address 49000 (Maine-et-Loire). Château d'Angers: Prom du Bout du Monde, 49100; 02 41 86 48 77 94; angers.monuments-nationaux. fr. Musée Jean-Lurçat et Tapisserie Contemporaine: 4 Blvd Arago, 49100; www.musees.angers.fr

🚗 **Train** from Nantes

ℹ️ **Visitor information** 7 Pl Kennedy, 49100; 02 41 23 50 00, www. angersloiretourisme.com

🕐 **Open** Château d'Angers: daily. Musée Jean-Lurçat et Tapisserie Contemporaine: Jun–Sep: daily; Oct–May: closed Mon

🍴 **Eat and drink** Snacks Crêperie du Château (21 Rue Saint Aignan, 49000; 02 41 88 53 87; www. creperieduchateau.fr) serves excellent crêpes. Family treat Au Restau-Théâtre (14 Rue Garnier, 49000; 02 41 72 84 26; www.au restau-theatre.com; closed Wed & Tue, and Sun eve) is popular for its delicious modern cuisine.

---

scenes were recovered and restored in the 19th century. Angers' 12th-century Cathédrale St-Maurice has an interior supported by the graceful Angevin vaulting; original stained glass lines the left side of the nave.

The Apocalypse tapestry inspired 20th-century artist Jean Lurçat to create his own masterpiece called the *Chant du Monde* (Song of the World), displayed in the **Musée Jean-Lurçat et Tapisserie Contemporaine** in the Gothic hospital, built in 1175.

Letting off steam
Head for the **Jardin des Plantes** (*Blvd Carnot*), or take bus 5, 3 km (2 miles) to the north, to **Terra Botanica** (*www.terrabotanica.fr*), a park with the flora of six continents and interactive attractions such as a 4D journey to the centre of a plant.

⑨ Le Mans
The noisiest and fastest 24 hours in Europe

Often used as a film set, evocative old Le Mans is still partly enclosed by its 3rd-century Roman walls. Begun in 1060, the Cathédrale St-Julien is one of the wonders of France, with its intricate web of flying buttresses, 11th-century stained glass and late 14th-century musical angels frescoed on the ceiling. Historical finds such as a

---

Uniquely designed cars on display at the Musée des 24 Heures, Le Mans

Gaulish drinking horn and the Plantagenet enamel of 1151, the oldest and biggest piece of its kind, fill the **Carré Plantagenêt**. Other treasures – including the reconstruction of two Egyptian tombs – are in the **Musée de Tessé**. Le Mans is, however, best known for its 24-hour endurance motor race, held every year on the Circuit de la Sarthe. The interactive **Musée des 24 Heures** covers its history with rare racing cars on display.

Letting off steam
Near the cathedral, the **Jardin d'Horticulture** (*Rue Premartine, 72000*), has a charming children's garden, or take the tram to **L'Arche de la Nature** (*www.arche-nature. org*) for walks in the woods, visits to a farm and children's activities.

The Lowdown

🌐 **Map reference** 7 D1
Address 72000 (Sarthe). Carré Plantagenêt: Rue Claude-Blondeau. Musée de Tessé: 2 Ave Paderborn. Musée des 24 Heures: Circuit des 24 Heures du Mans, Pl Luigi Chinetti

🚗 **Train** from Nantes, Angers & Paris

ℹ️ **Visitor information** 16 Rue de l'Etoile, 72000; 02 43 28 17 22; www.lemanstourisme.com

🕐 **Open** Carré Plantagenêt & Musée de Tessé: closed Mon. Musée des 24 Heures: 15 Apr–Sep: daily; Oct–mid-Apr: Wed–Sun; Dec–Jan: Fri–Sun

🍴 **Eat and drink** Real meal Le Jardin sur le Pouce (83 Blvd Marie et Alexandre Oyon, 72000; 02 43 86 11 20; www.jardin-pouce-restaurant.com; closed Sat lunch, Sun & Aug) offers exotic cuisine and salads. Family treat La Table d'Owen (4 Rue du Vert Galant, 72000; 02 43 20 57 24; latable dowen.canalblog.com; closed Sun dinner & Mon) has classic French dishes, with a good kids' menu.

🎪 **Festival** 24 Heures du Mans (Jun)

---

⑩ Tours

The Loire's historic capital

The metropolis of the Loire Valley, Tours is a lively university city with a history that dates back to Roman times. St Martin of Tours made the city a religious centre, and for a while in the turbulent 15th century it was the capital of France. Tours' modern economy co-exists with a lovely historic centre. The city lives up to its status as a laid-back place, full of gardens, open-air markets, and choral singers; it is the site of the annual European Choral Singing championship.

Half-timbered buildings in Place Plumereau

Key Sights

① **Muséum d'Histoire Naturelle** Begun in 1780, this museum is housed in the 18th-century Ancien Présidial de Tours. It features animals from the Tourraine region and from around the world.

⑦ **Rue Nationale**

0 metres 200
0 yards 200

② **Place Plumereau** Popularly known as "Place Plum", this charming café-filled square is the centre of action in Vieux Tours, lined with medieval half-timbered houses.

③ **Hôtel Goüin** One of the town's finest buildings, this ornate 15th-century palace of a silk merchant has an Italian Renaissance façade. It now holds regular art exhibitions.

④ **Musée du Compagnonnage** This museum gives the history of *compagnonnage*, a medieval apprentice system still in existence. It displays some of the *compagnons'* masterpieces.

⑤ **Cathédrale St-Gatien** Flamboyant-Gothic in style, it has lofty towers and exceptional stained glass. It is hard to believe it has caught fire eight times.

⑥ **Musée des Beaux Arts** This museum houses an impressive collection, featuring Grand Masters such as Rubens, Rembrandt and works from other periods.

⑦ **Rue Nationale** This busy main street and its stately commercial buildings look historic, but were redesigned and rebuilt after the Nazis bombed it in June 1940.

The Lowdown

🌐 **Map reference** 8 E2
Address 37000 (Indre-et-Loire). Muséum d'Histoire Naturelle: 3 Rue du Président Merville; *www.museum.tours.fr*. Hôtel Goüin: 25 Rue du Commerce; *www.musee-gouin.fr*. Musée du Compagnonnage: 8 Rue Nationale; 02 47 21 62 20. Musée des Beaux Arts: 18 Pl François-Sicard; 02 47 05 68 73. Cathédrale St-Gatien: Pl de la Cathédrale; 02 47 70 21 00. Jardin Botanique de Tours: 33 Blvd Tonnellé; 02 47 70 37 37

🚆 **Train** from Paris and Orléans

ℹ️ **Visitor information** 78 Rue Bernard Palissy, 37000; 02 47 70 37 37; *www.tours-tourisme.fr*

🕐 **Open** Muséum d'Histoire Naturelle: 10am–noon Tue–Fri, 2–6pm Sat & Sun, 2–6pm hols. Musée du Compagnonnage: mid-Jun–mid-Sep: 9am–12:30pm & 2–6pm daily; mid-Jun–mid-Sep: 9am–noon & 2–6pm Wed–Mon. Musée des Beaux-Arts: 9am–12:45pm & 2pm–6pm Wed–Mon

💶 **Prices** Muséum d'Histoire Naturelle: €9–19; under 12s free. Musée du Compagnonnage: €20–30; under 12s free. Musée des Beaux Arts: €12–22; under 12s free

🎟️ **Skipping the queue** The tourist office offers a Carte Multivisite (€24–34) for admission to most sights and discounts on hotels, bike rentals and more.

🚩 **Guided tours** Contact the tourist office for details.

👫 **Age range** 5 plus

⏱️ **Allow** A day and a half

🎭 **Festival** Festival de la Bande Dessiné, a comic book fest (Sep)

Good family value?
Tours is a big lively city full of interest, especially for the culturally inclined, but a bit expensive.

⑧ **Jardin Botanique de Tours** Created in 1843, this is the city's oldest park, with huge trees, a herb garden, greenhouses, an orangerie and two winsome wallabies.

Prices given are for a family of four

Letting off steam

Go canoeing or kayaking on the Loire river at the **Pôle Nautique du Cher** (5 Ave de Florence, 37000; 02 47 63 13 98), suitable for kids aged 7 plus. Head for a swim to the indoor and outdoor pools of **Centre Aquatique du Lac** (275 Ave Granmont, 37000; 02 47 80 78 10).

Cheese stall in the covered market of Les Halles

Eat and drink

Picnic: under €20; Snacks: €20–45; Real meal: €45–90; Family treat: over €90 (based on a family of four)

PICNIC Aux Trois Petits Cochons (142, Ave de la Tranchée, 37100) is famous for its pâtés. Les Halles (Pl Gaston-Paillhou, 37000), a covered market south of Place Plumereau, is great for picnic supplies. Picnic in the parks on the Île Simon or the Île Aucard in the Loire.

SNACKS Hansel et Gretel (107 Rue Colbert, 37000; 02 47 05 58 65) is a tea room with ice cream, cakes and sweets to pamper the little ones.

REAL MEAL La Souris Gourmande (100 Rue Colbert, 37000; 02 47 47 04 80; lasourisgourmande.com; closed Sun & Mon) is partially located in a vaulted cellar. This friendly restaurant serves cheesy *tartiflettes*

(a dish made of potatoes, bacon and cheese) and omelettes, as well as salads and meat dishes.
FAMILY TREAT L'Estrade (123 Rue Colbert, 37000; 02 47 20 80 20; www. restaurant-lestrade.fr; closed Sat & Sun) serves well-prepared market cuisine and a superb choice of fish, with a great selection of Loire wines. Menu is seasonal and good value.

Shopping

Valeur en Plus (71 Rue Colbert, 37000; 02 47 61 65 94) specializes in natural clothing and gifts. **America Latina** (68 Rue Colbert, 37000; 02 47 64 57 45) has interesting imports from South America. Head for **La Chocolatière** (4 Rue de la Scellerie, 37000; www.la-chocolatiere.com) for gorgeous chocolates and cakes.

Next stop...

CHÂTEAUX AND CAVE HOUSES Two of the Loire's great Renaissance gems are just west of Tours. Take the bus (www.tourainefilvert.com) west to Villandry to the **Château de Villandry** (www.chateauvillandry.com). It is full of art and its gardens include a garden for children, a maze of 1,200 beech trees and a greenhouse. Take the same bus to Azay-le-Rideau, just south of Villandry, to see the **Château d'Azay-le-Rideau** (www.azay-le-rideau.monuments-nationaux.fr). With its lace-like façade and pointy towers mirrored in its lagoon, it is one of the prettiest.

The nearby **Vallée Troglodytes des Goupillières** (www.troglodytedes goupillieres.fr) is a village of cave-houses that has been restored to evoke the life of 19th-century farmers.

The jewel-box-like Château d'Azay-le-Rideau, surrounded by its moat

⑪ Chinon
The Loire's most war-like castle

The Chinonais like to refer to Chinon as a "little town of great renown". This lovely medieval town, with its blue slate roofs and towers, is the place where noted Renaissance writer François Rabelais was born, King Henry II of England died and Joan of Arc met Charles VII. High on a rocky spur, the enormous, partly ruined **Fortresse Royale de Chinon** dominates the town. It was mostly built by Henry II of England in the 12th century. In 1308, the Grand Master of the Knights Templar, Jacques de Molay, and many of his top men were imprisoned in this fort, before de Molay was burnt at the stake in Paris. After years of restoration, eight rooms in the fortress's Logis Royaux were reopened in 2010, with films and interactive displays on Chinon's eventful history and historical figures.

Visit the **Musée d'Art et d'Histoire**, in the handsome 15th-century Hôtel des Etats-Généraux, where highlights include a famous portrait of Rabelais, a plume in hand

The majestic walls of Chinon's castle rising above the Vienne river

and a beautiful piece of medieval Arabian silk embroidered with leopards. The charming **Musée Animé du Vin** has hand-crafted automated figures that explain everything about wine-making.

Letting off steam

Chinon has a covered and an open pool on Quai Danton. Or take a taxi to St-Benoît-la-Forêt, located 4 km (3 miles) north, to visit **St-Benoît Aventure** (www.saintbenoitaventure. com), an adventure park where kids aged 4 plus can swing through the trees like Tarzan in perfect safety.

⑫ Château d'Ussé
Sleeping Beauty's castle

Ever since the 6th century, a fort has controlled the river traffic on the Loire and Indre at Rigny-Ussé. The fort was known to the Romans as Renacium. Its first recorded lord,

The pretty chapel set in the grounds of of the Château d'Ussé, Rigny-Ussé

The Lowdown

🌐 **Map reference** 7 D3
Address 37500 (Indre-et-Loire). Fortresse Royale de Chinon: Rue de la Fontaine; 02 47 93 13 45; www.forteressechinon.fr. Musée d'Art et d'Histoire: 44 Rue Haute-St-Maurice. Musée Animé du Vin: 12 Rue Voltaire; 02 47 93 25 63

🚗 **Train** from Tours

ℹ **Visitor information** 1 Pl d'Hofheim, 37500; 02 47 93 17 85; www.chinon-valdeloire.com

🕐 **Open** Fortresse Royale de Chinon: daily. Musée d'Art et d'Histoire: mid-Feb–Apr & Oct–mid-Nov: Fri–Mon pm; May–Sep: daily pm. Musée Animé du Vin: mid-Mar–Sep daily

🍽 **Eat and drink** Snacks Jadis Salon de Thé (23 Pl de l'Hôtel de Ville, 37500; 02 47 93 35 23) serves pies and simple lunches and great hot chocolate. Real meal Côté Jardin (30 Rue du Commerce, 37500; 02 47 93 10 97; closed Mon) specializes in local favourites such as coq au vin (cock stewed in wine) and succulent meats; good list of Loire wines.

🎪 **Festival** Marché Medieval, street market with troubadours, dancers and medieval entertainment (Aug)

The Lowdown

🌐 **Map reference** 7 D2
Address 37420 (Indre-et-Loire). 37420 Rigny-Ussé; 02 47 95 54 05; www.chateaudusse.fr

🚗 **Train** from Tours to Chinon, then a 15-min drive by car or taxi

ℹ **Visitor information** BP 5, 37190 Azay-le-Rideau; 02 47 45 44 40

🕐 **Open** mid-Feb–mid-Nov: daily

💶 **Price** €34–44; under 8s free

🍽 **Eat and drink** Picnic Intermarché (Route de Tours, 37420 Chinon; 02 47 98 11 37) stocks supplies. The surrounding Forêt de Chinon is good for picnics. Family treat Le Moulin Bleu (7 Rue du Moulin Bleu, 37140 Bourgueil; 02 47 97 73 13; www.lemoulinbleu.com) offers refined traditional cuisine.

in 1004, was the Viking Gueldon I, better known as "Gueldon the Devil". The construction of the majestic Château d'Ussé was begun in the 15th century. The rooms contain period furnishings, wax figures in period costume, and include an exceptional ensemble of Flemish tapestries showing extraordinarily detailed scenes of village life.

Outside, there are stables, with a collection of antique carriages, and a beautiful Renaissance chapel, as well as formal gardens designed by the greatest known French landscape architect, Andre Le Nôtre, who also created the gardens at Versailles. Ussé's real glory came when writer Charles Perrault, supposedly inspired by its beauty, wrote down the tale of La Belle au Bois Dormant – otherwise known as Sleeping Beauty – a story retold by life-sized figures in the château.

Letting off steam

There is plenty of room to scamper about in the château's gardens. For playgrounds, mini-golf and an artificial lake, take a 20-minute taxi ride north to the **Parc Capitaine de Bourgueil** *(www.bourgueil.fr)*, set in the vine-clad landscapes of Pays de Borgueil.

⑬ Château de Chenonceau

Palace of many intrigues

The most romantic and the most-visited of all the Loire châteaux, the Château de Chenonceau stretches across the Cher river on a row of graceful arches. It was spared during the Revolution thanks to the wise Madame Dupin who had made it a salon for writers and philosophers.

It is famous for the six women who lived here, beginning with Diane de Poitiers, the mistress of Henri II, who gave it to her. But, after his sudden death in 1559, his wife Catherine de Medici expelled Diane from the château and grabbed it for herself. Beautifully restored, the grounds include glorious formal gardens, flower and vegetable gardens, a 16th-century farm, a maze designed by Catherine de Medici, a tea room, and a play area for kids.

Letting off steam

Hire canoes from **Canoe Company** *(www.canoe-company.fr)* or take a cruise on the Cher river with **La Bélandre** *(www.labelandre.com)*, passing underneath the château. Take a taxi to the town of St-Martin-le-Beau, located halfway between Chenonceaux and Tours, where

Catherine de Medici's richly decorated bedroom in Château de Chenonceau

The Lowdown

🌐 **Map reference** 8 E2
Address 37150 (Indre-et-Loire). Pl de la Mairie; 02 47 23 90 07; www.chenonceau.com

🚃 **Train** from Tours

ℹ️ **Visitor information** 1 Rue Docteur Bretonneau, 37150; 02 47 23 94 45; www.chenonceaux-blere-tourisme.com

🕐 **Open** daily

💲 **Price** €38–48; under 7s free

🍽️ **Eat and drink** *Snacks* Self Service Restaurant *(in the old royal stables of the château, 37150; 02 47 23 91 97; Mar–mid-Nov)* serves salads, hamburgers and simple lunches. *Real meal* Hostel du Roy *(9 Rue Docteur Bretonneau, 37150 Chenonceaux; 02 47 23 90 17; www.hostelduroy.com)* is a local favourite with a good kids' menu and also vegetarian dishes.

🎪 **Festival** Promenade Nocturnes, a sound and light show (Jun–Aug)

Family Park *(www.familypark.com)* offers a water park and games, 37 tree sports, pony rides, bouncy castles and more to entertain kids.

Boating on the Cher river by the magnificient Château de Chenonceau

Picnic under €20; **Snacks** €20–45; **Real meal** €45–90; **Family treat** over €90 (based on a family of four)

⑭ Château Royal de Blois
Royal splendour and royal murder

One of the most splendid of the Loire Valley châteaux, the 13th- to 17th-century Château Royal de Blois was home to seven kings, ten queens and one famous assassination. Its regal residents left behind a stunning complex that offers a one-stop architectural tour of France. Inside are 564 rooms and over 35,000 works of art. In 1845 it was the first royal palace in France to be restored. The town of Blois itself is full of interest – especially the Maison de la Magie Robert-Houdin.

Equestrian statue of King Louis XII

Key Sights

Aile François I Begun in 1515, this wing is the first Renaissance masterpiece in France, with a façade showing a strong Italian influence.

Chambre de Catherine de Medici

Son et Lumière On summer evenings, a sound and light show illuminates the château in brilliant colours while tracing its equally colourful history.

The spiral stair This splendid three-storey external spiral staircase is believed by some to be the work of King François' friend Leonardo da Vinci.

Aile Louis XII

Aile Gaston d'Orléans In 1626, Louis XIII gave the château to his brother, the Duke of Orléans. Architect François Mansart completed the extension, using three classical orders of columns.

Musée des Beaux Arts This museum, in the Louis XII wing, houses a rich collection of paintings that was gathered by generations of royalty.

Aile Louis XII The wing of Louis XII (born here in 1462) shows the beginnings of Renaissance architecture in France, mixed with traditional Gothic.

Chambre de Catherine de Medici The queen had 237 little cabinets built into the wall of her study. She is said to have used poisons, but no one knows for sure what she stored here.

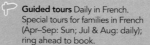

The Lowdown

🌐 **Map reference** 8 F2
Address 41000 (Loir-et-Cher). Pl du Château; 02 54 90 33 33; www.chateaudeblois.fr

🚃 **Train** from Tours and Orléans

ℹ️ **Visitor information** 23 Pl du Château, 41000; 02 54 90 41 41; www.bloispaysdechambord.com

🕐 **Open** Jan–Mar & Nov–Dec: 9am–12:30pm & 1:30–5:30pm daily; Apr–Jun & Sep: 9am–6:30pm daily; Jul–Aug: 9am–7pm daily; Oct: 9am–6pm daily. Son et Lumière: Apr–Sep: 10:30pm Wed (in English)

💶 **Price** €36–46; under 6s free

👫 **Skipping the queue** Buy a joint ticket (€59–69) for the château, the Maison de la Magie Robert Houdin and also the son et lumière show.

🚩 **Guided tours** Daily in French. Special tours for families in French (Apr–Sep: Sun; Jul & Aug: daily); ring ahead to book.

👫 **Age range** 4 plus

👫 **Activities** See Blois from a horse and carriage (€20 plus tip) from Apr–Sep. Trips begin in Place du Château. From May–Aug, book trips for €26–60 (family ticket) on a futreau (traditional wooden

river boat with a sail) at the tourist office to see the city. The guide will point out waterfowl along the way and may also stop outside town to look for beavers.

⏱️ **Allow** Half a day for the château; a day or more to see all of Blois

☕ **Café** La Duchesse Anne on Place Victor Hugo just outside the château.

👫 **Toilets** Near château entrance

Good family value?
Blois and its surroundings balance fun and culture nicely, with plenty of inexpensive activities.

Letting off steam

Scamper in the gardens of **Hôtel de Ville** in Blois. The château-laden countryside around Blois is ideal for cycling. Rent one at **Traîneurs de Loire** (www.traineursdeloire.com) that also has kids' bikes and tandems.

Outdoor café and Maison de la Magie Robert Houdin on Place du Château

Eat and drink

Picnic: under €20; Snacks: €20–45; Real meal: €45–90; Family treat: over €90 (based on a family of four)

PICNIC Le Bistrot de Léonard *(8 Rue du Maréchal de Lattre de Tassigny, 41000; 02 54 74 83 04; www.lebistrotdeleonard.com)* does takeaway versions of its classic French dishes. There are picnic tables in the Jardin du Roi, just opposite the château.

SNACKS Au Croissant d'or *(4 Pl, Victor Hugo, 41000; 02 54 74 77 10)* sells a wide range of hot snacks, salads and sandwiches.

REAL MEAL Le Castelet *(40 Rue St-Lubin, 41000; 02 54 74 66 09)* is an attractive family-run restaurant serving traditional dishes, with menus for kids and vegetarians as well.

FAMILY TREAT Au Rendez-vous des Pêcheurs *(27 Rue du Foix, 41000; 02 54 74 67 48; www.rendezvousdes pecheurs.com)* is not just for seafood, but also for other delectable dishes. An extensive wine list and a kids' menu are available too.

Shopping

For fancy chocolates and pralines, visit **Max Vauché** *(50 Rue du Commerce, 41000; 02 54 78 23 55)*. Head for **Au Paradis des Enfants** *(24 Rue Porte Chartraine, 41000; 02 54 51 98 86)*, a toy shop started in 1930. The **Maison de la Magie Robert-Houdin** *(see below)* has a gift shop with magic tricks and DVDs.

Take cover

Located next to the château, the **Maison de la Magie Robert-Houdin** *(Pl du Château, 41000; www.maison delamagie.fr)* is not to be missed. This museum of magic, is dedicated to the first great stage magician. Robot magicians introduce visitors to a world of illusions, special effects, automata and curiosities from the early days of magic to the present.

Next stop...

MORE STATELY CHÂTEAUX
A shuttle bus Navette des Châteaux links Blois to **Château de Chambord** *(www.chambord.org)*, the "Mini Paris on the Loire" begun by François I and finished by Louis XIV. The château contains a double helix staircase, designed by Leonardo da Vinci. Visit **Les Ecuries de Chambord** *(www.ecuries-chambord.com)* in the château stables for a carriage ride around the château or to watch the equestrian show in historical costume from May to September.

The same bus continues to the **Château de Cheverny** *(www. chateau-cheverny.com)*, the model for "Marlinspike Hall", the home of Captain Haddock in the Tintin series. Check out the expo on Tintin, watch hunting dogs being fed, visit the gardens, or tour the grounds in an electric car and on canal boats.

The grand Château de Chambord with its roof full of chimneys, spires and turrets

Above Gardens in bloom outside the Château de Clos Lucé, Amboise
Below An ornately furnished salon in the Château de Clos Lucé, Amboise

⑮ Château d'Amboise

Leonardo da Vinci's last home

Another lovely château overlooking the Loire river, Château d'Amboise became a royal residence when Charles VIII went off to invade Italy (1494–8) and brought back artists and architects to rebuild it in the Renaissance style. The château has been restored; there are beautiful gardens and a 15th-century chapel.

A later Italian visitor to the château was Leonardo da Vinci, who spent the rest of his life in the town and died in the arms of François I, his patron, at the nearby **Château de Clos Lucé**. This is the château where Leonardo da Vinci stayed as a guest; it displays exhibits on his life and life-size models of his flying machine and other inventions.

Letting off steam

There is an adventure playground by the Château de Clos Lucé, or head to **Pagode de Chateloup** (Route de Bléré, 37400; 02 47 57 20 97; www.pagode-chanteloup.com) and climb its 44-m (144-ft) stone pagoda overlooking a lake. There are old-fashioned wooden games for kids, such as skittles, tops and jev de la grenoville (an early form of pinball).

⑯ Bourges

A medieval mastermind

The former capital of the wealthy province of Berry, Bourges is an elegant city. Its centre is full of half-timbered buildings from the 15th century, arranged around one of France's greatest Gothic works, the Cathédrale de St-Étienne. A treasure house of medieval sculpture and 13th-century stained glass, it contains an astronomical clock. Climb the 396 steps of the Tour de Beurre, the "butter tower" that was paid for like Rouen's (see pp144–5), for a view over the city. Other sights include the magnificent 15th-century **Palais de Jacques Coeur**, named after the richest businessman of medieval France, the master of the mint

Intricately painted ceiling in the Palais de Jacques Coeur, Bourges

The Lowdown

🌐 **Map reference** 8 G3
Address 18000 (Cher). Palais de Jacques Coeur: 10 bis Rue Jacques-Coeur; 02 48 24 79 42; palais-jacques-coeur.monuments-nationaux.fr. Musée du Berry: 4 Rue des Arènes; 02 48 70 41 92; www.ville-bourges.fr. Musée des Arts Décoratifs: 6 Rue Bourbonnoux; 02 48 57 81 17; www.ville-bourges.fr

🚃 **Train** from Tours, Orléans and Paris

ℹ️ **Visitor information** 21 Rue Victor Hugo, 18000; 02 48 23 02 60; www.bourges-tourisme.com

🕐 **Open** Palais de Jacques Coeur: guided tours daily. Musée du Berry: closed Tue & Sun am. Musée des Arts Décoratifs: closed Mon & Sun am

🍵 **Eat and drink** Snacks Bar du Château d'Eau (35 Rue Séraucourt, 18000, 02 48 20 09 46; closed Sun), a welcoming neighbourhood café, it has an outdoor terrace and serves very inexpensive lunches. Real meal La Pasta (6 Rue Littré, 18000; 02 48 65 60 30; closed Sun & Mon) serves the city's best pizzas and other Italian dishes, which make this a firm family favourite.

🎭 **Festivals** Le Printemps à Bourges, a week of all kinds of French music in the streets (Apr). Un Eté à Bourges, concerts and animations in a different location almost every night (21 Jun–21 Sep)

The Lowdown

🌐 **Map reference** 8 E2
Address 37400 (Indre-et-Loire). Château d'Amboise: 60 Rue de la Concorde; 02 47 57 00 98; www.chateau-amboise.com. Château de Clos Lucé: 2 Rue du Clos Lucé; 02 47 57 00 73; www.vinci-closluce.com

🚃 **Train** from Tours and Blois

ℹ️ **Visitor information** Quai Général de Gaulle, 37400 Amboise; 02 47 57 09 28; www.amboise-valde loire.com

🕐 **Open** Château d'Amboise & Château de Clos Lucé: daily

🍵 **Eat and drink** Real meal La Trattoria (2 Rue Jean Jacques Rousseau, 37400; 02 47 57 67 57) is popular for its fresh pasta dishes and quick service. There is a play area. Family treat Les Remparts (2 Rue Paul Louis Courier, 37400; 02 47 57 20 43; www.restaurant-lesremparts-amboise.com) serves refined fish and meat dishes. Desserts are works of art and there is a menu for kids.

🎭 **Festival** A la Cour du Roy François, 350 actors put on a Renaissance son et lumière (sound & light) show with fireworks (Jul & Aug)

under Charles VII and ambassador to sultans and popes. Bourges has excellent museums such as the **Musée du Berry**, with a rich history and archaeological collection, and the evocative **Musée des Arts Décoratifs**, with a fine *belle époque* toy collection among the furnishings. The museum is housed in a striking mansion, the Hôtel Lallemant, dating from 1500.

Letting off steam

Head for the **Centre Nautique** *(Ave du 11 Novembre, 18000)*, which has two covered pools, a wading pool and an outdoor summer pool.

⑰ Orléans
The city of Joan of Arc

It was from Orléans that Joan of Arc saved France from the English in 1429. She is remembered in a statue on the cathedral, while the half-timbered **Maison de Jeanne d'Arc** has multimedia displays telling her story. The **Musée des**

Statue of Joan of Arc on the Cathédrale Ste-Croix, Orléans

Participants in medieval costumes during Les Fêtes Jeanne d'Arc, Orléans

Beaux Arts has an impressive collection of art from the 16th–20th centuries. The Renaissance Hôtel Cabu houses the **Musée Historique et Archéologique**, with remarkable Celtic bronzes and medieval relics.

Take a bus or train to the **Château de la Ferté**, located 20 km (12 miles) away, in the village of La Ferté-St-Aubin. There are indoor and outdoor games, working kitchens and stables that re-create the 18th century, as well as a rail museum with restored Orient Express carriages.

Letting off steam

Head for the **Parc Floral de La Source** *(Ave du Parc Floral, 45000; www.parcfloraldelasource.com)*, an enormous botanical garden with a butterfly conservatory and a menagerie of animals.

The Lowdown

🌐 **Map reference** 8 G1
Address 45000 (Loiret). Maison de Jeanne d'Arc: 3 Pl de Gaulle, 45000; 02 38 42 25 45; *www.orleans.fr*. Musée des Beaux Arts: Pl Ste-Croix, 45000; 02 38 79 21 55; *www.orleans.fr*. Musée Historique et Archéologique: Pl de l'Abbé Desnoyers, 45000; 02 38 79 25 60; *www.orleans.fr*. Château de la Ferté: Route d'Orléans, 45240 La Ferté St Aubin; 02 38 76 52 72; *www.chateau-ferte-st-aubin.com*

🚆 **Train** from Paris

ℹ️ **Visitor information** 2 Pl de l'Etape, 45000; 02 38 24 05 05; *www.tourisme-orleans.com*

🕐 **Open** Maison de Jeanne d'Arc & Musée des Beaux Arts: Tue–Sun.

Musée Historique et Archéologique: May–Sep: Tue–Sun pm; Jul & Aug: Tue–Sun; Oct–Apr: Wed & Sun afternoon. Château de la Ferté: Feb–Easter & Oct–mid-Nov: daily pm; closed mid-Nov & Jan

🍴 **Eat and drink** *Real meal* Les Fagots *(32 Rue du Poirier, 45000; 02 38 62 22 79)* is a local favourite for grilled meats. *Family treat* La Parenthèse *(26 Pl du Châtelet, 45000; 02 38 62 07 50; www.restaurant-la-parenthese.com; closed Sun & Mon)* offers excellent cuisine in a cheerful setting.

🎪 **Festival** Les Fêtes Jeanne d'Arc is marked by military parades, historical re-enactments, concerts, medieval market (29 Apr–9 May)

Picnic under €20; **Snacks** €20–45; **Real meal** €45–90; **Family treat** over €90 (based on a family of four)

⑱ Chartres Cathedral
The most perfect Gothic cathedral

An important pilgrimage site and a great centre of medieval learning, Chartres's pride and joy is the Cathédrale Notre Dame – the most perfect Gothic cathedral in France – completed in AD 1260 after an earlier Romanesque church was damaged by fire. Spared by the ravages of war, its sculpted portals and colour-drenched stained glass depict over 5,000 figures. There is more to Chartres than the cathedral, including attractive old quarters and museums of art and stained glass.

Statues on the Royal Portal

Key Features

Northwest Tower Climb this Gothic pinnacle for great views.

Southwest Tower

Vaulted Ceiling

South Porch

Crypt This crypt houses a famous relic, the *Sancta Camisia*, or tunic of the Virgin Mary.

Labyrinth Believers saw this maze as a symbolic pilgrimage to Jerusalem.

Royal Portal

Musée des Beaux-Arts Housed in the former bishops' palace, near the cathedral, it has on show French paintings and art from Oceania.

Rose windows There are three spectacular flowers, one over each portal. The West and North roses depict scenes of saints.

Stained glass Surviving for over 800 years, these windows have never been replaced.

Royal (West) Portal Begun in 1145, it shows Christ at the Last Judgement and the statues of Old Testament kings.

The Lowdown

🌐 **Map reference** 4 F6
Address 28000 (Eure-et-Loire). Cathedral: 24 Cloître Notre-Dame; cathedrale.chartres. free.fr. Crypt: Pl de la Cathédrale: www.chartres-tourisme.com. Musée des Beaux-Arts: 29 Cloître Notre Dame; www.ville-chartres.fr

🚋 **Train** from Paris Montparnasse and Le Mans

ℹ️ **Visitor information** Pl de la Cathédrale, 28000; 02 37 18 26 26; www.chartres-tourisme.com

🕐 **Open** Cathedral and crypt: 8:30am–7:30pm daily, no visits during Mass. Northwest Tower: Sep–Apr: 9:30am–noon & 2–4:30pm Mon–Sat, 2–4:30pm

Sun; May–Aug: 9:30am–noon & 2–5:30pm Mon–Sat, 2–5:30pm Sun. Musée des Beaux-Arts: Nov–Apr: 10am–noon & 2–5pm Wed–Sat & Mon, 2–5pm Sun; May–Oct: 10am–noon & 2–6pm Wed–Mon, 2–6pm Sun

💶 **Price** Cathedral: free. Crypt: €10–20; under 7s free. Northwest Tower: €23–33; under 18s free. Musée des Beaux-Arts: €6–16; under 18s free

👭 **Skipping the queue** Buy the Chartres Pass at the tourist office to see a number of sights.

👇 **Guided tours** Contact the tourist office for details.

👫 **Age range** 4 plus

🏃 **Activities** Walk the labyrinth of the cathedral on Fridays, between Lent and mid-October, when it is not covered by chairs.

⏱️ **Allow** A day

☕ **Cafe** Le Serpente, just across the road from the cathedral, has ice creams and milkshakes.

🚻 **Toilets** No

🎭 **Festivals** Festival de Pâques features a children's book fair (Apr). Chartres en Lumières (May–Sep)

Good family value?
This is one of the world's great sights and it is free. Children will especially enjoy the labyrinth.

Letting off steam

Rent a canoe or pedal boat at **La Petite Venise** (*50 Blvd de la Courtille, 28000; 02 37 91 03 65; Apr–Oct*) for a ride on the Eure through the centre of the city. For year-round fun, visit **Odyssée** (*Rue du Médecin Général Beyne, 28000; 02 37 25 33 33; www.vert-marine.com*) – the largest pool complex in France, which has Europe's biggest indoor river, wave pool, wading pool and slides, as well as an ice-skating rink.

Family fun at the indoor wading pool at Odyssée

Eat and drink

Picnic: under €20; Snacks: €25–45; Real meal: €45–90; Family treat: over €90 (based on a family of four)

PICNIC Monoprix (*21 Rue Noel Ballay, 28000; closed Sun*), a 15-minute walk from the cathedral, stocks ingredients for picnics that can be enjoyed just behind the cathedral, in the Jardins de l'Evêché, overlooking the Eure.
SNACKS La Mie Caline (*36 Rue Bois Merrain, 28000; 02 37 21 95 24; closed Sun*) offers a good choice of sandwiches, cakes and pastries, and ice cream to eat in or take away.
REAL MEAL La Picoterie (*36 Rue des Changes, 28000; 02 37 36 14 54; www.picoterie.com; open daily*) is a cheerful place that serves soups, crêpes, omelettes and salads.
FAMILY TREAT Les Feuillantines (*4 Rue du Bourg, 28000; 02 37 30 22 21; closed Sun*) offers well-prepared French classics, served with the Loire's wines. There is a pretty terrace and an excellent set price menu.

Shopping

Visit the **Galerie du Vitrail** (*17 Cloître Nôtre-Dame, 28000; 02 37 36 10 03*), the specialists in stained glass, who have a collection of historic works and modern pieces that are small enough to take home. For dolls, toys, antiques and miniatures of all kinds, go to **Tuvache et Fils** (*34 Rue des Changes, 28000; 02 37 21 60 43*).

Find out more

DIGITAL Go to *www.labyrinthos.net/ chartresfaq.html* for the real story behind the cathedral's labyrinth. For more detail on every aspect of the cathedral, visit *www.tinyurl.com/ 3vapnoq*.

Next stop...

FARMING AND ART Chartres has another masterpiece made by a single man: **La Maison Picassiette** (*22 Rue du Repos, 28000; 02 37 34 10 78*). Born in 1900, Raymond Isidore was a street sweeper, who spent 26 years (1938–64) covering his house, gardens and furniture and even his wife's sewing machine with bizarre, colourful mosaics of broken tiles and crockery. Visitors can also check out the **Conservatoire de l'Agriculture** (*Pont de Mainvilliers, 28000; 02 37 84 15 00; www.le compa.fr*), an interactive museum on the history of farming. The **Musée du Vitrail** (*Rue Cardinal Pie, 28000; 02 37 21 65 72; www.centre-vitrail. org*) has stained glass from all periods and various exhibits on the history of the art; they also provide live demonstrations.

Unique courtyard of La Maison Picassiette, covered with multi-coloured mosaics

Where to Stay in the Loire Valley

With hotels and B&Bs in elegant châteaux, traditional *gîtes* (cottage rentals), city hotels, seaside apartments and fully equipped camp sites – some open year-round – the Loire Valley has something to suit every family's need and budget.

AGENCIES

Experience Loire
www.experienceloire.com
The directory lists *gîtes*, B&Bs, self-catering cottages and other types of accomodation in all price ranges, with websites of owners.

Pays de la Loire
www.westernloire.com
This site lists nearly all the available places to stay for all budgets on the Atlantic side of the Loire.

Angers   Map 7 C2

HOTELS
Hôtel du Mail
8 Rue des Ursules, 49100; 02 41 25 05 25; www.hoteldumail.fr
A short walk from the city centre, this hotel, with a massive iron gate draped in wisteria, was once an 18th-century town mansion. It retains a lot of its original character, including high ceilings that keep it cool in summer.
 P   €€

Hotel L'Océane
RN 23, 49140 Villeveque; 02 41 32 93 34; www.hotelaloceane.com
This is a friendly two-star motel in the suburbs, convenient for families touring by car. Pleasant rooms come with Wi-Fi. There is a small garden, playground and also a restaurant specializing in grilled dishes.
 P ✳   €€

The entrance of centrally located Le Christina, Bourges

CAMPING

Camping Port Caroline
Rue du Pont Caroline, 49800 Brain-sur-l'Authion; 02 41 80 42 18; www.campingduportcaroline.fr
One of the nicest camp grounds in the region, Port Caroline is set by the river under big trees. Besides pitches, they offer a wide range of tents, wood chalets and mobile homes. Apart from games such as table tennis, they also rent bikes.
🚐 🏠 **P** ⊘   €

Blois   Map 8 F2

HOTEL
Côté Loire
2 Pl de la Grève, 41000; 02 54 78 07 86; www.coteloire.com
This is an unpretentious budget choice by the river, a short walk from the Château Royal de Blois. The Wi-Fi-equipped rooms are simple, but comfortable enough for a day or two. The excellent courtyard restaurant is a local favourite and has a good kids' menu.
🚐 **P**   €€

CAMPING

La Grande Tortue
3 Route de Pontevoy, 41120 Candé-sur-Beauvron; 02 54 44 15 20; www.la-grande-tortue.com
A large complex, 12 km (7 miles) southwest of Blois, it offers a wide choice of chalets and mobile homes with a playground and other games for kids. In summer, there are staff to organize activities and bikes, as well as pedal karts to rent.
🚐 🏠 **P** ⊘   €

Bourges   Map 8 G3

HOTEL
Le Christina
5 Rue de la Halle, 18000; 02 48 70 58 13; www.le-christina.com
Centrally located, this hotel has stylish black and grey rooms equipped with Wi-Fi. There is

no restaurant, but there are quite a few at walking distance. The staff is friendly and helpful.
🚐 **P** ✳   €€

Chambord   Map 8 F2

CAMPING
Château des Marais
27 Rue de Chambord, 41500 Muides-sur-Loire; 02 54 87 05 42; www.chateau-des-marais.com
This château offers chalet and mobile-home accomodation in its grounds. There is a giant water-park playground for kids, as well as games such as mini-golf. Bikes, kayaks and canoes are also available to rent.
P ⊘   €–€€

Basket of assorted bread with jam for breakfast at Diderot, Chinon

Chinon   Map 7 D3

HOTEL
Diderot
4 Rue du Buffon, 37500; 02 47 93 18 87; www.hoteldiderot.com
This family-run hotel is set in a lovely 15th-century building with a pretty courtyard and rooms furnished with antiques. There are 65 different flavours of home-made jams on offer at breakfast. Babysitting available.
🚐 **P**   €€

Le Mans   Map 7 D1

HOTEL
Hotel Green7
447 Ave Georges Durand, 72100; 02 43 40 30 30; www.hotelgreen7.com
On the edge of town, this is a great place to stay on race days as it is

located close to the start and finish points. The hotel has bright modern rooms. The restaurant is good and has a decent kids' menu.

🛏️ P   €

Les Espesses
Map 7 C3

HOTEL
Le Puy du Fou
85590 Grand Parc Puy du Fou; 08 20 09 10 10; www.puydufou.com
The park has three different wonderfully tacky theme hotels on the Îles de Clovis grounds in re-created Dark Ages huts on stilts over a lagoon, a Roman villa, and an 18th-century house, the Logis de Lescure. See website for offers.

🛏️ P   €€

Les Sables d'Olonne
Map 7 A4

HOTEL
Arc en Ciel
13 Rue Chanzy, 85100; 02 51 96 92 50; www.arcencielhotel.com
Near the beach, this hotel has a grim exterior but the rooms, some with balconies, are comfortable and colourful. The breakfast room is a surprising belle époque fantasy.

🛏️ P   €€

Nantes
Map 7 B2

HOTELS
Hotel Cholet
10 Rue Grasset, 44000; 02 40 73 31 04; www.hotelcholet-nantes.com
Centrally located near the Musée d'Histoire Naturelle, the hotel has elegant red and black rooms and an unusual Indo-Chinese touch to the decor. Rooms are equipped with Wi-Fi and free cots are available for kids under two. Buffet breakfast is served, but there is no restaurant.

🛏️   €€

Hotel de la Régate
155 Route de Gachet, 44300; 02 40 50 22 22; www.hotel-nantes-laregate.com
Located 15 minutes from the city centre, this modern eco-friendly hotel has spacious, airy rooms with all conveniences. The restaurant is good for seafood. There are special offers during off-season months and weekends; see their website for details.

🛏️ P   €€€

A themed room in Un Coin Chez Vous, Nantes

SELF-CATERING
Un Coin Chez Vous
Various locations, Nantes, 44000; 06 64 20 31 09; www.uncoinchezsoi.com
This organization offers unique city-centre flats. The themed accommodation ranges from "childhood memories" and "cuisine" to "Jules Verne". All flats can be rented by the week or for one night only. Some of the flats can accomodate four and most are inexpensive; breakfast is included.

🛏️   €–€€€

Orléans
Map 8 G1

HOTEL
Hôtel de l'Abeille
64 Rue Alsace-Lorraine, 45000; 02 38 53 54 87; www.hoteldelabeille.com
This well-maintained hotel has been in the same family for almost a century. It offers well-appointed rooms and a small garden terrace with fine views. Wi-Fi available.

🛏️   €€

Saumur
Map 7 D2

BED AND BREAKFAST
Château de Beaulieu
Route de Montsoreau, 49400; 02 41 51 19 01; www.chateaudebeaulieu.fr
Located 2 km (1 mile) from the city centre, the château was built in 1727 and boasts exquisite grounds and a terraces. The amiable Irish owners will help arrange horse-riding, boating and other activities.

🛏️ P ⊙   €€€

Château de la Coutancière
Route de la Coutancière, 49650 Brain-sur-Allonces; 02 41 40 37 13; www.chateaudelacoutanciere.com
This serene early 19th-century château, 10 km (6 miles) from Saumur,

is set in a huge park. The spacious rooms are furnished with antiques. There is a giant outdoor chess set.

🛏️ P ⊙   €€

Tours
Map 8 E2

HOTELS
La Héraudière
60 Rue Ronsard, 37100; 02 47 72 94 47; www.la-heraudiere.fr
This handsome family mansion is 10 minutes by bus north of the centre. Rooms have Wi-Fi. There is a playground and games for kids. A babysitting service is provided, as are table d'hôte (communal dining) dinners on weekdays.

✕ 🛏️ P   €€

Hotel Trianon
57 Ave de Grammont, 37000; 02 47 05 35 27; www.hoteltrianontours.com
Just south of the centre near the train station, this hotel is basic but with well-kept rooms with Wi-Fi and satellite TV. The pleasant terrace is suited for breakfast and lounging in the afternoon. The staff are helpful.

🛏️ P   €€

CAMPING
Camping Les Acacias
Rue Berthe Morisot, 37700 La Ville-aux-Dames; 02 47 44 08 16; www.camplvad.com
The leafy camp site is set on the eastern edge of Tours, but close enough to take bus 50 into the town. It offers accomodation in heated mobile homes. A playground, laundry and Wi-Fi are available.

🛏️ 🍽️ P   €

Price Guide
The following price ranges are based on one night's accommodation in high season for a family of four, inclusive of service charges and any additional taxes.

€ Under €100 €€ €100–200 €€€ over €200

Key to symbols see back cover flap

Central France
and the Alps

This vast area in the heart of France is bursting with historical and cultural gems, the heritage of the Romans and the powerful Dukes of Burgundy, and of its location at a pilgrimage route crossroads. It is also a magnificent land of wide, open spaces, with forests, river gorges, the volcanic mountains of the Massif Central and the snowy Alps – a perfect blend of art and history surrounded by the great outdoors.

Highlights

Dijon
Explore the splendid capital of the Dukes of Burgundy and discover its gastronomic heritage (see pp200–201).

Parc Naturel Régional du Morvan
The splendid outdoors for all the family – hiking, watersports, along with stirring tales of the French Resistance in World War II (see pp206–207).

Gorges du Tarn
Explore these craggy gorges in a canoe to see some of the most beautiful scenery and varied wildlife in the area (see p242).

Le Puy-en-Velay
Visit this spectacular town set in rolling country, where religious monuments perch on jagged volcanic outcrops (see pp244–5).

Chamonix
Take the world's highest vertical ascent cable car up the Aiguille du Midi for a close-up look at Mont Blanc, as well as hiking and skiing (see pp224–5).

Gorges de l'Ardèche
Starting at the natural arch at Pont d'Arc, kayak down a long stretch of the Ardèche river beneath towering 300-m (1,000-ft) limestone cliffs (see pp232–3).

Left Monument to Dr Michel Paccard, who first climbed Mont Blanc, Chamonix
Above left Grazing cows at Les Hautes-Combes, Parc Régional Naturel du Haut-Jura

The Best of
Central France and the Alps

Central France has diverse landscapes and cultural attractions to explore. The Alps, the Auvergne and the Gorges de l'Ardèche make for superb outdoor adventures, while the museums of Dijon and Lyon and the churches and châteaux of Burgundy and the Massif Central delight young and old with their cultural treasures. The cuisine varies from the rich dishes and wines of Burgundy and the Rhône to cheeses of the Massif Central.

Culture vultures

Savour the heritage of the Dukes of Burgundy in the palaces of **Dijon** (see pp200–201) and **Beaune** (see p202) and learn the story of crusaders and pilgrims in **Vézelay** (see pp204–205). In **Cluny** (see pp208–209), discover how the ruins of the abbey, set in a backwater, were once the home of Europe's most powerful monastic order. Watch the world's first film and learn about the history of film-making at the Musée Lumière in **Lyon** (see pp220–21), along with puppet shows at the Théâtre de La Maison de Guignol. The Musée d'Art Moderne in **St-Étienne** (see p222) houses a fine art collection. The Romanesque Abbaye de Ste-Foy in **Conques** (see pp246–7) has a treasury museum where

Left The carved tympanum of the Abbaye de Ste Foy, Conques
Below The extraordinary hilltop chapels of Le-Puy-en-Velay

Above *Canoeists paddling in the river at the beach by the Pont d'Arc, the Gorges de l'Ardèche*

St Foy's relics are kept in a dazzling gold statue. A display of the world's oldest cave paintings, from the Grotte Chauvet, is held at Vallon-Pont-d'Arc in the **Gorges de l'Ardèche** *(see pp232–3)*.

In a week

In Burgundy and Franche-Comté, spend a couple of days in **Dijon** and **Beaune**, then see a farmers' market in action in **Louhans** *(see p211)*. Explore the abbey in **Cluny** and then head north to hike by the **Lac des Settons** *(see p207)* in the Morvan and see the Romanesque pilgrims' church, the Basilique Ste Madeleine, in **Vézelay**.

During a week in the Rhône Valley and Alps, soak up the atmosphere of **Lyon** in the quarters of Vieux Lyon, Croix-Rousse and Fourvière Hill. See the **Gorges de l'Ardèche** by car or kayak. Alpine adventures await in **Chamonix** *(see pp224–5)*, from hikes to rides up the Aiguille du Midi in a cable car and to the glaciers of the Mer de Glace in the Train du Montenvers.

In the Massif Central, tour the volcanoes of the picturesque **Parc Naturel Régional des Volcans d'Auvergne** *(see p250)* and have fun at

Vulcania *(see p250)*. Head south to **Le Puy-en-Velay** *(see pp244–5)* to see churches perched on rocky peaks and the pilgrims' Cathédrale de Notre-Dame. Get active with a day's rafting down the **Gorges du Tarn** *(see p242)*. Go underground amid stalagmites and stalactites in the **Aven Armand** *(see pp240–41)* cavern.

Outdoor action

Chamonix is at the heart of one of the world's great outdoor playgrounds – perfect for winter sports, and walking or climbing in summer. The **Parc National de la Vanoise** *(see p230)* is a quieter option for fun in the snow; in summer, hike across the Col d'Iséran, Europe's highest mountain pass. In Burgundy, walk, cycle and canoe among the forest trails, hills and lakes of the **Parc Naturel Régional du Morvan** *(see pp206–207)*, or hire bikes and pedal around châteaux and vineyards on the car-free paths of the *Voie Verte*. Stay in St Claude or Les Rousses in the **Parc Régional Naturel du Haut-Jura** *(see pp212–13)* and hike around its waterfalls, valleys and peaks.

Gastronomic delights

Turn the kids into budding foodies with top-class dining and wine in Burgundy's heartland, home to *boeuf bourguignon* (Burgundy beef stew), *coq au vin* (cockerel cooked in wine) and Dijon's gingerbread. Kids can learn how to cook at Le Chabichou in Courchevel, in **Les Trois Vallées** *(see pp230–31)*. See how cheese is made at Beaufort des Montagnes in **Moûtiers** *(see p230)*. Try the famous walnuts of **Grenoble** *(see p231)* in a yummy cake called L'Olympique at the Patisserie Les Ecrins. Enjoy the tour of Musée du Nougat in **Montélimar** *(see pp234–5)*, to taste some fine nougats.

Left *A scrumptious selection of the region's finest gourmet cheeses in a shop in Chamonix*

Central France and the Alps

Splendid, contrasting scenery lies in the heart of France. The lush winelands of Burgundy and the Rhône are crisscrossed by placid canals and dotted with historic treasures. The old towns of Dijon, Beaune and Lyon have narrow, mysterious alleys. Around them are dramatic mountains: the Jura, the Massif Central and the Alps. Superb transport facilities, whether switchback highways, shuttle buses or mountain railways, make high Alpine valleys accessible.

Giraffes at the massive Parc de la Tête d'Or, Lyon

Haunting ruins of the Château de Murol

Places of interest

The unique bubble-shaped cable car in transit, Grenoble

The Lowdown

 Getting there and around
Air (see p198). **Train** TGV high-speed trains from Paris or Lille to Dijon, Grenoble, Lyon, Chambéry, Bourg St-Maurice and Geneva. Slower Intercité trains run from Paris to the Massif Central, especially Limoges and Clermont Ferrand. Each region has TER local train lines (www.ter-sncf.com) with services to many small towns. **Bus** Contact tourist offices for local bus services and local buses running from main towns to nearby villages. Lyon has superb public transport, with metro lines, tramways, hillside funiculars and buses (www.tcl. fr). Grenoble and Clermont Ferrand have local tramways. **Car** Europcar (www.europcar. com) has offices across France; Rentacar (www.rentacar.fr) offers rentals at low prices.

 Supermarkets Essentials can be bought from Intermarché, Carrefour, Super U and Leclerc. In the countryside, there is at least one supermarket in the main town of each district. **Markets** Many cities and large towns have a main market, often indoors, open most of the week except Monday. Tourist offices have details of local market days.

 Opening hours Large stores and supermarkets are open Mon–Sat. Many small shops, mostly in small towns and villages, still close for lunch (noon–2pm). Very few shops and petrol stations away from tourist areas open on Sundays, except some supermarkets (often Sunday mornings only) and pâtisseries, as well as boulangeries (bread shops).

 Pharmacies There is at least one pharmacy, identified by a green cross outside, in each town and many villages. A list in the window will give details of the nearest pharmacie de garde open outside normal hours (on Sundays and at night). They are also listed in local newspapers and on www. pharmaciesdegarde.com.

 Toilets Large supermarkets, shopping centres and markets have public toilets. Cities have pay or free street toilets that clean themselves after every use.

A brightly painted merry-go-round in a town square, Beaune

Key to symbols *see back cover flap*

Central France and the Alps Regional Airports

Lyon's St-Exupéry airport is the main air gateway to central France, with its own TGV rail station and excellent rail and road links to Lyon and every part of the region. Alpine winter sports enthusiasts often prefer Chambéry or Grenoble, which have many low-cost flights from the UK and other parts of Europe, especially in winter. Dijon airport has limited international flights.

Dijon-Bourgogne

Dijon's small airport, 6 km (4 miles) south of the city, has low-cost flights from Southampton with Eastern Airways and services from several French cities, as well as charter flights. Rental cars or taxis (€20) are the main transport; buses are fairly infrequent. A restaurant and ATM are on site.

Lyon-St-Exupéry

Lyon's airport is located 20 km (13 miles) east of the city. It has Air France services to many French and European destinations, as well as flights with British Airways from London, with Aer Lingus from Dublin, and from all parts of Europe and North Africa with a range of other airlines. There is also a seasonal service from Montréal. Low-cost services include easyJet flights from London (Gatwick or Stansted), Edinburgh and other European cities.

The airport has its own station on the Paris–Marseille TGV high-speed rail line, which also offers direct connections to Chambéry, Annecy and Grenoble. Altibus (www.altibus. com) operates regular bus shuttle services to these and other Alpine resorts. The best way to get into Lyon is the Rhônexpress tram (www. rhonexpress.fr), which reaches the city centre in 25 minutes, with services daily every 15 minutes (see

Inside the departure terminal of Chambéry-Savoie airport

website for timings and fares). Taxis (€40) are plentiful and there are car rental desks in the Arrivals terminal.

The airport has been extensively renovated and has a wide range of restaurants, from the smart Espace Le Bec to brasseries, cafés and pizza restaurants. There is a wide range of hotels and several shops, including a post office and a pharmacy.

Chambéry-Savoie

Chambéry-Savoie airport, located 8 km (5 miles) from Chambéry, has low-cost flights with Flybe, Jet2 and bmibaby from many UK airports; British Airways flights from London-City and charter flights from the UK, as well as several other European cities. Most services only operate during the ski season. There is a taxi (€20) rank and car rental desks, and in winter, Trans'Neige provides shuttle buses to the town and other ski resorts. It has fairly limited facilities, with a café-restaurant and shop.

Grenoble-Isère

Located 45 km (29 miles) northwest of Grenoble city, Grenoble-Isère airport mainly has low-cost flights in the winter season from UK, Irish and northern European airports, particularly with easyJet (from Bristol, Birmingham, Edinburgh, Liverpool

and different London airports) and Ryanair (from London Stansted and Dublin). There is a bus service (€12.50) to the train and bus station in Grenoble. In winter, Altibus and other companies run shuttle buses to alpine resorts. Local taxi companies provide transfers all over the area. It has a café-restaurant and shops.

Limoges

Situated 6 km (4 miles) northwest of the town, Limoges is a popular airport for low-cost airlines such as Flybe (from Newcastle and Southampton) and Ryanair (from East Midlands, Liverpool and Stansted), as well as domestic flights with Air France. More destinations are available in summer. Taxi (€20) transfers are available to Limoges train station and there are several car rental desks. The airport has been modernized, with a restaurant and an on-site hotel.

Rodez-Marcillac

Located 11 km (7 miles) from Rodez town, the airport is largely served by Ryanair, with low-cost flights from Stansted, Porto and Dublin (seasonal only), but also has French domestic flights. Taxis (€25 to Rodez) are the only form of public transport, but there are car rental desks.

The Lowdown

Chambéry-Savoie 04 79 54 49 54; www.chambery-airport.com

Dijon-Bourgogne 03 80 67 67 67; www.aeroport.dijon.cci.fr

Grenoble-Isère 04 76 65 48 48; www.grenoble-airport.com

Limoges 05 55 43 30 30; www.aeroportlimoges.com

Lyon-St-Exupéry 08 26 80 08 26; www.lyonaeroports.com

Rodez-Marcillac 05 65 76 02 00; www.aveyron.cci.fr

The futuristic TGV station adjacent to Lyon-St-Exupéry airport

Burgundy and Franche-Comté

Rich in landscape, history, art and good living, Burgundy has rolling gold-and-green hills that produce world-famous wines and also many of France's most celebrated foods. Towns and countryside boast a range of historic buildings, from the giant abbey at Vézelay to Beaune's amazing Hôtel-Dieu. Franche-Comté has the Jura mountains, ideal for active exploration.

Vézelay
p204

Dijon
p200

Cluny
p208

Parc Naturel
Régional du
Haut-Jura
p212

Below *Patchwork of rolling fields, Vézelay*

① Dijon
Gothic gargoyles and gingerbread

The city of Dijon had its golden age in the 14th and 15th centuries, thanks to the powerful Dukes of Burgundy, who left behind plenty of medieval art treasures and splendid architecture such as the Palais des Ducs, whose Gothic halls and towers are concealed behind 18th-century Classical columns. Dijon has surged into the 21st century as a vibrant centre of culture and top-class food and wine. The compact historic centre with cobbled streets is made for exploring on foot or by bike, and it has beautiful parks and squares.

View of the city from the tower in Palais des Ducs

Key Sights

Notre-Dame The façade of this 13th-century Gothic church is richly decorated with gargoyles. When the hour chimes, the Jacquemart family of mechanical figures come out of the clock on the right-hand steeple.

Hôtel de Vogüé This 17th-century mansion showcases a colourful tiled roof and fancy Renaissance decoration of carved fruit garlands.

Palais des Ducs The palace of the Dukes of Burgundy houses the Musée des Beaux Arts, with the sculpted tomb of Phillip the Bold in the Salle des Gardes. Climb for impressive views from its Tour de Phillipe-le-Bon.

Musée de la Vie Bourguignonne The museum has re-created a 19th-century street, including a beauty salon whose equipment looks more like instruments of torture.

RUE ODEBERT
RUE QUENTIN
RUE VERRERIE
RUE MUSETTE
RUE JEANNIN
RUE DES FORGES
RUE LAMONNOYE
PL STE CHAPELLE
RUE DE LA LIBERTE
PL DE LA LIBÉRATION
PL DU THEATRE
R VAILLANT
PL ST MICHEL
RUE CHABOT CHARNY
RUE LEGOUZ GERLAND
RUE BUFFON

← **Parc de l'Arquebuse** 1 km (half a mile)

Musée de la Vie Bourguignonne 450 m (400 yards)

Palais des Ducs

Parc de l'Arquebuse These botanical gardens have two shallow pools for paddling and a Musée d'Histoire Naturelle.

The Lowdown

🌐 **Map reference** 9 D2
Address 21000 (Côte d'Or). Notre-Dame: 9 Pl Notre Dame; 03 80 30 40 42. Hôtel de Vogüé: 8 Rue de la Chouette; 03 80 74 51 51. Musée de la Vie Bourguignonne: Monastère des Bernardines, 17 Rue Ste-Anne; 03 80 48 80 90. Palais des Ducs: Pl de la Libération; 03 80 74 51 51. Musée des Beaux Arts: 03 80 74 52 09. Tour de Phillippe-le-Bon: 03 80 74 52 71. Parc de

l'Arquebuse: Ave Albert 1er; 03 80 48 82 00

🚗 **Train** TGV from Paris

ℹ️ **Visitor information** 11 Rue des Forges, 21000; 08 92 70 05 58; www.visitdijon.com

🕐 **Open** Musée de la Vie Bourguignonne: May–Sep: 9am–12:30pm & 1:30–6pm; rest of the year: 9am–noon & 2–6pm; closed Tue. Tour de Phillippe-le-Bon: Apr–Nov: 9am–noon & 1:45–5:30pm (every 45 mins);

Dec–Mar: 9am–5:30pm Sat & Sun (every 1 hour). Musée des Beaux Arts: May–Oct: 9:30am–6pm; 10am–5pm rest of the year; closed Tue. Parc de l'Arquebuse: Muséum d'Histoire Naturelle: currently closed for renovation

💰 **Prices** Tour de Phillippe-le-Bon: €10–20. Museums: free

👥 **Skipping the queue** The Dijon Côte de Nuits pass gives access to 30 attractions and unlimited transport. Contact tourist office

Prices given are for a family of four

Letting off steam

Head for the **Parc de la Colombière** (156 Rue de Longvic, 21000; 03 80 65 42 33), where kids can try their skill at ropes and zip lines high in the trees. For strolling, swimming and canoeing, take bus 30 to Lac Kir, a summertime "beach" located 11 minutes west of Dijon.

La Causerie des Mondes, an Asian café-restaurant on Rue Vauban

Eat and drink

Picnic: under €20; Snacks: €20–45; Real meal: €45–90; Family treat: over €90 (based on a family of four)

PICNIC Marché Central (Pl des Halles, 21000; closed Sun) is a 19th-century ironwork and glass market hall that is the best place to stock up on local goodies such as cheese, ham and bread. Go for an open-air feast in one of the leafy parks or on the pedestrianized Place de la Libération, where the pavement fountains are a magnet for kids on warm summer days.
SNACKS La Causerie des Mondes (16 Rue Vauban, 21000; 03 80 49 96 59; www.lacauseriedesmondes. fr; closed Sun & Mon) is a cosy Asian-themed tea room that serves

dozens of exotic teas, coffees and chocolates to sip, as well as light meals and cakes.
REAL MEAL Le Bistrot des Halles (10 Rue Bannelier, 21000; 03 80 49 94 15; www.jeanpierrebilloux. com; closed Sun & Mon) serves classic French bistro food and local specialities such as snails, jambon persillé (jellied ham with parsley) and bouef bourguignon (hearty stew of beef braised in wine).
FAMILY TREAT Le Pré aux Clercs (13 Pl de la Libération, 21000; 03 80 38 05 05; www.jeanpierrebilloux. com; closed Sun dinner & Mon) is Burgundian super-chef Jean-Pierre Billoux's flagship restaurant offering top-class dining with an al fresco terrace facing the Palais des Ducs.

Shopping

Go to **Mulot & Petitjean** (13 Pl Bossuet, 21000; 03 80 30 07 10; www.mulotpetitjean.fr), a palatial timbered shop selling gingerbread, one of Dijon's unmissable treats. The **Maille Mustard** (32 Rue de la Liberté, 21000; 03 80 30 41 02; www.maille. com) has over 30 exotic flavours of mustard. Kids can visit the Musée de la Vie Bourguignonne museum shop to buy old-fashioned toys.

A walkway fringed by trees along the Ouche river, Canal de Bourgogne

Next stop...

CANAL DE BOURGOGNE Head for the Canal de Bourgogne (www. burgundy-canal.com) located 14 km (9 miles) from Dijon, which is part of France's huge interconnecting network of waterways that allows boats to travel between the Atlantic and Mediterranean. Hire a boat from **Locaboat** (www.locaboat.com).

KIDS' CORNER

Things to do...
1 Can you see the gargoyles on the façade of the Notre-Dame? Try to mimic their expressions!
2 Find the little figure of the chouette (owl) on the Notre-Dame façade. If you stroke it with your left hand and make a wish, it is supposed to bring good luck.
3 Call in at the chocolatier Maison Carbillet (www. chocolat-carbillet.com), and take home a box of dark, milk and white chocolate escargots (snails) as a souvenir of Dijon.

GINGERBREAD FAME
Ever wondered why Dijon is famous for gingerbread? Its French name, pain d'épice (spice bread), is a clue. The town was on the historic spice route from Asia to Europe.

Robot family
Look at the clock on top of Notre-Dame. The mechanical man who strikes the bell is named Jacquemart and he arrived in 1500. After a 100 years on his own, the people of Dijon felt sorry for him and gave him a wife in 1610. A 100 years later, they added a son, Jacquelinet, who strikes the bell for the half-hours. Finally, in 1881, a daughter named Jacquelinette came along to strike the quarter hours.

🪧 **Guided tours** Contact tourist office for details
🧍‍♂️🧍 **Age range** 5 plus
⏱ **Allow** 2 days
🧍🧍 **Toilets** Near Les Halles and the Darcy, Grangier, Condorcet and Ste-Anne car parks.

Good family value?
Dijon's atmospheric old town, kid-friendly museums and leafy parks make it a superb family destination.

② Beaune
Roof-eating monsters and rampart walks

Flanked by the beautiful vineyards in Burgundy, the ancient centre of Beaune is a rewarding place to explore on foot. Its highlight is the palatial hospice known as the **Hôtel-Dieu**, which was founded in 1443 by the Duke of Burgundy's chancellor Nicolas Rolin to help Beaune's suffering citizens after the Hundred Years' War. The intact medieval gem is roofed with colourful geometric glazed tile mosaics. The Great Hall of the Poor has a carved and painted roof with beams held in monsters' mouths. An amazing nine-panelled painting of the *Last Judgement* by Flemish artist Rogier van der Weyden reminded the poor of what would happen to them if they did not lead good lives.

Continue the Middle Ages mood with a wall walk around parts of the ramparts above the cobbled streets. Finish by learning what makes a true Burgundy mustard at the **Moutarderie Fallot**, a mustard mill that has been in business since 1840 and is one of the last independent manufacturers.

Letting off steam

Head for the **Parc de la Bouzaise** (Rue du Docteur Bouley, 21200; 03 80 24 57 23) on the edge of town, in a lovely spot at the foot of the vineyards. It has a small zoo, a kids' playground and boating lake. Pick up a brochure of marked trails at the tourist office for hikes into the hills of the Montagne de Beaune.

The stunning glazed-tile roof of the Hôtel-Dieu, Beaune

③ Vallée d'Ouche Steam Railway, Bligny-sur-Ouche
Steam trains and canal boats

Steam and diesel trains of the Vallée d'Ouche steam railway run on a section of the Épinac to Dijon line, which is one of France's oldest railway routes. The trip runs for 9 km (6 miles), through a valley of wooded hillsides and meadows, from Bligny-sur-Ouche to Pont d'Ouche, where the Ouche river and the Burgundy Canal meet. Take bicycles – it is possible to rent them from the tourist office in Bligny – and do a one-way trip on the train, returning by bike from Pont d'Ouche. Take a break in the little riverside café that is popular with boaters on the canal

who moor up for a drink and bite to eat. Alternatively, cycle along the canal towpath to the pretty village of La Bussière-sur-Ouche, 13 km (8 miles) north of Bligny, to see the barges moored on the canal and have lunch in its posh abbey hotel.

Take cover

Head for the **Château du Clos de Vougeot** (www.closdevougeot.fr), 22 km (14 miles) east of Bligny, to learn about how wine has been made on the Côte d'Or since Cistercian

A Vallée d'Ouche steam railway train arriving at the station, Bligny-sur-Ouche

The Lowdown

🌐 **Map reference** 9 C3
Address 21360 (Côte d'Or). Chemin de Fer de la Vallée d'Ouche; 06 30 01 48 29; www. thetouristrailwayoftheouche valley.blogspot.com

🚌 **Bus** Transco bus 47 from Dijon and bus 72 from Beaune

ℹ **Visitor information** 21 Pl de L'Hôtel de Ville, 23160; 03 80 20 16 51; www.ot-cantondebligny surouche.fr

🕐 **Open** May–Sep: 2:45pm & 4:30pm (departs Bligny) and 3:15pm & 5pm (departs Pont d'Ouche) Sun & bank hols; extra trains in Jul–Aug: also 3:30pm Mon–Sat (diesel trains)

💲 **Prices** Round trip: €21–30 & one-way: €14–25; under 3s free

🍴 **Eat and drink** *Real meal* Auberge du Val d'Ouche (Pl de l'Hôtel de Ville, 21360 Bligny; 03 80 20 12 06; www.auberge-val-ouche. com; daily) is a simple restaurant that offers *coq au vin* (cockerel cooked in wine) and pizzas. *Family treat* Abbaye de la Bussiere (33 Route Departementale, 21360 La Bussière-sur-Ouche; 03 80 49 02 29; www.abbaye-dela-bussiere. com; open daily) is a 12th-century Cistercian abbey turned country hotel that serves gourmet lunch in its bistro.

The Lowdown

🌐 **Map reference** 9 C3
Address 21203 (Côte d'Or). Hôtel-Dieu: Rue de l'Hôtel Dieu; 03 80 24 45 00; www. hospices-de-beaune.com. Moutarderie Fallot: 31 Rue du Faubourg-Bretonnière; 03 80 22 10 02; www.fallot.com

🚗 **Train** TGV (www.ter-sncf.com/ bourgogne) & local express trains from Dijon. **Bus** 44 from Dijon

ℹ **Visitor information** 6 Blvd Perpreuil, 21203; 03 80 26 21 30; www.ot-beaune.fr

🕐 **Open** Hôtel-Dieu: daily. Moutarderie Fallot: guided visits only. Mar–Nov: 10am & 11:30am Mon–Sat (Jun–Aug also 3:30 & 5pm)

🍴 **Eat and drink** *Picnic* Charcuterie Raillard (4 Rue Monge, 21203; 03 80 22 23 04) stocks picnic supplies such as *jambon persillé* (jellied ham with parsley), quiches and slabs of *pâté en croûte* (pâté in a pastry crust). Enjoy the picnic in the Jardin Anglais across the road. *Real meal* Caveau des Arches (10 Blvd de Perpreuil, 21203; 03 80 22 10 37; www.caveau-des-arches. com; closed Sun & Mon) serves classic Burgundy dishes such as snails and *boeuf bourguignon* (beef casserole cooked in red wine) in a vaulted dining room.

Prices given are for a family of four

KIDS' CORNER

Find out more...

1 What ingredients are a must for genuine Burgundy mustard?
2 How many flavours of sweets can you find in Flavigny?
3 Which countries do the aniseeds used in Flavigny's sweets come from?
4 How long does it take to turn an aniseed into a sweet?

Answers at the bottom of the page.

Above Flavigny-sur-Ozerain, surrounded by fields and trees
Below Attractively packaged tins of aniseed sweets, Flavigny-sur-Ozerain

monks started cultivating vines here in the 12th century. It is now home to the **Confrérie des Chevaliers du Tastevin** (www.tastevin-bourgogne.com) who organize prestigious wine tasting events. The château is surrounded by huge vineyards.

④ Flavigny-sur-Ozerain

Aniseed sweets and *Chocolat*

Everyone in France knows the pretty little oval tins of aniseed sweets from Flavigny. France's famous pea-sized aniseed balls have been made in the former Benedictine Abbaye de St-Pierre, set in ancient tiny streets of stone houses, since 1591. The abbey was founded in the 8th century and has an eerie Carolingian **crypt** to visit, as well as the Troubat family's tiny **factory**, where visitors can take a short peek at the workshop and breathe in the lovely fragrances of orange blossom, rose petals and liquorice used to flavour the sweets. Afterwards, wandering around Flavigny is a step back to another age. The fortress

village perches on a rocky spur above the vineyards and has winding cobbled streets of well-preserved and restored medieval houses – featured in the movie *Chocolat* (2000). Look out for the shop where Vianne opened her chocolate boutique on the Place de l'Église.

Letting off steam

Explore the defences with a walk round the remaining ramparts. Visit the **Parc de l'Auxois** (www.parc-auxois.com), 8 km (5 miles) south of Flavigny, in the town of Arnay-sous-Vitteaux, with exotic animals, swimming pools and water slides, as well as jungle adventure activities.

The Lowdown

🌐 **Map reference** 9 C2
Address 21150 (Côte d'Or). Factory: Rue Abbaye; 03 80 90 20 88; www.anis-flavigny.com. Crypt: within the factory

🚗 **Train** SNCF from Les Laumes-Alesia and TGV from Montbard

ℹ **Visitor information** Pl Bingerbrück, 21150 Venarey-les-Laumes; www.alesia-tourisme.net

🕐 **Open** Factory: Mon–Fri. Crypt: daily

🍽 **Eat and drink** *Snacks* La Grange (Pl de l'Église, 21150; 03 80 96 20 62; closed Mon) serves home-made terrines or rabbit in mustard sauce. *Real meal* Le Relais de Flavigny (Pl des Anciennes Halles, 21150; 03 80 96 27 77; www.le-relais.fr; open daily) offers local specialities, such as *oeufs en meurette* (eggs in red wine sauce) or frogs' legs.

THE PAUPER'S PALACE

Back in the 15th century, the poor had little chance of medical care and so the sumptuously decorated Hôtel-Dieu hospice in Beaune became known as the "pauper's palace". Lucky patients were cared for in four-poster beds, but they often had to share them with several others!

Peek inside the pots

There are weird medicines in the porcelain pots of the pharmacy in Beaune's Hôtel-Dieu. See if you can find:
1 Woodlouse powder (*Poudre de cloportes*)
2 Vomit nut powder (*Poudre de nux vomica*)
3 Crayfish eyes (*Yeux d'écrevisses*)

Answers: 1 Mustard seeds grown in Burgundy and white aligoté wine from the same region. **2** Nine: blackcurrant, lemon, orange blossom, mint, liquorice, rose, violet, ginger and mandarin in the organic range. **3** Spain, Tunisia, Turkey and Syria. **4** 15 days.

⑤ Vézelay
Crusaders, pilgrims and holy relics

Since the 11th century, pilgrims have travelled to Vézelay's Basilique Ste-Madeleine to pay respects to the relics of St Mary Magdalene before setting off on the scallop-signed route to Santiago de Compostela in Spain. St Bernard of Clairvaux preached the Second Crusade here, and Richard the Lionheart came to meet French king Philippe-Auguste before embarking on the Third Crusade. Today this UNESCO World Heritage Site is thronged with tourists and pilgrims, attracted by its history and the medieval atmosphere of its streets.

The lofty ceiling of Basilique Ste-Madeleine

Key Features

The façade Built in 1150, this Romanesque and Gothic masterpiece was on the point of collapse when architect and master restorer of medival ruins Viollet-le-Duc rescued it in 1840.

The crypt Located beneath the basilica, it was reputed to house the remains of Mary Magdalene. Then in the 13th century, belief spread that the true relics were in St Maximin (in Provence) and Vézelay's fame faded.

Musée de l'Oeuvre Viollet-le-Duc

Nave of Ste-Madeleine

Main portal

Tour St-Michel

Capitals

The narthex This is where pilgrims have gathered for centuries before setting off on the "Way of St James".

Entrance

The capitals These fancy tops decorating the columns inside the nave and narthex have carvings of monsters. Use binoculars to spot David chopping off Goliath's head.

The main portal The beautiful sculpture on top of the door, called a tympanum, shows Christ with the apostles, the zodiac and a mythical menagerie of men with dog's heads and feathered bodies.

Musée de l'Oeuvre Viollet-le-Duc Named after the architect Eugène Emmanuel Viollet-le-Duc, the museum displays original medieval carvings preserved during the 19th-century restoration work.

The Lowdown

🌐 **Map reference** 9 B2
Address 89450 (Yonne). Basilique Ste-Madeleine: Presbytère; www.vezelay.cef.fr. Musée de l'Oeuvre Viollet-le-Duc: Pl du Cloître; 03 86 33 24 62

🚗 **Train** TGV from Paris to Montbard, then bus to Vézelay via Avallon. **Bus** from Avallon and Clamecy

ℹ **Visitor information** Rue St-Étienne, 89450; www.vezelaytourisme.com

Prices given are for a family of four

Letting off steam

Follow the 30-minute trail around the old town ramparts – the Promenade des Fossés – for grand views over the valleys of the densely forested region of Morvan. Look out for the gold scallop shells marking the pilgrimage trail to Compostela. From the southern ramparts, a lovely path leads to the village of St-Père, located 2 km (1 mile) from Vézelay.

One of the quaint, steep streets in the old town of Vézelay

Eat and drink

Picnic: under €20; Snacks: €20–45; Real meal: €45–90; Family treat: over €90 (based on a family of four)

PICNIC Au Tastevin (28 Rue St-Étienne, 89450; 03 86 33 22 08) offers picnic supplies such as sausages, charcuterie, pâtés and cheese. There are also plenty of places on Rue St-Étienne and Rue St-Pierre that sell local delicacies.

SNACKS Cabalus (Rue St-Pierre, 89450; 03 86 33 20 66; www.cabalus. com/hotellerie/hotellerie.html; closed Tue) is an arty tea shop that serves cakes and light snacks in the vaulted rooms of an ancient pilgrims' hostelry.

REAL MEAL Le Bougainville (26 Rue St-Étienne, 89450; 03 86 33 27 57; closed Tue & Wed), a charming old

house on the high street, is where diners can sit down for a proper meal of local dishes.

FAMILY TREAT L'Espérance (25 Grande Rue, 89450 St-Père-sous-Vézelay; 03 86 33 39 10) offers serious gastronomy from legendary chef Marc Meneau.

Find out more

DIGITAL Take a closer look at the Basilique Ste-Madeleine on whc. unesco.org/en/list/84, which has photos and videos of the basilica.

Next stop...

CHÂTEAU DE BAZOCHES Zip off to the 12th-century Château de Bazoches (www.chateau-bazoches. com/accueil.htm), 13 km (8 miles) south of Vézelay, once home to Louis XIV's military architect and fort builder Vauban. The château is an atmospheric place where visitors can imagine Vauban at work, designing his fortresses in the Grand Gallery. He also designed the citadel of Besançon (see p214), which is now a UNESCO World Heritage Site.

Le Bougainville, an elegant restaurant in a lovely old house on Rue St-Étienne

---

⏰ **Open** Basilique Ste-Madeleine: 6am–8pm daily; winter 7am–dusk. Musée de l'Oeuvre Viollet-le-Duc: Jul & Aug: 2–6pm daily; Easter–Jun & Sep: 2–6pm Sat & Sun

💰 **Prices** Basilique Ste-Madeleine: free. Musée de l'Oeuvre Viollet-le-Duc: €12–22; under 12s free

Skipping the queue Visit early morning or late afternoon after tour groups have left.

Guided tours Contact the tourist office for one-hour tours of the

basilica (adults €3.50) and also of the village in English.

👫 **Age range** 5 plus

⏱ **Allow** A day

☕ **Café** Many along Rue St-Étienne

🚻 **Toilets** In the tourist office

Good family value?
A great place to learn about crusaders and the pilgrimage to Santiago de Compostela.

⑥ Avallon

Battlement walks and Roman mosaics

Perched on a rocky spur above the Vallée du Cousin, the tranquil fortified town of Avallon is encircled by ancient ramparts. The ramparts make for a fine walk back through time, along with streets of houses dating from the 15th century. But remember that the defensive walls are there for a reason: things were not always this peaceful in the Middle Ages, when Avallon was the scene of many a battle. The main sight is the 12th-century Romanesque Église St-Lazare, where signs of the zodiac, images of the apocalypse and the labours of the months are carved

Horses grazing freely in the fields of the Morvan

into the beautiful doorway. Admire the fine old mansion next door, the Maison des Sires de Domecy, and visit the **Musée de l'Avallonnais** to see a Roman mosaic of Venus, and the dramatic 20th-century art by the French Fauvist and Expressionist artist Georges Rouault.

Letting off steam

Take a taxi or drive 6 km (4 miles) to **Parc Aventure des Châtelaines** (www.loisirsenmorvan.com/index. htm), an adventure park for kids aged 5 plus with tree-top trails, ropes, climbing, canoeing, rafting and more.

⑦ Parc Naturel Régional du Morvan

Wartime heroes and outdoor action in a nature park

A vast hilly wilderness of forest and lakes, the Morvan region is perfect for walking, cycling, swimming, fishing and watersports. But life in this densely forested heart of Burgundy has not always been about fun and leisure. The local people once had a hard life trying to make a living as woodcutters and cowherds. During World War II, the deep woodland and sparse population of the Morvan made it a perfect place for the French Resistance movement, known as the *maquis*, to hide out in isolated farms and carry out operations against the Nazi war machine. The **Musée de la Résistance en Morvan** in the park's information centre tells the moving story of the wartime occupation and resistance. The British parachuted in supplies, weapons and radios to help the *maquis*, while the local population suffered terribly at the hands of the Germans, who arrested and executed people and burnt down farms and villages. In the same building, the **Maison des Hommes et des Paysages** has exhibits on the region's traditional way of life in the days when men cut trees down and floated them away

The Lowdown

🌐 **Map reference** 9 B2
Address 89200 (Yonne). Musée de l'Avallonnais: 4 Rue du College; www.museeavallonnais.fr

🚗 **Train** TGV from Paris to Montbard & Dijon, then bus to Avallon and Saulieu

ℹ️ **Visitor information** 6 Rue Bocquillot, 89200; 03 86 34 14 19; www.avallonnais-tourisme.com

🕐 **Open** Musée de l'Avallonnais: Apr–Jun: Mon & Wed–Sat pm; Jul–Sep: Mon & Wed–Sat pm, Sun am

🍽️ **Eat and drink** *Snacks* Dame Jeanne *(59 Grande Rue, 89200; 03 86 34 58 71; damejeanne.fr; closed Thu),* a palatial *salon de thé* in a grand 17th-century house, serves 27 types of tea and tasty snacks such as snail tarts. *Real meal* Hostellerie de la Poste *(3 Pl Vauban, 89200; 03 86 34 16 16; www.hostelleriede laposte.com; closed Mon & Sun)* is the best table in town with snails, Morvan trout in a creamy wine sauce; includes a kids' menu.

The Lowdown

🌐 **Map reference** 9 B3
Address 58000 (Nièvre), 21000 (Côte-d'Or), 71000 (Saône-et-Loire) & 89000 (Yonne). Musée de la Résistance en Morvan & Maison des Hommes et des Paysages: in Maison du Parc, 58230 St-Brisson; www.museeresistancemorvan.fr

🚗 **Train** TGV to Montbard and Dijon, then bus to Salulieu, then car to St-Brisson

ℹ️ **Visitor information** Maison du Parc, 58230 St-Brisson; 03 86 78 79 00; www.parcdumorvan.org

🕐 **Open** Musée de la Résistance en Morvan & Maison des Hommes et des Paysages: May–Sept: closed Tue & Sat am. Jul & Aug: daily

🍽️ **Eat and drink** *Picnic* Marché du Samedi Matin *(Pl Monge, 21210 Saulieu)* is a superb place from where excellent Morvan charcuterie, cheese and bread can be picked for a picnic in the clear air of the Morvan. *Real meal* L'Auberge Ensoleillée *(Route du Vieux Dun, 58230 Dun-les-Places; 03 86 84 62 76; open daily)* is a pretty family-run country inn serving local dishes such as *crapiaux* (thick pancakes with bacon) or *oeufs en meurette* (poached eggs in red wine sauce).

The 12th-century Romanesque Église St-Lazare, Avallon

Prices given are for a family of four

along lakes and rivers all the way to Paris or joined seasonal cattle drives to market, while local women were in demand as wet nurses.

Letting off steam

The Morvan is one big outdoor adventure playground. The Maison du Parc, in the park information centre of St-Brisson, offers short and long walking trails in the Regional Nature Park. Head for the **Lac des Settons** (*www.mouxenmorvan.fr*), 9 km (6 miles) south, in the town of Montsauche-les-Settons. The **Base Nautique des Settons** here offers watersports and walking, as well as cycling trails around the lake.

Exhibits in the Maison des Hommes et des Paysages, St-Brisson

⑧ Autun

Medieval treasures and a visit to a Roman theatre

With a superb cathedral and one of Burgundy's best museums, Autun is a cultural gem. The town's name comes from Augustodunum, which is a clue to its illustrious past back in Roman times. It was also an important city in the Middle Ages, when Nicolas Rolin, Chancellor to the Duke of Burgundy, Philip the Good, made sure his hometown did well from his prestige. His son Cardinal Jean Rolin also put his weight behind the city's fortunes, turning it into an important centre of religion and learning, and adding Gothic grandeur to the Romanesque Cathédrale St-Lazare.

Autun's fortunes took a turn for the worse during the French Revolution, when the cathedral was damaged. Luckily, its Romanesque sculptures by the 12th-century artist Gislebertus got off lightly – the tympanum over the main doorway depicting the *Last Judgement* is a masterpiece. His *Temptation of Eve*

The Lowdown

- 🌐 **Map reference** 9 C3
  Address 71400 (Saône-et-Loire). Musée Rolin: 5 Rue des Bancs; 03 85 52 09 76
- 🚆 **Train** TGV to Le Creusot, then bus to Autun. **Bus** from Chalon-sur-Saône
- ℹ️ **Visitor information** 13 Rue Général Demetz, 71400; 03 85 86 80 38; *www.autun-tourisme.com*
- 🕐 **Open** Musée Rolin:1 Apr–30 Sep: closed Tue; timings vary rest of the year
- 🍵 **Eat and drink** *Snacks* Café des Tilleuls (*6 Rue du Général-Demetz, 71400; 03 85 52 51 44; open daily*) offers good local cooking and live music in the evening. *Real meal* Hotel Les Ursulines (*14 Rue de Rivault, 71400; 03 85 86 58 58; www.hotelursulines.fr; dinner daily, Sat & Sun lunch*) is a classy restaurant in a former convent by the ramparts.
- 🎭 **Festival** Free cultural events in the evening, including music, poetry and art, in the Cathédrale St-Lazare (Jul & Aug)

also survived and is a highlight of the great collection of medieval art in the **Musée Rolin**.

Stroll the cobbled streets around the cathedral and Place Terreau in the upper town. The Roman remains are a bit scattered, but Autun has the ruins of the biggest Roman theatre in Gaul; it is a short stroll from the lower town's main square, the Place du Champ de Mars.

Letting off steam

Drive along the D978 towards Mont Beuvray to pick up the forest trail near St-Prix, 17 km (10 miles) west of Autun. Climb to the top of Haut-Folin, the highest point in the Morvan at 900 m (3,000 ft).

The awe-inspiring curve of Autun's Roman theatre

KIDS' CORNER

In Autun's Cathédral St-Lazare, look out for...

1 Devils. They are on the right hand of the tympanum above the main doorway, catching sinners with their claws.

2 An artist's signature. Under Christ, in the centre of the tympanum, it says *Gislebertus hocfecit.* Can you guess what it means?

3 The steps leading to the top of the belltower. How many are there?

....

Answers at the bottom of the page.

THE ASTERIX OF GAUL

While cartoon character Asterix held out in Brittany, real life Gallic chieftain Vercingetorix gathered his army at Bibracte in Morvan, in a last attempt to stop the Romans from taking Gaul. He was defeated by Julius Caesar in the battle of Alesia in 52 BC.

Military magnificence

A statue of Vauban stands in the Place Vauban in Avallon. Do you know who he was? A Marshal of France and a military engineer, Vauban was born in a Burgundian village just 10 km (6 miles) from Avallon called St-Léger-de-Fourcheret. It was renamed St-Léger-Vauban in his honour.

An expert in building and destroying fortifications, he designed hundreds of citadels and defences all over France for Louis XIV, the Sun King.

....

⑨ Cluny
The church that disappeared

Founded in 910, the now ruined Ancienne Abbaye de Cluny was once the most powerful monastery in Europe, and its church was Europe's biggest until St Peter's Basilica in Rome was built in the 16th century. The abbots of Cluny were bigwigs of the Middle Ages, as important as kings and popes. Learn about them, the abbey and what went wrong in the Musée d'Art et d'Archéologie, and by exploring the old town.

A display outside the abbey, Cluny

Key Features

① **Musée d'Art et d'Archéologie** Housed in a 15th-century palace are medieval sculptures and decorations from the abbey, as well as audio-visual displays and a 3D reconstruction of the abbey in the 13th century.

② **Tour des Fromages** Climb to the top of the oddly named 11th-century "Cheese Tower" for the best view over the town and to get an idea of how huge the abbey once was. A superb display here shows what the streets looked like before the abbey was destroyed.

③ **Abbey church ruins** Walk around to spot bits and pieces of the church appearing among the later buildings, including the south transept. Their size gives an idea of how enormous the church was, before it was demolished after the French Revolution.

④ **Clocher de l'Eau-Bénite** Of the five towers that once crowned the south transept, only the imposing octagonal Belfry of the Holy Water and a smaller clocktower remain.

Entrance

Le Haras National

⑤ **Farinier** This flour store, beneath a splendid oak roof dating from the 13th century, displays the beautifully carved stone capitals – the crowns on top of columns – salvaged from the abbey church.

The Lowdown

🌐 **Map reference** 9 C4
Address 71250 (Saône-et-Loire). Pl de l'Abbaye; www.cluny-tourisme.com. Musée d'Art et d'Archéologie: Palais Jean de Bourbon; 03 85 59 12 79; www.cluny.monuments-nationaux.fr

🚗 **Train** TGV from Paris to Mâcon Loché or regular train to Mâcon Ville, then bus 7 (Mâcon to Chalon-sur-Saône via Cluny) or bus 9 (Mâcon to Digoin via Cluny)

ℹ️ **Visitor information** Tour des Fromages, 6 Rue Mercière, 71250; 03 85 59 05 34

🕐 **Open** Abbey: May–Aug: 9:30am–6:30pm; Sep–Apr: 9:30am–noon & 1:30–5pm. Musée d'Art et d'Archéologie: mid-Feb–Mar: ring ahead; rest of the year: daily (ticket office shuts 30 mins before closing time). Tour des Fromages: Jan–Apr & Nov–Dec: Mon–Sat; May–Oct: daily

💶 **Prices** Abbey & Musée d'Art et d'Archéologie: €16–26 (combined ticket); EU residents under 26 free. Tour des Fromages: €6–16; under 12s free

👥 **Skipping the queue** Early morning or late afternoon are the best times to visit.

🎫 **Guided tours** In French and German only

👫 **Age range** 5 plus

⏱️ **Allow** Half a day

☕ **Café** Café du Centre "Chez Sissis" near the Tour des Fromages

🚻 **Toilets** By the tourist office on the Place de l'Abbaye

Good family value?
The ruined abbey Abbaye de Cluny is a fascinating and educational visit for kids aged 5 plus.

Cyclists on the picturesque Voie Verte *trail near Cluny*

Letting off steam

Pick up the "follow the lamb" leaflet from the tourist office and walk the route marked with bronze lamb symbols through the town. Hire bicycles from **Ludisport** (*www.ludisport.com*), located by the old railway station, and ride on the Voie Verte (Green Lane) trail from Cluny to the village of Cormatin, which is 13 km (8 miles) north of Cluny to visit the **Musée de Velo** (*www.envies develo.com*), a bicycle museum.

Organic bread and croissants displayed at Le Pain sur la Table

Eat and drink

Picnic: under €20; Snacks: €20–45; Real meal: €45–90; Family treat: over €90 (based on a family of four)

PICNIC Le Pain sur la Table (*Pont de l'Étang, 71250; 03 85 59 24 50; autrementbio.free.fr/index.html; bakery: open daily & café: noon–2pm daily*) is a riverside bakery and café near the *Voie Verte* trail, with organic bread, croissants and *pain au chocolat*. Picnic along the *Voie Verte*.
SNACKS Germain (*25 Rue Lamartine, 71250; 03 85 59 11 21; closed Mon*) is a patisserie-tea shop that serves great cakes and quiches.
REAL MEAL Auberge du Cheval Blanc (*1 Rue Porte de Mâcon, 71250; 03 85 59 01 13; www.chevalblanc-auberge.com; open daily*) is a classic *auberge* (inn) that cooks up excellent Burgundian dishes.

FAMILY TREAT Hôtel de Bourgogne (*Pl de l'Abbaye, 71250; 03 85 59 00 58; www.hotel-cluny.com; closed Tue & Wed*) offers Burgundian heritage cuisine, such as Charolais beef in Mâcon red wine sauce, in the traditional dining room of the hotel.

Find out more

DIGITAL Go to *www.cluny.monuments-nationaux.fr* not only to read more on the abbey, but also to watch an excerpt from a 3D film featuring the abbey.

Next stop...

LE HARAS NATIONAL Visit **Le Haras National** (*2 Rue Porte des Prés, 71250; www.haras-nationaux.fr*), the National Stud Farm, to see magnificent thoroughbred stallions. Built with stone from the ruined Ancienne Abbaye de Cluny, the farm was founded by Napoleon in 1806 to breed horses for his military campaigns. The farm offers guided visits of the stables and there are various displays of the stallions through the year, as well as show-jumping competitions.

Thoroughbred stallions at Le Haras National, Cluny

An old-fashioned carousel facing the Saône riverfront in Mâcon

⑩ Mâcon

Waterside walks and hunting cavemen

Sandwiched between the Saône river and hillsides carpeted with vineyards lies the town of Mâcon. Start exploring along the café terraces of the riverfront promenade, Quai Lamartine, and enjoy the view of the town from the Pont St-Laurent.

A great market is hosted Tuesday to Saturday mornings, on the Place aux Herbes. While here, take time to admire the weird animals and

The Lowdown

🌐 **Map reference** 9 D4
Address 71000 (Saône-et-Loire). Musée des Ursulines: 5 Rue des Ursulines; 03 85 39 30 98. Hôtel-Dieu: 34 Rue des Épinoches; 03 85 39 90 38

🚃 **Train** from Dijon, Beaune, Chalon-sur-Saône and Lyon. **Bus** 7 & 9 from Cluny

ℹ️ **Visitor information** 1 Pl St-Pierre, 71000; 03 85 21 07 07; *www.macon-tourism.com*

🕑 **Open** Musée des Ursulines: Tue–Sat, Sun pm. Hôtel-Dieu: Jun–Sep: Tue–Sun

🍽️ **Eat and drink** *Snacks* Le 88 (*39 Pl aux Herbes, 71000; 03 85 38 00 06; closed Wed & Sun and Tue dinner*) offers good-value traditional brasserie dining. *Real meal* Le Poisson d'Or (*Allée du Parc, Port de Plaisance, 71000; 03 85 38 00 88; www.lepoisson dor.com; closed Wed & Sun and Tue dinner*) serves fresh fish and frog's legs on a riverside terrace.

🎆 **Festival** L'été frappé, free concerts and events (mid-Jun & Aug)

Antiques and ceramic pots for sale at a shop in Tournus

characters sculpted into the fantastic Renaissance façade of the Maison de Bois. Take a look at the ruins of Cathédrale St-Vincent, then visit the **Musée des Ursulines** to learn about the prehistoric finds from the Roche de Solutré, where skeletons of 100,000 horses were discovered. Finish in the apothecary's shop in the **Hôtel-Dieu** to see an old-style pharmacy that is more like a magician's laboratory. Inside its 18th-century walnut cabinets are delicate ceramic pots of lotions and potions, including opium, powdered ivory and adderwort.

Letting off steam

Drive 17 km (10 miles) northwest of Mâcon to explore the caverns of the **Grottes d'Azé** (*www.grotte-aze. com*), where bears and lions once lived 300,000 years ago. Burgundy's largest cave system, it has limestone formations and an underground river.

⑪ Tournus

A monk's life and a special nature ramble

Located on the Saône river between Mâcon and Chalon, Tournus is a lovely riverside town. The star of the town is the **Abbaye de St-Philibert**, one of the oldest Romanesque buildings in Burgundy, founded in the 9th century, where children will enjoy learning what life was like for the monks 1,000 years ago. They brought with them the relics of their patron saint, Philibert; pay respects to him in the choir. The old town around the abbey is a charming place with antiques and art galleries, made for gentle browsing. On the first Sunday

The Lowdown

🌐 **Map reference** 9 D4
Address 71700 (Saône-et-Loire). Abbaye de St-Philibert: Pl de l'Hôtel de Ville. Hôtel-Dieu & Musée Greuze: 21 Rue de l'Hôpital; 03 85 51 23 50

🚃 **Train** Tournus is on the main SNCF Paris-Lyon train line and served by TER Dijon-Lyon trains. TGV from Mâcon-Loché and Le Creusot. **Bus** from Chalon-sur-Saône, Mâcon, Cluny and Louhans

ℹ️ **Visitor information** 2 Pl de l'Abbaye, 71700; 03 85 27 00 20; *www.tournugeois.fr*

🕑 **Open** Hôtel-Dieu & Musée Greuze: Apr–Oct: Wed–Mon

🍽️ **Eat and drink** *Picnic* Fromagerie Giroud (*63 Rue du Docteur-Privey, 71700; closed Mon*) stocks goodies for a gourmet riverside picnic. *Real meal* Aux Terrasses (*18 Ave du 23 Janvier, 71700; 03 85 51 01 74; www. aux-terrasses.com; closed Mon & Sun dinner and Tue lunch*) is a well-known restaurant in an old roadside inn that serves traditional Bourguignon cuisine and has a kids' menu.

🎆 **Festival** Saint Philibert's fireworks display on the Saône quays (third weekend in Aug)

of the month, a lively flea market takes over the quays along the Saône river. Visit the **Hôtel-Dieu**, a hospice with an apothecary and a garden of medicinal plants. Move about the hospice building, which houses the **Musée Greuze**, dedicated to artist Jean-Baptiste Greuze.

The garden of medicinal plants in the Hôtel-Dieu, Tournus

Letting off steam

Drive 6 km (4 miles) south of Tournus to the **Réserve de la Truchère** *(Pont de Seille, 71290 Truchère; 03 85 51 35 79)*, situated at the confluence of the Saône and Seille rivers. A magical nature reserve, it has walking and cycling trails around its lake, dunes, peat marshes and oak forest.

Interior of the 17th-century Hôtel-Dieu with its beautifully lit chapel, Tournus

⑫ Louhans

Blue-footed chickens at a special country market

The Bresse region, located south of Burgundy, is poultry country. Louhans's livestock market on Mondays is the place to see the Bresse chickens, considered the best in the world, not just by the French. It is a sight that seems to belong to medieval times, with the arcaded high street, Grande Rue, lined with stalls selling chickens, ducks and geese, and the country folk buying them. The 157 archways lining the street date from the 15th century and help to keep the sun and rain off shoppers while they browse their way along the market and the shops. Around town, visit

the landmark Église St-Pierre, with its pretty tiled steeple. See the workshop where the town's local newspaper *L'Indépendant* was printed for a century until it closed in 1984. It is preserved as the **Musée de l'Imprimerie** and its ancient rotary presses still work. The **Hôtel-Dieu**, a former hospital and now a museum, is especially atmospheric, with its grand wards of curtained beds and the beautiful curvy Hispano-Moorish jars in the apothecary. They contain things that are not seen on prescriptions these days, such as billy goat's dried blood.

Letting off steam

Set off from the river port of Louhans for pleasant strolls along the towpaths of the Seille river where pleasure boats chug along and anglers fish for carp. About 5 km (3 miles) west is the lock at Branges, a lovely village. Visit the **Maison de la Volaille de Bresse** *(www.pouletbresse.com)*, a poultry house, in the Bois de Chize à Branges to learn about the chickens.

Signage outside a poultry house indicating free entry in Louhans

The Lowdown

🌐 **Map reference** 9 D4
Address 71500 (Saône-et-Loire). Musée de l'Imprimerie: 29 Rue des Dodânes; 03 85 76 27 16. Hôtel-Dieu: Rue du Capitaine Vic; 03 85 75 54 32

🚆 **Train** TGV and regional train to Mâcon, then bus 14 to Tournus, followed by bus 11 to Louhans

ℹ️ **Visitor information** Pl St-Jean, 71500; 03 85 75 05 02; www.bresse-bourguignonne.com

🕐 **Open** Musée de l'Imprimerie: 6 Jan–14 May & 1 Oct–19 Dec: Mon–Fri; 15 May–30 Sep: daily. Hôtel-Dieu: guided visits (in French) 1 Feb–31 Mar &

1 Nov–15 Dec: 2:30pm & 4pm; 1 Apr–15 June & 16 Sep–31 Oct: 10:30am, 2:30pm, 4pm; 16 Jun–15 Sep: 10:30am, 2:30pm, 4pm, 5:30 pm, closed Tue

☕ **Eat and drink** *Picnic* The Grande Rue has plenty of shops selling local organic produce. Picnic by the Seille river. Try the local cake speciality *corniottes* (a cheese pastry) from one of the pâtisseries. *Real meal* La Mère Jouvenceaux *(26 Rue Lucien Guillemaut, 71500; 03 85 75 00 51; closed Tue & Wed)* serves Bresse chicken, fresh *sandre* (pike-perch) and frog's legs.

⑬ Parc Régional Naturel du Haut-Jura
Nature's splendour and a gem of a train ride

Just a stone's throw from Switzerland, near Geneva and Lac Léman, the Parc Régional Naturel du Haut-Jura is an exciting playground for year-round outdoor action. Hike and mountain bike its trails along rocky crests, through forests and up to its high peaks and plateaux. In winter, put on snow shoes or zip off on a dog sleigh adventure. There is plenty of artisan heritage in its stonecutting workshops and cheese-makers' cooperatives.

Pungent cheeses at Les Rousses

Key Sights

① **St Claude** The town is known for its craftsmen, who created its famous pipes. Visit the Musée de la Pipe et du Diamant whose collection is from the 18th century.

② **Ligne des Hirondelles** This picturesque 123-km (77-mile) long track from St Claude to Dole passes through 36 tunnels and 18 viaducts, through the Forêt de Chaux and vineyards of Arbois.

③ **Les Hautes-Combes** This 1,000-m (3,300-ft) high plateau offers jaw-dropping views over the Jura's highest peaks. Head for the Coopérative Fromagère du Haut-Jura to see how local cheeses are made.

④ **Maison du Haut-Jura** Work out the lie of the land and stock up leaflets for hikes and things to see and do in the park information centre, with interactive displays for kids to learn more about the region.

Prices given are for a family of four

[Map showing the Parc Régional Naturel du Haut-Jura region with locations including Dole, Bois d'Amont, Morez, Doucier, Lac des Rousses, Ligne des Hirondelles, Le Fort des Rousses, Les Rousses, Prémanon, St Claude, Chaumont, Lamoura, Maison du Haut-Jura, Divonne-les-Bains, Les Moussières, Colomby de Gex, Gex, Cessy, Les Hautes-Combes, Ségny, La Pesse, Crêt de la Neige 1720m, Ferney-Voltaire, Crêt de Chalam 1545m, St-Genis-Pouilly, St-Jean-de-Gonville, SWITZERLAND]

⑥ **Le Fort des Rousses** Learn about Comté cheeses as 50,000 of them mature in the caves of Juraflore inside this old military fort. Follow a trail of zip wires, assault course and tree-top trails.

⑤ **Les Rousses** Four villages – Les Rousses, Prémanon, Bois d'Amont and Lamoura – make up this ski resort. In summer, the Lac des Rousses is perfect for swimming and watersports.

The Lowdown

🌐 **Map reference** 10 E4
Address 39140 (Jura), 25300 (Doubs) and 01000 (Ain). Musée de la Pipe et du Diamant: 1 Pl Jacques Faizant, 39200 St Claude; 03 84 45 17 00. Coopérative Fromagère du Haut-Jura: 39310 Les Moussières; 03 84 41 60 96; *www.fromagerie-haut-jura.fr*. Maison du Haut-Jura: 39310 Lajoux; 03 84 34 12 27; *www.parc-haut-jura.fr*. Le Fort des Rousses: 39220 Les Rousses; 03 84 60 02 55; *fort-des-rousses.com*

🚗 **Train** TGV from Paris to Besançon, then SNCF to St Claude. SNCF

from Dole to Morez, then bus to Les Rousses (*www.jurabus.fr*)

ℹ️ **Visitor information** Office du Tourisme Haut-Jura: 1 Ave de Belfort, 39200 St Claude; 03 84 45 34 24; *ot-saint-claude.com*. Office du Tourisme Les Rousses: 495 Rue Pasteur, 39220; 03 84 60 02 55; *www.lesrousses.com*

🕐 **Open** Musée de la Pipe et du Diamant: May–Sep: 9:30am–noon & 2–6:30pm daily; 2–6pm rest of year, closed Sun. Coopérative Fromagère du Haut-Jura: daily. Maison du Haut-Jura: Jul & Aug:

Letting off steam

From St Claude, head for the nearby village of Chaumont for a hike to the Cascade de la Queue de Cheval, the "horse's tail" waterfall. It is about an hour's walk to the waterfall and back from Chaumont.

The Swiss-French themed Hôtel Arbez Franco-Suisse

Eat and drink

Picnic: under €20; Snacks: €20–45; Real meal: €45–90; Family treat: over €90 (based on a family of four)

PICNIC Le Marché du Jeudi Matin (*39200 St Claude; 7am–1pm Thu*) has Bresse chickens roasting on the spit and splendid displays of cheese and other local goodies for a picnic near the Cascade de la Queue de Cheval.
SNACKS Pâtisserie Jérôme Simon (*33 Rue de Pré, 39200 St Claude; 03 84 45 00 55*) has a tea room that serves scrumptious sweet treats.
REAL MEAL Ferme-Auberge La Combe aux Bisons (*L'Embossieux, 30370 La Pesse; 03 84 42 71 60; closed Mon & Tue*) is 12 km (7 miles) south of St Claude. It raises Canadian bisons that are served as *pierrade* (steaks and kebabs cooked on a hot stone) and cheesy treats such as fondue as well as *raclette* (made

of thick slices of melted cheese with potatoes, gherkins, pickled onions and dried meat).
FAMILY TREAT Hôtel Arbez Franco-Suisse (*77 Rue Ferme La Cure, 39220; 03 84 60 02 20; www.arbezie-hotel.com; open daily*) is a border-straddling restaurant, located 2 km (1 mile) to the south of Les Rousses, with a brasserie in France and wood-panelled restaurant in Switzerland.

Next stop...

CASCADES DU HÉRISSON The village of Doucier, located 31 km (19 miles) north of St Claude, is the starting point for the valley of the Hérisson river. Head out for Doucier to check out the spectacular fall of the Cascades du Hérisson, a 15-km (9-mile) long trail of waterfalls. Leave the car at the park by the Moulin Jacquand, then pick up the woody trail to visit the 65-m (220-ft) high waterfall Cascade de l'Éventail and walk behind the curtain of water at the nearby 60-m (200-ft) high Cascade du Grand Saut.

The 65-m (220-ft) high, breathtaking waterfall of Cascade de l'Éventail

---

10am–1pm & 2–7pm Tue–Fri, 2–7pm Sat & Sun; timings vary rest of year. Le Fort des Rousses: Contact tourist office for information on visits.

Prices Musée de la Pipe et du Diamant: €20–30; under 6s free. Ligne des Hirondelles: €19 (one-way ticket – St Claude to Dole).

Skipping the queue The Juramusées Pass (*juramusees.fr/le-pass.html*) offers admission to 29 sites in the area at a discount.

Guided tours Contact tourist office for details.

 Age range 5 plus

Activities Take a train ride on the Ligne des Hirondelles (*lignedeshirondelles.fr*).

Allow 2 or 3 days

Toilets In St Claude, Les Rousses and Maison du Haut-Jura in Lajoux and by the Lac des Rousses

Good family value?
The park offers top-class outdoor fun for active families and also activities of local cultural interest.

⑭ Arc-et-Senans

A salty story

In 1773, Louis XV's government decided to build the **Saline Royale**, or royal saltworks, and appointed the architect Claude-Nicolas Ledoux to do the job at Arc-et-Senans. The idea was to pump out the salty water 24 km (15 miles) from the mineral springs at Salins-les-Bains to the factory at Arc-et-Senans and extract salt by evaporating it, using wood from the Chaux forest. But the saltworks were closed in 1895 as it never made as much salt as was planned. Ledoux's visionary plans for a futuristic town built in circles around the central works, led it to be declared a UNESCO World Heritage Site. Inspired by advances of the Industrial Revolution, this was to have been a utopian model town

The grand central building of the saltworks at Arc-et-Senans

for the workers. Housed in the Saline Royale, the Musée Claude Nicolas Ledoux explains it all in the old Coopers' workshop.

Letting off steam

Drive 14 km (9 miles) north to the **Forêt de Chaux**, France's second largest forest, to walk on its vast network of marked trails. It is home to deer, wild boar, foxes and weasels.

⑮ Besançon

Clocks and ramparts

The city of Besançon sits in a loop of the Doubs river beneath a rocky spur crowned by the fortification expert Vauban's mighty 17th-century **Citadelle**. This historic fortress contains museums, including quirky local arts and crafts in the Musée Comtois, as well as a zoo and the best views over the town. The charming old St-Jean quarter at the foot of the citadel is pedestrianized,

which makes for relaxed wandering around its grand stone townhouse mansions and inviting cafés. Look up to see the fantastic **Horloge Astronomique**, an astronomical clock in the 12th-century Cathédrale St-Jean; when it chimes the hour, mechanical figures come out to dance. Continue along the Grande Rue, where writer Victor Hugo was born at No.140, to the Renaissance Palais Granvelle, which has the family-friendly **Musée du Temps**, with a superb collection of clocks and timepieces.

Letting off steam

Take a walk along the ramparts of the Chemins de Ronde, or take a scenic boat trip on the Doubs river with **Vedettes Paroramiques** (www.vedettes-panoramiques.com) to the Saut du Doubs waterfall.

Walking along the ramparts of the 17th-century Citadelle, Besançon

The Lowdown

🌐 **Map reference** 10 E3
Address 25610 (Doubs).
Saline Royale: Ave de la Saline; 03 81 54 45 45; www.saline royale.com

🚗 **Train** Ligne des Hirondelles from St Claude. TGV from Mouchard

ℹ️ **Visitor information** Saline Royale, 25610; 03 81 57 43 21; www.ot-arcetsenans.fr

🕐 **Open** Saline Royale: year round; timings vary throughout the year

🍴 **Eat and drink** Snacks Bar-Restaurant de la Saline (35 Grande-Rue, 25610; 03 81 57 49 49) does plats du jour (daily special) and sandwiches. Real meal Relais d'Arc-et-Senans (9 Pl de l'Église, 25610; 03 81 57 40 60; www.le-relais-darc-et-senans.com; closed Sun & Mon) offers good-value dining; includes a kids' menu.

The Lowdown

🌐 **Map reference** 10 E2
Address 25000 (Doubs).
Citadelle: 99 Rue des Fusillés; www.citadelle.com. Horloge Astronomique: Rue de la Convention; 03 81 81 12 76. Musée du Temps: Palais Granvelle, 96 Grand Rue; 03 81 87 81 50

🚗 **Train** from Dijon, Lyon, Dole, Belfort and Lons-le-Saunier. **Bus** (www.montsjura-autocars.fr) from Pontarlier, Vesoul, Montbéliard, Gray and Ornans

ℹ️ **Visitor information** Parc Micaud, Pl de la Première Armée Française, 25000; 03 81 80 92 55; www.besancon-tourisme.com

🕐 **Open** Citadelle: Mar–end-Oct: daily (Jul & Aug: till 7pm); timings

vary rest of the year. Horloge Astronomique: Apr–Sep: Wed–Mon; winter: Thu–Mon; last entry 10 mins before closing time (10am–noon & 3–6pm). Musée du Temps: Tue–Sat

🍴 **Eat and drink** Snacks Traiteur Courbet (71 Rue de Dole, 25000; 03 81 52 02 16; www.courbet-traiteur.com) offers two categories of gourmet food platters to take away. Real meal Brasserie du Commerce (31 Rue des Granges, 25000; 03 81 81 33 11; www.brasserie-ducommerce.com) serves brasserie classics and also has a kids' menu.

🎉 **Festival** Festival International de Musique de Besançon, Besançon's biggest cultural event (Sep)

The elegant Renaissance courtyard of the Musée du Temps, Besançon

Prices given are for a family of four

Bartholdi's massive lion sculpture below the Citadelle de Belfort

⑯ Belfort

Underground tunnels and a giant lion

The history of Belfort has been shaped by its position between the valleys of the Rhine and the Rhône, a natural route for invading armies. Louis XIV ordered Vauban to build the impregnable **Citadelle de Belfort**, which withstood many sieges, including the big one in 1870, when 40,000 Germans besieged Belfort for months. Commemorating this is a colossal red sandstone lion, below the fortress walls, by the famous sculptor Frédéric Bartholdi, who later built New York's Statue of Liberty. A visit to the citadel is essential to experience what it must have been like for the defenders living in the underground world of the **Grand Souterrain** – a maze of huge tunnels, as Prussian shells rained on it. Follow it up with a view from the **Terrasse du Lion**, a walk round the moats and walls of the fortress, and then enter the colourful old town through the Porte de Brisach to browse through the restaurants, shops and cafés.

Take a bus from Belfort to the town of Ronchamp, located 18 km (11 miles) to the west, which boasts

Cannons outside the Citadelle de Belfort, the history museum

the white and curvy **Chapelle Notre-Dame-du-Haut**, designed by the architect Le Corbusier in 1955. A peaceful spot, it looks more like a modern sculpture than a building.

Letting off steam

Explore the excellent nature trail around the **Étang des Forges** lake (*www.etangdesforges.fr*), 2 km (1 mile) northeast of Belfort.

The Lowdown

🌐 **Map reference** 10 F1
Address 90000 (Territoire de Belfort). Citadelle de Belfort: Le Château, 90000. Grand Souterrain & Terrasse du Lion: inside Citadelle de Belfort. Chapelle Notre-Dame-du-Haut: 13 Rue Chapelle, 70250 Ronchamp; *www.chapellede ronchamp.fr*

🚆 **Train** from Lyon, Mulhouse, Strasbourg, Montbéliard, Nancy Besançon and Épinal. **Bus** (*www. optymo.fr*) from Montbéliard, Mulhouse and Strasbourg

ℹ️ **Visitor information** 2 Rue Clemenceau, 90000; 03 84 55 90 90; *www.belfort-tourisme.com*

🕐 **Open** Citadelle de Belfort: year round. Grand Souterrain: Jul & Aug: daily, timings vary rest of year. Terrasse du Lion: Jun–Sep: daily; timings vary rest of year

🍵 **Eat and drink** Picnic Marché Fréry (*Rue Fréry, 90000*), a covered market, stocks local produce for a perfect picnic. *Real meal* Le Pot au Feu (*27 bis Grand Rue, 90000; 03 84 28 57 84; closed Sat, Sun & Mon lunch*) is a cosy stone-vaulted restaurant in the old town that offers refined regional cooking, including a hearty *pot au feu* stew made with Montbéliard sausage.

Picnic under €20; **Snacks** €20–45; **Real meal** €45–90; **Family treat** over €90 (based on a family of four)

Where to Stay in Burgundy and Franche-Comté

The lush abundance of the Burgundy countryside provides an ideal setting for much of its most enjoyable accommodation. In towns, many hotels are in magnificent historic buildings, full of period details, while around the villages, gorgeous B&Bs and camp grounds can be found amidst woods and vineyards.

AGENCIES

Gîtes de France
www.gites-de-france.com
The website lists a vast selection of self-catering properties, from simple country cottages to villas with pools and historic châteaux.

Bienvenue à la Ferme
www.bienvenue-a-la-ferme.com
This is a huge network of farms across the country, offering B&B, self-catering and camping options.

Arbois   Map 10 E3

HOTEL
Hôtel des Messageries
2 Rue de Courcelles, 39600;
03 84 66 15 45;
www.hoteldesmessageries.com
This characterful old coaching house has a creeper-clad stone façade and spacious, newly renovated bedrooms, including connecting rooms that are great for families.

🛏️ P   €€

CAMPING
Camping Les Vignes
Ave du Général Leclerc, 39600; 03 84 66 14 12; tinyurl.com/3ck5n59
This pleasant camp site has shaded pitches arranged in terraces at the edge of the vineyards that produce the grapes for the renowned Arbois *vin jaune*. There is a bar, a snack bar and shops. There are walking and biking trails through the vineyards.

P 🌀   €

Avallon   Map 9 B2

HOTEL
Le Relais Fleuri
1 La Cerce, 89200 Avallon, 03 86 34 02 85, www.relais-fleuri.com
Just a 5-minute drive from Avallon, this charming traditional hotel sits in vast, fabulous gardens in glorious countryside. Three-and four-bed

family rooms are on offer. Tennis courts and swimming pool on site. Try the beamed restaurant.

🛏️ P ❄️ 🌀   €€

SELF-CATERING

Domaine Le Grand Bois
Magny-Cours   Map 9 A3
Route de Fertot, 58470 Gimouille;
03 86 21 09 21; www.grand-bois.eu
Near Nevers and the Magny-Cours racing circuit, this expansive complex offers 66 fully equipped cottages spread around a green and leafy area with its own lake and adventure park. The wooden cottages are newly built and eco-friendly. Watersports, tennis, go-karting and bike rental available.

🗄️ P 🌀   €€

CAMPING

Camping du Lac   Map 9 C2
58230 St-Agnan; 03 86 78 73 70;
www.campingbourgogne.fr
Located by the lake of St Agnan in the Parc Naturel Régional du Morvan, this is suited for active family holidays spent spent walking, cycling, kayaking and windsurfing. Besides tents and caravans, the 18th-century château, restored by the British owners, offers simple rooms with tiled floors and marble fireplaces.

P 🌀   €

Beaune   Map 9 C3

HOTEL
Hotel des Remparts
48 Rue Thiers, 21200; 03 80 24 94 94;
www.hotel-remparts-beaune.com
Just a short stroll from the Hôtel-Dieu and the city centre, this is a stylish 17th-century mansion. Rooms retain original features – terracotta-tiled or parquet floors, marble fireplaces and stone walls – and look out over the flowery courtyard or the rampart walkway. Babysitting service can be provided.

P ❄️   €€

A delicious breakfast spread at Nuits d'Etape, Beaune

BED & BREAKFAST

Nuits d'Etape
21 Rue Paul Cabet, 21700 Nuits-St-Georges; 06 19 92 41 07; www.nuits detape.com
In the centre of a famous wine-producing village, this is a lovely self-contained two-bedroom *gîte*. Cafés, shops and restaurants are nearby. Its location mid way between Dijon and Beaune makes it a great base for exploring the Côte d'Or.

🛏️ 🗄️ P   €€

Belfort   Map 10 F1

HOTEL
Hôtel Vauban
4 Rue du Magasin, 90000 Belfort; 03 84 21 41 67; www.hotel-vauban.com
Just across the Savoureuse river from Belfort's old town and citadel, this peaceful small hotel has a lovely riverside garden and colourful, well-maintained rooms. The hands-on owner lends the place the feel of a friendly guesthouse.

🛏️ P   €

CAMPING
Camping L'Étang des Forges
Rue du Général Béthouart, 90000; 03 84 22 54 92; www.camping-belfort.com
Located on the outskirts of town and by the side of a lake, this camp

site offers pitches, chalets and mobile homes, as well as bungalows to rent. Bar, snack bar and grocery on site. Activities for kids include basketball, canoeing, hiking and biking trails. Visitors need to bring their own gear.

P ☉ €

Besançon
Map 10 E2

HOTEL
Hôtel du Nord
8 Rue Moncey, 25000; 03 81 81 34 56; www.hotel-du-nord-besancon.com
Comfortable, well-kept and great-value family rooms, right in the heart of the historic quarter, make this a perfect base for exploring Besançon.

🛏 P €

Cluny
Map 9 C4

HOTEL
Hôtel de Bourgogne
Pl de l'Abbaye, 71250; 03 85 59 00 58; www.hotel-cluny.com
Formerly a 19th-century mansion where poet Alphonse de Lamartine stayed, this is now a classy hotel. It has a lounge adorned with antiques, a tranquil patio and an excellent restaurant. The three apartments are perfect for families.

🛏 P ❊ €€

BED & BREAKFAST
La Maison des Gardes
18 Ave Charles de Gaulle, 71250; 03 85 59 19 46; www.lamaisondes gardes.com
This ancient house in the medieval heart of Cluny offers a fully equipped family-sized *gîte* and charming B&B rooms. It has been in the family of Hélène (who speaks English) since 1703. It has exposed beams, stone walls and expansive leafy grounds.

🛏 🍴 P €€

Ferme Auberge des Collines
Le Bourg, 71800 Amanzé; 03 85 70 66 34; www.fermeaubergedes collines.com
Set in rolling Brionnais countryside just 34 km (21 miles) from Cluny, this is a real working farm where several generations of the Paperin family have bred Charolais cattle. The simple rustic bedrooms sleep up to four. The grand farm buildings now consist of a *ferme-auberge* restaurant serving the farm's produce.

🛏 P €

CAMPING
Camping Saint-Vital
30 Rue des Griottons, 71250; 03 85 59 08 34; camping-cluny. blogspot.com
Shaded by trees, this site has a free swimming pool. Cluny is a short stroll away and the *Voie Verte* (Green Lane) trail passes right by the camp site.

P €

Dijon
Map 9 D2

HOTELS
Hotel Wilson
Pl Wilson, 21000; 03 80 66 82 50; www.wilson-hotel.com
A short stroll from the old centre, this smart 17th-century post house has plenty of character. Bright rooms are arranged around a central courtyard.

🛏 P ❊ €€

Hostellerie le Sauvage
61 Rue Monge, 21000; 03 80 41 31 21; www.hotellesauvage.com
A 10-minute walk from the Palais des Ducs, this 15th-century coaching house is a peaceful bolthole with a delightful vine-shaded courtyard. Rooms are colourful with many period features.

🛏 P €

An aesthetically furnished room in La Maison des Gardes, Cluny

BED & BREAKFAST
Chambres d'Hôtes des Marcs d'Or
9 Rue des Marcs d'Or, 21000; 03 80 43 30 44; chambre-hote-dijon.com
A short walk from the heart of Dijon, the old stables of this 19th-century winemaker's house have been converted into stylish guest rooms, with tasteful colour schemes, wooden floors and antiques.

🛏 P €

CAMPING
Camping du Lac Kir
3 Blvd Chanoine-Kir, 21000; 03 80 43 54 72; www.camping-dijon.com
This lovely camp site boasts a great location by Kir lake, the Ouche river

Flowers adorning the balconies of Hotel Wilson, Dijon

and the Burgundy Canal. Campers need to bring their own gear or book one of the eight self-catering cabins with their private lawned area and car parking. On offer are canoes, pedalos, swimming in the lake and great walking, as well as biking trails.

🛏 P ☉ €

Camping La Grappe d'Or
Map 9 C3
2 Route de Volnay, 21190 Meursault; 03 80 21 22 48; www.camping-meursault.com
Set amidst verdant Burgundy vineyards, this friendly family-run camp site is 42 km (26 miles) from Dijon. Mobile homes are available and there is also a *gîte* sleeping up to seven, just outside the camp site.

🛏 🍴 ☉ €

Flavigny-sur-Ozerain
Map 9 C2

HOTEL
Gîtes de la Licorne Bleue
Rue de la Poterne, 21150; 03 80 96 20 59; www.licorne-bleue.net
Two options here in the heart of the time-warp village of Flavigny where the film *Chocolat* was shot: the "Maison du Vigneron", an old wine producer's house converted in a tasteful contemporary rustic-chic style with exposed oak beams, and the Jean Dampt apartment above the Licorne Bleue art gallery. Perfect peace, and rolling Burgundian landscapes all around.

🛏 🍴 P €

> **Price Guide**
> The following price ranges are based on one night's accommodation in high season for a family of four, inclusive of service charges and any additional taxes.
> € Under €100 €€ €100–200 €€€ over €200

Key to symbols *see back cover flap*

Haut-Jura
Map 10 E4

HOTEL
Hotel du Commerce
01410 Chézery-Forens; 04 50 56 90 67; www.hotelducommerce-blanc.fr
An old-school hotel in the Valserine valley south of St-Claude that has been run by five generations of the Blanc family, it offers good-value accommodation, with eight charming, traditional bedrooms. The outdoor terrace looks over the Valserine river. There is a lovely beamed restaurant with an open fireplace.
P €€

SELF-CATERING
Les Eterlous
Haut-Crêt, 39200 St-Claude; 03 84 45 08 63; www.grand-gite-haut-jura.fr
A family-run auberge 3 km (2 miles) from Lamoura, this property sits at an altitude of over 1,000 m (3,281 ft) on the old stagecoach route from Paris to Geneva. Rooms are simple and spotless. Restaurant on site. A great base for hiking and biking in the Parc Régional Naturel du Haut-Jura.
P €

Lac des Settons
Map 9 B2

CAMPING
Camping La Plage des Settons
Rive Gauche, 58230 Les Settons; 03 86 84 51 99; www.settons-tourisme.com
This camp ground offers leafy, shaded pitches and wooden cabins for hire on the shores of the Lac des Settons in the Parc Naturel Régional du Morvan. Good site for watersports and exploring the great outdoors.
P €

Les Hautes-Combes
Map 10 E4

BED & BREAKFAST
La Pourvoirie
Sous-La-Joux, 39310 Les Moussières; 03 84 41 64 91; www.gite-la pourvoirie.com
This farm up on a wild mountain plateau in the Parc Régional Naturel du Haut-Jura has log-cabin rooms, with all modern facilities. Donkeys, reindeer and dog-sledding on offer for kids. The independent "Kota" is a superb octagonal-shaped Nordic pine cabin suited for a family. Rates are half-board as it is a remote spot.
P €€€

Les Rousses
Map 10 E4

HOTEL
Hôtel Le Lodge
309 Rue Pasteur, 39220; 03 84 60 50 64; www.hotellelodge.com
Built of stone and wood, this 150-year-old mountain-style hotel sits at the heart of Les Rousses, near all the restaurants and slopes. Comfortable rustic-chic bedrooms. Geneva is 40 minutes away by bus or car, making this a great base to explore the Jura.
P ✳ €€

BED & BREAKFAST
Gîte d'Étape Le Grand Tétras
705 Route des Rousses d'Amont, 39220; 03 84 60 51 13; www.grand tetras.com
This friendly, family-run *gîte* lies a few minutes outside the town centre. It has simple rustic pine-clad rooms and a self-contained apartment sleeping four to six. Half-board and full-board options available.
P €

Louhans
Map 9 D3

BED & BREAKFAST
La Ferme des Fourneaux
Les Chizes, 71500 St-Usuge; 03 85 72 18 12; www.fermedesfourneaux.com
This idyllic red brick and timber Bressane farmhouse, 6 km (4 miles) west of Louhans, dates from 1785. Rooms are spacious and done up in a rustic style, with cheerful fabrics and summery colour schemes. Breakfast is a treat for lovers of local cheeses.
P ✳ O €€€

Mâcon
Map 9 D4

HOTEL
Hotel d'Europe et d'Angleterre
92–109 Quai Jean-Jaurès, 71000; 03 85 38 27 94; www.hotel-europe angleterre-macon.com
An 18th-century former convent, this splendid old dame of the Saône river quays has been renovated to high standards. It has a grand staircase and public rooms, as well as bedrooms in all shapes and sizes.
P €

Tournus
Map 9 D4

CAMPING
Domaine de L'Épervière
9 Domaine du Château de L'Épervière, 71240 Gigny-sur-Saône; 03 85 94 16 90; www.domaine-eperviere.com
Set in the wooded grounds of a 16th–18th-century château, with its own lake, the camp site offers mobile homes, cabins and three spacious apartments to rent in a side wing of the château. It has a superb restaurant and activities for kids.
P O €

Vézelay
Map 9 B2

HOTEL
Hotel Poste et Lion d'Or
Pl du Champ-de-Foire, 89450; 03 86 33 21 23; www.laposte-liondor.com
This grand old coaching house has communicating rooms, triples and family suites, all catering for family groups. The rooms are big, with views of either the Basilique Ste-Madeleine or the lush valley. Great restaurant with a panoramic terrace.
P ✳ €€

The impressive façade of the Hotel Poste et Lion d'Or, Vézelay

Key to Price Guide *see p217*

The Rhône Valley and French Alps

Two natural features dominate the area: mountains and water. From the snowy heights of Mont Blanc to the watery depths of Lac d'Annecy, there are plenty of perfect spots for outdoor activities in winter and summer. Its cultural gems, Lyon and Briançon, are the proud caretakers of UNESCO World Heritage Sites. It also boasts some of France's finest regional produce.

Below *Hikers trekking uphill, the Alps towering majestically in the background, Mont Blanc*

① Lyon
Film, food and football

France's second city after Paris, Lyon was founded by the Romans; the remains of their settlement on Fourvière hill include an amphitheatre. The city was built around the Rhône and Saône rivers, which helped make it a major centre for business and trading, notably silk-making. Today, Lyon is best known for its famous chefs, excellent restaurants and a successful football team. The world's first film was made here in 1895 by the Lumière brothers.

Sculpture at the entrance to the city of Lyon

Key Sights

0 metres 500
0 yards 500

① **Place Bellecour** This vast square with an equestrian statue of Louis XIV in its centre is on the Presqu'île, which was an island in Roman times.

② **Basilique Notre-Dame de Fourvière** This 19th-century basilica stands at Fourvière hill, the site where Romans settled in 43 BC. Nearby is the amphitheatre and a museum of Gallo-Roman art and objects.

③ **Musée Gadagne** This fascinating museum housed in a 16th-century mansion traces the history of Lyon and also houses puppets from around the world.

④ **Musée des Beaux Arts** This museum, housed in a 17th-century abbey, takes visitors on a tour of fine arts from antiquity to modern times. The ancient Egyptian exhibits are always popular with families.

⑤ **Opéra Nouvel** Named after French architect Jean Nouvel, the grand opera house was redesigned by him in the late 1980s.

⑥ **Maison des Canuts** The 19th-century former silkworker's house in the hilly Croix Rousse district is now a museum. Visitors can learn about the industry and see how silk was woven on antique looms.

⑦ **Musée Lumière** This museum occupies the Lumière brothers' former home, where visitors can watch their films and see the camera they invented.

Letting off steam

Take Métro Line A to Masséna, then bus C1 to Lyon's **Parc de la Tête d'Or** (Blvd Stalingrad, 69000; www.loisirs-parcdelatetedor.com), an urban park with a zoo, pony rides and pedalos, or walk along the left bank of the Rhône, a Voie Verte (Green Lane) for walking and cycling.

Eat and drink

Picnic: under €20; Snacks: €20–45; Real meal: €45–90; Family treat: over €90 (based on a family of four)

PICNIC Les Halles Paul Bocuse (102 Cours Lafayette, 69003; 04 78 62 39 33; closed Sun pm & Mon), Lyon's magnificent market, is named after

a famous chef and sells top-quality regional food. Enjoy a picnic with a view on Place Abbé-Larue.

Giraffes and wild cattle in the zoo in Parc de la Tête d'Or

SNACKS La Dinette (3 Rue Sala, 69002; 09 52 83 59 11; closed Mon) is a retro-looking café-tea room with highchairs, toys, games and a place to park pushchairs. Try the spicy hot chocolate or a Carambar cookie.
REAL MEAL Le Bouchon de l'Opéra (11 Rue des Capucins, 69001; 04 78 28 49 47; bouchonde lopera.com; dinner only; closed Sun) is a family-friendly restaurant specializing in traditional regional dishes such as quenelles de brochet (pike dumplings) and andouillette au St Marcellin (tripe sausage with cheese).
FAMILY TREAT Le Pavillon de La Rotonde (3 Ave du Casino, 69260 Charbonnières-les-Bains; 04 78 87

Prices given are for a family of four

The Lowdown

🌐 **Map reference** 9 D5
Address 69000 (Rhône). Basilique Notre-Dame de Fourvière: 8 Pl de Fourvière, 69005; 04 78 25 13 01. Musée Gadagne: 1 Pl du Petit Collège, 69005; www.gadagne.musees. lyon.fr. Musee des Beaux Arts: 20 Pl des Terreaux, 69001; www. mba-lyon.fr. Opéra Nouvel: Pl de la Comédie, 69000; www.opera-lyon.com. Maison des Canuts: 10–12 Rue d'Ivry, 69004; www. maisondescanuts.com. Musée Lumière: Pl Ambroise Courtois, 69008; www.institut-lumiere.org

🚗 **Train** TGV from Paris

ℹ️ **Visitor information** Pl Bellecour, 69002; 04 72 77 69 69; www. lyon-france.com

🕐 **Open** Musée Gadagne: 11am–6:30pm Wed–Sun. Musee des Beaux Arts: closed Tue. Opéra Nouvel: box office noon–7pm Tue–Sat, timings vary Sun & Mon. Maison des Canuts: 10am–6pm Mon–Sat, guided tours 11am & 3:30pm, closed public hols. Musée Lumière: 10am–6:30pm Tue–Sun

💶 **Prices** Musée Gadagne: €12–16; under 26s free. Musee des Beaux Arts: €14–32; under 18s free. Maison des Canuts: €12–24; under 12s free. Musée Lumière: €12–22; under 7s free

👫 **Skipping the queue** The Lyon City Card (€67–77) is available for 1–3 days and includes trips on public transport, entry to museums, guided tours and activities.

🚩 **Guided tours** With the tourist office and local greeters' (www. lyoncitygreeter.com) in English.

👫 **Age range** All ages

👫 **Activities** The left bank of the Rhone river has been turned into a Voie Verte (Green Lane) for cycling and walking. Go for puppet shows at the Théâtre de la Maison de Guignol (www. lamaisondeguignol.fr).

⏱️ **Allow** 2 days

👫 **Toilets** By the flower stalls in Place Bellecour and in the car park in the Place de la République

✈️ **Festivals** Les Musicades, an international fest of chamber music (Sep). La Fête des Lumières, the festival of lights (Dec)

Good family value?
Lyon has indoor and outdoor activities to suit all ages, with superb restaurants and a sensory market to get fussy eaters interested in food.

79 79; www.pavillon-rotonde.com; closed Sun & Mon) is a Michelin-starred restaurant in a luxury hotel. Kids under 12 have their own menu from Tuesday to Friday.

Tempting desserts on sale at Les Halles Paul Bocuse

Shopping
Drop in to **Village des Créateurs** (Passage Thiaffait, 19 Rue René Leynaud, 69001; 04 78 27 37 21; www.villagedescreateurs.com; closed Sun & Mon) for clothes and accessories for all the family by local upcoming designers.

Find out more
DIGITAL Go to www.soierie-vivante. asso.fr to know more about Lyon's silk industry. Learn about puppetry at www.gadagne.musees.lyon.fr, the website of Lyon's puppet museum.

Next stop...
A PALACE AND A WINE VILLAGE
Hop on to a train to the town of St-Vallier-sur-Rhône, then a bus to Hauterives to visit the **Palais Idéal** (www.facteurcheval.com). It is an amazing 19th-century folly built in a range of exotic styles by a postman, Ferdinand Cheval. The "palace" took 33 years to build as Cheval worked on the project alone. The building is now regarded as a superb example of Naïve art. Take a train to Romanèche-Thorins, 49 km (24 miles) northwest of Lyon, to see how wine is made and to explore Beaujolais vineyards in **Le Hameau du Vin** (www.hameauduvin.com).

A sculpture at the entrance of the Parc de l'Europe, St-Étienne

② St-Étienne

From arms to art

Located 60 km (37 miles) southwest of Lyon, the town of St-Étienne was at the forefront of France's Industrial Revolution in the 19th century. It all started in the 16th century when the city became the country's centre for arms manufacturing; the abundant coal in the area was heated to create coke, which was used to smelt iron to make the arms. It was the need to transport coal that led to France's first military line being built here in 1823. The city was also well known for producing ribbons and bicycles. To find out more about the town's industrial heritage, head to the **Musée d'Art et d'Industrie** and visit the **Musée de la Mine** to explore the world of miners. The **Musée d'Art Moderne** houses the second-largest collection of contemporary art in France.

Letting off steam

Take bus 4 or 6 and head to the **Parc de l'Europe** *(Rue de Coventry, 42100)* in St-Étienne. The park has a merry-go-round, a little train and various play areas set amongst lots of greenery. It is also a popular place for picnics on fine days.

③ Vienne

Roman around the Rhône

Like Lyon, Vienne has well-preserved Roman remains. The town was founded by the Gauls next to the Rhône, but it did not really become a major settlement until Julius Caesar came here in 47 BC. The most impressive remnants are Le Temple d'Auguste et de Livie and La Pyramide du Cirque Romain de Vienne. The circus was used for chariot races and other sporting events and La Pyramide was a copy of the Egyptian pyramids erected in the major circuses of the Roman Empire. The town's Roman theatre, the **Théâtre Antique**, dates back to the time of ancient Gaul and is still

An exhibition of bicycles at the Musée d'Art et d'Industrie, St-Étienne

used for concerts. Across the river from Vienne is St-Roman-en-Gal, an impressive archaeological site, which houses the **Musée Gallo Romain**. Showcasing the remains of an ancient Roman town, the site provides a snapshot of daily life and includes mosaics, outlines of houses and a granite road.

Letting off steam

Vienne's public garden, located behind the tourist office, has a play area for young children. Take bus 51 from Vienne 14 km (9 miles) east to **Cimes Aventures** *(www.cimes-aventures.com)*, an adventure park

Fun on a treetop at Cimes Aventures in Septème, Vienne

Humboldt penguins sunbathing in their enclosure at the Parc des Oiseaux, Les Dombes

in the village of Septème. The park offers tree-top activities to families, for kids aged 3 plus. The rope bridges, nets and death slides will keep everyone entertained for half a day. Or hire mountain bikes and enjoy exploring the forest.

④ Les Dombes
Something fishy, something "fowl"

The Dombes plateau extends north of Lyon towards Bourg-en-Bresse, a town well known for the quality of its chickens, the Poulets de Bresse *(see p211)*. These chickens can be found on the menus of many top restaurants. In fact, Les Dombes also produces some of the best game bird meat in the world and is a leading centre for hunting. The **Parc des Oiseaux** in Villars-les-Dombes is a large ornithological park, which houses more than 400 species (2,000 birds) from around

the world; the baby bird nursery and the "birds in flight" show are popular with kids.

The plateau has more than 1,000 lakes and is France's main region for the breeding of freshwater fish and frogs. It is also the perfect place to go horse-riding, as there are many riding schools; the area is France's second centre for horse breeding. The well-preserved medieval village of Pérouges is well worth a visit, especially in June, when it hosts La Fête Médiévale.

Take cover
Take bus 181 from Villars to Belleville-sur-Saône, then bus 113 to the **Château de Fléchères** (www.chateaudeflecheres.com) in the village of Fareins. Swoon over the countess' pink dream of a bedroom, find Hercules and study interesting perspectives among the famous 17th-century frescoes. Play hide and seek in the park and maze.

The Lowdown

🌐 **Map reference** 9 D5
Address 01330 (Villars-les-Dombes). Parc des Oiseaux: RD 1083, Villars-les-Dombes; 04 74 98 00 54; www.parcdesoiseaux.com

🚂 **Train** from Lyon to Meximieux and Villars-les-Dombes. **Bus** 132 from Lyon to Perouges or bus 102 from Lyon to Villars-les-Dombes

ℹ **Visitor information** 3 Pl de l'Hotel de Ville, 01330; 04 74 98 06 29; www.villars-les-dombes.com; www.ain-tourisme.com; www.perouges.org

🕐 **Open** Parc des Oiseaux: Mar–Nov: daily

🍴 **Eat and drink** *Real meal* Le Petit Carpe (RD 1083, 01330 Villars-les-Dombes, 04 74 98 05 54; www.parcdesoiseaux.com) serves traditional dishes in a shady setting, which overlooks the largest lake of the Parc des Oiseaux. *Real meal* La Grenouille (135 Rue du Commerce, 01330 Villars-les-Dombes; 04 74 98 05 10; closed Mon) specializes in local produce, including frogs' legs, carp and game. There is a play area for kids as well.

🎪 **Festival** Fête des Dombes celebrates local life through activities and displays (Oct)

Picnic under €20; **Snacks** €20–45; **Real meal** €45–90; **Family treat** over €90 (based on a family of four)

⑤ Chamonix
Home of the first Winter Olympics

The most famous ski resort in the French Alps and with a strong claim to be the home of winter sports, Chamonix sits in a valley at the foot of Mont Blanc, the highest peak in Western Europe at 4,808 m (15,774 ft). The town first became known internationally when two Englishmen, Richard Pococke and William Windham, came here to see the glaciers in 1741. Chamonix hosted the first Winter Olympics in 1924, and now combines its spectacular location with the facilities of a mountain resort.

Town centre with Mont Blanc in the backdrop

Key Sights

② **Musée Alpin** This museum charts the history of Chamonix as a ski resort via a fascinating display of exhibits, from early skis to relief maps.

④ **Musée des Cristaux** Colourful crystals found in the Mont Blanc area, as well as in other parts of the world, are on display in this museum.

① **Place Balmat** The bronze sculpture of Horace Saussure, the renowned Swiss climber, the founder of "alpinism", and Jacques Balmat, the first man to climb Mont Blanc, is the main attraction of this square.

③ **Maison de la Montagne** This is the headquarters of around 200 highly qualified mountain guides whose services include taking small groups on an ascent of Mont Blanc.

⑤ **Mer de Glace** Admire the "Sea of Ice", France's longest glacier at 14 km (9 miles), aboard the Train du Montenvers.

⑥ **Aiguille du Midi** The ascent to the top of this peak, the "Needle of Midday", is made via the world's highest vertical ascent cable car.

⑦ **Mont Blanc** Western Europe's highest mountain was first conquered by two local men, Jacques Balmat and Dr Michel Paccard, in 1786.

The Lowdown

🌐 **Map reference** 10 F5
Address 74400 (Haute-Savoie). Musée des Cristaux: Esplanade St-Michel, 615 Allée du Recteur Payot; 04 50 55 53 93. Maison de la Montagne: by the tourist office; www.ohm-chamonix. com. Musée Alpin: Ave Michel Croz; 04 50 53 25 93

ℹ **Visitor information** 85 Pl du Triangle de l'Amitié, 74400; 04 50 53 00 24; www.chamonix.com

🚗 **Train** from St-Gervais-les-Bains to and from Chamonix. It is best to use a car to explore this area.

🕐 **Open** Musée des Cristaux & Musée Alpin: 2–7pm daily; school hols 10am–noon & 2–7pm. Maison de la Montagne: 9am–noon & 3pm–6pm Mon–Sat

💶 **Price** Musée des Cristaux & Musée Alpin: €12–22; under 18s free

👪 **Skipping the queue** In summer, a free *carte d'hôte* (guest card) is available from hotels and other accommodation providers, allowing free local bus travel and discounts on attractions and activities. In winter, a family ski pass gives a 50 per cent reduction (to ski

lifts) to the first child and the other kids go free.

🚩 **Guided tours** Tours of the town arranged by the tourist office and of the mountains by specialist guides (in English). Kids can go for mountain walks, but Mont Blanc climbs are suited for those aged 16 plus

👫 **Age range** 3 plus. High-altitude walks are not suitable for younger children.

🎿 **Activities** Hop on to the Train du Montenvers (35 Pl de la Mer de Glace, 74400; www. compagniedumontblanc.fr;

Letting off steam

Children aged 8 plus can try tandem paragliding from one of the lower peaks. However, all kids will love spending time with the huskies of **Husky Dalen** *(74 Chemin des Falete, 74400; 04 50 47 77 24; www.huskydalen.com)* – try sledging in winter or hiking with the dogs in summer. **The Centre Sportif Richard Bozon** *(214 Ave de la Plage, 74400; 04 50 53 23 70; timings vary)* is a sports centre with an indoor and outdoor ice rink, a swimming pool and a climbing wall.

The sign for Boulangerie Patisserie St-Hubert, Place de l'Église

Eat and drink

Picnic: under €20; Snacks: €20–45; Real meal: €45–90; Family treat: over €90 (based on a family of four)

PICNIC Boulangerie Patisserie St-Hubert *(31 Pl de l'Église, 74400; 04 50 53 01 46; open daily)* is an artisan bakery offering sandwiches and cakes. Take a gondola from La Tour up to La Balme for stunning views over Switzerland to enjoy a good picnic.
SNACKS Aux Petits Gourmands *(168 Rue du Docteur Paccard, 74400; 04 50 53 01 59; open daily)* serves superb hot chocolate and cakes in a treasure trove of cocoa-based concoctions.

€90–100), which offers scenic views. In winter, visit the ice grotto to see ice sculptures and a display of mountain animals.

🕐 **Allow** 2 days or longer

🚻 **Toilets** At the tourist office and on the Rue du Lyret

🎭 **Festival** Fête des Guides features parades, dinners, music and a mass (Aug)

Good family value?
Chamonix is an excellent year-round destination for outdoorsy families as it offers activities to suit all ages, tastes and budgets.

REAL MEAL La Bergerie de Planpraz *(232 Ave Michel Croz, 74400; 04 50 53 05 42; daily lunch in season)* can be reached by the Planpraz gondola, a ski lift. Local cuisine, including *tartiflette* (a dish made of potatoes, cheese, cream and bacon), are served on a terrace with great views over mountain tops. There is a special menu for *petits bergers* (little shepherds).
FAMILY TREAT Le Bistrot Hotel Le Morgane *(151 Ave Aiguille du Midi, 74400; 04 50 53 57 64; www. lebistrotchamonix.com; open daily)* serves Michelin-starred food in stylish yet unstuffy surroundings. Kids can enjoy a main course and dessert at an affordable price.

Shopping

Le Refuge Payot *(166 Rue Joseph Vallot, 74400; 04 50 53 18 71; www. refugepayot.com)* is the place to go for local gourmet specialities, including cooked meats, sweets, liqueurs and cheese.

Sausages and champagne for sale at Le Refuge Payot at Rue Joseph Vallot

Find out more

FILM The mountain scenes in the James Bond adventure *The World Is Not Enough* (1999) were filmed in the nearby village of Argentière. A documentary *Touching the Void* (2003), based on a book about a man's survival in the Andes, was also shot around Chamonix.

Next stop...

OUTDOOR FUN Head for the **Parc de Loisirs** *(351 Chemin du Pied du Grépon, 74400; www. chamonixparc.com)*, with more than 15 activities such as luge, trampolines and electric motorbikes. Animal lovers should visit the **Parc de Merlet** *(www.parcdemerlet.com)* in the village of Les Houches, located 14 km (8 miles) from Chamonix, to see Alpine animals.

The old-fashioned fishing village of Yvoire on the shore of Lac Léman

⑥ Samoëns

Stonemasons, Alpine plants and summer waterfalls

The pretty mountain village of Samoëns, about 60 km (37 miles) north of Chamonix, is best known for the legacy of its stonemasons. The Giffre valley, in which Samoëns is located, is made up of limestone, and local farmers eventually took to stone cutting to supplement their income. Their skills were renowned throughout France and many were employed by the celebrated 17th-century military engineer Vauban to build fortifications. Not everything here is about stone though. **La Jaÿsinia**, a botanical garden, has more than 5,000 species of mountain plants from around the world.

Samoëns is a great resort for families in both summer and winter. No summer visit would be complete without a trip to the Cirque du Fer à Cheval, a limestone corrie (a horseshoe-shaped rock formation

at the head of a valley caused by glacial erosion) renowned for its waterfalls. Nearby is Sixt-Fer-à-Cheval, a picturesque village, with the largest nature reserve in Haute-Savoie. Samoëns and Sixt-Fer-à-Cheval are part of the Grand Massif ski area: a good place for beginners.

Letting off steam

Take a helicopter ride (*Mont Blanc Helicoptères; www.mbh.fr*) to enjoy splendid aerial views of the Alps. In winter, hurtle down a slope in a toboggan. The **Base de Loisirs des Lacs aux Dames** (*74340 Samoëns; 06 89 83 18 84*) offers a host of fun activities such as paragliding, golf, football and fishing.

⑦ Yvoire

An old-fashioned fishing village

This beautiful 14th-century former fishing port is the perfect place to mess about in water. Yvoire stands on the banks of Lac Léman (Lake

The Lowdown

- 🌐 **Map reference** 10 E4
  Address 74140 (Haute-Savoie). Jardin des Cinq Sens: Rue du Lac; 04 50 72 88 80; *www.jardin5sens.net*
- 🚗 **Train** from Annecy and Cluses to Thonon-les-Bains, then bus 152
- ℹ️ **Visitor information** Pl de la Mairie, 74140; 04 50 72 80 21; *www.yvoiretourism.com*
- 🕙 **Open** Jardin des Cinq Sens: mid-Apr–mid-Oct: daily (times vary)
- 🍽️ **Eat and drink** *Snacks* Le Chardon (*Rue des Boulangers, 74140; 04 50 72 81 71; open daily*) is a little stone house that serves sandwiches, ice creams and cakes. *Real meal* Restaurant des Pêcheurs (*Rue Principale, 74140; 04 50 72 80 26; closed Tue*), a lively bar-restaurant, is known for its delicious lake-caught perch served with a lemon and butter sauce.
- 🎉 **Festival** Jeud'Yvoiriens presents entertainment for all tastes and ages on Thu nights (Jul & Aug)

Kids playing in the sand at one of the beaches, Lac d'Annecy

Geneva), almost 60 per cent of which is in southern Switzerland. Boat trips across the lake are a must-do. Along with regular cruisers, small solar-powered boats can be hired from Helionaute (*www.helionaute.com*) for 30-minute guided tours.

Wander around the ancient streets and admire the flower-bedecked houses before taking the *Voie Verte* (Green Lane) to picturesque Le Domaine de Rovorée for lakeside walks beneath the age-old chestnut trees. The **Jardin des Cinq Sens**, once the kitchen garden of the village's privately owned castle, has been transformed into a medieval garden. Families can play hide and seek among the hedges and follow a trail designed to awaken the five

The Lowdown

- 🌐 **Map reference** 10 F5
  Address 74340 (Haute-Savoie). La Jaÿsinia: 04 50 34 49 86
- 🚗 **Train** from Annecy and Thonon to Cluses, then bus 94. **Bus** 91 from Thonon to Cluses or bus 82 from Chamonix to Cluses, then bus 94
- ℹ️ **Visitor information** Pl de L'autogare, 74340; 04 50 34 40 28; *www.samoens.com*
- 🕙 **Open** La Jaÿsinia: year round (Nov–Apr: till 4:30pm), closed in snowy weather
- 🍽️ **Eat and drink** *Snacks* Boulangerie Tiffanie (*Ave du Giffre, 74340; 04 50 34 42 62*) is an artisan bakery

known for great baguettes, biscuits and fruit tarts. Enjoy them on the terrace overlooking the river. *Real meal* Le Monde à l'Envers (*Pl du Criou, 74340; 04 50 34 19 36; closed Tue*) serves inventive cuisine, using local and seasonal produce, as well as value-for-money lunch and "proper food" for kids.

- 🎉 **Festivals** Fest'Nordic, free trial sessions of winter sports, including dog sledding (Jan). Samoëns American Festival, a celebration of the Wild West with country music, horse rides, equestrian displays and a mechanical bull (Jul)

Prices given are for a family of four

The shore of Lac d'Annecy, popular with swimmers and picnickers

senses. A film and written information about the garden are also available in English.

Letting off steam

Head for Excenevex, a sandy beach about 3 km (2 miles) southeast of Yvoire. The beach is safe for kids and has activities for 6 to 16-year-olds in July and August.

⑧ Lac d'Annecy
Europe's cleanest lake

Renowned for its beauty as well as its exceptionally clean water, Lac d'Annecy is a perfect summer holiday kind of place, with great watersports opportunities. Its banks are dotted with beaches; the ones at Annecy-le-Vieux and Talloires are the most popular with families who have children. The second largest lake in France, it is 14 km (9 miles) long and 3 km (2 miles) wide and has an average depth of 41 m (134 ft).

A cycle path runs along the left bank, passing through traditional villages. Rent bikes from Roul' ma poule (*www.annecy-location-velo. com*). The main town around the lake is Annecy, which is the capital of the Haute-Savoie *département*. The town's turbulent history saw it being owned by the Kingdom of Sardinia, whose Italian influence is still evident in the architecture, especially in Rue Ste-Claire with its arcades. The main sights in town are the **Musée-Château d'Annecy**, a 16th-century castle transformed into a museum, which houses the Observatoire Régional des Lacs Alpins and the Musée d'Art Populaire Alpin, and the **Palais de l'Île**, a 12th-century former prison, built on an islet in the centre of the Thiou canal.

Take cover

Take bus 61 to Menthon to visit the **Château de Menthon** (*www. chateau-de-menthon.com*), a fairy-tale castle, seated high above Lac d'Annecy. It was the birthplace of St Bernard, who lent his name to the brandy-carrying dogs. Costumed guides welcome visitors during weekends from May to September.

The Lowdown

🌐 **Map reference** 10 E5
Address 74000 (Haute-Savoie). Musée-Château d'Annecy: Pl du Château; 04 50 33 87 30; www.musees.aglo-annecy.fr. Palais de l'Île: 3 Passage de l'Île; 04 50 65 08 14

🚆 **Train** from Chamonix, Thonon-les-Bains and Cluses

ℹ **Visitor information** 1 Rue Jean Jaurès, 74000; 04 50 45 00 33; www.lac-annecy.com

🕙 **Open** Musée-Château d'Annecy & Palais de l'Île: Jun–Sep: daily; Oct–May: Wed–Mon

🍽 **Eat and drink** *Real meal* Café Brunet (*18 Pl Gabriel Fauré, 74940 Annecy-le-Vieux; 04 50 27 65 65; www.closdessens.com; closed Sun & Mon*) serves traditional French fare in the 14th-century house or on its lovely terrace. *Family treat* Auberge du Père Bise (*Route du Port, 74290 Talloires; 04 50 60 72 01; www.perebise.com; opening days and timings vary according to season*) is a luxury hotel and restaurant that offers Michelin-starred food.

🎉 **Festival** La Fête du Lac, a fireworks extravaganza (Aug)

⑨ Briançon
A fortress frontier town

At 1,326 m (4,300 ft) it may be the highest town in the European Union, but Briançon is also the lowest resort in the Serre Chevalier ski area. Located on the Italian border near the Col de Montgenèvre mountain pass, it is a UNESCO World Heritage Site for its 18th-century fortification built by Vauban, the famous military engineer of Louis XIV. The surrounding area is great for skiing, rafting and walking.

The sundial on the Collégiale Notre Dame

Key Sights

① Collégiale Notre-Dame The design and building of this early 18th-century parish church was overseen by Vauban. One of the four sundials in the fortified upper town is in front of this church.

② Centre d'Art Contemporain This contemporary art gallery is housed in La Maison du Roi, a 17th-century building, which also accommodates the law courts. The art gallery holds temporary art exhibitions.

RUE CHAMP DE MARS
CHEMIN DU BARRY
AVENUE VAUBAN
Collégiale Notre-Dame ①
RUE DU TEMPLE
PLACE DU TEMPLE
RUE
Fort du Château ③
RUE HAUTE DE CASTRE
CHEMIN DE LA RONDE
RUE PORTE MÉANE
GRANDE RUE
Centre d'Art Contemporain ②
RUE PERCHÈRE
RUE DE ROCHE
RUE DU PONT D'ASFELD
Pont d'Asfeld 200 m (220 yards) ⑥
Place d'Armes ④
⑥ Parc de la Schappe 300 m (330 yards)
Église de Cordeliers ⑤
RUE DE L'ASPIRANT-JAN

0 metres   200
0 yards   200

③ Fort du Château Briançon's medieval castle, which was fortified between 1835 and 1845, dominates the upper town, also known as Cité Vauban. It offers scenic views across the area.

④ Place d'Armes The square has always been a popular meeting place for locals, but in the 18th century it was used as a parade ground for soldiers.

⑤ Église de Cordeliers This church, noted for its 15th-century frescoes, is the only medieval building left in Briançon as all the others were destroyed by fire.

⑥ Parc de la Schappe This pleasant park in Ste-Catherine, the lower town, was created on the site of a 19th-century silk factory.

The Lowdown

🌐 **Map reference** 14 F1
Address 05100 (Hautes Alpes). Collégiale Notre-Dame: Ave Vauban. Centre d'Art Contemporain: Pl d'Armes; 04 92 21 08 50. Fort du Château: via Chemin de la Ronde; 04 92 21 08 50. Église de Cordeliers: Rue de l'Aspirant-Jan. Parc de la Schappe: 1 Chemin Schappe; 04 92 46 16 91

🚗 **Train** from Paris, local train from Turin, Grenoble or Lyon
Bus from Oulx and Grenoble.

ℹ **Visitor information** 1 Pl du Temple, 05100; www.ot-briancon.com

🕐 **Open** Collégiale Notre-Dame: daily. Centre d'Art Contemporain: 3–7pm Wed–Mon. Fort du Château: Jun–Sep. Église de Cordeliers: guided tours only (ring ahead). Parc de la Schappe: daily

💰 **Prices** Fort du Château: €20–30; under 12s free

🚩 **Guided tours** In English. Service du Patrimoine (*Porte de Pignerol, 05100; 04 92 20 29 49*) offers guided tours of the Fort du Château (ring ahead).

👫 **Age range** 4 plus

👟 **Activities** Go kayaking and white-water rafting on the Durance river south of the town, with Eaurigine (www.eaurigine.net).

⏱ **Allow** A day to explore the town, but more for exploring the surrounding area.

👫 **Toilets** In the two car parks at Champ de Mars and Avenue de la Libération.

Good family value?
Briançon is historically interesting and has plenty of summer and winter activities for all ages.

⑦ Pont d'Asfeld Completed in four months in 1731, this stone bridge crosses the Durance river and links the upper town with Fort des Têtes, which is one and a half times the size of Briançon's upper town.

Letting off steam

Head for the **Parc 1326** (*37 Rue Bermon-Gonnet, 05100; 04 92 20 04 04*), a leisure centre with an Olympic-sized skating rink and outdoor and indoor swimming pools. There is also a 65-m (213-ft) long waterslide.

Playing in one of the many pools at Parc 1326

Eat and drink

Picnic: under €20; Snacks: €20–45; Real meal: €45–90; Family treat: over €90 (based on a family of four)

PICNIC Letinturier (*1 Chemin Vieux, lower town, 05100; 04 92 21 13 21; closed Tue & Sun pm*) is the place to buy cakes and sandwiches made with woodfire-baked bread. Head to the Parc de la Schappe for an al fresco lunch next to the Durance river with views up to the old town.

SNACKS L'Étage (*35 Grande Rue, upper town, 05100; 04 92 23 09 22; open daily*) is a characterful crêperie in the heart of the upper town where savoury and sweet pancakes revive weary visitors.

REAL MEAL La Caponnière (*12 Rue Commandant Carlhan, upper town, 05100; 04 92 20 36 77; closed Tue & Wed*) has costumed staff serving up authentic regional dishes, featuring pigeon and trout. The recipes on the Menu Vauban date from the 17th century. Try the nutty Gâteau de Voyage for dessert.

FAMILY TREAT Le Pêché Gourmand (*2 Route de Gap, 05100; 04 92 21 33 21; closed Tue & Wed*), a child-friendly restaurant, is located in an old mill opposite the lower town. Long been regarded as one of the best in the region, the restaurant serves beautifully presented dishes such as scallops with meat gravy and a tobacco-flavoured dessert.

Shopping

Visit **Les Poteries de Virginie** (*51 Rue des Tabellions, Centre Activités Sud, 05100; 06 80 51 37 65; www.poterievirginie.com*) to see Virginie at work in her pottery studio. Choose from a wide variety of styles and designs; those from the fir tree collection make perfect Christmas presents. Ring ahead of visit.

Find out more

DIGITAL Older kids can browse through *www.sites-vauban.org* for more information (in English) about Marshal Vauban, France's celebrated 17th-century military engineer.

Next stop...

PARC NATIONAL DES ECRINS Head west of Briançon to France's largest national park in the Massif des Ecrins (*www.ecrins-parcnational.fr*). The park is noted for its glaciers, as well as its diverse wildflowers. With more than 100 peaks over 3,000 m (9,842 ft) high, it is a year-round destination attracting skiers, walkers and climbers. Drop in to the **Maison du Parc** (*Pl Général Blanchard, 05100; 04 92 21 42 15*), the park's discovery centre in Briançon, to learn about the heritage of the area, including skiing.

KIDS' CORNER

Look out for...

1 The sundials in Briançon's upper town. How many are there?

2 The 15th-century Église des Cordeliers is the oldest building in Briançon. What does its doorway look like?

3 The sundial in front of the Collégiale Notre-Dame church. Check the time against the clocks on the two clocktowers (or your watch). Do they agree?

4 Fort des Têtes. How did it get its name and what does Tête mean in French?

Answers at the bottom of the page.

CLASSIC SUNDIALS

A sundial is a kind of clock, which tells the time by the position of the sun in the sky. As the earth moves around the sun, a gnomon (rod) casts a shadow on the dial that lands on the corresponding hour.

Extreme terrain

Thanks to its challenging geography, Briançon has regularly been a stage in the Tour de France. Launched in 1903, the Tour de France is the world's most famous cycle race. It lasts for three weeks, covers around 3,600 km (2,200 miles) and takes riders through the length and breadth of France.

Answers: 1 Four. **2** It is arched with several narrow columns either side of the wooden door. **4** It is named after the rocky plateau on which it is built. In French, Tête means head.

Magnificent snow-capped peaks in the Parc National des Ecrins

⑩ Parc National de la Vanoise

Rare animals

This beautifully rugged national park of Vanoise was created in 1963. Located east of Les Trois Vallées, it was France's first national park and its purpose was to protect the region's few remaining Alpine ibex (capra ibex), which were being wiped out by hunters; there are now about 2,000 of them. The area is popular among hikers and climbers of all abilities who come for its glaciers, mountain lakes, protected plants and flowers, and to perhaps glimpse one of the 20 pairs of golden eagles.

Most visitors base themselves in Pralognan-la-Vanoise nearby, which has an Olympic-sized skating rink. In 1992, the village hosted the curling competition in the Winter Olympics. An alternative is the village of Champagny-en-Vanoise, where **Espace Glacialis** tells visitors all that they need to know about glaciers. Tourist offices in both villages advise on the best walks for families and beginners' climbing courses. On

Adult male Alpine ibex in the Parc National de la Vanoise

the eastern edge of the park is Bonneval-sur-Arc, a pretty village of rustic stone chalets nestling at the foot of Col d'Iséran. This pass, which is Europe's highest at 2,770 m (9,088 ft), is open to cars from July to September.

Take cover

Beaufort cheese is a speciality of this region. Head to the milk co-operative **Beaufort des Montagnes** (www.beaufortdesmontagnes.com) in the town of Moûtiers on weekday mornings to see how the cheese is made and of course to taste some. There is an informative film with English subtitles and also a shop.

⑪ Les Trois Vallées

Family-friendly outdoor fun

Spread over 600 km (373 miles) and made up of eight resorts, Les Trois Vallées is the world's largest ski area. The best resorts for families are

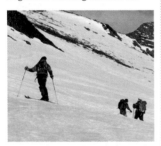

Skiing in Les Trois Vallées, the largest ski area in the world

The Lowdown

- 🌐 **Map reference** 10 F6 **Address** Savoie
- 🚗 **Train** from Grenoble and Modane to Moûtiers, then bus from Moûtiers to Les Trois Vallées see www.altibus.com for details
- ℹ️ **Visitor information** Visit www.les3vallees.com for details
- 🍴 **Eat and drink** Real meal La Ferme (Reberty Village, 73440 Les Menuires; 04 79 00 77 01) is a traditional restaurant that offers a good-value kids' menu. Family treat Le Chabichou (Rue des Chenus, 73121 Courchevel 1850; 04 79 08 00 55; www.chabichou-courchevel.com; daily) is a Michelin-starred restaurant. Kids are welcomed in the dining room and on the cookery courses.
- 🎆 **Festival** International Fireworks Festival in Courchevel (Feb & Mar)

Courchevel, Les Menuires and Val Thorens, of which Courchevel is the best known and comprises four villages. One of them is the traditional hamlet of Le Praz, which was the site of ski jumping in the 1992 Winter Olympics. Another one is the super-glitzy Courchevel 1850, a favourite with billionaires and celebrities. Watch the private planes landing and taking off from its "altiport". For beginners and kids, the modern Les Menuires is a good place. The sports centre here has a swimming pool and a fun park with bouncy castles. At 2,300 m (75,456 ft), Val Thorens, Europe's highest ski resort, offers skiing from November to May and has one of France's longest toboggan runs.

The Lowdown

- 🌐 **Map reference** 10 F6 **Address** 73320 (Tignes). Espace Glacialis: 73350 Champagny-en-Vanoise; 04 79 01 40 28; www.espace-glacialis.fr
- 🚗 **Train** from Grenoble and Modane to the park and Moûtiers. **Bus** from Moûtiers to Pralognan and Champagny and from Modane to Bonneval-sur-Arc
- ℹ️ **Visitor information** See www.parcnational-vanoise.fr for details
- 🕐 **Open** Espace Glacialis: Sun–Thu pm
- 🍴 **Eat and drink** Snacks Le Criou (Top of Vallonnet chairlift; 73480 Bonneval-sur-Arc; 04 79 05 97 11; winter: lunch daily; Jul & Aug timings vary) is a mountain restaurant that serves tasty planche du criou (a platter of local cheese and charcuterie). Real meal Les Glières (Lotissement de Planchamp, 73350 Champagny-en-Vanoise; 04 79 55 05 52; www.hotel-glieres.com; open daily) offers traditional Savoyard wine and food such as diots (sausages) served with crozets (small pasta squares) in a cheese sauce.
- 🎆 **Festivals** La Grande Odyssée, a dog sled race in Bonneval (Jan). Special "children's weeks" of fun activities in Pralognan (Jul & Aug)

Take cover
Take bus T3 from Moûtiers to the village of St-Martin-de-Belleville near Les Menuires, to visit the **Musée St-Martin** (www.st-martin-belleville.com), which traces the village's history from its farming origins to the creation of the ski resorts.

⑫ Grenoble
The capital of the Alps
Located at the confluence of the Drac and Isère rivers, Grenoble is the perfect place to combine a city break with time spent in the great outdoors: the Parc National du Vercors to the west and Les Trois Vallées, Parc National de la Vanoise and Serre Chevalier to the east. The two rivers were responsible for the city's industrial growth, including glove making, cement production

Children's play area in the Jardin des Dauphins, Grenoble

and paper mills. Today, the city is an important centre for science and technology.

On arrival, the first thing that visitors notice are *Les Bulles* (bubbles), the unusual bubble-shaped cable cars that take passengers up to **La Bastille**, a series of fortifications built on a mountaintop overlooking the city. Here, the **Musée des Troupes de Montagne** focuses on the history of mountain troops. Head back down on foot via the Parc Guy-Pape and Jardin des Dauphins, where kids can dash off to the play area. Also worth visiting is the **Musée de Grenoble** for its important collection of 16th- to 20th-century artworks.

Letting off steam
Make sandcastles or play beach sports such as volleyball at **La Plage de Grenoble** (2 Rue Gustave Flaubert; 04 76 23 57 16; www.plage degrenoble.com), a very urban piece of sand. On Saturday mornings, from May to September, the beach hosts special sessions for families, with sand sports and picnics.

Grand view of the town from the bubble-shaped cable car, Grenoble

The Lowdown
Map reference 10 E6
Address 38000 (Isère). La Bastille: reached by cable car at Quai Stéphane Jay; 04 76 44 33 65; www.bastille-grenoble.fr. Musée des Troupes de Montagne: 19 Rue Hébert; 04 76 00 93 41. Musée de Grenoble: 5 Pl de Lavalette; 04 76 63 44 44; www.museedegrenoble.fr

Train from Moûtiers and Modane; TGV from Paris. **Bus** LER bus 35 from Briançon.

Visitor information 14 Rue de la République, 38000; 04 76 42 41 41; www.grenoble-tourisme.com

Open La Bastille: days and timings vary throughout the year; cable car:

closed Jan. Musée des Troupes de Montagne: Tue–Sun; closed Jan. Musée de Grenoble: Wed–Mon

Eat and drink Snacks Patisserie les Ecrins (11 Rue de Bonne, 38000; 04 76 46 48 22; www.patisserie-lesecrins.com; open daily) serves fabulous chocolates, ice creams and cakes to eat indoors or take away. Real meal La Ferme à Dédé (1 Pl aux Herbes, 38000; 04 76 54 00 33; www.restaurantlafermeadede.com; open daily) is renowned for its regional specialities – try the green salad with walnut, accompanied by charcuterie and cheesy ravioli.

Festival Le Grenoble Jazz Fest (Mar)

Picnic under €20; **Snacks** €20–45; **Real meal** €45–90; **Family treat** over €90 (based on a family of four)

⑬ Gorges de l'Ardèche

Paddle down a river and explore a huge cave

The Ardèche gorges are a meandering part of the Ardèche river, stretching for about 30 km (19 miles) southeast of Vallon-Pont-d'Arc to St-Martin-d'Ardèche. This wild, protected site offers activities such as caving and climbing, but most visitors come here to descend the river by canoe, whether accompanied or self-guided. The area has several intriguing caves including the Aven d'Orgnac, where visitors can explore one of the world's largest underground caverns.

Signposts to attractions in a town in the Ardèche

Key Sights

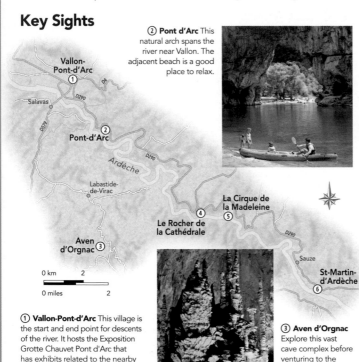

② **Pont d'Arc** This natural arch spans the river near Vallon. The adjacent beach is a good place to relax.

④ **Le Rocher de la Cathédrale** Overlooking the river, this pointed rock formation resembles a cathedral – hence the name.

⑤ **La Cirque de la Madeleine** The ruins of a Templar hospital can be seen at this horseshoe-shaped bend in the river. It is best viewed from the Balcon des Templiers.

① **Vallon-Pont-d'Arc** This village is the start and end point for descents of the river. It hosts the Exposition Grotte Chauvet Pont d'Arc that has exhibits related to the nearby Grotte Chauvet. Discovered in 1994, the cave is home to the earliest known cave paintings, but is closed to the public.

③ **Aven d'Orgnac** Explore this vast cave complex before venturing to the on-site Musée de Préhistoire to find out about early man's life here.

⑥ **St-Martin-d'Ardèche** The southernmost point of the gorges, this village hosts lively morning and evening markets.

Map labels:
Vallon-Pont-d'Arc ①
Salavas
Pont-d'Arc ②
Ardèche
Labastide-de-Virac
Le Rocher de la Cathédrale ④
La Cirque de la Madeleine ⑤
Aven d'Orgnac ③
Sauze
St-Martin-d'Ardèche ⑥

0 km   2
0 miles   2

Take cover

Drive to the village of Labastide-de-Virac to visit the 14th-century **Château des Roure** (www.chateaudesroure.com), a fortified manor. It played a major role during the Wars of Religion in the 16th century, as it was owned by a Protestant nobleman. There are great views of the countryside from the round tower, a "ghost" to scare kids and a reconstructed 17th-century silk workshop, where visitors can work the looms and see wriggly silk worms.

The fortified Château des Roure, Labastide-de-Virac

Prices given are for a family of four

Eat and drink

Picnic: under €20; Snacks: €20–45 Real meal: €45–90; Family treat: over €90 (based on a family of four)

PICNIC Boulangerie Lichière (Rue des Maquisards, 07150 Vallon-Pont-d'Arc; 04 75 88 03 52; closed Wed) stocks sandwiches, quiches and cakes, including *Lou Pisadou*, a crisp, flat cake made with chestnut cream. Picnic at a nearby beach.
SNACKS Le 14 (14 Blvd Peschaire Alizon, 07150 Vallon-Pont-d'Arc; 04 75 94 78 55; open daily), housed

The Lowdown

🌐 **Map reference** 13 C2
Address 07150 (Ardèche).
Exposition Grotte Chauvet
Pont d'Arc: Rue du Miarou,
Vallon-Pont-d'Arc; www.
prehistoireardeche.com.
Aven d'Orgnac: Orgnac l'Aven;
www.orgnac.com

🚗 **Train** TER from Paris to
Montélimar, then bus to Vallon.
Bus 15 from Avignon, Balazuc
and Vogüé

ℹ️ **Visitor information** Pl de la Gare,
07150 Vallon-Pont-d'Arc; www.
vallon-pont-darc.com

🕐 **Open** Exposition Grotte Chauvet
Pont d'Arc & Aven d'Orgnac:
timings vary. St-Martin-d'Ardèche
(markets): Jul–Aug: Fri pm, Sun
am; Jun–Sep: Wed am; year
round: Thu am

💶 **Prices** Exposition Grotte Chauvet
Pont d'Arc: €17–27; under 6s

free. Aven d'Orgnac: €32–42;
under 6s free

👪 **Skipping the queue** Visit in Sep
when it is not so crowded.

🚩 **Guided tours** Tour the cave
complex of Aven d'Orgnac;
walking or canoeing

👫 **Age range** 4 plus

👨‍👩‍👧 **Activities** Opt for canoeing,
caving, horse-riding, canyoning
& Via ferrata (mountain climbing
using iron ladders fixed into the
rockface; suitable for grownups

⏱️ **Allow** At least 3 days

🚻 **Toilets** In the car park in the
Grand Plage, behind the Mairie.

Good family value?
The area is good for families who
enjoy outdoor activities and offers
a glimpse into prehistory too.

---

in a renovated 19th-century building,
this café serves salads, crêpes,
waffles and ice cream. There is
also free Wi-Fi.
REAL MEAL Coeur d'Ardèche (8 Pl
du Verger, 07150 Vallon-Pont-d'Arc;
04 75 87 27 52; daily in season) is the
place to go to sample fine regional
cuisine; many dishes are based on
chestnuts, the local speciality.

Shopping
Visit **Moulin des Gorges** (Rond point
des Gorges, 07150; 04 75 88 07 46;
www.moulindesgorges.com) where
they sell their own olive oil and
other regional produce, including
tasty chestnut goodies.

Find out more
DIGITAL Go to earlyhumans.mrdonn.
org/caveart.html to learn about cave
paintings and www.kinderart.com/
arthistory/cave paintings.html for how
to make one.

Signboard showing hiking trails in the
Bois de Païolive forest of Ardèche

Delicious desserts at Boulangerie
Lichière, Vallon-du-Pont-d'Arc

Next stop...
EXPLORE THE OUTDOORS The
Ardèche is famous for its chestnuts,
which have been awarded the AOP
label of quality. Drive to the town of
Joyeuse, 27 km (17 miles) north
of Vallon-Pont-d'Arc, to visit the
Musée de la Châtaignerie (www.
musee-chataignerie.fr) to learn more
about the fruit. From Joyeuse, drive
15 km (9 miles) southwest to the
forest of Bois de Païolive, near the
village of Les Vans. This is a wood of
petrified trees, eroded into unusual
shapes such as a lion and a bear
fighting. Several footpaths run
through this protected area. From Les
Vans, head 20 km (12 miles) west to
the village of St-Alban-Auriolles to
explore the gorges on horseback
with **Chavetourte** (04 75 39 66 73).
They offer treks ranging from an
hour to a week, which include river
crossings and beach breaks.

⑭ Balazuc and Vogüé

Castles and knights

Balazuc and Vogüé have been officially declared two of *Les Plus Beaux Villages de France*. Balazuc slopes down to the Ardèche river, where there is a small beach that is suitable for paddling on hot days. Wander around the narrow, cobbled streets, through vaulted passages, and imagine what it must have been like to be a knight in the medieval days of the Lords of Balazuc. For the best view of the village, walk across the bridge over the river and look back; then follow the river for 15 minutes to the once-abandoned silk workers' hamlet of **Le Viel Audon** – visitors can volunteer with the eco-friendly restoration work or simply check out the animals and browse local produce in the shop.

Vogüé, 6 km (4 miles) north by car, is built into the side of a cliff, which rises up from the Ardèche river. Its main feature is the **Château de Vogüé** whose current form with four round towers dates from the 17th

century. The castle, privately owned by the Marquis Pierre de Vogüé, regularly hosts art exhibitions. Visitors can also admire the wonderful views from its "hanging gardens". In July and August, a Monday morning market takes place in the village.

Letting off steam

Take the tourist train (*www.viaduc07. fr*) dating from 1963, which runs along a disused SNCF line from Vogüé, 14 km (9 miles) north, to the village of St-Jean-le-Centenier (Jul & Aug: daily). The route goes over several viaducts and offers stunning views.

Above *The village of Balazuc*
Below *Enjoying the summer at the beach in Balazuc*

The Lowdown

🌐 **Map reference** 13 C2
Address 07120, 07200 (Ardèche). Le Viel Audon: 07120 Balazuc; *vielaudon.free.fr*. Château de Vogüé: 07200 Vogüé; *www. chateaudevogue.net*

🚈 **Train** from Vallon to Balazuc & Vogüé. **Bus** 15 from Vallon to Balazuc & Vogüé

ℹ️ **Visitor information** Balazuc: Rue Alphonse Daudet, 07120 Ruoms; 04 75 93 91 90; *www.ot-pays-ru omsois.com*. Vogüé: Pl de Heyd, 07200; 04 75 37 01 17; *www.ot-vogue.com*

🕐 **Open** Château de Vogüé: mid-Jun–mid-Sep: daily; Easter–Nov: Wed–Sun

🍽️ **Eat and drink** *Snacks* Chez Paulette (*Rue Pons, 07120 Balazuc; 04 65 88 85 50*) is an authentic *bistro du pays* (regional bistro) offering crêpes, pizzas and regional specialities. *Real meal* Le Mas de Mon Père (*off RN 102, 07580 St-Jean-le-Centenier; 04 75 36 71 23; www.lemasdemonpere. com*) has a *menu du terroir* (regional menu) offering trout, goats' cheese and chestnuts, with a good selection of local wines.

⑮ Montélimar

Nougat and fighter jets

Located northeast of the Gorges de Ardèche, Montélimar is named after the aristocratic Adhémar de Monteil family who used to live in the 12th-century **Château des Adhémar** overlooking the town; the castle now houses a contemporary art

centre. Montélimar is best known as the capital of nougat, a chewy sweet made from egg whites, almonds, honey and pistachios. To see how this treat is made and to taste some, head over to the **Musée du Nougat Arnaud Soubeyran**; the company has been making nougat since 1837. That is not the only speciality in Montélimar: the fields around this

The Lowdown

🌐 **Map reference** 13 D2
Address 26200 (Drôme). Château des Adhémar: Plateau de Narbonne; 04 75 00 62 30. Musée du Nougat Arnaud Soubeyran: ZC Sud, off RN7, 26204; *www.nougat soubeyran.com*. Musée Européen de l'Aviation de Chasse: Chemin Aérodrome Montélimar; *www. meacmtl.com*

🚈 **Train** from Vallon, Balazuc & Vogüé

ℹ️ **Visitor information** Allées Provençales, 26200 Montée St-Martin; 04 75 01 00 20; *www. montelimar-tourisme.com*

🕐 **Open** Château des Adhémar: daily; Nov–Mar: closed Tue. Musée du

Nougat Arnaud Soubeyran & Musée Européen de l'Aviation de Chasse: daily

🍽️ **Eat and drink** *Snacks* Goutez-y (*34 Rue Quatre Alliances, 26200; 09 50 02 10 66*) offers over 50 ice cream flavours including balsamic vinegar, lavender, cactus and nougat to eat in or take away. *Family treat* Aux Gourmands (*14 Pl du Marché, 26200; 04 75 01 16 21; www.aux-gourmands.fr; closed Sun & Mon*) serves local dishes made with seasonal produce, accompanied by a good wine list.

🎪 **Festival** Couleur Lavande, lavender festival (Jul)

town are filled with lavender from mid-June to September. The tourist office provides details of driving routes where visitors can see some fine examples. On the edge of town is the **Musée Européen de l'Aviation de Chasse** (MEAC), where visitors can take a look at some of the world's most famous fighter jets including Mirages and MiGs.

Letting off steam

Fly in a micro-light aircraft with a pilot instructor to see Gorges de l'Ardèche and the lavender fields from above. **ULM Montélimar** (Aérodrome, 26200; 04 75 53 76 73; www.espace-aerien.com) offers flights ranging from 10 minutes to a couple of hours. On the ground, families can visit **Mistral Kart** (Route du Teil, 26200; 04 75 01 46 33; open daily), a fun place for kids aged 3 plus. It is good for go-karting.

Honey pots on display at the Musée du Nougat Arnaud Soubeyran, Montélimar

⑯ Nyons

Famous for its black olives

Medieval Nyons is known throughout France for its black olives, which have an AOP label of quality; in fact, the town is a *site remarquable du goût*, a French town or area that produces a superior foodstuff. The olives are harvested in December and January and turned into oil or *tapenade* (a paste spread on bread). To find out more about olives and their uses, pay a visit to the **Musée de l'Olivier**, then head to the **Moulin Ramade** to watch how the oil is extracted and taste the products.

The most impressive sight in town is the 18-m (59-ft) high 14th-century stone bridge that straddles the Eygues river for 43 m (141 ft). The Place des Arcades is a charming medieval square, which hosts the Thursday morning market and is a popular place to stop for a coffee.

The Lowdown

🌐 **Map reference** 13 D2
Address 26110 (Drôme). Musée de l'Olivier: Pl Olivier-de-Serres; 04 75 26 95 00; www.vignolis.fr. Moulin Ramade: 7 Impasse du Moulin; 04 75 26 08 18; www.moulinramade.com

🚌 **Bus** 36 from Montélimar

ℹ️ **Visitor information** Pl de la Libération, 26110; 04 75 26 10 35; www.paysdenyons.com

🕐 **Open** Musée de l'Olivier: daily. Moulin Ramade: Mon–Sat

🍽️ **Eat and drink** Snacks Miss Maple (8 Pl Buffaven, 26110; 04 75 27 64 56; open daily) is a quirky tea room that serves home-made cakes, snacks, smoothies and, of course, a variety of teas. *Real meal* La Farigoule (26 Rue des Déportés, 26110; 04 75 26 07 01; www.lafarigoule-nyons.com; closed Tue, Wed & Thu dinner) is a small restaurant where diners can sample the local olives in a variety of dishes, including omelettes, and as accompaniment to goat cheese. Book in advance.

🎪 **Festivals** Les Olivades celebrates black olive oil through guided walks, markets and tastings (Jul). Festival l'Alicoque celebrates the new season's oil (Feb).

Letting off steam

The countryside around Nyons offers plenty of opportunities to get back to nature. Climb through the trees along rope bridges at **Les Barons Perchés** (Col de la Croix, 26110; www.les-barons-perches.com) that is suitable for kids aged 5–12 years, with an adult. Take bus 36 to **Camp Anes** (www.campanes.fr), which is 6 km (4 miles) north from Nyons, village of Les Echirons. Here, families can explore olive fields on a donkey.

A model of the olive oil making process at Musée de l'Olivier, Nyons

Picnic under €20; **Snacks** €20–€45; **Real meal** €45–€90; **Family treat** over €90 (based on a family of four)

Where to Stay in The Rhône Valley and French Alps

From historic châteaux to riverside camp sites and from luxury spa hotels to traditional wooden chalets, the Rhône-Alpes region has something to suit all tastes and budgets. Farm stays allow visitors to get to know the countryside and its inhabitants – including furry ones.

AGENCIES
Gîtes Rhône-Alpes
www.gites-rhone-alpes.org
This website lists accommodation options, from big country houses to small camp sites on farmland.

Peak Retreats
www.peakretreats.co.uk
This award-winning British tour operator offers self-catering accommodation throughout the Alps in both winter and summer.

Annecy
Map 10 E5

HOTEL
Les Grillons
Angon, 74290 Talloires; 04 50 60 70 31; www.hotel-grillons.com
This 32-room, traditionally furnished three-star hotel on the right bank of Lac d'Annecy offers great views over the lakes and mountains. The restaurant has a kids' menu. There is a large garden to run around in; babysitting service is provided.
🐾 P ⊘ €€

CAMPING
Camping de la Ravoire
Route de la Ravoire, 74210 Doussard; 04 50 44 37 80; www.camping-la-ravoire.com
Besides pitches for tents and caravans, this four-star camp site in a pretty location on the left bank of Lac d'Annecy also has small, individual chalets. Bring bikes and race along the cycle path to Annecy.
🏕 P ⊘ €

Briançon
Map 14 F1

BED & BREAKFAST
La Joie de Vivre
Hameau de Salé, 05100 Névache; 04 92 21 30 96; www.la-joie-de-vivre.fr
Stays at this attractive chalet 18 km (11 miles) from Briançon are on a half-board basis. The owner Claire

is a trained chef with a passion for alpine cuisine. Work up an appetite with a trek through the mountains accompanied by the family llamas.
🐾 P €€€

SELF-CATERING
Résidence du Temple
3 Pl du Temple, 05100; 04 92 50 19 97; www.residencedutemple.com
In the heart of the Cité Vauban, these boutique-style apartments housed in a recently renovated building sleep up to eight people. The smallest apartments have a double and a sofa-bed, while those for six have added bunk beds. Breakfast, lunch and dinner available at the restaurant.
🐾 🍽 €

Chamonix
Map 10 F5

HOTEL
Auberge du Bois Prin
69 Chemin de l'Hermine, Les Moussoux, 74400; 04 50 53 33 51; www.boisprin.com
There are ten rooms and suites at this luxurious mountain retreat, with traditional timber decor. Balconies or terraces have wonderful views over Mont Blanc. Spa for adults, and a play area for kids. Guests can also visit the restaurant chef's organic vegetable garden in summer.
🐾 P €€€

CHALET
Chalet in Chamonix
08 45 89 00 362 (UK); www.chalet-in-chamonix.co.uk
This British-run company offers catered and self-catering lodging in several chalets here. While Chalet Vincent is the more luxurious option with bunk rooms for kids, Chalet Les Pelerins is popular amongst eco-friendly families. There are four small chalets-cabins on the Île des Barrats.
🍽 P €€

Contemporary-style interior of the salon in Les Grillons, Annecy

Gorges de l'Ardèche
Map 13 C2

HOTEL
Le Clos des Bruyères
07150 Vallon-Pont-d'Arc; 04 75 37 18 85; www.closdesbruyeres.fr
Near the river, this Provençal-style modern hotel has rooms on the ground floor that open directly onto the garden, complete with kids' play area. Guests can tuck into local dishes on the shaded terrace. The owners can also arrange canoe hire.
🐾 P ☀ ⊘ €€

SELF-CATERING
Le Mas de la Bastide
Les Grads de Perret, 07260 Joyeuse; 04 75 39 49 60; www.masdela bastide.com
These pretty stone *gîtes*, on an estate dotted with olive trees, sleep up to eight. Fresh bread and croissants are delivered direct to the door each morning. Organized kids' activities and themed meals in summer.
🐾 🍽 P ⊘ €€

CAMPING
Camping Beau Rivage
Les Mazes, 07150 Vallon-Pont-d'Arc; 04 75 88 03 54; www.beaurivage-camping.com
A family-oriented camp site next to the river, offering pitches and mobile homes for hire. Guests can hire canoes and learn how to paddle.

Sandy-floored play area for kids; both old and young can participate in the boules and karaoke competitions.

 €

Grenoble
Map 10 E6

HOTEL
Hotel Splendid
22 Rue Thiers, 38000; 04 76 46 33 12; www.splendid-hotel.com
This two-star hotel in the city centre is the ideal place for a short family break. There is an enclosed garden and table tennis for children, as well as hydro-massage showers for grown-ups. Room service is 24/7 and it is only a short walk from the tram stop.

€€

SELF-CATERING
Ferme de Namière
38120 Mont-St-Martin; 04 76 75 55 72; lejardindesdaines.pages perso-orange.fr
Located in the heart of the Parc Naturel Régional de Chartreuse, this deer farm is about 20 minutes' drive from Grenoble. The *gîte* is an old stone outbuilding that has been restored in contemporary style. There are plenty of walks in the area. Be sure to try the venison for dinner.

€

Les Dombes
Map 9 D5

HOTEL
Hotel et Golf du Gouverneur
Château du Breuil, 01390 Monthieux; 04 72 26 42 00; wwwgolfgouverneur.fr
The remains of a 15th-century château houses this three-star hotel. The accommodation is attached to one of the finest golf courses in the region. Rooms are furnished in contemporary style. Swimming, tennis and horse-riding are available.

€€

The seating area in front of Hotel Manali, Les Trois Vallées

Enjoying a splash in the swimming pool at Camping Indigo, Lyon

BED & BREAKFAST
Ferme du Clos
01400 Neuville les Dames; 04 74 55 65 24; www.auclos.com
Kids will love feeding the animals in the heart of one of France's main agricultural areas. Rooms are basic, but the property is noted for its meals made with local produce.

€

SELF-CATERING
Château de Joyeux
01800 Joyeux; 04 74 98 20 31; www.chateaudejoyeux.net
One of Les Dombes' grand houses; this 19th-century pile can be rented by the week. Or opt for a more modest *chambre d'hôtes* stay or one of the self-catering *gîtes* in the château grounds, with views onto the gardens. There is a tennis court.

€€€

Les Trois Vallées
Map 10 F6

HOTEL
Hotel Manali
Rue de la Rosière, 73120 Courchevel 1650; 04 79 08 07 07; www.hotelmanali.com
One of the best family options in the area, this is the only five-star hotel and spa in Courchevel 1650, the slightly less pricey part of this ski resort. Family rooms come with bunk beds and colouring books, and the restaurant has a special kids' menu and dining area. Nursery for tots.

€€€

CHALET
Green Mountain Chalets
La Combe, 73440 St-Martin-de-Belleville; 06 85 50 21 49; www. greenmountainchalets.co.uk
There are two attractive wood and stone British-run catered chalets with 32 beds. There are toys, books,

Wii and also board games to occupy all ages. Special children's meals and mealtimes.

€€

Lyon
Map 9 D5

HOTELS
Hotel Central
26 Cours de Verdun, 69002; 04 78 71 17 47; www.hotel-central.fr
Behind Perrache railway station, this two-star hotel has had a makeover in recent years. Rooms are attractively decorated in a bright, contemporary style. Suited for late arrivals or early starts by train. Public car parks nearby.

€€

Hotel Lyon Metropole
85 Quai Joseph Gillet, 69004; 04 72 10 44 44; www.lyonmetropole.com
This four-star hotel, overlooking the Rhône just north of the city centre, is the perfect place for families seeking rest and relaxation. The hotel boasts France's largest urban spa and an outdoor Olympic-sized swimming pool. Welcome gifts and special buffet for kids.

€€€

CAMPING
Camping Indigo
Allée du Camping-Porte de Lyon, 69570 Dardilly; 04 78 35 64 55; www.camping-indigo.com
In a wooded site on the outskirts of Lyon, this camp site is ideally situated for exploring the city and surrounding area. Wooden caravans, mobile homes and tents available. There are swings and arcade games for kids.

€

> **Price Guide**
> The following price ranges are based on one night's accommodation in high season for a family of four, inclusive of service charges and any additional taxes.
> € Under €100 €€ €100–200 €€€ over €200

Key to symbols *see back cover flap*

Montélimar
Map 13 D2

BED & BREAKFAST
Domaine de Paissy
176 Route de Sauzet, 26200; 04 75 46 04 08; www.domainede paissy.com
A charming B&B in a 15th-century manor house, on the outskirts of town, it is decorated with antiques and traditional furnishings. Fans of architecture will be impressed by the staircase and fireplace. There is a huge garden for kids to run around in.
🚫 �> P ⊘ €€

CAMPING
Camping de l'Ile Blanc Map 9 C2
1205 Chemin de l'Ile Blanc, 26200 Ancône; 04 75 51 20 05; www. camping-montelimar.com
A small camp site 3 km (2 miles) northwest of Montélimar with the Rhône on one side and plenty of greenery on the other, it offers 80 spaces for tents and caravans; it is possible to rent statics. There is plenty to amuse all ages, from table tennis and canoeing to live music and themed meals.
P ⊘ €

Nyons
Map 13 D2

HOTEL
La Bastide des Monges
Route d'Orange, 26110; 04 75 26 99 69; www.bastidedes monges.com
This traditional Provençal manor house in the heart of the Drôme countryside has eight individually furnished rooms. A perfect place to relax, there is a pool to lie by and a boules pitch. There are scenic views over the surrounding fields and Mont Ventoux.
🚯 P ⊘ €€€

SELF-CATERING
Camp'Anes
Quartier Les Echirons, 26110 Venterol; 04 75 26 37 09; www. campanes.fr
Besides hiring out donkeys for walks, this peaceful farm just outside Nyons also does B&B in the main house and self-catering in a *gîte* or wooden caravan. Fine views from the terrace. Kids will enjoy petting the animals.
🚫 🚯 P €

Parc National de la Vanoise
Map 10 F6

HOTEL
Le Grand Bec
Rue Aiguille du Mey, 73710 Pralognan-la-Vanoise; 04 79 08 71 10; www.hoteldugrandbec.fr
Located in the Vanoise's main village, this is a traditionally furnished chalet-style hotel. In winter, there is pool or board games and in summer there are swings, tennis and boules. The Jacuzzi is popular year round. Excellent regional cuisine in the rustic restaurant.
🚯 P ⊘ €€€

CAMPING
Camping Le Chenantier
73500 Sollières-Sardières; 04 79 56 73 30; www.camping-lechenantier.com
In a stunning location in the south of the Vanoise, this camp site offers yurts, tipis and pitches for families bringing their own tent or caravan. There is a lake for swimming and many outdoor activities in the area.
🚫 🛖 P €

Outdoor activities at the Sixt Alpine Chalet, Sixt-Fer-à-Cheval

Samoëns and Sixt-Fer-à-Cheval
Map 10 F5

CHALETS
Sixt Alpine Chalet
L'Alpée, La Chaletaz, 74740 Sixt-Fer-à-Cheval; 04 50 89 06 18; www.sixtal pinechalet.com
A British-run chalet, which sleeps ten, it overlooks the pretty village of Sixt and offers catered or self-catering stays in cosy, rustic rooms. Special rates for activities, including white-water rafting, from a local provider.
🚫 🚯 🛖 P €€€

Chalet La Source
La Combe, 74340 Samoëns; www. greenadventureretreats.com
This stylish eco-friendly chalet runs Family Adventure Weeks in July and August. The former 19th-century hay barn now has five bedrooms, a playroom and a wood-fired hot tub.
🚯 P €€€

St-Étienne
Map 9 D6

HOTEL
Hotel Continental
10 Rue François Gillet, 42000; 04 77 32 58 43; www.hotelcontinental42.fr
A former coaching inn in the city centre has been transformed into an award-winning two-star "design hotel", with muted, minimalist rooms. Free Wi-Fi throughout.
🚯 P €

Vienne
Map 9 D6

HOTEL
Grand Hotel de la Poste
47 Cours Romestang, 38200; 04 74 85 02 04; www.hotel delapostevienne.com
This yellow-fronted two-star hotel on one of the town's busiest routes dates from the 18th century. Rooms overlooking the courtyard are quieter but all are brightly decorated and well kept. Free Wi-Fi.
🚯 ❄ €

Yvoire
Map 10 F4

HOTEL
Château de Coudrée
74140 Sciez-Bonnatrait; 04 50 72 62 33; www.coudree.fr
On the banks of Lac Léman east of Yvoire, this ivy-clad four-star hotel dates from the 12th century and has been run by the same family for three generations. Best known for its excellent restaurant, it has a private beach, large garden and kids' games.
🚯 P ⊘ €€€

CAMPING
Camping La Pinède
74140 Excenevex Plage; 04 50 72 85 05; www.camping-lac-leman.info
This three-star camp site just outside Yvoire has direct access to the sandy beach on Lac Léman. Rent a tent or a mobile home or pitch up with a caravan. There is a playground.
🚫 🛖 P €

The Massif Central

An area of mountains, plateaus and fierce beauty, the Massif Central is one of France's least spoilt regions. The dramatic landscape is peppered with dormant volcanoes and pitted with gorges, as well as crater lakes. Besides canoeing or hiking, there are many fine Romanesque churches and medieval castles to visit, all with something to fire a child's imagination.

Château de Murol
p248

Le Puy-en-Velay
p244

Aven Armand
p240

Below *Dramatic view of the Puy de Dôme towering above the plateau of the Auvergne*

① Aven Armand
A journey into the earth

Beneath a meadow on the Jurassic limestone plateau known as the Causse Méjean, Aven Armand is an enormous cavern – so large that Notre-Dame (see pp90–91) in Paris could fit inside it. For years, sheep, goats and even some unfortunate travellers had disappeared into the gaping hole on the surface. The cave was eventually explored in 1897 by Edouard Alfred Martel and Louis Armand, who found a forest of towering shapes formed from 400 individual stalagmites.

Key Features

Entrance

Funicular

Shaft Martel and Armand climbed through the swallow hole and lowered themselves down the 75-m (246-ft) deep vertical shaft using mountaineering techniques.

Limestone

Great Hall

Stalactites Stalactites hang down from the roof like icicles. They are formed from deposits of calcium carbonate, a crystalline salt that builds up when rain water drips continuously through limestone.

Funicular The tour starts with a 90-second ride on a funicular railway, which travels 60 m (197 ft) down into the cool, moist air of the underground cavern.

Great Hall The oval-shaped chamber is bigger than most football pitches. The acoustics are remarkable and concerts are sometimes held here.

The Lowdown

🌐 **Map reference** 13 B3
Address 48150 (Lozère). Meyrueis; 04 66 45 61 31; www.aven-armand.com

🚗 **Bus** D35 from Millau to Meyrueis, then a 15-min taxi ride

ℹ️ **Visitor information** Pl Sully, 48150 Meyrueis; 04 66 45 60 33; www.meyrueis-office-tourisme.com

🕐 **Open** Mar–mid-Jul & Sep–early-Nov: 10am–noon & 1:30–5pm daily; mid-Jul–Aug: 9:30am–6pm

💶 **Price** €30–40

Skipping the queue Buy a pass at the ticket office that includes up to nine sights in the area.

Guided tours Obligatory; the tour leaves every 25 mins. On Fri in summer by arrangement,

adults and kids aged 8 plus can descend through the shaft into the cave, using ropes and accompanied by a speleologist.

👫 **Age range** 5 plus

Activities Think of good names for the different stalagmites.

⏱️ **Allow** 45 mins

☕ **Café** Snack bar on site (see p241)

🚻 **Toilets** In the upper station building

Good family value?
A visit to this cave is educational and fun. The intriguing shapes formed over millennia will delight children and adults alike. Be sure to wear warm clothes as it is chilly and damp underground.

Lower shaft A build-up of stones and clay obstructs the entrance to this shaft, which plunges 87 m (285 ft) into the earth.

Stalagmites Growing like tree trunks from the cave floor, the stalagmites are known as the Forêt Vierge (Virgin Forest). Due to their unusual shapes, some have been given names such as Frog and Jellyfish.

Shepherds herding sheep at Le Villaret d'Hures, near Aven Armand

Letting off steam

Go for a walk on the rugged Causse Méjean and look out for vultures, which have been reintroduced into the region. Or drive 10 minutes for a ramble around **Le Villaret d'Hures** *(Le Villaret, 48150 Hures-la-Parade; 04 66 45 64 43)*, which is home to a herd of Przewalski horses. They were relocated here from zoos to roam and breed semi-free, in an attempt to preserve the last surviving species of wild horse, long since extinct in its native Mongolia.

Variety of cheese on sale at Le Fédou, Hures-la-Parade

Eat and drink

Picnic: under €20; Snacks: €20–45; Real meal: €45–90; Family treat: over €90 (based on a family of four)

PICNIC Le Fédou *(Hyelzas, 48150 Hures-la-Parade; 04 66 45 66 74; Sep–Jun: closed noon–2pm)* offers sheep's cheese, charcuterie and other farm products from its shop attached to the cheese dairy. Buy bread from the next door **Boulangerie Pacaud** and picnic on the Causse Méjean or in the picnic area at Aven Armand.

SNACKS Aven Armand Café *(on site)* is a good-value café-bar that serves pizzas, salads, ice creams and pastries.

REAL MEAL Ferme-Auberge Baret *(Les Hérans, 48150 Hures-la-Parade; 04 66 45 64 42)* is a traditional inn that uses ingredients fresh from the farm in its dishes. Sausages are a speciality here and the desserts are filling and delicious.

FAMILY TREAT Château d'Ayres *(Ayres, 48150 Meyrueis; 04 66 45 60 10; www.hotel-restaurant-meyrueis. com)* is a fine château located in a wooded parkland, with a restaurant offering kids' menus. Table tennis, table-football and a pool keep boredom at bay.

Find out more

DIGITAL Find photos, facts, puzzles, experiments, quizzes and art projects at *www.caverntours. comKIDSPAGE_Formations.html*. For tips on how to grow stalactites and stalagmites, visit *www.tlc.how stuffworks.com/ family/science-experiments-for-kids13.htm.*

Next stop...

PEEK INTO MUSEUMS Head for Millau, but skirt the town and drive under the spectacular modern viaduct. At 343 m (1,125 ft) to the top of its highest mast and 2,460 m (8,070 ft) in length, it is the tallest and longest cable-stayed bridge in the world, and cost €400 million to build. In town, visit the **Musée de Millau** *(www.museede millau.fr)* to discover how rough skins are turned into soft leather.

Drive east from Aven Armand to the village of Hyelzas to visit **Ferme Caussenarde d'Autrefois** *(ferme.caussenarde.free.fr)*, a farm museum that offers an insight into how farmers lived years ago. Head to St-Pierre-des-Tripiers, which is a 25-minute drive from Hyelzas, to visit **Le Belvédère des Vautours** *(www.vautours-lozere.com)*. Perched high above the Jonte gorges, the building contains a vulture museum, observation terrace and also a live video stream from cameras located by the nests of the local vulture colony.

A family enjoying the banks of the Tarn river, Ste-Enimie

A breathtaking view of the spectacular Gorges du Tarn

② Gorges du Tarn

Cliffs, canyons and canoes

Formed by the Tarn river, these spectacular gorges cut through the limestone plateaux of the Cévennes. Plunging 500 m (1,640 ft) from the clifftop, they are some of the deepest canyons in Europe. For the most dramatic view, climb up to Point Sublime, perched high above the gorges, just west of the picturesque village of La Malène. Other pretty villages such as Castelbouc and St-Chély-du-Tarn dot the route.

A great way to enjoy the scenery is in a canoe or kayak. There are many placid stretches, particularly the one from Le Rozier to Peyrelade. Descents run from an hour to several days. The tourist office offers a list of companies who rent canoes *(www. gorgesdutarn.net)* or try **Aigue Vive** *(www.canoekayakgorgesdutarn.com)*. If the kids are young, let the boatman

take the strain on the hour-long barge tour from La Malène offered by **Les Bateliers des Gorges du Tarn** *(www.gorgesdutarn.com)*. An accompanied donkey ride with **Les Ânes du Causse** *(www.bourricot. com/anesducausse)*, a 15-min drive from La Malène, is also an option.

Take cover

Among the unspoilt medieval buildings and steep cobbled alleys of Ste-Enimie, the central town of the gorges, **Le Vieux Logis** *(www. gorgesdutarn.net/Museum-Le-Vieux-Logis; mid-Jun–mid-Sep)* re-creates the interiors of a traditional dwelling before the arrival of modern amenities such as running water and electricity.

③ Florac

Travels with a donkey

Hugging the banks of the Tarnon river, Florac is a small town on the route followed by 19th-century writer Robert Louis Stevenson and his donkey, Modestine. Smitten with Florac's "quaint street-corners" and "handsome women", Stevenson spent the night at an inn before setting off the next afternoon. He also remarked on the town's castle,

The Ste-Enimie bridge and a grand view of the town

Château de Florac, which was built in 1652 on the site of a 13th-century castle destroyed during the Wars of Religion. This castle was used for storing salt during the French Revolution – an essential and valuable commodity for preserving food in the time before people had refrigerators. In the early 19th century, it became a prison. Later, in 1976, it was taken over by the Parc National de Cevennes, whose information centre is now housed here.

Stroll through Le Planet, the town's old quarter of medieval lanes and plane-shaded avenues. A stream flows through its centre and opens out into several ponds. The stream is used for trout breeding, with the baby fish kept here until they are ready to be released into the wild.

The brightly painted exterior of the pizzeria P'tit Loup, Marvejols

Letting off steam

Rent mountain bikes from **Cévennes Evasion** (www.cevennes-evasion. com) and cycle along the nearby footpaths and forest trails. A 45-min drive away is **Vallon du Villaret** (www.levallon.fr), a discovery park with a difference. The park is filled with sculptures by contemporary artists, all of them intended to be clambered over and explored.

④ Marvejols
Legacy of a bloodthirsty beast

Inside three medieval stone gates lies the pedestrian-only centre of this modest but attractive town, which keeps its bloodthirsty past under wraps. During the Wars of Religion, the Catholic and inappropriately named Admiral Joyeuse (French for joyful) employed his troops to ransack and burn the town in 1586, massacring many of its inhabitants as punishment for their Protestant faith. Look out for two statues by the noted local sculptor Emmanuel Auricoste (1908–55). The first statue, which is of Henri IV, celebrates the

king's role in rebuilding much of the town in 1601. The second statue, of an evil-looking wolf, crouched and ready to pounce, marks another bloodcurdling event. From 1764 to 1767, the town was terrorized by the so-called *Bête du Gévaudan* (Beast of Gévaudan) who was held responsible for slaughtering 99 people in the area, most of them children. Although never proven, the culprit was believed to be a wolf.

Letting off steam

Go for a splash in La Colagne river or take a 10-minute drive north to **Les Loups du Gévaudan** (www. loupsdugevaudan.com), a large wildlife park where more than 100 wolves live in semi-freedom. Wolves are shy by nature so the best chance of seeing them is on a guided tour. An exhibition demolishes many of the myths about them.

A wolf relaxing in the shade at Les Loups de Gévaudan, Marvejols

The Lowdown

- 🌐 **Map reference** 13 A2 **Address** 48100 (Lozère).
- 🚆 **Train** from Mende, Clermont-Ferrand and Millau. **Bus** from Mende and Rodez
- ℹ️ **Visitor information** Porte du Soubeyran, 48100 Marvejols; 04 66 32 02 14; www.ville-marvejols.fr
- 🍴 **Eat and drink** *Snacks* P'tit Loup Pizza (3 Pl du Soubeyran, 48100; 04 66 32 47 94; closed Sun lunch & Mon) offers a selection of pizzas. *Real meal* Les Rochers (27 Ave Pierre Semard, 48100; 04 66 32 10 58; www.hoteldesrochers. com) offers steak *haché* (ground steak), *frites* and a good-value *menu du terroir* (menu of the region) for children and parents.
- 🎭 **Festivals** Festival en Scène, a festival of street theatre (late-Jul). Festival Henri IV, costume parades, night markets and games for children (Aug)

Statue of Henri IV at the gate to the old town, Marvejols

Picnic under €20; **Snacks** €20–45; **Real meal** €45–90; **Family treat** over €90 (based on a family of four)

The Lowdown

🌐 **Map reference** 13 B1
Address 43000 (Haute-Loire). Statue de Notre-Dame-de-France: Rocher Corneille. Cathédrale de Notre-Dame: 2 Rue Manécanterie; *www. cathedraledupuy.org*. Musée des Croyances Populaires: 26 Rue Raphaël; *loeildela salamandre.com*. Musée Crozatier: Jardin Henri Vinay Chapelle St-Michel d'Aiguilhe: 1 Rue Crozatier; *www.rocher saintmichel.fr*.

🚗 **Train** from Lyon and Clermont-Ferrand. **Bus** from Mende, Brioude and Craponne

ℹ️ **Visitor information** 2 Pl du Clauzel, 43000; 04 71 09 38 41; *www.ot-lepuyenvelay.fr*

🕐 **Open** Statue de Notre-Dame-de-France: Feb–mid-Nov & Christmas hols: daily; mid-Nov–late-Dec & Jan: Sun pm only. Musée des Croyances Populaires: Jun–Sep: Tue–Sun. Musée Crozatier: closed for renovation till 2014

💶 **Prices** Statue de Notre-Dame-de-France & Chapelle St-Michel d'Aiguilhe: €9–19; under 6s free. Cathédrale de Notre-Dame: free. Musée des Croyances Populaires: €12–22. Buy adult passes (€7.50 per person) to visit the cloister, chapel and statue at any of these sights or tourist office.

👫 **Skipping the queue** The sights are not usually very crowded.

👉 **Guided tours** In the cloister of the cathedral (in French)

👫 **Age range** 5 plus

🧒 **Activities** Buy glove puppets at Le Chat Perché *(chat-perche. net)* or improvise with socks and put on a puppet show in the Jardin Henri Vinay.

⏱️ **Allow** A day

🎭 **Festival** Roi de l'Oiseau, Festival of the Bird King, with jugglers, stilt-walkers, musicians, archery contests and parades of local people in costume (mid-Sep)

Good family value?
Le Puy has lots for families, from its Romanesque cathedral to the puppet shows staged at the Musée des Croyances Populaires.

⑤ Le Puy-en-Velay
Weary pilgrims and lofty pinnacles

The approach to Le Puy-en-Velay is an amazing sight: the town sits in a volcanic bowl with dark basalt spurs erupting from it, each topped with a building or statue. It looks rather like Middle Earth in *The Lord of the Rings*. Le Puy is famous as one of the starting points of a major pilgrimage route to the Spanish town of Santiago de Compostela and for producing lace, lentils and a sticky green liqueur called *verveine*, made from the herb verbena.

Key Sights

② **Cathédrale de Notre-Dame** Decorated with striped stonework, this soaring medieval cathedral houses a black Madonna dressed in Le Puy lace. Almost hidden above the arches in the 12th-century cloister is a cornice, carved with monsters and mythical beasts.

③ **Musée des Croyances Populaires** Puppet shows are the highlight of this museum, even for non-French speakers. Three actor-musicians perform mime and plays based on local folklore.

④ **Musée Crozatier** The unique collection of exhibits include samples of the finest lace, handmade over five centuries, and some fascinating early lace-making machines.

① **Statue de Notre-Dame-de-France** It is possible to climb up inside this colossal red statue of Mary and Jesus, perched on the pinnacle of Rocher Corneille. It was cast in 1860 from 213 cannons seized in Sevastopol during the Crimean War.

⑤ **Chapelle St-Michel d'Aiguilhe** A flight of 268 steps, carved out of rock, lead to this 10th-century chapel, balanced on a rocky 85-m (279-ft) high pinnacle.

Kite flying in the Jardin Henri Vinay in Le Puy-en-Velay

Letting off steam

Head to **Jardin Henri Vinay** (04 71 04 07 74) in Le Puy-en-Velay for wide open spaces, three playgrounds and an animal park. Or take bus 1 or 2 to **Planet'air** (Plaine d'Audinet, 43700 Brives-Charensac), a fun place for the whole family, with a mini-golf course and bouncy castles for tots. In St-Christophe Dolaizon, a ten-minute drive, there is ten-pin bowling at **Complexe L'Odyssée** (www. bowlingodyssee.com).

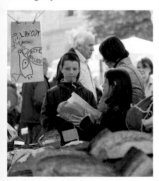

Bread for sale at the busy Marché du Samedi on Place du Plot

Eat and drink

Picnic: under €20; Snacks: €20–45; Real meal: €45–90; Family treat: over €90 (based on a family of four)

PICNIC Marché du Samedi (Pl du Plot, 43000; Sat only) offers a choice of local farmers' produce. On other days, buy provisions at **Petit Casino** (8 Rue St-Gilles, 43000; 04 71 09 03 51). Picnic in the Jardin Henri Vinay. **SNACKS Au 3B** (8 Pl de la Halle, 43000; 04 71 02 01 48) has a terrace where a sandwich, cheese or a local dish can be sampled. The three Bs

of this restaurant's name stand for *Bonjour, Bienvenue* and *à Bientôt* (hello, welcome and see you soon). **REAL MEAL Marco Polo** (46 Rue Raphaël, 43000; 04 71 02 83 11) is a friendly restaurant, with warm orange and red interiors. Large portions of tasty homecooked pasta are standard fare here. **FAMILY TREAT Tournayre** (12 Rue Chênebouterie, 43000; 04 71 09 58 94; www.restaurant-tournayre. com; closed Jan & first week Sep) is housed in a 16th-century chapel, with stone walls, vaulted ceilings and frescoes. It serves superb regional and seasonal cuisine.

Find out more

DIGITAL The website www.learner. org/interactives/volcanoes provides answers to questions and excellent video clips related to volcanoes. Go to www.fema.gov/kids/volcano.htm for fascinating facts and figures, as well as an interactive game.

Next stop...
A FORTRESS AND A FRESCO

Take bus 9 from Le Puy to the atmospheric 12th-century fortress, **Château de Polignac** (04 71 04 06 04; Jul–mid-Sep) that once housed the most powerful family in the region. Hop on to a bus (www.ter-sncf.com) or drive 50 km (31 miles) northwest to the Gothic **Abbaye de la Chaise-Dieu** (www.abbaye-chaise-dieu.com). Check out the spine-chilling 15th-century fresco depicting a *Danse Macabre* (Dance of Death), a procession of figures, partnered by skeletons, which served to remind people of their mortality. Drive to **Parc Aquatique et Sportif des Portes d'Auvergne** (04 71 00 51 89; late-Jun–Aug) at St-Paulien, 20 minutes by car, for thrills such as a 68-m (223-ft) slide, gushing waves and a waterfall.

Fresco portraying the Danse Macabre at Abbaye de la Chaise-Dieu

A horse-drawn carriage at Les Bisons d'Europe

⑥ Les Bisons d'Europe
A shaggy bison tale

The largest European mammal, the bison can weigh up to 1 ton (1 tonne), the same as an elephant, a hippo or a Formula 1 racing car. They run free in this wild, wooded reserve created as a breeding centre in 1991. Unlike their American cousins, who prefer plains, European bison favour forests. In summer, tour the reserve on foot or by a horse-drawn carriage along a 2-km (1-mile) long trail or in winter by sleigh. End up at the **Musée des Bisons d'Europe**, which investigates the origin and lifestyle of the bison through audio-visual displays and a reconstructed prehistoric cave.

Take cover
Head west to the town of St-Chély d'Apcher to visit the **Musée des Papillons** (15 Rue des Penitents,

The Lowdown

🌐 **Map reference** 13 A1
Address 48000 (Lozère) 48120 Ste-Eulalie-en-Margeride; 04 66 31 40 40; www.bison europe.com

🚗 **Train** to St-Chély-d'Apcher, then a 20-min taxi ride

ℹ️ **Visitor information** 48 Rue Théophile Roussel, 48200 St-Chély d'Apcher; 04 66 31 03 67; www.ot-saintchelydapcher.com

🕐 **Open** year round

💶 **Prices** €20–24 on foot; €39–50 by carriage; €45–58 by sleigh; €14–16 for museum

🍽️ **Eat and drink** *Picnic* Supermarché Champion (Blvd Guérin d'Apcher, 48200) in St-Chély d'Apcher, located12 km (7 miles) from the reserve, stocks picnic supplies. Eat at the reserve's picnic area. *Snacks* Bisons d'Europe Bar (on site) sells sandwiches and fast food.

48200; 04 66 31 17 95). The free exhibition here displays more than 2,700 species of butterflies from across the world; some surprisingly large and many dazzlingly coloured.

⑦ St-Flour
Ups and downs

Located on a crucial trade route, St-Flour once rivalled Aurillac as capital of the Auvergne. Today, it is a town divided into two parts: the high town climbs the abrupt volcanic outcrop of Planèze and the lower town hugs the banks of the Ander river. Climb up to the higher part to explore its charming huddle of old, narrow streets, and peek into the 14th-century **Cathédrale St-Pierre**. It has a life-sized statue of a black Christ inside and a terrific view from its cliff-edge terrace. The **Musée de la Haute-Auvergne** will captivate kids with its Gallo-Roman weapons, colourful ceremonial costumes, amazing headdresses and a 10th-century shrine made from bones.

Letting off steam
Go for a splash at the nearby **Le Centre Aqualudique** (Route de Chaudes-Aigues, 15110; 04 71 60 76 86), a water park, or head for **Margeride Aventure** (www.

The imposing structure of the Abbaye de Ste Foy, Conques

The Lowdown

🌐 **Map reference** 13 A1
Address 15100 (Cantal). Cathédrale St-Pierre: Pl d'Armes; 04 71 60 61 90. Musée de la Haute-Auvergne: 1 Pl d'Armes; 04 71 60 22 32

🚗 **Train** from Mende, Millau and Clermont-Ferrand. **Bus** from Clermont-Ferrand, Massiac and St-Flour-Chaudes-Aigues station

ℹ️ **Visitor information** 17 bis Pl d'Armes, 15100; 04 71 60 22 50; www.saint-flour.com

🕐 **Open** Musée de la Haute-Auvergne: early-May–Sep: daily; Oct–early-May: Mon & Wed–Sat

🍽️ **Eat and drink** *Picnic* La Ferme Sanfloraine (Zone Commerciale de Montplain, Rue Léopold Chastang, 15100; 04 71 60 06 97) stocks bread, cheese and pâté. Picnic in the lower town or at Margeride Aventure. *Real meal* Les Iles du Cantal (61 Rue des Lacs, 15100; 04 71 60 76 70; www.lesilesducantal. com) is a modest restaurant with panoramic views that serves hearty regional dishes and crêpes.

🎪 **Festival** Christmas market (mid-Dec)

margeride-aventure.fr). A 15-minute drive away, this is a woodland adventure park for all ages, with fun activities such as tunnels to squeeze through and bouncy trampolines.

⑧ Conques
Bone rustling monks

In this medieval town of cobbled streets and half-timbered houses, the splendid **Abbaye de Ste-Foy** has origins that link Dadon, an 8th-century hermit and St Foy, a 3rd-century teenage martyr. Dadon founded a community of monks, one of whom stole St Foy's remains from the town of Agen in a bid to put Conques on the map. With her remains stored in its abbey, Conques soon became an important stop on the Santiago pilgrimage route. Her relics are still here, in a 9th-century gold-encased statue in the Treasury Museum. Above the abbey doors, teeming with monstrous figures, the tympanum depicts the Last Judgement. Do not miss the creatures writhing in hell and the 15 tiny faces peeping out from the stonework above the arch.

Letting off steam

Walk down to the river and join the well-signed GR 65, part of the pilgrims' route. Drive 8 km (5 miles) south to the village of St-Cyprien-sur-Dourdou and cool off at the pleasant aquatic centre, with a 25-m (82-ft) swimming pool and paddling pool for tots, surrounded by terraces and lawns.

The Lowdown

🌐 **Map reference** 12 G2
Address 12320 (Aveyron). Abbaye de Ste-Foy: Pl de l'Église; 08 20 82 08 03

🚌 **Train** to St-Christophe, then shuttle bus. **Bus** from Rodez

ℹ️ **Visitor information** Conques, 12320; 05 65 72 85 00; www. tourisme-conques.fr

🕐 **Open** Abbaye de Ste-Foy: church & Treasury Museum: daily

🍽️ **Eat and drink** Snacks Les Rives du Lot (Les Pélies, 12320 Grand-Vabre; 05 65 72 84 96; mid-Apr–Oct) is a simple riverside café, 10 minutes northwest of Conques, that serves salads, pizzas and frites (chips). Real meal Au Parvis (Le Bourg, 12320; 05 65 72 82 81) offers tasty regional dishes, crêpes and ice creams.

⑨ Salers
Cloak and dagger country

Dark volcanic stone buildings and lush surroundings have lent this mountain village the description, "a black diamond on a green carpet". Salers was an administrative centre in the 16th century, and although a small place, the town boasts grand architecture; intricate carvings decorate the large houses around Place Tyssandier d'Escous. Try and find demonic faces on the façade

The quaint-looking Au Parvis opposite the Abbaye de Ste-Foy, Conques

Witch dolls adorning a window at Place Tyssandier d'Escous, Salers

of the Musée Maison des Templiers. Look out for the turrets, each one fashioned like a giant pepper pot. The 16th-century Église St-Mathieu has carvings in stone of pairs of dogs, goats and birds huddling at the top of the porch pillars. Look inside at the eerily life-like *mise au tombeau*, a statue of Jesus lying on his shroud, surrounded by onlookers.

Letting off steam

Walk around the 15th-century ramparts of Salers or drive to Tournemire and go for a scramble around the knights and dragons-style **Château d'Anjony** (www.anjony. com). Owned at different times by the feuding Tournemire and d'Anjony families, once when the d'Anjonys sent a spy into the Tournemire camp, he was sent back with his ears cut off and sewn to his bottom!

The Lowdown

🌐 **Map reference** 12 G1
Address 15140 (Cantal).

🚌 **Train** to Aurillac, then bus from Aurillac to Les Quatre Routes (on the Borg-les-Orgues route) and then a 10-min taxi ride

ℹ️ **Visitor information** Pl Tyssandier-D'Escous, 15140; 04 71 40 58 08; www.salers-tourisme.fr

🍽️ **Eat and drink** Snacks Chez La Préfète (Pl Tyssandier d'Escous, 15140; 04 71 40 70 55; closed Jan–mid-Feb & Mon in low season), located in the main square, is famous for its tartines (open sandwiches) and ordinary sandwiches. Real meal La Diligence (Rue de Beffroi, 15140; 04 71 40 75 39; www.ladiligence-salers.com) is a cosy restaurant, bar and crêperie rolled into one, which serves Auvergnat dishes and snacks, as well as salads; includes a kids' menu.

Picnic under €20; **Snacks** €20–45; **Real meal** €45–90; **Family treat** over €90 (based on a family of four)

⑩ Château de Murol
A knight's tale

In the Middle Ages, a lord's castle was not just his home but also a symbol of his power. It needed to protect him from foreign and religious enemies, unruly neighbours and rebellious peasants. The sturdy keep in Murol, with its multi-sided design to spot attackers from all directions, shows what was needed to stay safe in the 14th century. The sight is brought to life by costumed guides and actors.

Children playing with swords on a castle bastion

Key Features

Entrance ———

① Chapels A 568-year-old skeleton, thought to be that of Guillaume de Murol, who built the castle in 1380, was unearthed in a chapel crypt.

② Spiral staircase Set within the thickness of the wall, this 13th-century staircase is particularly cramped. Medieval builders had them built like this to stop an armed attacker from using his sword.

⑥ Living quarters There is a kitchen with a fireplace and cooking pots, a room with coats of arms, where vassals came to swear loyalty, and a knight's bedroom.

④ Wall-walk This fortified walkway at the top of the castle, circles the top of the keep's inner curtain wall. It protected defenders as they shot arrows at attackers and dropped cannon balls or rocks on them.

⑤ Guardroom The guardroom protected three crucial areas: the cellars, where vital supplies for use during a long siege were kept; the armoury, which held stocks of spare weapons and arrows; and the access to the wall-walk, the castle's last defence.

③ Keep Designed to protect the castle's interior and repel cannon balls, the keep's massive inner curtain wall is 10-m (33-ft) high and 3-m (10-ft) thick in places.

The Lowdown

🌐 **Map reference** 9 A6
Address 63790 (Puy-de-Dôme). Maison du Pré Long, Murol; 04 73 26 02 00; www.chateau demurol.fr

🚗 **Train** to Clermont-Ferrand, then bus (Tue all year; Jul & Aug also Sat) or taxi

🕐 **Open** Apr–Jun & Sep: 10am–6pm daily; Jul & Aug: 10am–6:30pm daily; Oct–Mar: 10am–5pm Sat & Sun & school hols; Feb–Mar & Oct: themed visits at 2:30pm & 3:30pm Wed during school hols & Sun; Apr–Jun: 2:30pm & 3:30pm Sun; Jul & Aug: re-enactments 10:30am–

6pm Mon, Tue, Thu, & Fri. *Son et lumière:* Jul & Aug: 8:30pm Tue & Thu (reservations advised); unaccompanied visits possible if no other event is scheduled.

💶 **Prices** €23–33; re-enactments €36–46. son et lumière: €42–52

👪 **Skipping the queue** Buy tickets in advance, by e-mail, phone or at local supermarkets.

🔫 **Guided tours** Tours in French (Jul & Aug) every 30 mins on Sun; book ahead for other days. For groups of 15 plus, tours can be reserved Sep–Jun. Tours in other languages are also available.

👫 **Age range** 4 plus

🤾 **Activities** Watch a re-enactment, then stand at the foot of the castle and plan an attack or climb up to the wall-walk to see how it can be best defended.

⏱ **Allow** 1–2 hours

☕ **Café** Nearby, in the village of Murol

🚻 **Toilets** Below the castle near the car park

Good family value?
A visit that includes re-enactments or displays of falconry and jousting gives children an insight into life in the Middle Ages.

Strolling along one of Lac Chambon's sandy beaches

Letting off steam

Although there is plenty of space to run around the château, if the weather is fine, Lac Chambon is great for a visit. It was formed when the Tartaret volcano erupted and lava blocked the Couze river. The calm, shallow waters of the lake make it ideal for swimming and watersports. It has two beaches that are patrolled by lifeguards in July and August. Canoes, windsurfers and pedalos are available for rent.

Eat and drink

Picnic: under €20; Snacks: €20–45; Real meal: €45–90; Family treat: over €90 (based on a family of four)

PICNIC Petit Casino (*Rue Pierre Celeirol, 63790; 04 73 88 80 13*), a supermarket in the village of Murol, is a great place for food shopping. Picnic near the castle or on one of Lac Chambon's beaches.
SNACKS La Petite Plage (*63790 Chambon-sur-Lac; 04 73 88 67 25*) is a lakeside café with a panoramic terrace that serves snacks all day as well as more substantial dishes.

Picnicking on the lawns by Lac Chambon

REAL MEAL Le Chalet de la Plage (*Plage du Lac Chambon, 63790; 04 73 88 82 31*) offers fresh regional food on its menu. This chalet-style restaurant has a large terrace right on the beach.
FAMILY TREAT Aux 500 Diables (*63790 Chambon des Neiges; 04 73 88 81 71; www.500diables.com*) is an attractively rustic mountain restaurant with tables surrounding a central wood fire. A popular family choice, it offers a good-value kids' menu and superb pastries.

Find out more

DIGITAL Go to *www.castles.org/ Kids_Section/Castle_Story/index. htm* for pages to print and colour and fun facts about castles and their inhabitants. Share stories on the creative and interactive website, *www.kidsonthenet.org.uk/castle*.

Take cover

If the weather turns nasty, take refuge in the **Patinoire-Centre Sportif et Culturel** (*tinyurl.com/3p2qyn5*), 20 km (12 miles) away in Le Mont-Dore, where there are six bowling lanes and an ice rink.

Next stop...
MONT-DORE AVENTURES

Drive 20 km (12 miles) west through the mountains to Le Mont-Dore spa and ski resort, where **Mont-Dore Aventures** (*www.montdore aventures.com*) offers a host of forest activities such as crossing rope bridges and swinging through the trees on zip lines. Supervised courses range from those designed for kids aged 4 to the "super black" for kids who are good climbers. Safety is taken seriously here.

⑪ Parc Naturel Régional des Volcans d'Auvergne

Sleeping giants

France's largest regional nature park (3,950 sq km/1,525 sq miles) boasts one of Europe's highest volcanoes, Puy de Sancy. Crowning the Mont-Dore, the park rises up to 1,886 m (6,185 ft). Climb up the steps and boardwalks to the summit or cheat by taking the cable car from Le Mont-Dore town. Also in the park are Monts Dôme and Mont du Cantal, and the volcanic Plateau du Cézallier. It is a stiff hike on an old mule track to the vast green crater at the top of the 1,465-m (4,792-ft) high Puy de Dôme, but worth it for the view. The Auvergne volcanoes have not erupted for years, but are

Breathtaking view of the Puy de Dôme, Parc Naturel Régional des Volcans d'Auvergne

still active underground; experts have classified them dormant and not extinct. The park is a centre for outdoor activities ranging from mountain-biking to skiing. Rent mountain bikes from VTT Evasion (*www.vtt-superbesse.com*) and ski equipment from Bessac Sports (*www.bessac-sports.fr*). The park is also crisscrossed by walking trails.

Take cover

Head west to Lanobre for **Château de Val** (*www.chateau-de-val.com*), a 15th-century fairy-tale castle on the Borg-les-Orgues lake, which stood on a hilltop until the dam was built and the valley filled with water. Stop for a view of the 120-m (394-ft) high dam, before heading to the lake.

The charming Château de Val on the Borg-les-Orgues lake

The Lowdown

🌐 **Map reference** 8 H5
Address 63000 (Puy-de-Dôme) & 15000 (Cantal).

🚗 **Train** from Clermont-Ferrand to Le Mont-Dore. **Bus** from Clermont-Ferrand to Le Mont-Dore and other towns

ℹ️ **Visitor information** Pl de la Victoire, 63000 Clermont-Ferrand; 04 73 98 65 00; *www.clermont-fd.com*

🍽️ **Eat and drink** *Picnic* Market St-Pierre (*Pl St-Pierre, 63000 Clermont-Ferrand*) is the best place to buy bread and Auvergne cheese. Picnic beside the crater lake, Lac Pavin. *Snacks* Crêperie le 1513 (*3 Rue des Chaussetiers, 63000 Clermont-Ferrand; 04 73 92 37 46; www.le1513.com*), in an ancient building with stone walls and bags of character, serves great savoury and sweet crêpes.

🎭 **Festival** Fête Médiévale de Montferrand (May–Jun)

Prices given are for a family of four

⑫ Vulcania

Shake, rattle and roll

Vulcania turns science into a pulsating adventure. Walk inside earth and experience its "hot spots"; recline on a revolving platform and learn the secrets of the solar system.

A dramatic caldera-shaped building in Vulcania

The Lowdown

🌐 **Map reference** 8 H5
Address Rue de Mazayes, 63230 St-Ours-Les Roches; 08 20 82 78 28; *www.vulcania.com*

🚗 **Train** or bus to Clermont-Ferrand, then a shuttle bus (in summer) or a 25-min taxi ride

🕐 **Open** Apr–Aug: daily; mid-Mar–end-Mar & Sep–mid-Oct: Wed–Sun; mid-Oct–mid-Nov: daily

💶 **Family ticket** €68–78; under 6s free

🍽️ **Eat and drink** *Snacks* Snack du Cratère (*on site*) has a large terrace perfect for a speedy snack. *Real meal* Brasserie du Bougnat (*on site*) has a decent menu, including *truffade* (a local speciality made with cheese and potatoes).

Feel the sensations of a tornado, an earthquake and volcanic eruptions, participate in experiments through games and hands-on activities that teach kids about earth sciences, including one where kids have to help save the town of Clermont-Ferrand from being engulfed in lava. Attractions such as "The Earth's Rage", "The Magical Odyssey" and the "Dragon Ride" involve an imaginary journey on board a simulator through magma to the bowels of the earth, meeting 3D mythical monsters on the way. There are amusements and play areas for younger kids too.

Letting off steam

Whizz down the waterslide and cool off with a plunge in the wave pool at **Centre Aquatique à Chamalière** (www.clermontcommunaute.net) in a Clermont-Ferrand suburb or head out to **Stade Nautique Pierre de Coubertin** (04 73 17 60 70), with a retractable roof over its lane pools. Both sights are 25 minutes by car.

⑬ Limoges
China, churches and chops

Start exploring at the Limoges station, Gare des Benedictins, with its splendid dome and stained-glass windows decorated with Limousin symbols. Head to the spooky 10th-century **Crypte St-Martial** – it is all that remains of an ancient abbey and contains the tombs of St Martial, Limoges' first bishop, and St Valerie, an early Christian martyr. Legend has it that St Valerie was beheaded for her faith and she carried her own head to the bishop.

The history of Limoges' butchers is on display in the tiny **Maison de la Boucherie**. Butchers formed a

A family interacting with a science exhibit in Vulcania

The splendid Gare des Benedictins, Limoges, from a well-manicured park

guild in the Middle Ages, and became so rich that aristocrats came to them for loans. Two museums are associated with the porcelain that made Limoges world famous – the **Musée des Beaux Arts** traces the history of porcelain production and the **Musée Adrien-Dubouché** displays some examples, including Napoleon's dinner service. The **Musée de la Résistance et de la Déportation** celebrates World War II courage through an exhibition of photos, documents and weapons. A fighter jet is one of the main highlights here.

Letting off steam
Take bus 1 to **Parc Victor Thuillat** (Rue Victor Thuillat, 87100; 05 55 34 46 87), which has a playground, plenty of lawns to run around and also duck ponds.

The Lowdown

🌐 **Map reference** 8 F5
Address 87000 (Haute-Vienne). Crypte St-Martial: Pl de la République. Maison de la Boucherie: Rue de la Boucherie; 05 55 34 46 87. Musée des Beaux Arts: Pl de l'Evêché; 05 55 45 98 10; www.museebal.fr. Musée Adrien-Dubouché: Pl Winston Churchill; 05 55 33 08 50; www.musee-adriendubouche.fr. Musée de la Résistance et de la Déportation: Rue de la Régle, Jardin de L'Evêché; 05 55 45 98 23

🚗 **Train** from Paris, Lyon & Bordeaux. **Bus** from St-Junien, Bellac, St-Yrieix-la-Perche & Treignac

ℹ️ **Visitor information** 12 Blvd de Fleurus; www.limoges-tourisme.com

🕐 **Open** Crypte St-Martial: daily. Maison de la Boucherie: Jul–Sep. Musée des Beaux Arts: Apr–Sep: Wed–Mon; Oct–Mar: closed Tue. Musée Adrien-Dubouché: Wed–Mon. Musée de la Résistance et de la Déportation: Wed–Mon

🍴 **Eat and drink** Snacks Le Glacier (12 Pl Denis Dussoubs, 87000; 05 55 77 23 81) is an ice cream parlour that serves omelettes and crêpes. Real meal Chez Alphonse (5 Pl de la Motte, 87000; 05 55 34 34 14; closed Sun), a Limousin institution, offers classic Limousin specialities.

🎡 **Festival** Fêtes des Ponts, festival of bridges, accompanied by a traditional cycle race (mid-Jun)

Picnic under €20; Snacks €20–45; Real meal €45–90; Family treat over €90 (based on a family of four)

Where to Stay in the Massif Central

The practical, good-value accommodation typical of this unspoilt region suits families well, whether in châteaux, traditional family-run hotels and inns, B&Bs, farmhouse *chambres d'hôtes* or self-catering *gîtes*. For families who enjoy camping, there is an excellent choice of high-end sites.

AGENCIES

Chez Nous
www.cheznous.com
The website offers a good range of self-catering accommodation in the Auvergne. Visitors can book directly from the owners.

Gîtes de France
www.gites-de-france.com
This nationwide organization offers a wide choice of rural and village family *gîtes* in the Massif Central.

Aven Armand
Map 13 B2

BED & BREAKFAST
Auberge du Chanet
Nivoliers, 48150 Hures-la-Parade; 04 66 45 65 12; www.aubergedu chanet.com
Within easy reach of Aven Armand, this Causse Méjean inn has four vaulted rooms with wooden floors and exposed stone walls. The dining room is popular with walkers. Donkeys can be hired for a day's hike.
� P €

Florac
Map 13 B2

CAMPING
Camping Le Pont du Tarn
Route du Pont-de-Montvert, 48400; 04 66 45 18 26; www.camping-florac.com
A three-star camp site, it offers 153 pitches and enjoys the twin benefits of the Tarn with its beaches and the town of Florac. A snack bar, fridges, barbecues, Wi-Fi, a laundrette and large-screen TV are available.
P 💧 €

Gorges du Tarn
Map 13 B2

HOTEL
Château de la Caze
Route des Gorges du Tarn, La Malène, 48210 Ste-Enimie; 04 66 48 51 01; www.chateaudelacaze.com
This 15th-century stone castle, with turrets, moat and private chapel

has a relaxed atmosphere. It stands above the Tarn with a backdrop of towering cliffs and all the activities of the river on hand.
🚶 P 💧 €€€

SELF-CATERING
Village Gîtes de Blajoux
Quézac, 48320 Blajoux; 04 66 49 46 00; www.village-gite-blajoux.com
At the heart of the Gorges du Tarn, these 28 newly built, well-equipped *gîtes* offer fishing, donkey- and horse-riding, climbing and mountain-biking. A paddling pool adds appeal for families with toddlers.
🍴🛏 P 💧 €€

CAMPING
La Blaquière
Map 13 A2
48210 Les Vignes; 04 66 48 54 93; www.campinggorgesdutarn.fr
A bit isolated, 6 km (4 miles) from La Malène, beside a pebble beach along the Tarn, this small camp site offers pitches, mobile homes and a playground; linen hire available.
🍴🛏 P €

Lanuéjols
Map 13 B3

CAMPING
Domaine de Pradines
Route de Millau, 30750; 04 67 82 73 85; www.domaine-de-pradines.com
A two-star camp site in pine woods on a former Templar site, it has 55 well-spaced pitches, as well as yurts, mobile homes, cabins and *gîtes* to rent. Tennis courts, playground, volleyball and *pétanque* on site.
P 💧 €

La Salle Prunet
Map 13 B2

BED & BREAKFAST
Ferme Auberge de la Borie
La Borie, 48400; 04 66 45 10 90; tinyurl.com/3vxcfpv
This is a working farm at the heart of the Parc National des Cévennes, with goats to milk, poultry to feed

and cheese to make. Families are encouraged to help. Accommodation is simple but tasteful. The home-produced organic food is superb.
🚶 P €

Le Pont de Montvert
Map 13 B2

BED & BREAKFAST
Auberge des Cévennes
48220 Jean Camus; 04 66 45 80 01; www.auberge-des-cevennes.com
In 1878, Robert Louis Stevenson stopped for Sunday lunch and flirted with the waitress at this charming inn. Pretty, simply decorated bedrooms, with bunks for kids.
🚶 P €

Le Puy-en-Velay
Map 13 B1

HOTEL
Appart' Hôtel des Capucins
29 Rue des Capucins, 43000; 04 71 04 28 74; www.lescapucins.net
Housed in a modern terracotta building, this is a family-friendly hotel in central Le Puy. The airy duplex rooms are especially suitable. The style is all-white minimalism, but sticky fingerprints are easily wiped off.
🚶🛏 P €€

Children on an Easter egg hunt at Camping du Pré Bas, Murol

BED & BREAKFAST
Les Jardins De Gisèle
Le Bourg, 43510 St Jean Lachalm;
04 71 57 56 11; tinyurl.com/3vk6aa5
Surrounded by splendid countryside
and less than 20 minutes from Le Puy,
this is a rustic, beautifully restored
14th-century fairy-tale house. Inside,
it bristles with beams and has three
bedrooms with galleries. There are
swings and two donkeys to befriend.
P ❂   €

CAMPING
Camping Rochelambert
Le Rochelambert, 43350 St-Paulien;
04 71 00 54 02; www.camping-
rochelambert.com
Just outside Le Puy, this 80-pitch
riverside site offers a range of terrific
activities, such as kids' treasure hunts,
painting workshops, archery and an
open-air cinema, as well as football
and video games. Library on site.
P ❂   €

Limoges
Map 8 F5

BED & BREAKFAST
Hôtel Familia
18 Rue du Général du Bessol, 87100;
05 55 77 51 40; www.hotelfamilia.fr
A 2-minute walk from the station
and handy for the main sights, this
hotel has a warm atmosphere. The
freshly decorated bedrooms are
arranged around a central patio
enlivened with plants and flowers.
P   €

Marchal
Map 8 H6

SELF-CATERING
Chalets de l'Eau Verte
Le Jagounet, 15270; 04 71 78 78 78;
www.auvergne-chalets.fr
Dotted around a large clearing,
these two-bedroom wooden chalets
provide comfortable accomodation
for a family of four. There are way-
marked hikes and cycle rides, on-site
fishing, and sailing and swimming.
P   €€

Murol
Map 8 H6

CAMPING
Camping du Pré Bas
Lac Chambon, 63790; 04 73 88 63 04;
www.leprebas.com
This four-star camp site on the banks
of Lac Chambon offers 80 pitches
and four kinds of mobile homes.

*A bright and attractive room in
Saluces, Salers*

There is an indoor soft play area for
younger kids, a giant water slide for
older ones and sauna for grown-ups.
P ❂   €

Orcines
Map 8 H5

BED & BREAKFAST
Le Domaine de Ternant
63870 Ternant; 04 73 62 11 20;
domaine.ternant.free.fr
A delightfully warm, informal place
to stay, this impressive-looking manor
house has a billiard room, a tennis
court and swings in the grounds. Two-
night minimum stay in high season.
P   €€

Salers
Map 12 G1

HOTEL
Saluces
*Rue de la Martille, 15140; 04 71 40
70 82; www.hotel-salers.fr*
A delightful 16th-century townhouse,
this hotel offers bright bedrooms.
Delicious breakfast and tea are served
in a snug room or the courtyard
garden – do not miss the heavenly
hot chocolate. No restaurant on site.
Most of the staff only speak French.
    €€

St-Flour
Map 12 H1

BED & BREAKFAST
Ferme Les Deux Vallées
*Le Bourg, 15110 Fridefont; 04 71 23
56 10; www.deuxvallees.com*
Located 20 minutes south of St-Flour,
this friendly shuttered, stone house
on a working farm is filled with toys,
games and baby equipment. Special
children's dishes are on offer. Rock
climbing, fishing and sailing nearby.
P   €

St-Gervais d'Auvergne
Map 8 H5

HOTEL
Le Relais d'Auvergne
*Route de Châteauneuf, 63390; 04 73
85 70 10; www.relais-auvergne.com*
A Logis de France for the 21st
century, it has been run by the same
family for almost two decades. The
bedrooms, decorated with kids in
mind, have splendid bathrooms with
monsoon showers. Well-placed for
a visit to Vulcania.
P   €

St-Martin Terressus
Map 8 F5

BED & BREAKFAST
Château Ribagnac
*Lieu dit Ribagnac, 87400; 05 55 39
77 91; www.chateauribagnac.com*
A stunning 16th-century château in
expansive grounds, it is designed
to cater to young families. Kids' teas
are at 6pm to leave parents time
to change before dinner; sterilizing
equipment and highchairs available.
P   €€

Tauves
Map 8 H6

BED & BREAKFAST
Les Escladines
*Escladines, 63690 Tauves; 04 73 21
13 02; www.escladines.fr*
A restored farmhouse in the Sancy
mountains, it has beamed rooms,
two interconnecting for families.
Book meals in advance (Mon–Fri).
P   €

*A family enjoying a meal at Ferme Les
Deux Vallées, near St-Flour*

Key to symbols *see back cover flap*

Southwest France

Southwest France offers sandy Atlantic beaches and lazy seaside days on the Île de Ré and Île d'Oléron. The Pyrenees are a fantastic summer and winter playground, while caves such as Lascaux and Niaux hold humanity's earliest artistic masterpieces. Historic cities – including Albi, Poitiers and Bayonne – boast museums and monuments, and many churches and castles date from the days of Eleanor of Aquitaine.

Poitou and Aquitaine

Périgord, Quercy and Gascony

The Pyrenees

Highlights

Futuroscope
Dance with robots or take an augmented-reality safari with creatures of the future at this theme park (see pp282–3).

La Rochelle
Take a stroll through this lively 17th-century city and visit its excellent aquarium and sandy beaches (see pp286–7).

Lascaux II
Descend into a replica of the most beautiful prehistoric painted cave in the world. See modern descendants of the animals painted on the walls of Le Thot nearby (see pp262–3).

The Pyrenees
Ski, snowboard, sled in the snow or hike to the spectacular sheer-sided Cirque de Gavarnie. Take Le Petit Train d'Artouste in the Vallée d'Ossau or the cableway to the observatory on Pic du Midi (see pp302–313).

Rocamadour
Explore this remarkable medieval, cliffside pilgrimage site built high over a gorge (see pp268–9).

Dune de Pyla
Climb this immense sand dune to the south of Arcachon bay and soak in the views before cooling off in the sea (see p295).

Left Hot-air balloons above the striking pilgrimage town of Rocamadour
Above left The splendid medieval clocktower overlooking the harbour of La Rochelle

The Best of
Southwest France

Framed by the Atlantic and the Pyrenees, where dozens of beautiful river valleys crisscross some of the prettiest, most unspoilt countryside in Europe, Southwest France is an ideal family destination. Combine outdoor activities with cultural forays, including visits to a stunning concentration of Palaeolithic caves, medieval towns and cathedrals, as well as cities packed full of interesting things to see and do.

Culture vultures

Start with **Lascaux II** (*see pp262–3*), a perfect replica of a 14,000-year old masterpiece. Pay a visit to nearby **Le Thot** (*see p263*), a discovery centre where kids can meet the animals

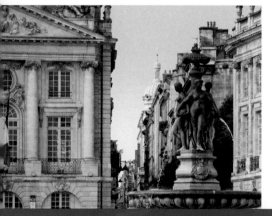

depicted on the cave walls. Near the **Grotte de Niaux** (*see pp310–11*), children can learn cave painting techniques in the **Parc de la Préhistoire** (*see p311*).

Many of the region's other great sites are medieval – the extraordinary pilgrimage town of **Rocamadour** (*see pp268–9*) built into a cliff, the spectacular Gothic brick cathedral of **Albi** (*see pp274–5*), or **Cahors** (*see p271*) with its beautiful towered Pont Valentre and secret devil. Children can spot the animals and monsters in the medieval carvings that adorn the great cathedrals of **Poitiers** (*see p284*) and **Toulouse** (*see p276*), or work out the stories at **St-Savin-sur-Gartempe** (*see pp284–5*), a World Heritage Site for its "comic strip" of 12th-century murals. They will also enjoy the Basque music and dance festival in **Bayonne** (*see pp302–303*).

Left Handsome buildings in Place de la Bourse, Bordeaux
Below The astronomical observatory on top of Pic du Midi

Above *The futuristic Kinémax and Futuroscope Digital City theatres in the Futuroscope theme park, near Poitiers*

The great outdoors

The Atlantic's sandy beaches and sheltered islands, the **Île de Ré** *(see p287)* and the **Île d'Oléron** *(see p288)*, are great for lounging, while in **Biarritz** *(see p303)*, kids as young as seven can take lessons with a surfboard. Children adore scrambling over Europe's largest sand pile, the **Dune de Pyla** *(see p295)*, and punting through the green waterways of the **Marais Poitevin** *(see p285)*. In summer, families can take a steam train back to the 19th century at **Eco-musée de la Grande Lande** *(see p297)* or ride **Le Petit Train d'Artouste** *(see p305)* dizzyingly high up into the Pyrenees. Here, resorts offer many activities for families, including a thrilling cable car ride up to the summit of the **Pic du Midi** *(see pp306–307)*.

In a week

Spend a couple of days in **Poitiers**, visiting its churches, the high-tech marvels of **Futuroscope** *(see pp282–3)* and waterways of the **Marais Poitevin**. Then head south, with a break at **Lascaux II**, before carrying on to the pretty Renaissance town of **Sarlat** *(see p266)*, a great base for three days to visit the incredible terrace settlement of **La Roque St-Christophe** *(see p266)*, **Beynac** *(see p267)* and the castles along the Dordogne, as well as **Rocamadour**. Be sure not to miss a superb boat journey on an underground river to **Gouffre de Padirac** *(see p270)*. On the sixth day, head west to **Arcachon** *(see p295)* for relaxing on the beach, with perhaps an outing to **Bordeaux** *(see pp294–5)*.

By season

In spring, spend the day outdoors exploring the Roman ruins at **Saintes** *(see pp292–3)* or solving the enigmas of the **Château d'Usson** *(see p293)*.

Summer is ideal for leisurely journeys in a boat down the Charente, Dordogne, or Lot rivers, or for trips to the **Cirque de Gavarnie** *(see p307)*. **La Rochelle** *(see pp286–7)* hosts Les Francofolies, a festival of French song for a week in July, while **Le Bournat** *(see p266)* offers great farm activities.

Autumn, when the vineyards and forests turn red, orange and yellow, is a lovely time to visit **Angoulême** *(see pp290–91)*, with its comic book museum as a centerpiece.

In winter, the family-oriented ski resorts in the Pyrenees are in full gear. December and February are good times to visit **Futuroscope**.

Right Spectacular cave paintings inside Lascaux II, part of the Vézère Valley UNESCO World Heritage Site

Southwest France

With lazy rivers winding through landscapes dotted with châteaux, medieval villages, fields of maize, wheat, sunflowers and vineyards, Southwest France is full of charm. Its Atlantic beaches and coastal lakes offer both sheltered swimming and surfing, and the Marais Poitevin is superb for boat rides under tree canopies. South of Bordeaux, the Landes contain Europe's biggest pine forest, while the Pyrenees tower up to the Spanish frontier. The road network is excellent, as is public transport to the most popular destinations.

Fountains in Clémenceau Square, at the heart of Pau's town centre

The Lowdown

🚗 **Getting there and around**
Air (see p260). **Train** TGV from Paris to Futuroscope and Poitiers (with a branch to La Rochelle), Angoulême, Agen, Bordeaux and Toulouse. From Bordeaux, TGVs continue to Dax, Bayonne, Biarritz, Orthez, Pau, Lourdes and Tarbes. TER trains provide links to towns in Poitou-Charentes, Aquitaine and Midi-Pyrénées; www.ter-sncf.com (in French only) lists links to the regional networks. **Bus** Buses have replaced trains on some routes, but the service is not regular or visitor-friendly; although Poitiers (www.vitalis-poitiers.fr), La Rochelle (www.rtcr.fr) and Bayonne (www.chronoplus.eu) have good city bus services. Toulouse has a great network of métro, tram and bus lines (www.tisseo.fr); Bordeaux has a superb tram and bus system (www.infotbc.com). **Car** Hire cars to visit places beyond the main cities. Hertz (www.hertz.fr) has branches in most towns.

🍴 **Supermarkets** Major chains in this part of France include Auchan, Intermarché, Carrefour, Leclerc and Casino.
Markets The bigger cities have *halles* (covered markets) daily except Monday. Many small towns and villages have markets on one set day each week. A list of such markets is available from the *Département* and local tourist offices.

🕐 **Opening hours** Many shops are closed on Monday, but open on Sunday morning.

➕ **Pharmacies** There is at least one pharmacy, identified by a green cross outside, in each town and many villages. A list in the window will give details of the nearest *pharmacie de garde* open outside normal hours (on Sundays and at night), and they are also listed in local newspapers, as well as on www.pharmaciesdegarde.com.

🚻 **Toilets** Towns have municipal public toilets, but be prepared for an emergency. Cities have pay or free street toilets that automatically clean themselves after every use.

*A sandy beach on the
Île d'Oléron*

*Ruins of the impressive
Château de Bonaguil*

Places of interest

● PÉRIGORD, QUERCY AND GASCONY
1 Lascaux II
2 Château de Hautefort
3 Château de Jumilhac
4 Périgueux
5 La Roque St-Christophe
6 Le Bournat
7 Sarlat
8 Beynac
9 Rocamadour
10 Gouffre de Padirac
11 St-Cirq-Lapopie
12 Cahors
13 Château de Bonaguil
14 Villeréal
15 Latour-Marliac
16 Albi
17 Toulouse
18 Auch
19 Condom
20 Larressingle

● POITOU AND AQUITAINE
1 Futuroscope
2 Poitiers
3 Angles-sur-l'Anglin
4 St-Savin-sur-Gartempe
5 Marais Poitevin
6 La Rochelle
7 Rochefort
8 Marennes and the Île d'Oléron
9 Royan
10 Angoulême
11 Château de La Rochefoucauld
12 Cognac
13 Saintes
14 Pons
15 Bordeaux
16 St-Émilion
17 Bazas
18 Eco-musée de la Grande Lande
19 Dax

● THE PYRENEES
1 Bayonne
2 Grottes d'Isturitz et Oxocelhaya
3 Sauveterre-de-Béarn
4 Pau
5 Le Petit Train d'Artouste
6 Pic du Midi de Bigorre
7 Parc National des Pyrénées
8 Parc Animalier des Pyrénées
9 Lourdes
10 Château de Mauvezin
11 Grotte de Niaux
12 Réserve Nationale d'Orlu
13 Montségur
14 Grotte du Mas d'Azil
15 St Bertrand-de-Commminges

Southwest France Regional Airports

This part of France is well served by regional airports, many offering low-cost links to the UK, Ireland and other cities in northern Europe, although many of these flights only operate from spring to autumn. For families arriving from outside of Europe, the two largest airports in the region are Toulouse and Bordeaux, served by national airlines with direct links to the major international European air hubs.

Brive Vallée de la Dordogne

The airport is just off the A20, 21 km (13 miles) north of Souillac and 40 km (25 miles) east of Montignac. It is served by City Jet, Jet2 and Airliner. Taxis and hire cars are available. Everything is easy to find in the airport. There is no restaurant.

Bergerac Dordogne Périgord

One of the busiest small airports in the southwest, it is located 3 km (2 miles) south of Bergerac. It has Ryanair, Jet2, Twin Jet and Flybe flights. There is a taxi stand and car hire is available. It is easy to get around and has a café.

Toulouse-Blagnac

Situated 8 km (5 miles) northwest of Toulouse, off the A620, this airport is served by several airlines, including Air France, Alitalia, British Airways and easyJet. It is linked by a regular shuttle (€4) every 20–40 minutes to Toulouse's bus station, a short walk from the city's main train station.

The airport is medium-sized and well signposted, with lifts. It closes after the last flight. There is a good but expensive restaurant, 8ème Ciel (05 61 16 70 40), overlooking the runways. Holiday Inn Express (05 61 31 06 00, www.hiexpress.com), is located two minutes from the airport.

Poitiers-Biard

Poitiers-Biard is 3 km (2 miles) west of Poitiers, a 10-minute drive from Futuroscope. It is served by carriers such as Airliner and Ryanair. There are taxis and hire cars available at the airport. It is small and easy to get around, but closes after the last flight. There is a bar-restaurant.

La Rochelle-Île de Ré

La Rochelle-Île de Ré is 5 km (3 miles) northwest of La Rochelle, with Flybe, Ryanair and Airliner flights. Bus 7 and

The entrance to La Rochelle-Île de Re airport

47 (€1.30) provide links to the city centre. Services are easy to find at the airport. There is a snack bar/café.

Bordeaux

Bordeaux, the biggest airport in the southwest after Toulouse, is 10 km (6 miles) west of the centre of town in Mérignac, off the rocade (bypass) that surrounds the city. It is served by easyJet, British Airways, Flybe, Air Transat, Ryanair, Veuling, Air France, Chalair, Aer Lingus Jet4you.The Jet' bus (€7) links the airport every 45 minutes to Bordeaux's St-Jean train station; The La Liane 1 city bus also runs every 10 minutes from the airport to central Bordeaux, connecting with Tram line A at Mérignac centre, and with Trams B and C at Bordeaux-Quinconces.

It is a medium-sized airport, with a 5-minute walk to the departure gates. It closes after the last flight until 5am. There is a brasserie, sandwich bar and café in the main terminal, as well as a snack bar/café in the Billi terminal (where low cost flights arrive). The All Seasons Bordeaux Aéroport hotel (05 56 55 93 42; www.accorhotels. com) is nearby.

Biarritz-Anglet-Bayonne

Only 2 km (1 mile) south of Biarritz, this airport is served by Air France, Ryanair, easyJet, Transavia and Darwin Airline-Baboo. Chronoplus shuttles (€1) run to Biarritz, Anglet and Bayonne; ATCRB buses run to St-Jean-de-Luz.

Pau-Pyrénées

Pau-Pyrénées is a small airport 7 km (4 miles) north of Pau off the A64. It has Air France, City Jet and Twin Jet. It is linked to the centre of Pau and the train station by Idelis shuttle (€1).

Tarbes-Lourdes-Pyrénées

This airport is 10 km (6 miles) from both Tarbes and Lourdes. It is served by Ryanair, Air France, bmibaby, Thomas Cook and Jetairfly. Bus 2 (€2) links it to Tarbes, Lourdes, Argelès-Gazost, Luz St-Sauveur and Barèges. It has snack bars and a restaurant.

The Lowdown

Bergerac Dordogne Périgord
05 53 22 25 25; www.bergerac.
aeroport.fr

Biarritz-Anglet-Bayonne 05 59 43
83 83; www.biarritz.aeroport.fr

Bordeaux 05 56 34 50 50;
www.bordeaux.aeroport.fr

Brive Vallée de la Dordogne
05 55 22 40 00; www.aeroport-
brive-vallee-dordogne.com

La Rochelle-Île de Ré 05 46 42
30 26; www.larochelle.aeroport.fr

Pau-Pyrénées 05 59 33 33 00;
www.pau.aeroport.fr

Poitiers-Biard 05 49 30 04 40;
www.poitiers.aeroport.fr

Tarbes-Lourdes-Pyrénées 05 62
32 92 22; www.tlp.aeroport.fr

Toulouse-Blagnac 08 25 38 00 00;
www.toulouse.aeroport.fr

Périgord, Quercy and Gascony

Together these three regions offer families the opportunity to experience some of France's most unspoilt countryside. There are gastronomic delights to sample and medieval discoveries to be made at every turn, with a slower pace of French life full of rustic charm. The area also has the Dordogne and Lot rivers, which provide extensive waterways to explore year round.

Lascaux II
p262

Rocamadour
p268

Albi
p274

Below *Soaring limestone walls of Gouffre de Padirac, an underground cave system*

① Lascaux II
Arts and crafts, prehistoric-style

The original Lascaux caves with their amazing paintings date back 17,000 years, and were rediscovered in 1940 by four teenage boys roaming over the hills in search of adventure, when their dog Robot fell into the caves. Opened in 1948, the caves were closed 15 years later since the rising carbon dioxide levels from the breath of visitors caused the artworks to fade. After years of painstaking work, Lascaux II, an exact replica of two of the most famous chambers, the Great Hall of Bulls and the Painted Gallery, was opened in 1983. It took 11 years, cost over €73 million and involved over 20 sculptors and artists to re-create these chambers.

Key Features

② **The largest prehistoric painting** This 5-m (16-ft) wide painting of the enormous "Bull" in the Great Hall of Bulls is believed to be the largest example of prehistoric art discovered. The centrepiece of the cave, it is Lascaux's most famous image.

③ **Diverticule Axial** The Painted Gallery, which has been termed the "Sistine Chapel of Prehistory", houses images including a falling cow and a frieze of ponies.

① **Salle des Taureaux**
The Great Hall of Bulls is one of the most impressive examples of prehistoric art. Each animal was painted and drawn in countless shades of charcoal, yellow and red. Modern-day artists used the same techniques and materials as the Palaeolithic painters to re-create the paintings.

La Scène du Puits There is only one drawing of a human, in the Shaft of the Dead Man. Next to him looms a bison and under him a bird. This is in the original Lascaux caves, which are closed to visitors.

Letting off steam

Splash off the cave dust paddling along the Vézère river. **Canoë Vallée Vézère** (www.canoesvalleevezere. com) organizes canoeing trips. Four-seater family kayaks are available, but kids aged under 12 years must be accompanied by an adult. Life jackets are provided. Or check out the bears at the **Site Préhistorique de Regourdou** (Regourdou, 24290 Montignac; 05 53 51 81 23; www. regourdou.fr), 450 m (1,476 ft) uphill from Lascaux. Discovered in 1954, it is said to have been the centre of a prehistoric bear cult. Today, 20 bears roam around in their natural habitat, but fenced off from humans.

Canoe rental along the calm Vézère river, perfect for families

Prices given are for a family of four

A variety of produce on sale at the Saturday market, Montignac

market, sells regional cheeses and freshly baked breads, as well as locally grown fruit and vegetables. Picnic at the tables at Lascaux II or on the banks of the river in Montignac. **SNACKS La Dolce Vita** (6 Pl de la Liberation, 24290 Montignac) serves delicious pizzas with a wide choice of toppings.

Eat and drink

Picnic: under €20; Snacks: €20–45
Real meal: €45–90; Family treat:
over €90 (based on a family of four)

PICNIC Marché Samedi (Pl Quai Merilhou, 24290 Montignac; 8am–1pm), the local Saturday morning

The Lowdown

🌐 **Map reference** 12 E1
Address Route de la Grotte de Lascaux II, 24290 Montignac; *www.semitour.com*

🚗 **Train** from Bordeaux to Condat-Le-Lardin, then taxi

ℹ️ **Visitor information** Mairie de Montignac, Pl Yvon Delbos, 24290 Montignac; 05 53 51 72 00; *www.ville-montignac.com*

🕐 **Open** Feb–Mar & Oct–Dec: 10am–12.30pm & 2–5.30pm Tue–Sun; Apr–Jun & Sep: 9am–6pm daily; Jul–Aug: 9am–7pm daily

💶 **Price** €30–40; under-5s free

👨‍👩‍👧 **Skipping the queue** Buy tickets ahead of time in Jul & Aug. In summer, tickets are only available at the tourist office in Montignac. Buy a combined ticket including Le Thot for €42–52. First visit

Le Thot and then go on to see Lascaux II.

🚩 **Guided tours** A 45-min tour is available in English. Contact the tourist office for details.

👫 **Age range** 6 plus

🎨 **Activities** Children can learn cave painting and more about archaeological excavation at Le Thot's prehistoric park.

⏱️ **Allow** An hour

☕ **Café** Basic refreshments are available at a stand Jul–Aug.

🚻 **Toilets** On site; larger public toilets are available in the centre of Montignac nearby.

Good family value?
An affordable day out for the family, with numerous activities to engage and educate children.

REAL MEAL Les Pilotis *(6 Rue Lafitte, 24290 Montignac; 05 53 50 88 15)*, a family-friendly restaurant located down by the Vézère river, serves simple, home-cooked fare.
FAMILY TREAT La Chaumière *(53 Rue 4 Septembre, 24290 Montignac; 05 53 50 14 24)* appears to be a small thatched cottage on the outside. But inside it is a thriving restaurant that serves an impressive array of regional dishes made with fresh local produce. The duck confit is highly recommended.

Shopping
Located next to Montignac's tourist office is an exhibition area with stalls selling goods produced in the region. Clothes and interesting knick-knacks – including Lascaux souvenirs for kids – can be bought here.

Find out more
DIGITAL Visit *www.lascaux.culture.fr* to find out more about Lascaux and take an interactive tour of the cave. Learn about the history of cave painting on *www.historyworld.net*.

Next stop...
AN ANIMAL PARK AND A CASTLE
Visit **Le Thot** *(www.semitour.com)*, a prehistoric animal park at Thonac, just 7 km (4 miles) south of Lascaux II. Discover animals resembling those that would have lived in the region during the time of the cave painters. Go to **Maison Forte de Reignac** *(www.maison-forte-reignac.com)*, 15 km (9 miles) south of Montignac, which is built into the rock itself. The most intact castle of its kind in France, it was ruled by a notorious tyrant. See over 60 medieval torture devices.

Replicas of the extinct woolly rhinoceros at Le Thot, Thonac

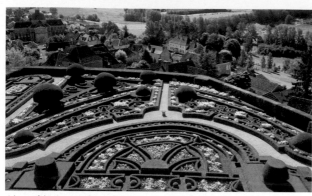

A beautiful topiary garden at the Château de Hautefort

The square and circular turrets of the Château de Jumilhac

② Château de Hautefort

A site for a Hollywood film

A listed historical monument, the Château de Hautefort was about to be destroyed in the Revolution, but was saved by villagers. It is grand in every sense and considered the most prestigious building in the Dordogne. Built in the 17th century, the castle fell into a state of disrepair before it was meticulously restored by the Baron and Baronesse de Bastard. The baron, however, died before the restoration was completed in 1968 and in a tragic turn of events, it was burnt to the ground shortly after the

work was finished. The baroness began the renovation process all over again. The end result is stunning with a splendid exterior and, inside, an impressive collection of 17th-century art and tapestries.

The château was a location for the Hollywood film *Ever After* (1998) starring Drew Barrymore.

Colonnade around the inner courtyard of the Château de Hautefort

Letting off steam

There is plenty of space for kids to scamper about in the grounds of the Château de Hautefort. There is a mix of well-manicured formal and informal gardens, with grasslands and wooded areas.

③ Château de Jumilhac

Ideal for a fairy tale

With its magnificent towers and turrets, the Château de Jumilhac resembles a castle out of a fairy tale. Originally built in the 12th century, it experienced a rebirth in the 17th century when new black tiled roofs were added, earning it the nickname of "Black Pearl" of the Green Périgord. Inside, visitors can peep into the legendary bedroom of the Lady of Jumilhac, who was also known as "the spinner". Imprisoned in her bedroom by her jealous husband who was away fighting, she spent 30 years with only a spinning wheel for company. She spun wool

The Lowdown

🌐 **Map reference** 8 E6
   Address 24390 (Dordogne).
   Château de Hautefort: Le Bourg
   d'Hautefort; 05 53 50 51 23; *www.chateau-hautefort.com*

🚆 **Train** from Bordeaux to Périgueux,
   then 40 km (25 mile) by car

ℹ️ **Visitor information** Pl Marquis
   Jacques François de Hautefort,
   24390; 05 53 50 40 27;
   ot-hautefort.com

🕐 **Open** Château de Hautefort:
   Mar & first two weeks Nov:
   Sat–Sun pm; Apr–Oct: daily

💲 **Price** €25–35; under 7s free

🍴 **Eat and drink** *Picnic* Marché du
   Mercredi Matin *(Pl Eugene Le
   Roy, 24390 Hautefort)* offers fresh
   breads, local fruits, vegetables
   and regional delicacies. Picnic
   in the château grounds. *Real
   meal* La Table d'Erillac *(Pl Eugene
   Le Roy, 23480; 05 53 51 61 49)*
   serves contemporary dishes and
   vegetarian options.

The Lowdown

🌐 **Map reference** 8 E6
   Address 24630 (Dordogne).
   Château de Jumilhac: Henry de La
   Tour du Pin; 06 09 61 78 40;
   jumilhac.net

🚆 **Train** from Limoges that connects
   with Paris, to La Coquille, then a
   20-min taxi ride

ℹ️ **Visitor information** Pl du Château,
   24630 Jumilhac-le-Grand; 05 53 52
   55 43; *jumilhac.fr*

🕐 **Open** Château de Jumilhac: spring
   & Nov school hols: daily pm; rest of
   the year: Sun pm

💲 **Price** €25–35 (additional charges
   for garden tours and visits to the
   roof); under 5s free

🍴 **Eat and drink** *Picnic* Marché de
   Producteurs *(Pl du Château,
   24630; Jul–Aug: 9am–1pm Sun)*
   is a farmer's market ideal for
   supplies. Picnic by the water
   fountain in front of the château.
   Snacks Café de Sport *(19 Pl du
   Chateâu, 24630; 05 53 52 50
   59)* serves bar food and is also
   a patisserie.

🎊 **Festival** Jour de Bastille (14 Jul)

with hidden romantic messages to her lover who lived in the grounds as the castle shepherd.

Letting off steam

Head to the nearby **Galerie de l'Or** *(Pl du Château, 24630; 05 53 52 55 43)*, which runs half-day gold panning lessons on the banks of the Isle river. After a run around, families can paddle and possibly find a nugget or two!

④ Périgueux

Architecture and visual tricks

Capital of the Périgord (or Dordogne) region, Périgueux was established in Neolithic times. Not much remains from its time as a Roman hub, but ruins of a Roman temple and an amphitheatre provide a fascinating insight into the beautiful French architecture through the centuries. A monumental entrance of the **Musée d'Art et d'Archéologie du Périgord** leads to the east and west galleries that are devoted to prehistoric, Gallo-Roman, medieval archaeology and non-European ethnography. There is also an impressive collection of 16th to 20th century fine art on display. The Musée Gallo-Romain de Vesunna, located in the heart of the ancient city, is also worth a visit. It houses the remains of a grand Gallo-Roman residence. The ruins have been enclosed within a large glass building, designed by award-winning architect Jean Nouvel.

Letting off steam

There are plenty of grassy areas along the river bank for stretching little legs. The *Voie Verte* (Green Lane), a safe trail along the river for walkers and cyclists through idyllic scenery, is perfect for family cycling. It runs all the way to Bordeaux in the west and Limoges in the east.

Traditional crafts on offer in the canopied market stalls of Périgueux

The Lowdown

- 🌐 **Map reference** 11 C1
  Address 24000 (Dordogne). Musée d'Art et d'Archéologie du Périgord: 22 Cours Tourny; 05 53 06 40 70.
- 🚆 **Train** from Paris
- ℹ️ **Visitor information** 26 Pl Francheville, 24000; 05 53 53 10 63; www.tourisme-perigueux.fr
- 🕐 **Open** Musée d'Art et d'Archéologie du Périgord: Wed–Mon
- 🍴 **Eat and drink** *Real meal* Aux Berges de L'Isle Restaurant *(2 Rue Pierre Magne, 24000; 05 53 09 51 50)* provides a riverside setting and offers French dishes; includes a kids' menu. *Family treat* Hercule Poireau *(2 Rue de la Nation, 24000; 05 53 08 90 76)* serves traditional French cuisine.
- 🎉 **Festival** Concerts de Jazz, jazz concerts in the streets (Aug)

Roman remains on display in the Musée Gallo-Romain de Vesunna, Périgueux

Picnic under €20; **Snacks** €20–45; **Real meal** €45–90; **Family treat** over €90 (based on a family of four)

⑤ La Roque St-Christophe

Stone Age housing complex

Resembling a giant beehive, La Roque St-Christophe is a huge troglodyte cave complex in the village of Peyzac-le-Moustier. There are 100 natural caves in five tiers, hollowed out of the rockface, which stand 250 m (820 ft) tall and 800 m (2,625 ft) in length. The caves could house up to 1,000 people, and excavations have proved that they were inhabited from the Upper Palaeolithic Age onwards. Within the rock's stronghold there would once have stood a town and an impressive fortress. Models on display show how the cave village would have looked when inhabited.

Letting off steam

For some fresh air after the rock caves, go for a little exploration around the picnic area and the duck pond. Neanderthal fossils have also been found in and around the cave complex, so keep an eye out for anything old and unusual.

The Lowdown

- 🌐 **Map reference** 12 E1
  Address 24620 (Dordogne). La Roque St-Christophe: off the D706, Le Moustier
- 🚗 **Car** own transport or hire a car from Sarlat. There is free parking available.
- ℹ️ **Visitor information** 3 Rue Tourny, 24203 Sarlat; 05 53 31 45 45; www.sarlat-tourisme.com
- 🕐 **Open** La Roque St-Christophe: mid-Nov–Jan: daily pm; self-guided tour available
- 💶 **Price** €23–33; under 5s free
- 🍵 **Eat and drink** Picnic Le Café (on site) is an outdoor stand serving refreshments with seats and a picnic area.

⑥ Le Bournat

Step back in time

French life from a bygone era is re-created in this outdoor museum, where time appears to have stood still since 1900. An old-fashioned rural community has been rebuilt, complete with chapel, farm and windmill. In each of the different village areas, traditional crafts are

A model of a caveman in La Roque St-Christophe, Peyzac-le-Moustier

demonstrated and both parents and children are invited to join in one of the many workshops on offer each day, from photography classes with a pinhole camera to breadmaking in a replica mill. Scattered among the exhibits are replicas of 100-year-old funfair attractions for kids to enjoy. Nearby, the **Parc Aquarium du Périgord Noir**, France's largest freshwater aquarium, has over 6,000 types of fish. There is much to see and do, like watching shark feeding and a guided tour with the resident marine biologist.

Letting off steam

There are plenty of open spaces for kids to run around in Le Bournat. Visit the old-fashioned funfair and enjoy the rides on offer. Head for the **St-Avit Loisirs** (www.saint-avit-loisirs. com), a 10-minute drive west in the town of Le Bugue. This holiday park has a kids' play area, camp site, crazy golf and water flumes.

A traditional windmill at the outdoor museum of Le Bournat

The Lowdown

- 🌐 **Map reference** 8 E6
  Address 24260 (Dordogne). Le Bournat: Le Bugue; 05 53 08 41 99; www.lebournat.fr. Parc Aquarium du Périgord Noir: Allee Paul-Jean Souriau, Le Bugue; 05 53 08 41 99; aquariumperigord noir.com
- 🚗 **Car** 30-min drive from Sarlat
- ℹ️ **Visitor information** Porte de la Vézère, 24260 Le Bugue; 05 53 07 20 48
- 🕐 **Open** Le Bournat: Mar–mid-Oct: daily. Parc Aquarium du Périgord Noir: mid-Feb–mid-Nov: daily, closed Dec & Jan
- 💶 **Price** €36–46; under 4s free
- 🍵 **Eat and drink** Picnic The village shop sells speciality foods from times gone, including bread, cheese and preserves. Real meal Chez Paul (Le Bournat, 24260 Le Bugue), a family-friendly restaurant, it serves substantial meals, including regional delicacies.

Shop selling foie gras in the medieval centre of Sarlat

⑦ Sarlat

France's most popular town

An incredibly attractive town with a maze of narrow lanes, yellow sandstone buildings and medieval, as well as Renaissance architecture, Sarlat has featured in quite a few films, including the Cinderella inspired Ever After (1998) and The Musketeer (2001). It is also very popular with tourists and gets extremely busy during the summer months, but it is still possible to soak up its atmosphere by getting purposefully lost among its winding streets. Just wander around, spot pretty gas lights, carved decorations and surprising statues. Eventually everyone ends up at the Place de la Liberté, full of cafés, and also, on Saturday mornings, the site of the region's finest market. Depending on season, stalls sell walnuts, foie gras, truffles and local delicacies.

The Lowdown

- 🌐 **Map reference** 12 F1
  Address 24200 (Dordogne).
- 🚗 **Train** from Bordeaux
- ℹ **Visitor information** Rue Tourny, 24200 Sarlat; 05 53 31 45 45; www.sarlat.com
- 🍽 **Eat and drink** *Real meal* Le Bistro de l'Octroi *(111 Ave Selves, 24000; 05 53 30 83 40)* is a popular haunt with local families. It provides a great opportunity to sample local delicacies, including truffles, duck and crème brulée. *Family treat* Restaurant Le Grand Bleu *(43 Ave de la Gare, 24000; 05 53 31 08 48)* is a Michelin-starred restaurant that serves innovative and modern French food. Try some of the more unusual dishes, such as the asparagus ice cream.
- 🎪 **Festival** Fête de la Truffe, an annual celebration of the glorious truffle (Jan)

Letting off steam

Head for the two tree-top adventure parks: **Indian Forest Périgord** *(www.indianforestperigord.com)* and **La Forêt des Ecureuil** *(www.laforetdesecureuils.com)*, located 2 km (1 mile) east of Sarlat. Rope bridges and zip lines strung between trees offer Indiana Jones-style adventure in the French countryside. Health and safety equipment are provided. There are courses of varying difficulty, some suitable for kids aged 4–8 years.

⑧ Beynac

Lights, camera, action

Beynac is a picturesque French town with a château that dates back to the Middle Ages. Perched high on a limestone cliff, which protected the town from potential invaders, the **Château de Beynac** overlooks the Dordogne river below. It was lovingly restored in the 1960s by Lucien Grosso and is now one of the best preserved in the region. Within the château walls lies a Romanesque keep and several Renaissance sculptures. Thanks to this château, Beynac has had an illustrious film career. It has provided the location for big budget movies that include *Les Visiteurs* (1993) and *Jeanne d'Arc* (1999).

Letting off steam

Hire some bicycles from any of the cycle shops in town and follow one of the recommended routes through the surrounding countryside. The area is stunning and there is no better way to see its full splendour than on a bike.

The Lowdown

- 🌐 **Map reference** 8 E5
  Address 24220 (Dordogne). Château de Beynac: Le Bourg, Beynac-et-Cazenac.
- 🚗 **Train** from Sarlat
- ℹ **Visitor information** La Balme, 24220 Beynac-et-Cazenac; 05 53 29 43 08
- ⏱ **Open** Château de Beynac: Sep–Jun: Mon–Sat; Jul–Aug: daily
- 🍽 **Eat and drink** *Real meal* Auberge Lembert *(Le Capeyrou, 24220 Beynac et Cazenac; 05 53 29 50 45)* serves traditional French dishes, including pies and *cassoulet* (rich bean stew) and also has a kids' menu. *Family treat* Café de la Riviere *(La Bourg, 24220 Beynac; 05 53 28 35 49)* offers great food along with al fresco dining and spectacular views over the Dordogne river.

A canoe and a gabare on the Dordogne river, overlooked by the Château de Beynac

Picnic under €20; **Snacks** €20–45; **Real meal** €45–90; **Family treat** over €90 (based on a family of four)

⑨ Rocamadour
From flocks of pilgrims to flocks of birds

Located in a gorge above the Dordogne river in the Parc Naturel Régional des Causses du Quercy, this small and almost vertical village, set into the cliffside, has been the destination of pilgrims for centuries. The apparently miraculous healing abilities of the church's Black Madonna have been the main draw. Today, it is France's second most visited tourist location outside Paris. At the summit sits the château, followed by the cluster of churches and the village itself, sweeping down towards the river below. Do not miss the exotic birds that soar freely above the Rocher des Aigles.

Black Madonna

Key Features

Croix de Jérusalem

Château de Rocamadour

Crypte de St Amadour

The uppermost point A final set of steps lead up to the château's ramparts, dating from the 14th century. From here, visitors can survey the countryside for miles around.

Chapelle de Notre Dame The statue of the Black Madonna depicts the Virgin Mary with dark skin. This chapel houses her wooden form and throne, carved from one single piece of walnut wood.

Grand Escalier This great stairway consists of 216 steps and leads from the village to the sanctuaries above. Earlier, pilgrims used to climb the steps on their knees.

Le Sanctuaire de Notre Dame This is a complex set of churches centred around the statue of the Virgin Mary and tomb of St Amadour, whose perfectly preserved body was discovered in the 12th century.

Grand Escalier

Main Street The village of Rocamadour has only one street and two fortified gateways: Porte du Figuier and the Porte Salmon.

Château de Rocamadour The château stands on the site of a fort that protected the sanctuary from the west.

Prices given are for a family of four

The Lowdown

🌐 **Map reference** 12 F1
Address 46500 (Lot). Château de Rocamadour: Rocamadour; 05 65 33 73 62

🚗 **Train** from Paris to Gramat, then taxi; TER from Rodez, Figeac & Brive

ℹ️ **Visitor information** L'Hospitalet, 46500; 05 65 33 22 00; *www.rocamadour.com* (opening hours vary)

Letting off steam

Head for the **Rocher des Aigles** (*46500 Rocamadour; 05 65 33 65 45; www.rocherdesaigles.com*), also known as Eagle's Rock, just past the Château de Rocamadour. Kids will love the spectacular air ballet here that is performed by birds of prey in free flight. There are over 400 types of birds and 60 species at the centre. Learn about how birds are trained as well as their mating and feeding habits.

Eat and drink

Picnic: under €20; Snacks: €20–45; Real meal: €45–90; Family treat: over €90 (based on a family of four)

PICNIC Leclerc (*Champbas, 46500 Gramat*) stocks grocery essentials along with fresh produce such as fruit and vegetables. Picnic on the river bank at the foot of the village.
SNACKS Café du Château (*Le Château, 46500; 05 65 33 62 31*) is an adequate choice for a light lunch after the grand ascent.
REAL MEAL L'Auberge le Roc de Berger (*Bois de Belveyre, Route de Padirac, 46500; 05 65 33 19 99*) specializes in wood-fire grilled meats such as duck and lamb, and seasonal fish. The desserts are a hit with kids as they mostly involve ice cream and chocolate.
FAMILY TREAT Restaurant Jehan de Valon (*Cité Médiévale Rocamadour, 46500; 05 65 33 63 08*) serves rich regional dishes, including truffles, on its terrace.

Shopping

Go to **Celeste Bazaar** (*Rue de la Couronnerie, 46500*) for traditional French craft and a range of fair trade products. Visit the **Rocamadour Boutique Iemanja** (*Pl Europe, 46500*),

a stylish little boutique with a great range of French styles and designer labels that may tempt mum or dad to treat themselves for a change!

Find out more

DIGITAL For further information on Rocamadour, go to *www.rocamadour.com*. Visit *www.sacred-destinations.com/france/rocamadour-shrine* for information on the Black Madonna.

Take cover

Grotte Préhistorique des Merveilles (*L'Hospitalet, 46500*) has 20,000-year-old cave paintings and rock formations. The nearby **Le Féérie Autour du Rail** (*L'Hospitalet, 46500; 05 65 33 71 06; www.la-feerie.com*) is a show that takes visitors on a magical journey through lights, music and animation.

A cave painting of spotted horses, Grotte du Pech Merle

Next stop...

PECH MERLE A 35-minute drive south of Rocamadour is the Grotte du Pech Merle. Discovered in 1922, the cave is 2 km (1 mile) in length, a third of which can be explored to reveal galleries of rich subterranean paintings that date back 25,000 years. Experts believe the caves may have been used as a refuge by prehistoric man during the Ice Age.

Open Château de Rocamadour: 8am–8pm daily

Skipping the queue Winter is the best time to visit as it is less crowded.

Guided tours Daily 90-min walking tours of Rocamadour can be arranged by appointment through the tourist office.

Age range All ages

Allow Half a day

Café Café du Château inside the Château de Rocamadour

Toilets There are public toilets in the village.

Good family value?
This is a good and inexpensive day out for the family with the main cost being for food and drink.

Underground caves at the Gouffre de Padirac

The village of St-Cirq-Lapopie on its ragged cliff top

⑩ Gouffre de Padirac

Going underground

A spectacular cave complex, the Gouffre de Padirac cannot fail to impress its visitors. Central to the experience is the eerie descent via stairs or lift into the gaping chasm, 103 m (338 ft) underground. The tour continues on board a gondola through the subterranean river system that links the network of caves below. The rest of the tour is on foot through the Great Dome, a large limestone chamber within the cave. This is an awe-inspiring underground adventure, sure to transport visitors back in time. Bring warm clothing, since it is chilly inside.

The Lowdown

🌐 **Map reference** 12 F1
Address 46500 (Lot). 46500 Padirac; 05 65 33 64 56; *www.gouffre-de-padirac.com*

�"**Train** to Rocamadour, then a 20-min taxi ride

ℹ️ **Visitor information** 3 Rue Tourny, 24203 Sarlat Cedex; 05 53 31 45 45; *www.sarlat-tourisme.com*

🕐 **Open** Apr–Oct: daily

💲 **Price** €31–40

🍽️ **Eat and drink** *Snacks* There is a snack bar (*on site; Jul & Aug*) with a park and a picnic area. *Real meal* L'Auberge du Gouffre (*on site; 05 65 38 48 53*) offers regional specialities from foie gras and truffles to Rocamadour cheeses.

Letting off steam

Head for the **Forêt des Singes** (*www.la-foret-des-singes.com*) in Rocamadour, a 20-ha (50-acre) forest home to 130 barbary apes. Families have the rare opportunity to see the apes playing freely in the forest or to visit the research centre on site to discover more about this species.

⑪ St-Cirq-Lapopie

A painter's paradise

Perched on a cliff above the Lot river, the picturesque village of St-Cirq-Lapopie provides spectacular views across the valley. Officially declared one of *Les Plus Beaux Villages de France*, it has inspired painters such as the Impressionist Henri Martin and writers including Andre Breton with its sheer beauty. In the Middle Ages, four feuding families were embroiled in fights over the village's ownership. This resulted in the construction of several castles and fortified houses. There are many opportunities to fuel the imagination of children as they explore the narrow cobbled streets running between the shops

The Lowdown

🌐 **Map reference** 12 F2
Address 46330 (Lot).

🚌 **Bus** or boat ride from Cahors (see opposite).

ℹ️ **Visitor information** Pl Sambral, 46330; 05 65 31 31 31; *www.saint-cirqlapopie.com*

🍽️ **Eat and drink** *Snacks* Bar Café La Peyroliere (*Pl Sombral, 46330; 05 65 24 34 66*) serves tasty affordable crêpes. Dine on the terrace. *Family treat* Le Gourmet Quercynois (*Le Bourg, 46330; 05 65 31 21 20*) is a more expensive option, offering traditional local dishes.

and houses and the medieval ruins along the riverbank. The village has also been proclaimed a natural heritage monument preventing any new building work.

Letting off steam

Head back down the hill to the Lot river below. On the riverbank there is a nice grassy area suitable for picnics and a kids' play park. Fishing workshops are available for kids aged 8 plus (*www.pechelot.com*).

A barbary ape basking in the sun at the Forêt des Singes, Rocamadour

⑫ Cahors

Bridging the past

The medieval capital of the Lot region, Cahors sits on the banks of the Lot river, which winds its way through this wine region and beyond for about 500 km (310 miles). The town is the birthplace of popes and poets and home to the 14th-century Pont Valentre, reputed to be France's most beautiful bridge and shrouded in myth and legend. This market town also has 29 secret gardens (hidden behind and between buildings) to explore – each garden has a different theme. A map of their locations is available at the tourist office. There is a statue of the famous 16th-century French poet Clément Marot in the town.

Letting off steam

Hire a canoe at the river or drive 25 km (16 miles) west to St-Cirq-Lapopie and canoe leisurely back to town. Families with younger children can board the **Bateau Promenade Valentre** (www.bateau-cahors.com) and take a cruise along the Lot. The boat's departure point is near the Pont Valentre. **L'Archipel** on the l'Île de Cabessut (www.tourisme-cahors.

Above Canoeing on the Lot river, Cahors
Below The fortified Pont Valentre spanning the Lot, Cahors

com/fr/cahors-ludique/loisirs.php) is a water park that has slides and also a toddler pool. It is only open in high season from June to September.

A view of multi-hued vineyards around Cahors

The Lowdown

- 🌐 **Map reference** 12 F2
  Address 46000 (Lot).
- 🚗 **Train** from Paris and Toulouse. **Bus** from Fumel in the west and Figeac in the east
- ℹ️ **Visitor information** Pl Francois Mitterrand, 46000; 05 65 53 20 65; www.tourisme-cahors.com
- 🍽️ **Eat and drink** *Snacks* Le Mephisto (10 Ave Jean Jaures, 46000; 05 65 53 00 77) has an entertaining owner and reasonably priced traditional lunch options. *Real meal* Au Fil des Douceurs (90 Quai de la Verrerie, 46000; 05 65 22 13 04) is a floating restaurant, just upriver from the Pont Cabessut. The desserts alone are worth the trip.
- 🎊 **Festival** Le Blues Festival de Cahors, an annual blues festival that attracts international performers (Jul)

MATTER OF INTEREST

Cahors was once France's main financial area with many of the country's bankers based here. It became famous for being the first place where bankers charged interest on their loans.

The devil's bridge

In the 14th century, the builder of the Pont Valentre promised to sell the devil his soul if he would help him finish the bridge. The builder, however, panicked and to delay the completion of the bridge, gave the devil a sieve to collect the last bucket of sand. The devil admitted defeat and the builder laid the final brick. But, the devil came back every night to knock out the corner stones at the top of the bridge's central tower. The bridge was finally completed after a restoration project by Paul Gout in 1879.

Breathtaking view of boats awaiting travellers at the dock, Luzech

⑬ Château de Bonaguil

Most fortified castle in France

Known as France's most magnificent folly, the Château de Bonaguil was begun in the 13th century, but was extensively fortified by the mighty Bérenguer de Roquefeuil (1444–1530), an infamous hunchbacked tyrant. He dedicated over 30 years of his life to building further towers, along with a bunker and no less than seven drawbridges. Further sections were added over the centuries. The castle eventually fell into disrepair and was sold in the 18th century for just 100 francs and a sack of walnuts. Since 1862,

The Lowdown

- 🌐 **Map reference** 12 E2
  Address 47500 (Lot-et-Garonne). Château de Bonaguil: 47500 St-Front-sur-Lémance; 05 53 71 90 33; www.bonaguil.org
- 🚃 **Train** from Bordeaux and Paris to Agen, then a 70-min taxi ride
- ℹ️ **Visitor information** Pl Georges Escande, 47500 Fumel; 05 53 71 13 70; www.tourisme-fumelois.htm
- 🕐 **Open** Mar–Oct: daily; Nov–Feb: daily, school hols pm only
- 💲 **Price** €22–32; under 6s free
- 🍽️ **Eat and drink** *Picnic* Marché du Dimanche (*Rue de la Republique, 47500*) is superb for picking up fresh produce. Picnic at the château. *Family treat* Villa Margaux (*1 Pl du Chateau, 47500; 05 53 75 15 70; www.lavilla margaux.fr*) offers award-winning French dining in a contemporary setting. It serves local produce; the praline lemon sorbet cacao is highly recommended.

however, it has been classified as a national monument and has undergone extensive restoration. During this process, graffiti from the Middle Ages was discovered. It is a fascinating insight into old France, illustrating the evolution of defence techniques between the Middle Ages and the Renaissance.

Letting off steam

Canoes can be hired from a number of places in the town of Fumel and the nearby towns of Puy l'Eveque and **Luzech**. Hire them by the hour or book a guided tour.

⑭ Villeréal

Bustling market and a leper's house

Dating back to the 13th century, this small town was originally founded by Alphonse de Poitiers as a *bastide* town, one of the hundreds of new

Above *Horse-riding through the lush green countryside near Villeréal*
Below *The Château de Bonaguil*

The Lowdown

- 🌐 **Map reference** 12 E2
  Address 47210 (Lot-et-Garonne).
- 🚃 **Train** from Bordeaux to Bergerac, then a 45-min taxi ride
- ℹ️ **Visitor information** Pl de la Halle, 47210; 05 53 36 09 65; www.villereal-tourisme.com
- 🍽️ **Eat and drink** *Real meal* Le Montecristo (*Bois de Madame, 47210 Bournel; 05 53 36 65 78*) is very family orientated and specializes in pizzas. It also has a kids' outdoor playground. *Family treat* La Dolce Vita (*31 Rue du Dropt, 47210; 05 53 71 64 02*) is a more expensive option offering a contemporary twist to local dishes, along with a range of tempting desserts.

towns built in the 13th and 14th centuries in a bid to colonize southwest France. On Saturdays, the town's original 14th-century market hall springs to life with local tradesmen selling their wares. People from far and near have flocked to this town market for over 700 years.

A guided walk leaflet is available from the tourist office that takes in the town's back streets, including the Leper's House – a refuge in medieval times for those suffering from leprosy – with its ornate sculpted door and the old station. Some town houses date back to the 16th century.

Letting off steam

Saddle up and see the countryside on horseback with **Les Ecuries de Lamouthe** (*www.ecuries-de-la mouthe.com*), located in the village of Mazières-Naresse 4 km (2 miles)

Plants for sale at the 14th-century market hall in Villeréal

west of Villeréal. This equestrian centre offers riding lessons for all levels and smaller ponies suitable for kids aged 6 plus.

⑮ Latour-Marliac
Monet's water lillies

This water lily nursery was founded in 1875 by lawyer Joseph Bory Latour-Marliac. Latour-Marliac's passion was plants and he devoted all his spare time to growing tropical plants in his purpose-built greenhouse. This led to him crossbreeding water lilies with other wild varieties of plants and exhibiting his results at the World Fair in Paris. Claude

The Lowdown

🌐 **Map reference** 12 E2
Address 47110 (Lot-et-Garonne). Latour-Marliac: Le Bourg, 47110 Le Temple-sur-Lot; 05 53 01 08 05; www.latour-marliac.com

🚗 **Car** (own transport required)

ℹ️ **Visitor information** Pl des Templiers, 47110; 05 53 01 08 04

🕒 **Open** Botanical gardens: May–mid-Oct. Nursery and gardens: mid-Mar–Oct: Tue–Sun

💶 **Price** €24–34; under 15s free

🍽️ **Eat and drink** *Picnic* Le Temple-sur-Lot has a Sunday morning market *(Pl Templiers, 47110; Jul–Aug)*. Picnic in the Latour-Marliac. *Real Meal* Café Marliacea *(Le Bourg, 47110; 05 53 01 08 05)* in the Jardin Botanique, is good for a snack. The restaurant offers regional fare; includes a kids' menu.

Monet, the renowned French Impressionist painter saw the exhibit and became captivated with water lilies. Monet made a pond in his garden home in the village of Giverny and ordered his plants directly from Latour-Marliac. It was these plants that would become the subject of Monet's famous water lily paintings.

Water lilies in full bloom in the nursery at Latour-Marliac

Letting off steam
At Latour-Marliac there are acres of open spaces to explore, with lawns, gardens, ponds and bridges. Or visit the colourful town of Damazan, which is located 27 km (17 miles) west of Latour-Marliac. Damazan is a good example of an "arcaded bastide" where residents are required by law to keep the façades of the buildings brightly coloured. For a fun evening, visit on a Tuesday (July and August) around 7pm when the night market is set up. Local families bring their own crockery, cutlery and glasses, buy local treats from market stalls and enjoy an open-air picnic with plenty of singing and dancing.

⑯ Albi

Lively carnivals and fabulous art

Albi is a vibrant city, rich in cultural heritage. It survived two world wars relatively unscathed, so many of its magnificent historical buildings remain intact. It is also the birthplace of Henri de Toulouse-Lautrec (1864–1901), the popular French artist best known for his paintings of *belle époque* cancan dancers; his works are on display in the 13th-century Palais de la Berbie – an artistic treat in the middle of this lively city.

Toulouse-Lautrec-inspired street art

Key Sights

② Le Vieil Albi
A pedestrianized area in the city centre, Le Vieil Albi has perfectly preserved buildings made of distinctive red bricks, built from red sands found in the Tarn river.

④ Musée Toulouse-Lautrec
The largest public collection of the work of Henri de Toulouse-Lautrec includes horses, cancan dancers and his trademark posters, housed in an impressive medieval palace.

③ Cathédrale Ste-Cécile
Looking like a mix of a fortress and an old power station, Albi's pink cathedral has parts dating to 1282 and a chunky 78-m (256-ft) belfry.

① Hôtel du Bosc
The privately-owned Hôtel du Bosc is where Toulouse-Lautrec was born. A commemorative plaque hangs on the wall.

⑤ Jardin du Palais de la Berbie These fabulous gardens were originally planted during the Renaissance. It is no wonder this area of the city has been added to the list of UNESCO World Heritage Sites.

⑥ Marché Couvert Opened at the turn of the 20th century, the market hall gives visitors a chance to experience French market life on a larger scale than most towns and villages.

⑦ Vieux Pont Originally built in AD 1035 from stone and clad with bricks, this bridge is still in use after almost a millennium.

⑧ Musée Lapérouse This museum depicts the life and travels of French naval officer Jean-François de Galaup Lapérouse, who led an expedition around the globe.

The Lowdown

🌐 **Map reference** 12 G3
Address 81000 (Tarn). Hôtel du Bosc: 14 Rue Toulouse-Lautrec Cathédrale Ste-Cécile: Pl Ste-Cécile. Musée Toulouse-Lautrec: Palais de la Berbie, Pl Ste-Cécile; *www.museetoulouselautrec.net*. Jardin du Palais de la Berbie: Pl Ste-Cécile; 05 63 49 72 42; Musée Lapérouse: 41 Rue Porta; *www.laperousefrance.fr*.

🚗 **Train** from Toulouse

ℹ️ **Visitor information** Pl Ste-Cécile, 81000; 05 63 36 36 00; *www.albi-tourisme.fr*

🕑 **Open** Musée Toulouse-Lautrec: closed for renovation. Musée Lapérouse: Mar–Jun: 9am–6pm, closed Mon; Jul–Aug: 9am–6pm daily; Sep–Oct: 9am–6pm, closed Mon; Nov–Feb: 10am–5pm, closed Mon; year round: closed noon–2pm

💶 **Price** Musée Lapérouse: €6–12; under 12s free

👪 **Skipping the queue** Pick up the Albi Pass for €6.50 or Junior Pass for €1.50 from the tourist office. It is valid for a guided tour of the Cathédrale Ste-Cécile and offers 20–40 per cent discount at other city attractions.

🚩 **Guided tours** Visit *www.albivisit.com* for walking tours. There are themed visits for kids in summer.

👫 **Age range** All ages

⏱️ **Allow** A day

🚻 **Toilets** Behind the cathedral, at Rue de Verdusse and inside the covered market, as well as the Gare de la Madeleine

🎊 **Festival** Carnaval d'Albi, with floats, music, parades (Feb–Mar)

Good family value?
There is plenty for everyone to do and some of the attractions are free. Families will enjoy it here.

Steps through Albi's historic centre, with Ste-Cécile in the background

Letting off steam

Take bus A from the city centre to go to **Espace Nautique Atlantis** *(Rue Pierre Brossolette, 81000; www. grand-albigeois.fr)* just north of Albi's centre. Kids will enjoy rollicking in its indoor and outdoor pools and slides.

Eat and drink

Picnic: under €20; Snacks: €20–45; Real meal: €45–90; Family treat: over €90 (based on a family of four)

PICNIC Place Marché Couvert is the place to pick up fresh supplies. Picnic at the grassy areas along the river.
SNACKS Le Solelhou *(13 Rue Plancat, 81000)* serves light food, including tasty tarts and quiches.
REAL MEAL Le Papillon *(1 bis Rue Henri de Toulouse-Lautrec, 81000; 05 63 43 10 77)* offers contemporary dishes, including vegetarian options drawn from California and Asia.
FAMILY TREAT Le Vieil Alby *(25 Rue Toulouse-Lautrec, 81000; 05 63 54 14 69)* is a nice little hotel located in the historic centre of Albi.

Tarts and other pastries on sale in the local market

It serves a range of traditional dishes that represent the best of the region.

Shopping

The main shopping area is east of the Cathédrale Ste-Cécile. Here there is a wide range of boutiques, antique shops and gift vendors. Kids will enjoy the souvenirs available at every turn. On a Saturday morning, visit the local flea market that takes place in the **Halle du Castelviel** *(Pl du Castelviel, 81000)*. There is lots of fun to be had rummaging for bargains.

Find out more

DIGITAL Log on to *www.lautrec.info* for the great French artist's life and works. Scroll through images of Lautrec's complete works at *www. toulouse-lautrec-foundation.org*.

Take cover

On a rainy day, head to the **Château du Bosc** *(www.aveyron.com/english/ tourism/boscUK.html)* in the village of Camjac, 41 km (25 miles) north of Albi. This was the summer home of Toulouse-Lautrec and his family. This is where the artist spent most of his childhood and also where he sustained the injuries that resulted in his stunted growth and the limited use of his legs. Guided tours of the château are available on a daily basis.

Houses of the town of Cordes-sur-Ciel climbing skywards up the hilltop

Next stop...

CORDES-SUR-CIEL Standing high on an isolated hilltop, 24 km (15 miles) west of Albi, is the town of Cordes-sur-Ciel. In spring and autumn, its rooftops glisten in the sunlight, while the low cloud and mist in the valley below shows it is floating. There is lots to do in this town for families – from annual medieval festivals to a visit to the Historama museum, which has over 80 life-sized waxworks.

KIDS' CORNER

Who was Henri de Toulouse-Lautrec?
The young Henri first started to show his true artistic talents at the tender age of 8 years. As a teenager, he suffered many accidents and illnesses that left him unable to compete in sports, so he threw himself further into his artwork. Although he died at only 36, he is one of France's most renowned and celebrated artists. In 2005, one of his paintings set a new record at Christie's auction house when it sold for a colossal €16 million!

PEACE OFFERINGS
To show his peaceful intentions, the French explorer Lapérouse took the following items with him to give to people he would meet en route as he sailed around the world: 600 mirrors, 2,600 combs and 50,000 sewing needles!

Vanished into thin air...
Lapérouse set sail on 1 August 1785, intending to return to France four years later. His two ships, *La Boussole* and *L'Astrolabe*, made good progress, going around Cape Horn, entering the Pacific in January 1786. The next year saw him visit Chile, Easter Island and Maui in the Hawaiian Islands. He sailed along the Asian coastline sending notes of the journey to King Louis XVI. The ships docked in Botany Bay in Australia and continued sailing on 10 March 1788. Soon after, the ships and crew vanished. What happened to them? Find out at the Musée Laperouse.

⑰ Toulouse
Space craft and pink houses

Toulouse is known as one of the "three pink cities" in the region – the other two being Montauban and Albi. This thriving red-bricked city has a significant part of its modern-day industry based around space technology. A visit to the **Cité de l'Espace** provides a fascinating insight into the mysteries of space via shows, interactive exhibitions and guided tours.

Toulouse is also considered to be the rugby capital of France so visitors are guaranteed an electric atmosphere when any of the major championship matches are being played at the Stadium Municipal de Toulouse located on the Île du Ramier, south of Toulouse. On the island, visitors will also find the Parc du Ramier with walking trails and cycle paths. Away from the bustling city centre, the park is a peaceful haven for nature lovers. Toulouse offers an impressive collection of museums. Visit the **Musée des Augustins de Toulouse**, housed in a stunning Gothic building dating from the 14th century, with a vast collection of medieval art.

The European rocket launcher Ariane 5 and other exhibits, Cité de l'Espace

A bronze statue of the legendary king's musketeer D'Artagnan, Auch

Letting off steam

Relax and run about in the **Jardin des Plantes** (Allée Frédéric Mistral, Allée Jules-Guesde, 31000), a public park and botanical garden.

⑱ Auch
One for all and all for one

The historical capital of Gascony, Auch is rich in local heritage. The old town is fascinating to explore on foot and a visit to the **Cathédrale Ste-Marie**, started some time in the 15th century and completed over two centuries, is a must. Climb over 200 steps to the top of the Escalier Monumental and be rewarded with spectacular views over the Gers valley. On the way down, be sure to nod respectfully to the statue of D'Artagnan, the legendary swordsman and king's musketeer. Born 45 km (28 miles) west of Auch in Lupiac in 1611, D'Artagnan captured the public's imagination in Alexandre Dumas' 1844 novel *The Three Musketeers*, an exciting

The Lowdown

🌐 **Map reference** 12 E4
Address 32000 (Gers). Cathédrale Ste-Marie: Rue Arnaud de Moles; 06 30 41 19 38

🚃 **Train** from Toulouse or from Bordeaux to Agen, then bus

ℹ️ **Visitor information** 1 Rue Dessoles, BP 174, 32003; 05 62 05 22 89; www.auch-tourisme.com

🍽️ **Eat and drink** *Snacks* Bistrot des Gourmandises (8 Rue de la Marne, 32000; 05 62 05 10 79) offers a very affordable three-course lunch menu. Arrive early for a table *Real meal* Le Daroles (4 Pl Libération, 32000; 05 62 05 00 51) serves tasty steaks and duck, the regional speciality.

🎭 **Festival** Eclat de Voix, singing festival (Jun)

fictionalized story of the life and adventures of Louis XIII's musketeers based on local folklore around the exploits of the real D'Artagnan.

Letting off steam

Picnic in the **Jardin Ortholan** (Quai Lissagaray, 32000) or the **Parc de Coulome** (5 Pl de la Libération, 32000). Down by the river, explore a 4-km (2-mile) discovery trail that winds its way along the riverbank.

⑲ Condom
Castles and brandy

Condom is an ancient town with its first recorded inhabitants dating back to before the Roman conquest in 27 BC. The town sits on the banks of the Baise river and is home to two 13th-century castles: the Château de Mothes and the Château de Puypardin, with its intact keep (the castle's tower and most fortified section), as well as two watermills. During the Middle Ages, Condom was an important religious centre, housing over 130 churches due to its position on the famous pilgrim route to Santiago de Compostela (see p244), ending in northwest Spain.

The town is also known as Condom-en-Armagnac. The **Musée de l'Armagnac** celebrates France's oldest distilled brandy. On display is a 17th-century frame with an 18-ton (16-tonne) wine press. More than 1,000 years ago, it was the pilgrims travelling through the town who would load up with bottles

The Lowdown

🌐 **Map reference** 12 F4
Address 31000 (Haute-Garonne). Cité de l'Espace: Ave Jean Gonord, 31506; 08 20 37 72 33; www.cite-espace.com. Musée des Augustins de Toulouse: 21 Rue de Metz, 31000; 05 61 22 21 82; www.augustins.org

🚃 **Train** from Paris and Bordeaux

ℹ️ **Visitor information** Square du General Charles de Gaulle, 31080; 08 92 18 01 80; www.toulouse-tourisme.com

🕐 **Open** Cité de l'Espace: Sep–Mar: Tue–Sun; Apr–Aug: daily; closed Jan. Musée des Augustins de Toulouse: 10am–6pm daily

🍽️ **Eat and drink** *Snacks* ZePléGraounde (20 Pl Occitane, 31000; 05 62 30 11 80; www.ze plegraounde.fr) serves home-made food with fresh juices. *Real meal* Eau de Folles (14 Allée du President Roosevelt, 31000; 05 61 23 45 50), one of the most family-friendly restaurants, offers ten choices of starters, main course and desserts.

🎭 **Festivals** C'est de la Danse Contempororaine celebrates the art of choreography (Jan). Festival International de Théâtre d'Enfants (Jun). Christmas Market held on the Place du Capitole (Dec)

The Grands Moulins de Condom, one of two mills overlooking the Baïse river

The Lowdown

🌐 **Map reference** 11 D3
Address 32100 (Gers).
Musee de l'Armagnac: 2 Rue
Jules Ferry; 05 62 28 47 17

🚆 **Train** from Bordeaux to Agen,
then a bus or taxi

ℹ️ **Visitor information** 50 Blvd
de la Libération, 32100; 05 62
28 00 80; www.tourisme-
tenareze.com

🕐 **Open** Musee de l'Armagnac:
Apr–Oct: Wed–Mon; Nov–Dec:
Wed–Sun; closed Jan. Guided
tours on request via the tourist
office (www.condom.org/index.
php/musee-de-larmagnac)

🍴 **Eat and drink** *Real meal* L'Origan
(4 Rue Cadeot, 32100) offers
an affordable menu and great
pizzas. *Family treat* La Table des
Cordeliers (1 Rue des Cordeliers,
32100; 05 62 68 43 82) has an
impressive menu with lots of
regional specialities.

🎪 **Festival** Festival de Bandas
y Penas, orchestras and brass
bands (May)

of Armagnac and export them
all over Spain as they continued
on their journey.

Letting off steam

Go to Condom's central **Parc de la
Gauge** (Chemin Argente, 32100),
where younger kids can play in the
large playground and families can
picnic along the river bank.

⑳ Larressingle

**Good things come in small
walled villages**

The boundaries of this picturesque
tiny village, which is the smallest
walled village in France, consists
of a 300-m (984-ft) circle of heavily
fortified 13th-century walls. It can

only be entered by crossing a moat
via a pretty little bridge and then
continuing through the village's only
gate. The village museum depicts the
life of the locals in the Middle Ages,
but to really fuel the imagination,
pay a visit to the exhibition of
medieval weaponry on display just
outside the village walls, at the **Cité
des Machines du Moyen-Age**. Here
a 13th-century siege camp has been
re-created complete with battering
rams and medieval armoury, making
it easy to go back in time and
imagine what life must have been
like while the village was under
siege centuries ago.

Letting off steam

Kids can run around the grassy areas
just outside the village walls. There
are also benches ideal for a picnic.

The Lowdown

🌐 **Map reference** 11 D3
Address 32100 (Gers).
Cité des Machines du Moyen-
Age: Camp de Siège Médiéval,
La Cité des Machines; 05 62 68
33 88

🚆 **Train** to Agen, then an hour's taxi

ℹ️ **Visitor information** Communauté
de Communes de al Tenarèze,
32100; 05 62 68 22 49; www.
tourisme-tenarze.com

🕐 **Open** Cité des Machines du
Moyen-Age: Jul & Aug: daily;
rest of the year pm only

€ **Price** €23–33 (see *larressingle.
free.fr* for details)

🍴 **Eat and drink** *Picnic* Marché
de Condom (Wed & Sat am)
has freshly baked breads, local
cheeses and delicacies on
sale. Picnic in the grassy area
outside the village's walls. *Snacks*
Larressingle Creperie (Château de
Larressingle, 32100; 05 62 68 48
93) serves a wide range of crêpes.

Where to Stay in Périgord, Quercy and Gascony

From child-friendly *gîte* complexes, traditional hotels and modern B&Bs to eco yurts, log cabins and tents, Périgord, Quercy and Gascony offer a wide range of accommodation options to families. Enjoy a taste of rural hospitality, sample a little luxury or experience the latest trend in glamping.

AGENCIES

Tots to Travel
www.totstotravel.co.uk
The website specializes in lodging for young families. There is a wide selection ranging from *gîte* complexes to rural farmhouses.

Gites de France du Gers
www.gers-gites-france.com
The official tourism website for *gîtes* in Gers lists family-friendly accommodation in Gascony.

Albi
Map 12 G3

HOTEL
Hotel du Parc
3 Park Ave, 81000; 05 63 54 12 80; www.hotel-du-parc-albi.com
Located in the heart of the city, this hotel is an affordable base for exploring the main attractions of Albi. Although the furnishings are basic, the facilities are clean and there is a small bar and restaurant. Ideal for a short stay. Friendly staff.
 €

CAMPING
Albirondack Park Camping Lodge et Spa
1 Allee de la Piscine, 81000; 05 65 60 37 06; www.albirondack.fr
Just 2 km (1 mile) from the centre of Albi, a riverside trail leads directly from this camp ground into the city centre. The site is modern and

Interior of the Albirondack Park Camping Lodge et Spa, Albi

luxurious, with a choice of chalets, wooden lodges or serviced pitches. A heated pool, kids' club and organized activities run during the summer months, with a spa and cooking lessons for grown-ups.
 €

Belves
Map 12 E1

SELF-CATERING
Domaine de Peyrecaty
24170 Belves; 05 53 29 16 83; www.peyrecaty.com
Set on a 23-ha (56-acre) estate, this family-friendly property offers nine cottages, each sleeping between four and 12. Tennis courts, an adventure playground, a play barn, organized activities and babysitting service are also available.
 €€€

Bergerac
Map 11 D1

SELF-CATERING
Ecovallée Yurts
LD Coste Perie, 24150 Couze et St Front; 05 53 57 94 41; www.ecovallee.com
With a vast woodland to explore, animals to feed, eggs to collect and hammocks to snooze in, this property offers two 5-m (18-ft) tall yurts for weekly hire, each with a double and two single beds. An outdoor safari-style kitchen and a kids' play yurt complete the set-up. Baby and toddler supplies are available.
 €

Beynac
Map 12 E1

CAMPING
Camping le Capeyrou
24220 Beynac; 05 53 29 54 95; www.campinglecapeyrou.com
A stone's throw from the village with its cafés and restaurants, this camp site sits in the shadow of the

A spacious and elegantly decorated family room at Le Chatenet, Brantome

Château du Beynac. Families can pitch their own tent here or hire a luxury tent or mobile home. There are two pools and a large play area on site, with access to the nearby beach, where bicycles, canoes and kayaks are available for hire. The perfect base for exploring the region's most famous châteaux
P ☻ €

Brantôme
Map 8 E6

HOTEL
Le Chatenet
24310 Brantôme; 05 53 05 81 08; www.lechatenet.com
Originally built in the 17th century by Seigneur de Giry, this is a small but luxurious hotel, in a tranquil setting, and Brantôme's largest private estate. This magnificent manor house has fabulous gardens and an outdoor pool, as well as tennis and badminton courts.
P ☻ €€

Cabrerets
Map 12 F2

BED & BREAKFAST
Un Jardin dans la Falaise
46330 Cabrerets; 05 65 30 85 35; www.unjardindansfalaise.com
With breathtaking views over the Célé valley below, this small and charming B&B is located in the

historical village of Cabrerets. It offers three rooms, including a family suite with its own small kitchen area. Ideal for exploring the Lot, including Cahors and the painted caves of Pech Merle.

 P   €

Cahors
Map 12 F2

HOTEL
Hotel de la Paix
30 Pl St Maurice, 46000; 05 65 35 03 40; www.hoteldelapaixcahors.com
Located off the market square, this Art Deco hotel has a prime location in the heart of Cahors' old town. It has been fully renovated and has 17 rooms, including four family suites. The staff is friendly, organizing tours and activities on request.

     €

Catus
Map 12 F2

SELF-CATERING
Pagel Holidays
46150 Catus; 05 61 21 69 19; www.pagel-france.com
A 20-minute drive from the medieval town of Cahors, Pagel offers child-centred holidays, exclusively for families with children aged under 10, in three painstakingly restored cottages in a tranquil setting. There are acres of woodland to explore, an Indian village complete with totem pole and wigwams, a pirate ship, a heated swimming pool and a play barn full of toys and dressing-up gear.

 P ✪   €€

Clermont-Pouyguilles
Map 11 D4

SELF-CATERING
Domaine la Douce   32300
Clermont-Pouyguilles; 05 62 61 88 92; www.domaineladouce france.nl
These luxurious safari tents stand on raised platforms, complete with large terraces for fine views of the extensive privately owned woodland. The furnishings are high-end and each tent has electricity and a fully equipped kitchen, as well as a bathroom. Forest trails, swimming pool, play area and lakes for fishing make it a superb base for a family holiday. Picnic baskets are available on request.

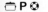 P ✪   €€

Duravel
Map 12 E2

CAMPING
Club de Vacances Duravel
Route de Vire, 46700; 05 65 24 65 06; www.clubdevacances.eu
This four-star camp site, on the banks of the Lot river, has a wide range of accommodation options, including pitches, mobile homes, tents and chalets. In summer, there are kids' clubs for ages 4–12 with daily activities, and cabaret shows for the whole family in the evening. There are swimming pools, water slides, a playground, football pitch and volleyball court on site, along with a bar and restaurant.

P ✪   €

Exterior of the beautiful Hostellerie La Roseraie, Montignac

Mirepoix
Map 12 F5

CAMPING
Belrepayre Airstream & Retro Trailer Park
09500 Manses; 05 61 68 11 99; www.airstreameurope.com
Guests can pitch their own tent or take their pick from a fleet of vintage Airstream American Trailers at this scenic camp site. The on-site diner is a converted Airstream, serving up tapas, grills and milk shakes. For grown-ups, there is a spa area, with hot tub for a little R&R.

 P   €

Montignac
Map 12 E1

HOTEL
Hostellerie La Roseraie
24290 Montignac; 05 53 50 53 92; www.laroseraie-hotel.com
Located on the riverside in the heart of Montignac, this is a completely

refurbished 19th-century mansion hotel. The large grounds have an outdoor swimming pool, a rose garden and terrace overlooking the river. There is an excellent restaurant, and babysitting service is offered; packed lunches on request.

P ✪   €€€

SELF-CATERING
Le Four à Sel
Le Port d'Aubas, 24290 Aubas; 05 53 51 39 87; www.lefourasel.com
Located 2 km (1 mile) outside the village, this is a group of three holiday homes set in vast private grounds. They vary in size and can accommodate groups ranging from two to 30 people. A playground and a covered play area for kids make it an ideal base for families.

P ✪   €

BED & BREAKFAST
Le Hameau Du Moulin
Chemin de Gourny, 24291 Montignac; www.le-hameau-moulin-montignac. federal-hotel.com
Situated on the outskirts of Montignac, this B&B is in a prime location for exploring Lascaux II and the surrounding area. It is child-friendly with a choice of family rooms in the main building or fully serviced maisonettes in the grounds. There is also a BBQ area and two heated outdoor pools.

P ✪   €€

Montcabrier
Map 6 C5

SELF-CATERING
Domaine de la Dolce
46700 Montcabrier; 05 65 31 62 90; www.domainedeladolce.com
Three family-friendly *gîtes* set in the rolling countryside. Each cottage is single storey and equipped with baby and toddler essentials such as highchairs, sterilizers and bouncy chairs. There is a heated swimming pool, shaded playground and a play cottage full of toys and books. Guided trips, parent pamper sessions and babysitting available.

P ✪   €€

Price Guide
The following price ranges are based on one night's accommodation in high season for a family of four, inclusive of service charges and any additional taxes.
€ Under €100 €€ €100–200 €€€ over €200

Key to symbols *see back cover flap*

Rustic Domaine de la Rhue, Rocamadour

Padirac
Map 12 F1

CAMPING
Les Chenes
*46500 Padirac; 05 65 33 65 54;
www.campingleschenes.com*
This is a large, family-oriented camp site with its own aquatic park. There is organized entertainment in high season. Bar, restaurant and pizzeria on site.

P ☉ €

Rocamadour
Map 12 F1

HOTEL
Domaine de la Rhue
*46500 Rocamadour; 05 65 33 71 50;
www.domainedelarhue.com*
Set in the Parc Naturel Régional des Causses du Quercy, this is a charming hotel with 14 rooms in a renovated stable block. Several options are available for family accomodation, including adjoining rooms, with kitchenettes and terraces.

🐾 🍴 P €€

BED & BREAKFAST
La Noyeraie
*46500 Rocamadour; 05 65 40 43 91;
www.lanoyeraierocamadour.com*
This beautiful B&B offers a choice of suites for families and a separate apartment sleeping four. Parquet floors, chandeliers and breathtaking views of the walnut orchards, make it a superb choice. The terrace café serves up a delicious walnut cake. Friendly owners; pets are welcomed.

🐾 🍴 P €€

Sarlat
Map 12 F1

BED & BREAKFAST
La Barde
*Montfort, 24200 Vitrac; 05 53 28
24 34; www.perigord-dordogne-sarlat.com*
Located 3 km (2 miles) from the bustling medieval town of Sarlat, this is a small, traditional B&B. There are four double or triple bedrooms and a family suite with two bedrooms. Games, a billiards table and a BBQ area are provided. Highchairs and cots are available on request.

🐾 P ☉ €€

CAMPING
Campsite Aqua Viva
*24200 Carsac-Aillac, 553 314 600,
www.campings.village-center.com*
This lakeside camp site offers pitches, eco-lodge tents and mobile homes, with kids' clubs for ages 4–17 years in summer. A small paddling pool with water slides provide outdoor fun, along with a play area and mini-golf. In high season, there is a shop, snack bar and restaurant on site. Bicycles are available for hire.

P ☉ €

St-Amand-de-Coly
Map 12 F1

CAMPING
Lascaux Vacances Camping
*24290 Yelloh Village; 04 66 73
97 39; www.yellohvillage.co.uk*
A family-oriented wooded camp site, it offers pitches, chalewts, log cabins and tents. There are plenty of leisure activities on site, including a volleyball court. In summer there are clubs for kids aged 5–17 years. Nearby are Lascaux II and outdoor activities such as horse-riding.

P ☉ €

St-Cirq-Lapopie
Map 12 F2

CAMPING
Camping de la Plage
*46330 St-Cirq-Lapopie; 05 65 30
29 51; www.campingplage.com*
In a stunning location beside the Lot river, in the shadow of one of France's most beautiful villages, this is a basic camp site. There are 98 pitches for tents, caravans and motor homes. Fishing lessons, kayaking trips, hiking trails and team sports are available.

P €

St-Jean-Poutge
Map 12 D3

BED & BREAKFAST
Château de Plehaut
*32190 St-Jean-Poutge; 05 62 64
68 06; www.chateaudeplehaut.co.uk*
Set in 5 ha (12 acres), this château provides two B&B options. Guests can stay in the main house or in the cottage by the pool. There is a family suite with adjoining bedrooms. Fishing on site.

🐾 🍴 P ☉ €€

Thégra
Map 12 F1

HOTEL
Hotel Restaurant Giscard
*46500 Thegra; 05 65 38 77 31;
www.hotel-giscard.com*
This small and traditional hotel, set in the medieval village of Thégra between Padirac and Rocamadour, offers spacious rooms and family suites. There is a superb restaurant serving regional dishes.

🐾 P ☉ €

Toulouse
Map 12 F4

HOTEL
Citadines Wilson Toulouse
*8 Blvd de Strasbourg, 31000; 05 34
41 75 00; www.citadines.com/en/
france/toulouse/wilson.html*
This clean and modern city-centre apartment-hotel offers studios and larger apartments with bathrooms and kitchens ideal for families. Cots and highchairs are available on request, and breakfast is included.

🐾 🍴 ❋ €€

Varen
Map 12 G3

CAMPING
Le Camp
*Arnac, 82330; 06 11 94 33 68;
www.lecamp.co.uk*
A small, stylish, family-run camp site, it offers fully equipped luxurious tents and yurts, which are elevated on wooden platforms, with panoramic views of the surrounding countryside. There is woodland to explore and a natural swimming pond.

🍴 P ☉ €€€

Poitou and Aquitaine

South of the Loire, this fertile Atlantic region of gentle hills and rivers starts in the north with the waterways of the Marais Poitevin and ends in the south with the sandy beaches and pine forests of Les Landes. While La Rochelle and Bordeaux are packed with history, Futuroscope offers a high-tech wonderland. Seaside resorts and camp sites line the coasts.

Below *The 15th-century Porte Cailhau with its fairy-tale belltower, Bordeaux*

① Futuroscope
Play with the future

Futuroscope makes the future fun. Dedicated to exploring current techniques in media, it offers 30 experiences that illuminate the world's past, present and future using the latest multimedia imagery, from IMAX and Omnimax to augmented reality and 4D rides. Now France's second-largest theme park, Futuroscope is a magnet for upcoming technological innovations; half the experiences in this unique park change every two years.

The double IMAX Travellers by Air and by Sea theatre

Key Features

Travellers by Air and by Sea

Entrance   Children's World

④ **Dynamic Vienne** Tour the villages and landscapes of the area around Futuroscope in a speeding train, hang-glider and Formula 3 car.

⑤ **The 8th Continent** Help scientists ride the ocean of trash on virtual scooters and shooting laser pistols in this life-sized video game.

⑥ **Arthur, the 4D Adventure** Don 3D glasses, hop in a "Ladybuggy" and go on a wild ride in an adventure created by film director Luc Besson.

⑦ **Dances with Robots** Hop on to ten, 7 m (23 ft) robots, while they do a breathtaking boogie woogie.

⑧ **Le Petit Prince** Inspired by Antoine de St-Exupéry's famous story, this 3D adventure uses special effects, such as mists and tickles, to make the on-screen action more life-like.

① **The Future is Wild** Take an augmented reality safari, with special binoculars and a sensor bracelet to stroke, feed and play with animals – 500 million years from now.

② **Cosmic Collisions** Made with the aid of NASA satellite images and narrated by Robert Redford, this film puts visitors in the chaotic centre of intergalactic space.

③ **Blue Note Mystery** This outdoor theatre hosts a 30-minute musical fairy-tale spectacle projected on water screens, dancing jets of fire and laser lights.

Prices given are for a family of four

The Lowdown

🌐 **Map reference** 7 D4
Address 86000 (Vienne). Blvd Léonard de Vinci, 86360 Chasseneuil-du-Poitou; 05 49 49 59 06; www.futuroscope.com

🚗 **Train** TGV from Paris to Futuroscope's own station. **Bus** 9 from Poitiers

🕐 **Open** Mar–Aug: daily. For other months, check website for details. The park opens at 10am and closes at dusk. The evening show starts 30 mins before the park closes.

€ **Price** One-day pass (includes evening show): €122–132; under 5s free; a two consecutive days pass: €226–236; evening tickets (summer) €54–64; under 5s free

👫 **Skipping the queue** Book tickets and packages online, including stay in one of the family-oriented chain hotels within a 10-minute walk of the entrance. Pick up the day's schedule of shows and start with the furthest and less crowded attractions. In July and August, arrive early to get a seat for the evening show.

🚩 **Guided tours** Spiral up the Gyrotour, a 45-m (150-ft) high shaft, for a 360° view of the park, with a commentary.

👫 **Age range** 2 plus; pushchairs available. Some rides have a minimum height restriction of 1 m (3 ft) or 1.2 m (4 ft).

⏱ **Allow** At least a day or, even better, two to see and do everything

☕ **Café** Inside the park (see p283)

🚻 **Toilets** Many inside the park

Good family value?
Futuroscope is great for kids, but expensive and there can be long queues in the summer.

Kids enjoying thrilling boat slides at Children's World

Letting off steam

Futuroscope's **Children's World** is ideal for 12-year-olds and younger, with boat slides, flying seats that are suspended on parachutes, cars to drive through the city of the future, foam ball fights and more. While some rides are suited for tots, some are for kids aged 8 plus with adult supervision. Head to the **Lac de St-Cyr** (www.lacdesaintcyr.com), a 10-minute drive north of the park, for calmer swims in a large lake, mountain bikes and kayaks.

Eat and drink

Picnic: under €20; Snacks: €20–45; Real meal: €45–90; Family treat: over €90 (based on a family of four)

PICNIC Supermarché Auchan (on the D3, 86360 Chasseneuil-du-Poitou), less than 2 km (1 mile) from the park, stocks ingredients for picnics. Picnic inside Futuroscope in the covered area; buy a good supply of water.

SNACKS Illico Resto (on site) is a snack bar that offers a wide choice of sandwiches, tortilla wraps, salads, crêpes, waffles, ice cream and drinks throughout the day. There are 10 outlets in the park.

Motorbikes on display in the Musée Auto Moto Vélo, Châtellerault

REAL MEAL La Crêpe Volante (on site), one of the seven restaurants in the park, specializes in crêpes with a flying saucer theme. There are salads and grilled meats on offer. Try **Comptoir du monde** (on site) for a wide choice of world cuisine.

FAMILY TREAT Le Cristal (on site, by lake; Apr–Jun: Sat & Sun; Jul & Aug: closed Mon) serves some colourful and often surprisingly good food of the future, overseen by Hervé This, a physical chemist and one of the fathers of molecular cuisine; kids are catered for as well. Book well in advance to dine here.

Shopping

There are eight gift shops in the park selling a variety of clothing, toys, games, souvenirs, books, fashion accessories, gadgets and a range of regional delicacies.

Outdoor seating at La Crêpe Volante, "the flying pancake"

Find out more

DIGITAL Go to www.lesanimaux dufutur.com to experiment with augmented reality at home.

Next stop...

A MUSEUM AND A CHÂTEAU
Take Vitalis bus 1 or E to the town of Châtellerault to see the Pont Henri IV, built in 1609, with its fairy-tale towers and the **Musée Auto Moto Vélo** (3 Rue Clément Krebs, 86100; tinyurl. com/4x7zdkr; closed Mon & Tue), which has bicycles, cars and engines dating back to 1818. From the town of Châtellerault, bus 210 goes to the town of Scorbé-Clairvaux, where the 15th-century **Château de Clairvaux** (7 Pl de Montbron, 86140) has a park, orangerie and a chess museum, featuring 150 chess sets from 70 countries, including one so tiny that it fits inside a Fabergé egg.

② Poitiers

Troubadours and colourful churches

Poitiers was France's third-largest city in the Middle Ages, and famous as the seat of Eleanor of Aquitaine's Court of Love. Her palace, with its great hall where troubadours once sang, is now part of the **Palais du Justice**. Poitiers is most famous for its medieval churches. Check out the façade of the 11th–12th-century Notre-Dame-la-Grande whose sculptures were originally brightly coloured. On summer evenings, a spectacular show, *Polychromies*, "re-paints" the church's sculptures with lights. Inside, the columns are painted in myriad geometric shapes. The 12th-century Cathédrale St-Pierre in Grand Place, still has its original stained glass, while the 6th-century **Baptistère St-Jean** contains Merovingian tombs. The **Musée de Ste-Croix** houses curious Upper Palaeolithic engravings from a nearby cave, sculptures by Camille Claudel, Roman finds and medieval capitals.

Letting off steam

Play in the **Parc de Blossac** (*Rue de la Tranchée, 86000; 05 49 41 39 37*) with streams and bridges. Visit **Royal

Noah's Ark, an exquisite 12th-century wall painting, in the Abbaye de St-Savin

Kids (*www.royalkids.fr*), an indoor games park for kids (1–10 years) with ball pools and giant LEGO blocks.

③ Angles-sur-l'Anglin

The hidden treasure under Wizard's Rock

A ruined **château** perches on the cliffs above the pretty village of Angles-sur-l'Anglin. More intriguing, however, is the find made in 1922, of a 13,000-BC Magdalenian-era settlement at the base of a local cliff called the Roc aux Sorciers (Wizards' Rock). In 1947, archaeologist Suzanne de Saint-Mathurin came to investigate and found a stunning 20-m (65-ft) Magdalenian frieze of horses, bison, goats, lions and human figures in motion, dubbed as the "Lascaux of Sculpture". The original, still under the cliff, is inaccessible to the public, but the **Centre d'Interprétation du Roc-aux-Sorciers** has a life-sized cast and a multimedia spectacle that explains everything.

Letting off steam

Run in the **Jardin Public** (*Rue de Église, 86260*), located by the Église St-Martin. Take a taxi or drive west to **Chauvigny**, a medieval village, where Vélo-Rail (*www.velorail-chauvigny.fr*)

The Lowdown

🌐 **Map reference** 7 D4
Address 86000 (Vienne).
Palais du Justice: Pl Alphonse-Petit; 05 49 50 22 00. Baptistère St-Jean: Rue Jean-Jaurès. Musée de Ste-Croix: 3 bis Rue Jean-Jaurès; *www.musees-poitiers.org*

🚆 **Train** from Paris and La Rochelle

ℹ️ **Visitor information** 45 Pl Charles de Gaulle, 86000; 05 49 41 21 24; *www.ot-poitiers.fr*

🕑 **Open** Palais du Justice: Mon–Fri. Baptistère St-Jean: Apr–Sep: Wed–Mon; July & Aug: daily; Oct–Mar: Wed–Mon pm. Musée de Ste-Croix: Jun–Sep: daily, closed Mon; Oct–May: closed Mon & Tue, Sat & Sun am

🍴 **Eat and drink** *Snacks* L'Oasis des Saveurs (*78 Rue de la Cathédrale, 86000; www.oasis-des-saveurs. com; closed Sun & Mon*) serves tasty kebabs and Moroccan pastries. *Real meal* Les Bons Enfants (*11 bis Rue Cloche Perse, 86000; 05 49 41 49 82; closed Sun night & Mon*) offers some of the best food at reasonable prices. Best to book ahead.

The Lowdown

🌐 **Map reference** 8 E4
Address 86260 (Vienne). Centre d'Interprétation du Roc-aux-Sorciers: 2 Route des Certeaux; *www.roc-aux-sorciers.com*

🚌 **Bus** 10313R from Poitiers to Chauvigny, then taxi

ℹ️ **Visitor information** 2 Rue du Four Banal, 86260; 05 49 48 86 87; *www.anglessuranglin.com*

🕑 **Open** Château d'Angles-sur-l'Anglin: Jul & Aug: Wed–Mon; May & Sep: Sat & Sun pm. Centre d'Interprétation du Roc-aux-Sorciers: French school hols, public hols & Jul–Aug: daily; Apr–Nov: Wed–Sun; Nov–Mar: Sat & Sun; closed Jan

🍴 **Eat and drink** *Snacks* Le Marsala (*38 Rue du Pont, 86260; 05 49 48 65 44; www.lemarsala.fr; closed Mon & Tue and Wed lunch*) serves grilled meats, pizzas and home-made *frites*. *Family treat* Le Relais du Lyon d'Or (*4 Rue d'Enfer, 86260; 05 49 48 32 53, www.lyondor.com; closed mid-Nov–mid-Mar*) offers beautifully prepared dishes perfectly matching the fine wines.

offers two-hour excursions through pretty landscapes on pedal bicycles fitted on old train tracks.

④ St-Savin-sur-Gartempe

A 900-year-old comic strip

In the 8th century, during the reign of Charlemagne, the discovery here of the relics of the martyrs Savin and Cyprian prompted the construction of a chapel, which by the 11th century grew into the vast **Abbaye de St-Savin**. The abbey church is nothing less than the "Sistine Chapel

Impressive façade of Notre-Dame-la-Grande, Poitiers

The Lowdown

🌐 **Map reference** 8 E4
Address 86310 (Vienne). Abbaye
de St-Savin: 26 Pl de la Libération;
www.abbaye-saint-savin.fr

🚌 **Bus** from Poitiers train station

ℹ️ **Visitor information** 20 Pl de l
a Libération, 86310; 05 49 48
11 00; www.saintsavin.com

🍽️ **Eat and drink** *Real meal* Le
Patisson (52 Pl de la République,
86310; 05 49 84 14 73; closed Tue
dinner & Wed) serves simple but
tasty dishes such scallops cooked
on a hot griddle. *Family treat*
Christophe Cadieu (15 Rue de
l'Abbaye, 86310; 05 49 48 17 69,
www.cadieu-86.com; closed Mon
& Wed) serves great gourmet
cuisine. Best for lunch, when it is
cheaper and dishes are simpler.

of Romanesque Art" – its early 12th-
century murals cover the Biblical
story from creation to apocalypse in
scenes presented like a comic strip.
Today, these are brought to life
with films, fiber optics and special
activities for kids.

Letting off steam

Go for a splash in St-Savin's **Centre
Aquatique de La Gassotte** (Allée
des Tilleuls, 86310; mid-May–Aug),
an open-air pool complex with
slides and a wading pool for tots.

⑤ Marais Poitevin
The green Venice of France

The Poitevin marshes offer a different
world altogether – an emerald
dreamland of tree-canopied canals

populated by frogs, dragonflies and
swans. Take a boat tour or hire a
batai (punt) to explore the green
labyrinth – the waterways are well
signposted and maps are available.
Start in pretty little Coulon, where
the **Maison des Marais Poitevin** has
displays on the history and traditions
of the region. At St-Hilaire La Palud,
in the heart of the marshes, punt or
take a boat tour through the **Parc
Ornithologique Les Oiseaux du
Marais Poitevin**, a sanctuary to
70 species of birds.

Letting off steam

Go for a pedal with the **La Bicyclette
Verte** (www.maraispoitevin-
bicyclette.com) on the 300-km
(186-miles) bike path to the town
of St-Hilaire. They offer all kinds of
bikes, including tandems, bikes
with child seats, and kids' bikes.

*Flat-bottomed batais moored at Coulon's
quayside in the Marais Poitevin*

The Lowdown

🌐 **Map reference** 7 C4
Address 17000 (Charente-
Maritime), 79000 (Deux Sèvres)
and 85000 (Vendée). Maison des
Marais Poitevin: Pl de la Coutume,
79510 Coulon; 05 49 35 81 04.
Parc Ornithologique Les Oiseaux
du Marais Poitevin: Le Petit
Buisson, 79210 St-Hilaire
La Palud; www.oiseauxmarais
poitevin.com

🚆 **Train** from Poitiers or La Rochelle
to Niort, then bus 20 or 21 to the
villages in the marshes

ℹ️ **Visitor information** Parc
Interrégional du Marais Poitevin,
2 Rue de l'Eglise, 79510 Coulon;
05 49 35 15 20; www.parc-marais-
poitevin.fr

🕐 **Open** Maison des Marais Poitevin:
Apr–11 Nov. Parc Ornithologique
Les Oiseaux du Marais Poitevin:
late-Mar–15 Sep: daily; mid-Sep–
1 Nov: closed Mon

🍽️ **Eat and drink** *Picnic* La Nappe à
Carreaux (178 Route des Bords de
Sèvre, Coulon 79510; 05 49 35
90 36; www.camping-laveniseverte.
fr) organizes picnics on booking.
Family treat Le Central (4 Rue
d'Autremont, 79510 Coulon; 05 49
35 90 20; www.hotel-lecentral-
coulon.com; closed Sun dinner,
Mon & Oct–Mar) offers a gourmet
splurge of local specialities such as
eels, snails and frogs' legs.

🎪 **Festival** Pentecost Crafts Festival at
the Maison de la Meunerie (Jun)

⑥ La Rochelle
Historic gateway to the west

Guarded by its landmark fat towers, La Rochelle bursts with character, proud mansions and arcaded streets. By the 16th century, it was making fortunes from the New World, while becoming a defiant Huguenot stronghold. Two revolts, in 1622 and 1625, led it to suffer the siege of 1627–8. La Rochelle regained prosperity through the Atlantic slave trade; today it boasts a spectacular aquarium and several fine museums.

Tour de la Lanterne

Key Sights

① **Muséum d'Histoire Naturelle** One of the best outside Paris, the museum's natural history exhibits include Zarafa, the country's first giraffe.

② **Musée du Nouveau Monde** The museum covers La Rochelle's settlement and trade with the New World and Native Americans, and also slavery.

③ **Hôtel de Ville** The Renaissance town hall houses mementos related to the 1627–8 siege.

④ **Rue de l'Escale** One of La Rochelle's oldest streets, it is paved with stones from Canada brought over as ballast. Nearby, seek out the gargoyles on Rue des Merciers and the arcaded Rue de Minage.

⑤ **Tour de la Lanterne** The last medieval lighthouse on the Atlantic, this 70-m (230-ft) high tower was also a prison.

⑥ **Tour de la Chaîne and Tour St-Nicolas** Built in the 15th century, these towers guard the entrance to the Vieux Port. Nearby is Le Gabut, the old fishermen's quarter.

⑦ **Aquarium** Some 12,000 creatures from the Atlantic, Mediterranean and Caribbean live here in stunning natural settings.

⑧ **Musée des Automates and Musée des Modèles Réduits** Antique clockwork figures reconstruct Montmartre in the Musée des Automates; the adjacent museum displays a miniature sea battle.

0 metres 500
0 yards 500

The Lowdown

🌐 **Map reference** 7 B5
Address 17000 (Charente-Maritime). Muséum d'Histoire Naturelle: 28 Rue Albert 1er; www.museum-larochelle.fr. Musée du Nouveau Monde: 10 Rue Fleuriau; 05 46 41 46 50. Hôtel de Ville: Pl de l'Hôtel de Ville; 05 46 41 14 68. Tour de la Lanterne: Rue sur les Murs; la-rochelle. monuments-nationaux.fr. Aquarium: Quai Louis Prunier; www.aquarium-larochelle.com. Musée des Automates & Musée des Modèles Réduits: Rue La Désirée, Ville-en-Bois; www.museeslarochelle.com

🚗 **Train** TGV from Paris, regular train from Bordeaux and Nantes. **Bus** Besides regular buses, sea buses link the Tour de la Chaîne to the Port des Minimes (Oct–Mar: Sat & Sun only) for €8–18; under 5s free. An electric shuttle boat Le Passeur links Tour de la Chaîne and Ville-en-Bois.

ℹ️ **Visitor information** 2 Quai Georges-Simenon, Le Gabut, 17000; 05 46 41 14 68; www. larochelle-tourisme.com

🕐 **Open** Muséum d'Histoire Naturelle: Tue–Fri, Sat & Sun pm. Musée du Nouveau Monde: Oct–Mar: 9:30am–12:30pm & 1:30–5:30pm; Sat & Sun: 2:30–6pm. Apr–Sep:

10:30–12:30pm & 2–6pm; 2–6pm Sun; closed Tue. Hôtel de Ville: June–Sep: 3pm daily, Oct–May 3pm Sat & Sun. Tour de la Lanterne: daily. Aquarium: Apr–Jun & Sep: 9am–8pm; Jul & Aug: 9am–11pm; Oct–Mar: 10am–8pm. Musée des Automates & Musée des Modèles Réduits: 10am–noon & 2–6pm daily; Jul & Aug: 9:30am–7pm

💰 **Prices** Muséum d'Histoire Naturelle: €8–18; under 18s free. Musée du Nouveau Monde: €8–18; under 18s free. Hôtel de Ville: €11–21. Tour de la Lanterne: €12–22. Aquarium: €50–60; under 3s free. Musée des Automates & Musée des

Letting off steam

Head for the **Parc Charruyer** *(Chemin des Remparts, 17000; 05 46 41 14 68)* for its canals and ducks. Go for a romp at the **Mini Golf du Mail** *(Ave de la Monnaie, 17000; 05 46 41 76 06; www.minigolf-larochelle.com)*, near the Vieux Port. It has an 18-hole mini-golf course, bouncy castles, bumper cars and a crêperie.

Boats docked at the tranquil inner harbour of La Rochelle

Eat and drink

Picnic: under €20; Snacks: €20–45; Real meal: €45–90; Family treat: over €90 (based on a family of four)

PICNIC Marché Couvert *(Pl du Marché, 17000; till 1pm daily)* is a covered market where goodies can be picked up. Head for the city's charming Parc Charruyer to enjoy the picnic.
SNACKS L'Hacienda *(22 Rue des Templiers, 17000; 05 46 41 03 89)* serves good sandwiches and kebabs. Try **Ernest Le Glacier** *(18 Rue du Port, 17000)* for home-made ice cream and sorbets in delicious flavours.
REAL MEAL L'Accademia Teatro Bettini *(1 Rue de Thiers, 17000; 05 46 41 07 03; open daily)* is located

Modèles Réduits: €25–35 each, or €35–45 together

Skipping the queue The tourist office's Pass'Rochelais *(www.pass partout17.org)* offers admission at discount to 13 sights, guided tour and free bus, sea or bike transport.

Guided tours Contact the tourist office for details.

Age range 4 plus

Allow At least a day

Good family value?

La Rochelle offers lots of things to see and do, with fascinating historical monuments, museums and an excellent aquarium.

in a former theatre. Dine on excellent pizza, generous portions of lasagne and other kinds of pasta dishes.
FAMILY TREAT Les Quatre Sergents *(49 Rue Saint-Jean du Pérot, 17000; 05 46 41 35 80; www. les4sergents.fr; closed Mon)* has a pretty winter garden setting and some of La Rochelle's tastiest cuisine. The restaurant also has a kids' menu.

Shopping

Head for **Icare Cerf-volant** *(1 Rue Lalo, 17000)* to check out a huge variety of kites. For new and antique toys, visit **Piccolo** *(16 Rue du Pas-du-Minage, 17000)*. Drop in to **Les Géants de la Miniature** *(14 Rue de la Ferté, 17000)* for model trains and cars, as well as miniatures.

Find out more

DIGITAL Download The Three Musketeers game from *www.dingo games.com/three-musketeers-game*.
FILM The siege of La Rochelle is shown in Alexandre Dumas' The Three Musketeers, which has been filmed many times over the years, the latest version in 2011.

Aerial view of the lighthouses at St-Clément des Baleines

Next stop...

ÎLE DE RÉ Take a bus from La Rochelle's train station over the 3-km (2-mile) long toll bridge to the Île de Ré, with its golden beaches, salt pans and vines. Rent a bike (child seats available) and aim for the port of La Flotte and the town of St-Martin-de-Ré, with fortifications by French military engineer Vauban. In Loix, visit the **Ecomusée du Marais Salant** *(www.marais-salant. com)* to learn about salt marshes. At St-Clément des Baleines, visit the two lighthouses (1682 and 1854) known as **Phare des Baleines** *(www. lepharedesbaleines.fr)* named for the whales frequently spotted here. There is also a whale museum.

⑦ Rochefort
Maritime marvels

A handsome 17th-century port near the mouth of the Charente river, Rochefort is home to the mighty arsenal set up under Louis XIV and his minister Colbert. **La Corderie Royale** recalls the town's shipbuilding past in an astonishing 374-m (1,224-ft) long building, where ropes for 500 frigates were made. It houses the **Centre International de la Mer**, while the nearby shipyard houses *Hermione*, the frigate used by the Marquis de Lafayette to sail to America from Rochefort in 1780. The ship is due to set sail across the Atlantic in 2012. Both offer films, games and audio guides for kids. The **Musée National de la Marine** has a fantastic collection of ship models, figureheads and cannons from the arsenal, while the **Musée des Commerces d'autrefoi** has re-created 20 French shops from 1900. Visit the **Maison de Pierre Loti**, the

Carefully sculpted ape enclosure at the delightful Zoo de La Palmyre

house of marine officer, novelist and travel writer Julien Viaud (1850–1923), who fell in love with Turkey and wrote under the name of Pierre Loti. For fun, cross the Charente on the **Pont Transbordeur**, France's last active transporter bridge, that carries a segment of "road", hanging from overhead wires, across the river.

Letting off steam

Play hide and seek in the yew labyrinth at La Corderie Royale. Take bus G to the Grande Plage de Fouras, 5 km (3 miles) west of Rochefort, for a mighty bounce with nets, helmets and harnesses at the **Attraction Trampoline** (*www.location-trampoline.com*), with activities for kids aged 4 plus.

Richly decorated interior of the Maison de Pierre Lotti, Rochefort

⑧ Marennes and the Île d'Oléron
Oyster city and oyster island

Two names that French oyster lovers know well are *Marennes* and *Oléron*. Learn about molluscs in the **La Cité des Huitres**, in Marennes, with audio visuals, games and oyster shacks. The museum is visited via a 3-km (2-miles) trail for which bikes are given. Over the viaduct is the Île d'Oléron. Hire bikes (*www.velos17 loisirs.com*) to visit its west coast beaches, small villages and nature reserves. Try the sheltered Anse de Gatseau beach, by St-Trojan-les-Bains. Architectural highlights on the island include the star-shaped **Citadelle du Château d'Oléron**, which is impressive in spite of being mostly destroyed by Allied bombs in World War II, and the **Phare de Chassiron**, the lighthouse on the island's northernmost point and local "world's end", with a museum and old-fashioned fish traps; the tide brings the fish in and imprisons them behind walls when it goes out.

Visitors to the oyster beds at La Cité des Huitres, Marennes

The Lowdown

🌐 **Map reference** 7 B5
Address 17300 (Charente-Maritime). La Corderie Royale & shipyard: Rue du Docteur-Pujols; *www.corderie-royale.com*. Musée National de la Marine: Pl de la Galissonnière; *www.musee-marine.fr*. Musée des Commerces d'autrefoi: 12 Rue Lesson; *www.museedescommerces.com*. Maison de Pierre Loti: 141 Rue Pierre Loti; *www.ville-rochefort.fr*. Pont Transbordeur: 05 46 83 30 86

🚗 **Train** from La Rochelle; TGV from Paris to Surgères, then shuttle

ℹ **Visitor information** Ave Sadi Carnot, 17300; 05 46 99 08 60; *www.rochefort-ocean.com*

🕐 **Open** La Corderie Royale & Musée des Commerces d'autrefoi: daily, closed Jan. Shipyard: daily, closed 25 Dec & Jan (combined tickets available with La Corderie Royale).

Musée National de la Marine: Feb–Apr & Oct–Dec: pm; May–Sep: daily. Musée des Commerces d'autrefois: Feb–Jun & Sep–Dec: Mon–Sat, Sun pm; Jul–Aug: daily. Maison de Pierre Loti: closed Tue & Sun am (limited guided tours; best to book). Pont Transbordeur: summer: daily, except Mon am; for other times, ring ahead.

🍽 **Eat and drink** *Snacks* Barolo *(15 Rue Lesson, 17300; 05 46 99 28 50)* serves excellent pizzas, pasta dishes and generous desserts. Book in advance. *Real meal* La Goule Benaise *(23 Ave Marcel Dassault, 17300; 05 46 83 19 17; closed Sun & Mon)* offers changing daily specials; friendly young owners and market-fresh cuisine.

🎵 **Festival** Résonances, a world music festival (Jul)

The Lowdown

🌐 **Map reference** 7 B5
Address 17560 (Charente-Maritime). La Cité des Huitres: Chenal de la Cayenne, 17320 Marennes; 05 46 36 78 98; www.cite-huitre.com. Citadelle du Château d'Oléron: Pl de la République, 17480; 05 46 47 60 51. Phare de Chassiron: St-Denis d'Oléron, 17650; www.chassiron.net

🚗 **Train** to Surgères, then bus to Marennes, Bourcefranc and Château d'Oléron. Viaduct to Île d'Oléron or passenger boats from Bourcefranc to Le Château d'Oléron or La Tremblade to St-Trojan-les-Bains

ℹ️ **Visitor information** Route du Viaduc, 17480 Bourcefranc-le-Chapus; 05 46 85 65 23; www.ile-oleron-marennes.com

🕐 **Open** La Cité des Huitres: Feb, Apr, Jul & Aug: daily; other months: Wed–Sun; closed Jan. Citadelle du Château d'Oléron: day and night tours arranged by the tourist office in Bourcefranc. Phare de Chassiron: daily

🍴 **Eat and drink** Real meal Le Drugstore (Pl de la République, 17480 Le Château d'Oléron; 05 46 85 02 66) has a kids' menu and offers picture books. Family treat Les Jardins d'Aliénor (11 Rue du Maréchal Foch, 17480 Le Château d'Oléron; 05 46 76 48 30; www.lesjardinsdalienor.com; closed Mon & Tue (winter) has chicken or fish on the kids' menu.

🎪 **Festival** Fête de Vent, kite flying at St-Denis-d'Oléron (Aug)

Letting off steam
Head for Dolus-d'Oléron's **Park Aquatique** (www.vert-marine.com) for indoor or outdoor fun. Splash in a lagoon, go down giant slides and float amid geysers, down a "river" and under waterfalls.

⑨ Royan
Beaches, butterflies and bonsai
Located near the northern tip of the Gironde estuary, the seaside resort of Royan became a popular bathing resort for its sheltered silky sands. It was, however, one of the last places held by the Nazis in France in World War II, and when the Allies tried to bomb them out in January 1945, they tragically hit the civilian population instead; Royan was not liberated until 18 April. Rebuilt with plenty of concrete in the 1950s, it

Colourful striped tents on the sandy beach at Royan

looks like no other French resort. Visit the surviving 19th-century *belle époque* mansions and **Les Jardins du Monde**, with bonsais, orchids, Japanese and English gardens, and a butterfly greenhouse. There is also an 1,800-year-old olive tree, 7 m (23 ft) in circumference, which was brought here from Spain. Kids can follow a treasure hunt, find their way out of a bamboo maze and ride electric boats.

Letting off steam
Play on the beaches of the Côte de Beauté in Royan or head west to the small town of La Palmyre to visit the **Zoo de La Palmyre** (www.zoo-palmyre.fr), with 1,600 animals and a giant ape enclosure.

The Lowdown

🌐 **Map reference** 7 B6
Address 17200 (Charente-Maritime). Les Jardins du Monde: 5 Ave des Fleurs de la Paix; www.jardinsdumonde.com

🚗 **Train** from Angoulême or Saintes, or directly from Paris in summer. Ferry from Le Verdon

ℹ️ **Visitor information** 1 Blvd de la Grandière, 17200; 05 46 05 04 71; www.royan-tourisme.com

🕐 **Open** Les Jardins du Monde: closed early-Jan–mid-Feb

🍴 **Eat and drink** Snacks La Coccinelle Carrée (51 Blvd de la République, 17200; 05 46 23 03 76; except Sun dinner & Mon in winter) serves tartiflette (potatoes, reblochon cheese, cream, and lardons), pizzas, ostrich steaks and has a kids' menu too. Real meal Le Lido (157 Blvd Frédéric Garnier, 17200; 05 46 05 12 00; restaurant lelido.monsite-orange.fr; Apr–mid-Nov) serves simple but tasty dishes – seafood, duck and beef.

🎪 **Festival** Rêve d'Icare, a festival of kites, balloons and gliders (Jun, every two years)

⑩ Angoulême
The world capital of comics

A medieval city divided into an aristocratic upper town and business-like lower town, Angoulême has a history intertwined with its river, the meandering Charente. The river's water was so pure that it was perfect for paper making. But as the local paper mills were replaced by big industrial plants, Angoulême decided to re-invent itself as the world capital of comic strips, hosting the prestigious Festival International de la Bande Dessinée.

Statue at Musée de la Bande Dessinée

Key Sights

0 metres 200
0 yards 200

④ Musée d'Angoulême Housed in the former archbishop's palace, it has excellent sections on history, geology, fine arts and one of France's top collections of African and Oceanic art.

① Musée du Papier-Le Nil Founded in 1792, this former mill houses a museum devoted to the Charente river and paper making then and now.

② Musée de la Bande Dessinée Comics, from the first ones of 1830 till the present, are interspersed with videos on how they are made.

③ Cathédrale St-Pierre Built in the 12th century, its huge façade has sculptural reliefs on the Ascension of Christ and the Last Judgment and the knight Roland fighting the Moors.

⑤ Château d'Angoulême Marguerite d'Angoulême, known for her writings and patronage of humanists, was born here in 1492. A tower and keep remain of the medieval castle, which are now used as the Town Hall.

⑥ Place des Halles This square occupies the spot of Angoulême's 10th-century fortress; today it is the location for a pretty 19th-century covered market.

⑦ Fonds Régional d'Art Contemporain Poitou-Charentes This art gallery in a big white building exhibits its collection of over 800 works by contemporary French and foreign artists from recent decades, in rotating exhibitions.

The Lowdown

🌐 **Map reference** 7 D6
Address 16000 (Charente). Musée du Papier-Le Nil: 134 Rue de Bordeaux; www.angouleme. fr/museep. Musée de la Bande Dessinée: Cité International de la Bande Dessinées, 121 Rue de Bordeaux; www.citebd. org. Musée d'Angoulême: 1 Rue Friedland, Square Girard II; www.angouleme.fr/ museeba. Fonds Régional d'Art Contemporain Poitou-Charentes: 63 Blvd Besson-Bey; www.frac-poitou-charentes.org

🚗 **Train** from Paris and Bordeaux

ℹ️ **Visitor information** Pl des Halles, 16000; 05 45 95 16 84; www.angouleme-tourisme.com

🕐 **Open** Musée du Papier-Le Nil: 10am–noon & 2–6pm Tue–Fri, 2–6pm Sat & Sun; Jul & Aug: noon–6:30pm Tue–Fri, 1–6:30pm Sat & Sun. Musée de la Bande Dessinée: Sep–Jun: 10am–6pm Tue–Fri, 2–6pm Sat & Sun; Jul & Aug: till 7pm. Musée d'Angoulême: 10am–6pm Tue–Sun. Fonds Régional d'Art Contemporain Poitou-Charentes: 2–9pm Tue–Sat & first Sun of month

€ **Prices** Musée du Papier-Le Nil, Musée d'Angoulême & Fonds Régional d'Art Contemporain Poitou-Charentes: free. Musée de la Bande Dessinée: €26–36; under 18s free

👥 **Skipping the queue** Visit the Musée de la Bande Dessinée in the morning when it is less crowded.

🚩 **Guided tours** Via Patrimoine (www.via-patrimoine.com) offers a range of guided tours and the Musée d'Angoulême has audio guides in English and French.

Prices given are for a family of four

Entrance to the Centre Aquatique Nautilis in St-Yrieix-sur-Charente

Letting off steam

Wander along the Charente river on Boulevard Besson-Bey or take bus 9 to the town of St-Yrieix-sur-Charente, located 6 km (4 miles) northwest, for a splash in the **Centre Aquatique Nautilis** (*www.grandangouleme.fr*). The park has seven pools, water slides, and an ice-skating rink near an artificial lake, where swimming is free.

Eat and drink

Picnic: under €20; Snacks: €20–45; Real meal: €45–90; Family treat: over €90 (based on a family of four)

PICNIC Les Halles (*Pl des Halles, 16000*) is the covered market from where picnic supplies can be bought. Picnic by the lily pond in the shady Place Beaulieu.

SNACKS Le Palet d'Or (*1 Pl Francis Louvel, 16000; 05 45 95 00 73*) serves sandwiches and light lunches to take away, as well as some of Angoulême's best cakes.

REAL MEAL La Braise (*5 Rue Trois Notre-Dame, 16000; 05 45 95 52 60; www.restaurant-angouleme.info; Wed–Sun*) serves grilled meats –

there are no fewer than 27 varieties to choose from, along with big salads and home-made desserts.

FAMILY TREAT Chez Paul (*8 Pl Francis Louvel, 16000; 05 45 90 04 61; www.restaurant-16.com; Nov–Mar: closed Sun*) has a pretty garden overlooking the ramparts, which is the perfect place to enjoy its market cuisine with exotic touches.

Shopping

Go to **Chocolaterie Letuffe** (*10 Pl Francis Louvel, 16000; chocolaterie-letuffe.fr*) for a range of chocolates and sweets. Take bus 21, to the west of Angoulême, to Trois-Palis, to visit the store's factory and gift shop. At the Librarie de la Bande Dessinée, pick up comic albums, DVDs, toys and figurines.

Next stop...

AUBETERRE-SUR-DRONNE Take a bus south to Montmoreau and then a taxi to the tiny village of Aubeterre-sur-Dronne. Similar to St-Émilion (*see p296*), the village is known for its curious *église monolith*, excavated out of the rock. **Église St-Jean** is the underground church with the highest nave in Europe – the work of Pierre de Castillon – who returned from the First crusade inspired by the cave-churches of Cappadocia. While only the façade remains, the 12th-century **Église St-Jacques** (*Pl Ludovic Trarieux, 16390*) has finely sculpted Spanish-Moorish portals. Watch puppet shows in the **Musée des Marionnettes** (*05 45 98 45 59*) in July and August. Explore the pretty Dronne river in a canoe hired from the **Club Canoë Kayak** (*Route du Pont de Riberac, 16390 Aubeterre; 05 45 98 51 72; snpa.aubeterre.pagesperso-orange.fr; May–Sep*).

👫 Age range 6 plus

⏱ Allow Half a day

🎏 Festivals Festival International de la Bande Dessinée (Jan). Coupe d'Europe de Montgolfières, world hot-air balloon rally (Jul-early-Aug, odd numbered years). Circuit des Remparts, Bugatti and other classic cars race (Sep).

Good family value?

An inexpensive and low-key town worth a leisurely day. Knowing French is a big plus here.

Château de la Rochefoucauld with its pepper-pot towers

⑪ Château de La Rochefoucauld

Keeping it in the family

Begun in the 11th century, this Renaissance château is still inhabited by La Rochefoucaulds, one of the oldest families in France. In the late 15th century, one ancestor, François, became godfather to the future king François I. Since then, as the portraits on the wall make clear, "Francois" has remained the favourite family name. Of all these, François VI was a witty writer, while number XII fought against slavery and introduced vaccines to France in 1800.

The Lowdown

⊕ **Map reference** 7 D5
Address 16110 (Charente). 1 Rue Tanneurs, 16110 La Rochefoucauld; 05 45 62 07 42; www.chateau-la-rochefoucauld.com

🚗 **Train** from Paris and Bordeaux to Angoulême, then taxi

ℹ **Visitor information** Rue des Halles, Ancien Couvent des Carmes, 16110; 05 45 63 07 45; www.bandiat-tardoire.fr

🕑 **Open** Apr–Dec: Wed–Mon; Jan–Mar: Sun pm only

💶 **Price** €28–38; under 12s free

🍽 **Eat and drink** *Real meal* Chez Steph (Pl du Champs de Foire, 16110; 05 45 62 09 11; closed Mon, book in summer) is a local favourite with friendly staff and succulent meat dishes. *Family treat* La Carpe d'Or (1 Route de Vitrac, 16110; www.hotel-restaurant-lavieilleauberge.com; closed Sun eve) serves classic French cuisine, including a rack of lamb and crème caramel. It has a kids' menu.

The arcaded courtyard has an Italian air; Leonardo da Vinci is said to have contributed to the design.

Letting off steam

Walk along the paths by the Tardoire river. Run about in the village's lovely **Le Jardin St-Florent** *(1 Rue St-Florent, 16110; 05 45 23 94 30)*. Or head for the outdoor **Piscine Municipale** *(Rue de la Piscine, 16110; 05 45 62 01 25)*. It is open from mid-June to August.

⑫ Cognac

Not just a drink

There is more to the handsome town on the Charente river than its famous namesake. Get an overview in the **Espace Découverte en Pays du Cognac**, with child-friendly activities such as illuminated models, 3D "magical books", films and the **Musée d'Art et d'Histoire**, which has treasures ranging from a Neolithic canoe to Art Nouveau glass by French artist Émile Gallé. Nearby is the **Château de Cognac**, now the Otard distillery, where François I was born. **Hennessey** is the most interesting for kids, with its museum, film tour and boat trips across the Charente river to the vines. Reward the tots with a trip on a wooden *gabare* (a traditional river boat) called *La Dame Jeanne*. Boat trips (www.tourism-cognac.com/fr_decouverte/04gabare.htm) are available from May to September.

Letting off steam

Head for the big playgrounds of **Base André Mermet** *(Allée Basse du Parc, 16100; 05 45 82 46 24)* on the banks of the Charente river, with sand pits, rope climbs and more.

Romanesque leaf carvings on columns in the church of St-Eutrope, Saintes

The Lowdown

⊕ **Map reference** 7 C5
Address 16100 (Charente). Espace Découverte en Pays du Cognac: Les Remparts, Pl de la Salle Verte; 05 45 36 03 65; www.espace-decouverte.fr. Musée d'Art et d'Histoire: 48 Blvd Denfert-Rochereau; 05 45 32 07 25; www.musees-cognac.fr. Hennessey: Rue de la Richonne; 05 45 35 72 68; www.hennessy.com

🚗 **Train** from Angoulême and La Rochelle

ℹ **Visitor information** 16 Rue du XIV Juillet, 16100; 05 45 82 10 71; www.tourism-cognac.com

🕑 **Open** Espace Découverte en Pays du Cognac: Mar–Nov: closed Mon except Jul & Aug. Musée d'Art et d'Histoire: closed Tue. Hennessey: May–Sep: daily; Oct–Dec, Mar–Apr: Mon–Fri (book tours online)

🍽 **Eat and drink** *Real meal* La Brasérade (23 Rue Pont Faumet, 16100; 05 45 82 00 45; Tue–Sat) serves Alpine-style dishes – raclettes, fondues and meats, cooked at the table on a hot stone. *Family treat* Les Pigeons Blancs (110 Rue Jules Brisson, 16100; 05 45 82 16 36; www.pigeons-blancs.com; closed Sun eve & Mon lunch) features bream in a lobster cream sauce and a delicious dessert cart. A gourmet kids' menu is available.

⑬ Saintes

From a Roman chariot to Louis XVI's slippers

Once the Roman capital of Aquitaine, Saintes is proud of its Arch of Germanicus, built in the 1st century AD to mark the completion of Via Agrippa across Gaul. In the nearby **Musée Archéologique** are remnants of a Roman chariot and horses' bridles which might have been used in Saintes' amphitheatre, which in its prime seated 15,000.

There is a splendid 11th-century pilgrimage church, St-Eutrope, and the **Abbaye aux Dames**, now dedicated to music. The **Musée Dupuy Mestreau** is filled with historical treasures, including slippers worn by Louis XVI before he lost his head.

Letting off steam

Play in the **Parc Pierre Mendès-France** *(Ave de la Saintonge, 17100)*. To explore the river, drive north to

The tree-lined drive to the majestic Château d'Usson in Pons

The Lowdown

🌐 **Map reference** 7 C5
Address 17100 (Charente-Maritime). Musée Archéologique: Esplanade André Malraux; 05 46 74 20 97; www.ville-saintes.fr. Abbaye aux Dames: 11 Pl de l'Abbaye; www.abbayeauxdames. org. Musée Dupuy Mestreau: 4 Rue Monconseil; 05 46 93 36 71; www.ville-saintes.fr

🚗 **Train** from Angoulême

ℹ️ **Visitor information** Pl Bassompierre, 17100; 05 46 74 23 82; www.saintes-tourisme.fr

🕐 **Open** Musée Archéologique & Musée Dupuy Mestreau: year round Tue–Sun; Apr–Sep: closed Sun am; Oct–Mar: closed daily am

🍴 **Eat and drink** *Snacks* Le Petit Bistrot *(7 Rue Victor Hugo, 17100; 05 46 91 56 24; lepetitbistrot. webobo.biz; closed Sun)* serves salades composées (mixed salad with cheese, meat or seafood). *Real meal* Le Mezzé *(9 Rue de la Comédie, 17100; 05 46 92 22 36; closed Sun & Mon)* is a Lebanese restaurant that also offers many vegetarian dishes.

the town of Port-d'Envaux, where families can hire bikes or canoes from **Les Canotiers** *(www.les-canotiers.fr).*

⑭ Pons
Into the castle of riddles

A massive **Donjon** (keep) towers over the medieval town of Pons. It was rebuilt in the 12th century after the original keep was razed by Richard the Lionheart in 1179, as a lesson to his uppity vassals, the Lords of Pons, for not toeing the line. The Hôpital des Pélerins, from the same time, was founded for pilgrims on their way to Santiago de Compostela.

For families, however, the big lure is the beautiful Renaissance **Château d'Usson** – the whole château was moved stone by stone from another village by its new owner and rebuilt in the 1880s. Kids get busy exploring the château, park and farm by way of games, puzzles and activities related to Knights Templars and musketeers.

Letting off steam

If the château adventure was not enough, run around the Donjon a couple of times.

The Lowdown

🌐 **Map reference** 7 C6
Address 17800 (Charente-Maritime). Donjon de Pons: 5 Pl de la République; Château d'Usson: Les Egreteaux; www.chateau-enigmes.com

🚗 **Train** from Angoulême, La Rochelle and Bordeaux

ℹ️ **Visitor information** 1 Rue des Pontils, 17800; 05 46 96 13 31; www.pons-tourisme.fr

🕐 **Open** Donjon de Pons: Easter–Jun, Sep–mid-Oct: Tue–Fri & Sun pm, Sat: all day; Jul–Aug: daily. Château d'Usson: mid-Apr–early-Nov: daily

🍴 **Eat and drink** *Real meal* Les Moulins de la Vergne *(9 Impasse du Moulin de la Vergne, 17800; 05 46 90 50 84; May–Sep)* is run by a welcoming Dutch couple and has a simple brasserie-style menu. *Family treat* Auberge Pontoise *(23 Ave Gambetta, 17800; 05 46 94 00 99; closed Sun eve & Mon lunch)* has a young chef who cooks tasty dishes from the region's oysters, duck, beef, fruit and vegetables.

🎪 **Festival** Sur un Air de Barouf, a rock festival (Aug)

⑮ Bordeaux
Wine and dukes around the Port of the Moon

Built along the banks of the Garonne, where the river forms the crescent called the "Port of the Moon", Bordeaux grew out of the prime Gallo-Roman city of Burdigalia. Its rulers were the powerful Dukes of Aquitaine, including William, the first ever troubadour. His grandaughter Eleanor's marriage to Henry II made Bordeaux the capital of English Aquitaine for three centuries. The town was largely rebuilt in the 18th century with money from France's colonies. Today, Bordeaux is most famous for some of the best wines in the world.

Monument des Girondins

Key Sights

① Place de la Bourse Elegant 18th-century buildings surround a giant reflecting pool with 900 misting jets, designed for frolicking.

② Bordeaux Monumental Located in the Quartier St-Pierre, Bordeaux's medieval core, this exhibition centre traces the city's evolution over the centuries.

③ Basilique St-Michel This Flamboyant-Gothic basilica has a landmark 47 m (154 ft) detached belltower, one of the tallest in France.

④ Musée d'Aquitaine The museum covers the history of Aquitaine, starting in 25,000 BC. Nearby, the huge bell in the 15th-century Grosse Cloche gate used to signal the start of the wine harvest.

⑤ Cathédrale St-André The city's huge Gothic masterpiece is where Eleanor of Aquitaine married Louis VII in 1137.

⑥ Musée des Beaux Arts Housed in the Palais de Rohan, this museum is rich in Dutch masters, but also has works by Bordeaux's Odilon Redon and Albert Marquet.

⑦ Musée d'Art Contemporain (CAPC) A former warehouse houses this edgy art museum in Quartier des Chartrons, the old wine merchants' quarter.

⑧ Monument des Girondins Located in the Place des Quinconces, this monument and fountain honours Bordeaux's revolutionaries killed in the Terror (1793–94).

The Lowdown

🌐 **Map reference** 11 C1
Address 33000 (Gironde). Musée d'Art Contemporain (CAPC): 7 Rue Ferrère; www.capc-bordeaux.fr. Bordeaux Monumental: 28 Rue des Argentiers. Basilique St-Michel: 45 Rue des Faures, 33800. Musée d'Aquitaine: 20 Cours Pasteur. Cathédrale St-André: Pl Pey-Berland. Musée des Beaux Arts: 20 Cours d'Albret

🚃 **Train** from Toulouse; TGV from Paris

ℹ️ **Visitor information** 12 Cours du XXX Juillet, 33000; 05 56 00 66 01; www.bordeaux-tourisme.com

🕐 **Open** Musée d'Art Contemporain (CAPC): 11am–6pm Tue–Sun, until 8pm Wed. Bordeaux Monumental: Nov–Apr: 10am–1pm & 2–6pm Mon–Sat, 2–6pm Sun; May–Oct: 9:30am–1pm & 2–6pm, 10am–1pm & 2–6pm Sun. Musée d'Aquitaine: 11am–6pm Tue–Sun. Musée des Beaux Arts: 11am–6pm Wed–Mon

💶 **Prices** Musée d'Art Contemporain (CAPC): €15–25; under 12s free. Bordeaux Monumental, Musée d'Aquitaine & Musée des Beaux Arts: free

🚻 **Skipping the queue** Book ahead during the city's big events, especially late-June–early-July.

🪧 **Guided tours** Contact the tourist office for details.

👫 **Age range** 4 plus

🤸 **Activities** Cruise on the Gironde estuary with Croisières Burdigala

Prices given are for a family of four

The traditionally elegant white and blue dining room at La Gabriel

Letting off steam

Play in the new park areas along the Garonne river or visit the **Jardin Public** (*Rue de Verdun, 33000*), which has a few playgrounds. Take bus 503 to the town of Cadaujac to the **Ferme Exotique** (*www.fermeexotique.com*), with donkey and dromedary rides.

Eat and drink

Picnic: under €20; Snacks: €20–45; Real meal: €45–90; Family treat: over €90 (based on a family of four)

PICNIC Marché des Grands Hommes (*Pl des Grands Hommes, 33000*) is a market from where supplies can be picked. Picnic by the Garonne river or in the Jardin Public.
SNACKS La Vie en Rose (*8 Rue Sicard, 33000; 05 56 48 03 44; closed Sun & Mon*) is a tea room serving home-made savoury tarts, salads and sandwiches, and delicious cakes.
REAL MEAL Le Plat dans l'Assiette (*8 Rue Ausone, 33000; 05 56 01 05 01; www.leplatdanslassiette.com; Mon, Wed & Sat lunch, closed Sun*) serves southwestern and Lyonnaise specialities with three courses (starter, main and cheese) on a plate. The kids' menu includes duck magret – deboned duck breast grilled like a steak. Order desserts separately.

(*www.evolutiongaronne.fr*). The tourist office offers a whole range of wine tours and tastings throughout the year.

⏱ **Allow** At least a day

🎉 **Festivals** Les Epicuriales, food festival (Jun)

Good family value?
A year-round destination with free or affordably priced attractions and near the beaches at Arcachon.

FAMILY TREAT Le Gabriel (*10 Pl de la Bourse, 33000; 05 56 30 00 70; restaurant.bordeaux-gabriel.fr; closed Sun & Mon*) offers François Adamski's exquisite Michelin-starred cuisine, but lunch in the bistro downstairs is more reasonably priced.

Shopping

L'Ecole Buissonière (*74 Rue des Trois-Conils, 33000; 05 56 79 12 86*) stocks every conceivable toy – from porcelain dolls to action heroes. Drop by **Cadiot Badie** (*26 Allées de Tourny, 33000; 05 56 44 24 22; www.cadiot-badie.com*) for some wonderful sweets from a master chocolate maker since 1826.

Find out more

FILM *The Lion in Winter* (1968), a historical drama starring Katherine Hepburn and Anthony Hopkins, is about Eleanor of Aquitaine and Henry II. She also features in *Robin Hood* (2010).

Footsteps crisscrossing on the immense sand dunes of the Dune de Pyla

Next stop...

ARCACHON AND DUNE DE PYLA
Several trains a day go to Arcachon, Bordeaux's beach playground, the source of its oysters, and site of the historic **Musée Aquarium** (*2 Rue Professeur Jolyet, 33120; 05 56 83 33 32*) created in 1865. Buses from the Arcachon bus station go around the bay to a mind-boggling sand mountain, the 107-m (351-ft) Dune de Pyla, 10 km (6 miles) from Arcachon. Carry on to La Hume in the adjacent village of Gujan-Mestras, home to the **Parc de la Coccinelle** (*www.la-coccinelle.fr*), with 800 animals, a petting zoo and rides for tots and **Kid Parc** (*www.kidparc.com*), a park for kids under 12.

Above Broad horizons across a vineyard at St-Émilion
Below Café terraces in the square in front of L'Église Monolithe, St Émilion

⑯ St-Émilion
Into the secret underground

On the surface St-Émilion is a lovely old wine town, but another world awaits underground. Book a visit with the tourist office to explore the cave of the hermit Emilion – going back to the 8th century – Chapelle de St-Trinité, catacombs and the 12th-century **L'Église Monolithe** – the second-largest subterranean church in the world. Climb the belltower, Le Clocher, or opt for the La Tour

du Château du Roy for great views. Elsewhere, quarries dating from the 12th century now house the **Musée Souterrain de la Poterie**, which has a fascinating collection of pots from Gallo-Roman times to the present.

Letting off steam

Explore St-Émilion's vine-covered countryside by foot, bicycle or petit train (www.visite-saint-emilion.com).

⑰ Bazas
Beef and holy blood

Bazas is synonymous with the beef that goes in the classic steak bordelais (grilled over vine cuttings) and for its 13th-century Gothic **Cathédrale St-Jean-Baptiste**. The cathedral, dedicated to St John the Baptist, has a beautifully sculpted triple portal, a massive rose window and a luminous interior. It houses a reliquary of the saint's blood supposedly collected by a local woman at his beheading. On the Place de la

The Lowdown

🌐 **Map reference** 11 D1
Address 33330 (Gironde). L'Église Monolithe: Pl Pierre Meyrat; 05 57 55 28 28. Musée Souterrain de la Poterie: 21 Rue André Loiseau, www.saint-emilion-museepoterie.fr

🚆 **Train** from Bordeaux to Libourne, then bus 315 to St-Émilion

ℹ️ **Visitor information** Pl des Créneaux, 33330; 05 57 55 28 28; www.saint-emilion-tourisme.com

🕑 **Open** L'Église Monolithe: underground tours year round (in English Apr–Oct); Le Clocher: key from tourist office; La Tour du Château du Roy: Apr–Sep. Musée Souterrain de la Poterie: daily

🍴 **Eat and drink** Real meal L'Envers du Décor (11 Rue du Clocher, 33330; 05 57 74 48 31; envers-du decor.com; open daily) offers excellent market cuisine, salads and wonderful cheeses that match the superb wines. Family treat Logis de la Cadène (3 Pl du Marché au Bois, 33330; 05 57 24 71 40; closed Sun dinner & Mon) features well-prepared steak bordelais served at tables beneath a magical wisteria.

🎉 **Festival** Fête de Solstice & La Jurade, ceremonial judgment on the wine of the previous year and whether it deserves to be labelled "St-Émilion" (Jun)

The Lowdown

🌐 **Map reference** 11 C2
Address 33430 (Gironde). Cathédrale St-Jean-Baptiste: Pl de la Cathédrale. Château de Roquetaillade: 33210 Mazères; 05 56 76 14 16; chateau roquetaillade.free.fr

🚆 **Train** from Bordeaux to Langon, then bus 512

ℹ️ **Visitor information** Pl de la Cathédrale, 33430; 05 56 25 25 84; www.tourisme-bazadais.com

🕑 **Open** Château de Roquetaillade: Jul & Aug: 11am–5pm; Easter–Jun & Sep–Oct: 3pm & 4pm, Nov–Easter: Sun & school holidays 3pm & 4pm

🍴 **Eat and drink** Snacks Café d'Oc (13 Rue Bragous, 33430; 05 56 25 96 08; www.cafedoc.com; closed Sun) serves excellent omelettes, salads and an enormous choice of savoury and sweet crêpes. Real meal Indigo (25 Rue Fondespan, 33430; 05 56 25 25 52; closed Sun & Mon) uses local ingredients with a twist (duck with mangoes) and fish and chips or burgers on the children's menu.

🎉 **Festival** Fête de St-Jean celebrates John the Baptist's feast day with huge bonfires (Jun)

Cathédrale, seek out La Maison de L'Astronome, with the carving of an astronomer in a pointy hat like that of a wizard. Take a taxi to the village of Mazères, 9 km (5 miles) northwest of Bazas, to visit the **Château de Roquetaillade**, a 700-year-old feudal estate – in the same family the whole time – restored in the 19th century by Viollet-le-Duc, who also fixed up Carcassonne (see pp324–5).

Letting off steam

Scamper around the lovely medieval garden next to the cathedral. Take a taxi west to the town of Belin-Belliet

Carved stonework on the Cathédrale St-Jean-Baptiste, Bazas

to canoe along the shady Leyre river, suitable for kids aged 6 plus (*www.canoesurlaleyre.com*).

⑱ Eco-musée de la Grande Lande

Go back in time

Landes was a sparsely populated moorland, where shepherds eked out a meager living, spending much of their time on stilts. Gradually, maritime pines were planted, which resulted in what is now the largest cultivated forest in Europe. In the middle, accessible only by a special historic train from the station in Sabres, Marquèze, an agricultural estate preserved as it was in 1836, is now the Eco-musée de la Grande Lande. The pavilion of Marquèze at the train station in Sabres offers an overview, while in Marquèze itself vistors can watch or even join the "locals" going about their lives. There are activities for kids too: allow up to half a day.

Hot thermal springs at La Fontaine Chaude, Dax

⑲ Dax

Hot mud and cow jumps

France's number one thermal resort, Dax is famous for the hot water that steams out of the earth in the central La Fontaine Chaude. Parents can soak in the mud at the **Thermes Borda**, while everyone can enjoy the **Musée de l'ALAT**'s collection of light aircraft and helicopters. Best of all, take in a *course landaise*. Dax and the nearby Mont de Marsan rival each other in their passion for this sport, where participants leap over charging cows.

Letting off steam

Take a bus to the Atlantic beaches of Hossegor. Or visit the anteaters and lemurs at **Oceafaunia** (*www.oceafaunia.com*), located south in Labenne. For big sploshy slides, go to **Atlantic Park** (*www.ville-seignosse.fr*), a water park north of Seignosse.

The Lowdown

🌐 **Map reference** 11 B3
Address 40100 (Landes). Thermes Borda: 30 Rue des Lazaristes; *www.thermes-borda.com*. Musée de l'ALAT: 58 Ave de l'Aérodrome; *www.musee helico-alat.com*

🚃 **Train** from Bordeaux

ℹ️ **Visitor information** 11 Cours Foch, 40100; 05 58 56 86 86; *www.dax-tourisme.com*

🕐 **Open** Thermes Borda: Mon–Sat. Musée de l'ALAT: Mar–Nov: Mon–Fri pm; Jul–Aug: Mon–Sat pm

🍽️ **Eat and drink** *Snacks* Au Fin Gourmet (*3 Rue Pénitents, 40100; 05 58 74 04 26*) serves the meaty specialities of the Landes and Basque Country. *Real meal* La Table de Pascal (*4 Rue de la Fontaine Chaude, 40100; 05 58 74 89 00; closed Sun & Mon*) is known for its upmarket market cuisine.

🎪 **Festival** Feria, a 6-day-long fun fair (Aug)

The Lowdown

🌐 **Map reference** 11 C3
Address 40630 (Landes). Eco-musée de la Grande Lande: Lande; 05 58 08 31 31; *www.parc-landes-de-gascogne.fr*

🚃 **Train** to Mont-de-Marsan, then taxi to Sabres, then train

🕐 **Open** Eco-musée de la Grande Lande: Apr–Oct: daily

🍽️ **Eat and drink** *Snacks* La Table de Marquèze (*40630 Marquèze; 05 58 07 59 44; French summer hols, Easter–Nov, Sun & hols lunch daily*) offers farm-raised chicken and duck dishes. *Real meal* Ô Mille et une Pâtes (*108 Ave du Marensin, 40550 Léon; 05 58 49 24 21; Jul–15 Sep: open daily; 16 Sep–Jun: closed Mon–Wed*) serves home-made pasta, grilled fish and beef with golden chips, and has a children's menu.

🎪 **Festival** La Fête du Printemps et des bergers, Gascon music, dancing and egg hunts (Apr)

Letting off steam

Take a taxi west to Léon for a boat tour with **Les Bateliers du Courant d'Huchet** (*www.bateliers-courant-huchet.fr*). Or go to Soustons Plage, where kids aged 11 plus can captain replica steamships at the **Port Miniature de Port d'Albret** (*www.loisirs-soustons.com*).

Where to Stay in Poitou and Aquitaine

For the most part, accommodation in Poitou and Aquitaine is oriented towards summer holidays near the ocean and, compared to France's other coasts, offers good value for money for families. Fancy villas and boutique hotels are rare, but camp sites and holiday apartments are easy to find.

AGENCIES

Discover Poitou-Charentes
www.discover-poitou-charentes.com
This website lists a wide range of self-catering accommodation and châteaux, B&Bs, as well as camp sites across Poitou-Charentes, most of it suitable for families.

Alternative Aquitaine
www.alternative-aquitaine.co.uk
A specialist agency, with focus on the west coast, it lists villas, beach houses, apartments and cottages in the Gironde and Landes.

Angoulême
Map 7 D6

HOTELS

Hôtel All Seasons Angoulême Nord
122 Rue des Meneaux, 16430 Champniers; 05 45 68 53 22; www.all-seasons-hotels.com
This chain hotel, 7 km (4 miles) off the Paris–Bordeaux motorway, is family friendly, with 30 rooms that come with the Disney channel, Wi-Fi, Vtech game consoles and crayons. Bottle warmers and baby shampoo are available. Breakfast is included.
🛏 P ✳   €

Le Palma
4 Rampe d'Aguesseau, 16000; 05 45 95 22 89
This renovated hotel has been in the same family since 1919 and offers a convenient base for visiting the city. The nine rooms have Wi-Fi and flat-screen TV. There is a restaurant. Parking is available, nearby.
✳   €

CAMPING

Les Gorges du Chambon
Map 7 D5
16220 Eymouthiers; 05 45 70 71 70; gorgesduchambon.fr
Located east of Angoulême towards La Rochefoucauld, this environment-friendly camp

ground occupies an old farming estate; tents to two-star *gîtes* are on rent. Club for kids aged 6–12 years, mini-golf and river swims, as well as a pool, games, pony rides, canoeing and hot-air balloon rides are provided.
🛏 🏠 P ☉   €

Arcachon
Map 11 B2

SELF-CATERING

Residhome Apart Hotel Plazza
49–51 bis Ave Lamartine, 33120; 05 57 15 48 00; www.residhome.com
Opened recently, these flats are in Arcachon's Ville d'Eté, a 5-minute walk from the beach and within walking distance of the train station, putting Bordeaux within easy reach. The apartments are in natural colours; babysitting and baby kits available.
🛏 🏠 ✳   €€

CAMPING

Camping de la Dune
Route de Biscarrosse, 33115 Pyla-sur-Mer; 05 56 22 72 17; www.camping deladune.fr
Located in the pine trees next to the Dune de Pyla, this camp site is where two French comedies: *Camping* and *Camping 2* were shot. There are mobile homes and chalets to rent and disposable bedding to buy; bicycle hire is also available.
🏠 P ☉   €–€€

Bordeaux
Map 11 C1

HOTELS

Au Comte d'Ornon
Allée de Mégevie, 33170 Gradignan; 05 56 75 26 85; www.aucomte dornon.com
This pleasant little Logis de France is in a peaceful area, a 15-minute drive south of the city centre. The rooms are equipped with Wi-Fi and satellite TV. There is a restaurant, which serves delicious regional French cuisine.
🛏 P ✳   €

Hôtel des 4 Soeurs
6 Cours du XXX Juillet, 33000; 05 57 81 19 20; www.hotel-bordeaux-centre.com
Right in the heart of Bordeaux, this hotel occupies an 18th-century town house and retains elegant features, in spite of a complete overhaul in the recent past. Rooms are soundproof and Wi-Fi-equipped. Underground parking nearby in Place Tourny.
🛏 ✳   €€

A well-furnished one-bedroom flat in Citadines Meriadeck , Bordeaux

BED & BREAKFAST

Natura Cabana
75 Rue la Fontaine, 33290 Le Pian Médoc; 05 56 46 29 48; www.natura cabana.fr
Located 14 km (9 miles) from Bordeaux, this is a delightful wooden house perched high in the trees of the enormous Parc du Château de Malleret. A mobile phone is essential in case of emergencies and kids have to be at least 3 plus to stay here.
P   €€

Ecolodge de Chartrons
23 Rue Raze, 33000; 05 56 81 49 13; www.ecolodgedeschartrons.com
In the old wine merchants' quarter, the Quartier des Chartrons, this is a B&B in an 18th-century stone building. Beautifully restored, using sustainable materials, equipped with solar power and water-saving devices, it has won the European Eco-label award. The friendly owners serve a healthy breakfast.
🛏 P   €€€

SELF-CATERING
Citadines Centre
Mériadeck Bordeaux
25 Rue Jean Fleuret, 33000; 05 57
01 62 70; www.citadines.com
Located just a few streets away
from the cathedral, overlooking the
Esplanade Charles de Gaulle, these
centrally located three-star high-rise
apartments have sofa beds in the one
bedroom flats. Rooms have high-
speed Ethernet. Baby equipment
and a laundrette are available.
🛏 🍽 P   €

Cognac
Map 7 C5

HOTEL
Cheval Blanc
6 & 8 Pl Bayard, 16100; 05 45 82
09 55; www.hotel-chevalblanc.fr
Housed in a former coach house,
a two-minute walk from the city
centre, these motel-style rooms
are suited for a brief stay in the
area. Rooms are soundproofed
and equipped with Wi-Fi, but the
hotel's parking spaces are limited;
be sure to reserve a parking space
when booking.
🛏 P ✳   €

BED & BREAKFAST
Les Yourtes
Charentaises
Map 7 C6
19 Rue de la Tonnellerie, 17800
Salignac; 05 16 20 48 87; www.
yourtescharentaises.com
This B&B is located 7 km (4 miles)
from Cognac in Salignac. Individual
toilets, along with solar heated Italian
showers are outside each yurt. The
yurts are heated, but bring warm
pyjamas in winter. Rates include
breakfast and the owner offers *table
d'hôte* meals, if booked in advance.
🛏 🛏 P   €€

Futuroscope/
Poitiers
Map 7 D4

HOTELS
Jules Verne Futuroscope
Ave Jean Monnet Téléport 3, 86961;
05 49 49 10 49; www.hoteljulesverne-
futuroscope.biz
This modern family hotel, located
near the entrance to Futuroscope,
has been inspired by Jules Verne's
Nautilus. See website for special
packages and ticket discounts.
There are free shuttle services to
the park during school holidays.
🛏 P   €

*Towers of the charming Château de la
Motte, Poitiers*

Le Bois de la Marche
D611, 86240 Ligugé; 05 49 53 10
10; www.bois-de-la-marche.com
A 15-minute drive from Futuroscope
and Poitiers, this sleek modern hotel
enjoys a peaceful setting surrounded
by a large forest. Free Wi-Fi and
phone calls to 23 countries, satellite
TV and Jacuzzis in some rooms are on
offer. A games room is also available.
🛏 P ✿   €€

Le Grand Hôtel
28 Rue Carnot, 86000;
05 49 60 90 60,
www.grandhotelpoitiers.fr
A delightful establishment in the
historic centre of Poitiers, this hotel
has big comfy beds. The buffet
breakfast is superb and served on the
patio in good weather. Rooms are
equipped with Wi-Fi and satellite TV.
There is no restaurant, but there are
many in easy walking distance.
🛏 P ✳   €€

Plaza Futuroscope
Ave du Futuroscope Téléport 1,
86960; 05 49 49 07 07; www.plaza-
futuroscope.com
A short walk from the entrance to
Futuroscope, this contemporary hotel
offers a wide variety of packages and
discounts for early booking. The
indoor pool is open all year. There
is a gym, billiards and an attractive
restaurant with a giant fish tank.
🛏 P ✿   €€

BED & BREAKFAST
Château de la Motte
Map 8 E3
2 La Motte, 86230 Usseau;
05 49 85 88 25; www.chateau-
de-la-motte.net
A short drive north of Futuroscope,
this wonderful 15th-century château,
with pointy towers, is set in a pretty

medieval garden. The charming
owners keep up the medieval
castle theme, and love telling
its stories to guests.
🛏 🛏 P ✿   €€

La Roseraie
78 Rue Armand Caillard, 86170
Neuville de Poitou; 05 49 54 16 72;
www.laroseraiefrance.fr
Located 11 km (7 miles) from Poitiers,
this impressive English-owned manor
house has two-room suites especially
fitted out for families. Rooms have
Wi-Fi. Breakfasts are delicious and
other meals are available on request.
🛏 🛏 P ✿   €€

CAMPING
Le Futuriste
St-Georges-les-Baillargeaux, 86130;
05 49 52 47 52; www.camping-le-
futuriste.fr
Just north of Futuroscope, this camp
ground offers pitches, chalets and
mobile homes. A lake for fishing,
playground and football pitch
are on offer. There is a restaurant.
🛏 🍽 P ✿   €

Hossegor
Map 11 B4

CAMPING
Camping du Lac
518 Rue du Janin, 40440 Ondres;
05 59 45 28 45, camping-du-lac.fr
South of Hossegor, this woodsy
camp site is perfect for visits to the
big beaches of the Landes, as well
as Bayonne and the Basque country
just to the south. Rentals range
from *roulottes* (wooden caravans)
to chalets. There are special "Kid
Camping" activities on weekdays.
🍽 P ✿   €

*Façade of the modern Plaza
Futuroscope, Poitiers*

Price Guide
The following price ranges are based
on one night's accommodation in high
season for a family of four, inclusive of
service charges and any additional taxes.
€ Under €100 €€ €100–200 €€€ over €200

Key to symbols *see back cover flap*

Île d'Oléron

Map 7 B5

HOTEL
Hôtel de la Plage
51 Blvd du Capitaine-Leclerc, 17310 St-Pierre d'Oléron; 05 46 47 28 79; www.oleronhotel.com
A short walk from the sandy beach and La Cotinière, the island's main fishing port, this hotel offers a mix of pleasant rooms and studios. Rooms have Wi-Fi and also high-tech anti-mosquito devices to keep pests at bay. Steep stairs in the studios are unsuitable for very young children.

 €€

BED & BREAKFAST
La Cabane
62 Route du Viaduc, 17480 Ors; 05 46 47 48 01; www.alacabane.fr
Just outside of Château d'Oléron, Ors is a traditional oyster-fishing hamlet on the south coast of the island. Families can stay in a stylish B&B room in the 200-year-old house of an oysterman. The helpful owner also has five *gîtes* all in the area, a short walk from the sea.

 €€

CAMPING
Sequoia Parc
La Josephtrie, 17320 St-Just-Luzac; 05 46 85 55 55; www.sequoiaparc.com
On the mainland near the bridge to Oléron, this award-winning family-friendly camp site, in a garden setting surrounding a spectacular water park, rents well-equipped modern chalets and mobile homes by the week. There are playgrounds, a pony club, kids' clubs, bike hire and a good restaurant, as well as a pizzeria on site, along with a full range of evening entertainment.

€–€€

Île de Ré

Map 7 B4

SELF-CATERING
Le Palais des Gouverneurs
Rue des Gouverneurs, 17410 St-Martin-de-Ré; 08 92 70 21 80; www.pv-holidays.com
Located in the centre of St-Martin-de-Ré, the Île-de-Ré's former governors' palace and two other buildings have been converted into elegant apartments. There is a children's playroom and free Wi-Fi

by the reception. It is a short walk to shops and restaurants; the Plage de Cible is nearby.

€€

Saint-Martin Club
Chemin des Maraises, 17410 St-Martin-de-Ré; 05 46 09 01 43; www.belambra.co.uk
This stress-free family vacation club amidst the pines, 3 km (2 miles) from St-Martin, offers self-catering chalets and bungalows with furnished patios. Flat-screen TVs, a playground and kids' club for ages 3–10 years and free baby kits for under two are on offer. Horse-riding and beaches are nearby. Thalassotherapy packages are also available.

€€

The no-frills exterior of Hôtel Saint-Nicolas, La Rochelle

La Rochelle

Map 7 B5

HOTELS
Les Brises
1 Chemin de la Digue Richelieu, 17000; 05 46 43 89 37; www.hotellesbrises.eu
Named for its sea breezes, this oceanfront hotel is near the Tour de la Laterne. The sea-view family room is especially lovely, with its balconies. Rooms have free Wi-Fi and there is a solarium. Although there is no restaurant, there are plenty to choose from a short walk away.

€€

Hôtel Saint-Nicolas
13 Rue Sardinerie, 17000; 05 46 41 71 55; www.hotel-saint-nicolas.com
Located in the heart of the Vieux Port near Place de la Solette, this family friendly hotel is a great base for exploring La Rochelle. Completely renovated, the hotel's rooms are comfortable and contemporary and

equipped with Wi-Fi and satellite TV. Discounts on kids' breakfast; free breakfast for kids aged under 6.

€€

CAMPING
Le Beaulieu
Map 7 C4
3 Rue du Treuil Gras, 17138 Puilboreau; 05 46 68 04 38; www.camping-la-rochelle.com
A 10-minute drive from La Rochelle's Vieux Port, this camp site rents out pitches bungalows, mobile homes and. Free club for kids aged 6 plus during summer holidays. Disposable sheets, laundrette, towels, bike hire and a playground are also available.

€–€€

Marais Poitevin

Map 7 C4

HOTEL
Maison Flore Hôtel Environnemental
25 Rue du Port, 79210 Arçais; 05 49 76 27 11; www.maisonflore.com
On the banks of one of the channels in the in the centre of the marshes, this solar-powered hotel has been renovated to be as ecologically sustainable as possible. The ten rooms are named after flowers and decorated accordingly. Breakfast is organic and features home-made jams; bikes and games are available.

€

BED & BREAKFAST
Château de l'Abbaye
Map 7 B4
Moreilles, 85450; 02 51 56 17 56; www.chateau-moreilles.com
A half-hour drive from both the beaches and La Rochelle, this grand, ivy-swathed house has five delightful guest rooms and a family apartment to rent. The charming hosts prepare superb *table d'hôte* meals. Free Wi-Fi in rooms; mountain bikes available.

€€

CAMPING
Le Lidon
Lieu-dit Lidon, 79210 St-Hilaire-La-Palud; 05 49 35 33 64; www.camping-le-lidon.com
Right in the centre of the Marais Poitevin, this lush, well-wooded camp ground also has a base for boats to explore France's "Green Venice". There are 136 shady pitches and chalets with kitchenettes, as well as tents sleeping four to rent. There is a playground too.

€

The Pyrenees

France's second-highest mountain range, running along the border with Spain, the Pyrenees offer spectacular scenery, easy access and a calendar full of activities. By contrast, the Basque country in the west has beaches, a unique culture and France's chocolate city, Bayonne. Families can enjoy scenic trains, animal parks and prehistoric painted caves high up in the mountains.

Below Hikers at the Cirque de Gavarnie, a UNESCO World Heritage Site

① Bayonne
The city of whales and chocolate

For centuries, Bayonne was the Basque country's window on the world, from where bold captains set sail on the oceans, forming Europe's first whaling fleets. The city's other claim to fame is the introduction of chocolate to France from the New World via Spain, thanks to trade links maintained by the Jewish community who settled here after their expulsion from Spain in 1492. Along with its walls, cathedral and museums, Bayonne offers access to the beaches of Anglet and Biarritz.

Surfers in the waters at Anglet beach

Key Sights

① **Fortifications** These are one of Louis XIV's military engineer Sébastien Vauban's masterworks. Still intact today, these walls have never been taken by an enemy.

② **Cathédrale Ste-Marie** Taking over 600 years to build, this Gothic cathedral houses a masterpiece of Renaissance stained glass in its chapel of St Jérôme.

③ **Le Cloître** Completed in the 14th century, this Gothic cloister was where citizens and town councillors met and where merchants used to cement business deals.

④ **Musée Basque** Through artefacts and reconstructions, it shows the lives of the Basque people in the olden days.

⑤ **Atelier du Chocolat** A shop full of treats, this place is also a museum of chocolate. Go on a tour and watch the chocolates being made.

The Lowdown

🌐 **Map reference** 11 B4
Address 64100 (Pyrénées-Atlantiques). Cathédrale Ste-Marie: 15 Rue des Prébendes; 05 59 46 01 46. Le Cloître: 1 Pl Louis Pasteur; 05 59 46 11 43. Musée Basque: 37 Quai des Corsaires; www.musee-basque.com. Atelier du Chocolat: 7 Allée de Gibéléou; 05 59 55 70 23.

🚗 **Train** SNCF trains from Bordeaux and Paris. **Bus** ATCRB buses to coastal towns. STAB, the city bus line, has a summer service (bus C) from the Mairie to all the Anglet & Biarritz beaches ending up eventually at the airport

ℹ️ **Visitor information** Pl des Basques, 64100; 08 20 42 64 64; www.bayonne-tourisme.com

🕐 **Open** Le Cloître: mid-Sep–mid-May: 9am–12:30pm & 2–5pm; mid-May–mid-Sep: until 6pm. Musée Basque: 10am–6:30pm Tue–Sun; Jul & Aug: 10am–6:30pm daily. Atelier du Chocolat: Sep–Jun: 9:30am–12:30pm & 2–6pm Mon–Sat; Jul–Aug: 9:30am–6:30pm (last visit 90 mins before closing)

€ **Prices** Musée Basque: €34–44; under 18s free. Atelier du Chocolat: €64–74

👫 **Skipping the queue** Beaches in Anglet and Biarritz are packed in July and August. Take bus C to avoid crowded car parks.

✂️ **Guided tours** Contact the tourist office for details

👫 **Age range** All ages

Activities Cruise on the Ardour river with Le Coursic (adourloisirs. free.fr), which offers one-hour to full day excursions, along with commentary.

Prices given are for a family of four

Letting off steam

If hanging out on the beaches of Anglet and Biarritz is not enough, the Bay of Biscay has some of the best waves for surfing in Europe, and the surf schools offer lessons to kids aged 7 plus. **Plums Surf School** (Rue Garderès, 64200 Biarritz; 05 59 24 10 79; www.touradour. com/shops/plums/gb/index.htm) has staff that speaks English.

Brightly striped tents lining the Grande Plage at Biarritz

Eat and drink

Picnic: under €20; Snacks: €20–45; Real meal: €45–90; Family treat: over €90 (based on a family of four)

PICNIC Les Halles (Quai du Commandant Roquebert, 64100) is full of Basque cheeses and cured Bayonne ham. Picnic in the Remparts de Mousserolles and explore the famous fortifications of France's military engineer Vauban.
SNACKS Patisserie Raux (7 Rue Bernadou, 64100; 05 59 59 34 61) offers home-made chocolates, sandwiches, plats du jour (daily special), tea and hot chocolate.

⏱ **Allow** A day for the city and more for the beach

🎭 **Festivals** Foire au Jambon, the Bayonne Ham Festival (Apr). Biarritz Surf Festival and championships (Jul). Other surf events (Aug). Fêtes de Bayonne, street music, bull fights and costumes (late-Jul–Aug)

Good family value?
Generally inexpensive and not very touristy, the city combines beach fun and sightseeing with a modest mix of things to see and do.

REAL MEAL Brasserie du Trinquet Saint-Andre (1 Rue Jeu de Paume, 64100; 05 59 25 76 81; brasserie-saint-andre.fr) offers salads, steaks, chops and Basque hamburgers.
FAMILY TREAT Auberge du Cheval Blanc (68 Rue Bourgneuf, 64100; 05 59 59 01 33) is a Michelin-starred restaurant famous for its seafood, especially its salmon.

Find out more

DIGITAL Families can download and play the three Chocolatier games on tinyurl.com/6ftuapb and learn about the international chocolate business.
FILM Le Voyage à Biarritz (1963) stars Fernandel as a station master who goes on a holiday to Biarritz. Un amour de sorcière or Witch Way Love (1997), starring Vanessa Paradis and Jean Reno, a comedy film, was shot in part just outside Bayonne.

Take cover

Visit the trinquet (indoor court) at **Trinquet St-André** (Rue des Tonneliers, 64100; 05 59 25 76 81; closed Sun) to watch pelota, the Basque national sport. A ball game played with the hand or a chistera (curved racket), pelota can also be played in a fronton (outdoor court).

Food counters selling local specialities at Les Halles

Next stop...

SARE Located south of Bayonne, in the Pyrenean foothills, is the village of Sare. Go to the **Grottes de Sare** and the **Musée et du Parc Mégalithique** (both www.sare.fr) to learn about Palaeolithic caves, Neolithic dolmens and the origins and myths of the Basques. Or take a ride on the **Petit Train de la Rhune** (www.rhune.com) up to the holy mountain of the Basque country.

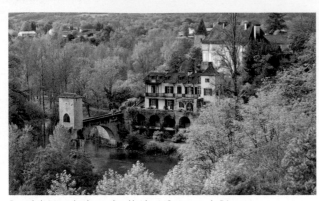

Pont de la Légende, the medieval bridge in Sauveterre-de-Béarn

② Grottes d'Isturitz et Oxocelhaya

An underground river and an ancient flute

Located in the heart of the French Basque country near Hasparren, a village southwest of Bayonne, these caves were inhabited as long ago as 80,000 BC. A guided tour follows the course of an underground river, through halls and grottos of brilliant stalactites, but the real wonders here are the relics and works of art left by early man. There are a huge number of finds – drawings and incisions picturing animals, tools and weapons, as well as a 40,000-year-old flute.

The Lowdown

- **Map reference** 11 B4
  Address 64240 (Pyrénées-Atlantiques). On the D251; 05 59 29 64 72; www.grottes-isturitz.com
- **Bus** from Bayonne or St-Jean-de-Luz to Hasparren, then taxi
- **Visitor information** 2 Pl St-Jean, 64240 Hasparren; 05 59 29 62 02; www.hasparren-tourisme.com
- **Open** Mar–May & Oct–Nov: daily pm
- **Price** €26–36; under 7s free
- **Eat and drink** *Snacks* Pizzas-Pat (6 Rue Pierre Broussain, 64240 Hasparren; 05 59 93 03 17; www.pizzas-pat.fr) offers takeaway pizzas, cooked dishes and panninis. *Real meal* Argia (32 Rue Jean Lissar, 64240 Hasparren; 05 59 29 60 24; www.hotel-restaurant-argia.fr) serves tasty dishes such as Basque-style poached eggs and grilled duck.

Letting off steam

Head 7 km (4 miles) to the south of Bayonne where the **Base de Baigura** (*www.mendionde.fr.gd/Base-de-loisirs-du-baigura.htm*) offers trampolines, mountain bikes and an initiation in hang-gliding, as well as a tourist train ride to the top of the 897-m (2,942-ft) Mount Baigura.

③ Sauveterre-de-Béarn

A medieval time capsule and a museum of salt

In the Middle Ages, this was a busy town on the main route to Spain. Medieval life is re-created in the **Maquette de la Cité Médievale**, an impressive model of the town, housed in the Chapelle St-Martin. The town's monuments include the original walls and gates, some fine Romanesque sculpture in the St-André church and an enchanting half of the Pont de la Légende (Bridge of Legend) whose tolls were once the town's main source of income. The legend involves the local viscountess who, in 1170, was accused of witchcraft, tied up and thrown off the bridge. She was alive

A 17th-century statue of Good King Henri, Pau

The Lowdown

- **Map reference** 11 B4
  Address 64390 (Pyrénées-Atlantiques). Maquette de la Cité Médievale: Chapelle de Sunarthe; 05 59 38 57 56. Musée du Sel: Rue Des Puits-Salants, 64390 Salies de Béarn; 05 59 09 31 99
- **Train** to Orthez on the Bayonne–Pau line, then bus 22 to Sauveterre and Salies de Béarn
- **Visitor information** Pl Royale, 64390; 05 59 09 31 99; www.tourisme-bearn-gaves.com
- **Open** Maquette de la Cité Médievale: Jul & Aug: Tue–Sat; Apr–Jun & Sep: Sat. Musée du Sel: mid-Apr–Oct: Tue–Sat
- **Eat and drink** *Snacks* Pub-Snack de la Mairie (Pl Royal, 64390; 05 24 37 11 85; Oct–May: closed Thu) is good for a quick bistro-style lunch, with *frites*, salads and *croque-monsieurs* (grilled ham and cheese sandwich). *Real meal* Au Fil du Temps (Blvd St-Guily, 64390 Salies-du-Béarn; 05 59 38 31 27; www.hotelcasinoduparc.fr), an elegant restaurant, offers lunch menus and a chance to look at a restored hotel from the 1890s.

when they found her downstream, so she was said to have passed the "test of innocence".

Just north of Sauveterre-de-Béarn is Salies de Béarn. This lovely old spa town, built on winding little rivers that resemble Venetian canals, is well known for its saline springs. Head for the **Musée du Sel** (salt museum) that is one of the landmarks of the town.

Letting off steam

Sauveterre-de-Béarn's Gave d'Oloron river is renowned for salmon fishing and whitewater rafting. The **Centre Nautique de Soeix** (05 59 39 61 00; www.soeix.com) offers rafting trips. It is suitable for kids aged 8 plus.

④ Pau

Birthplace of Good King Henri

East of the Basque country, Béarn is a little enclave of mountains and dairy farms that for centuries was a proudly independent Gascon state, ruled by its own viscounts. Its capital Pau is a lively city that became a Victorian-era resort popular with the British, who gave it the continent's first golf course. Take in the famous view from the promenade, the

"Balcony of the Pyrenees" and visit the **Musée National du Château de Pau**, where Pau's favourite son and France's most amiable king, Henri IV, was born in 1553; his mother, according to legend, rubbed his lips with garlic to make him a good Gascon. The star exhibit is his famous tortoiseshell cradle.

Letting off steam

Pau's elegant Parc Beaumont is a good place to play, or have year-round family water fun in **Calicéo** (Blvd du Cami Salié, 64000; 08 26 30 36 64; www.caliceo.com/pau/pages/pau/default.asp), a spa.

The Lowdown

- 🌐 **Map reference** 11 C4
  Address 64000 (Pyrénées-Atlantiques). Musée National du Château de Pau: 2 Rue du Château; www.musee-chateau-pau.fr
- 🚃 **Train** from Bordeaux & Toulouse
- ℹ️ **Visitor information** Pl Royale, 64000; 05 59 27 27 08; www.pau-pyrenees.com
- 🕐 **Open** Musée National du Château de Pau: daily
- 🍴 **Eat and drink** Snacks La Brochetterie (16 Rue Henri IV, 64000; 05 59 27 40 33; www.labrochetterie.com) is popular for grilled meats and fish. Real meal La Fourchette à Soupe (12 Blvd Champetier de Ribes, 64000; 05 59 90 14 70; www.la-fourchette-a-soupe.com; closed Sun & Mon) uses locally sourced and organic ingredients in tasty soups, vegetarian and meat dishes, as well as pretty desserts.
- 🎎 **Festivals** Carnaval Biarnés, wild week-long festivities (Feb). Festival des Pyrénées hosts traditional dancers and musicians from all over the world (Jul)

⑤ Le Petit Train d'Artouste

Europe's highest train ride

At Artouste, in the Vallée d'Ossau, hop aboard the open-top Petit Train d'Artouste. At 2,000 m (6,561 ft), this is Europe's highest train. The spectacular trip goes right up to the Lac d'Artouste on the Spanish border. At the top, hike around the mountain lakes or take a 20-minute walk to the Artouste dam. Ride the cableway the skiers use in winter, or

Le Petit Train d'Artouste in the Vallée d'Ossau

visit a shepherd in his bergerie (sheep pen) to see how he makes cheese. Prolong the fun by camping or booking a bed in a refuge to spend a night on the mountain. In winter, the Station de Ski d'Artouste has a special park for kids and a luge run, as well as a ski school.

Take cover

Head north to Aste-Béon, the site of the **Falaise aux Vautours** (Vulture Cliffs). Cameras built into the cliffs allow a look at the big scavengers and their chicks in the nests on the screens in the information centre (www.falaise-aux-vautours.com).

The Lowdown

- 🌐 **Map reference** 11 C5
  Address 64440 (Pyrénées-Atlantiques).
- 🚌 **Bus** from Pau to Laruns, then summer bus or taxi to Artouste
- ℹ️ **Visitor information** Maison de Fabrèges, 64440 Artouste-Fabrèges; 05 59 05 34 00; www.ossau-pyrenees.com
- 🕐 **Open** late-May–late-Sep: train departs every hour; Jul & Aug: every 30 mins. Book at 05 59 05 36 99; www.altiservice.com/236-36723-Tarifs-et-horaires.php
- 💰 **Price** €70–80; under 4s free
- 🍴 **Eat and drink** Snacks Le Panoramic (Station Altitude, 64440 Artouste Fabrèges; 05 59 05 42 56; open daily) offers sandwiches and ice cream with spectacular views. Real meal L'Embaradère (13 Ave de la Gare, 64440 Laruns; 05 59 05 41 88; www.gite-embaradere.com; closed Tue) serves filling garbure (bacon and vegetable soup) and grilled meats.
- 🎎 **Festival** Montagnes en Chansons, a mountain song festival in Laruns (May)

Picnic under €20 Snacks €20–45 Real meal €45–90 Family treat over €90 (based on a family of four)

⑥ Pic du Midi de Bigorre
A ride through the air to the top of the Pyrenees

The Pyrenees were born when Iberia smashed into France 100 million years ago and right in the heart of the mountains towers the Pic du Midi de Bigorre. At 2,877 m (9,438 ft), this is one of the highest peaks in the world that can be accessed by cable car. Known as the "last stop before the stars", its pinnacle is crowned with an astronomical observatory and a 104-m (341-ft) television antenna broadcasting radio and television signals across much of Southwest France.

Wildflowers on the slopes of the Pic Du Midi

Key Features

La Lunette Jean Rösch This observatory houses a refractor telescope that studies the surface of the sun.

Terraces The views alone were enough to give the Pic du Midi de Bigorre its designation as a "site classé national" in 2003. Often, the other Pyrenees resemble floating islands.

Musée des Etoiles Learn about discoveries made in the observatory and current projects with the weather service on climate change.

Téléphérique This cable car was built in 1952: from La Mongie, it is a 15-minute ride to Pic du Midi de Bigorre. It rises 1,000 m (3,280 ft) from start to finish.

Coupole du Télescope DIMM Added in 2009, this instrument measures the level of turbulence in the atmosphere at night.

La Lunette Jean Rösch

Terraces

Cabine du téléphérique

Télescope Bernard Lyot Set in a 28-m (91-ft) tower, this is the largest telescope in France.

Observatoire Astronomique A weather station was first built on the Col de Sencours in 1873. The construction of the observatory began in 1881.

Coupole Gentili The 106-cm (42-in) telescope in this dome was financed by NASA in 1963. It was used to map the moon's surface for the Apollo missions.

The Lowdown

🌐 **Map reference** 11 D5
Address 65200 (Hautes-Pyrénées). Pic du Midi de Bigorre: Bagnères-de-Bigorre

🚗 **Train** from Toulouse to Tarbes, then bus to La Mongie for the cable car

ℹ️ **Visitor information** 3 Allée Tournefort, 65200 Bagnères-de-Bigorre; 05 62 95 50 71; www.picdumidi.com

🕐 **Open** Apr–Mar, Jun–Sep & Dec: daily; May, Oct, Jan & Feb: Wed–Mon. Cable car departure (every 15 mins): Oct–May: 10am–3:30pm; Jun–Sep: 9am–4:30pm

💶 **Price** Family pass €84–94; under 6s free (including cable car round trip)

👫 **Skipping the queue** The cable car gets crowded in the ski season and August. Buy tickets online (www.skipass-npy.com).

👉 **Guided tours** Book online (www.picdumidi.com) well in advance for a sunset–night visit and a look at the stars and planets.

👫 **Age range** 3 plus for the cable car, as it can be a bit scary. The ride is not recommended for pregnant women or people with heart problems.

🤸 **Activities** Attend a workshop (in French and English) on constellations, telescopes and talks with astronomers ending at 11:30 pm. A starry evening with or without dinner

⏱️ **Allow** Half a day

☕ **Café** There is a café at the top.

🚻 **Toilets** At the top and bottom cable-car stations

Good family value?
The cable car and astronomical site are great, but as a result, the area is extremely popular and expensive. Be sure to dress warmly.

Prices given are for a family of four

Gearing up to ski outside the Col du Tourmalet, Tourmalet

Letting off steam

Drive 16 km (10 miles) south to the **Ski Station Grand Tourmalet** (*www.n-py.com*) at the villages of La Mongie and Barèges. In season, this is the biggest ski area in the Pyrenees, with snow crèches for kids aged 3–11 years if the parents want to hit the big slopes.

Eat and drink

Picnic: under €20; Snacks: €20–45; Real meal: €45–€90; Family treat: over €90 (based on a family of four)

PICNIC The ski resorts Le Bagnères and Mongie have plenty of shops with picnic supplies that are open every morning. Eat on the terrace of Pic du Midi de Bigorre.

SNACKS Le Killarney (*Pl des Monge, 65200 La Mongie-Tourmalet; 05 62 91 99 24*) sells sandwiches, salads and *clocherade* (meats cooked on a bell) and takeaways.

REAL MEAL Le Cantalou (*16 Pl des Thermes, 65200 Bagnères-de-Bigorre; 05 62 95 07 72; www.restaurant-lecantalou.com; closed Mon*) serves generous, home-style cuisine and pizzas, as well as pasta dishes for kids.

FAMILY TREAT L'Auberge Gourmande (*Blvd de l'Hypéron, 65200 Bagnères-de-Bigorre; 05 62 95 52 01; Wed–Sun; Jul & Aug: also Mon*) serves Gilles Béal's gastronomic delights, such as pork baked in the oven for 12 hours. Be sure to book.

Shopping

Bagnères is a centre for traditional handmade clothing. **Ateliers B** (*12 Rue Justin Daléas, 65200 Bagnères-de-Bigorre*) carries a range of high-design and high-quality goods in Pyrenean wool, leather and deerskin. **Val d'Arizes** (*65200 Cieutat*), 9 km (5 miles) from Bagnères, is also good for woollens.

Find out more

DIGITAL Get your own planetarium, with a free download application called Stellarium from *www.stellarium.org*. Beautifully designed and easy to use, it shows everything in the sky for a specific time and location.

Take cover

Les Grottes de Médous in Bagnères (*60 Route des Cols, 65200 Asté; 05 62 91 78 46; www.grottes-medous.com; Apr–Oct*) is one of the most beautiful stalactite caves in France. Visitors are taken through part of it in boats on an underground river.

Breathtaking view of the cascade and snowpatches, Cirque de Gavarnie

Next stop...

CIRQUE DE GAVARNIE Take a bus from Lourdes to the Cirque de Gavarnie (*www.gavarnie.com*), a UNESCO World Heritage Site – a 4-km (2-mile) mountain wall, with Europe's highest waterfall and the famous 100-m-(328-ft) gash called the Brèche de Roland. Legend has it that Roland, nephew of Charlemagne and the subject of the medieval epic, *La Chanson de Roland*, struck the mountain with his sword Durendal after his heroic defeat at the pass of Roncevaux, hoping to destroy it to keep it from falling into enemy hands. Get there by a 45-minute walk from the Hôtel du Cirque or ride on horseback with **Club Vignemale** (*www.cheval-gavarnie.com*).

Lac de Gaube located inside the Parc National des Pyrénées

⑦ Parc National des Pyrénées
Snowshoes and mountain bikes

The spectacular scenery in the Pyrénées National Park competes with the exciting activities on offer here. The best place to start is in Cauterets, a gracious old spa town that has become the gateway to the park. Its **Maison du Parc** has information on the park's flora and fauna and on hiking, mountain biking, skiing, ice-skating and other sports. Inside the park, the 1,496-m (4,908-ft) high Pont d'Espagne offers waterfalls, splashing, snow-shoeing and the chance to take a chairlift up to the Lac de Gaube. Take the cableway up to the Cirque du Lys, where there is skiing in winter. Mountain bikes can be hired in Cauterets in summer and are suitable for kids aged 7 plus.

The Lowdown

🌐 **Map reference** 11 C5
Address 65110 (Hautes-Pyrénées). Maison du Parc, 65110 Cauterets; 05 62 92 52 56 59; www.parc-pyrenees.com

🚐 **Bus** SNCF buses from the train station in Lourdes to Cauterets

ℹ️ **Visitor information** Pl Foch, 65110 Cauterets; 05 62 92 50 50; www.cauterets.com

🕐 **Open** Maison du Parc: daily

🍽️ **Eat and drink** *Picnic* Carrefour (5 bis Ave de Général Leclerc, 65110; 08 99 1952 77; closed Sun pm) is great to pick up supplies from. Picnic by the Cirque du Lys cableway. *Real meal* Les Trois Couronnes (Galerie Aladin, 65110 Cauterets; 05 62 92 02 14) offers local treats, with good kids' menus.

Prices given are for a family of four

Take cover
From Cauterets, take a taxi or drive 10 km (6 miles) north to **Aquarium Tropical** (www.aquarium-tropical-pierrefitte.com) in Pierrefitte-Nestalas, which has freshwater and saltwater species from across the world.

⑧ Parc Animalier des Pyrénées
A day with birds and beasts

This animal park, in Argelès-Gazost, offers visitors a chance to meet bears, otters, lynxes and other fauna of the Pyrenees. Huge enclosures house over 100 species in their natural surroundings. Playful marmots steal the show, offering photo ops with the kids. There is a footprint trail, restaurant and picnic area. End the day with a visit to the **Donjon des Aigles** at Beaucens, where eagles, falcons, owls and parrots, among others, put on an aerial spectacle to music above an 11th-century castle.

Letting off steam
A shuttle bus links Argelès to Hautacam, the local sports centre, which offers skiing, snow-shoeing and the chance to zip down the mountain on an all-season luge.

A boy playing with marmots at the Parc Animalier des Pyrénées, Argelès-Gazost

The Lowdown

🌐 **Map reference** 11 D5
Address 65400 (Hautes-Pyrénées). Parc Animalier des Pyrenees: 60 Ave des Pyrenées, Argelès-Gazost; www.parc-animalier-pyrenees.com. Donjon des Aigles: Beaucens; 05 62 97 91 07; www.donjon-des-aigles.com

🚐 **Bus** Shuttle bus from the train station in Lourdes

ℹ️ **Visitor information** Pl de la République, 65400 Argelès-Gazost; 05 62 97 00 25; www.argeles-gazost.com

🕐 **Open** Parc Animalier des Pyrénées: Apr–Sep: daily; Oct: pm only; closed Nov–Mar. Donjon des Aigles: Apr–Sep: daily, shows at 3:30pm & 5pm; Aug: 3pm, 4:30pm & 6pm

💲 **Price** €40–50; under 3s free

🍽️ **Eat and drink** *Picnic* Melchoir (4 Ave Pierre de Coubestin, 65400 Argelès-Gazost; 05 62 46 19 86) is a good place to pick up picnic goodies. Enjoy them at the park's picnic area. *Real meal* Auberge de l'Arrioutou (Route de Hautacam, 65400; 05 62 97 11 32; Sat, Sun & school hols only) has home-made pâtés, garbure (thick vegetable and bacon soup) and other mountain dishes.

🎪 **Festival** Festa Muchas Bandas, musicians play on the streets (Aug)

Activities are suitable for children aged 3 plus and accompanied by a parent.

⑨ Lourdes
Pilgrims and wax works

In 1858, in a grotto in Lourdes, a "small young lady" appeared 18 times to Bernadette Soubirous, the 14-year-old daughter of a miller. At one point, the lady instructed her to drink from a spring that was soon found to have healing properties. The Catholic church investigated the "miracle" and it was not long before Lourdes became France's most important pilgrimage destination, with a reputation for miraculous cures.

Besides an ocean of kitsch souvenirs, which leads up to the famous grotto and church, there are also plenty of opportunities for family fun. The petit train, which departs every 20 minutes from Place Mons Laurence, offers a good overview. Seated on a lofty outcrop is the Château Fort that was begun in the

11th century, which houses the **Musée Pyrénéen**, with exhibits on traditional life in the mountains from the 18th to the 20th centuries as well as a botanical garden housing miniature buildings. The **Musée de Cire** has over a 100 life-sized waxwork figures that represent stories of St Bernadette, Leonardo's *Last Supper* and more.

Letting off steam

Take bus 3 from Place Peyramale, 3 km (2 miles) west to the Lac du Lourdes for playgrounds, mountain bikes or to hire horses.

The town of Lourdes with the Château Fort in the background

The Lowdown

🌐 **Map reference** 11 D5
Address 65100 (Hautes-Pyrénées). Musée Pyrénéen: 25 Rue du Château Fort; 05 62 42 37 37; *www.lourdes-visite.com*. Musée de Cire: 87 Rue de la Grotte; 05 62 94 33 74; *www.museede cireslourdes.com*

🚗 **Train** SNCF from Tarbes and Pau. **Bus** Limited bus services to the Pyrenean valleys

ℹ️ **Visitor information** Pl Peyramale, 65100; 05 62 42 77 40; *www. lourdes-infotourisme.com*

🕐 **Open** Musée Pyrénéen: daily Musée de Cire: Apr–Oct: daily

☕ **Eat and drink** *Real meal* Grill Alexandra (3 Rue Fort, 65100; 05 62 94 31 43; open Sat, Sun & school hols) serves duck, seafood and good desserts. *Family treat* Le Magret (10 Rue des 4 Frères Soulas, 65100 Lourdes; 05 62 94 20 55; www.lemagret.com) serves some of the best traditional Pyrenean dishes in the region, based on local ingredients such as trout, duck and lamb; includes menu for vegetarians and kids. Book 24 hours in advance.

🎭 **Festival** Festival de Théâtre, singers and theatre personalities take part in this weekend festival (Jul)

⑩ Château de Mauvezin
Where the Middle Ages live on

Located in little Mauvezin, east of Bagnères-de-Bigorre, the perfectly restored Château de Mauvezin was begun around the year 1000 and later belonged to a hell-raiser of the Hundred Years' War, Count Gaston Fébus. Today, it has everything that a medieval castle should have: collections of swords, halberds, axes, crossbows, armour and even a catapult. On summer Sundays, the château puts on shows of medieval music and dance, acrobatics, juggling and many other evocations of everyday medieval life.

The Lowdown

🌐 **Map reference** 11 D5
Address 65130 (Hautes-Pyrénées). Château de Mauvezin: 10 Rue du Château; 05 62 39 10 27; *www.chateaudemauvezin.com*

🚗 **Train** to Tarbes, then bus to Bagnères-de-Bigorre and then taxi

ℹ️ **Visitor information** 3 Allées Tournefort, 65130 La Mongie; 05 62 95 50 71; *www.bagneresde bigorre-lamongie.com*

🕐 **Open** Year round

💰 **Price** €20–30; under 4s free

☕ **Eat and drink** *Real meal* Auberge Gourmande (1 Blvd de l'Hypéron, 65130 Bagnères-de-Bigorre; 05 62 95 52 01; closed Nov) specializes in local treats such as pork baked for 12 hours. *Family treat* L'Atelier (33 Allée des Coustous, 65130; 05 62 95 02 06; closed Sun out of season) is a modern brasserie offering creative cuisine such as fresh pasta with duck and *gambas* (large prawns).

🎭 **Festival** La Pourcailhade, an annual pig-calling contest in Trie-sur-Baïse, north of Mauvezin, involves pork roasts and pig races (mid-Aug).

Letting off steam

Take a bus from La Mongie, 40 km (25 miles) west of Château de Mauvezin, to Tarbes, capital of the Hautes Pyrénées. Run around the **Jardin Massey** (Pl Henri Bordes, 65000; www.ville-tarbes.fr) and play in the pool at the **Centre Nautique Paul Boyrie** (www.legrandtarbes.fr; Jun–Aug). Watch equestrian shows in summer at the **Haras National de Tarbes** (www.haras-nationaux.fr).

KIDS' CORNER

Look out for…
Spot these great birds of prey in the Parc National des Pyrénées:

1 Golden eagle
Dark brown with straight tail feathers and 85-cm (33-in) long wings, they have extremely powerful talons and can catch large prey.

2 Peregrine falcon
Black and tan mottled breast, pointed 43-cm (17-in) long wings, these birds nest on cliffs. They are the fastest creatures in the world, clocking up to 320 kmph (200 mph) when they swoop down for their prey.

3 Griffon vulture
Dual-tone grey with 100-cm (39-in) long wings, these birds have white bald heads. They lay one egg a year and can live up to 118 years.

4 Lammergeyer
These rare "bearded vultures" have 110-cm (43-in) long wings, and a big curved beak. They drop bones on the rock to break them open for the marrow.

VANISHING BEARS
The Pyrenees were famous for bears – but chances are you won't see any outside the Parc Animalier. Only a handful of the native Pyrenean bears remain and attempts to reintroduce mountain bears from Slovenia have caused big battles between animal lovers and local farmers.

Oink, oink
It started out as a joke, but the annual pig noise-making contest in Trie-sur-Baïse, where people compete to see who can make the best pig noises, has become one of France's most famous festivals.

Picnic under €20; **Snacks** €20–45; **Real meal** €45–90; **Family treat** over €90 (based on a family of four)

⑪ Grotte de Niaux
Amazing caveman cartoons

The most beautiful cave in the Pyrenees, the Grotte de Niaux is dazzling, its vast chambers decorated with paintings of bison, mountain goats, horses and deer. These were made by great hunters of the Magdalenian era (around 11,000 BC), who lived above the valley in the Grotte de la Vache. Like many modern artists, the hunters sketched animals in charcoal before painting them. The Parc de la Préhistoire in nearby Tarascon brings it all vividly to life.

Key Sights

④ Les Galeries Profondes
Only experts can enter this gallery housing mysterious signs and 15,000-year-old footprints.

⑤ Salon Noir This enormous "Black Hall" has over 100 drawings of animals – bison, deer and horses, but also fish and a weasel.

Information centre

① Entrance The cave can be spotted from a distance because of its 55-m (180-ft) high and 50-m (165-ft) wide porch set high above the valley.

② Entrance sculpture In 1994 the Italian sculptor Massimilliano Fuskas erected this sculpture in raw steel that echoes the mountains and draws the eye into the cave.

③ Entrance passages The passages are full of strange symbols, which are mostly a series of dots and dashes that seem to relay a message. Scholars have been trying to decode them for decades.

Letting off steam
Head to the **Base Nautique de Mercus** (www.basenautiquemercus. fr) in the town of Mercus-Garrabet, 11 km (7 miles) north of the village of Niaux. Swimming and boating with pedal boats, wakeboarding and "téléski nautique", in which eight water-skiers at a time are pulled across the lake with a giant cable, are on offer to visitors here.

Eat and drink
Picnic: under €20; Snacks: €20–45; Real meal: €45–90; Family treat: over €90 (based on a family of four)

PICNIC La Mie Dorée Ariégeoise (12 Rue St-Roch, 09040 Tarascon-sur-Ariège) offers sandwiches and pizzas. There is a picnic area with a play ground at the Parc de la Préhistoire.

Prices given are for a family of four

Lake by the Base Nautique de Mercus, Mercus-Garrabet

SNACKS La Bécane (28 Ave de Sabart, 09400 Tarascon-sur-Ariège; 05 61 03 61 72; la.becane.free.fr) is an American 1950s-style diner, which serves hamburgers and ribs, with an unlimited supply of coffee.

REAL MEAL La Mandoline (2 Ave Sabart, 09400 Tarascon-sur-Ariège; 05 61 05 15 75; closed Mon) tempts with delicious lasagne and pizzas baked in a wood-fired oven, along with steaks and seafood.
FAMILY TREAT Auberge de la Grotte (Pl du Village, 09040 Bédeilhac; 05 61 02 84 68; www. restaurant-auberge-de-la-grotte. com) is regarded as the best in the area, where a highly-rated young chef serves lobster and other seafood dishes, as well as more traditional mountain fare.

Shopping
Visit **Les Trésors de Pyrene** (Ave de la République, 09040 Tarascon-sur-Ariège) to pick up cheese, honey, hazelnut oil, pottery and crafts

The Lowdown

🌐 **Map reference** 12 F5
Address 09040 (Ariège). Grotte de Niaux: south of Tarascon-sur-Ariège on the D8; *www.sesta.fr/grotte-de-niaux.html*

🚗 **Train** from Toulouse via Foix for Tarascon-sur-Ariège, then taxi to Grotte de Niaux *(05 61 05 97 71)*

ℹ️ **Visitor information** Ave Paul-Joucla, 09040 Tarascon-sur-Ariège; 05 61 05 94 94; *www.montagnesdetarasconetduvicdessos.fr*

🕑 **Open** Feb–Oct: daily; Jan: Sat & Sun; Nov: Wed–Sun; Dec: school hols. Daily tours; book in advance *(05 61 05 88 37; www.ariege.com/niaux)*

💶 **Price** €27–37

🚩 **Guided tours** Visits are by guided tours only. From Apr–Oct, there are tours in English.

👫 **Age range** 5 plus. It is a 2-km (1-mile) walk and is slippery in some places.

⏱️ **Allow** A day to see Niaux, the Grotte de la Vache and the Parc de la Préhistoire.

🚻 **Toilets** At the ticket office at the entrance to the cave.

Good family value?
Besides the caves, there is plenty to interest children in the area. The prices for food and accommodation are also very reasonable.

from the Pyrenees. Or head for **Hypocras**, *(Pl Ste-Quitterie, 09400 Tarascon-sur-Ariège; 05 61 05 60 38; www.hypocras.com; open Tue–Sat)* to watch *hypocras* – a spicy cinnamon, cardamom and ginger alcoholic drink being made. Attributed to ancient Greek doctor Hippocrates, the drink arrived in France with the crusaders.

Find out more
DIGITAL Get information, pictures about Niaux and other Palaeolithic art on *www.bradshawfoundation.com*. The Bradshaw Foundation is dedicated to online learning about art, archaeology, and in particular, rock art from around the world.

Next stop...
BACK TO THE STONE AGE Pay a visit to the **Grotte de la Vache** *(09040 Alliat; 05 61 05 95 06; www.grotte-de-la-vache.org)* located on

the hill opposite Niaux. This cave sheltered a settlement that offers fascinating insights into the life of the Stone Age hunters in 14,000 BC. After visiting the cave, drive 4 km (2 miles) west to the **Parc de la Préhistoire** *(09040 Tarascon-sur-Ariège; 05 61 05 10 10; www.sesta.fr/parcdelaprehistoire.html)*. This has reconstructions of Palaeolithic shelters, along with demonstrations of Stone Age skills such as fire-making and painting.

Above Trying a hand at cave painting
Below Learning about cave painting techniques at the Parc de la Préhistoire

KIDS' CORNER

Unravel the mystery of cave paintings
Think of the cave paintings as a puzzle. Why were they made and what does it all mean? When you visit Niaux, take a notebook. Copy down the symbols you see and make up a map of their locations. See if you can find any clues and patterns. Why did they paint inside caves? Why some animals and not others? What did people actually do down in the caves?

FORGED CAVE ART
As far back as 1602, people visited Niaux and carved their names in the walls, but no one "recognized" cave art until 1906. When the Palaeolithic paintings were discovered in 1880 at Altamira, Spain, people accused the man who found them of forging them!

Enjoy the underground
There are two other fascinating caves around Niaux. The Grotte de Bédeilhac, 5 km (3 miles) north of Tarascon, has a huge entrance: a plane has been flown out of it. Inside it has beautiful stalactites and a smattering of cave art. Just 3 km (2 miles) south in Ussat-les-Bains, a little train goes up to the biggest cave in Europe: the Grotte de Lombrives.

Haunting ruins of the Château de Montségur

⑫ Réserve Nationale d'Orlu

Scenic mountains, golden eagles and wolf parks

Stretching eastwards from the ski-and-spa resort of Ax-les-Thermes, the Réserve Nationale d'Orlu covers one of the most scenic corners of the Pyrenees, where it is not unusual to see golden eagles floating overhead. The **Observatoire de la Montagne** is the headquarters for exploring wildlife, with an information centre and an interactive museum in French. It is also the base for nature walks or a visit to a hydroelectric dam. From here it is not far to the **Maison des Loups**, a park dedicated to wolves, who live in large natural enclosures.

Letting off steam

In summer, explore the mountains with a donkey. Hire one from **La Ferme des Anes** (www.la-ferme-aux-anes.com) at Unac, north of Ax-les-Thermes, for full-day or half-day excursions (parents walk and children ride).

⑬ Montségur

The last stand of the Cathars

Set vertiginously on a mountain top, the **Château de Montségur** was a witness to the demise of the heretical Cathars, who took refuge here at the end of the Albigensian Crusade (see p326). After a 10-month siege, it fell in 1244; the surviving 225 Cathars leapt into a huge bonfire rather than convert. Today, thousands visit the ruined site each year, drawn by the legends of the Cathars and the lost treasure that was smuggled out just before the fall of Montségur, possibly to Rennes-le-Château (see pp326–7). The steep climb can be

A European grey wolf on an outcrop, Réserve Nationale d'Orlu

tough for children aged under 8. The **Musée Archéologique** down in the village displays everyday objects used in the Middle Ages.

Letting off steam

Drive 13 km (8 miles) north to **Base de Loisirs Le Kart'are** (www.kartare-09.com) at Aigues-Vives, which has a first-rate karting track. Also on offer are mountain biking and paintball, with a playground for smaller children.

⑭ Grotte du Mas d'Azil

A drive-through cave

The D119 that goes from Sabarat or Lescure to Mas d'Azil also runs right through the Grotte du Mas d'Azil. This cave is a natural 150-m (429-ft) gallery in the rock and so important to prehistorians that it gave its name to the Azilien period (9,000 BC). The galleries have late Palaeolithic etchings, bear bones and memories of oppressed Protestants who made the cave into a fortress. In 1625, around 1,000 Protestants are believed to have held out here against an army of 14,000 during the Wars of Religion. The **Musée de la Préhistoire**

The Lowdown

🌐 **Map reference** 12 F5
Address 09300 (Ariège). Château de Montségur & Musée Archéologique: Montségur

🚗 **Train** to Foix, then CAP Pays Cathare bus to Lavelanet, then taxi

ℹ️ **Visitor information** 32 Rue du Village, 09300; 05 61 03 03 03; www.montsegur.fr

🕐 **Open** Château de Montségur & Musée Archéologique: daily; closed Jan

🍽️ **Eat and drink** *Real meal* À Table, (63 Ave Léon Blum, 09300; 05 61 64 61 73) has good lunch choices and a kids' menu. *Family treat* Costes (52 Le Village, 09300; 05 61 01 10 24; www.chez-costes. com) is a cosy old inn with a pretty terrace, with lots of duck on the menu; their *cassoulet* (bean and duck stew) is made from an old family recipe.

🎭 **Festival** Les Feux de la St-Jean, summer celebrations with "devils" and troubadour songs (22 Jun)

The Lowdown

🌐 **Map reference** 12 F6
Address 09110 (Ariège). Observatoire de la Montagne: Les Forges d'Orlu; 05 61 03 06 06; www.observatoire-montagne.com. Maison des Loups: Les Forges d'Orlu; 05 61 64 02 66; www.maisondesloups.com

🚗 **Train** from Toulouse to Ax-les-Thermes, then taxi

ℹ️ **Visitor information** 6 Ave Delcassé, 09110 Ax-les-Thermes; 05 61 64 60 60; www.vallees-ax.com

🕐 **Open** Observatoire de la Montagne: Apr–Jun & Sep–

Oct: closed Mon & Tue; Jul–Aug: daily. Maison des Loups: late-Apr–Oct: daily; May–Jun: closed Wed; Sep–Oct: closed Mon & Tue

🍽️ **Eat and drink** *Real meal* Le P'tit Montagnard (6 Pl Roussel, 09110 Ax-les-Thermes; www.leptitmontagnard.fr) offers more seafood than usual for a mountain restaurant, and also grilled meats, salmon and cheese fondues. *Family treat* Le Chalet (Ave Turrel, 09110 Ax-les-Thermes; www.le-chalet.fr) offers refined cuisine with a menu for children.

The Lowdown

- 🌐 **Map reference** 12 F5
  Address 09290 (Ariège).
  Grotte du Mas d'Azil & Musée
  de la Préhistoire: Mas d'Azil; 05 61
  69 97 22; www.grotte-masdazil.com.
  Forêt des Dinosaurs: Route de
  Sabarat, Castagnès; 05 61 60 03
  69; www.ariege-dinosaure.com
- 🚗 **Train** to Foix, then taxi or car
- ℹ️ **Visitor information** 17 Ave de la
  Gare, 09290 Mas d'Azil; 05 61 69
  99 90; www.tourisme-arize-leze.com
- 🕐 **Open** Grotte du Mas d'Azil &
  Musée de la Préhistoire: Apr–Jun
  & Sep: Tue–Sun; Jul–Aug: daily;
  other times: Sun only, daily during
  school hols (ring tourist office for

schedule). Forêt des Dinosaurs:
Jul & Aug: daily; Jun: pm daily;
Sep–Mar: Wed, Sat & Sun pm
- 🍴 **Eat and drink** *Picnic* Proxi
  Alimentation *(Rue Mouret, 09290
  Mas d'Azil; 05 61 60 44 58)* is a
  good place for picnic supplies.
  Real meal Le Jardin de Cadettou,
  *(09290 Faubourg St-Ferréol; 05 61
  69 95; 23; closed Mon & Tue, Sat
  lunch & Sun dinner)* serves dishes
  such as sheep cheese and spinach
  in pastry and crispy duck with fruit.
- 🎉 **Festival** Fête du Mas d'Azil,
  a village fête (Sep)

exhibits artefacts from the cave,
including unique works of art such
as harpoons, sculptures, a throwing
stick carved with a fawn and birds,
and a famous skull.

There are Neolithic dolmens
(megalithic table tombs) in the area
and the **Forêt des Dinosaurs**, which
reconstructs a dinosaur fossil dig
that took place in the 1920s. Kids
will enjoy the chance to play
palaeontologist here.

Letting off steam

Drive 11 km (7 miles) north to the
village of Carla-Bayle, to visit **Sequoia
Vertigo** *(www.sequoia-vertigo.com)*,
a tree adventure park with 13 routes
and 134 things to do. Set among a
vast woodland of majestic sequoias
planted over a century ago, it is
suitable for kids aged 5 plus and
over 4 ft (48 in) tall.

⑮ St Bertrand-de-Comminges

**Roman ghosts, ruins and
medieval mysteries**

This was once the flourishing Roman
city of Lugdunum Convenarum, until
the barbarian invasions destroyed it
in the 6th century. The city's fortunes

*One of the curious carved images in the
Basilique de Ste-Marie, St Bertrand*

changed in the 11th century, when
Bertrand de l'Île-Jourdain – the
cousin of Count Raymond IV of
Toulouse, who was the leader of the
First Crusade – was appointed bishop
and built the Romanesque **Basilique
de Ste-Marie**, nicknamed the
Cathedral of the Pyrenees. This
cathedral is filled with intriguing
details that include superbly carved
capitals and choir stalls.

Letting off steam

Run around in the Roman ruins
of Lugdunum or take a bus 12 km
(7 miles) north to the town of
Montréjeau, to the **Grottes de
Gargas** *(grottesdegargas.free.fr)*.
The caves have animal decorations
and 231 handprints; nearly all of
them are missing at least one finger.

The Lowdown

- 🌐 **Map reference** 12 E5
  Address 31510 (Haute-Garonne).
  Basilique de Ste-Marie: Pl de
  la Cathédrale; www.cathedrale-
  saint-bertrand.org
- 🚗 **Train** to Montréjeau, then SNCF
  bus to Labroquère, 2 km (1 mile)
  from St-Bertrand-de-Comminges
- ℹ️ **Visitor information** Ave des
  Thermes, 31510 Barbazan;
  05 61 88 35 64; www.tourisme-
  barbazan.com
- 🍴 **Eat and drink** *Snacks* La Bergerie
  *(Rue de la Porte Majou, 31510;
  05 61 89 60 33; Apr–Sep: open
  daily)* offers galettes (savoury
  pancakes). *Real meal* La Vieille
  Auberge *(Ville Basse, 31510;
  05 61 88 36 00; vieilleauberge.
  free.fr)* has duck à l'orange (duck
  in orange sauce) and lemon
  tart as specialities.

Where to Stay in the Pyrenees

Away from the Basque coast, accommodation in the Pyrenees tends to be more functional than glamorous. Self-catering apartments in the winter and summer resort areas are a popular choice for families, but there are also plenty of *gîtes* (cottage rentals), hotels and B&Bs.

AGENCIES
Alternative Aquitaine
www.alternative-aquitaine.co.uk
The website lists self-catering properties on the coast and in the mountains in all price ranges.

French Entrée Midi-Pyrenees
www.frenchentree.com/holiday-pyrenees
This website lists *gîtes*, apartments and B&Bs throughout the Hautes-Pyrénées and Ariège.

Bagnères-de-Bigorre
Map 11 D5
BED & BREAKFAST
Au Chat Ronfleur
3 Rue Cazalas, 65200; 05 62 95 42 87;
www.bagneres-chambredhote.com
The "Snoring Cat" is located in the heart of the Bagnères. The three large rooms are basic, but the breakfasts are good. The English-speaking owners are friendly and offer sound advice for visiting the region.

 €

CAMPING
Camping Monloo
Route de la Plaine, 65200; 05 62 95 19 65; www.lemonloo.com
Located in a quiet setting on the edge of the Bagnères, this camp site has mobile homes and chalets to let. There is a heated pool, waterslides, a playground, tennis and fishing to keep the kids busy. In summer, there are sports tournaments, themed evenings and other entertainment.

P ◎ €

Bayonne
Map 11 B4
HOTELS
Hotel Côte-Basque
2 Rue de Maubec, 64100; 05 59 55 10 21; www.hotel-cotebasque.fr
An atmospheric establishment right in the centre of Bayonne's St-Esprit quarter, this hotel offers attractive modern rooms, done up in natural

colours, with wooden floors. Some rooms have air conditioning, and all have double glazing and Wi-Fi.

€€

Hotel Loustau
1 Pl de la République, 64100; 05 59 55 08 08; www.hotel-loustau.fr
Housed in a charming old building just across the Adour river from the city centre, this hotel has splendid views over the river towards Bayonne. Rooms are soundproof and have Wi-Fi; there is a good restaurant too.

€€

Contemporary decor in Hotel Côte-Basque, Bayonne

Biarritz
Map 11 A4
HOTEL
Hôtel de l'Océan
9 Pl Ste-Eugénie, 64200; 05 59 24 03 27; www.biarritz-hotel-ocean.com
Located in the centre near the beach, this hotel has 24 rooms done up in bold colours and equipped with Wi-Fi; balconies of some rooms overlook the sea. The restaurant is good. Discount packages are on offer for golf and other attractions.

P €€€

CAMPING
Camping Le Ruisseau
Rue Burruntz, 64210 Bidart; 05 59 41 94 50; www.camping-le-ruisseau.fr
This big camp site south of Biarritz offers mobile homes, bungalows and a tree lodge; free shuttles to the beach in July and August. Mini-golf, watersports and other games available. Bar and restaurant on site.

P ◎ €

Cauterets
Map 11 C5
HOTEL
Village de Vacances Les Marroniers
Ave du Mamelon Vert, 65110; 05 62 92 12 12; www.marronniers-vacances.com
This resort complex is ideal for both outdoor summer sports and skiing, with an emphasis on family activities. The en-suite rooms are simple and modern. There is a playground and children's clubs for those aged 4 plus run during school holidays.

P ◎ €€

SELF-CATERING
Hotel-Résidence Le Lys
Rue de la Feria, 65110; 05 62 92 11 11; www.hotelresidencelelys.com
A bright, modern property near the cable cars, it offers attractive rooms and suites, with balconies and Wi-Fi on request. There is a small garden, activities for kids and laundry facilities. A spa and reflexology are also on offer.

€

Foix
Map 12 F5
HOTEL
Auberge des Myrtilles
Col du Marrous, 09000 Le Bosc; 05 61 65 16 46; www.auberge-les-myrtilles.com
Just west of Foix, this secluded hotel has modern-rustic rooms, a pleasant *gîte* and a restaurant specializing in traditional home cooking. There is a Jacuzzi, garden terrace and acres of woods to roam around in.

P ◎ €€€

Gavarnie
Map 11 D5
HOTEL
Le Compostelle
Rue de l'Eglise, 65120; 05 62 92 49 43; www.compostellehotel.com
Located on the pilgrimage route to Santiago de Compostela, this recently remodelled hotel has

comfortable and well-appointed rooms, some with great views of the cirque. There is a game room for kids.

🚫 €

SELF-CATERING
Gîte du Clot
Rue Principale, 65120; 05 62 92 40 49; www.leclot.fr
Set on the slopes of Mont Perdu, this *gîte* is a converted stone barn that sleeps up to 11. It can be divided into two independent units, including one sleeping four. It also has a pretty garden with a pond.

🚫 🛏 P €€

CAMPING
Le Pain du Sucre
65120 Gavarnie; 05 62 92 47 55; www.camping-gavarnie.com
Just ten minutes from the Gavarnie-Gèdre ski station, it offers 50 pitches, wooden cottages and mobile homes. A bar, shop, pizzeria, playground and laundry service are on offer.

🚗 🛏 P €

Lourdes
Map 11 D5

HOTEL
Villa Bon Repos
Ave du Stade, 65400 Argelès-Gazost; 05 62 97 01 49; www.bonrepos.com
A seven-minute drive from Lourdes, this old manor house is a family-run Logis de France, with stone walls and wooden beams. Comfortable and well-kept, all rooms have Wi-Fi; some have balconies and air conditioning. There is a garden and Jacuzzi outside.

🚗 P €

SELF-CATERING
Victoria Garden
13 Ave du Maréchal Foch, 65100; 05 62 92 77 67; www.victoriagarden.com
A good-value city-centre apartment hotel, close to the sanctuaries, it offers studio and larger junior suites for families, some with balconies. Wi-Fi,

Brick-red apartment building of Victoria Garden, Lourdes

Beautiful façade of the Manoir d'Agnès, Tarascon-sur-Ariège

optional breakfast, laundry service and free parking are available. See website for special offers.

🛏 P ✳ €

CAMPING
La Bergerie
8 Chemin de la Bergerie, 65400 Argelès-Gazost; 05 62 97 59 99; www.camping-labergerie.com
Just north of Argelès, at the crossroads of three valleys, this camp site offers cabins and two *gîtes* to let by the week. There is a playground.

🚫 🚗 P €

Montségur
Map 12 F5

BED & BREAKFAST
L'Oustal
46 Le Village, 09300; 05 61 02 80 70; tinyurl.com/4xfx985
This property offers four comfortable rooms and also a well-furnished *gîte*, with a garden and a terrace with great views. Friendly owners.

🚫 🚗 P €€

St-Bertrand-de-Comminges
Map 12 E5

HOTEL
Hôtel du Comminges
Ville Haute, 31510; 05 61 88 31 43; www.hotelducomminges.fr
This peaceful 15th-century pilgrims' hospice right by the Basilique de Ste-Marie was converted into a hotel over a century ago. Rooms are furnished with antiques. Breakfast available, but no restaurant.

🚫 P €

CAMPING
Camping Es Pibous
D26, 31510; 05 61 88 31 42; www.es-pibous.fr
This small, well-manicured camp site sits right on top of the ruins of the

Roman city under St-Bertrand. There are chalets and a mobile home on offer. A playground is on site.

🚗 P ⊙ €

Salies de Béarn
Map 11 B4

HOTEL
Hôtel du Parc
Blvd St-Guily, 64270; 05 59 38 31 27; www.hotelcasinoduparc.fr
A beautifully restored grand hotel of the 1890s, it has a spectacular glass-roofed lobby. Some rooms are simple and modern, others a little sleeker. There is an elegant restaurant and a casino; special deals for families.

🚗 P ✳ €€

BED & BREAKFAST
Demeure de la Presqu'Île
22 Ave des Docteurs-Foix, 64270; 05 59 38 06 22; www.demeure presquile.com
This peaceful 18th-century country house, surrounded by gardens, has en-suite rooms, with old parquet floors, tastefully painted in different colours. Excellent breakfasts and home-cooked dinners on request.

🚫 🚗 P €€

Tarascon-sur-Ariège
Map 12 F5

HOTEL
Manoir d'Agnès
2 Rue St-Roche, 09400; 05 61 02 32 81; www.manoiragnes.com
This charming 17th-century mansion looks like a gingerbread house outside; inside it is sharp and modern. A well-run and welcoming place, with Wi-Fi and a spa, it has one of the area's best restaurants.

🚗 P ✳ €€€

CAMPING
Le Pré Lombard
Map 12 F5
09400 Capoulet-Junac; 05 61 05 61 94; www.prelombard.com
This camp ground on the banks of the Ariège river offers pitches and a range of tents and cottages; game rooms and watersports available.

🚗 P ⊙ €

Price Guide
The following price ranges are based on one night's accommodation in high season for a family of four, inclusive of service charges and any additional taxes.
€ Under €100 €€ €100–200 €€€ over €200

The
South of France

With long sandy beaches, wild mountains and Mediterranean landscapes, the South of France and Corsica are great for a family holiday. The Cathar castles of Languedoc and the Roman Theatre at Orange bring history to life, while a boat ride along the pretty Canal du Midi, or the art and glitter of the Côte d'Azur show other aspects of the region. The cuisine is world famous and the climate perfect for outdoor activities.

Provence and the Côte d'Azur

Languedoc-Roussillon

Corsica

Highlights

Nice
Enjoy some of France's most delightful contemporary art in the capital of the Côte d'Azur. Be sure not to miss the Fondation Maeght in nearby St-Paul-de-Vence (see pp358–9).

Pont du Gard
Walk over, kayak under, have a swim and a picnic next to the world's best-preserved Roman aqueduct (see pp334–5).

The Camargue
Ride a white pony in the Camargue, home to pink flamingos, black bulls and French cowboys (see p345).

Palais des Papes, Avignon
Visit the medieval citadel of the popes in one of Provence's most beautiful cities, then seek out scenes painted by Van Gogh in Arles (see pp342–3 & 344–5).

Corsica
Build sandcastles on the beaches of the "Île de Beauté" and explore its magnificent forests, mountains and old granite villages (see pp365–75).

Carcassonne
Time-travel to the Middle Ages in Europe's strongest citadel. Walk along the ramparts and watch a joust in summer (see pp324–5).

Left The busy Quai des Martyrs de la Libération, Bastia, Corsica
Above left Barges cruising along the lush tree-lined waterway of the 240-km (149-mile) long Canal du Midi

The Best of
The South of France

The South of France conjures up images of villages immersed in vines, olive groves, sunflowers and lavender, sunny Mediterranean beaches and a breathtaking hinterland of mountains and dramatic gorges. It provides an idyllic setting for France's most striking Roman monuments and medieval castles, alongside cities filled with art and culture from all eras.

Culture vultures

Spend a day exploring the **Pont du Gard** (see pp334–5) and the interactive Discovery Centre, whetting appetites for the Maison Carrée – a superbly preserved Roman temple – and the amphitheatre in nearby **Nîmes** (see p336). Stand on stage to test the Roman theatre's acoustics in **Orange** (see p345).

Travel to the Middle Ages in **Carcassonne** (see pp324–5) and the Palais des Papes in **Avignon** (see pp342–3) – both offer tours. Pay a visit to **Les Baux** (see p344), where catapults are a vivid reminder of its feisty warlords, and medieval **Bonifacio** (see pp370–71) teetering over the sea. In **Arles** (see pp344–5) and **St-Rémy-de-Provence** (see p344) discover the scenes immortalized by Van Gogh, or follow Matisse's trail through **Collioure** (see p328), **St-Tropez** (see pp354–5) and **Nice** (see pp358–9).

Right Artworks for sale on a street in St-Tropez
Below Beach near the town of Ajaccio, Corsica

The great outdoors

The beaches are great, from the long sands near **Aigues-Mortes** (see pp336–7) to the *plages* (beaches) of **St-Tropez**. Bring binoculars to watch the pink flamingos of the **Camargue**

The petit train crossing a bridge, with the imposing ramparts of the medieval citadel of Carcassonne in the background

(see p345). Kayaking is great fun on the Sorgue, down from the mysterious **Fontaine-de-Vaucluse** *(see pp346–7),* in the heart of some of Provence's most idyllic landscapes. Be sure to take a barge along the tree-canopied ribbon of the **Canal du Midi** *(see pp330–31).* For families that love nature, Corsica offers magnificent mountain scenery and forests; fantastical rock formations around the **Golfe de Porto** *(see pp366–7)* are a World Heritage Site, and the beaches around **Porto-Vecchio** *(see p371)* as well as **St-Florent** *(see pp368–9)* are dazzlingly beautiful.

In a week

Start with two days in lively **Nice**, visiting the city, the delightful and often playful art in the **Fondation Maeght** *(see p359)* in St-Paul-de-Vence and Marineland in **Antibes** *(see p360).* Head west to **Avignon** to tour the Palais des Papes, then use Avignon as a base for a two-day trip to **Les Baux**, **Nîmes** and the **Pont du Gard**, with a swim in the Gardon river in the afternoon. On the sixth day, continue west to **Carcassonne**, taking in a joust in the afternoon, before ending with a lazy day along the **Canal du Midi**.

By season

Spring is a good time for exploring Corsica's **Balagne** *(see p368)* or the classic Provençal landscapes of Luberon such as in **Apt** *(see pp348–9)* and Cézanne's **Aix-en-Provence** *(see p352)* as well as **Monaco** *(see p360).* In early June, go to **Céret** *(see pp328–9)* for its luscious cherries. Summer is a time when fresh produce floods the markets and restaurants and festivals

start to fill the calendar – from the theatre festival in **Avignon** to lively water jousts in **Sète** *(see p332).* Some of the biggest summer festivals take place in **Beaucaire** *(see p336),* and often include the city's acrobatic *courses* or bloodless bullfights. If it gets too hot, go to the chestnut forests of the **Cévennes** *(see pp336–7)* or cool, windy Mount Ventoux above **Vaison-la-Romaine** *(see p348)* or splash in the rock pools of the **Gorges de Spelunca** *(see p366).*

By autumn, the huge chestnut forest of the **Castigniccia** *(see p369)* in Corsica glows with colour. On the island's more sheltered beaches, the sea is warm enough for a dip well into October, as it is around **Perpignan** *(see p328)* and **Antibes**. In winter, take **Le Petit Train Jaune** *(see p329)* into the Pyrenees for skiing or head for a sunny city break to **Nice** or **Marseille** *(see pp350–51).* For lively carnival celebrations, head to **Limoux** *(see p325),* which hosts Los Fécos with music, costumes and confetti battles every weekend from January to March.

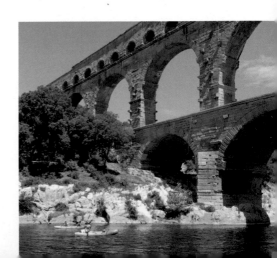

Kayaking on the Gardon river under the mighty Roman Pont du Gard

The South of France

Curving around the Mediterranean, the South of France is lined with beaches and lagoons, with the Camargue – the delta of the Rhône – in the centre. Mountains are never far, hugging the shore east of Nice, and the Pyrenees in the west. Road and rail networks are excellent along the coast and between cities. France's largest island, Corsica, is a mountain in the sea, with narrow roads and limited public transport, but extraordinary scenery and fabulous beaches.

Fresh produce at a covered market in Aix-en-Provence

Summer crowds at one of the many beaches in St-Tropez

Places of interest

The fortified old town of Bonifacio, Corsica, with the harbour in the foreground

Ruins of the Roman Théâtre Antique, Orange

Place de l'Horloge, one of the main squares in Nîmes

The Lowdown

🚗 **Getting there and around**
Air (see p322). **Ferry** (www.corsica-ferries.fr) from Toulon, Marseille and Nice to Corsica. **Train** TGV (www.voyages-sncf.com) serve major cities, including links from Paris. TER provides regional train service in Provence and the Côte d'Azur and Languedoc-Roussillon; www.ter-sncf.com (in French only) lists links to the regional networks. **Bus** Service varies from excellent to poor; the further from the coast, the less regular the public transport. Marseille (www.rtm.fr), Montpellier (www.montpellier-agglo.com/tam/index2.php) and Nice, as well as the towns on the Côte d'Azur (TAM, www.cg06.fr) have useful métro, trams and bus lines. Lignes d'Azur (www.lignesdazur.com) also provides bus connections in this area. For all train and bus timetables on Corsica, see www.corsicabus.org/Train_services.html. **Car** Rent from Europcar (www.europcar.fr); compare ticket prices on www.travelsupermarket.com.

🛒 **Supermarkets** Major chains include Monoprix, Intermarché, Carrefour, Super U and Casino. **Markets** Larger cities have daily markets, either outdoors or halles (covered markets), nearly all of which are closed on Monday. Many small towns and villages have markets on one set day each week. A list of markets is available from the local tourist and Département offices.

🕐 **Opening hours** Many shops are closed on Monday, but open on Sunday morning.

➕ **Pharmacies** There is at least one pharmacy, identified by a green cross outside, in each town and many villages. A list in the window will give details of the nearest pharmacie de garde open outside normal hours (on Sundays and at night). They are also listed in local newspapers and on www.pharmaciesdegarde.com.

🚻 **Toilets** Every city, town and village has generally decent toilets. Cities have pay or free street toilets that automatically clean themselves after each use.

The South of France Regional Airports

One of France's main holiday destinations for both the French and people from around the world, the south of France is well served by regional airports with links across Europe. While most are fairly small, Nice is the busiest airport in France after Paris, serving around 8 million passengers a year. Mountainous Corsica has four airports, two of which are primarily served by charters.

Wave-like roof of Béziers Cap d'Agde airport, close to the Languedoc beaches

Languedoc-Roussillon

The **Montpellier Méditerranée** is located off the D66, 9 km (5 miles) southeast of Montpellier. It is served by Air France, Ryanair, easyJet, Alitalia and bmibaby. A shuttle bus (€1.50) links it to the Place de l'Europe tramway station. It is medium-sized, easy to get around and closes at night. The airport has a café and two restaurants. Aéroport Hôtel (04 67 20 07 08; www.r-hotel34.com) is right next to the airport.

There are several other airports in this part of France that are suited to reaching different parts of the region. **Carcassonne Pays Cathar** is located just west of Carcassone off the A61, and offers Ryanair flights. **Béziers Cap d'Agde** is off the E80, 16 km (19 miles) east of Béziers and served by Ryanair and Flybe. **Perpignan-Rivesaltes**, 7 km (4 miles) north of Perpignan, is served by Aer Lingus, Ryanair, bmibaby and Flybe. **Nîmes-Alès-Camargue**, 11 km (7 miles) south of Nîmes, offers Ryanair flights.

Provence and the Côte d'Azur

At the west end of the Promenade des Anglais, **Nice Côte d'Azur** has flights with Air France, Aer Lingus, easyJet, Ryanair, British Airways, Lufthansa, Iberia, Air Corsica, Alitalia, Delta, Emirates and Qatar. Bus 23 (€1) goes to Nice's centre and Express Bus 99 (€4) to the train station.

There are two restaurants, sandwich/snack bars and Quick fast food in both terminals, as well as play areas in the departure areas of Terminal 1, at the Méli-Mélo Food Court, and in T2, at the Quick. It is a big airport – be sure to go to the right terminal. Allow ten minutes to take the free shuttle between terminals, and 15 minutes to get to the gate. The airport closes from midnight to 6am. The Novotel Nice Aeroport Cap 3000 (04 93 19 55 55; www.novotel.com) is linked to the airport by a five-minute free shuttle.

Provence and the Côte d'Azur are served by numerous other airports. **Marseille Provence**, located 20 km (12 miles) north of Marseille, just off the A7 and A55, offers flights by Air France, Ryanair, Twin Jet, easyJet, Lufthansa, Aer Lingus, Air Transat and Air Corsica. **Avignon** is off the A7 in Montfavet, 10 km (6 miles) from the city and is served by City Jet and Flybe. **Toulon-Hyères** is 3 km (2 miles) south of Hyères and 23 km (14 miles) east of Toulon. Flights are operated by Ryanair, Transavia, City Jet, Jetairfly and Air France.

Corsica

Located 7 km (4 miles) east of Ajaccio, off the N193, **Ajaccio Napoleon Bonaparte** has flights with easyJet, Air Corsica, Air France, Transavia,

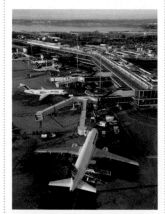

Aerial view of the busy Marseille Provence airport

Lux Air and Jetairfly. There are buses (€4.50) every hour linking the airport to the Ajaccio bus and train station. It has a snack bar, restaurant and an ice cream parlour. The airport is compact, easy to get around and closes at night.

Besides Ajaccio, Corsica has airports in Bastia, Figari and Calvi as well. **Bastia Poretta** is 22 km (14 miles) south of Bastia, off the N193, with flights operated by Air Corsica, Air France and easyJet. **Figari Sud-Corse** is situated 21 km (13 miles) north of Bonifacio and served by Ryanair and Air Corsica. Located 7 km (4 miles) south of Calvi on the Route des Artisans, **Calvi Sainte-Catherine** is served by Air Corsica, Air France and Niki.

The Lowdown

Ajaccio Napoleon Bonaparte 04 95 23 56 56; www.2a.cci.fr

Avignon 04 90 81 51 51; www.avignon.aeroport.fr

Bastia Poretta 04 95 54 54 54; www.bastia.aeroport.fr

Béziers Cap d'Agde 04 67 80 99 09; www.beziers.aeroport.fr

Calvi Sainte-Catherine 04 95 65 88 88; www.calvi.aeroport.fr

Carcassonne Pays Cathar 04 68 71 96 46; www.aeroport-carcassonne.com

Figari Sud-Corse 04 95 71 10 10; www.2a.cci.fr

Marseille Provence 04 42 14 14 14; www.marseille.aeroport.fr

Montpellier Méditerranée 04 67 20 85 00; www.montpellier.aeroport.fr

Nice Côte d'Azur 08 20 42 33 33; www.nice.aeroport.fr

Nîmes-Alès-Camargue 04 66 70 49 49; www.nimes-aeroport.fr

Perpignan-Rivesaltes 04 68 52 60 70; www.perpignan.cci.fr

Toulon-Hyères 08 25 01 83 87; www.toulon-hyeres.aeroport.fr

Languedoc-Roussillon

Stretching between the Pyrenees and the Rhône, this rugged region offers sandy beaches, a sunny climate and affordable prices. The ancient Romans left their remarkable legacy in the Pont du Gard and Nîmes, while Cathar castles, including the fantastic Carcassonne, evoke the Albigensian Crusade. Boating on the Canal du Midi or many rivers is a fun activity for kids.

Pont du Gard
p334

Canal du Midi,
Béziers
p330

Carcassonne
p324

Below *Alfresco tables in front of the remarkably preserved Roman amphitheatre, Nîmes*

① Carcassonne
The unconquered citadel

Dominating the Aude valley – the main Atlantic-Mediterranean trade route – Carcassonne has been the key to the south of France since prehistoric times. Its medieval *cité*, the most powerful in Europe, was never conquered; its Viscount Roger Trencavel was only captured in 1209 by treachery. Abandoned in the 1700s, the *cité* was about to become a stone quarry in the 1850s when the restorer Eugène Viollet-le-Duc stepped in and brought it back to life.

Boat moored on the Canal du Midi

Key Features

Basilique St-Nazaire

Château Comtal

R DU MOULIN D'AUDE

PLACE ST-JEAN

R PORTE D'AUDE

RUE ST LOUIS

ROMME CROS

R VIOLLET LE DUC

RUE TRENCAVEL

K RUE TRESAU

LICES BASSES

RUE DU PLO

PL MARCOU

LICES HAUTES

Porte Narbonnaise

Entrance

Gallo-Roman walls Made in 4th century AD, these protected the *cité* till 1209.

Le Grand Puits This is the largest of the 22 wells that supplied the *cité*. Legend says there is a hidden treasure here.

Basilique St-Nazaire Finished in 1330, this church is home to spectacular gargoyles and two enormous rose windows.

Porte Narbonnaise Two portcullises and a drawbridge defend the only road entrance to the *cité*.

The walls Two rings of walls (the outer one added in 1226) surround the *cité*.

Lices These easily defended spaces between the inner and outer ramparts were used for jousting and crossbow practice.

Château Comtal The castle in the *cité* was built by French kings to protect their *seneschal* (governor) from the locals.

The Lowdown

🌐 **Map reference** 12 G5
Address 11000 (Aude). Le Grand Puits: 8 Pl Grand Puits. Basilique St-Nazaire: Pl Auguste Pierre Point; 04 68 25 27 65 Château Comtal: cité de Carcassonne; *www.carcassonne.monuments-nationaux.fr.*

🚗 **Train** from Toulouse and Montpellier

ℹ️ **Visitor information** 28 Rue de Verdun, 11890; 04 68 10 24 30; *www.carcassonne-tourisme.com*

🕐 **Open** Château Comtal: Apr–Sep: 10am–6:30pm daily. Oct–Mar: 10am–5pm daily

💶 **Price** Château Comtal: €34–44 (audio guides €18); under 18s free

👫 **Skipping the queue** Arrive early in the morning – the citadel gets crowded in July and August.

👉 **Guided tours** For a tour of the towers and walls, ring Château Comtal for hours and languages. Audio guides available; contact the tourist office for details. Petit Train (*www.petit-train-cite-carcassonne.com*) and horse-drawn carriage tours (*www.carcassonne-caleches.com*) depart from Porte Narbonnaise.

👫 **Age range** 5 plus

🎭 **Activities** Hire boats from Hélios & Lou Gabaret (*www.carcassonne-croisiere.com*) for trips down the Canal du Midi (*see pp330–31*).

⏱️ **Allow** A day

🚻 **Toilets** Inside Porte Narbonnaise

🎪 **Festivals** Chevaliers de la Foi, jousting tournament full of broken lances and charging horses (Jul–Aug). La Fête Nationale, fireworks display (14 Jul). Le Marché de Noël, Christmas fair and markets (Dec)

Good family value?
This town is out of a storybook – kids simply adore it. The jousting tournaments are of special interest.

Letting off steam

Take bus 1 to Montlegun, with the option of lots of tree-top fun with **O2 Aventure** (www.02aventure. spaces.live.com). Bus 1 also goes to **Le Parc Australien** (www.leparc australien.wifeo.com), which has kangaroos, wallabies, ostriches and traditional Australian games such as boomerangs.

Swinging through the trees at O2 Aventure, Montlegun

Eat and drink

Picnic: under €20; Snacks: €20–45; Real meal: €45–90; Family treat: over €90 (based on a family of four)

PICNIC Le Break du Terroir (2 Rue du Grand Puits, 11000; 04 68 72 17 82; open daily) is a good place to pick up cold and warm sandwiches, chips and salads in the heart of the *cité*. There are picnic spots along the Chemin des Anglais outside the walls.

SNACKS Les Terrasses de Café (Pl Marcou, 11000; 04 68 72 07 99; www.lesterrassesdelacite.com) is a delightful al fresco café in the *cité*.

REAL MEAL Le Saint-Jean (1 Pl St-Jean,11000; 04 68 47 42 43; www.le-saint-jean.fr; closed Tue & Jan) offers a hot *chèvre* salad and salmon and a *croque monsieur* (grilled ham and

The chic bar area of Le Saint-Jean, Carcassonne

cheese sandwich) in the kids' menu. Sit in the garden and enjoy fine views of the Château Comtal. **FAMILY TREAT Le Trivalou** (69 Rue Trivalle,11000; 04 68 71 23 11; summer closed Mon for lunch; winter closed Mon & Tue for lunch; book ahead) is a restaurant on the road up to the *cité*. It serves *cassoulet*, lamb and traditional dishes, with matching wines and accommodates kids too.

Shopping

For a special treat, visit **L'Art Gourmand** (13 Rue St Louis, 04 68 25 95 33; Feb–Dec: daily) that sells delicious caramels, toffees, fudge, chocolate and over 30 kinds of ice cream. Take some time out to visit the fun, private museum of chivalry next door. Buy handmade arts and crafts from around Languedoc-Roussillon at **Le Vieux Lavoir** (11 Rue de Plô, 11000; 04 68 71 00 04).

Find out more

DIGITAL Download Carcassonne, a board game at carcassonneapp. com. The game is suitable for children aged 8 plus.
FILM Carcassonne's medieval gates and streets have been used in *Robin Hood: Prince of Thieves* (1991), which stars Kevin Costner and Morgan Freeman.

A still from the film Robin Hood: Prince of Thieves, shot in Carcassonne

Next stop...

LIMOUX Trains from Carcassonne go to Limoux, which is famous for its fizzy Blanquette de Limoux wine and Los Fécos (Jan–Mar: Sat & Sun), a carnival of satire, costumes and dancing. Do not miss the paintings at the **Musée Petiet** (www.limoux.fr). Take a taxi to the **Abbaye de St Hilaire**, off the D118, where a monk first added bubbles to wine, in 1531. The abbey has an exquisitely carved sarcophagus and a 16th-century painted ceiling.

A life-sized skeleton of a dinosaur in Dinosauria, Espéraza

② Cathar castles

Catapults, crusaders and castles in the sky

In 1210, Albigensian Crusaders (*see p312*) led by Simon de Montfort turned their trebuchets and catapults on Minerve, a beautiful old village located on a rocky outcrop where many Cathars had taken refuge. After two months, it fell, and 140 Cathars were burnt at the stake, a sign of things to come in Montségur, which was one of the last strongholds of the Cathars. Minerve has a full-size replica of a catapult on the opposite side of the ravine from the village as a reminder. To the west, bands of Cathars held out in castles so lost in the clouds that not even Simon de Montfort tried to attack them. **Château de Peyrepertuse**, teetering on a ridge, was abandoned only in 1240. **Château de Quéribus**, on top of a pinnacle, held out for 11 years after Montségur, till 1255. Both are ruined – but still breathtaking.

Letting off steam

Drive west through the dramatic Gorges de Galamus; the road is so narrow that it is controlled by a one-way signal in summer. Take a scenic tour on the **Train du Pays Cathar et du Fennouillèdes** (*www.tpcf.fr*) from the town of St-Paul-de-Fenouillet, just south of the gorge.

③ Dinosauria, Espéraza

Discovering dinosaur fossils

In the 19th-century town of Espéraza is a museum entirely dedicated to dinosaurs, displaying finds from a site nearby where bones and other remains have been dug out since the 1980s. The star attraction is a nearly complete skeleton of an *Ampelosaurus Atacis*, one of the four new species discovered here. In July and August, visitors can watch volunteers unearth new fossils. Espéraza was once the

world's second-largest producer of wool hats and the **Musée de la Chapellerie** shows how they were made.

Letting off steam

Drive or take a taxi 12 km (8 miles) south to the village of St-Martin-Lys, where **Pyrenees Outdoor** (*www.pyrenees-outdoor-sports.com*) offers rafting excursions down the Aude, which are gentle enough but only for children who can swim.

④ Rennes-le-Château

A village with hidden secrets

This tiny hilltop village has become famous thanks to a mystery that has inspired many conspiracy stories about the lost treasures and the

Rennes-le-Château overlooking mountainous terrain

The Lowdown

- 🌐 **Map reference** 12 G5
  Address 11260 (Aude). Dinosauria: Ave de la Gare; 04 68 74 26 88; *www.dinosauria.org*. Musée de la Chapellerie: Ave de la Gare; 04 68 74 00 75; *www.museedelachapellerie.fr*
- 🚗 **Train** from Carcassonne
- ℹ️ **Visitor information** Pl André Tricoire, 11500 Quillan; 04 68 20 07 78; *www.aude-pyrenees.fr*
- 🕐 **Open** Dinosauria & Musée de la Chapellerie: daily; closed Dec & Jan
- 🥤 **Eat and Drink** *Snacks* Le Tyrex (*Pl de la Gare, 11260 Espéraza; 04 68 20 53 96*) has steak *frites*, pasta and pizza. *Real meal* Relais de la Vallée Haute (*46 Ave du Languedoc, 11260 Campagne-sur-Aude; www.haute-vallee.fr*) serves tasty prawns, steak and Languedoc's lovely wines.
- 🚩 **Festival** Corse de Cote, rally race on the mountain roads (late-May–early-Jun)

The Lowdown

- 🌐 **Map reference** 12 H5
  Address 11190 (Aude). Château de Peyrepertuse: 11350 Duilhac-sous-Peyrepertuse; *www.chateaupeyrepertuse.com*. Château de Quéribus: 11350 Cucugnan; *www.cucugnan.fr*
- 🚗 **Train** from Carcassonne to Lézignan-Cobières, then taxi to Minerve. Peyrepertuese & Quéribus: Train from Carcassonne to Quillan, then taxi
- ℹ️ **Visitor information** Pl André Tricoire, 11500 Quillan; 04 68 20 07 78; *www.aude-pyrenees.fr*. Rue des Martyrs, 34210 Minerve;

04 68 91 81 43; *www.minervois-tourisme.fr*
- 🕐 **Open** Château de Peyrepertuse & Château de Quéribus: daily
- 🥤 **Eat and drink** *Picnic* Tudi (*20 Rue Promenade, 11350 Cucugnan; 04 68 45 49 44*) is a supermarket with all the ingredients for a picnic. Take them to the picnic area by the Château de Peyrepertuse. *Real meal* Auberge du Vigneron (*2 Rue Achille Mir, 11350 Cucugnan; 04 68 45 03 00; www.auberge-vigneron.com; closed 15 Nov–late-Mar*) serves excellent *cassoulet* (rich bean stew) and fine wines on its terrace.

Holy Grail, popularized by *The Da Vinci Code*. They are based around a poor parish priest Bérenger Saunière, who started to restore the church of Ste-Mary Magadeleine in the 1890s, then he was seen digging in the cemetery; he went on to spend an estimated €2.5 million before he died in 1917. Did Saunière find a treasure or discover a powerful secret and use it to blackmail the church? Over the church door, he inscribed "This is a Terrible Place". The parish house that he built, **Le Domaine de l'Abbé Saunière**, is now a museum.

Letting off steam

Play in the belvedere gardens of Rennes-le-Château. Or head 7 km (4 miles) east to **Rennes-les-Bains** (www.renneslesbains.org), a village spa with an outdoor warm mineral water pool, which is suitable for kids aged 3 plus.

The Lowdown

- **Map reference** 12 G5
  Address 11190 (Aude). Le Domaine de l'Abbé Saunière: Rue de l'Église; 04 68 31 38 85; www.renneslechateau.com
- **Train** from Carcassonne to Couiza, then take a taxi
- **Visitor information** Le Domaine, 11190; 04 68 31 38 85; www.rennes-le-chateau.fr
- **Open** Le Domaine de l'Abbé Saunière: daily
- **Eat and drink** *Snacks* Le Fournil (Z.A de l'Horte, 11190 Luc-sur-Aude; 04 68 31 47 75; www.du graindupain.com) has organic sandwiches, snacks and drinks served on a terrace. *Real meal* Hostellerie de Rennes les Bains (Rue des Bains Forts, 11190; 04 68 69 88 49; www.hotel-renneslesbains.com; closed Nov–mid-Mar) serves meat dishes and pasta.
- **Festival** Festival International de Folklore (Jul)

⑤ Forteresse de Salses

Spain's state-of-the-art fortress

For centuries, Salses was just on the Spanish side of the French–Spanish border. France's interest in the town caused King Ferdinand and Queen Isabella of Spain to order the construction of this vast state-of-the-art fortress, which housed 1,500

Column of stately rugged arches in the Forteresse de Salses

men and 300 horses on a narrow strip of land between sea and mountain. The Forteresse de Salses is the opposite of Carcassonne (see pp324) – it looks like a huge bunker – with rounded 32-ft (10-m) thick walls to deflect 15th-century cannons. Everything was carefully thought out, down to the hot baths for the officers. Despite this, the French captured it, Spain took it back, and after the Treaty of the Pyrenees in 1659, the frontier moved to where it is today.

Letting off steam

Take a taxi 11 km (7 miles) east from Salses to the town of **Port Barcarès** (www.portbarcares.com/tourisme. html). The town has a beach and hosts a summer Luna Park fun fair.

The Lowdown

- **Map reference** 12 H5
  Address (66600) Pyrénées-Orientales. Forteresse de Salses, Salses-le-Château; 04 68 38 60 13; monuments-nationaux.fr
- **Train** from Carcassonne
- **Open** Forteresse de Salses: year round
- **Price** €14–24; under 18s free
- **Eat and drink** *Real meal* Restaurant-Pizzeria du Fort de Salses (D900 Planal Salses, 66600; 04 68 38 70 72; closed Wed & out of season) has seafood *parillades*, (mixed grill). *Family treat* Rocher des Pirates (6 Rue Georges Méliès, 66600 Riversaltes; 04 68 57 15 84; www.rocherdespirates.com) is a pirate-themed restaurant with a show every evening.
- **Festival** Setmana per la Llengua, Catalan theatre and music (May)

⑥ Perpignan
Impressive Catalan castle

Part of Catalonia until 1659, Perpignan was the capital of a short-lived Catalan kingdom and has the **Palais des Rois de Majorque** (1276) to show for it, with ornate rooms in the keep. Unlike the soaring northern Gothic style, Catalan Gothic is best known for its remarkably wide buildings; the 15th-century **Cathédrale St-Jean** is a good example. Nearby in Place de la Loge, look out for the ship sticking out of the handsome Loge de Mer and the three arms poking out of the Hôtel de Ville. The city's best-known symbol is its castle-like gate, Le Castillet, housing the **Casa Pairal**, a museum showcasing local traditions.

Letting off steam
Head to the leafy Promenade des Platanes or take bus 22 to the sandy **Canet Plage**. Or go to **Aqualand**

The stone and red-brick walls of Cathédrale St-Jean, Perpignan

The Lowdown

🌐 **Map reference** 12 H6
Address 66000 (Pyrénées-Orientales). Palais des Rois de Majorque: Rue des Archers. Cathédrale St-Jean: Pl Léon Gambetta, 66000; 04 68 51 33 72. Casa Pairal: Pl du Verdun

🚗 **Train** from Carcassonne, change at Narbonne

ℹ️ **Visitor information** Pl Armand Lanoux, 66002; 04 68 66 30 30; www.perpignantourisme.com

🕐 **Open** Palais des Rois de Majorque: daily. Casa Pairal: Wed–Mon

🍽️ **Eat and drink** *Real meal* Grand Café de la Bourse (*2 Pl de la Loge, 66000; 04 68 34 25 05; open daily*) offers Catalan grilled meats, salads and *crème catalan*. *Family treat* Aux Reflets du Liban (*12 Rue Pierre Rameil, 66000; 04 68 51 71 29; closed Sun*) has tasty Lebanese dishes, mezés and honey desserts.

The beach of Port d'Avall, Collioure

(www.aqualand.fr) at St-Cyprien Plage, located 21 km (13 miles) south of Perpignan, separated from Canet Plage by a dune-lined lagoon.

⑦ Collioure
"Wild Beasts" and anchovies

A pretty anchovy fishing port, Collioure is located on the rugged Côte Vermeille. It was to this port that Henri Matisse and André Derain came to paint in 1905. The result was 242 paintings and drawings that so shocked art critics in Paris, they called the artists *fauves* (wild beasts). Art would never be the same again: learn more about it in the **Espace Fauve** and along the town's Fauvism trail. The seaside church of Notre-Dame-des-Anges, which the artists loved to paint, has an extraordinary Catalan Baroque altarpiece. The **Château Royal**, the imposing summer palace of the Kings of Mallorca, is used for special exhibitions. As for the anchovies, they are big business here: learn more at **Anchois Desclaux**.

The entrance to the Musée d'Art Moderne in Ceret

The Lowdown

🌐 **Map reference** 12 H6
Address 66190 (Pyrénées-Orientales). Espace Fauve: Ave Camille Pelletan; 04 68 98 07 16; www.collioure.com. Château Royal: Vieux Port. Anchois Desclaux: D914; www.anchois desclaux.com

🚗 **Train** from Perpignan. **Bus** from Perpignan

ℹ️ **Visitor information** Pl du 18 Juin, 66190; 04 68 82 15 47; www.collioure.com

🕐 **Open** Espace Fauve, Château Royal & Anchois Desclaux: daily

🍽️ **Eat and drink** *Snacks* Le Clocher (*Pl de L'Église, 66190; 04 68 82 22 94*) offers hot or cold tapas. *Real meal* El Capillo (*22 Rue St Vincent, 66190; 04 68 82 48 23*) has classic Catalan hams, anchovy dishes and brochettes.

🎆 **Festival** Fêtes de la St Vincent, great fireworks (Aug)

Letting off steam
Kick up sand on Collioure's beach at Port d'Avall, or take bus 400 to **Banyuls-sur-Mer** (www.obs-banyuls. fr) and its aquarium that showcases the marine biodiversity of the region. There are over 200 species of aquatic plants and animals from all over the Pyrénées-Orientales in 40 basins.

⑧ Céret
Three bridges, three Cubists and a ton of cherries

The Fauves went to Collioure, but the great Cubists – Picasso, Braque and Juan Gris – and their friends hung out in handsome old Céret. There is an art trail through town, while the **Musée d'Art Moderne**

The Lowdown

- **Map reference** 12 H6
  Address 66400 (Pyrénées-Orientales). Musée d'Art Moderne: 8 Blvd Maréchal Joffre; *www.musee-ceret.com*
- **Train** from Perpignan
- **Visitor information** 1 Ave Georges Clémenceau, 66400; 04 68 87 00 53; *www.ot-ceret.fr*
- **Open** Musée d'Art Moderne: daily; Oct–Apr: closed Tue
- **Eat and drink** *Real meal* La Fontaine (*Pl des Nou Raigts, 66400; 04 68 87 23 47*) serves home-style French dishes. *Family treat* Del Bisbe (*4 Pl Soutine, 66400; 04 68 87 00 85; www.hotelceret.com*) offers creative Catalan cuisine.
- **Festival** La Fête de la Cerise, cherry festival (May)

Colourful bunting on a square in Villefranche-de-Conflent, Têt valley

displays Matisse drawings from Collioure, Picasso's ceramics on bullfighting and works by Chagall and others. Do not miss the three bridges over the Tech river, including the 14th-century Pont du Diable, with a single 45-m (147-ft) high arch. Céret is also France's cherry capital from late May to June.

Letting off steam

Play in the car-free squares of Céret's medieval centre or take bus 340 or 341, to the town of Arles-sur-Tech, located 13 km (8 miles) southwest, where visitors don hard hats to walk along metal gantries into the **Gorges de la Fou** (*les-gorges-de-la-fou.com*), one of the narrowest canyons in Europe. Suitable for kids aged 5 plus.

⑨ Villefranche-de-Conflent

Forts in tight spots

The walled Villefranche-de-Conflent is a masterpiece created by Louis XIV's military genius, Sébastien Vauban, in the 1680s. Squeezed into the Têt valley, the covered **Ramparts** are fascinating to explore, as is **Fort Libéria**, built to defend the heights; the fort is reached by an underground staircase with 1,000 steps. Look out for the spectacular stalactite **Grotte des Grandes Canalettes** nearby and from June to September, Garage Villacèque in Verent-les-Bains offers a 4WD excursion to the lower slopes of

Canigou, a mountain that has been a pilgrimage spot since the Middle Ages. Rumour has it that the Holy Grail is hidden in the mountain.

Letting off steam

Run in the parks outside Villefranche's walls or take a ride into the Pyrenees on **Le Petite Train Jaune** (*www.trains-touristiques.sncf.com*) to Mont Louis, another Vauban citadel. Get off at **Font Romeu** (*www.font-romeu.fr*), an all-season resort that offers skiing, snow-shoeing, dog sledding and lovely walks in the summer.

The Lowdown

- **Map reference** 12 G6
  Address 66500 (Pyrénées-Orientales). Ramparts: 32 Rue du St-Jean. Fort Libéria: Villefranche de Conflent; *www.fort-liberia.com*. Grotte des Grandes Canalettes: 2 Rue St-Jacques; *www.grotte-grandes-canalettes.com*
- **Train** from Perpignan
- **Visitor information** 2 Rue St-Jean, 66500; 04 68 96 22 96; *www.villefranchedeconflent.fr*
- **Open** Ramparts: daily. Fort Libéria: daily (4WD available). Grotte des Grandes Canalettes: open Apr–Nov & French school hols; winter: Sat & Sun
- **Eat and drink** *Real meal* Café le Canigou (*Pl du Génie; 04 68 96 12 19; www.bistrot-villefranche.com; open daily*) offers Catalan salads, charcuterie and *escalivada* (roast vegetables). *Family treat* Grill la Senyera (*81 Rue St Jean; 66500, 04 68 96 17 65; closed Wed in winter*) offers refined cuisine and a kids' menu. Best to book.
- **Festival** Journées Médiévales (Jul)

⑩ Canal du Midi, Béziers
Up and down the locks

Completed in 1681, the Canal du Midi is a marvel of engineering that links the Mediterranean to the Atlantic via the Garonne river. Before it existed, cargo ships had to sail around the Straits of Gibraltar, facing pirates and other perils. With the building of the canal, transport became much easier and safer, and many inland towns along its banks profited too. One of these is Béziers, birthplace of the canal's chief builder Pierre-Paul Riquet. Today freight is moved by train, and boats cruise gently down the beautiful canal, with 63 locks and 130 bridges adding excitement.

Statue of Paul Riquet, Béziers

Key Sights

0 km / 1
0 mile / 1

② Musée des Beaux Arts
The mansion and paintings attest to Béziers's wealth. Many of the 20th-century works belonged to famous Resistance leader Jean Moulin, a native of Béziers.

④ Pont-Canal de l'Orb
Added in 1857, this 240-m (787-ft) aqueduct carries the Canal du Midi over the Orb river, eliminating the need for two of the Fonsérannes locks (see below).

⑤ Malpas Tunnel Riquet, the engineer behind the canal and its locks, also dug the world's first canal tunnel. Walk the towpath through its 170 m (557 ft) length and seek out the Roman Via Domitia nearby.

① Cathédrale St-Nazaire
Climb up to the terrace of Béziers's great Gothic cathedral for stunning views, reaching as far as the Massif Central.

③ Écluses de Fonsérannes The most impressive of Riquet's innovations, the 312-m (1,023-ft) staircase of nine locks raises boats from the Mediterranean to the level of the Orb river.

The Lowdown

🌐 **Map reference** 12 H4.
Address 34500 (Hérault). Cathédrale St-Nazaire: Plan des Albigeois; 04 67 76 84 00. Musée des Beaux Arts: Hôtel Fabrégat, Pl de la Révolution; 04 67 28 38 78

🚗 **Train** from Toulouse, Montpellier and Carcassonne

ℹ **Visitor information** 29 Ave St-Saëns, Béziers, 34500; 04 67 76 84 00; www.beziers-tourisme.fr

🕐 **Open** Musée des Beaux Arts: Apr–Jun & Sep–Oct: 10am–6pm

Tue–Sun; Nov–Mar: 10am–5pm Tue–Sun

💶 **Price** Musée des Beaux Arts: €9–19

👫 **Skipping the queue** Prices for boat hire soar in summer – visit out of season, if possible.

🛈 **Guided tours** Béziers' tourist office offers one of Canal du Midi and one devoted to Paul Riquet. Book in advance.

👫 **Age range** 4 plus

👫 **Activities** Hire canal boats (€425 plus per week). Les Bateaux de

Soleil (www.bateaux-du-soleil.com) offers a choice of day cruises around Béziers. The tourist office offers a Geo-caching treasure-hunt game (using GPS) in the city centre.

⏱ **Allow** A day to a week

🚻 **Toilets** At Place Pierre Semard in Béziers, Fonsérannes and Malpas Tunnel

Good family value?
Although not suitable for toddlers, the Canal du Midi is a calm, relaxing place to explore together as a family.

Letting off steam

There is plenty of room to run around and cycle along the banks of the canal. Head south of Béziers to Valras-Plage which, besides a sandy beach, has the **Palais de la Maquette** (www.palaisdelamaquette. com), housing world record-breaking LEGO and K'nex models. There are playrooms where visitors can build their own.

A wealth of fresh farm produce awaiting shoppers in Les Halles, Béziers

Eat and drink

Picnic: under €20; Snacks: €20–45; Real meal: €45–90; Family treat: over €90 (based on a family of four)

PICNIC Les Halles (Pl Pierre Semard, 34500) sells ingredients for picnics that can be enjoyed at shady spots along the canal.
SNACKS Allo'thentic (74 Blvd Georges Clémenceau, 34500; 04 67 28 59 93; www.allothentic. com; lunch & dinner daily) is a local favourite for its scrumptious pizzas, salads and sandwiches, as well as paninis.
REAL MEAL Le P'tit Semard (13B Pl Semard, 34500; 04 67 80 31 04; www.leptitsemard-beziers.com; closed Mon & Sun dinner) offers dishes prepared with fresh ingredients from Béziers's market, just opposite the restaurant. Specialities include seafood cassoulet (rich bean stew) and tender Charolaise steak, along with home-made frites (chips).
FAMILY TREAT La Maison de Petit Pierre (22 Ave Pierre Verdier, 34500; 04 67 30 91 85; www.lamaisonde petitpierre.fr; Mon–Wed lunch & Thu–Sat lunch & dinner) is a welcoming "country house" with a garden terrace. It is the realm of Top Chef winner Pierre Auge and serves refined, quite pricey modern fare.

Shopping

Visit **King Jouet** (Rue de la Ginesse, 34500; 04 99 47 49 90), a huge toy store that stocks many international toy brands. Delectable chocolates and cakes that look almost too pretty to eat tempt everyone in **Maison CarraTié** (49 Ave Jean Moulin, 34500; 04 67 31 13 25; www.maison-carratie.fr). For a variety of locally made cheese, wine and other goodies, head to **Maison de Malpas** (Route de l'Oppidum, next to the Malpas tunnel, 34440; 04 67 32 88 77; www.lemalpas.com).

Find out more

DIGITAL Play lock-keeper online on www.terrax.org/sailing/locks/lockflightjs.aspx.

Take cover

Head for Béziers' excellent history museum, the **Musée du Bitterois** (Caserne Saint-Jacques, Rampe du 96ème, 34500; 04 67 36 81 61), with its antiquities and displays on how the Canal du Midi made Béziers world famous for its wine.

Next stop...

PÉZENAS Take bus 216 northeast to Pézenas, a quaint 17th-century town, where famous playwright and actor Molière and his troupe performed for the governors of Languedoc. Learn all about him in 3D at **Scénovision Molière** (www.scenovisionmoliere. com). Look out for the little tower-shaped, sweet-savoury meat pies, the petits pâtés Pézenas, supposedly introduced by Lord Clive of India – a must-try!

Charming 17th-century mansions lining a quiet street, Pézenas

Inside the unfinished Cathédrale St-Just-et-St-Pasteur, Narbonne

⑪ Narbonne
A rutted Roman highway and half a cathedral

In Roman times, Narbonne was the principal city in southern Gaul, and it continued to prosper until the catastrophic 14th century when, on top of plague and wars, the harbour silted up. But with the construction of Canal de la Robine in 1787, which linked up with Canal du Midi, trade returned. The canal flows under the Pont des Marchands, one of the only bridges in France lined with houses. Nearby, on Place de l'Hôtel de Ville, is a section of the Via Domitia, once

The Lowdown

🌐 **Map reference** 12 H5
   Address 11100 (Aude). Musée d'Art et d'Histoire & Musée Archéologique: both in Pl de l'Hôtel de Ville; 04 68 90 30 54; www.narbonne.fr. Cathédrale St-Just-et-St-Pasteur: 7 Rue Armand Gauthier; 04 68 32 09 52

🚗 **Train** from Montpellier, Nîmes, Paris and Béziers

ℹ️ **Visitor information** Rue Jean Jaurès, 11100; 04 68 65 15 60; www.narbonne-tourisme.com

🕐 **Open** Musée d'Art et d'Histoire & Musée Archéologique: closed Mon. Cathédrale St-Just-et-St-Pasteur: daily; Oct–Jun: pm only

🍽️ **Eat and drink** *Snacks* En Face (27 Cours République, 11100; 04 68 75 16 17; closed Tue pm & Wed) cooks up bourrides (a tasty fish stew). The kids' menu has frites (chips). *Real meal* La Flambée des Mille Poètes (2 bis, Ave Elie Sermet, 11100; 04 68 65 15 87; closed Sat & Sun) serves Breton crêpes and pizzas.

---

the main Roman highway in Gaul – the deep ruts left by chariots and wagons over the centuries can still be spotted. More Roman remains can be seen in **Musée Archeologique**, which is housed in the 13th-century archbishop's palace together with the **Musée d'Art et d'Histoire**. Behind it, the half-finished Gothic **Cathédrale St-Just-et-St-Pasteur**, begun in 1272, has a splendid cloister and a soaring 40-m (130-ft) choir – but construction stopped due to bad times, leaving a glorious stump. The treasury has fine 16th-century tapestries, one depicting the Creation.

Letting off steam
The shady pedestrian promenades along the canal are perfect for stretching the legs, or hire electric boats by the Pont de la Liberté.

⑫ Agde
The Black Pearl

Sitting on a volcanic bubble, Agde was the ancient Greek town of Agathé Tyché or "Good Luck". The many ships that sank nearby were not lucky, but they preserved bronzes, including a superb 4th-century BC statue of Alexander the Great that is on display in the **Musée de l'Ephèbe** devoted to underwater archaeology.

Agde is nicknamed the "Black Pearl" for its unique basalt buildings. By far the largest of these, the 12th-century **Cathédrale St-Étienne d'Agde** is fortified with 3-m (10-ft) thick walls and a towering keep-belltower, which was built over a temple dedicated to Diana.

Letting off steam
Agde merges into Le Cap d'Agde, Languedoc-Roussillon's most fashionable resort, with a variety of sports and activities and 14 km (8 miles) of sandy beaches. Take bus 10 to **La Tamarissière** (4 Rue Commandant Malet, 34300; 04 67

Roman amphorae on display at the Musée de l'Ephèbe, Agde

The Lowdown

🌐 **Map reference** 13 B4
   Address 34300 (Hérault). Musée de l'Ephèbe: Mas de la Clape; 04 67 94 69 60. Cathédrale St-Étienne d'Agde: Rue de l'Hotel du Cheval Blanc

🚗 **Train** from Béziers. **Bus** Capbus 3 & 4 link Agde & Le Cap d'Agde

ℹ️ **Visitor information** Rond-Point du Bon Accueil, 34305 Le Cap d'Agde; 04 67 01 04 04; www.capdagde.com

🕐 **Open** Musée de l'Ephèbe: closed Tue

🍽️ **Eat and drink** *Snacks* Sea Side (3 Pl Terrisse, Le Cap d'Agde, 34300; 04 67 01 71 58) is a terrace restaurant that offers mussels, frites, pizzas and crêpes. *Real meal* L'Ami Louis (Quai Di Dominico, 11 Rue de la Gabelle, 34300; 04 67 26 25 48; www.ami-louis.com; closed Mon & Thu lunch & Wed) has a variety of surf and turf menus for parents and kids.

🎭 **Festival** Festival des Marionnettes (May)

Travellers aboard a colourful cruise boat on Sète's Grand Canal

94 79 46). This nature reserve, where an ancient pine forest backs the sands, is a good bet for families.

⑬ Sète
Canal cruises and dolls

Once the Canal du Midi was finished, it needed a defensible port. In 1666, Louis XIV's minister Colbert founded Sète, by channelling the surrounding wetland swamps into canals and then building a fake cardboard town to lure in residents. Today, it is one of the biggest fishing ports on the Mediterranean: **Sète Croisières** offer cruises through the canals to the local oyster farms. For a giggle, visit **Musée International des Arts Modestes** (MIAM), where exhibits include the likes of plastic Bart Simpson and Scooby-Doo dolls!

Letting off steam

Jump around in the **Fantasy Park** (www.fantasypark.fr), a bouncy castle park on Plage de la Corniche, the nearest to the centre of Sète's many beaches. Bus 320 goes to the town of Mèze, where dinosaurs once roamed. Today, the **Musée Parc des Dinosaurs** (www.musee-parc-dinosaures.com) has life-sized models of the giant lizards to gawp at.

The Lowdown

Map reference 13 B4
Address Hérault 34200.
Sète Croiseres: Quai du Général-Durand; 04 67 46 00 46; www.sete-croisieres.com. Musée International des Arts Modestes: 23 Quai du M de Lattre de Tassigny; www.miam.org

Train from Béziers, Narbonne or Montpellier

Visitor information 60 Grand Rue Mario Roustan, 34200; 04 99 04 71 71; www.ot-sete.fr

Open Sète Croisières: cruises Apr–Nov. Musée International des Arts Modestes: closed Mon

Eat and drink *Snacks* Royal Juice (5 Rue Gambetta, 34200; 04 67 18 72 14; www.royaljuice.fr; closed Sun) has fresh fruit juices and offers the chance to create smoothies, sandwiches or salads from a list of ingredients. *Real meal* Monte-Christo (31 Quai Général Durand, 34200; 04 67 51 95 65; daily summer, closed Wed dinner & Thu out of season) offers good-value fresh food and colouring books.

Festival Fête de St-Louis, water jousting championships (Aug)

⑭ Montpellier

A buzzing capital

No city in Languedoc-Roussillon can match the buzz and boutiques of Montpellier, or the fantastic collection of art by Gustave Courbet and other 19th-century artists in the **Musée Fabre**, a short walk from the vibrant Place de la Comédie. Highlights include Courbet's famous *Bonjour M. Courbet* and Berthe Morisot's *L'Eté*. The €12 million **Amazonian Greenhouse** in the Parc Zoologique de Montpellier, built in conjunction with a nature reserve in French Guiana, has sloths, armadillos and much more. The **Aquarium Mare Nostrum**, on the other side of the town, displays 300 species in its tanks. There are virtual tours on offer

A stack of brightly painted toy cars outside a store, Montpellier

too: ride a cargo boat in a storm, descend into an ocean abyss and visit an ice cave.

Letting off steam

Run around the arty playgrounds near Place de la Comédie, along the Esplanade Charles du Gaulle.

The Lowdown

Map reference 13 B4
Address Hérault 34000. Musée Fabre: 39 Blvd de Bonne Nouvelle, 34000; 04 67 14 83 00; www.museefabre.montpellier-agglo.com. Amazonian Greenhouse: 50 Ave d'Agropolis, 34000; 04 67 54 45 23; www.zoo.montpellier.fr. Aquarium Mare Nostrum: Allée Ulysse, Odysseum, 34960; 04 67 13 05 50; www.aquariummarenostrum.fr

Train from Béziers

Visitor information Pl de la Comédie, 34000; 04 67 60 60 60; www.ot-montpellier.fr

Open Musée Fabre: closed Mon. Amazonian Greenhouse: closed Mon except school hols. Aquarium Mare Nostrum: daily

Eat and drink *Snacks* Le Dilemme (12 Rue Farges; 04 67 69 02 13; open daily) offers affordable refined cuisine, with prawns, chicken and *cassoulet* (rich bean stew). The restaurant's relaxed mood has made it a big favourite. *Real meal* Place O Goût (5 Pl de la Chapelle Neuve; 04 67 29 90 45; open daily) is centrally located and serves dishes such as exquisite cheese soufflé and duck burgers in olive bread; kids are welcomed.

All Hail the Water Knight!

Agde claims to have held the first modern *joutes nautiques* (water jousts) in 1601. The crusaders at Aigues-Mortes (see p336) jousted on boats because there were not many horses available. It is one of the most popular summer sports in Languedoc; children start jousting at the age of six. To be a water knight, you need:

1 A boat with a special platform high over the bow.
2 A small wooden shield and a long wooden lance.
3 A team of eight to ten rowers, a bowman to direct them, a drummer and an oboe player. Everyone must wear white.
4 Charge! Stand on the platform as oarsmen row furiously, the musicians play and you lunge at your opponent's shield. The first to fall in the water loses!

ALL THAT GLITTERS IS NOT GOLD

Bronze was so valuable in ancient times that nearly all the surviving statues today come from ship wrecks. The rest of the metal was melted down.

The hill of broken pots

In the Musée de l'Ephèbe, try to spot the different types of amphorae. These were used as shipping containers in ancient times. Wine, olive oil, grains and other foods were sent in such pots, mostly to Rome – where there is a hill named Testaccio that is made of nothing but broken pots, dropped by butterfingered dock workers!

Picnic under €20; **Snacks** €20–45; **Real meal** €45–90; **Family treat** over €90 (based on a family of four)

⑮ Pont du Gard
Built to last – and without cement

In AD 45, the growing Roman colony of Nîmes was thirsty. The nearest water source was in Uzés – far away across rugged country and the Gardon river – so Roman engineers brought water to Nîmes instead. In 15 years, a thousand workers built a 50-km (31-mile) aqueduct, carried over the Gardon on a 49-m (160-ft) high bridge known today as the Pont du Gard. This marvel has lasted 2,000 years.

Grafitti on the Pont du Gard

Key Features

Middle tier In the 18th century, this was widened to carry a road that was eventually closed in 1998. A flood that year prompted restoration work, for which stone from the original quarries was used.

The piles Wide and shaped like prows, they support the bridge and help the aqueduct to stand up to the Gardon's floods.

Upper tier For over five centuries, water flowed through the top channel carrying up to 40,000 cubic metres (over 10.5 million gallons) a day at its peak.

Left bank (towards Uzès)

The piles

Lower tier

Right bank (towards Nîmes)

Middle tier

Cavities and protruding stones The Romans knew that nothing lasts forever. The holes and stones were left to support scaffolding for future repairs.

The stones Although weighing up to 6 tons (5 tonnes), these were cut so perfectly that the Pont du Gard was constructed without using any mortar.

Discovery Centre Opened in 2000, this complex on the right bank puts the Pont du Gard in context with a cinema, museum, children's activities, an open-air exhibition on the local *garrigue* (the surrounding scrub-covered hills) and also a 25-minute Cinemascope film on the bridge's history.

The Lowdown

🌐 **Map reference** 13 C3.
Address 30210 (Gard). Pont du Gard & Discovery Centre: 400 Route du Pont du Gard, 30210 Vers-Pont-du-Gard; *www.pontdugard.fr*

🚗 **Train** to Nîmes, then bus 168 or 169. **Bus** 205 from Avignon

ℹ **Visitor information** Pl des Grands Jours, 30210 Remoulins; 04 66 37 22 34; *www.ot-pontdugard.com*

🕐 **Open** Pont du Gard: year round. Discovery Centre: Mar–Oct: 9am–5:30pm (May–Sep: until 7pm), closed Mon am. There are entrances to the Pont du Gard

and Discovery Centre on both banks.

💶 **Prices** Discovery Centre: €10–20 (Nov–Feb) for a family of up to five & €15–25 (Mar–Oct)

👫 **Skipping the queue** Arrive early as the car park fills up fast.

🏇 **Guided tours** Contact the tourist office for details.

👫 **Age range** 4 plus

🧩 **Activities** Ludo, in the Discovery Centre, has activities for ages 5–12 years, such as Roman role playing, observing nature and archaeology.

⏱ **Allow** A day

☕ **Café** In the Discovery Centre

🚻 **Toilets** In the Discovery Centre and the left bank entrance

🎭 **Festivals** Garrigue en Fête, a rural festival with shows and tastings (Easter weekend). Nuit de la Chouette, "night of the owl" to learn about owls and other birds of prey (mid-March)

Good family value?
An educational and inexpensive day out, especially with the family-oriented activities in the Discovery Centre and on the Gardon river.

Letting off steam

Go for a dip in the calm, clear waters of the Gardon, or, on condition that the kids know how to swim, take an unforgettable canoe ride under the Pont du Gard with **Kayak Vert** (www.canoe-france.com/gardon), based just upstream in Collias.

Visit the **Estel Quarries** on the left bank, which provided the easily cut golden limestone that was used to build the aqueduct. Enjoy the three easy family walks that have been set up by the Maison de la Pierre. One of the walks follows the path used by the ancient engineers to bring the stone to the building site.

The family-friendly beach along the Gardon near the Pont du Gard

Eat and drink

Picnic: under €20; Snacks: €20–45; Real meal: €45–90; Family treat: over €90 (based on a family of four)

PICNIC Buy supplies in one of the supermarkets in the nearby town of Remoulins and have a picnic along the botanical trail that follows the Gardon river by the Pont du Gard.
SNACKS Le Cafeteria (Pont du Gard right bank), in the Discovery Centre, serves sandwiches, snacks, quick lunches and ice cream.
REAL MEAL Les Terrasses (Pont du Gard left bank; 04 66 37 50 88; summer daily, winter Thu–Sun) is a brasserie that serves Mediterranean cuisine – not just dishes such as tomato and asparagus soup, lamb provençale, but also apple pie, along with teas and snacks. Kids' menus are available.
FAMILY TREAT Le Moulin des Artistes (14 Ave du Pont du Gard; 04 66 22 44 28, 30210 Remoulins; www. lemoulindesartistes.fr) is housed in a 15th-century mill, filled with paintings and sculptures. This well-priced gastronomic restaurant has three terraces shaded by willows. It serves traditional French fare, with an exotic touch.

Shopping

The Discovery Centre's three shops (two on the left bank and one on the right) offer a huge range of books, colouring books, games, comic books and clothing. Other goodies include varieties of honey, olive oil, savoury delicacies and wines, as well as ceramics and pottery that display the arts and crafts of the region.

Find out more

DIGITAL Go to www.pbs.org/wgbh/ nova/lostempires/roman/aqueduct java.html to construct an aqueduct.

Take cover

Head west of the Pont du Gard to Arpaillargues-et-Aureillac, where the Moulin de Chalier houses the **Universal Museum** (www.moulin-de-chalier.fr), with thousands of antique toys dating from 1900 to 1960, including old cars and trains that kids can actually play in. In April, they host the annual Great Bear fair, devoted to European dolls and teddy bears.

Next stop…

UZÈS Ride bus 205 or drive 11 km (7 miles) southeast to the town of Uzès, where the belltower, the **Tour Fenestrelle**, looks like an upright Tower of Pisa. Take a guided tour of the **Duché** (www.uzes.com). This handsomely furnished Renaissance castle served as the residence of the 17th duke of Uzès. Follow it up with a visit to the renowned confectioner Haribo's **Musée des Bonbons** (www. haribo.fr), with interactive exhibits, games and of course candy tasting.

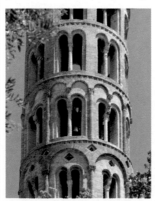

Exquisite tiers of windows on the Tour Fenestrelle in Uzès

Les Arènes in Nîmes, where gladiators fought in Roman times

⑯ Beaucaire

A medieval castle and a Roman farm

An important river port, Beaucaire has an impressive medieval castle towering over the Rhône. Inside the castle walls are gardens and the **Musée Auguste Jacquet**, which has archaeological finds and artefacts recalling Beaucaire's celebrated ten-day Foire de la Ste-Madeleine that drew merchants from across Europe. Just 4 km (2 miles) west of town, the **Mas des Tourelles** is located on the site of a Roman villa and an amphora factory. It produces wine the ancient

way – a film on a giant screen shows how they do it. There is also a reconstructed Roman wine cellar.

Letting off steam

Kids aged 7 plus can go for a spin at Beaucaire's **Karting Circuit Julie Tonelli** (*Chemin des Melettes, 30300; 04 66 59 60 13; www.circuitjulie tonelli.com*). A short distance 6 km (4 miles) south is **Le Vieux Mas** (*www.vieux-mas.com*), where tots can run around a 1900s farm, with friendly animals and costumed craftspeople.

⑰ Nîmes

The Rome of France

Nîmes earned its nickname, the "Rome of France" thanks to two exceptional buildings. The **Maison Carrée**, an intact ancient temple, shows a 3D film to further boost the imagination. **Les Arènes**, the world's best surviving amphitheatre, demonstrates its purpose in the *Espace Gladiateur*, which shows virtual combats. The **Castellum Divisorium**, where water from the Pont du Gard

was distributed in ten lead pipes across the city is a rare survivor. Look out for crocodiles. A crocodile chained to a palm, celebrating Augustus's defeat of Antony and Cleopatra, is the symbol of Nîmes. The symbol is even on sewer lids.

Letting off steam

Let the kids tear around the **Jardins de la Fontaine** (*6 Ave Jean Jaurès, 30000; 04 66 58 38 00*) one of the oldest public gardens in France, built in 1735 around the spring that served Nîmes before the Pont du Gard. There is a ruined temple of Diana, and a path up Mont Cavalier leads to the **Tour Magne** (*Cadereau, 30000; 04 66 58 38 00*), a 32-m (101-ft) high Roman tower.

Jet skis on the Rhône with the Château de Beaucaire in the background, Beaucaire

⑱ Aigues-Mortes

Through the salt mountains

The mighty **Ramparts** of Aigues-Mortes rise out of the salty marshes of the Camargue (*see p345*) that gave this medieval town its name – "Dead Waters". King Louis IX made it a base for his crusades, setting sail from here in 1248 with 1,500 ships bound for the Holy Land. Remains of his

---

The Lowdown

- 🌐 **Map reference** 13 C3
  Address 30300 (Gard).
  Musée Auguste Jacquet: Ave Marius Gardiol; 04 66 59 90 07.
  Mas des Tourelles: 4294 Route de Bellegarde; 04 66 59 19 72; www.tourelles.com

- 🚗 **Train** from Nîmes. **Bus** from Nîmes

- ℹ️ **Visitor information** 24 Cours Gambetta, 30300; 04 66 59 26 57; www.ot-beaucaire.fr

- 🕐 **Open** Musée Auguste Jacquet: closed Tue. Mas des Tourelles: pm (Jul & Aug also am); Nov–Mar: closed Sun

- 🍽️ **Eat and drink** *Snacks* La Brasserie du Château (*30 Rue Maréchal Joffre, 30300; 04 30 67 84 25; open daily*) serves sandwiches, chips, salads and ice cream. *Real meal* Auberge de l'Amandin (*1076 Chemin de la Croix de Marbre, 30300; 04 66 59 55 07; www.auberge-amandin.com; closed Sun dinner & Mon*) is the place for artistic Provençal dishes; includes an excellent kids' menu.

The Lowdown

- 🌐 **Map reference** 13 C3
  Address 30000 (Gard).
  Maison Carrée: Pl de la Maison Carrée and Les Arènes: Pl des Arènes; www.arenes-nimes.com. Castellum Divisorium: Rue de la Lampèze

- 🚗 **Train** from Montpellier

- ℹ️ **Visitor information** 6 Rue Auguste, 30020; 04 66 58 38 00; www.ot-nimes.fr

- 🕐 **Open** Maison Carrée, Les Arènes & Castellum Divisorium: daily

- 🍽️ **Eat and drink** *Real meal* Les Bartavelles (*4 Rue de l'Ecole, 30000; 04 66 21 30 18; closed Mon*) tempts with the local *gardianne de taureau* (beef stew); kids adore the *crème brûlée au Carambar*. *Family treat* Aux Plaisirs des Halles (*4 Rue Littré, 30000; 04 66 36 01 02; www.aux plaisirsdeshalles.com; closed Sun & Mon*) is one of the gourmet delights of Nîmes and pricey. Weekday adult and kids' menus are reasonable.

- 🎪 **Festival** Feria de Pentecôte features bull fights (Jun)

The Lowdown

🌐 **Map reference** 13 C4
Address 30220 (Gard).
Ramparts & Tour de Constance:
Pl Anatole France; *aigues-mortes.*
monuments-nationaux.fr. Salins
du Camargue: Route du Grau-du-
Roi; 04 66 73 40 24; *www.visites*
alinsdecamargue.com

🚗 **Train** from Nîmes. **Bus** from Nîmes

ℹ️ **Visitor information** Pl St-Louis,
30220; 04 66 53 73 00; *www.ot-*
aiguesmortes.fr

🕐 **Open** Ramparts & Tour de
Constance: daily. Salins du
Camargue: Mar–Oct: tours daily

🍽️ **Eat and drink** *Real meal* L'Eden
(8 Rue Denfert Rochereau, 30220;
04 66 53 69 45; www.eden
restaurant.fr; closed Sun dinner &
Mon) serves *foie gras* with melon,
steaks and grilled seafood.
Family treat Restaurant Le "S"
(38 Rue de la République, 30220;
04 66 53 74 60; www.le-s.fr; closed
Thu lunch summer & Sun dinner,
Mon lunch & Thu in winter) serves
elegant Mediterranean cuisine,
using the fresh herbs of the
south. Book ahead.

---

castle can be seen in the **Tour de
Constance**, which in the 17th century
was used as a prison for Protestants.
Sea salt has for long been a mainstay
of the town; the **Salins du Camargue**
can be visited on *petit train* rides
through mountains of salt and pink
lagoons. Look out for the Tower of
the Salted Burgundians located left
of the south exit of the town.

Letting off steam

Kids will love running around the walls
of the town. Take a taxi or drive to
Domaine de Listel *(Domaine de*

*The old town of Aigues-Mortes, fortified
with medieval ramparts*

Jarras, 30220; *www.chevaux-listel.
camargue.fr)* for riding safaris and
pony rides. Play on the beach in **Le
Grau-du-Roi** *(www.ville-legrauduroi.
fr)*, 8 km (5 miles) from Aigues-Mortes.

⑲ St-Hippolyte-du-Fort

Hungry little caterpillars

Most people associate silk with
China, but for centuries it has been
a mainstay of the lush hills of the
Cévennes. One of the main centres
of silk production is the village of
St-Hippolyte-du-Fort. The **Musée
de Soie** demonstrates how silk is
made – from silkworm to cocoon
to cloth. Kids can try a hand at
untangling the threads. Count the
sundials while walking through the
village (there are at least 20). Like
most towns in the Cévennes, St-
Hippolyte was once Protestant and
it claims to have the biggest Temple
(Protestant church) in France.

The Lowdown

🌐 **Map reference** 13 B3
Address 30170 (Gard).
Musée de Soie: Pl du 8 Mai;
04 66 77 66 47; *www.museede
lasoie-cevennes.com*

🚗 **Bus** D40 from Nîmes

ℹ️ **Visitor information** Les Casernes,
30170; 04 66 77 91 65; *www.
cevennes-garrigue-tourisme.com*

🕐 **Open** Musée de Soie: Apr–Nov:
daily

🍽️ **Eat and drink** *Real meal*
L'Auberge Cigaloise *(Route de
Nîmes, 30170; 04 66 77 64 59;
www.aubergecigaloise.fr; closed
Wed)* does seafood, lamb and
pies, plus a kids' menu. *Family
treat* L'Amourier *(Route de
Monoblet, 30170; 04 66 77 26 19;
www.amourier.free.fr; closed Sun
dinner & Mon)* offers food with
exotic touches; vegetarian and
kids' menus too.

🎪 **Festival** Folies des Fils,
needlework festival (Oct)

Letting off steam

There is plenty of room to run around
in sleepy St-Hippolyte. Or take bus
715 to the town of Anduze, which
is famous for its bamboo gardens,
Bambouseraie *(www.bambouseraie.
com)*. Catch the **Cévennes steam
train** *(www.trainavapeur.com)* from
Anduze to St-Jean-de-Gard.

Picnic under €20; **Snacks** €20–45; **Real meal** €45–90; **Family treat** over €90 (based on a family of four)

Where to Stay in Languedoc-Roussillon

With its warm climate, beaches, beautiful scenery and laid-back attitude, Languedoc-Roussillon is an especially popular region for camping in the great outdoors, although rates of its luxury hotels and villas tend to be more affordable than elsewhere in Mediterranean France.

AGENCIES
Crème de Languedoc
www.creme-de-languedoc.com
This website offers an extensive list of luxury villas, cottages, B&Bs and apartments in all price ranges, across Languedoc-Roussillon.

Languedoc Holiday Rentals
www.languedoc-holiday-rentals.com
A good selection of self-catering properties and B&Bs for all budgets, many with pools, are listed here by their owners.

Aigues-Mortes   Map 13 C4
HOTEL
Hotel les Croisades
2 Rue du Port, 30220; 04 66 53 67 85; www.lescroisades.fr
In the centre of town, overlooking the Tour de Constance and the marina, this pleasant hotel's rooms on the ground floor are especially designed for families with children. Rooms are equipped with Wi-Fi. Breakfast offers good value and is served on the verandah much of the year.
🛏 ❄   €

CAMPING
Yelloh! Village La Petite Camargue
30220 Aigues-Mortes; 04 66 53 98 98; www.yellohvillage-petite-camargue.com
Located near the beach, this camp site offers three different kids' clubs, including one for teens, and a horse-riding centre with lessons. Shuttles to the beaches of Le Grau du Roi and La Grande Motte are available.
🛏 P 🌀   €–€€

Beaucaire   Map 13 C3
HOTEL
Hôtel Robinson
Route de Remoulins, 30300; 04 66 59 21 32; www.hotel-robinson.fr
Just 2 km (1 mile) northwest of the centre of Beaucaire, this 31-room

Mediterranean-style hotel is set in the hills and woods. Facilities include two pools, ping pong and a playground. The restaurant offers a kids' menu.
🛏 P ❄ 🌀   €€

Béziers   Map 13 A4
HOTELS
Hôtel des Poètes
80 Allées Paul Riquet, 34500; 04 67 76 38 66; www.hoteldespoetes.net
This little hotel, a short walk from the train station, overlooks the romantic garden right in the centre of Béziers, where the leafy lawns offer plenty of room to scamper about. Rooms are modern, functional and comfortable. Wi-Fi is free and bikes are available.
🛏 P   €

Château de Lignan
Pl de l'Église, 34490 Lignan-sur-Orb; 04 67 37 91 47; www.chateaulignan.fr
Located on the banks of the Orb river, just ten minutes from the city centre, this elegant château is set in a huge park full of old trees. Rooms are peaceful and modern. The restaurant serves exceptional cuisine.
🛏 P ❄ 🌀   €€

Elegant entrance to the Hôtel des Poètes, Beziers

Hôtel Résidence
35 Ave de la Cave, 34440 Nissan-les-Enserune; 04 67 37 00 63; www.hotel-residence.com
Housed in a 19th-century winemaker's mansion near the Canal du Midi, this attractive hotel has a pretty courtyard garden. The nearest Mediterranean beaches are a ten-minute drive away. It has a superb restaurant with a kids' menu.
🛏 ❄ 🌀   €€

SELF-CATERING
Résidences Port Minervois-Les Hauts du Lac   Map 12 H4
Route du Lac, 11200 Homps; 04 67 26 07 90; www.coralia-vacances.com
Located near the Canal du Midi, this complex offers 2–5-room villas ideal for families, with a communal playground, tennis, beach volleyball, mini-golf and spa. Some of the villas have private pools. Wi-Fi is available at the reception. Linen and towel hire and baby kits are also available.
🛏 P 🌀   €

CAMPING
Le Sérignan Plage
34410 Sérignan; 04 67 32 35 33; www.leserignanplage.com
On the sandy beach south of Béziers, this large camp site has unusually well-equipped mobile homes and chalets (minimum stay a week). The more luxurious ones are equipped with air conditioning, bedding, TV, dishwashers and bicycles. There are mini-clubs and games for kids.
🛏 P 🌀   €€

Le Cap d'Agde   Map 13 B4
HOTEL
Hôtel Hélios
Mont St-Martin, 12 Rue du Labech, 34300; 04 67 01 37 68; www.hotel-helios.com
This low-rise hotel, recently remodelled in an Art Deco style, is in the centre of action in Le Cap d'Agde and within walking distance

Outside tables in the courtyard of Hôtel de la Cité, Carcassonne

of the beaches and golf course. There is an apartment just for families and a playground in the garden.

🚐 P ❄ ❂   €€

CAMPING
Camping La Tama
4 Rue du Cadet Malet, 34300; 04 67 94 79 46; www.camping-latama.com
This camp site on the big sandy La Tamissière beach, 5 km (3 miles) west of the town centre, offers attractive pitches amidst a pine grove. They provide tents on wooden platforms, sleeping four, or chalets with kitchens. A play area, table tennis, launderette, barbecues and a shop are on offer.

🚐 🛏 P   €

Carcassonne   Map 12 G5
HOTELS
La Bastide
81 Rue de la Liberté, 11000; 04 68 71 96 89; www.hotel-bastide.fr
A 20-minute walk from the medieval citadel, near the train station, this hotel has well-kept rooms. A number of good restaurants are located nearby. Internet is available for a fee.

🚐 P ❄   €

Hôtel de la Cité
Pl Auguste-Pierre Pont, 11000; 04 68 71 98 71; www.hoteldelacite.com
One of Languedoc's most luxurious hotels occupies the former bishop's palace in the heart of the citadel, with canopied beds and other medieval trimmings. Many rooms overlook the romantic garden. The restaurant has a Michelin star. Special family packages are available.

🚐 ❄ ❂   €€€

SELF-CATERING
Les Gîtes de Cabardès   Map 12 G4
7 Rue des Jardins, 11610 Ventenac-Cabardès; 04 68 24 08 23; www.carcassonne-holidays.com
Located 8 km (5 miles) northwest of the city on the edge of a traditional village, these three tidy *gîtes* built over enormous ancient wine vats enjoy a peaceful feel. They come equipped with DVD players, TV and Wi-Fi, as well as baby cots and highchairs.

🛏 P ❂   €

Domaine de la Bouriette   Map 12 G4
11290 Arzen; 04 68 24 61 77; www.carcassonne-gite-wine.com
Set amidst the vineyards, a short drive on the D119 west of the city, these two stone-built family *gîtes* sleeping four are a relaxing retreat. The vineyard also has a petting zoo of farm animals and perhaps the only vine maze in France.

✕ 🛏 P ❂   €€

CAMPING
Domaine d'Arnauteille
Arnauteille, 11250 Montclar; 04 68 26 84 53; www.camping-arnauteille.com
Located 14 km (7 miles) south of the city, this camp site has mobile-home cottages and chalets, with incredible shower and toilet facilities, done up in Greco-Roman style. Morning kids' club for ages 4–12 years; horse-riding excursions are offered as well.

🚐 P ❂   €€

Collioure   Map 12 H6
CAMPING
Les Criques de Porteils
Corniche de Collioure D114, 66701 Argelès-sur-Mer; 04 68 81 12 73; www.lescriques.com
A half-hour walk from Collioure, this stylish camp ground is set on terraces above the rugged coast, with steps leading down to the coves. It has playgrounds, a mini-farm and music, art and sports activities. Highchairs and cots available.

🛏 P ❂   €–€€

Narbonne Plage   Map 12 H6
HOTEL
Hotel de la Clape
4 Rue des Fleurs, 11100 Narbonne Plage; 04 68 49 80 15; www.hoteldelaclape.com
A short walk from the big sandy beach, this eco-friendly hotel has a lovely patio and a great restaurant; half-pension terms offer a good deal. Staff is welcoming.

🚐 P ❄ ❂   €€

Nîmes   Map 13 C3
HOTEL
Acanthe du Temple
1 Rue Charles Babut, 30000; 04 66 67 54 61; www.hotel-temple.com
A 5-minute walk from the Maison Carrée and 2 minutes from the airport shuttle stop, this is a friendly little hotel in a 17th-century mansion. It offers free Wi-Fi and a reasonably priced breakfast; the nearby garage is available for a fee.

🚐   €

SELF-CATERING
Le Cheval Blanc
1 Pl des Arènes, 30000; 04 66 76 05 22; www.lechevalblanc-nimes.com
Housed in a former denim factory, these large apartments enjoy a superb location looking out over Les Arènes. It retains several original features. The apartments come with stylish furnishings and flat-screen TV, as well as Internet access.

🚐 🛏 ❄ ❂   €€

Price Guide
The following price ranges are based on one night's accommodation in high season for a family of four, inclusive of service charges and any additional taxes.
€ Under €100 €€ €100–200 €€€ over €200

Key to symbols *see back cover flap*

Perpignan
Map 13 A6

BED & BREAKFAST
La Maison Haute
17 Impasse Drancourt, 66000; 04 68 34 76 64; www.lamaisonhaute-perpignan.fr
Conveniently located between the train station and the centre of Perpignan, this relaxed, welcoming *chambre d'hôtes* has a suite ideal for two adults and two kids. The owner knows all about Perpignan and treats visiting families like her own.

 €

Pont du Gard & Uzès
Map 13 C3

HOTELS
Hôtel Restaurant Le Gardon
9 Rue de Campchesteve, 30210 Collias; 04 66 22 80 54; www. hotel-le-gardon.com
In the heart of the Gardon gorges, this hotel offers a relaxed atmosphere along with good cooking using local ingredients. There are many places of interest around, such as the Pont du Gard, Roman villages, great walks and rivers to paddle or swim in.

🚫 🛏 P ⊗ €€

Château d'Arpaillargues
Route du Château, 30700 Arpaillargues; 04 66 22 14 48; www.chateaudarpaillargues.com
Just west of Uzès, set in a park of century-old trees, this beautiful 18th-century residence was once home to Franz Liszt's beloved Marie de Flavigny. Run by a young couple, it has an outdoor Jacuzzi, tennis, table tennis and bikes to rent, as well as an elegant restaurant.

🛏 ⊗ €€€

SELF-CATERING
Résidence le Mas des Oliviers
1 Rue des Cedres, 30700 Uzès; 04 79 65 08 41
Located in a quiet neighbourhood, a short walk from the historic centre of Uzès, these modern and well-maintained apartments with terraces offer an excellent and affordable option for families. Linen can be hired and Wi-Fi is available on the ground floor.

 P ✳ ⊗

Mas des Sagnes
68 Chemin de la Draille, 30210 Collias; 04 66 22 85 62; www.lemas dessagnes.fr
This collection of newly built *gîtes*, set amidst olives and mulberries, is immersed in the countryside, with views over the *garrigue*-covered hills stretching all the way to Mont Ventoux in Provence. Pastel rooms are simply furnished; the owners are helpful and provide linen; cots and highchairs are also available.

🚫 🛏 P ⊗ €€

Le Mazet
D981, 30700 Uzès; 06 10 42 15 23; www.mazet-uzes.com
Only 2 km (1 mile) from the centre of Uzès, yet enjoying a charming rural setting, this stone *bergerie* (sheepfold) has been beautifully restored into a villa accommodating up to six. The pretty garden is perfect for lazing around the pool. Internet access is available and board games are provided for rainy days.

🚫 🛏 P ⊗ €€

The fully-equipped modern kitchen of Le Mazet, Uzès

CAMPING
Camping Gorges-Gardon
762 Chemin Barque Vieille, 30210 Vers-Pont-du-Gard; 04 66 22 81 81; www.camping-gorges-gardon.fr
Located on the banks of the Gardon river and not far from the famous aqueduct, this camp ground offers shady pitches and a choice of mobile homes and chalets. Kids love the pool with its giant slides and there is a playground and games room, too. The restaurant offers takeaways and there is free Wi-Fi at the bar.

🚫 🛏 P ⊗ €–€€

Sète
Map 13 B4

HOTEL
Hôtel Venezia
Les Jardins de la Mer, 20 La Corniche de Neuburg, 34200; 04 67 51 39 38; www.hotel-sete.com
A rare affordable family lodging in Sète, this modern 18-room hotel is located near the beach and a short bus hop into the city centre. Each room has a patio, where the friendly owners deliver breakfasts. Restaurants are within walking distance.

🛏 P €€

CAMPING
Le Castellas
RN 112, 34200; 04 99 57 21 21; campings.village-center.com
Located 15 km (9 miles) southwest of Sète, this large and popular camp ground is right on the beach and offers a variety of activities, entertainment and clubs for kids aged 4 plus in July and August. There are pitches but the chalets and mobile homes are preferable; half board is available.

🛏 P ⊗ €–€€

Villefranche-le-Conflent
Map 12 G6

BED & BREAKFAST
Casa Penalolen
3 Domaine Ste-Eulalie, 66500; 04 68 96 52 35; casa-penalolen.com
Built in 1910, this handsome pink granite and marble villa, by the Têt river and surrounded by a lush meadow and mountains, is only a few minutes from Villefranche. The rooms are decorated with a smattering of antiques; the friendly owners serve a generous breakfast on the summer terrace.

🚫 🛏 P ⊗ €€

SELF-CATERING
Chalets Quazemi
Blvd St-Martin, 66820 Casteil; 04 68 05 55 11; www.cuisine-produits-catalans.com/location.htm
In a stunning setting on the slopes of Canigou, the sacred mountain of the Catalans, these basic wooden chalets are a good choice for families who love nature. Villefranche is a short drive away and there are picturesque mountain paths in every direction. Meals are provided on request.

🚫 🛏 🛏 P €

Provence and the Côte d'Azur

This region, extending from the Rhône river to the Italian Riviera, has inspired some of the greatest 19th- and 20th-century artists with its sun-soaked landscapes. Avignon boasts the splendid Palais des Papes, Marseille has great museums and St-Tropez has France's most famous beaches. Kids will enjoy spotting real French cowboys in the Camargue.

Below *Sunbathers and swimmers at one of the many beaches of St-Tropez*

Fontaine-de-Vaucluse *p346*
Palais des Papes, Avignon *p342*
Nice *p358*
St-Tropez *p354*
Marseille *p350*

① Palais des Papes, Avignon
Splendour and intrigue

In 1309, after French King Philip IV bribed cardinals to elect the French pope Clement V, he convinced Clement to flee Rome, a city of warring gangs, and come to Avignon. The next six popes stayed here, bringing it 70 years of corruption; in 1340, the poet Petrarch called Avignon "the sewer of the earth". The popes' palace, begun in 1335, proclaims the power of the medieval church – the largest Gothic palace ever built.

The Avignon Cathedral

Key Features

Belltower

Grand Tinel All original decorations in this banqueting hall were lost in a fire in 1413. Cardinals met here to elect a new pope.

St Martial Chapel Matteo Giovanetti's frescoes show the life of Martial, one of the first saints to bring Christianity to France.

Pope's Chamber

Angel's Tower

Stag Room

Champeaux Gate

Great Chapel Built in four years during the Black Death (1348–52), this chapel is 52 m (170 ft) in length.

Stag Room Ceramic tiles and colourful frescoes of hunting and fishing in a forest adorn Clement VI's study.

Petit Palais Located to the north of the Palais des Papes, the former archbishop's palace contains a fine collection of Italian art, including Botticelli's *Virgin and Child*.

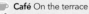

Military architecture The ten towers of the palace ensured it was virtually unconquerable.

The Lowdown

🌐 **Map reference** 13 D3
Address 84000 (Vaucluse). Palais des Papes: 3 Pl du Palais; *www.palais-des-papes.com*. Petit Palais: 3 Pl du Palais des Papes; *www.petit-palais.org*

🚗 **Train** from Nîmes and Marseille

ℹ️ **Visitor information** 41 Cours Jean Jaure, 84000; 04 32 74 32 74; *www.ot-avignon.fr*

🕐 **Open** Palais des Papes: Nov–Feb: 9:30am–5:45pm; 1–14 Mar: 9am–6:30pm; 15 Mar–Jun: 9am–7pm; Jul: 9am–8pm; Aug: 9am–9pm; 1–15 Sep: 9am–8pm;

16 Sep–Oct: 9am–7pm. Petit Palais: 10am–1pm & 2–6pm Wed–Mon

💰 **Price** Palais des Papes: €38–48 (including audio guides); under 8s free. Petit Palais: €12–22; under 18s free

🚻 **Skipping the queue** Get the Avignon Passion pass. Pay full fare at one monument and receive discounts at others. Contact the tourist office for details.

🚩 **Guided tours** Contact the tourist office for details

👫 **Age range** 6 plus

⏱️ **Allow** 2 hours

☕ **Café** On the terrace

🚻 **Toilets** On the ground floor

🎭 **Festivals** Festival d'Avignon, the biggest theatre festival in France (Jul). The Festival d'Avignon Off features street performances and alternative productions (Jul)

Good family value?
Kids with imagination who like history will enjoy it. The guided tours really help bring it to life.

Letting off steam

Dance to the tune of *Sur le pont d'Avignon* on the Pont St-Bénezet, below the Palais des Papes. Legend says the original wooden bridge was built by the shepherd Bénezet. When it collapsed, a new one, with 22 arches, was built of stone in 1172, which lasted for 600 years. Four arches remain, enough for a little dance. Ride the antique carousel in the nearby Place d'Horloge.

The Pont St-Bénezet bridge located just under the Palais des Papes

Eat and drink

Picnic: under €20; Snacks: €20–€45; Real meal: €45–€90; Family treat: over €90 (based on a family of four)

PICNIC Les Halles *(Pl Pie, 84000; www.avignon-leshalles.com; closed Mon)* offers fresh ingredients every morning in a building with a garden growing on the façade. Enjoy food on the Île de la Barthelasse – free shuttle boats, from the landing just up the river from the Pont St-Bénezet, cross over every 15 minutes from April to December.
SNACKS Encas de Plaisir *(5 Rue des Fourbisseurs, 84000; 04 90 85 59 48; closed Sun)* offers delicious *quiches*, Sicilian *arancini* (deep fried rice balls) and *spitini* (filled meat parcels on a skewer), either to eat in or take away.
REAL MEAL Tapalocas *(15 Rue Galante, 84000; 04 90 82 56 84; www.tapalocas.com; open daily)*, a Spanish theme restaurant, remains

Diners enjoying an evening at Tapalocas, a popular choice for its tapas

a firm favourite for its wide choice of hot and cold *tapas* (all available at the same price) and its big lunch specials.
FAMILY TREAT La Petite Pêche *(13 Rue St-Étienne, 84000; 04 90 86 02 46; closed Sun)*, an informal little restaurant, serves perfectly cooked fresh seafood and offers an affordable wine list.

Shopping

Visit **Librerie Boutique Palais des Papes** *(6 Rue Pente-Rapide, 84000; 04 90 27 50 87)* for educational toys and books with a medieval theme. Go to **La Carte a Jouer** *(6 Rue De La Rappe, 84000; 04 90 16 98 75)* for games and stuffed toy flamingos.

Find out more

DIGITAL Families can download a self-guided walking tour of Avignon at *www.gpsmycity.com/iphone/avignon-walking-tours-269.html*.

A street performance at the Palais des Papes during the Festival d'Avignon

Take cover

Walk south to the **Musée Calvet** *(65 Rue Joseph Vernet, 84000; www.musee-calvet.org)*, with an eclectic collection of exhibits. Or the **Musée Angladon** *(5 Rue Laboureur, 84000; www.angladon.com)*, where Van Gogh's only painting in Provence keeps good company with others by Picasso, Degas and Cézanne.

Next stop...

TARASCON Take a train south from Avignon to the town of Tarascon to visit "Good King" René's **Château Royal de Provence** *(tinyurl.com/6av2f95)* high over the Rhône. A medieval legend tells how St Martha saved the town from a man-eating monster called the Tarasque, now Tarascon's symbol. See it at the train station, public buildings and in the Place Charles de Gaulle.

Pink flamingos in the Parc Ornithologique in the Camargue

② St-Rémy-de-Provence

Where Vincent van Gogh painted *The Starry Night*

Under the jagged peaks of the Alpilles, delightful St-Rémy-de-Provence has been an artists' town ever since 1889, when Vincent van Gogh checked himself into a local asylum. The **Hôtel Estrine: Centre d'Art Presence** covers this period, while the hospital where Van Gogh painted the hypnotic *The Starry Night* occupies the Romanesque monastery of **St-Paul-de-Mausole**, a 15-minute walk south from the art centre. Just opposite the monastery is Les Antiques – a triumphal arch and cylindrical mausoleum – erected to honour Roman emperors Julius Caesar and Augustus. They belong to the predecessor of St-Rémy: the evocative Celtic-Greek-Roman city of **Glanum**, preserved for 1,700 years under a layer of silt from the Alpilles.

Letting off steam

For some stunning ruins, take bus 59 to Les Alpilles and Les Baux, where the **Château des Baux** (*www.chateau-baux-provence.com*) was once home to troublemaking lords. Three catapults, including Europe's largest trebuchet, are fired several times a day (Apr–Sep). In the old bauxite quarries, the **Cathédrale d'Images** (*www.cathedrale-images.com*) holds sound and light shows.

③ Arles

Gateway to the Camargue

Like St-Rémy, Arles was home to Van Gogh for a year. The tourist office distributes a map of a Vincent van Gogh Walk, taking in places where he set up his easel (much has changed, but the Pont de Langlois still looks the same). The city's Mediathèque doubles up as the **Espace Van Gogh**, with many reproductions of the artist's works. But there is more to Arles, known in ancient times as Arelate (Bog Town). Under the Place du Forum, explore the underground galleries of the 1st-century BC Cryptoporticus (under restoration), entered by way of the

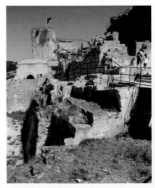

Ruins of the fortified 10th-century Château des Baux, Les Baux

The passageways of the old Roman Amphithéâtre in Place du Forum, Arles

elegant Hôtel de Ville in the Place de la République. This square features another masterpiece – the 11th-century sculpted portal of the Cathédrale de St Trophime, with more great sculptures in the cloister – find St Martha and the Tarasque.

Dating back to AD 80, Arles' **Amphithéâtre**, which is 3 m (10 ft) wider than Nîmes' Arènes, hosts mock gladiator combats on Tuesdays and Thursdays in July and August. On the edge of the town, the excellent **Musée d'Arles et de la Provence Antiques** exhibits artefacts and models of how things worked during Roman times.

Letting off steam
Relax in the Jardin d'Été, located between St-Trophime and the Amphithéâtre, or take bus 20 to the **Camargue**, the delta of the Rhône, and the largest delta in western Europe. Do not miss the French *gardiens* (cowboys), who ride a special breed of white horses, herding black bulls. Head for the **Parc Ornithologique** (*www.parc ornithologique.com*) in the Camargue and spot pink flamingos and 400 other species of birds.

④ Orange
Be a star on an ancient stage
Built by the Emperor Augustus in the 1st century AD, Orange's **Théâtre Antique** or Roman Theatre is the best preserved of its kind – with seats for 10,000 spectators, the stage and the rarest survival of all, its back wall. The wall makes the acoustics

extraordinary – just stand on the stage and test them! Built around the same time, Orange's equally well-preserved Arc de Triomphe on Rue Victor Hugo, celebrates the victory of the Second Gallic Regiment over the Gauls.

Letting off steam
Steps from the theatre lead up to the **Colline de St-Eutrope**, a park with views, play areas and more ruins. For a biology lesson, take a taxi to Sérignan-le-Comtat, 8 km (5 miles) to the north of Orange and visit **L'Harmas** (*tinyurl.com/3z4dzlq*), where 19th-century writer Jean-Henri Fabre, known as the "Virgil of insects", lived and planted a huge variety of plants to attract insects he loved. Nearby is the science centre **Naturoptère** (*www.naturoptere.fr*), dedicated to his life and insects.

Exhibits at Naturoptère, the science centre at Sérignan-le-Comtat

The Lowdown

🌐 **Map reference** 13 D3
Address 84100 (Vaucluse). **Théâtre Antique:** Rue Madeleine Roch; 04 90 51 17 60; *www. theatre-antique.com*

🚆 **Train** from Avignon

ℹ️ **Visitor information** 5 Cours Aristide Briand, 84100; 04 90 34 70 88; *www.otorange.fr*

🕐 **Open** Théâtre Antique: daily (free kids' activity books available)

🍽️ **Eat and drink** *Real meal* Le Garden (6 Pl de Langes, 84100; 04 90 34 64 47; closed Sun lunch & Mon) offers traditional Provençal dishes in a wide choice of fixed-price menus. *Family treat* Au Petit Patio (58 Cours, Aristide Briand, 84100; 04 90 29 69 27) is an attractive restaurant offering a number of gourmet delights. Book in advance.

🎪 **Festival** Les Chorégies, opera festival (Jul)

Picnic under €20; **Snacks** €20–45; **Real meal** €45–90; **Family treat** over €90 (based on a family of four)

⑤ Fontaine-de-Vaucluse
A mysterious spring

Squeezed in the narrow *vallis clausa* ("closed valley"), Fontaine-de-Vaucluse and the wonder of its mysterious "bottomless" spring have long fascinated visitors. In ancient times, water gods were worshipped here; in the Middle Ages, stories spoke about how it was guarded by a fierce dragon. Today, scientists try to explain how an average of 60,000 litres (15,850 gallons) of water per second flows year round into a green pool at the base of a cliff.

The shimmering green pool of Fontaine-de-Vaucluse

Key Sights

④ **Musée Pétrarque** Petrarch, the Italian poet, spent summers writing his *De Vita Solitaria* (On the Solitary Life) in this villa.

① **Source** The source of the Sorgue river, this spring is the fifth strongest in the world. In 1989, a tiny robot submarine descended 308 m (1,010 ft), but could not uncover its watery secrets.

② **Musée d'Histoire L'Appel de la Liberté** This covers the history of France during World War II with interactive exhibits and vignettes of life during the war years.

③ **Moulin à Papier Vallis Clausa** Fontaine-de-Vaucluse once had seven paper mills along the Sorgue river. This mill, which dates back to the 15th century, still makes paper the old-fashioned way.

⑤ **Château des Evêques de Cavaillon** This romantic 14th-century ruin on a rocky outcrop occupies the site of a 7th-century town. Climb up for the great views.

⑥ **Église de Fontaine-de-Vaucluse** This Romanesque church was built over an ancient temple. Its crypt houses the 6th-century tomb of St Véran. Legend says the saint slew the dragon who lived near the source.

The Lowdown

🌐 **Map reference** 13 D3
Address 84899 (Vaucluse). Musée d'Histoire L'Appel de la Liberté: Chemin de la Fontaine, 84800; 04 90 20 24 00. Moulin à Papier Vallis Clausa: Chemin de la Fontaine, 84800; www.vallis-clausa.com. Musée Pétrarque: Rive Gauche de la Sorgue, 84000; www.vallis-clausa.com. Château des Evêques de Cavaillon: 84800 Fontaine-de-Vaucluse. Église de

Fontaine-de-Vaucluse: Ave Robert Garcin, 84800

🚗 **Train** from Avignon to L'Isle-sur-la-Sorgue, then the Voyages Raoux bus

ℹ **Visitor information** Chemin de la Fontaine, 84800; 04 90 20 32 22; www.oti-delasorgue.fr

🕐 **Open** Musée d'Histoire L'Appel de la Liberté: Apr–Jun, Sep & Oct: Wed–Mon; Mar, Nov & Dec: Sat & Sun; closed Jan & Feb.

Moulin à Papier Vallis Clausa: Jul & Aug: daily; May, Jun & Sep: daily; Mar & Oct: daily; Feb & Nov: daily; Jan & Dec: daily. Musée Pétrarque: Wed–Mon

💶 **Prices** Musée d'Histoire L'Appel de la Liberté & Musée Pétrarque: €10–20; under 12s free. Moulin à Papier Vallis Clausa: free

👪 **Skipping the queue** Come in spring or after autumn rains, when the source is at its most dramatic.

Letting off steam

Spend a couple of hours canoeing down the limpid, emerald Sorgue river with **Kayak Vert Aqueduc** (84800 Fontaine-de-Vaucluse; 04 90 20 35 44; www.canoe-france. com/sorgue; late-Apr–Oct). This is suitable for kids aged 6 plus.

Canoe and kayaking trips on the Sorgue river

Eat and drink

Picnic: under €20; Snacks: €20–45; Real meal: €45–90; Family treat: over €90 (based on a family of four)

PICNIC Super U (Route de Carpentras, 84800 L'Isle-sur-la-Sorgue) is an ideal place to stock up on goodies. Picnic at the nearby Partage des Eaux, a lovely spot with picnic tables by the river.
SNACKS A qui Sian Ben (Quartier la Baume, 84800; 04 90 20 35 44; Apr–Oct) is an informal family snack bar and restaurant on the Sorgue river offering sandwiches and *plats du jour* (specials of the day).
REAL MEAL Hostellerie le Château (Quartier Château Vieux, 84800; 04 90 20 31 54; open daily) allows diners to sit on the riverfront terrace. It serves mouthwatering *foie gras* with honey and succulent lamb.
FAMILY TREAT Chez Dominique (6 Pl de la Colonne, 84800; www. chezdominique.com; open daily) offers superb no-fuss Mediterranean dishes (try stuffed mini-vegetables) to accompany a delightful, affordable wine list. Book a table on the flower-filled balcony.

👫 **Age range** 4 plus
⏱ **Allow** Half a day
🎏 **Festival** Festival de la Sorgue, boat races from the L'Isle-sur-la Sorgue (Jul)

Good family value?

Along with great natural attractions, there are interesting shops and craft workshops as well. Prices are kind.

Shopping

Visit **La Marmite des Saveurs** (Ave Robert Garcin; www.lamarmitedes saveurs.com) for a wide range of Provençal goodies, including jams and *tapenades* (olive spreads).

Find out more

DIGITAL See what the spring looks like at full force on www.wat.tv/ video/fontaine-vaucluse-en-crue-19cod_2g3dt_.html.

Take cover

Duck into **L'Ecomusée du Santon** (Pl de la Colonne, 84150; 04 90 20 20 83; www.musee-du-santon. org) and see over 2,000 Christmas nativity scene figurines made out of everything from bread to wax.

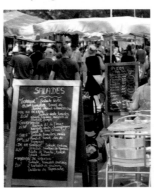

Sunday market at L'Isle-sur-la-Sorgue, Fontaine-de-Vaucluse

Next stop...

WATERWHEELS, CAVES AND PAPER MILLS Visit **Le Monde Souterrain** (Chemin de Gouffre, 84899; 04 90 20 34 13; www.monde souterrain.fr), a museum that displays cave carvings and geological findings. It also retells endeavours of marine explorer Jacques Cousteau to find the bottom of the source of the Fontaine-de-Vaucluse. Beyond Fontaine-de-Vaucluse, the Sorgue river splits to form L'Isle-sur-la-Sorgue, an island town of canals, footbridges and waterwheels that once powered textile and paper mills. Today, antique shops have taken their place, joined on Sunday mornings by a flea market. Visit the **Musée de l'École d'Autrefois** (musecole. vaucluse.pagesperso-orange.fr), a historic French schoolhouse, which traces school life from 1880.

⑥ Gordes
Underground labyrinths and stone igloos

With its golden stone houses piled up high on a steep hill, Gordes is called the "Acropolis of Provence". The **Château de Gordes** crowns the summit, housing the second-largest fireplace in France and a collection of paintings by Belgian avant-garde artist Pol Mara in the **Musée Pol Mara**. Don headlamps to explore the subterranean side of Gordes, with sound and light effects, in the **Caves du Palais de St-Firmin**, also near the summit.

Some 4 km (3 miles) north of Gordes, the Abbaye de Sénanque is a spectacular sight, set among fields of lavender. The Cistercian monks make lavender oils, honey and liqueurs, for sale in the abbey shop.

Letting off steam
Visit the **Village des Bories** (www.gordes-village-des-bories.com), 3 km (2 miles) southwest of Gordes, to explore the stone igloos. They are perfect for playing hide and seek.

The Lowdown

🌐 **Map reference** 13 D3
Address Vaucluse 84220. Château de Gordes & Musée Pol Mara: Pl Genty Pantaly; 04 90 72 02 75. Caves du Palais de St-Firmin: Rue du Belvédère, 84220; www.caves-saint-firmin.com

🚗 **Train** to Cavaillon, then taxi to Gordes

ℹ️ **Visitor information** Pl de Château, 84220; 04 90 72 02 75; www.gordes-village.com

🕐 **Open** Château de Gordes & Musée Pol Mara: daily; closed Dec 25 & Jan 1. Caves du Palais de St-Firmin: May–Sep: Wed–Mon; Oct–Apr: book ahead

🍴 **Eat and drink** Real meal Les Cuisines du Château (Pl du Château, 84220; 04 90 72 01 31; closed mid-Nov–early-Mar) is a charming restaurant in a 19th-century grocer's that features home-style Provençale cooking such as lamb, stews and patés, as well as yummy desserts. Family treat Auberge de Carcacille (Route de Apt; 84220; 04 90 72 02 63; www.auberge-carcacille.com; closed Fri lunch) serves tasty Provençale cuisine in a relaxed garden setting, with a play area. There are two kids' menus.

🎭 **Festival** Soirées d'été à Gordes, evening concerts (Aug)

Château de Gordes looking out over the sunlit village

⑦ Vaison-la-Romaine
The devil in the church

Vaison was a Roman city with a mouthful of a name, Vasio Vocontiorum. Its remains are in two sections: La Villasse has public baths and two posh villas; while Puyrmin has a theatre that could seat 7,000, "Pompey's Portico", an enclosed garden, and the **Musée Archéolgique Théo Desplans**, where objects from statues to lead pipes are explained by audio guides.

On the western end of the town, the **Cathédrale Notre-Dame-de-Nazareth** sports a spectacular apse and a stone devil. Cross Vaison's Roman bridge to the medieval Haute Ville, a steep maze of streets leading to the ruined 12th-century Château Comtal, which offers a bird's-eye view of the town.

Letting off steam
Play in Vaison's **Jardin des Neuf Damoiselles** (Route de Roaix; 04 90 36 11 30) or drive up the 1,912-m (6,272-ft) Mont Ventoux, Provence's

Display of candied fruits at the Kerry Aptunion factory, Apt

The Lowdown

🌐 **Map reference** 13 D2
Address Vaucluse 84110. Musée Archéolgique Théo Desplans: Pl du Chanoine, 84110; 04 90 36 50 38.

🚗 **Bus** Lieutaud bus from Avignon & Orange

ℹ️ **Visitor information** Pl du Chanoine Sautel, 84110; 04 90 36 02 11; www.vaison-la-romaine.com

🕐 **Open** Musée Archéolgique Théo Desplans: daily

🍴 **Eat and drink** Snacks L'Annexe Café (3 Pl Montfort, 84110; 04 90 36 00 03) offers crêpes, salads, sandwiches, plats du jour (daily special) and a kids' menu in the heart of the town. Real meal Le Bonheur Suit Son Cours (20 Cours Taulignan, 84110; 04 90 46 45 27) is a small restaurant that serves excellent, fresh and mostly organic food, with a superb choice of unusual local wines.

🎭 **Festival** Festival International de Danse features dancers from various parts of the world (Jul)

highest mountain. At the **Mont Serein** (www.stationdumont serein.com), a sports centre, families can ski on snow in winter and on grass in summer. For kids, there is go-karting, pony rides and bouncy castles.

⑧ Apt
World capital of candied fruit

Capital of the Luberon region, Apt shows its Roman origins in its street plan. Remains of a Roman building dating back to the 1st century AD can be found in the lower crypt of the **Cathédrale Ste-Anne**. Begun in the late 12th century, the cathedral is full of precious things, including the Veil of St Anne and ivories brought back by the crusaders, which are now housed in the treasury. After that, pay a visit to the **Musée de l'Aventure Industrielle**, which explores the traditional trades of Apt's region – ochre mining, ceramics and candied fruit. Learn more about the latter during a tour of **Kerry Aptunion**, the world's biggest candied fruit factory. The town is also famous for its Saturday market.

The Lowdown

- 🌐 **Map reference** 13 D3
  Address Vaucluse 84400. Cathédrale Ste-Anne: Rue St-Anne, 84400; 04 90 04 85 44; www.apt-cathedrale.com. Musée de l'Aventure Industrielle: Pl du Pastal, 84400; 04 90 74 95 30. Kerry Aptunion: Quartier Salignan, 84400; 04 90 76 31 31; www.kerryaptunion.com
- 🚆 **Train** from Avignon & Cavaillon
- ℹ️ **Visitor information** 20 Ave Philippe de Girard, 84400; 04 90 74 03 18; www.ot-apt.fr
- 🕐 **Open** Musée de l'Aventure Industrielle: Oct–May: closed Tue. Kerry Aptunion: ring ahead to visit
- 🍴 **Eat and drink** *Snacks* Les Gourmands Disent *(17 Pl du Septier, 04 90 74 27 97; closed Sun)* serves tarts and pastries. *Real meal* Le Royal's *(18 Pl de la Bouquerie, 84400; 04 90 04 77 69; daily)* offers *steak au poivre* (steak with peppercorns).
- 🎉 **Festival** La Cavalcade d'Apt, floats and music (May)

Letting off steam

Apt has a beautiful **Jardin Public** *(Pl Lauze de Perret, 84400)*. Or take a bus or taxi 11 km (7 miles) west to the village of Roussillon, located on a hill of ochre. Walk through the quarries on the Ochre Quarry Trail.

⑨ Lourmarin
Gargoyles and a Nobel prize winner

The beautiful village of Lourmarin is built around a medieval tower where the village clock keeps track of things. Pay a visit to the Renaissance **Château de Lourmarin** to see the gargoyles, the remarkable twisting spiral stair and strange fireplace with its "Aztec" faces made during the Renaissance, when the New World seemed very exotic. The château

A bird's-eye view of the red cliffs of the ochre quarries, Roussillon

frequently hosts superb exhibitions. Lourmarin's most famous resident was Nobel-prize-winning author Albert Camus, who always said the most absurd way to die would be in a car crash. In 1960, Camus died at the age of 46 in a car crash after accepting a lift from his publisher; he was found with an unused train ticket in his pocket. He is buried in the local cemetery.

Letting off steam

Run around the fields by the château or drive north 12 km (8 miles) on the D36 to Bonnieux to stroll through the cedar forest planted in 1861.

The Lowdown

- 🌐 **Map reference** 13 D3
  Address Vaucluse 84160. Château de Lourmarin: Impasse Pout du Temple, 84160; 04 90 68 15 23; www.chateau-de-lourmarin.com
- 🚌 **Bus** from Avignon, Apt & Aix-en-Provence
- ℹ️ **Visitor information** Pl Henri Barthélémy, 84160; 04 90 68 10 77; www.lourmarin.com
- 🕐 **Open** Château de Lourmarin: daily; closed Dec 25 and Jan 1
- 🍴 **Eat and drink** *Real meal* Le Ratelier *(2 Rue Albert Camus, 84160; 04 90 68 23 33; closed Wed, Mon and Sat lunch)* offers grilled meats, salads and pizzas. *Family treat* L'Antiquaire *(9 Rue du Grand Pré, 84160; 04 90 68 17 29; www.restaurant-antiquaire.com; closed Sun night and Mon)* serves classy cuisine in the heart of the village, with a gorgeous terrace.
- 🎉 **Festival** Festival Sun Art de Lourmarin, art, rock music (Jul)

⑩ Marseille
Saints, sailors and fish stew

Sunny, exuberant, multi-ethnic Marseille buzzes with excitement. The city began as a Greek colony in 600 BC and quickly grew into a major port city. Louis XIV himself ordered the opening of the main street, La Canebière, in 1666. Nearby, the Marché des Capucins offers scents from around the world, while the Vieux Port is the perfect place to try the city's famous *bouillabaisse* (fish stew).

Fort St-Jean towering over the marina, Vieux Port

Key Sights

① Museum d'Histoire Naturelle Over 300 stuffed animals and interactive displays are housed in the magnificent Palais Longchamps, surrounded by fountains and gardens.

② Musée d'Histoire de Marseille This houses the ancient Roman merchant ship that was found near the port.

③ Vieille Charité This 17th-century poorhouse has two museums: one with spookily expressive African masks and funny Mexican animal sculptures and the other with Egyptian mummies.

④ Musée Cantini This superb collection of 20th-century art features works by the leading Fauves, Cubists and Surrealists, and abstract artists.

⑤ Musée Marcel Carbonel Watch *santons* (little saints) being produced in Musée Marcel Carbonel's workshop, which makes over 600 figures.

⑥ Abbaye St-Victor Founded by St Jean Cassien in 416, this fortress-like church contains a 1,500-year-old crypt full of strange carvings and ancient sarcophagi.

⑦ Notre-Dame-de-la-Garde Marseille's landmark church has magnificent views. Touching votive paintings made by sailors saved from drowning crowd the interior.

The Lowdown

🌐 **Map reference** 13 D4
Address 13000 (Bouches-du-Rhône). Museum d'Histoire Naturelle: 21 Blvd Claude Charles Guillaume Philippon, 13004; www.museum-marseille.org. Musée d'Histoire de Marseille: Pl Belsunce, Centre Bourse, 13001; 04 91 90 42 22. Vieille Charité (Musée d'Archeologie Méditerranéenne & Musée des Africains, Océanien & Amerindien): 2 Rue de la Charité, 13002; 04 91 54 77 75. Musée Cantini: 19 Rue Grignan; 04 91 54 77 75. Musée Marcel Carbonel: 47 Rue Neuve Ste Catherine, 13007; www.santonsmarcelcarbonel.com. Abbaye St-Victor: 3 Rue de l'Abbaye; www.saintvictor.net. Notre-Dame-de-la-Garde: Rue

Fort du Sanctuaire, 13006; www.notredamedelagarde.com

🚗 **Train** from Paris, Nice, Lyon and Toulouse

ℹ️ **Visitor information** 4 La Canebière, 13000; 08 26 50 05 00; www.marseille-tourisme.com

🕐 **Open** Museum d'Histoire Naturelle: 10am–5pm Tue–Sun. Musée d'Histoire de Marseille: currently closed for restoration. Vieille Charité (Musée d'Archeologie Méditerranéenne & Musée des Africains, Océanien and Amerindien): Oct–May: 10am–5pm, closed Mon. Jun–Sep: 11am–6pm, closed Mon. Musée Cantini: Oct–May: 10am–5pm, closed Mon; Jun–Sep: 11am–6pm, closed Mon. Musée Marcel

Carbonel: 10am–12:30pm & 2–6:30, closed Mon. Abbaye St-Victor: 3pm–7pm Mon–Fri. Notre-Dame-de-la-Garde: daily

💶 **Prices** Museum d'Histoire Naturelle: €8–18; under 21s free; free Sun am. Vieille Charité (joint admission charge for Musée d'Archeologie Méditerranéenne & Musée des Africains, Océanien & Amerindien): €6–16; under 18s free; free Sun am. Musée Cantini: €6–16; under 18s free. Musée Marcel Carbonel: free. Abbaye St-Victor: crypt €4–14; under 18s free

👪 **Skipping the queue** The Marseille City Pass offers a boat trip to the Château d'If, a guided tour, a ride on the *petit train*, admission to 14 museums and

Letting off steam

Take bus 83 along the Corniche John F Kennedy to the **Plages du Prado**, with a long stretch of beach, lawns and playgrounds. For a treat, take a boat trip to the Calanques, 12 km (7 miles) east of Marseille, with **Bleu Evasion** (www.visite-bateau-calanques-marseille-cassis.fr). They offer child-friendly excursions and good places to swim and snorkel.

Vendors selling fruits and vegetables at the Marché des Capucins

Eat and drink

Picnic: under €20; Snacks: €20–45; Real meal: €45–90; Family treat: over €90 (based on a family of four)

PICNIC Marché des Capucins *(Pl des Capucins, 13001)* is an ideal place to stock up on goodies. Take bus 83 to Parc Borély for a picnic.
SNACKS Le Splendid *(1 Blvd Garibaldi, 13001; 04 96 12 06 69)* offers sandwiches and kebabs on the sidewalk terrace. For dessert, there is ice cream and sorbets at **Maison de la Glace** *(94 Rue Sainte, 13007).*
REAL MEAL Beach Café *(214 Quai du Port, 13002; 04 91 91 55 40; beach-cafe.net; lunch only)* is a

child-friendly bar-restaurant located on the north side of the Vieux Port. It serves good seafood and has a reasonably priced choice of menus.
FAMILY TREAT Chez Fonfon *(140 Vallon des Auffes, 13007; 04 91 52 14 38; www.chez-fonfon.com)* in a stunning setting above the port, cooks up an excellent version of *bouillabaisse.* It also has a kids' menu.

Shopping

Visit Marseille's oldest bakery, **Le Four des Navettes** *(136 Rue Sainte, 13007; 04 91 33 32 12; www.four desnavettes.com),* which opened in 1791 and specializes in boat-shaped "navette" pastries, associatied with St Victor. For Marseille's famous olive oil and soap, go to **La Savonnerie du Sérail** *(50 Blvd Anatole de la Forge, 13001; www.savon-leserail.com).*

Find out more

FILM *The Count of Monte Cristo* (many versions, last 2002), adapted from Alexander Dumas's novel, *My Father's Glory* and *My Mother's Castle* (both released in 1990 and based on books written by Marcel Pagnol), are all set in Marseille.

Next stop...

CHATEAU D'IF Take the **Frioul Express boat** *(www.frioul-if-express. com)* from the Quai des Belges to the Château d'If (www.monuments-nationaux.fr) built by François I in 1529 to defend Marseille from his enemy the Holy Roman Emperor Charles V. In Alexandre Dumas's renowned novel, *The Count of Monte Cristo,* Edmund Dantès was imprisoned here for 14 years. See his "cell" complete with his escape hole, along with spectacular views of Marseille.

Sheer white cliffs and stunningly blue creeks at the Calanques

free public transport for 1 or 2 days (€22 or €29 per person).
Guided tours Marseille Le Grand Tour (www.marseillelegrandtour. com) offers hop-on hop-off double-decker bus tours with an English audio guide.
Age range 5 plus
Allow A day
Festivals Carnaval de Marseille, carnival celebrations and parades (Mar). Fête du Vent has kite flying competitions (Sep)

Good family value?
Marseille is larger than life – has good transport, a warm climate and a warm heart, but does not have many sights for young kids.

⑪ Aix-en-Provence

Cézanne paintings and hot water

Once home to the art-loving 15th-century King René of Provence, the handsome city of Aix is still refined and arty. The Cathédrale St-Sauveur is filled with paintings, including the Renaissance *Triptych of The Burning Bush* by Nicholas Froment. Next door, in the archbishop's palace, the **Musée des Tapisseries** houses three sets of "merry" Beauvais tapestries, including a series on Don Quixote. Carefully hidden under the rafters from revolutionaries, the tapestries were only rediscovered in the 1840s.

Aix was the birthplace of artist Paul Cézanne (1839–1906), whose visionary paintings paved the way for the 20th-century artistic revolutions of Fauvism and Cubism, even though he was jeered at during his lifetime in

The téléphérique (cable car) going up Mount Faron, high above Toulon

his hometown. Now the repentant city runs tours of **Atelier Cézanne**. Dinosaur fossils await in the **Museum d'Histoire Naturelle**, located close to the outdoor market in the Place des Prêcheurs. Here, the Église-Ste-Marie-Madeleine has another Renaissance masterpiece *The Annunciation*. Natural hot springs steam out of the fountains along the Cours Mirabeau. Just south is the **Musée Granet**. Eight Cézanne paintings were given to this museum by the French government in 1984 to cover up the fact that no one in Aix had bought his work while he was alive. Also housed in the museum are archaeological finds, including the sculptures of decapitated heads from the Celtic settlement of Entremont.

Letting off steam

Visit the playground in **Parc Rambot** *(67 Cours Gambetta, 13100)* or find Cézanne's favourite haunts by car

Copies of Cézanne's paintings on sale at Aix-en-Provence

along the sign-posted Route de Cézanne, east of Aix towards Mont Ste-Victoire, a mountain he painted 87 times. Or take a 35-minute drive south to Carry-le-Rouet beach with its family-oriented sands.

⑫ Bandol

The city that sank in the sea

Famous for its wine, Bandol is a sunny resort. Tall cacti grow in the **Jardin Exotique Sanary Bandol**, sheltering monkeys, flamingos, toucans and Vietnamese pigs.

In ancient times, this coast belonged to Tauroentum, "the city of the bull", founded by the Cretans around 500 BC, which sank into the sea during an earthquake. The **Musée Tauroentum**, west of Bandol, in St-Cyr-sur-Mer, is centred around a Roman villa with beautiful mosaics. St-Cyr is also proud over its Statue of Liberty in Place Portalis – one of the original models by Bartholdi before making the big one in New York. On nearby Île des Embiez, **L'Institut Océanographique Paul Ricard** showcases endangered marine species.

Colourful birds at the Jardin Exotique Sanary Bandol

The Lowdown

🌐 **Map reference** 14 E4
  Address 13100 (Bouches-de-Rhône). Musée des Tapisseries: 28 Pl Martyrs de la Résistance, 13100; 04 42 23 09 91. Atelier Cézanne: 9 Ave Paul Cézanne, 13090; 04 42 21 06 53; www.atelier-cezanne.com. Museum d'Histoire Naturelle: 6 Rue Espariat, 13100; 04 42 27 91 27; www.museum-aix-en-provence.org. Musée Granet: Pl St Jean de Malte, 13100; 04 42 52 88 32; www.museegranet-aixenprovence.fr

🚕 **Train** from Marseille

ℹ️ **Visitor information** 2 Pl du Général de Gaulle, 13100; 04 42 16 17 61; www.aixenprovence tourism.com

🕐 **Open** Musée des Tapisseries: Feb–end-Dec: closed Tue; closed Jan.

Atelier Cézanne: 1 Oct–end-Mar: daily (visits in English: 4pm); Apr–Sep: daily (visits in English: 5pm). Museum d'Histoire Naturelle: daily. Musée Granet: closed Mon.

🍽️ **Eat and drink** *Real meal* Le Comté d'Aix *(17 Rue Coronne, 13100; 04 42 26 79 26; closed Sun & Mon lunch)* offers dishes from various regions of France. *Family treat* Mitch: *(26 Rue des Tanneurs, 13100; 04 42 26 63 08; www.mitch restaurant.com; Mon–Sat dinner only, closed Sun)* serves chic gourmet market cuisine to diners.

🎉 **Festivals** Festival du Tambourin, music in the streets (Mar). Festival d'Aix, concerts and theatre (Jun–Jul).

The Lowdown

- **Map reference** 14 E5
  Address 83110 (Var).
  Jardin Exotique Sanary Bandol: 83100 Sanary-sur-Mer; 04 94 29 40 38; www.zoosanary.com. Musée Tauroentum: 131 Route Madrague, 83270; 04 94 26 30 46; www.saintcyrsurmer.com. L'Institut Océanographique Paul Ricard: Île des Embiez, 83140 Le Brusc; 04 94 34 02 49; www. institut-paul-ricard.org

- **Train** from Marseille or Toulon. **Ferry** from Six-Fours-les-Plages to Île Embiez.

- **Visitor information** Allées Vivien, 83110; 04 94 29 41 35; tourisme. bandol.fr

- **Open** Jardin Exotique Sanary Bandol: May–end-Oct: daily; Dec–Feb: Sat, Sun & school hols. Musée Tauroentum: Jun–Sep: Wed–Mon; Oct–May: Sat & Sun. L'Institut Océanographique Paul Ricard: daily

- **Eat and drink** Real meal Pizzeria della Stazione (151 Ave de la Gare, 83150; 04 94 94 77 82) offers Italian-style pizzas and salads on the terrace. Family treat Ti Punch (10 Rue Voltaire, 83150; 04 94 32 31 32; closed Sun in winter) serves seafood with a Caribbean flair.

- **Festival** Fête du Millésime, wine festival in Bandol (Dec)

Letting off steam

Bandol has great beaches as does St-Cyr-sur-Mer, whose Les Leques is huge, sandy and gently shelving. Or pay a visit to the nearby **Aqualand** (www.aqualand.fr).

⑬ Toulon

Big ships, little ships

Boasting one of the finest natural harbours on the Mediterranean, Toulon is France's biggest naval port. Its **Musée National de la Marine** has a collection of ships' models and figureheads. The **Musée des Arts Asiatiques** showcases treasures the sailors brought home from their adventures. Take the *téléphérique* to Mount Faron, a 584-m (1,916-ft) limestone massif for great views, walks, picnic grounds and the **Musée Mémorial du Débarquement en Provence**, covering the August 1944 Allied landings in the south of France. Close by is the **Zoo du Mont Faron**, whose tigers and other big cats are being prepared for a life in the wild.

A life-sized model of a ship at the Musée National de la Marine, Toulon

Letting off steam

There are playgrounds in the central **Jardin Alexandre 1er** (Blvd Général Leclerc, 83000) or take bus 3 or 13 to the Plage du Mourillon just by the 16th-century Tour Royal and its park. Take a boat tour with the **Bateliers de la Rade** (Quai Constradt, 83000; 04 94 46 24 65) to get close to the aircraft carriers anchored in the harbour.

The Lowdown

- **Map reference** 14 E5
  Address 83000 (Var).
  Musée National de la Marine: Pl Monsenergue, 83000; 04 22 42 02 01; www.musee-marine.fr. Musée des Arts Asiatiques: Villa Jules Verne, 169 Littoral Frederic Mistral, 83000. Musée Mémorial du Débarquement en Provence: Route du Faron, 83200; 04 94 88 08 09; www.telepherique faron.com. Zoo du Mont Faron: 83200; 04 94 88 07 89; www. telepherique-faron.com

- **Train** from Marseille. **Bus** 40 to the téléphérique

- **Visitor information** 12 Pl Louis Blanc, 83000; 04 94 18 53 00 www.toulontourisme.com

- **Open** Musée National de la Marine: closed Tue except in Jul & Aug; closed Jan. Musée des Arts Asiatiques: closed Mon. Musée Mémorial du Débarquement en Provence & Zoo du Mont Faron: Sep–Mar: closed Mon

- **Eat and drink** Real meal Le Pascalou (3 Pl à l'Huile, 83000; 04 94 62 87 02; lunch only; Sep– Mar: closed Mon) serves delicious family-style seafood dishes. Family treat La Bouche et l'Oreille (1 Ave de l'Infanterie de Marine, 83000; 04 94 46 38 47; www. labouchetloreille.com) offers classic cuisine and tapas.

- **Festival** Festival de Jazz (Jul)

⑭ St-Tropez
From pirate ships to millionaires' yachts

Isolated on its peninsula, St-Tropez suffered pirate attacks for centuries. The locals did not pay taxes in exchange for defending the coast, and in 1637 they beat off 22 Spanish galleons. In the 20th century, life changed radically when artists, writers and film stars converged on St-Tropez, making it one of the world's most famous resorts. If the pirates returned today, they would find plenty of loot in the luxury yachts, villas and boutiques!

Sculpture of St Torpès

Key Sights

① **Place des Lices** Once used for practicing military skills, this big square now hosts a colourful market on Tuesdays and Saturdays and endless games of *pétanque* under the plane trees.

② **Musée de l'Annonciade** This chapel boasts a collection of Fauvist and Pointillist paintings by artists such as Matisse.

③ **Maison des Papillons** Entomologist Dany Lartique runs this fascinating butterfly museum in his house, beautifully displaying some 20,000 different species.

④ **Château de Suffren** This tower is all that remains of the castle of Admiral Pierre-André de Suffren, who fought the British in America's War of Independence.

⑤ **Église de St-Tropez** This 18th-century Italian-style Baroque church houses the statue of patron saint St Torpès that goes on parade during the Bravade celebrations.

⑥ **Place d'Ormeu** With the Église de St-Tropez and ochre coloured belltower of Église de Notre-Dame, this is one of the most photogenic squares in town.

⑦ **Musée de la Citadelle** Housed in the 16th-century royal citadel that was often attacked by the independent-minded locals, this museum's exhibits focus on the town's colourful naval history.

⑧ **Plage des Graniers** Located below the citadel, this beach is a family favourite. It is also one of St-Tropez's few free beaches. Bouillabaisse and Jumeaux beaches are also options for kids.

The Lowdown

🌐 **Map reference** 14 F4
Address 83990 (Var). Musée de l'Annonciade: Pl Georges Grammont; 04 94 17 84 10. Maison des Papillons: 9 Rue Étienne Berny; 04 94 97 63 45. Église de St-Tropez: 6 Rue du Commandant Guichard, 83990. Musée de la Citadelle: Rue de la Citadelle, 83990; 04 94 97 59 43

🚍 **Train** to St-Raphaël, then bus 7601

ℹ️ **Visitor information** Quai Jean Jaurès; 04 94 97 45 21; www.ot-saint-tropez.com

🕐 **Open** Musée de l'Annonciade: Jun–Sep: 10am–1pm & 2–10pm Wed–Mon; Oct–May: 10am–noon & 2–6pm Wed–Mon; closed Nov. Maison des Papillons: May–Nov: 10am–noon & 3–7pm Mon–Sat. Musée de la Citadelle: 10am–12:30pm & 1:30–5:30pm daily

💶 **Prices** Musée de l'Annonciade: €16–26; under 12s free. Maison des Papillons: €12–22; under 10s free. Musée de la Citadelle: €19–30; under 8s free

👫 **Skipping the queue** Pick up a €8 pass to see all three museums.

🚩 **Guided tours** Contact the tourist office for details.

👫 **Age range** 3 plus

⏱️ **Allow** A day

🎆 **Festivals** Fête de la Bravade (May) and Fête des Espagnols (Jun). Both festivals feature costumes, processions and loud muskets, celebrating historic victories.

Good family value?
St-Tropez has a laid-back atmosphere and great beaches, but gets very crowded during July and August and is also very expensive.

Prices given are for a family of four

A snorkelling lesson in progress at the Domaine du Rayol, Le Rayol-Canadel

Letting off steam

Zip off to the nearby village of Gassin for a thrilling time in the **Azur Park** (www.azurpark.com), a massive fun fair. Drive or take a taxi 27 km (17 miles) west of St-Tropez to the Mediterranean gardens of the **Domaine du Rayol** (www.domaine durayol.org) in Le Rayol-Canadel, which are a part of the coastal nature reserve. Book ahead for a guided snorkelling tour of the underwater flora and fauna in its Jardin Marin, suitable for kids aged 8 plus.

Eat and drink

Picnic: under €20; Snacks: €20–45; Real meal: €45–90; Family treat: over €90 (based on a family of four)

PICNIC La Tarte Tropézienne (Pl des Lices, 83990; 04 94 97 04 69) offers the local sweet yeast bread and cream tart. Picnic by the Plage des Graniers.
SNACKS Pizzeria Bruno (2 Rue de l'Eglise, 83990; 04 94 97 05 18; Apr–Nov) bakes pizzas, with plenty of choices for kids and also creamy mussels and savoury tarts.
REAL MEAL La Part des Anges (Rue de l'Eglise, 83990; 04 94 96 19 50; closed Sun) is a warm and friendly little bistro, with tasty food and reasonably priced menus displayed on chalkboards.
FAMILY TREAT La Pesquière-Le Mazagran-Lou Revelen (1 Rue des Remparts, 83990; 04 94 97 05 92; www.restaurant-pesquiere.fr; late-Mar–late-Oct: open daily) offers Provençal cuisine on a pretty terrace near the sea; includes a kids' menu.

Shopping

The classic store **Galeries Tropéziennes** (56 Rue Gambetta, 83990; 04 94 97 02 21) stocks a range of unique gift items, clothes, fabrics and espadrilles for the whole family. Check out **Rondini** (16 Rue Georges-Clemenceau, 83990; 04 94 97 19 55; www.rondini.fr), the inventor of handmade *sandales tropézinnes*. The shop has been around since 1927 and is renowned for elegant sandals, including versions for kids.

Find out more

FILM *Le Gendarme de Saint-Tropez* (1964), a French comedy about a sergeant, and other Louis de Funès comedies were filmed in St Tropez. The beach scenes in the children's musical *Chitty Chitty Bang Bang* (1964) were also shot in St-Tropez.

Winding canals in the popular resort of Port-Grimaud

Next stop…

PORT-GRIMAUD In summer, boats (www.bateauxverts.com) cross over to Port-Grimaud, Provence's "Little Venice" created in the 1960s out of a swamp by architect François Spoerry. The canals, beaches and lack of cars make it fun to explore. Hire bikes from **Amiral Services** (51 Grande Rue, 83310; 04 94 43 47 32) or a boat for half a day from **Presta Marine** (Quai de Fossés, 83310; 04 94 56 19 93; presta-marine.com).

⑮ Hyères
Cubism and sand dunes

A balmy micro-climate has enabled the city of Hyères to make a living out of growing palms and selling them around Europe. Sadly the trees have been laid low by grubs and weevils, but a few have survived amidst lush plantations in the **Jardins Olbius-Riquier**. In 1924, during the height of the palm boom, Charles de Noailles, a patron of writers and artists such as Salvador Dalí, Jean Cocteau, Picasso and Man Ray, built **Villa Noailles**, a "Château Cubiste," with a Cubist garden and an indoor pool. It hosts exhibitions and the annual Festival International de Mode et de Photographie à Hyères.

A 35-minute drive up in the hills is the **Village des Tortues**, a fascinating Hermann's tortoise sanctuary in the town of Gonfaron, located 27 km (17 miles) northeast of Hyères.

Letting off steam

Head to the vibrant **Magic World** (*www.magicmaman.fr*), for a variety of amusements at the fun fairs and shows. For a sand and beach outing, take the bus to the unique Giens Peninsula, located south of Hyères. Made up of two *tomobos* (sand dune ridges) that enclose salt

The beach on Porquerolles island, near Hyères

marshes, the peninsula is favoured by pink flamingoes. The more sheltered east side is better for sunbathing. TLV and TVM boats (*www.tlv-tvm.com*) shuttle off from Giens's Tour Fondue pier to the car- and cigarette-free island of Porquerolles, which is now a national park. Hire bicycles to explore its beaches and cliffside scenery, its fort and windmill.

⑯ Ste-Maxime
Babar on the beach

The city of Ste-Maxime may not have the glitter of St-Tropez, but it has long sandy beaches and Jean de Brunhoff (1899–1937), author of the Babar books. His *Voyage de Babar* eternalized the Plage des Eléphants, located east of the centre, although it is hard to imagine Babar on the jet skis that buzz there today.

Housed in the 16th-century tower of Ste-Maxime, the **Musée de la Tour Carrée** focuses on local history. The **Musée du Phonographe et de**

Remains of an impressive Roman aqueduct, Fréjus

The Lowdown

🌐 **Map reference** 14 F5
Address 83400 (Var). Jardins Olbius-Riquier: Ave Ambroise Thomas, 83400; 04 94 00 78 65. Villa Noailles: Parc St-Bernard, 83400; 04 98 08 01 98; *www.villanoailles-hyeres.com*. Village des Tortues: Quartier les Plaines, 83590; 04 94 78 26 41; *www.villagetortues.com*

🚗 **Train** from Toulon

ℹ **Visitor information** 3 Ave Ambroise Thomas, 83400; 04 94 01 84 50; *www.ville-hyeres.com*

🕐 **Open** Jardins Olbius-Riquier: daily until sunset. Villa Noailles: closed Mon, Tue & school hols year round. Village des Tortues: daily

🍽 **Eat and drink** *Real meal* La Belle Epoque (*14 Rue de Limans, 83400; 04 94 28 69 82; www.la belleepoque-hyeres.com; closed Mon & Sun*) changes its menu seasonally. *Family treat* Les Jardins de Bacchus (*32 Ave Gambetta, 83400; www.bacchushyeres. com; closed Sun dinner*) serves Mediterranean cuisine.

The Lowdown

🌐 **Map reference** 14 F4
Address 83120 (Var). Musée de la Tour Carrée: Pl de l'Eglise; 04 94 96 70 30. Musée du Phonographe et de la Musique Méchanique: Route du Muy; 04 94 96 50 52; *www.phono.org/Maxime*

🚗 **Boat** from St-Tropez. **Bus** (*www. bateauxverts.com*) from St-Tropez

ℹ **Visitor information** 1 Prom Simon Lorière, 83120; 04 94 55 75 55; *www.ste-maxime.com*

🕐 **Open** Musée de la Tour Carrée: closed Tue. Musée du Phonographe et de la Musique Méchanique: Easter–Jun & Sep: 10am–noon (Jul & Aug: also 4–6:30pm Wed–Sun)

🍽 **Eat and drink** *Real meal* Mahi Plage (*53 Ave Gen Touzet du Vigier, 83120; 04 94 96 25 57; www.mahiplage.fr; open daily*) on the beach, ranges from seafood to paninis. *Family treat* L'Endroit En Provence (*40 Rue Paul Bert, 83120; 04 94 49 19 71*) serves stylish Mediterranean dishes; best to book.

🎊 **Festival** Festival de Printemps, the spring festival (Jun)

la Musique Méchanique, located 6 miles (10 km) north, in a toy-like building in the Parc St-Donat, exhibits inventions of all kinds, including some of Edison's original phonographs.

Letting off steam

Take water-skiing classes and lots more at the **Water Glisse Passion** (*Plage de La Nartelle, 83120; 06 61 85 59 27; www.water-glisse-passion. com*) or enjoy exhilarating water rides in **Aqualand** (*www.aqualand.fr*).

Tree-top thrills await those aged 5 plus in **Arbre et Aventure** (*www.arbreetaventurestemaxime.com*).

⑰ Fréjus

Julius Caesar was here

Founded by Julius Caesar, Fréjus was the first Roman colony in France, but suffered a major setback when its huge port silted up. It was raided at least seven times by Saracens, but the Roman **Amphithéâtre** and aqueduct survived. Fascinating finds include a beautiful mosaic and a two-faced statue of Hermes, on display in the **Musée Archéologique**.

The **Cité Episcopale** is built around an early Gothic cathedral. Take a guided tour to see splendid Renaissance doors, a rare 5th-century baptistery and the unique cloister, where the ceiling is covered with 300 14th-century paintings of daily life and imaginary animals.

The Lowdown

- 🌐 **Map reference** 14 F4
  Address 83600 (Var).
  Roman Amphithéâtre: Rue du Theatre Roman; 04 94 53 58 75.
  Musée Archéologique: Pl Calvini.
  Cité Episcopale: 58 Rue de Fleury; 04 94 51 26 30; *www.cathedrale-frejus.monuments-nationaux.fr*

- 🚗 **Train** from Nice and Toulon

- ℹ **Visitor information** 249 Rue Jean Jaurès, 83600; 04 94 51 83 83; *www.frejus.fr*

- 🕐 **Open** Amphithéâtre & Musée Archéologique: closed Mon. Cité Episcopale: daily; Oct–May: closed Mon

- 🍴 **Eat and drink** *Snacks* L'Absolu (Pl Paul Vernet, 83600; 04 94 17 19 19; summer daily, winter lunch daily & dinner Fri and Sat only) offers cuisines from all over the world. *Real meal* Le Lagon Bleu (57 Quai Cléopâtre, 83600; 04 94 53 30 90) does delicious traditional steaks and profiteroles.

- 🎏 **Festivals** La Bravade (Apr–May). Fréjus Festival de l'Air, massive kite flying festival (Oct)

Letting off steam

If Fréjus's long beach is not enough, go to **Aqualand** (*www.aqualand.fr*), the biggest water park on the Côte d'Azur. Or feel the chills at **Luna Park** (*www.lunapark-frejus.com*), with its terrifying Magic Mountain and the massive Ferris wheel.

The orange-tiled roofs of the city centre, St-Raphaël

⑱ St-Raphaël

Mysteries under the sea

For decades people talked of a sunken city, perhaps even Atlantis, off the coast of St-Raphaël. Divers kept finding bricks, but it was oceanographer Jacques Cousteau who found a Roman shipwreck that had been carrying building materials. The finds are housed in the **Musée d'Archéologie Sous-marine**, along with the reconstruction of a Roman galley and a room on the dolmens, as well as menhirs of the area.

Today a charming seaside resort, St-Raphaël was badly damaged during World War II and underwent extensive restoration. Only Église St-Rafèu, built in 1150, and its Templar tower recall that this was once an important medieval town.

Letting off steam

Head to one of St-Raphaël's several beaches or drive or take a taxi east to the porphyry cliffs and creeks of Massif de l'Esterel. The **Parc Naturel de la Pointe de l'Aiguille** in Théoule-sur-Mer has picnic tables with superb views over the Baie de Cannes.

The Lowdown

- 🌐 **Map reference** 14 F4
  Address 83700 (Var).
  Musée d'Archéologie Sous-marine: Rue des Templiers; 04 94 19 25 75

- 🚗 **Train** from Nice and Toulon

- ℹ **Visitor information** Quai Albert 1er, 83700; 04 94 19 52 52; *www.saint-raphael.com*

- 🕐 **Open** Musée d'Archéologie Sous-marine: Tue–Sat

- 🍴 **Eat and drink** *Snacks* Maître Julien (171 Ave Général du Leclerc, 83700; 04 94 53 87 27) has home-made pizzas and cakes. *Real meal* L'Espace Bleu (Port Santa Lucia, 83700; 04 94 82 34 44) serves tagliatelle with prawns.

Picnic under €20; **Snacks** €20–45; **Real meal** €45–90; **Family treat** over €90 (based on a family of four)

⑲ Nice

France's southern capital of sun, fun and art

Popularly known in the local dialect as "Nizza la Bella", or "Nice the Beautiful", Nice was founded by the Greeks and was a part of the Italian kingdom of Sardinia until 1860. The second-most visited city in France after Paris, it offers semi-tropical gardens, great food and fine modern art museums. A superb network of public transport makes it an ideal base for touring the Côte d'Azur. Be sure to pack jelly shoes for the pebbly beach.

Wooden fishing boats at Nice's port

Key Sights

① **Musée Matisse** The museum exhibits a collection of Matisse's joyful collages, sculptures and paintings, which he left to Nice.

② **Musée Chagall** While living in nearby Vence in 1966, Chagall donated 17 colour-drenched canvases on Old Testament themes to the French state.

0 km   1

0 mile   1

⑥ **Musée International d'Art Naif Anatole-Jakovsky** The "perfume king" François Coty's villa houses an irresistible collection of art by Naïve artists such as Frederic Lanovsky.

③ **Musée d'Art Moderne et d'Art Contemporain** This collection is rich in the playful art of the 1960s and 70s by Ben, Warhol, Klein and Christo.

④ **Palais Lascaris** The 17th-century Baroque palace was built and decorated by Genoese architects. It houses rare and antique instruments.

⑤ **Cathédrale Ste-Réparate** This 17th-century cathedral in Vieux Nice is a fine example of pure Italian Baroque.

⑦ **Parc Phoenix** Wander amidst the flora and fauna of seven tropical climates in the "Green Diamond" greenhouse, and watch the musical fountain put on a free show.

The Lowdown

🌐 **Map reference** 14 G3
Address 06000 (Alpes-Maritimes). Musée Matisse: 164 Ave des Arènes de Cimiez, 06000; www. musee-matisse-nice.org. Musée Chagall: Ave Docteur Ménard, 06000; www.musees-nationaux-alpesmaritimes.fr. Musée d'Art Moderne et d'Art Contemporain: Prom des Arts 06364; www. mamac-nice.org. Palais Lascaris: 15 Rue Droite, 06300; www. palais-lascaris-nice.org. Cathédrale Ste-Réparate: 3 Pl Rossetti, 06300; www.cathedrale-nice. com. Musée International d'Art Naif Anatole-Jakovsky: Ave de Fabron, 06200; 04 93 71 78 33. Parc Phoenix: 405 Prom des

Anglais, 06200; www.parc-phoenix.org

🚗 **Train** from Marseille

ℹ️ **Visitor information** 5 Prom des Anglais, 06302; 08 92 707 407; www.nicetourisme.com

🕐 **Open** Musée Matisse, Palais Lascaris & Musée International d'Art Naif Anatole-Jakovsky: 10am–6pm Wed–Mon. Musée Chagall: 10am–5pm Wed–Mon; May–Oct: till 6pm. Musée d'Art Moderne et d'Art Contemporain: 10am–6pm Tue–Sun. Parc Phoenix: Apr–Oct: 9:30am–7:30pm daily; Oct–Mar: till 6pm

€ **Prices** Musée Matisse, Palais Lascaris, Musée d'Art Moderne

et d'Art Contemporain & Musée International d'Art Naif Anatole-Jakovsky: free. Musée Chagall: €14–24; under 18s free. Parc Phoenix: €16–26; under 12s free

👬 **Skipping the queue** The French Riviera Pass (www.frenchriviera pass.com) offers admission to the main sights in and around Nice; there are discounts for children.

🚩 **Guided tours** The Nice Le Grand Tour (under 4s free) and tramway tour (in English and French) are available. Contact tourist office for details.

👫 **Age range** 3 plus

👟 **Activities** Rent bikes at Roller Station (49 Quai des Etats Unis,

Nice's pebbly beach, backed by the famous Promenade des Anglais

Letting off steam

Go for a swim at Nice's public and private beaches. Among the latter, Neptune and Hi! Beach are family oriented, with special play areas. Climb the steps or pay a small fee for the lift from the Quai des Etats-Unis up the **Colline du Château** *(Parc du Château, 06000; 04 93 85 62 33)*, the Greek acropolis of Nice and now a park with a playground and scenic views.

Eat and drink

Picnic: under €20; Snacks: €20–45; Real meal: €45–90; Family treat: over €90 (based on a family of four)

PICNIC Cours Saleya hosts a great food market *(closed Mon)*. Try *socca* (a crispy chickpea pancake), eaten hot from a paper cone at Thérèse's stall. Head for the beach or picnic tables in Parc Phoenix.

SNACKS La Banane a Doume *(6 Rue de la Poissonnerie, 06300; 04 93 79 09 54; www.labananadoume.com; closed Wed)* is a bright-yellow snack bar that offers panninis and salads.

06000; 04 93 62 99 05; www. roller-station.fr) to cycle along the seaside on the celebrated Promenade des Anglais.

⏱ **Allow** 2 or 3 days

🎭 **Festivals** Carnaval de Nice, one of the biggest celebrations in France (Feb). Festival de Jazz and Musicalia, a world music festival (Jul)

Good family value?

Although most of the museums are free, Nice can be expensive. With a pleasing climate and plenty to see, the city makes for a superb winter break as it is warm and sunny.

REAL MEAL La Voglia *(2 Rue St François de Paule, 06300; 04 93 80 99 16; www.lavoglia.com; open daily)* serves pizzas, ravioli, *gnocchi* (dumplings) and heavenly desserts in generous portions.

FAMILY TREAT La Taverne Alsacienne *(49 Rue de l'Hôtel des Postes, 06000; 04 93 62 24 04; www. latavernealsacienne.com; open daily)* is a historic brasserie that not only prepares a variety of French classics, but also hot dogs and fish and chips.

Shopping

Head for the **Confiserie Florian** *(12 Quai Papacino, 06300; 04 93 55 43 50)* for home-made sweets and chocolates, with free tours of the workshop. A variety of model trains, cars and more awaits shoppers at **Love Modelisme** *(8 Blvd Lech-Walesa, 06300; 04 93 62 31 27; www.love-modelisme.com)*.

The bustling market area of Cours Saleya lined with a variety of stalls

Find out more

DIGITAL Download the audio guide *Nice: mp3cityguides Walking Tour* at www.audible.co.uk.
FILM *To Catch a Thief* (1955) starring Carry Grant and Grace Kelly is set on the French Riviera. *Return of the Pink Panther* (1975), starring Peter Sellers, was also shot in Nice.

Next stop...

ST-PAUL-DE-VENCE Take bus 400 west to the scenic town of St-Paul-de-Vence to visit the **Fondation Maeght** (www.fondation-maeght.com), an amazing and often amusing gallery of modern art. Built in 1964, the museum is fantastic for kids. The foundation's garden, adorned with Giacometti's stick-thin human and animal statues, Miró's maze, Chagall's mosaic and Bury's hypnotic fountain, has a magic all of its own.

⑳ Monaco
The second-smallest country in the world

Smaller than New York's Central Park, Monaco is famed for its casino, Formula 1 Grand Prix, millionaires and actress Grace Kelly, who married into the royal family of Grimaldi. Her son, Prince Albert II, opens his **Palais Princier** to visitors; the changing of the guard takes place at the entrance to the palace daily at 11:55am.

In 1910, the scientifically inclined Prince Albert I built the **Musée Océanographique**, a stone cliff of a building, with a 90-tank aquarium, including a shark and coral lagoon. He also planted the unique **Jardin Exotique**, on the mountainside with crazy-looking cacti. A visit to these gardens includes the Observatory Cave, which is filled with unusual stalactites, and also the Musée d'Anthropologie Prehistorique. The **Nouveau Musée National de Monaco-Villa Sauber** has a huge collection of dolls and their houses.

The Musée Oceanographique perching on its cliff, Monaco

Letting off steam

Hit the beach – Larvotto is the only public beach in Monaco, but the fee-charging Note Bleue offers fun attractions and a playground for kids.

㉑ Biot
Home of the fat noodly Tubist

In 1955, Fernand Léger bought land in the hill town of Biot to build a giant ceramic garden, but he died two weeks later. Instead, his widow built the **Musée Fernand Léger** to house his paintings and mosaics. Léger was nicknamed the "Tubist" for his love of fat, noodly and colourful art forms. Next to the museum is the Okonek family's Japanese gardens and Europe's biggest bonsai forest at the **Musée du Bonsaï**. Biot is also noted for its bubbly glass, made at the **Verrerie de Biot**, where visitors can watch the glassblowers at work.

Letting off steam

Head south to **Marineland** (*www. marineland.fr*) in the town of Antibes. It comprises four parks – Marineland, with an aquarium, polar bears and dolphin and seal shows; the Ferme du Far West, with fun rides and vast playgrounds; Adventure Golf,

Colourful bubbly glasses for sale in the shops in Biot

The Lowdown

🌐 **Map reference** 14 G4
Address 06410 (Alpes-Maritimes). Musée Fernand Léger: Chemin du Val de Pome; 04 92 91 50 20; *www.musee-nationaux-alpes martitime.fr*. Musée du Bonsaï: 299 Chemin du Val de Pôme; 04 93 65 63 99; *museedu bonsai.free.fr*. Monaco Verrerie de Biot: Chemin des Combes; 04 93 65 03 00; *www.verreriebiot.com*

🚆 **Train** to Antibes, then Envibus 7 or 10

ℹ️ **Visitor information** 46 Rue St-Sébastien, 06410; 04 93 65 78 00; *www.biot.fr*

🕐 **Open** Musée Fernand Léger & Musée du Bonsaï: closed Tue. Verrerie de Biot: daily

🍽️ **Eat and drink** *Snacks* Cucina Vera (44 Impasse St-Sébastien, 06410; 04 92 91 06 44; *closed Tue & Wed*) offers superb tagliatelle. *Real meal* La Pierre à Four (15 Route de Valbonne, 06410; 04 93 65 60 00; *closed Sun dinner & Mon*) serves Provençal cuisine and a cheese platter.

🎉 **Festival** Mimosa Festival (Feb)

a crazy-golf course; and the Aquasplash water park. Pick and choose, or visit all the attractions with a two-day pass.

㉒ Cannes
Stars by the sea

Oozing glitz and glamour, Cannes is synonymous with the Cannes Film Festival, when movie stars converge every May on the red carpet of the **Palais du Festival**, on the seafront boulevard of La Croisette. Wander along the Allée des Stars to see over 300 terracotta handprints of celebrities. Hop on to Le Petit Train du Cinéma (*www.cannes-petit-train. com*) for a guided tour of Cannes.

Steps lead up to the citadel which houses the **Musée de la Castre**, with paintings, Tibetan masks, Inuit art and antique instruments. For a free family beach, head to Port Canto and Plage Gazagnaire.

Letting off steam

Take a 15-minute boat ride to the car-free **Île Ste-Marguerite** (*www. trans-cote-azur.com*), a nature reserve with beaches and picnic sites. The Musée de la Mer here, which houses the prison cell of the Man in the Iron Mask, is a must-visit.

The Lowdown

🌐 **Map reference** 14 G3
Address 98030 (Monaco). Palais Princier: Monaco-Ville, 98000; 00377 93 25 18 31; *www.palais. mc*. Musée Océanographique: Ave St-Martin, 98000; 00377 93 15 36 00; *www.oceano.mc*. Jardin Exotique: 62 Blvd du Jardin Exotique, 98002; *www. jardin-exotique.mc*. Nouveau Musée National de Monaco-Villa Sauber: 17 Ave Princesse Grace, 98000; *www.nmnm.mc*

🚆 **Train** or RCA bus 100 from Nice

ℹ️ **Visitor information** 2a Blvd des Moulins, 98030; 04 92 16 61 16; *www.visitmonaco.com*

🕐 **Open** Palais Princier: Apr–Oct: daily. Musée Océanographique, Jardin Exotique & Nouveau Musée National de Monaco-Villa Sauber: daily

🍽️ **Eat and drink** *Real meal* La Pizzeria Monegasque (4 Rue Terrazzani, 98000 98000 La Condamine; 00377 04 93 30 16 38) offers pizza, steaks and duck maigret. *Family treat* Il Terrazzino (2 Rue des Iris, 98000; 00377 04 93 50 24 27; *Mon–Sat*) has daily pasta, meat specials and an antipasti bar.

🎉 **Festivals** Festival International du Cirque de Monte-Carlo (Jan–Feb). International Gran Prix de Monaco (May)

Prices given are for a family of four

The Lowdown

- 🌐 **Map Reference** 14 G4
  Address 06400 (Alpes-Maritimes).
  Musée de la Castre: Pl de la
  Castre, 06400 Le Suquet; 04 93
  38 55 26; www.cannes.com
- 🚆 **Train** or TAM bus 20 from Nice
- ℹ️ **Visitor information** Palais des
  Festivals, 1 Blvd de la Croisette,
  06400; 04 92 99 84 22;
  www.cannes.travel
- 🕐 **Open** Musée de la Castre: Jul &
  Aug: daily; Sep–Jun: closed Mon
- ☕ **Eat and drink** *Real meal* Bistrot
  Margaux (*14 Rue Helene Vagliano,
  06400; 04 93 38 68 68*) has herby
  lamb and creamy dauphinoise
  potatoes. *Family treat* IX-Nove
  (*24 Rue Pasteur, 06400; 04 93 43
  20 37; www.ix-nove.com*) offers
  pastas, Florentine steaks and
  vegetarian dishes.
- 🎏 **Festival** Festival de Cannes (May)

㉓ Grasse

France's most fragrant town

In the 16th century, the tanneries
of Grasse started making perfumed
gloves – one of the status symbols of
the Renaissance period – for Queen
Catherine de Medici. Although the
gloves went out of fashion with time,
the scent industry continued to
grow. Known as the World Capital of
Perfume, Grasse has 30 *parfumeries*,
three of which, **Fragonard**, **Galimard**
and **Molinard**, offer daily guided
tours. The **Musée International de
la Parfumerie** highlights 3,000 years
of the history of perfumes: buy a
joint ticket to see, or rather smell, the
museum's **Perfume Garden** in the
nearby town of Mouans-Sartoux.

Letting off steam

Head to Castellane, an hour's ride
by car or taxi, to Europe's deepest
limestone canyon, the **Gorges du
Verdon**, which at certain points drops
to a depth of 700 m (2,296 ft) from
the rim to the Verdon river. Enjoy the
thrill of scary bridges and dizzying
views on the circular route to the
village of Moustiers-Ste-Marie.

The Lowdown

- 🌐 **Map reference** 14 G3
  Address 06130 (Alpes-Maritimes).
  Fragonard: 20 Blvd Fragonard,
  06130; 04 92 42 34 34; www.
  fragonard.com. Galimard: 73
  Route de Cannes, 06130; 04 93
  09 20 00; www.galimard.com.
  Molinard: 60 Blvd Victor Hugo,
  06130; 04 92 42 33 28; www.
  molinard.com. Musée
  International de la Parfumerie:
  8 Pl du Cours, 06130 & Perfume
  Garden: 979 Chemin des
  Gourettes, 06370 Mouans-
  Sartoux; 04 97 05 58 00;
  www.museesdegrasse.com
- 🚌 **Bus** 500 from Nice
- ℹ️ **Visitor information** Cours Honoré
  Cresp, 06130; 04 93 36 66 66;
  www.grasse.fr
- 🕐 **Open** Fragonard: daily; Nov–Jan:
  closed 12pm–2:30pm. Galimard:
  daily; Oct–Mar: closed 1–2pm
  Sun. Molinard: daily. Musée
  International de la Parfumerie:
  Oct–May: closed Tue
- ☕ **Eat and drink** *Real meal* La Voute
  (*3 Rue du Thourun, 06130; 04 93
  36 11 43*) offers stuffed courgette
  flowers. *Family treat* Au Fil du
  Temps (*83 Ave Auguste Renoir,
  Magagnosc, 06520; 04 93 36 20
  64; www.restaurantaufildutemps.
  com; closed Sat lunch, Wed & Sun
  dinner*) serves Provençal cuisine.

A funny sand sculpture of Shrek on the beach of otherwise stylish Cannes

Picnic under €20; **Snacks** €20–45; **Real meal** €45–90; **Family treat** over €90 (based on a family of four)

Where to Stay in Provence and the Côte d'Azur

From celebrated hotels, villas and B&Bs to city apartments, self-catering resorts and camping sites, the range of accommodation in Provence and the Côte d'Azur is staggering, but often expensive. Families able to travel outside of July and August will find significant discounts.

AGENCIES

South of France Villas
www.southfrancevillas.com
This agency offers a selection of villas in Provence and the Côte d'Azur; all either have a pool or are located on the beach.

Côte d'Azur Maison
www.coteazurmaison.com
The website lists a wide range of properties – villas, apartments, *gîtes* and B&Bs that can be rented directly from the owners.

Aix-en-Provence Map 14 E4

HOTEL
Le Mas des Ecureuils
1170 Petite Route des Milles, 13090; 04 42 24 40 48; www.lemasdes ecureuils.com
Southwest of the centre of Aix, this hotel offers well-equipped rooms with Wi-Fi and satellite TV. There are hammocks for adults, a *hammam* (Turkish bath) and a *pétanque* court. Good restaurant with a kids' menu.
🐟 P ❋ ⊘　　　　　　€€

CAMPING
Camping Chantecler
13100 Val St-André; 04 42 26 12 98; www.campingchantecler.com
Only 2 km (1 mile) from Aix's centre, this camp site has shaded pitches, chalets and mobile homes. There is a playground, and a restaurant/snack bar open in July and August.
🏕 ⌂ P ⊘　　　　　　€

Rooms at the old farmhouse in Bastide de la Brague, Antibes

Antibes Map 14 G4

SELF-CATERING
Bastide de la Brague
55 Ave Numéro 6, 06600 La Brague; 04 93 65 73 78; www.bbchambre antibes.com
Located near the sea and set amidst olive trees, this old farmhouse has five rooms with Wi-Fi and individual entrances. Meals are available and the owner who knows the area well, offers excursions along the coast.
🐟 P ❋　　　　　　€€

Pierre & Vacances Premium Port Prestige
1 Ave Frédéric Mistral, 06600; 01 58 21 55 84; www.pv-holidays.com
Surrounding a garden, this complex of five buildings is within easy walking distance of the city centre. All the apartments have a balcony or terrace, Wi-Fi; baby kits for under 2s; and, for rainy days, PlayStation hire, board games and comic books.
🐟 ⌂ ❋ ⊘　　　　　　€€

CAMPING
Camping du Pylone
Ave La Brague, 06600; 04 93 74 94 70; www.campingdupylone.com
Located near the beach, this is a friendly camp site, with games and activities, and fishing in the river. There is a restaurant, bakery, shop and a swimming pool. Besides their pitches, their website lists companies and individuals who rent out cottages and mobile homes.
🏕 ⊘　　　　　　€–€€

Apt Map 13 D3

CAMPING
Camping Le Luberon
Route de Saignon, 84400; 04 90 04 85 40; www.camping-le-luberon.com
A short drive south of Apt, this leafy and friendly camp ground offers a range of cabins, chalets and mobile

Entrance to the centrally located Hotel de l'Horloge, Avignon

homes to choose from. For kids, there is a playground and an activity a day such as cooking or juggling.
🏕 ⌂ P ⊘　　　　　　€€

Arles Map 13 C4

HOTELS
Hotel Régence
5 Rue Marius Jouveau, 13200; 04 90 96 39 85; www.hotel-regence.com
On the quays of the Rhône, a few minutes walk from central Arles, this hotel has rooms painted in rich Provençal colours. Reasonably priced buffet breakfast and Internet connections are available.
🐟 P ❋　　　　　　€

Hôtel de l'Amphithéâtre
5–7 Rue Diderot, 13200; 04 90 96 10 30; www.hotelamphitheatre.fr
Centrally located, this hotel combines old-world charm and comfortable furnishings. Rooms have Wi-Fi and there are computers to share in the public rooms downstairs.
🐟 ❋　　　　　　€€

SELF-CATERING
Mas Saint Germain
13200 Villeneuve-Camargue; 04 90 97 00 60; www.massaintgermain.com
Just outside Arles, in the middle of the Camargue, kids will love their stay on this organic farm. The family breeds local horses, bulls and Merino sheep. Horse-riding is also available.
🏕 🐟 ⌂ P　　　　　　€

Avignon
Map 13 D3

HOTEL
Hotel De l'Horloge
Map 13 D3

Pl de l'Horloge, 84000; 04 90 16 42 00; www.hotel-avignon-horloge.com

A short walk from the Palais des Papes, this handsome hotel in a 19th-century stone building has Wi-Fi-equipped rooms with satellite TV. There is a pay-parking lot nearby.

⇔ P ✳ €€

BED & BREAKFAST
La Bastide des Anges

1634 Chemin des Vignes, 84000 Île de la Barthelasse; 04 90 82 56 04; www.la-bastide-des-anges.com

This old stone family house makes a good base for exploring Avignon, 5 km (3 miles) away. Rooms are well-furnished and spacious. There is a communal room, with TV, library, Wi-Fi and a kitchen for guests.

✉ ⇔ 🖙 P ⊙ €€

Domaine de Rhodes

486 Chemin de Rhodes, 84000 Île de la Barthelasse; 04 90 82 40 11; www.domainederhodes.com

This 16th-century country house has a family suite with two bedrooms furnished with antiques, and a self-catering apartment where four can sleep. The hosts offer bicycles to explore the Île de la Barthelasse.

⇔ P ⊙ €€

CAMPING
Camping l'Isle des Papes

30400 Villeneuve-lès-Avignon; 04 90 15 15 90; www.avignon-camping.com

Located 6 km (4 miles) north of Avignon on the Île de la Barthelasse, this family-friendly camp site has mobile homes and bungalows to rent, and playgrounds. Free shuttle bus to Avignon in July and August.

⇔ P ⊙ €

Cannes
Map 14 G4

SELF-CATERING
Villa d'Estelle

12–14 Rue des Belges, 06400; 04 92 98 44 48; www.villadestelle.com

A minute's walk from La Croisette and the sea, this property has cheerful apartments with terraces, satellite TV and Internet access. Staff is helpful. See website for special discount offers.

⇔ 🖙 ⊙ €€€

Fontaine-de-Vaucluse
Map 13 D3

HOTEL
Hôtel de la Source

Quartier Châteauvieux, Route de Cavaillon, 84800; 04 90 20 31 84; www.hoteldessources.com

A short walk from the city centre of Fontaine-de-Vaucluse, on the banks of the Sorgue, this hotel offers spacious Wi-Fi-equipped rooms with fine views overlooking the river. There is a restaurant and rates include a continental breakfast.

⇔ P ⊙ €€

BED & BREAKFAST
Domaine de la Fontaine

920 Chemin du Bosquet, 84800 L'Isle-sur-la-Sorgue; 04 90 38 01 44; www.domainedelafontaine.com

A short drive from Fontaine-de-Vaucluse, this charming home has two family suites, furnished in sunny colours. The garden, full of century-old planes and cypresses, is a great place to play and laze, as well as have breakfast. Meals are available only on Tuesdays and Saturdays.

✉ ⇔ P ⊙ €€€

CAMPING
Camping La Coutelière

D24 Route de Fontaine, 84800 Lagnes; 04 90 20 33 97; www.camping-la-couteliere.com

A 5-minute drive from Fontaine-de-Vaucluse, on the river, this camp ground offers a choice of shaded pitches, mobile homes, wooden bungalows and cabins on stilts; linen can be hired. There is a snack bar, a shop, basketball and tennis courts, a playground, table tennis and special activities for kids aged 6–12 years.

🖙 P ⊙ €

SELF-CATERING
La Bastide des Beaumes Rouges

84800 Chemin des Beaumes Rouges; 04 90 20 34 18; www.bastidedesbeaumesrouges.com

Decorated in Provençal yellows and blues, this apartment occupies the ground floor of an old stone manor house, with views of the cliffs and ruined castle, a short walk from the town's main spring. It has a private sunny terrace; linen can be hired. The owners also have a family B&B room.

✉ 🖙 P €

Pool at the Camping La Coutelière, Fontaine-de-Vaucluse

Gordes
Map 13 D3

HOTEL
Mas de la Sénancole

84220 Les Imberts; 04 90 76 76 55; www.mas-de-la-senancole.com

Located 4 km (3 miles) southwest of Gordes, in a residential area, this hotel makes a peaceful base for exploring the Luberon. Rooms can be interlinked to form family rooms. There are pretty gardens and a spa for relaxing. The excellent restaurant serves contemporary cuisine.

⇔ P ✳ ⊙ €€€

BED & BREAKFAST
La Guillone

84220 Murs; 04 90 72 06 43; www.guillone-luberon.com

Located 5 km (3 miles) from Gordes, this beautiful B&B in an 18th-century *bastide* has been in the same family for five generations. Rooms are painted in Provençal colours and there is a special suite for four. Breakfasts are sumptuous.

✉ ⇔ 🖙 P €€

Marseille
Map 13 D4

BED & BREAKFAST
La Bastide De Roucas

5 Rue Etienne Mein, 13007; 04 91 31 79 83; www.bastide-roucas.com

In the heart of Marseille, in a calm and authentic part of the city and two steps away from the Prophète beach, this B&B has a garden and swimming pool. Breakfast can be eaten under the plane trees in the garden.

⇔ ⊙ €€

Price Guide

The following price ranges are based on one night's accommodation in high season for a family of four, inclusive of service charges and any additional taxes.

€ Under €100 €€ €100–200 €€€ over €200

Key to symbols *see back cover flap*

SELF-CATERING
Adagio Marseille République
30 Rue Jean Trinquet, 13002; 04 96 11 67 00; www.adagio-city.com
A short walk from two Métro stations, this apartment hotel offers 33 family rooms, with high-speed Internet and television. Infant cots are available as well. There is an indoor and outdoor public parking nearby, and a laundromat.

🛏 🍽 ❄   €€

Monaco
Map 14 G3

HOTEL
Novotel Monte Carlo
16 Blvd Princesse Charlotte, 98000; 00377 99 99 83 00; www.novotel.com
This modern hotel in the heart of Monaco is a great-value option for families; two kids under 16 can stay for free in a family room and Wi-Fi is available at a charge. The hotel has play areas, a *hammam* (Turkish bath) and a fitness centre. The restaurant offers good menus for kids. See website for discount offers.

🛏 P ❄ ☺   €€

A pleasantly shaded tree house in Orion, St-Paul-de-Vence

Nice
Map 14 G3

HOTELS
Nice Garden Hotel
11 Rue du Congrés, 06000; 04 93 87 35 62; www.nicegardenhotel.com
This is a friendly nine-room hotel on the ground floor of a 19th-century townhouse, just a small walk from the beach. The windows are double glazed and overlook a charming little garden. There are triple rooms, where guests can add a cot.

❄   €€

La Pérouse
11 Quai Rauba Capeu, 06300; 04 93 62 34 63; www.hotel-la-perouse.com
Built right into the cliff by the sea and only a short walk from the lively

---

market in Cours Saleya, this boutique hotel offers suites for families done up in light Mediterranean colours. Most of these suites come with big terraces. There is Wi-Fi in the rooms and an excellent buffet breakfast. The staff is friendly and helpful.

🛏 P ❄ ☺   €€€

SELF-CATERING
Goldstar Resort & Suites
45 Rue Maréchal Joffre, 06000; 04 93 16 92 77; www.hotel-gold star-nice.com
Centrally located for the sights and just a 2-minute walk from the Promenade des Anglais, this contemporary high-rise building has suites suitable for families. The roof-top pool and stunning views over Nice are the main attraction. Rooms have free Wi-Fi and satellite TVs.

🍽 P ❄ ☺   €€

St-Paul-de-Vence
Map 14 G3

BED & BREAKFAST
Orion
Impasse des Peupliers, 2436 Chemin du Malvan, 06570; 04 93 24 87 51; www.orionbb.com
Set in peaceful surroundings, this property offers lodging in tree houses in an old oak grove outside St-Paul. The pool is designed like a mountain lake, with water filtered by plants.

🏊 🛏 ☺   €€€

St-Tropez
Map 14 F4

HOTELS
Hôtel des Lices
Ave Grangeon, 83993; 04 94 97 28 28; www.hoteldeslices.com
A short distance from the Place des Lices, this lovely hotel makes visitors feel as if it were in the countryside with a pretty garden and pool terrace. Rooms are spacious and furnished with St-Tropez chic. Baby cots are available. Helpful staff.

🛏 P ❄ ☺   €€€

L'Orangeraie
Route de Ramatuelle, 83420 La Croix Valmer; 04 94 55 27 27; www.hotel-lorangeraie.com
Out on St-Tropez's peninsula, this hotel housed in an early 20th-century mansion converted into a grand hotel, is packed with character. The rooms, all completely renovated, are

---

Pool terrace with sun beds lined up at the Hôtel des Lices, St-Tropez

big and airy with high ceilings and many have lovely sea views. Have breakfast in the lush park dominated by towering palms.

🛏 ❄ ☺   €€€

CAMPING
Camping Les Cigalons
34 Ave du Croiseur Leger le Malin, 83120 Ste-Maxime; 04 94 96 05 51; www.campingcigalon.com
A boat ride from St-Tropez and a stone's throw from the sea and the sandy Plage de Nartelle – with Water Glisse, its water park – this popular no-frills camp site offers pitches amidst parasol pines and bungalows, as well as chalets, with terraces, to rent. There is a playground and a Wi-Fi point.

🍽 P   €

SELF-CATERING
Le Mas des Oliviers
Quartier de la Croisette, 83120 Ste-Maxime; 04 94 96 13 31; www. hotellemasdesoliviers.com
This handsome complex is just a boat ride away from St-Tropez and a few minutes walk from a sandy beach. It offers hotel rooms and studio apartments, accommodating up to four, along with bunk beds, designed for week-long rentals. There are tennis courts. Linen can be hired.

🍽 ❄ ☺   €€

Résidence Les Bastide de Grimaud
Lieu-dit La Castellane, Route de Collobrières, 83310 Grimaud; 04 42 97 58 00; www.odalys-vacances.com
Located in one of the most expensive corners of France, this purpose-built family vacation centre offers studio apartments just outside Grimaud, 4 km (3 miles) from St-Tropez. Arranged in eight low-rise buildings, all flats come with terraces; many offer lovely views over the gulf.

🍽 P ☺   €€€

Corsica

Wild and beautiful, Corsica has been inhabited since prehistoric times, but did not become part of France until 1769. Earlier Italian influences survive in its architecture, and also in the Corsican language and cuisine. It is famous as the birthplace of Napoleon, but nature steals the show – beaches, mountains, rivers, forests and coastal scenery.

Below Splendid view of Calvi from Notre-Dame de la Serra

Golfe de Porto
p366

Bonifacio
p370

① Golfe de Porto
Where Mother Nature rocks and rolls

The coastline here borders on fantasy – the deepest red rocks blaze next to the intense blue of the sea. The savage porphyry cliffs of the Calanche de Piana and the wild coast of Scandola dwarf the little port of Porto, an outpost of civilization with its eucalyptus grove and pebbly beaches. Inland, mountains rise abruptly, offering spectacular views of gorges and waterfalls. At sunset, the light makes the red rocks glow like embers.

Sailing in the picturesque Golfe de Porto

Key Sights

① **Girolata** Accessible by sea or foot, the fishermen's hamlet of Girolata has a dream-like location next to its 16th-century Genoese tower. In winter the population here is less than 10.

② **Réserve Naturelle de Scandola** A World Heritage Site, Scandola's cliffs, sea and grottoes are home to rare fish, birds, seaweed and algae.

③ **La Poudrière** Once a gunpowder factory, this is now the Aquarium de la Poudrière, housing octopi and moray eels.

④ **Plage de Porto** This rocky town beach is set dramatically under the cliffs behind the Genoese tower.

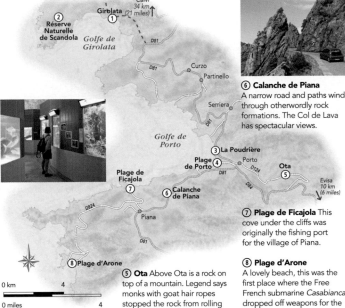

⑥ **Calanche de Piana** A narrow road and paths wind through otherwordly rock formations. The Col de Lava has spectacular views.

⑦ **Plage de Ficajola** This cove under the cliffs was originally the fishing port for the village of Piana.

⑤ **Ota** Above Ota is a rock on top of a mountain. Legend says monks with goat hair ropes stopped the rock from rolling down and crushing the village.

⑧ **Plage d'Arone** A lovely beach, this was the first place where the Free French submarine *Casabianca* dropped off weapons for the Maquis during World War II.

Letting off steam

Swim at Porto beach or take the Corte bus east to Evisa and the nearby Forêt d'Aïtone, which has a majestic stand of Larico pines. Make the easy hour's walk to the Grotte des Bandits, or continue up to the Col de Vergio for the 10-minute walk to the beautiful Cascades d'Aïtone. From Evisa there is also an easy two-hour walk down the old mule path through the spectacular Gorges de Spelunca to Ota with the chance for dips in the Porto river. Signs explain the key features along the way.

A winding path through the tall, slender pines in the Forêt d'Aïtone

Prices given are for a family of four

Eat and drink
Picnic: under €20; Snacks: €20–45; Real meal: €45–90; Family treat: over €90 (based on a family of four)

PICNIC Hibiscus (*Bypass, Porto-Vecchio, 20137; 04 95 70 02 26; mid-Apr–Oct*) offers Corsican cheese and charcuterie and cold drinks.

The well-preserved square Genoese tower at Porto

There are picnic spots by the Genoese bridges, 2 km (1 mile) up from Ota off the D124.

The Lowdown

- **Map reference** 1 A3
  Address 20150 (Corse-du-Sud).
  Aquarium de la Poudrière: Porto
  la Marine; 04 95 26 19 24
- **Bus** Autocars SAIB from Ajaccio
  and Calvi (May–Sep). Mordocini
  buses from Corte (Jul–Aug).
- **Visitor information** Quartier de
  la Marine, 20150; 04 95 21 10 55;
  www.porto-tourisme.com
- **Open** Aquarium de la Poudrière:
  Jul & Aug: 8am–9pm daily;
  Sep–Jun: 8am–7pm daily
- **Price** Aquarium de la Poudrière:
  €17–27; under 7s free
- **Skipping the queue** Porto is
  small and very crowded in
  August. Try and visit in May,
  June or September.
- **Guided tours** Several companies
  offer boat tours to the Réserve

Naturelle de Scandola and the
Calanche de Piana. Nave Va
(Route de Mezzavia 20090; 04
95 26 15 16; www.naveva.com)
offers a three-hour tour;
under 5s free.

- **Age range** 4 plus
- **Activities** Hire small boats for
  exploring the coast from Le
  Goéland (Port de Plaisance,
  Rive Gauche 20150; 06 81 06
  88 08). A half-day rental is €75.
- **Allow** At least a day
- **Toilets** In cafés
- **Festival** Fête de la Châtaigne,
  chestnut festival in Evisa (Nov)

Good family value?
Spectacular nature concentrated
in a small area; outdoor-loving
families cannot ask for more.

SNACKS Le Golfe (La Marine,
20150; 04 95 26 13 33; Apr–Oct) is a
portside snack bar with sandwiches,
paninis, salads and ice cream.
REAL MEAL Le Mini-golf (Plage de
Porto, 20150; 04 95 26 17 55; Apr–
Sep) offers pizza and full Corsican
meal. Diners can follow this up with
a rousing round of mini-golf.
FAMILY TREAT Le Bélvèdere (Port
of Porto, 20150; 04 95 26 82 13;
Apr–Oct) serves delicious Corsican
and French classics, which guests
can enjoy while taking in the
gorgeous views.

Take cover
Even if it is not raining, Porto's
landmark Genoese tower is
interesting to visit. Located on the

headland, this is one of the very few
square towers built around Corsica
(the other 90 are mostly round).
It houses exhibits on the coastal
defenses of the island.

Next stop...
CALVI Head 34 km (21 miles) north
to Calvi, a jolly resort with a vast
sandy beach by a pinewood and a
Genoese citadel located on a huge
rock above the sea. A monument by
the citadel boasts that Christopher
Columbus was born here. Another
famous seafarer Admiral Horatio
Nelson, is also linked to Calvi. When
Nelson attacked the town in 1794,
a piece of shrapnel took out his
eye and he had to wear an eye
patch ever after.

The beach in Calvi, overlooked by the Genoese citadel

② The Balagne
Music and crafts

Known as the "Garden of Corsica", the Balagne is an amphitheatre made up of *villages perchés*, olive groves, vineyards and orchards overlooking the coves on Corsica's northwestern coast. Just getting down to the beaches – Algajola is a good one – is fun; flag down the Balagne tram that runs between Calvi *(see p367)* and Île-Rousse.

Away from the coast, many of the Balagne hill towns are devoted to preserving traditional crafts and farming. Chief among these is Pigna, the centre for Corsican music and its unique and haunting multi-harmonied singing. Here **Ugo Casalonga** makes *cetere*, a traditional Corsican guitar; Marie Darneal creates music boxes

Canoes lying on Algajola beach in the Balagne

at the **Scat'A Musica** and **A Casa Musicale** presents live music. Other villages include Sant'Antonino, famous for lemons – taste the treats in the Maison de Citron; Aregno with Poterie d'Art de Praoli, a ceramics workshop, and a 11th-century Pisan church with a mysterious façade sculpture of a man pulling a thorn out of his foot; and Felicitu, site of the Ange Campana glass blowers.

The Balagne tram arriving from Calvi at the L'île-Rousse station

The Lowdown

🌐 **Map reference** 1 B2
Address 20217 (Haute Corse).
Ugo Casalonga: Pigna; 04 95
61 77 15; *ugocetera.monsite-orange.fr*. Scat'A Musica: Pigna;
04 95 61 77 34. A Casa Musicale:
20220 Pigna; 04 95 61 77 31;
www.casa-musicale.org

🚋 **Tram** The Balagne tram during summers; car or taxi for hill villages

ℹ️ **Visitor information** Port de Plaisance, 20217 Calvi; 04 95 65 16 67; *www.balagne-corsica.com*

🕐 **Open** Ugo Casalonga: daily.
Scat'A Musica: May–Oct: daily.
A Casa Musicale: daily; book ahead for Tue & Fri night concerts

☕ **Eat and drink** *Real meal* La Padulla (*Plage d'Aregno, 20217 Algajola;
04 95 60 75 22; www.restaurant-algajola-padula.com; Apr–Oct:
daily*) offers paella and pizzas.
Family treat A Caserella (*20220 Pigna; 04 95 61 78 08; Apr–Sep: daily*) serves organic tapas,
Corsican charcuterie. Book ahead.

🎭 **Festival** Festivoce, Corsican song festival in the Balagne (Jul)

Letting off steam

Take a walk with Corsica's donkeys in Calenzana, 13 km (8 miles) south of Calvi. English-speaking **Fasgianu** (*fasgianu.free.fr/ane*) offers a 4-hour family excursion that allows kids under 40 kg (88 lbs) to ride the donkeys. There is also a stop for lunch and a swim by a waterfall.

③ St-Florent
Between white sands and a zebra church

St-Florent is a sunny laid-back resort, with yachts bobbing in the marina and locals playing *pétanque* non-stop

in the square. Like most coastal towns, its landmark is a Genoese tower – now used for art exhibits – but it also has an exquisite Pisan church, the 12th-century **Église de**

The Lowdown

🌐 **Map reference** 1 C2
Address 20217 (Haute-Corse).
Église de Santa-Maria-Assunta:
9 Cours Général de Gaulle, 20100
Sartène. Église de San Michele de Murato: 20239 Murato

🚗 **Bus** Santini buses from Bastia

ℹ️ **Visitor information** Bâtiment Adminstrative, 20217; 04 95 37 06 04; *www.corsica-saintflorent.com*

☕ **Eat and drink** *Real meal* Brasserie La Caravelle (*Pl Porta, 20217;
04 95 37 00 27; open daily*) has al fresco tables. *Family treat* U Trogliu (*Rue Centrale, 20217;
04 95 37 20 73; www.utrogliu.com*) serves fresh pasta, home-made the same day.

🎭 **Festivals** Porto Latino, Latin music festival (Aug). Festival des Nuits de la Guitare, annual guitar festival in nearby Patromonio (mid-Jul)

Yachts at the marina in St-Florent

Santa-Maria-Assunta. The Pisans also built Corsica's most famous church, **Église de San Michele de Murato**, 17 km (10 miles) southeast in Murato. Dressed in green and white stripes and checks, the façade is decorated with reliefs of Adam and Eve, but also bizarre ones of cut-off hands and scissors, which recall that in the Middle Ages, Corsican churches often doubled as law courts.

Letting off steam
Bask on St-Florent's beach, Plage de la Roya, where **Sun Folies** (www.sunfolies.com) hire out equipment, from inflatable boats to sea scooters. Take the 15-minute boat ride on **Le Popeye** (www.lepopeye.com) to the soft white sands of Loto and Saleccia beaches, arguably the most beautiful and unspoilt in France.

The striped façade of the Église de San Michele de Murato, near St-Florent

④ Bastia
A town bombed by mistake
With its charming old port and tall, colour-drenched houses, Baroque Bastia is Corsica's most Italian-looking town. Only a few ruins recall one of the worst mistakes of World War II, when the Allies failed to learn that the Nazis had actually withdrawn from town, before they dropped bombs and killed hundreds of the locals who were celebrating their recent liberation in the streets.

High up over the old port, the Palais des Gouverneurs, seat of Corsica's 15th–18th century Genoese rulers, is being restored as a museum, the **Musée de Bastia**, but now holds temporary exhibitions and offers tours of the gardens. A little train makes the circuit around town

Boats docked in the magnificient old port of Bastia

The Lowdown

🌐 **Map reference** 1 C2
Address 20200 (Haute-Corse). Musée de Bastia: Pl du Donjon, La Citadelle; 04 95 31 09 12; www.musee-bastia.com

🚆 **Train** from Corte and Ajaccio. **Bus** Santini buses from St-Florent and Les Rapides Bleues from Aléria and Porto-Vecchio

ℹ️ **Visitor information** Rue José Luccioni Port Toga, 20200; 04 95 54 20 40; www.bastia-tourisme.com

🕐 **Open** Musée de Bastia: Tue–Sun

🍴 **Eat and drink** *Real Meal* La Réserve (Port de Toga, 20200; 04 95 31 05 35; closed Sun), located by the marina, serves juicy burgers, risotti and seafood, excellent fruit salads, as well as desserts. *Family treat* A Scaletta (4 Rue St-Jean, 20200; 04 95 32 28 70), a small, popular restaurant with a superb view over the old port, serves freshly cooked vegetables and local ingredients. Book in advance.

🎊 **Festivals** A Notte di a Memoria, historical pageant (Jul). Les Musicales, a music festival (Oct)

from Place St Nicolas, but best of all is the bird's-eye view over Bastia from the village of Cardo – take bus 3 from the Palais du Justice.

Letting off steam
Tear around Bastia's central Place St Nicolas. Or take bus 5 south from the Palais du Justice to **Le Paradis des Enfants** (www.parcloisirs.com), a water park with mini-quads, trampolines and a small farm in the village of Biguglia. Continue further south towards the Castagniccia, Europe's biggest chestnut forest, and stroll among the giant trees and to the waterfall along the Corniche de la Castagniccia, on the D330, between San Nicolao and Cervioni.

Picnic under €20; Snacks €20–45; Real meal €45–90; Family treat over €90 (based on a family of four)

⑤ Bonifacio

Emperors and plague, sieges and shipwrecks

Known as "Corsica's Gibraltar", Bonifacio looks like no other place on earth. Massive ramparts defend it from land; while tall Genoese houses teeter precariously over sheer white cliffs. But the real danger for this town lay with enemy navies and pirates, including the notorious blood-thirsty Dragut, who attacked its walls (and sometimes got in); raging tempests that sank ships and deadliest of all, the plague.

An ornate tomb in Cimetière Marin

Key Features

0 metres 200
0 yards 200

Baie de Bonifacio

Boat Tours ①

QUAI JÉRÔME COMPACTIT
QUAI SOTTA PORTIGLIOLU
RUE SAUVEUR-PAULE TIENNE
QUAI BANDA DEL FERRO
AVENUE CHARLES DE GAULE
HAUTE VILLE
③ Porte de Gênes
④ Église Ste-Marie-Majeure
R. ST-DOMINIQUE
St-Dominique ⑦
⑥ Il Torrone
⑧ Cimitière Marin
⑤
Escalier du Roy d'Aragon
Le Grain de Sable ②

⑤ Escalier du Roy d'Aragon Legend says these 187 steps, cut into the cliff, were carved in one night in 1420 during the siege of Bonifacio by the king of Aragon.

⑥ Il Torrone This 35-m (115-ft) high lookout tower was of no use to the Pisans in 1181, when the Genoese took Bonifacio from them.

⑦ St-Dominique Inside this Gothic church are the lavish Baroque sculptures that are carried around town during the Holy Week.

① Boat tours Explore Bonifacio's spectacular sea caves and cliffs on tours that depart from the town harbour.

③ Porte de Gênes This zig-zag gate was designed to slow down attackers. Scenes from Bonifacio's history are displayed in the museum in Bastion de l'Étendard, which offers tours of the walls.

④ Église Ste-Marie-Majeure Town meetings took place in the Loggia located in front of this church. The altar holds relics of St Bonifacio.

⑧ Cimitière Marin Watch beautiful sunsets from this picturesque cemetery, filled with ornate white memorials.

② Le Grain de Sable This chunk of cliff split from Bonifacio in the 13th century. See it from Chapelle St-Roch.

The Lowdown

🌐 **Map reference** 1 C6
Address 20169 (Corse-du-Sud). Bastion de l'Étendard: Pl des Armes. Église Ste-Marie-Majeure: Rue de St-Sacrement. Escalier du Roy d'Aragon: Rue des Pachas. St-Dominique: Rue de St-Dominique; 04 95 73 11 88

🚌 **Bus** Eurocorse buses link Bonifacio to Ajaccio, Sartène and Porto Vecchio. A mini-train links the port to Haute Ville.

ℹ️ **Visitor information** 2 Rue Fred Scamaroni, 20169; 04 95 73 11 88; www.bonifacio.fr

🕐 **Open** Bastion de l'Étendard: daily. Escalier du Roy d'Aragon: Jun–Sep: 11am–5:30pm. St-Dominique: Apr–Oct: 9am–7pm

💶 **Price** Bastion de l'Étendard & Escalier du Roy d'Aragon: €7–14; under 12s free

👪 **Skipping the queue** Visit during spring and autumn; very crowded in summer.

👉 **Guided tours** Contact the tourist office for details.

👫 **Age range** 4 plus

👫 **Activities** Vedettes Thalassa (www.vedettesthalassa.com)

offers tours of Bonifacio's cliffs, sea caves and islets; under 8s free

⏱️ **Allow** A day

🚻 **Toilets** At Bastion de l'Étendard

Festivals Holy week processions by the medieval confraternities (Apr). Festival Nautic et Music, a festival dedicated to sailing boats and music (Oct)

Good family value?
Bonifacio's settings are unique – a place that sets imaginations alight. The nearby beaches are heavenly.

Letting off steam

Bonifacio's Haute Ville is mostly pedestrian, with more open spaces at the Cimitière Marin. Or take a taxi to the delightful and sheltered beaches east of Bonifacio: Plage de Santa Manza and Plage de Maora around the Golfe de Santa Manza, and Rondinara, with a near perfect circle of sand, for kids of all ages.

Eat and drink

Picnic: under €20; Snacks: €20–€45; Real meal: €45–90; Family treat: over €90 (based on a family of four)

PICNIC AGS (*4 Quai Jérôme Comparetti, 20169; 04 95 73 11 49*), located by the port, stocks basic food items for picnics that can be enjoyed on the shady Piantarella beach.
SNACKS Sandwicherie du Port (*Quai Comparetti, 20169; 06 10 32 18 50; May–Oct*) offers tasty takeaway sandwiches.
REAL MEAL Cantina Grill (*3 Quai Banda del Ferro, 20169; 04 95 70 49 86*) is a good-value restaurant that serves fish and meat dishes. It is situated next to the port and has a covered terrace.
FAMILY TREAT Kissing Pigs (*15 Quai Banda del Ferro, 20169; 04 95 73 56 09; open daily*) is a wine bar that offers a great choice

View of the old town as seen from the belvedere below the Porte de Gênes

Above *The Plage de Rondinara*
Below *Montée Rastello, the steps linking the port with the Haute Ville*

of bottles to match its exquisite Corsican charcuterie, salads, quiches and even bacon and eggs.

Shopping

Visit **Les Terrasses d'Aragon** (*21 Rue St-Dominique, 201691; 04 95 73 54 91*) for Bonifacio's famous good luck charms in the form of hands – a traditional present given to a baby by its godparents, to ward off the evil eye.

Take cover

Housed in a natural cave by the port, **Bonifacio Aquarium** (*71 Quai Jérôme Comparetti, 20169; open daily*) has 13 tanks of mostly Mediterranean fish, caught in the surrounding waters.

Next stop...

PORTO-VECCHIO Located north of Bonifacio, Porto-Vecchio is Corsica at its most chic. Its dreamy beaches, including Santa Giulia, Palombaggia and Cala Rossa, are perfect for kids. Two remarkable Bronze Age forts offer inspiration: the 2,000-BC **Casteddu d'Araghju** is a steep walk up a hill north of Porto-Vecchio, and the easier-to-reach 3,500-BC **Casteddu de Tappa** is in a field to the southwest of Porto-Vecchio.

⑥ Filitosa
3,600-year-old stone warriors

In 1946, the owner of an ancient olive grove called Filitosa began finding stones carved with strange faces and swords. The archaeologist Roger Grosjean found some more – 70 statue-menhirs in all, mostly of warriors, dated 1400 BC. Most of the stones were deliberately broken soon after they were made and were then reused in structures that were nearly as old. Grosjean believes Filitosa's warriors were sculpted by the Shardanes, the mysterious sea people – mentioned in the pyramids of Egypt – who conquered the local Bronze Age people, the Torréens. When the Torréens kicked out the Shardanes, they took great pleasure in breaking their stone warriors and reusing the stone to build Filitosa's three towers. Now re-erected amidst oaks and olives, the statue-menhirs are haunting and strange. Each is individual; in fact they may be the oldest portraits in the world.

Letting off steam

Head to the nearby Porto-Pollo beach, or go to Propriano, 20 km (12 miles) from Filitosa, a town with kid-friendly beaches. Families can go sailing with the **Centre Nautique Valinco** (www.centre-nautique-valinco.com).

⑦ Ajaccio
The ups and downs of Napoleon Bonaparte

Born in Ajaccio in 1769, just three months after Corsica became part of France, Napoleon Bonaparte

Above A family relaxing by a river near the Col de Bavella above Aléria
Below Ajaccio's petit train showing visitors around the city

supported Pasquale Paoli, the leader of Corsican independence – until the French Revolution. In contrast to most Corsicans, Napoleon was full of enthusiam for the "new" France and in 1793 started a little war against Paoli in Ajaccio. As a result, he and his family had to flee for their lives, with Napoleon escaping ignobly through the trap door in the **Maison Bonaparte**. Eleven years later, he was to become the emperor of France. Today, Ajaccio remembers Napoleon with plenty of statues in Places Austerlitz, Charles de Gaulle and Foch – and lots of memorabilia in the **Salons Napoléoniens** of the Hôtel de Ville and **Musée Fesch**, which contains a collection of Grand Masters – Botticelli, Rembrandt and Titian – donated by Napoleon's great-uncle, Cardinal Fesch.

Letting off steam

The Jardin Elisa playground is by the Hôtel de Ville, or take bus 5 to a string of beaches off the Route des Sanguinaires. To see Europe's largest collection of turtles and tortoises, catch the bus to Bastia and get off at **Parc A Cupulatta** (www.acupulatta.com), on the N193, 21 km (13 miles) northeast of Ajaccio.

The Lowdown

🌐 **Map reference** 1 B5
Address 20140 (Corse-du-Sud). Petreto-Bicchisano; 04 95 74 00 91; www.filitosa.fr

🚌 **Bus** Eurocorse buses from Bonifacio or Ajaccio to Propriano, then taxi

🕐 **Open** Apr–Oct: daily

🍴 **Eat and drink** Snacks Filitosa brasserie (on site) serves cold drinks and snacks. Family treat Ferme-Auberge Comte Abbatucci (Pont de Calzola Lieu dit Chiesale, 20140; 04 95 24 36 30; www.domaine-comte-abbatucci.com; May–Sep) offers a farm lunch.

🎪 **Festival** Fiera di Filitosa (Aug)

The Lowdown

🌐 **Map reference** 1 B4
Address 20000 (Corse-du-Sud). Maison Bonaparte: 18 Rue St-Charles; 04 95 2143 89; www.musee-maisonbonaparte.fr. Salons Napoléoniens: Ave Antoine Serafini; www.ajaccio.fr/Salons-Napoleoniens_a50.html. Musée Fesch: 50 Rue Cardinal Fesch; www.musee-fesch.com

🚆 **Train** from Bastia and Corte. **Bus** Eurocorse bus from Bonifacio

ℹ️ **Visitor information** 3 Blvd du Roi Jérôme, 20000; 04 95 51 53 03; www.ajaccio-tourisme.com

🕐 **Open** Maison Bonaparte: closed Mon. Salons Napoléoniens: closed Sat–Mon. Musée Fesch: closed Tue

🍴 **Eat and drink** Real meal Le Temps des Oliviers (1 Rue des Halles, 20000; 04 95 28 36 72) serves Italian dishes and pizzas. Family treat Le 20123 (2 Rue Roi-de-Rome, 20000; 04 95 21 50 05; www.20123.fr; closed Mon) offers good Corsican dishes.

🎪 **Festivals** Festival Musical d'Ajaccio (Jul). Festival d'Art Contemporain (Aug)

⑧ Aléria
Roman baths, Greek vases and a dog-headed cup

The Greeks, who called Corsica Kalliste (the most beautiful), founded Aléria in 565 BC. Over the centuries, the city grew to become the Roman capital of Corsica, counting 20,000 inhabitants. The 15th-century Genoese Fort de Matra houses the **Musée Archéologique Jérôme Carcopino**, displaying beautiful Greek vases – status symbol for the rich in Roman times. Note the dog's

The Lowdown

🌐 **Map reference** 1 D4
Address 20270 (Corse-du-Sud).
Musée Archéologique Jérôme
Carcopino: Fort de Matra; 04 95
57 00 92

🚌 **Bus** from Porto-Vecchio or Bastia

ℹ️ **Visitor information** Casa Luciani,
20270; 04 95 57 01 51; www.
aleria-corse.fr

🕐 **Open** Musée Archéologique
Jérôme Carcopino & Site
Archeologique d'Aléria: 9am–
noon & 2–7pm daily

🍴 **Eat and drink** Real meal
Cendrillon (20270 Catteragio;
04 95 57 07 42) serves pizzas.
Family treat Au Coquillages de
Diana (20270 Étang de Diane;
auxcoquillages-dediana.fr) offers
seafood by an oyster-filled lagoon.

*The courtyard of the Musée Fesch,
Ajaccio, with a statue of the Cardinal*

and mule's head *rhytons* or drinking
cups, a crystal dodecahedron (12-
sided figure), dice, and Etruscan
helmets and swords. A path leads
to the **Site Archeologique d'Aléria**,
where the Roman city's forum,
houses and some baths have been
excavated. Ninety per cent of it
still awaits future archaeologists.

Letting off steam

Play at Aléria's beach or take a taxi
to see the fabled "needles" of the
Col de Bavella, a mountain pass. Or
go to the nearby village of Ospedale.
Here, **Xtreme-sud** (www.xtremsud.
com) offers outdoor activities such as
rock climbing and an adventure
park for kids aged 3–8 years.

⑨ Corte
Town of Corsican heroes

A statue in Place Paoli honours
Pasquale Paoli, who made the town
his capital in 1755–69, during his
battle for independence (a fight that
also inspired the revolutionaries in

*The 15th-century citadel, perched
high above Corte*

America). In Place Gaffori, a statue
of former independence fighter
Dr Gian' Pietro Gaffori stands in front
of his house, still full of Genoese
bullet holes. Walk up to the 15th-
century citadel's **Musée de la
Corse** for its exhibits on the island's
traditions and music. Even higher
up sits the "Eagle's Nest" viewpoint
that gives Corte a fairy-tale air from
a distance. Far below is the Restonica
valley, a remarkable beauty spot –
although its narrow single-lane
road is not for the faint hearted.

Letting off steam

Take a taxi north through Asco Valley
to spot eagles in the Carrozzica
forest. **Asco Vallée Aventure** (www.
interracorsa.fr.) offers zip wires and
canyoning designed for 4–8-year old
kids who are over 3 ft (90 cm) height.

The Lowdown

🌐 **Map reference** 1 C3
Address 20350 (Haute-Corse).
Musée de la Corse: La Citadelle,
20250; www.musee-corse.com

🚆 **Train** from Ajaccio and Bastia. **Bus**
Eurocorse buses from Ajaccio and
Bastia (summer only). Autocars
Cortenais to the Restonica valley

ℹ️ **Visitor information** La Citadelle
de Corte, 20350; 04 95 46 26 70;
www.corte-tourisme.com

🕐 **Open** Musée de la Corse: daily

🍴 **Eat and drink** Real meal U
Museu (Rampe Ribanelle, 20350;
04 95 61 08 36; closed Nov–Mar)
cooks Corsican food. Family treat
Le 24 (24 Cours Paoli, 20350;
04 95 46 02 90; closed Jan) offers
gourmet dishes and Corsican
wines in a vaulted dining room.

🎉 **Festival** San Ghjuva, cultural
festivities (Jun)

Where to Stay in Corsica

Accommodation in Corsica varies from luxury villas and hotels to camp grounds with basic chalets, while resort areas often have family-oriented complexes of apartments and mini-villas with shared pools. Expect higher prices than on most of the mainland, especially during July and August.

AGENCIES
Direct Corsica
www.directcorsica.com
This agency offers a wide choice of accommodation in Corsica, from cottages and apartments for small families, to villas with pools.

Corsican Places
www.corsica.co.uk
The website lists villas, apartments and residences, with self-catering mini-villas in all price ranges.

Ajaccio
Map 1 B4

HOTELS
San Carlu
8 Blvd Danielle Casanova, 20000; 04 95 21 13 84; www.hotel-sancarlu.com
This is one of central Ajaccio's most pleasant hotels, with sound-proof rooms overlooking the citadelle and located only steps away from the sandy Plage St-François and several restaurants. Flat-screen satellite TVs and Wi-Fi in all the rooms. A suite on the top floor accommodates four.

€€

Hôtel Stella di Mare
Route des Sanguinaires, 20000; 04 95 52 01 07; www.hotel-stelladimare.com
Overlooking a beach 7 km (4 miles) west of Ajaccio's city centre, this hotel is perfect for combining a beach holiday with visits to the Napoleonic sites in the city; there is a bus stop in front. Take in views of the Îles Sanguinaires from the pool.

€€€

CAMPING
Les Mimosas
Route d'Alata, 20090; 04 95 20 99 85; www.camping-lesmimosas.com
This is a peaceful, basic camping option in the shade of a eucalyptus grove, 3 km (2 miles) north of the city centre. There are five chalets, one mobile home to rent, and linen available for hire. A playground, snack bar and shop are also on site.
€

Bonifacio
Map 1 C6

HOTELS
Hôtel des Etrangers
Ave Sylvère Bohn, 20169; 04 95 73 01 09
This friendly inn, in the same family for generations, is within walking distance of the marina and a real treasure in expensive Bonifacio. Located near the main road into town, its spacious rooms have double glazing and come en suite with showers; Wi-Fi in the reception.
€

Hôtel A Madonetta
5 Rue Paul Nicolaï, 20169; 04 95 10 36 39; www.amadonetta.com
A 2-minute walk from Bonifacio's port and its many restaurants, this modern hotel with free parking is a good bet for touring families. All rooms have private terraces, bathtubs and Wi-Fi. There is also a *hammam* (Turkish bath) and Jacuzzi for relaxing. The hotel is open all year.
€€€

Solemare
Nouvelle Marine, 20169; 04 95 73 01 06; www.hotel-solemare.com
This modern low-rise hotel offers a truly breathtaking view over the bobbing yachts up to the citadel of Bonifacio. Rooms are not very large but all have balconies and there are a dozen restaurants near, at hand. The helpful, friendly management is a good source of information for the activities in the area.
€€€

The comfortable lobby of exclusive La Signoria, Calvi

One of the modern double rooms in Hôtel A Madonetta, Bonifacio

CAMPING
Camping La Rondinara
20169 Suartone; 04 95 70 43 15; www.rondinara.fr
Located between Bonifacio and Porto-Vecchio, this site offers pitches under the pines and mobile homes. A track leads to Plage de Rodinara, safe even for the youngest child. There is a playground, volleyball, grocers, a bakery and snack bar.
€€

SELF-CATERING
Residence Casarina
20169 Golfe de Santa Manza; 04 95 73 57 01; www.casarina-village.com
Just 5 km (3 miles) east of Bonifacio, these chalets and mini-villas – rented by the week – are a short walk from Plage de Maora in the Golfe de Santa Manza. All of them come with private terraces and barbecues and cable TV. An added bonus is the excellent restaurant.
€€€

Calvi
Map 1 B2

HOTELS
La Caravelle
Route de la Plage, 20260; 04 95 65 95 50; www.hotel-la-caravelle.com
This hotel is located on Calvi's long white Marco Plage, with shallow waters and sands perfect for castle building. Rooms have views across to the citadelle; other rooms look on to a Mediterranean garden. The hotel's beach restaurant is excellent and the family in charge is helpful.
€€€

La Signoria
Route de la Forêt de Bonifato, 20260;
04 95 65 93 00; www.hotel-la-
signoria.com
One of Corsica's most luxurious
hotels, La Signoria is an exclusive
hideaway in an 18th-century mansion
surrounded by a magnificent garden.
It has its own manicured sandy beach,
exquisitely furnished rooms, and
owners who make sure families have
a good time. The restaurant is superb.
🛏 P ✳ ⊙   €€€

CAMPING
Camping Les Castors
Route de Pietramaggiore, 20260;
04 95 65 13 30; www.camping-les-
castors.fr
Set in a eucalyptus grove, this camp
site provides a choice of self-catering
chalets and apartments. For kids,
the big lure is the mini-water park.
The large sandy beach is a short
walk away. Wi-Fi is available for a
fee, and there is a basic shop, pizza
van and live music two nights a week.
P ⊙   €€

SELF-CATERING
Gîtes de Paradella
20214 Calenzana; 04 95 65 31 61;
www.paradella.fr
On an agricultural estate along the
Figarella river– a 5-minute drive
south of Calvi – these three *gîtes*
are built to high environmental
standards and stay cool in summer.
Sheets and towels may be hired;
highchair, baby bath and a cot are
also available.
🛏 🛋 P ⊙   €€€

Porto   Map 1 B3

HOTELS
Hôtel l'Aïtone
20120 Evisa; 04 95 26 20 04;
www.hotel-aitone.com
Located in the mountains above
Porto, this hotel in one of Corsica's
most beautiful forests has staggering
views; the sunsets from the restaurant
are unforgettable. Rooms are a bit
dated, but families can enjoy easy
access to trails, waterfalls and river
pools. There is a play area for kids.
🛏 P ⊙   €€€

Hôtel Eden Park
20147 Serriera; 04 95 26 10 60,
www.hotels-porto.com
Hidden amidst the trees, near the
Plage de Bussalgia, this is a relaxing

36-room hotel on the Gulf of Porto.
Rooms are staggered along paths
on the slopes, offering privacy, and
there is a playground, table tennis,
mini-golf and bike hire. Breakfast
is included in the room rates.
🛏 P ✳ ⊙   €€€

CAMPING
Camping Les Oliviers
20150 Porto; 04 95 26 14 49;
www.camping-oliviers-porto.com
Along with its pitches, Les Oliviers
offers wooden family chalets with
terraces spread out amidst the
trees and gorgeous views over the
mountains. The pool, set among the
rocks, is delightful, but there is also
the option of swimming in the river.
Playground and tennis courts on site.
🛏 🛋 ✳ ⊙   €–€€

SELF-CATERING
Hôtel Residence Cabanaccia
20147 Serriera; 04 95 26 14 46;
www.residence-cabanaccia.com
Immersed in the maquis and trees
5 km (3 miles) north of Porto and
2 km (1 mile) from Bussaglia beach,
Cabanaccia offers guests a choice
of modern mini-villas and studios
with verandahs. It is a peaceful
retreat but a car is essential.
🛏 🛋 ✳ ⊙   €€

Porto-Vecchio   Map 1 C5

HOTEL
Kilina
Route de Cala Rossa, 20137; 04 95
71 60 43; www.kilina.net
This sleek hotel is near some of
Corsica's most beautiful beaches,
with rooms lodging up to six people.
One of the pools has a garden islet
in the centre. Washing machines, an
afternoon kids' club, Wi-Fi and buffet
breakfast included in rates; minimum
week's stay in July and August.
🛏 P ✳ ⊙   €€€

CAMPING
Camping U Pirellu   Map 1 C6
Route de Palombaggia, 20137;
04 95 70 23 44; u-pirellu.com
A few minutes drive from the toddler-
friendly Plage de Palombaggia, this
camp site offers sea views and simple
chalets, as well as pitches. There
are activities for kids, Wi-Fi, a solar
heated cascade pool, a shop, as well
as musical evenings at the bar.
🛏 🛋 P ⊙   €€

SELF-CATERING
Les Bungalows de Palombaggio   Map 1 C6
20137 Palombaggio; 06 22 04
55 63; www.palombaggia.cc
Located near the enchanting
Plage de Palombaggia, these
seven attractive bungalows 12 km
(7 miles) from the centre of town,
are among the cheapest high-
season rentals for a family.
🛏 🛋 P   €€

Swimming pool with a garden islet in Hotel Kilina, Porto-Vecchio

St-Florent   Map 1 C2

CAMPING
Camping La Pinède
Lieu dit Serrigio, 20217; 04 95 37
07 26; www.camping-la-pinede.com
This pleasant family camp ground
is located by the Aliso river, with
direct motor boat access to the
sea. Most visitors stay in the chalets,
which offer bunk beds for the kids
and are set back in the shade. Note
that linen is not supplied.
🛏 🛋 P ⊙   €

SELF-CATERING
E Caselle
Lieu Dit Calvello, 20253 Patrimonio;
04 95 37 19 19; www.villas-
caselle.com
Set in the hills of Patrimonio, only
a 5-minute drive from St-Florent's
Plage de la Roya, these comfortable
modern villas in a garden setting
come with modern conveniences,
including Wi-Fi, barbecues and all
the services of a hotel. By request,
they even pre-stock the fridge
with groceries.
🛋 P ✳ ⊙   €€€

Price Guide
The following price ranges are based
on one night's accommodation in high
season for a family of four, inclusive of
service charges and any additional taxes.
€ Under €100 €€ €100–200 €€€ over €200

Key to symbols *see back cover flap*

Grid of medieval streets surrounding the Gothic Cathédrale Notre-Dame in the historic heart of Strasbourg

France

MAPS

France Maps

3 **4** **5** **6**

LE NORD
AND PICARDY

2

NORMANDY

PARIS AND
ÎLE DE FRANCE

ALSACE AND
LORRAINE

CHAMPAGNE

BRITTANY

7 **8** **9** **10**

THE LOIRE VALLEY

BURGUNDY AND
FRANCHE-COMTÉ

POITOU
AND
AQUITAINE

THE MASSIF
CENTRAL

THE RHÔNE
VALLEY AND
FRENCH ALPS

11 **12** **13** **14**

PÉRIGORD,
QUERCY AND
GASCONY

LANGUEDOC-
ROUSSILLON

PROVENCE AND
THE CÔTE D'AZUR

THE PYRENEES

1

CORSICA

KEY TO MAPS 1–14

═•═	Motorway with junction
──	Dual carriageway
▦▦▦	Road under construction
──	Main road
⋯⋯	Minor road
──	Railway
─ ─	Ferry route
──	National border

──	Regional border
▢	Urban area
✈	Airport
⚓	Ferry port

◇	Place of Interest
△	Summit
✕	Pass

MAP (1)

0 km   10

0 miles   10

MAPS (2–14)

0 km   20

0 miles   20

Paris City Maps

18

| 17 | 18 | 19 | 20 |

MONTMARTRE

19

| 15 | 16 |

NEUILLY-
SUR-SEINE

PIGALLE

17

MONCEAU

9

PORTE-
DAUPHINE

CHAMPS-
ELYSÉES

8

OPÉRA

10

BELLEVILLE

| 23 | | 24 | 25 | | 26 |

2

TUILERIES

1

BEAUBOURG

20

| 21 |

16

CHAILLOT

| 22 |

3

THE MARAIS

11

PASSY

La Seine

ÎLE DE
LA CITÉ

4

INVALIDES

7

ST-GERMAIN-
DES-PRÉS

ÎLE ST-
LOUIS

BASTILLE

La Seine

GRENELLE

| 27 | | 28 | 29 | | 30 |

6

5

LATIN QUARTER

BERCY

12

15

MONTPARNASSE

La Seine

GOBELINS

GARE

DENFERT-
ROCHEREAU

13

14

KEY TO MAPS 15–30

▪	Major sight	🚌	River boat stop	──	Railway line
▫	Place of interest	**P**	Parking	---	*Arrondissement* boundary
▫	Other building	**i**	Visitor information		
🚉	Train station	🚓	Police station		
RER	RER station	📞	Playground		**MAPS (15–30)**
M	Métro station	▤	Motorway		
🚠	Cable car/Funicular station	▥	Pedestrian street		

0 m   200

0 yards   200

Rosslare, Cork   Plymouth

Sark

Guernsey

Channel
Islands

1

Jersey

3

Îles d'Er
Trégastel   Tourony   Île de Bréhat
Île Grande   Ploubazlanec   Pointe de l'Arcouest
Trébeurden   Perros-   Paimpol
Île de Batz   Guirec   Pontrieux   Tréguier   Plouézec
Roscoff   Lannion   Saint-Quay-   Cap
Plouescat   Saint-Pol-   Pontrieux   Lanvollon   Portrieux   Frébel
Landeda   Goulven   de-Léon   Plestin-les-   Étables   Sables-d'Or-   St-Cast-
Le Folgoët   Lesneven   St-Vougay   Taulé   Grèves   D767   Bégard   Pordic   les-Pins   le-Guildo
Ploudalmézeau   Morlaix   Plouaret   Guingamp   Le Val-   Fréhel
Plabennec   Landivisiau   N12   Belle-Isle-   Plouagat   André   Ploubalay
Saint-Renan   Brest ✈   Plougonven   Plouigneau   en-Terre   St-Brieuc   N12   Plancoët
Brest   Bretagne   Landerneau   Bourbriac   Lamballe   N176
Le Conquet   Océanopolis   Sizun   Callac   Jugon-Les-
Plougastel-   N165   Huelgoat   Corlay   Moncontour   Lacs
Daoulas   Logonna-Daoulas   Monts d'Arrée   Maël-Carhaix   Gouarec   Plouguenast   Collinée   Broons
Camaret-sur-Mer   Landévennec   Carhaix-   Mur-de-   Loudéac   N164   Saint-Méen-
Crozon   Presqu'île   Plouguer   Rostrenen   Bretagne   Merdrignac   D166   le-Grand
Châteaulin   de Crozon   Pleyben   Châteauneuf-   D768   Rohan   La Trinité-   Château
Douarnenez   N164   du-Faou   Montagnes Noires   Porhoët   de Comper
Pointe   Aulne   Gourin   Pontivy   Mauron   Paimpont
du Raz   Pont-Croix   Locronan   Guéméné-   Josselin   Forêt de   Guer
Audierne   Coray   Scaër   sur-Scorff   Bubry   Brocéliande
Plonéour-   Quimper   Bannalec   Kernascléden   Plouay   Ploërmel
Lanvern   Pays Bigouden   Scaër   Locuno lé   Baud   Locminé   Lizio   Malestroit
Pont-l'Abbé   Bénodet   Fouesnant   Pont-Aven   Hennebont   Saint-Jean-   Oust   La Gacilly
Penmarc'h   Concarneau   Trégunc   Pont-Scorff   Landévant   Brévelay   N166   Rochefort-
Pointe de   Lesconil   Lann Bihoué ✈   Lanester   Grand-   Elven   en-Terre
Penmarc'h   Lorient   Port-Louis   Auray   Champ   Questembert   Redon
Larmor-Plage   Îles de Groix   Erdeven   Vannes   Parc Animalier et   Saint-Gildas-
Plouharnel   Alignements   Golfe du   Botanique de Brenféré   des-Bois
Carnac   de Carnac   Larmor-   Morbihan   Muzillac
Saint-Pierre-Quiberon   Baden   Arzon   N165   La Roche-   Pontchâteau
Quiberon   Bernard
Sauzon   Piriac-sur-Mer   Montoir-de-
Belle-Île   Le Palais   Guérande   Bretagne
Le Croisic   Saint-
Batz-sur-Mer   La   Nazaire
Baule   St-Marc-   Saint-
sur-Mer   Brévin-
Pointe du St-Gildas   les-Pins
Pornic

BRETAGNE

N24

Landes de Lanvaux

Odet
Blavet
Scorff
Laïta
Isole

Océan

Atlantique

Noirmoutier-en-l'Île   7
Île de Noirmoutier   D38   Beauvoir-
sur-Mer

Fromentine

Saint-Jean-de-Monts   6

Île d'Yeu

France Maps Index

Paris Maps Index

Index

Page numbers in **bold** type refer to main entries.

Acknowledgments

Dorling Kindersley would like to thank the following people whose help and assistance contributed to the preparation of this book.

Main Contributors

Dana Facaros has lived in France since 1989. She is the author and co-author of over 40 guides. She and her husband, along with their two children, have travelled all over the world.

Leonie Glass has been a travel writer and editor for more than 25 years. She is the co-founder of *thehotel guru.com*, a successful online independent hotel guide.

Antony Mason is the author of about 80 books on travel, geography, exploration, history, the history of art and current affairs and has also contributed articles featured in publications by *Reader's Digest*, *National Geographic*, *The Daily Telegraph* and *Condé Nast Traveller*.

Mike Pedley is a freelance travel writer who has spent several years living and working in France, mainly in Provence, Languedoc-Roussillon and the Alps. He freelances as a writer for several French publications.

Ally Thompson is an ex-BBC producer based in Northern Ireland. She freelances as a journalist and travel guide author. She and her family like to spend the summers in the medieval town of Montcuq in the Lot region.

Rosie Whitehouse has spent over 20 years travelling with her five children. With family in Paris, Rosie has explored every nook and cranny of the French capital.

Editorial Consultant
Fay Franklin

Additional Photography
David Abram; Max Alexander; Marc Dubin; Philippe Giraud; Alex Havret; John Heseltine; Roger Hilton; Paul Kenward; Neil Lukas; Eric Meacher; Roger Moss; Ian O'Leary; John Parker; Cecile Treal and Jean-Michel Ruiz; Rough Guides: Demetrio Carrasco, Marc Dubin, Jean-Christophe Godet, James McConnachie, Greg Ward; Kim Sayer; Tony Souter; Clive Streeter; Rollin Verlinde; Alan Williams; Jerry Young.

Design and Editorial
PUBLISHER Vivien Antwi
LIST MANAGER Christine Stroyan
SENIOR MANAGING ART EDITOR Mabel Chan
SENIOR CARTOGRAPHIC EDITOR Casper Morris
CARTOGRAPHIC EDITOR Stuart James
SENIOR EDITOR Michelle Crane, Georgina Palffy
JUNIOR EDITOR Vicki Allen
JACKET DESIGN Tessa Bindloss, Louise Dick
ICON DESIGN Claire-Louise Armitt
SENIOR DTP EDITOR Jason Little

PICTURE RESEARCH Chloe Roberts, Ellen Root
PRODUCTION CONTROLLER Rebecca Short
READERS Nick Rider, Anna Streiffert
FACT CHECKERS Anna Brooke, Catherine Gauthier, Robert Harneis, Lyn Parry
PROOFREADER Lucy Ratcliffe
INDEXER Vanessa Bird

Additional Editorial Assistance
Vanessa Cerchia

Photography Permissions
Dorling Kindersley would like to thank all the museums, galleries, churches and other sights that allowed us to photograph at their establishments.

58 Tour Eiffel, Aquarium at Cinéaqua, Le Café du Palais, The Castle of Fontainebleau, Château de Chenonceau, Château Fort de Sedan, Cité de l'Automobile, Cité des Sciences et de l'Industrie, Fort des Rousses, L'abbaye de la Chaise-Dieu, La Maison des Hommes, Les Machines de l'Île, Le Musée d'Art et d'Industrie, Musée d'Angoulême, Musée de l'Oliver, Musée Grévin, Nausicaá, Nyons.

Works of art have been reproduced with the kind permission of the following copyright holders: *Birdie* 1997, resin & fiberglass, polyurethane paint, © Frederic Lanovsky, *http://www.lanovsky.com* 358cra.

Picture Credits
Key: a-above; b-below/bottom; c-centre; f-far; l-left; r-right; t-top

The publisher would like to thank the following for their kind permission to reproduce their photographs: ALAMY IMAGES: The Art Archive 125tc, 126cla; Camera Lucida Lifestyle 162cb; Culliganphoto 1c; Liz Garnett 166ca; Chris Hellier 189bl; Hemis 11br, 158cl, 174cl, 179bl, 233bl, 257br, 272c, 301; Eric James 183bl; JTB Photo Communications, Inc 12tr; Michael Juno 14br; Marion Kaplan 270br; Moviestore Collection Ltd 325cb; Noble Images 341; Photosilta 264c; Jordi Puig 266bc; Paul Shawcross 209tl; Kumar Sriskandan 132cl; Jack Sullivan 90crb; Gregory Wrona 342cra. ALBIRONDACK PARK CAMPING LODGE ET CAMP: 278bl. L'ATELIER DU CHOCOLAT: Paul Martinez 302crb. LA BASTIDE DE LA BRAGUE: 362bl. THE BRIDGEMAN ART LIBRARY: *Vercingetorix Threw his Arms at the Feet of his Conquerors'*, plate from *The Story of France* by Mary MacGregor, 1920 (coloured litho), Rainey, William (1852–1936) (after)/Private Collection/The Stapleton Collection/36cr. BRITTANY COTTAGES: 170cl. CAMPING INDIGO: 237tr. CAMPING LA COUTELIÈRE: 363tr. CHÂTEAU DE LA MOTTE: 28bl, 299tc. CHÂTEAU FORT DE SEDAN: 64cra. LE CHATENET BRANTÔME: 278cra. CITADINES CENTRE MÉRIADECK BORDEAUX: 298cra.